We the People

of the United States, in order to form a more perfect Union, establish Justice, insure domestic Tranquility, provide for the common defence, promote the general Welfare, and secure the Blessings of Liberty to ourselves and our Posterity, do ordain and establish this Constitution for the United States of America.

Article I

Section 1. All legislative Powers herein granted shall be vested in a Congress of the United States, which shall consist of a Senate and House of Representatives.

Section 2. The House of Representatives shall be composed of Members chosen every second Year by the People of the several States, and the Electors in each State shall have the Qualifications requisite for Electors of the most numerous Branch of the State Legislature.

[illegible]

We the People

of the United States, in Order to form a more perfect Union, establish Justice, insure domestic Tranquility, provide for the common defence, promote the general Welfare, and secure the Blessings of Liberty to ourselves and our Posterity, do ordain and establish this Constitution for the United States of America.

Article I

Section. 1. All legislative Powers herein granted shall be vested in a Congress of the United States, which shall consist of a Senate and House of Representatives.

Section. 2. The House of Representatives shall be composed of Members chosen every second Year by the People of the several States, and the Electors in each State shall have the Qualifications requisite for Electors of the most numerous Branch of the State Legislature.

No Person shall be a Representative who shall not have attained to the Age of twenty five Years, and been seven Years a Citizen of the United States, and who shall not, when elected, be an Inhabitant of that State in which he shall be chosen.

Representatives and direct Taxes shall be apportioned among the several States which may be included within this Union, according to their respective Numbers, which shall be determined by adding to the whole Number of free Persons, including those bound to Service for a Term of Years, and excluding Indians not taxed, three fifths of all other Persons. The actual Enumeration shall be made within three Years after the first Meeting of the Congress of the United States, and within every subsequent Term of ten Years, in such Manner as they shall by Law direct. The Number of Representatives shall not exceed one for every thirty Thousand, but each State shall have at Least one Representative; and until such enumeration shall be made, the State of New Hampshire shall be entitled to chuse three, Massachusetts eight, Rhode-Island and Providence Plantations one, Connecticut five, New-York six, New Jersey four, Pennsylvania eight, Delaware one, Maryland six, Virginia ten, North Carolina five, South Carolina five, and Georgia three.

When vacancies happen in the Representation from any State, the Executive Authority thereof shall issue Writs of Election to fill such Vacancies.

The House of Representatives shall chuse their Speaker and other Officers; and shall have the sole Power of Impeachment.

Section. 3. The Senate of the United States shall be composed of two Senators from each State, chosen by the Legislature thereof, for six Years; and each Senator shall have one Vote.

Immediately after they shall be assembled in Consequence of the first Election, they shall be divided as equally as may be into three Classes. The Seats of the Senators of the first Class shall be vacated at the Expiration of the second Year, of the second Class at the Expiration of the fourth Year, and of the third Class at the Expiration of the sixth Year, so that one third may be chosen every second Year; and if Vacancies happen by Resignation, or otherwise, during the Recess of the Legislature of any State, the Executive thereof may make temporary Appointments until the next Meeting of the Legislature, which shall then fill such Vacancies.

No Person shall be a Senator who shall not have attained to the Age of thirty Years, and been nine Years a Citizen of the United States, and who shall not, when elected, be an Inhabitant of that State for which he shall be chosen.

The Vice President of the United States shall be President of the Senate, but shall have no Vote, unless they be equally divided.

The Senate shall chuse their other Officers, and also a President pro tempore, in the Absence of the Vice President, or when he shall exercise the Office of President of the United States.

The Senate shall have the sole Power to try all Impeachments. When sitting for that Purpose, they shall be on Oath or Affirmation. When the President of the United States is tried, the Chief Justice shall preside: And no Person shall be convicted without the Concurrence of two thirds of the Members present.

Judgment in Cases of Impeachment shall not extend further than to removal from Office, and disqualification to hold and enjoy any Office of honor, Trust or Profit under the United States: but the Party convicted shall nevertheless be liable and subject to Indictment, Trial, Judgment and Punishment, according to Law.

Section. 4. The Times, Places and Manner of holding Elections for Senators and Representatives, shall be prescribed in each State by the Legislature thereof; but the Congress may at any time by Law make or alter such Regulations, except as to the Places of chusing Senators.

The Congress shall assemble at least once in every Year, and such Meeting shall be on the first Monday in December, unless they shall by Law appoint a different Day.

Section. 5. Each House shall be the Judge of the Elections, Returns and Qualifications of its own Members, and a Majority of each shall constitute a Quorum to do Business; but a smaller Number may adjourn from day to day, and may be authorized to compel the Attendance of absent Members, in such Manner, and under such Penalties as each House may provide.

Each House may determine the Rules of its Proceedings, punish its Members for disorderly Behaviour, and, with the Concurrence of two thirds, expel a Member.

Each House shall keep a Journal of its Proceedings, and from time to time publish the same, excepting such Parts as may in their Judgment require Secrecy; and the Yeas and Nays of the Members of either House on any question shall, at the Desire of one fifth of those Present, be entered on the Journal.

Neither House, during the Session of Congress, shall, without the Consent of the other, adjourn for more than three days, nor to any other Place than that in which the two Houses shall be sitting.

Section. 6. The Senators and Representatives shall receive a Compensation for their Services, to be ascertained by Law, and paid out of the Treasury of the United States. They shall in all Cases, except Treason, Felony and Breach of the Peace, be privileged from Arrest during their Attendance at the Session of their respective Houses, and in going to and returning from the same; and for any Speech or Debate in either House, they shall not be questioned in any other Place.

No Senator or Representative shall, during the Time for which he was elected, be appointed to any civil Office under the Authority of the United States, which shall have been created, or the Emoluments whereof shall have been encreased during such time; and no Person holding any Office under the United States, shall be a Member of either House during his Continuance in Office.

Section. 7. All Bills for raising Revenue shall originate in the House of Representatives; but the Senate may propose or concur with Amendments as on other Bills.

Every Bill which shall have passed the House of Representatives and the Senate, shall, before it become a Law, be presented to the President of the

We The People

CIVICS IN THE UNITED STATES

TEACHER'S ANNOTATED EDITION

Robert A. Carter
Social Studies Coordinator
Midland Independent School District
Midland, Texas

John M. Richards
Corpus Christi State University
Corpus Christi, Texas

Coronado Publishers

San Diego • New York • Chicago • Dallas

Cover: We the People, collage on wood by Fred Otnes (American, 1926—). Coronado Publishers collection. Photographed for printing by Stephen McCarroll.

Printed in the United States of America ISBN 0-15-771001-7

TEACHER'S PREFACE

This section is intended for use by you, the teacher. It does not appear in the students' edition, and it is separated from the text itself by being printed on a colored background. The Teacher's Annotated Edition consists of this 46-page Introduction plus page-for-page annotations that appear throughout the student section.

We the People: A Complete Program

We the People is a complete program in civics, or American citizenship. It consists of two basic components. The first is the student text, which is made up of thirty-two chapters divided into eight units. The second is a teacher's "resource package," which is made up of this Teacher's Annotated Edition, plus three support items—a Test Book, an Activity Book, and an Audio Program.

Contents of the Teacher's Introduction

The Teacher's Introduction is intended to familiarize you with *We the People* and to explain how it can be used. It begins with a series of reproductions of pages from the text, exemplifying the various features of the book. This is followed by an explanation of each of these features, and then by general suggestions for teaching strategy. Also included are a list of books and other materials that you can incorporate into your course. The Introduction concludes with an answer key for the activities that appear in the student text.

The Support Items

The Test Book consists of one test for each unit and each chapter, plus a mid-term and a final, for a total of forty-two tests in all. (This is in addition to the tests in the textbook itself.) The Activity Book consists of a series of activities that are related to the text but not directly connected to the specific chapters. Both of these books are available as blackline masters. The Audio Program consists of dramatic readings of great documents from our history, such as the Declaration of Independence and the Gettysburg Address.

These three support items may or may not be part of your course. Therefore, the accompanying materials for such an item—teacher's notes, table of contents, answers key, etc.—appear as a part of the support item itself rather than as a part of this introduction.

The Organization of We the People

Apart from the obvious device of units and chapters, there are two ways in which *We the People* is organized. The first involves the concept of great documents. Since it is crucial to the existence of a free society that it have "a government of laws, not men," the curriculum of *We the People* is built upon the foundation of the Constitution and other documents that have shaped our system of government. Each chapter begins with an excerpt from an actual document, and the content of the chapter unfolds according to the nature of that document.

The other method of organization involves a "three-part" concept. Our system of government is unique in that it divides into three parts both horizontally (Executive; Legislative; Judicial) and vertically (Federal; State; Local). Throughout *We the People*, the structure and the operation of our government is analyzed in terms of both of its three-part divisions, horizontal and vertical. For example, the Activity Book presents a variety of materials on a federal executive, a state legislator, and a local judicial officer.

Teaching Strategies for We the People

We the People is a flexible program that can be used in a variety of classroom situations by a variety of teachers. The section entitled "Suggestions for Teaching" is just that—*suggestions*, not rules. We hope that this book will be used as profitably as possible by you in the classroom, and thus we do not intend to set down restrictions that might inhibit its use. Therefore you will note that this Introduction does not contain a timetable indicating how many hours or days should be spent on each element of the program. Nor do we make recommendations as to material that can be omitted—if we didn't think something was important, it wouldn't have been included in the first place.

We the People is an element in a civics course—we hope the most important element. But it is not a total course in itself. The total course is shaped by you and by your institution, using our book as a tool. Therefore we leave to you the question of how much time and attention to give to the various parts of *We the People*, since only you fully know the realities of your classroom and the needs of your students.

Goals of We the People

Just as we do not presume to tell you how to manage your civics classroom, we also do not presume to state one or two finite, exclusive goals for a civics course. However, we feel that it is generally agreed that a successful civics course provides students with two things: an understanding of the rights and duties of a citizen, and the skills needed to appreciate these rights and carry out these duties. In order to achieve this second goal, that of such skills as comprehending and retaining information, expressing one's ideas, and evaluating points of view, *We the People* provides a complete curriculum of skills development, including a set of four full pages of activities at the conclusion of each chapter, two of which are intended as skill builders and two of which serve as a test.

With respect to the first goal, an awareness of citizenship, Thomas Jefferson said:

> "I know of no safe depository of the ultimate powers of society but the people themselves; and if we think them not enlightened enough to exercise their control with a wholesome discretion, the remedy is not to take it from them, but to inform their discretion"

The purpose of the *We the People* program is to provide students with this "discretion" that Jefferson mentions. By informing them about the nature of our government and the way in which it works, we hope that we can help your students to "exercise their control" of our society in a responsible and intelligent manner.

The American System

There is no such thing as a truly neutral textbook—such a book would probably be too boring to motivate students. As we state in the Preface to the Student Edition, we are certainly not neutral about the American system. Rather, we are very positive about it. We believe that patriotism, respect for the law, and civic responsibility are values worth instilling in students and indeed in any citizen of this country or any other free society. Throughout the text, students are reminded that living in a free society involves certain obligations if freedom is to be maintained.

We the People does not, of course, imply that the American system is absolutely perfect or that patriotism is equivalent to unquestioning obedience. We repeatedly stress the role of minority opinion and the value of responsible dissent. We also point out conflicts that have taken place in our society and changes that have resulted from this.

The scientist Isaac Newton said that he was able to achieve his momentous discoveries because he "stood on the shoulders of giants." We have emphasized the traditional aspects of American citizenship so that students will understand that they, too, stand on the shoulders of giants. These "giants" are not only the great men and women of our history, but even more important, the great documents, laws, court decisions, and other actions that have created the American system. In time, today's civics students will take on their role as adult citizens. Then, they in turn must be, and will be, the giants on whose shoulders the generations that follow them will stand.

FEATURES OF *WE THE PEOPLE*

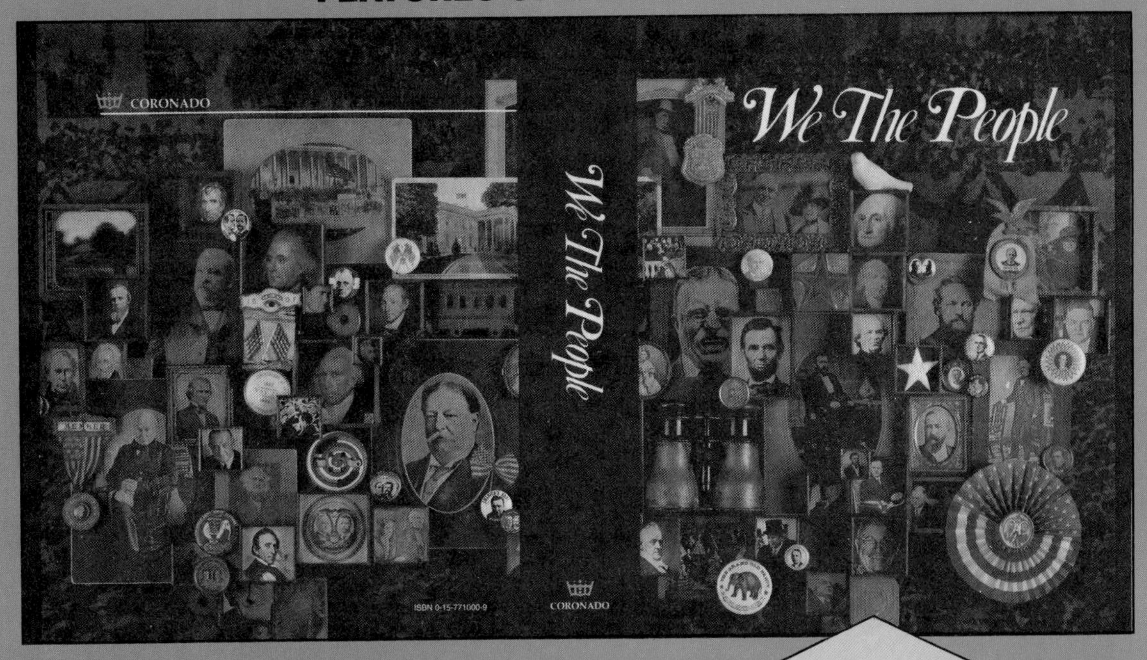

Cover (See Page T11)

The cover is a reproduction of an original artwork from the publisher's collection, entitled *We the People*. It is a collage on wood by the noted American artist Fred Otnes. It consists of authentic period photographs and other historical items, and it depicts the Presidents of the U.S. and other leading political figures. The backdrop is a photo of the inauguration of Grover Cleveland. A key identifying all the people who appear in the collage is included on the inside cover of the Activity Book that accompanies this text.

Unit Two
Our American Government

The Constitution was written by the founders of our country to ensure basic freedoms for their own generation and for all generations to come. As a citizen of the United States, you are protected each day of your life by the laws set forth in the original document, as well as by the Amendments that have been added since the Constitution was signed. Because the Constitution established a framework for our democratic government while also providing for the future, it is known as a "living document"—one that is constructed in such a way that it can continue to adapt to the needs of changing times.

73

Unit Opener (See Page T11)

Unit titles and thematic illustrations reflect the general concepts of the upcoming text.

A brief introduction summarizes the theme of the unit as a whole and serves as a complement to the illustration above.

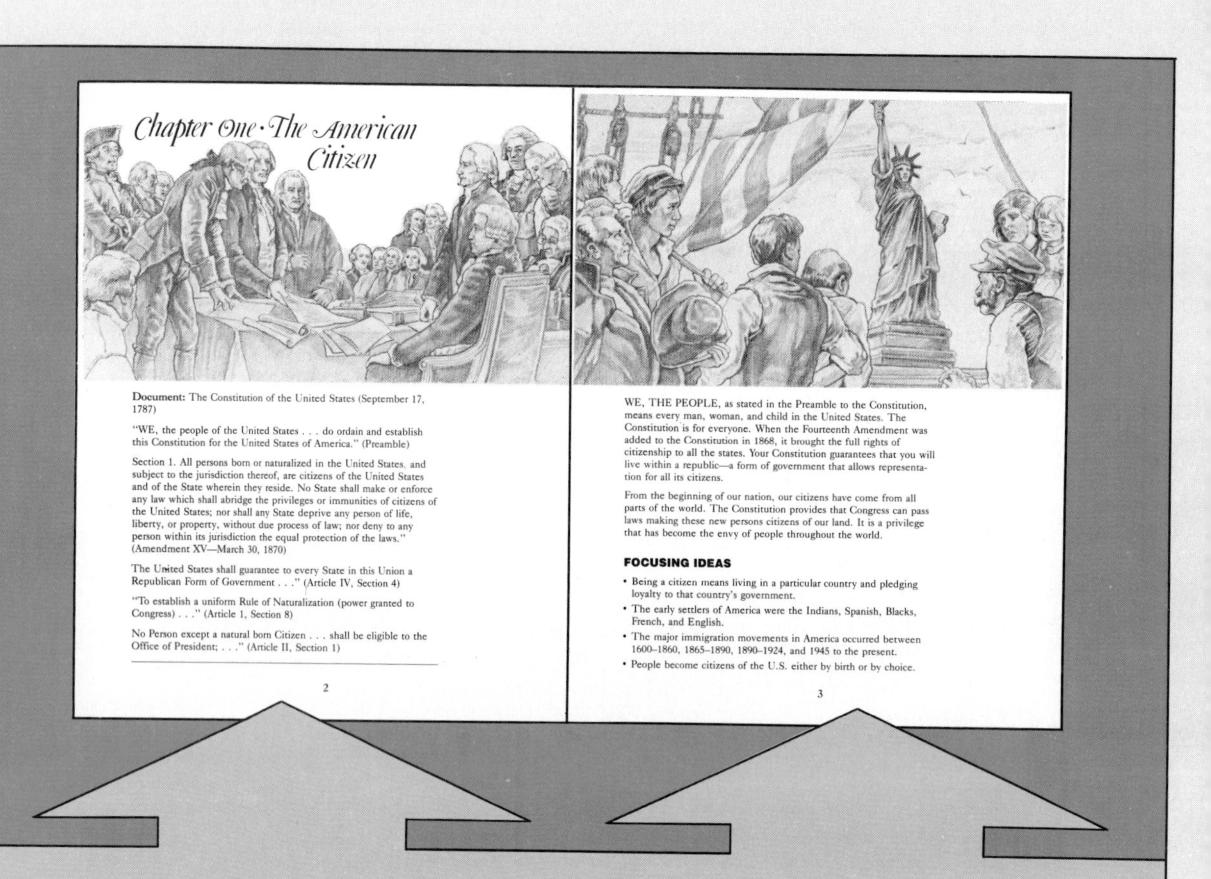

Chapter One · The American Citizen

Document: The Constitution of the United States (September 17, 1787)

"WE, the people of the United States . . . do ordain and establish this Constitution for the United States of America." (Preamble)

Section 1. All persons born or naturalized in the United States, and subject to the jurisdiction thereof, are citizens of the United States and of the State wherein they reside. No State shall make or enforce any law which shall abridge the privileges or immunities of citizens of the United States; nor shall any State deprive any person of life, liberty, or property, without due process of law; nor deny to any person within its jurisdiction the equal protection of the laws." (Amendment XV—March 30, 1870)

The United States shall guarantee to every State in this Union a Republican Form of Government . . ." (Article IV, Section 4)

"To establish a uniform Rule of Naturalization (power granted to Congress) . . ." (Article 1, Section 8)

No Person except a natural born Citizen . . . shall be eligible to the Office of President; . . ." (Article II, Section 1)

2

WE, THE PEOPLE, as stated in the Preamble to the Constitution, means every man, woman, and child in the United States. The Constitution is for everyone. When the Fourteenth Amendment was added to the Constitution in 1868, it brought the full rights of citizenship to all the states. Your Constitution guarantees that you will live within a republic—a form of government that allows representation for all its citizens.

From the beginning of our nation, our citizens have come from all parts of the world. The Constitution provides that Congress can pass laws making these new persons citizens of our land. It is a privilege that has become the envy of people throughout the world.

FOCUSING IDEAS

- Being a citizen means living in a particular country and pledging loyalty to that country's government.
- The early settlers of America were the Indians, Spanish, Blacks, French, and English.
- The major immigration movements in America occurred between 1600–1860, 1865–1890, 1890–1924, and 1945 to the present.
- People become citizens of the U.S. either by birth or by choice.

3

Chapter Opener
(See Page T11)

Specially-commissioned illustrations open each chapter. They visually depict the theme of the chapter and serve as a means of stimulating discussion.

The chapter begins with an excerpt from the Constitution or another great document from our nation's history. These documents serve as the foundation upon which the material in the text rests.

The presentation of the original document is followed by a short commentary on the meaning of the document and on the way it relates to the upcoming text.

"Focusing Ideas" list the major concepts to be dealt with in the chapter. They provide answers to the Pre-Test questions that appear at the beginning of the running text.

Unit 6 • Justice Under the Law

PRE-TEST

1. What steps are involved in the making of a Supreme Court decision?
2. What legal rights do individuals in our society have?
3. What are the major rights of free speech that all individuals in our country are entitled to?
4. What major rights do individuals have regarding search and seizure?
5. What are the rights involved in the trial and arrest process?

'OW ARE SUPREME COURT DECISIONS MADE?

This symbol of "blind justice" has been used since ancient times to represent the legal process.

Objectives: After you read this section, you will be able to:

- Understand how a case comes to be heard by the Supreme Court.
- Describe the process by which the Supreme Court arrives at its decision.
- See why electronic equipment is a valuable aid to the Supreme Court.

Ideal justice, meaning equal treatment for both sides in a dispute, is something people have sought since ancient days. Justice is often represented as a woman with a blindfold over her eyes and a pair of scales in one hand. What do you think this representation is meant to say about justice?

The Supreme Court of the United States is the final body to hear an appeal from a lower court. The real meaning of justice to all the people is often decided in this Court. Thus, the manner in which a decision is reached is important to us.

Building vocabulary:
Writ of Mandamus *(415)* • appellate jurisdiction *(415)* • original jurisdiction *(415)* • dissenting opinion *(416)* • concurring opinion *(416)* • due process *(417)* • procedural right *(424)*

414

Pre-Test
(See Page T11)

Each chapter begins with a Pre-Test. The content of the questions is identical to that of the "Focusing Ideas" section on the preceding page.

The questions in the Pre-Test are repeated as the headings within the chapter. The headings appear in the same sequence as the questions.

Unit 5 • Our Nation's Executives

PRE-TEST

1. What function does a state executive perform?
2. What are the usual duties and responsibilities of a country executive?
3. What role does a city executive play in our government?

The finest laws in the world are of little value if they are not enforced. So we look to executives and administrators to carry out the will of our legislators. The two words, executive and administrator, are generally used interchangeably. However, there is a fine distinction between them. The *executive* might be called the "top boss", and the *administrator* the one who carries out his orders.

HOW DO STATE EXECUTIVES WORK?

Objectives: After you have read this section, you will be able to:

- Describe the work of the governor.
- Name three powers of the governor.
- Describe the state bureaucracy.

From the time people first began living in groups, someone had to be the leader and direct the activities of the group. From before the time of historical records, this leader made the rules and then enforced them. Much of the time this ruler was called a "governor."

One dictionary definition of governor is "the chief executive of a dependent or component unit in a political system." Before the thirteen colonies were formed into the United States, Great Britain sent governors to administer the affairs of the various states. Much of the colonial resentment and friction was caused by, and directed toward, these governors. This resentment and the frictions of the Civil War have been carried over into the constitutions of the states. The framers of the state constitutions chose to keep the power to the hands of the lawmakers rather than put it in the hands of the governor.

Edward Winslow served three terms as governor of the colony of Massachusetts.

Building Vocabulary:
executive *(346)* • administrator *(346)* • sunset law *(348)* • ombudsman *(348)* • sheriff *(350)* • city manager *(352)* • special district *(353)*

346

Vocabulary
(See Page T11)

Key vocabulary items are identified by *italic type* as they appear in the text.

At the bottom of the first page of the chapter text, all the vocabulary words in the chapter are listed separately.

Words appear in the Vocabulary List according to the order in which they occur in the text. All vocabulary items are listed alphabetically in the Glossary, along with a full definition.

Unit 2 • Our American Government

PRE-TEST

1. How is the organization of state government different from that of the federal government? How is it similar?
2. How do people participate directly in state government?
3. How do the states provide for local self-government?
4. What are the different types of municipal government?

HOW ARE STATE GOVERNMENTS ORGANIZED?

Objectives: After you have read this section, you will be able to:

- Explain how state governments are similar to the national government.
- Describe the way in which state legislatures are organized.
- Provide the titles that are equivalent to President and Vice President in state government.

When someone speaks of the "government," you probably think of the federal government in Washington, D.C. Actually, there are thousands of governments in the United States.

There are fifty state governments, thousands of county governments, and thousands more city governments in the United States. There are also districts and authorities that perform specific services. In a certain city the citizens might live under eight different kinds of governmental authority. The laws these various governments pass, and the services they provide, are very important in the daily lives of all citizens.

State governments are similar in form to the federal government. Each state government has legislative, executive, and judicial branches. But while all states are organized with three branches, they all have many different rules. When you study state and local governments, you will need special information to find out the organization, rules, and powers in your own state and city or county.

Legislative branches

The lawmaking branch of the state government is called the legislature. Except in Nebraska, all legislatures have two houses. The names of the two houses vary among the states. Some states call one the House of Representatives or the Assembly and the other the Senate. In Nebraska the legislature has only one house, the Senate. A lawmaking body of this kind is called a "unicameral" legislature. Unicameral is a Latin word meaning "one house or chamber." Other states have bicameral, or two houses, legislatures. The various states have different rules as to when the legislature meets. In most states there is one session each year.

Building vocabulary:
initiative *(142)* • referendum *(143)* • recall *(143)* • county board *(144)* • municipality *(146)* • ordinance *(146)* • home rule *(147)* • district *(149)*

140

Chapter 9 • State and Local Governments

The state legislatures pass more laws than Congress. These laws affect our daily lives very closely. The state lawmakers regulate traffic. They set aside funds to build highways and bridges. They provide for public education. They affect our lives in many other ways.

Executive officers

The chief executive officer of each state is called the governor. He or she manages most of the state's institutions and may veto bills passed by the legislature. In case of the governor's death, disability, or removal from office, the lieutenant governor becomes governor. States have other officers as well. There is a secretary of state to keep the records. A treasurer keeps financial accounts for the state. An attorney general oversees the enforcement of laws. And a superintendent of education directs the educational program of the state.

In most states, the lieutenant governor, the secretary of state, the treasurer, and other officers are not appointed by the governor. They are elected separately in the same election in which the governor is chosen. Each state also has a number of boards or commissions. Usually the governor of the state appoints the members of these boards. Such appointments may be subject to approval by the upper chamber of the legislature.

Check for Understanding: Now that you have completed this section, you should be able to answer these questions:

1. How are state governments similar to the national government?
2. How are state legislatures organized?
3. What is the equivalent of the President and Vice President at the state level?
4. In what way is Nebraska different from all other states?

141

Objectives/Check for Understanding
(See Page T12)

Headings relate directly to the questions in the Pre-Test (and also relate directly to the "Focusing Ideas" items).

Each section contains three Objectives to be mastered by the students.

The order of the Objectives indicates the order in which the information relating to them will be found in the text.

Each section concludes with a "Check for Understanding" activity.

"Check for Understanding" always includes four questions. The first three relate directly to the Objectives and evaluate mastery of those goals.

The fourth question is not directly related to an objective. It is a "wild card" that tests knowledge of a specific point of information within the text.

Planning for the Future

When the Founding Fathers wrote the Constitution, there is no way that they could have imagined what life would be like 200 years later.

The Founding Fathers of our country faced a similar problem. Yet they wrote a living document. How could these people have written such a document without knowing what was to happen in the future?

It contains only important things

There are several reasons why the Constitution is a living document. Its authors were concerned only with things that were necessary to the process of establishing a strong democratic government. The structure of government and the law of the land were clearly defined. How the constitutional laws should be applied or the government administered were not included. For example, the Constitution gave Congress the control of trade between states. If it had limited the control to goods that traveled by oxen or by boat—the most common forms of transportation in the 1780's—the Constitution would have had to be changed each time a new means of transportation was invented.

It allows for change

In addition, the authors planned for the Constitution to be amended, or changed. Shortly after the Constitution was adopted, ten *amendments*, or additions, were attached to it. These ten amendments listed certain basic rights of people. They also prohibited the government from denying people these rights. The first ten amendments are called the Bill of Rights.

Methods of transportation have changed greatly from the time of the Constitution to the present day.

Check for Understanding: Now that you have completed this section, you should be able to answer these questions:

1. Why is it difficult to write a document that has to apply for many years in the future?
2. What are two reasons why the Constitution has remained effective?
3. What is the meaning of the term "amendment"?
4. Why is the Constitution referred to as a "living document"?

SUMMARY

The Constitution was written by a group often called the Founding Fathers. They faced a great many disagreements as to what should be in the document. The final Constitution consisted of the Preamble, the Articles, and the Amendments.

The Preamble introduces the Constitution. It defines the main premise of American democracy, that government's power comes from the power of the people.

The Articles establish a separation of power among the legislative, executive, and judicial branches. Each has powers that check and balance the others. Delegates to the Constitutional Convention argued about how states should be represented. A compromise was reached by establishing a Congress of two houses.

The Constitution is a living document. It establishes a framework and basic laws for our democratic government. But it leaves to each generation of Americans the task of applying the laws and administering the government which it has created. This quality has allowed the Constitution to meet the needs of people in different times. For this reason, we still have a strong democratic government in the United States.

The amendment process that is part of the Constitution allows new ideas and needed changes to be made peacefully. This provision for orderly change in the government has made the United States Constitution one of the greatest documents in the world.

Illustrations
(See Page T12)

We the People contains hundreds of illustrations in a variety of styles to support and complement the information in the text.

Subheadings present main ideas and help students develop valuable skimming skills.

Summary
(See Page T12)

Each chapter concludes with a summary that restates the important facts that were presented in the chapter.

Illustrations include both contemporary and historic subject matter, emphasizing that *We the People* deals with current issues in civics in relation to their historic context.

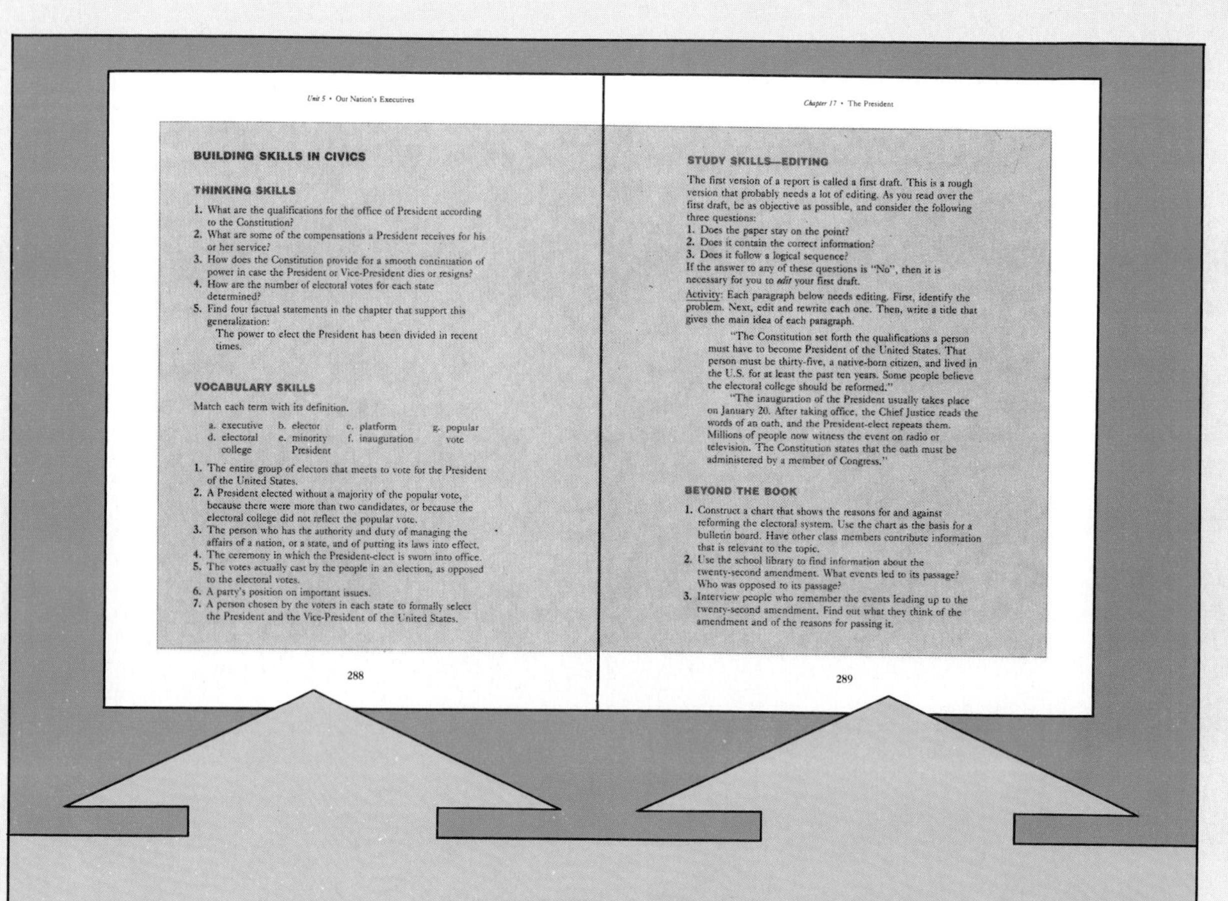

Unit 5 • Our Nation's Executives

BUILDING SKILLS IN CIVICS

THINKING SKILLS

1. What are the qualifications for the office of President according to the Constitution?
2. What are some of the compensations a President receives for his or her service?
3. How does the Constitution provide for a smooth continuation of power in case the President or Vice-President dies or resigns?
4. How are the number of electoral votes for each state determined?
5. Find four factual statements in the chapter that support this generalization:
   The power to elect the President has been divided in recent times.

VOCABULARY SKILLS

Match each term with its definition.

a. executive	b. elector	c. platform	g. popular vote
d. electoral college	e. minority President	f. inauguration	

1. The entire group of electors that meets to vote for the President of the United States.
2. A President elected without a majority of the popular vote, because there were more than two candidates, or because the electoral college did not reflect the popular vote.
3. The person who has the authority and duty of managing the affairs of a nation, or a state, and of putting its laws into effect.
4. The ceremony in which the President-elect is sworn into office.
5. The votes actually cast by the people in an election, as opposed to the electoral votes.
6. A party's position on important issues.
7. A person chosen by the voters in each state to formally select the President and the Vice-President of the United States.

288

Chapter 17 • The President

STUDY SKILLS—EDITING

The first version of a report is called a first draft. This is a rough version that probably needs a lot of editing. As you read over the first draft, be as objective as possible, and consider the following three questions:
1. Does the paper stay on the point?
2. Does it contain the correct information?
3. Does it follow a logical sequence?
If the answer to any of these questions is "No", then it is necessary for you to *edit* your first draft.

Activity: Each paragraph below needs editing. First, identify the problem. Next, edit and rewrite each one. Then, write a title that gives the main idea of each paragraph.

"The Constitution set forth the qualifications a person must have to become President of the United States. That person must be thirty-five, a native-born citizen, and lived in the U.S. for at least the past ten years. Some people believe the electoral college should be reformed."

"The inauguration of the President usually takes place on January 20. After taking office, the Chief Justice reads the words of an oath, and the President-elect repeats them. Millions of people now witness the event on radio or television. The Constitution states that the oath must be administered by a member of Congress."

BEYOND THE BOOK

1. Construct a chart that shows the reasons for and against reforming the electoral system. Use the chart as the basis for a bulletin board. Have other class members contribute information that is relevant to the topic.
2. Use the school library to find information about the twenty-second amendment. What events led to its passage? Who was opposed to its passage?
3. Interview people who remember the events leading up to the twenty-second amendment. Find out what they think of the amendment and of the reasons for passing it.

289

Building Skills In Civics
(See Pages T12-T13)

Each chapter concludes with a four-page activity section. These pages are set off by a colored tint to distinguish them from the text itself.

The first two pages of the activity section are entitled "Building Skills in Civics".

There are always four skill-building activities—two on the left-hand page and two on the right.

The "Thinking Skills" section reviews the important concepts of the chapter. The "Vocabulary Skills" section includes each of the vocabulary items that has been presented in the chapter.

"Study Skills" deals with a different social studies skill in each chapter. "Beyond the Book" is a special feature that enables students to use what they have learned to expand their citizenship awareness outside of the Civics course itself.

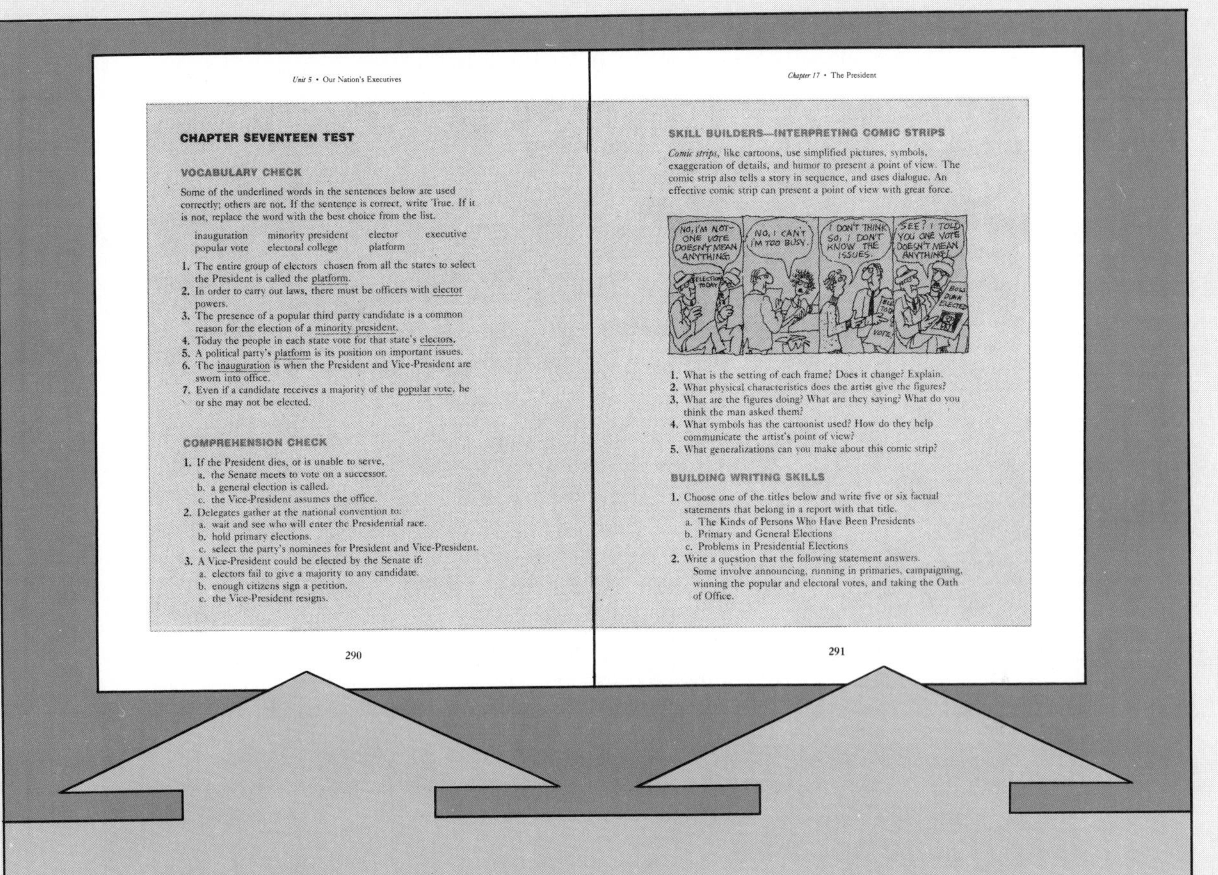

Unit 5 • Our Nation's Executives

CHAPTER SEVENTEEN TEST

VOCABULARY CHECK

Some of the underlined words in the sentences below are used correctly; others are not. If the sentence is correct, write True. If it is not, replace the word with the best choice from the list.

inauguration minority president elector executive
popular vote electoral college platform

1. The entire group of electors chosen from all the states to select the President is called the platform.
2. In order to carry out laws, there must be officers with elector powers.
3. The presence of a popular third party candidate is a common reason for the election of a minority president.
4. Today the people in each state vote for that state's electors.
5. A political party's platform is its position on important issues.
6. The inauguration is when the President and Vice-President are sworn into office.
7. Even if a candidate receives a majority of the popular vote, he or she may not be elected.

COMPREHENSION CHECK

1. If the President dies, or is unable to serve,
   a. the Senate meets to vote on a successor.
   b. a general election is called.
   c. the Vice-President assumes the office.
2. Delegates gather at the national convention to:
   a. wait and see who will enter the Presidential race.
   b. hold primary elections.
   c. select the party's nominees for President and Vice-President.
3. A Vice-President could be elected by the Senate if:
   a. electors fail to give a majority to any candidate.
   b. enough citizens sign a petition.
   c. the Vice-President resigns.

290

Chapter 17 • The President

SKILL BUILDERS—INTERPRETING COMIC STRIPS

Comic strips, like cartoons, use simplified pictures, symbols, exaggeration of details, and humor to present a point of view. The comic strip also tells a story in sequence, and uses dialogue. An effective comic strip can present a point of view with great force.

1. What is the setting of each frame? Does it change? Explain.
2. What physical characteristics does the artist give the figures?
3. What are the figures doing? What are they saying? What do you think the man asked them?
4. What symbols has the cartoonist used? How do they help communicate the artist's point of view?
5. What generalizations can you make about this comic strip?

BUILDING WRITING SKILLS

1. Choose one of the titles below and write five or six factual statements that belong in a report with that title.
   a. The Kinds of Persons Who Have Been Presidents
   b. Primary and General Elections
   c. Problems in Presidential Elections
2. Write a question that the following statement answers.
   Some involve announcing, running in primaries, campaigning, winning the popular and electoral votes, and taking the Oath of Office.

291

Chapter Test
(See Page T13)

The "Building Skills" section is followed by a two-page Chapter Test. There is also a Unit Test at the conclusion of each unit (not shown here).

The Chapter Test also includes four different activities, two per page.

The Vocabulary Check evaluates understanding of each of the Vocabulary items in the chapter. The Comprehension Check measures awareness of the key ideas in the chapter.

"Skill Builders" tests the ability to interpret a visual device, such as a map, chart, graph, photo, and so on. "Building Writing Skills" develops composition techniques within the context of Civics and also serves as an enrichment activity similar to the "Beyond the Book" section.

PREAMBLE

WE THE PEOPLE of the United States, in Order to form a more perfect Union, establish Justice, insure domestic Tranquility, provide for the common defence, promote the general Welfare, and secure the Blessings of Liberty to ourselves and our Posterity, do ordain and establish this Constitution for the United States of America.

ARTICLE I

THE LEGISLATIVE DEPARTMENT

SECTION 1. All legislative Powers herein granted shall be vested in a Congress of the United States, which shall consist of a Senate and House of Representatives.

[How the House of Representatives Is Formed]

SECTION 2. The House of Representatives shall be composed of Members chosen every second Year by the People of the several States, and the Electors in each State shall have the Qualifications requisite for Electors of the most numerous Branch of the State Legislature.

No Person shall be a Representative who shall not have attained to the Age of twenty five years, and been seven Years a Citizen of the United States, and who shall not, when elected, be an Inhabitant of that State in which he shall be chosen.

The Appendix
(See Page T13)

The Appendix includes the complete text of the Constitution, the Declaration of Independence, and other important documents in our history.

Susan B. Anthony (1820–1906): Here, in the Declaration of Independence, is the assertion of the natural right of all to the ballot; for how can "the consent of the governed" be given, if the right to vote be denied?

Ulysses S. Grant (1822–1885): I know no method to secure the repeal of bad or obnoxious laws so effective as their stringent execution.

Oliver Wendell Holmes, Jr. (1841–1935): If there is any principle of the Constitution that more imperatively calls for attachment than any other it is the principle of free thought—not free thought for those who agree with us but freedom for the thought that we hate.

Woodrow Wilson (1856–1924): The flag is the embodiment, not of sentiment, but of history. It represents the experiences made by men and women, the experiences of those who do and live under that flag.

Theodore Roosevelt (1858–1919): No man is above the law and no man is below it; nor do we ask any man's permission when we require him to obey it. Obedience to the law is demanded as a right, not asked as a favor.

Albert Einstein (1879–1955): My political ideal is democracy. Everyone should be respected as an individual, but no one isolated.

Franklin D. Roosevelt (1882–1945): The truth is found when men are free to pursue it.

Adlai Stevenson (1900–1965): The most American thing about America is the free common school system.

John F. Kennedy (1917–1963): And so, my fellow Americans, ask not what your country can do for you; ask what you can do for your country.

The Appendix also presents a variety of other information, such as a map of the U.S., tables on the Presidents and on the states, a chart of levels of government, and this unique "Thoughts on Free Government" section.

charter A document issued by the state government that sets the boundaries, governmental powers and functions, and method of finance of a city. [266]
checks and balances Limits of power placed on each of the executive, legislative, and judicial branches of the government by the other two branches. [303]
chief of state The President's role as the leader of the country. [301]
circuit court One of the courts presided over by a district judge. There is usually one in each county, each of which the district judge visits. [386]
citizenship The state of being a citizen, which provides certain rights and requires certain duties and responsibilities. [6]
city manager A person who is hired to run a city. [352]
civics The study of government and the rights and duties of citizens. [23]
civil case A suit between people, brought
compulsory Required or demanded by law. [472]
concurrent powers The powers held by both the states and the federal government. [129]
concurring opinion An opinion written by a Supreme Court justice who agrees with the majority in deciding a case, but who disagrees with the reasoning of their decision. [416]
confederation A national government in which states keep most of the power and give the central government only limited authority. [124]
congressional districts The areas into which states are divided according to population, each of which sends one representative to the house. [211]
conservative A person who prefers that government change society slowly or not at all. [181]
conserve To save, or use as little as possi-

The Glossary section includes all the vocabulary items presented in the text, along with definitions.

CHAPTER	STUDY SKILLS	VISUAL SKILLS
1	Using a Glossary	Graphs
2	Using Facts to Support Generalizations	Maps
3	Using an Index	Illustrations
4	Using Forms	Tables
5	Using Documents	Time Lines
6	Outlining	Charts
7	Using an Appendix	Time Charts
8	Using a Card Catalog	Maps
9	Outlining	Illustrations
10	Using an Encyclopedia	Graphs
11	Recognizing Techniques of Persuasion	Advertisements
12	Using the Newspaper	Illustrations
13	Topic Outlining	Illustrations
14	Using the Almanac	Flow Charts
15	Editing	Flow Charts
16	Making a Formal Outline	Atlases
17	Editing	Comic Strips
18	Making a Sentence Outline	Postage Stamps

The Civics skills presented in the Building Skills in Civics and Chapter Test Sections are listed here for reference.

HOW *WE THE PEOPLE* WORKS

The Cover

The artwork that is reproduced on the cover of *We the People* was chosen for this purpose because it is symbolic of two great strengths of the United States: our tradition of free government, as represented by the Presidents and other leaders who appear in the artwork, and the diversity of our society, as represented by the variety of materials that the artist used to compose the work.

The cover can be used to stimulate discussion about those two concepts of tradition and diversity, and also to lead in to an analysis of the contributions of the various people who are depicted.

The Unit Opener

Each unit begins with a one-page introduction consisting of an illustration and one or two paragraphs of text. Although the illustration always relates to the unit's theme, it is meant to be evocative rather than literal, and students can interpret it in various ways. Similarly, the text is intentionally brief and general, because its purpose is to promote discussion of the central ideas of the unit.

You might have students discuss the relationship between the unit title and illustration. Or, they could suggest other subjects that can be used to illustrate the same theme.

The Chapter-Opening Illustration

Like the unit illustrations, these are intended to evoke the theme of the text to come, rather than to provide an exact visual equivalent of the printed information on the page. For this reason, these illustrations do not have captions, although their content and purpose is explained in the teacher's annotations.

Chapter illustrations can be used in the same way as unit illustrations—students can speculate as why a particular subject was chosen, and also suggest alternative ways of illustrating the same idea.

The Original Document

The Constitution and other great documents appear in their actual wording, because we believe students should be exposed to the original source material. The Constitution, the Declaration of Independence, and other great documents are reproduced in their entirety in the Appendix, beginning on page 557.

The documents can form the basis for a class discussion. Students can also refer back to them as they proceed through the chapter itself to evaluate the relationship between the two elements.

The Chapter Introduction

Following the original document is a brief introduction to the chapter. This introduction is not a paraphrase or an interpretation of the document, but rather a general statement that, like the unit introduction, is meant to "set the stage" and provoke discussion of the themes of the chapter.

The "Focusing Ideas" Section

Each chapter-opening section concludes with a section entitled "Focusing Ideas." This section is a summary of the major points that will be presented in the chapter. It consists of a series of items set off by black circles (●). There are four (occasionally three or five) of these items; the number corresponds to the number of sections within the chapter. Students can comment on these Focusing Ideas, based on their previous knowledge, and they can suggest other central ideas that may apply to the chapter.

The Pre-Test

The Pre-Test opens the actual text of the chapter. It consists of three to five questions that correspond to the section headings within the chapter.

We do not expect students to be able to answer the Pre-Test questions precisely at this point; the questions are intended to focus their thinking on the themes of the chapter. However, you might want to have your students answer as best they can, based on their previous knowledge. They can then go back later and compare their preliminary answers with what they have learned in the chapter.

The Vocabulary List

The Vocabulary List includes the terms that are essential for an understanding of American government and citizenship. The number in parentheses after the word indicates the page on which the word is first presented in the text. Each chapter contains either seven or eight vocabulary items.

Students can discuss how the various words in a chapter relate to each other. They might also comment on what the selection of words for a chapter reveals about the content of the chapter.

The Objectives

A set of three objectives begins each section of the chapter. These objectives are specific and represent the major points covered in the section.

We do not intend that the students concentrate only on the information that fulfills the objectives, but we do recommend that you emphasize these points and ask students to watch for them as they read.

The "Check for Understanding" Section

This section serves as an internal test within the chapter; it appears at the end of each section. Because, as mentioned above, we don't intend that students should concentrate only on the three objectives, we have included a fourth "wild card" question that evaluates another concept, usually one that appears at the end of the section and that does not relate directly to the three objectives.

The Illustrations

In addition to the original paintings that introduce each unit and each chapter, illustrations also appear throughout the rest of the text. These illustrations are in three forms: photographs; cartoons; and charts, maps, or diagrams. Photographs are used to illuminate a specific point within the text. Cartoons are used to depict general principles—such as the duties of citizenship, the democratic process, and methods of political campaigning. Charts and the like are used for concepts that are best understood through a schematic presentation—levels of government, consumer spending, county administration, the federal court system, and so on.

There are many ways in which these illustrations can be used in the teaching process. They are the flexible elements in this book, as opposed to the more finite nature of the printed text. Students can discuss the content of an illustration, evaluate its subjective "message," suggest alternate illustrations for the same concept, create their own captions, and so on.

The Summary

Each chapter ends with a summary that recapitulates the preceding text. This can be used as a review, and students can also refer back to it at a later point to reinforce important concepts. It can also serve as preparation for the chapter-end activities that follow.

The "Building Skills" Section

Two pages of "Building Skills" activities follow each chapter summary in *We the People.* The four parts that make up this section are as follows:

THINKING SKILLS

Three to seven comprehension questions promote retention of the chapter content and provide opportunities to use this information. Each "Thinking Skills" section also contains at least one question asking students to either identify a generalization, determine a main idea, arrange a set of statements, or use various parts of the textbook.

VOCABULARY SKILLS

Four different kind of activities appear throughout the book to provide practice with key civics vocabulary:

- Given a list of terms and incomplete sentences, the student uses context clues to select the correct term for each sentence.
- Given an incomplete sentence and a choice of two or three terms to complete that sentence, the student uses context clues to select the appropriate term for the sentence.
- Given a sentence with an underlined term, the student decides if the sentence is true or false as written. If false, the student replaces the underlined term with the correct term from a given list of words.
- Given a list of terms and a list of definitions, the student matches the term with its correct definition.

STUDY SKILLS

An expository paragraph tells students how to utilize the different parts of their textbook or various media sources in order to locate, gather, organize, and communicate certain information. A complementary activity follows, asking students to use the information above to perform a particular task.

BEYOND THE BOOK

This section is composed of two to four questions that ask students to do one of the following:

- Construct or make a chart, graph, poster, map, bulletin board or other visual aid relating to a concept in civics.
- Use different sources of information in order to fulfill a particular objective.
- Collect or analyze a cartoon, article, editorial, chart, graph; or interview a resource person.

- Write an opinion paragraph, a letter to the editor, or a book report; give an oral report, participate in a debate, or dramatize an event.

The Chapter Test

Following the "Building Skills" section in each chapter of *We the People* is a two-page Chapter Test designed to provide students with an intensive review of text material, and to enable you to determine students' retention capabilities. The four parts of the Chapter Test are as follows:

VOCABULARY CHECK

Students further reinforce their knowledge of technical vocabulary by completing activity questions similar in nature to those found in the "Building Skills" vocabulary section.

COMPREHENSION CHECK

Several types of activities allow you to test students' retention and comprehension of factual material:

- Given a set of questions, each followed by an answer, the student determines if the question and answer match. If an incorrect answer is given, the student writes the correct answer to match the question.
- Given a series of multiple choice tasks, the student follows the directions in each task to select the correct answer.
- Given a series of statements, the student decides if they are true or false.
- Given several topics and a set of statements, the student matches each statement with its related topic.
- Given one topic and several statements, the student selects the statement(s) that pertain to the topic.

SKILL BUILDERS—INTERPRETING VISUALS

This part of the test asks students to use visual sources of data such as graphs, tables, cartoons, charts, illustrations, photos, and maps in order to gain information and complete tasks.

BUILDING WRITING SKILLS

The final portion of the test asks students to combine their writing and comprehension skills in order to complete these kinds of activities:

- The student writes a paragraph that explains, summarizes, compares, describes, fits a title, gives advantages or disadvantages, or reflects a personal opinion.
- Given a specific purpose and a set of sentences, the student selects and writes the sentences that enable him or her to meet the given purpose.
- Given a topic and a paragraph, the student edits the paragraph, eliminating irrelevant material.
- Given a topic, the student lists several sentences that match the topic.
- Given several pairs of words, the student selects one pair and writes sentences to explain the difference between the two terms.

The Unit Test

A one-page visual/verbal test appears on the last page of each unit in *We the People.* Each test features a visual such as a diagram, chart, graph, cartoon, painting, or map, and a set of related questions for the purpose of student interpretation. Subsequent questions ask students to write, create, speak, or think about a concept in civics.

Many of the unit test questions are conjectural in nature, asking students to express an opinion based on their acquired knowledge. As such, there may be quite a bit of variation in students' answers. You might wish to use students' varying responses as the basis for class discussion of student debate.

The Appendix

A list of the material presented in the 60-page Appendix appears in the Table of Contents of the Students' Edition. The Appendix contains many different kinds of information and can be used in a variety of ways. Students can employ it as a reference when they deal with portions of the text to which it is relevant, and also consult it independently for enrichment or for background information.

The Teachers' Annotations

You will find annotations on the majority of the Teacher's Edition text pages. They will facilitate your teaching of the course, as well as providing suggestions for extending the reach of given text materials. Annotations suggest questions to ask your students in order to clarify certain concepts that they may have trouble comprehending, and they point out significant details in the text that could conceivably be overlooked. Annotations with the heading *Issues in Civics* give you the opportunity to raise a question of a controversial or debatable nature that relates specifically to the material being studied.

SUGGESTIONS FOR TEACHING *WE THE PEOPLE*

Teaching begins with the assumption that students can learn. Working from that assumption, the teacher plans lessons and selects learning experiences for students. However, an activity that is appropriate for one student may be too difficult for another, and too easy for others.

As a teacher, you work with students who have different abilities, different predispositions for learning, and different rates of learning. To accommodate those individual differences, you need different kinds of learning activities. *We the People* is designed to meet that need. The activities in the text not only accommodate the students' individual learning needs and styles, but they also can be used to accelerate students' learning of content and building of skills.

Learning Styles

Contemporary research into the functions of the human brain has defined the predisposition of individuals for particular approaches to learning. Some individuals learn best by reading or writing or talking. Others learn best by doing something or making something or seeing what they are expected to understand. These differences present a challenge to the teacher who recognizes their existence. *We the People* promotes the presentation of different forms of information. The authors' goal is to help all students use verbal and visual forms of information with ease.

Thinking Skills

Complex thinking depends on an individual's recall and comprehension of information. Students must understand information before they can use it in new and creative ways. They need to develop thinking skills at different levels of cognition. *We the People* is written and organized to develop those skills, as well as a solid foundation of knowledge. The text has a comprehensive questioning strategy and activities that can be used to help students develop the following skills:

- Comparing and identifying similarities and differences.
- Changing information into different forms.
- Interpreting information.
- Perceiving relationships.
- Classifying information.
- Analyzing information.
- Identifying irrelevant items.
- Identifying sequence errors.
- Editing information.
- Identifying main ideas.
- Organizing information as needed.
- Transferring and applying knowledge to new situations.
- Selecting information.
- Citing evidence to support opinions and generalizations.
- Bringing together information that was gained in new and creative ways.

Teaching Controversial Issues

Controversial issues can evoke considerable learning if students discuss and examine the issues and their associated conflicting points of view. However, the students' exploration of issues can be productive only if they are encouraged and helped to seek and evaluate evidence concerning the issues. The evidence they collect must be clearly identified as either fact, opinion, or a combination of fact and opinion.

Guidelines are needed for selecting appropriate issues for discussion and exploration in class. When you select issues for your class, consider the following questions:

- Is the issue appropriate for Civics class?
- Do your students have the necessary content background?
- Does the issue help to reinforce and clarify the content that your class is currently learning?
- Is the issue significant to your students?
- Does the issue relate to their environment, needs, and current interests?
- Are your students able, at their maturity level, to comprehend that a conflict on the issue can exist?
- Can they identify the different viewpoints on the issue and understand them?
- Does your school library, the local library, or community agencies contain the necessary resources for the students' collection of evidence?
- Or, will *you* be your students' primary source of information?
- Can the available resources provide sufficiently different viewpoints?

Dealing with Controversial Issues

There are many different models for teaching controversial issues. Although the models differ in the number of teaching steps they use, they generally share the following key steps:

- Presenting the conflicts and issues.
- Defining the conflicts and issues.
- Identifying the different viewpoints.
- Collecting and examining evidence to support the differing viewpoints.
- Identifying additional relevant information.

Using Primary Sources

Social scientists learn about a society by studying primary sources of information. They examine documents, letters, artifacts, paintings, photographs, and posters. They probe the personal communication found in interviews and eyewitness accounts.

The same kind of primary sources are reproduced in *We the People*. With it, you can turn your students into young social scientists. You can help them to detect the ideas, events, and feelings that have created and are still shaping the American government.

Excerpts from great documents, such as the Constitution and the Declaration of Independence, introduce each chapter in *We the People*. Entire documents are printed in the Appendix of the book. Other written sources are within the chapters for your students to analyze and discuss. Through this experiental process, your students can gain a better understanding of our country's past and present. We hope that through this process they will become better equipped to manage the concerns and challenges of citizenship in the future.

Suggestions for Using Primary Sources

The degree of preparation needed for using a primary source depends on your student's familiarity with the subject matter and on their reading abilities. Such preparation can include the following:

- Identifying the source to be used and its origin.
- Studying background information to mentally set the stage for the historic time and social concerns that existed when the source was created.
- Examining and analyzing the usage of language in the source that may be unfamiliar to your students.
- Developing the students' understanding of the specialized vocabulary contained in the source.
- Identifying questions that can be answered with this source.

The Value of Practice

Without one critical attribute—the learner's intent—practice cannot succeed. The learner must intend to do something better, faster, easier, or better—and to improve. Without this intent, the individual is merely doing something again and again. The gains of this repetition, if any, will be minimal.

On the other hand, when practice sessions are well-planned and the students' intent has been enlisted, practice sessions can result in improvement. The planning and analyzing of an effective practice session can be guided by the following questions.

What Needs to be Practiced?

Students often have limited incentive to practice. For that reason, they should be taught to analyze what they need to practice. Here are two examples of such analysis:

- As students review or prepare for tests or discussions, they can use the questions within the chapters to determine what they need to practice (reread and review).
- When students plan to practice vocabulary, they should first classify the words according to how well they know them. They could divide the words into these three groups:

  1. Words I Know Well
  2. Words I'm Hesitant About
  3. Words I Don't Know

Intensive practice could be devoted to only the last two categories. Students should know that the second category, "Words I'm Hesitant About," would be easier for them to learn than the third. As practice continues, each student can reclassify vocabulary words.

How Much Can Be Practiced?

The amount of content that is practiced must be enough to be meaningful and yet it should not overwhelm the learner. Content should be divided into segments that allow the learner to practice productively. In addition, a plan is needed for the sequence or priority of those practice segments. What must be learned first, in order for the next segment to be understood?

How Long and How Often Should Students Practice?

Short, frequent practice sessions pay the highest dividends for a student working on new learning. As practice continues, the time between sessions can bė slowly increased, and the student will still retain the learning.

The length of a practice session is directly influenced by the content requirements, the immediate purpose for practice, the availability of resources, and the time required to set up the practice session. If your students are going to retain the content they have practiced and learned, they will need to regularly review that content.

Questioning Strategy

There are questions within the student's text and in the teacher's annotations that can be used in the continuous evaluation of your student's learning.

Questions can be found at the end of each section of content within the chapter. These questions can be used by your students to check their own learning of content. When students are hesitant and unsure in answering a question they can reread that content section for help. This regimentation of learning keeps the students from being overwhelmed by trying to locate content within the total chapter. The questions help the students to determine whether to continue into the next section or to review and reread the current section.

The Comprehension Check and Vocabulary Check activities at the end of each chapter provide practice and another measurement tool for student self-checking and for teacher use.

You can maintain a continuous check on your students' progress by using these questions and the ones in the teacher's annotations. During oral discussions, the questions provide a focus for students to demonstrate their present knowledge. The questions also are a valuable aid for determining the content areas that need additional teacher guidance and instruction.

Writing Skills

At the end of each chapter is a section called "Building Writing Skills." Such writing tasks can help students to learn the content and to give evidence of their learning.

Traditionally, teachers have used writing and essay questions as an important evaluative tool. In the process of writing, students reveal the following:

- How they are forming relationships among bits of information.
- Their processing and organization of information.
- How they can apply the information they have acquired to meet the specific demands and requirements of a given task.

Evaluation

Activities and tests in *We the People* are both related and transferable to formal standardized testing situations. For example, tasks require the following skills:

- The recalling of information.
- The use of a multiple choice format.
- The analysis of written content.
- The identification of main ideas.
- The analysis and interpretation of graphics.
- The recognizing of relationships.
- The selection of data to meet a specific purpose.
- The following of directions.
- The comprehension and application of specialized vocabulary.

BIBLIOGRAPHY

Unit One

Acheson, Patricia C. *Our Federal Government: How It Works.* Dodd, Mead

Asimov, Isaac. *Our Federal Union.* Houghton Mifflin

Barber, James. *Citizen Politics: An Introduction to Political Behavior.* Markham

Beaty, Patricia. *Lupita Manana.* Morrow

Bentley, Judity. *American Immigration Today: Pressures, Problems, Policies.* Messner

Black, Max. *Critical Thinking: An Introduction to Logic and the Scientific Method.* Prentice-Hall

Butts, R. Freeman. *The Revival of Civic Learning.* Phi Beta Kappa Educational Foundation

Cavanagh, Frances (Ed.). *We Came to America.* Macrae Smith Co.

Eaton, Jeanette. *Gandhi: Fighter Without a Sword.* Morrow.

Garver, Susan, and McGuire, Paula. *Coming to North America: From Mexico, Cuba, and Puerto Rico.* Delacorte

Hartmann, Edward G. *The Movement to Americanize the Immigrant.* AMS Press

Howe, Irving. *World of Our Fathers.* Harcourt Brace Jovanovich

Huxley, Aldous. *Brave New World.* Harper & Row.

Kennedy, John F. *A Nation of Immigrants.* Harper & Row

Lerner, Max. *America As a Civilization: Life and Thought in the United States Today.* Simon & Schuster

Massie, Robert K. *Nicholas and Alexandra.* Atheneum

Marzio, Peter (Ed.) *A Nation of Nations.* Harper & Row

Raskin, Joseph and Raskin, Edith. *The Newcomers: Ten Tales of American Immigrants.* Lothrop

Ross, George E. *Know Your U.S.A.* Rand Mc-Nally

Ruchlis, Hy. *Clear Thinking.* Harper & Row

Shaver, James P. (Ed.) *Building Rationales for Citizenship Education.* National Council for the Social Studies

Vincent, William S. *Roles of the Citizen: Principles and Practices.* Harper & Row

Wade, Richard (Ed.) *Life in America Series.* Houghton Mifflin

Weiss, Ann E. *We Will Be Heard: Dissent in the United States.* Messner

Unit Two

Acheson, Patricia C. *Our Federal Government: How It Works.* Dodd, Mead

Adrian, Charles R. *State and Local Government.* McGraw-Hill

Bates, Elizabeth B. *The Making of the Constitution.* Viking Press

Becker, Carl. *The Declaration of Independence: A Study in the History of Political Ideas.* Random House

Bowen, Catherine D. *Miracle at Philadelphia: The Story of the Constitutional Convention, May to September 1787.* Little, Brown

Boyce, Burke. *Man from Mt. Vernon.* Harper & Row

Brant, Irving. *The Bill of Rights: Its Origin and Meaning.* Mentor

Cooke, Donald E. *America's Great Document—The Constitution.* Hammond

Davis, Burke. *Heroes of the American Revolution.* Random House

Dos Passos, John. *The Men Who Made the Nation.* Doubleday

Fast, Howard. *Citizen Tom Paine.* Random House

Ferguson, John H., and McHenry, Dean E. *Elements of American Government.* McGraw-Hill

Fesler, James W. (Ed.) *The Fifty States and Their Local Government.* Knopf

Kohn, Bernice. *The Spirit & the Letter.* Viking Press

Liston, Robert A. *Defense Against Tyranny: The Balance of Power in Government.* Messner

Padover, Saul. *The Living U.S. Constitution.* New American Library

Wade, Richard C. (Ed.) *Life in America Series.* Houghton Mifflin

Warren, Roland L. *Studying Your Community.* Macmillan

Unit Three

Barber, James. *Citizen Politics: An Introduction to Political Behavior.* Markham

Binkley, Wilfred. *American Political Parties: Their Natural History.* Knopf

Campbell, Angus. *The American Voter.* Wiley

Key, Vladamir O. *Politics, Parties, and Pressure Groups.* Crowell

McGinness, Joe. *The Selling of the President 1968.* Trident.

Murphy, William, and Schnier, Edward. *Vote Power.* Doubleday

Neal, Henry Edward. *Diary of Democracy: The Story of Political Parties in America.* Messner

Neuberger, Richard. *Adventures in Politics: We Go to the Legislature.* Oxford

Patrick, J. J., and Glenn, A.D. *The Young Voter: A Guide to Instruction About Voter Behavior and Elections.* National Council for the Social Studies.

Perry, James M. *The New Politics.*

Practical Political Action: A Guide for Young Citizens. Houghton Mifflin

Ribicoff, A. and Newman, J.O. *Politics: The American Way.* Allyn & Bacon

Stone, Irving. *They Also Ran.* New American Library.

Unit Four

Askell, Bernard. *The Senate Nobody Knows.* Doubleday

Berman, Daniel M. *A Bill Becomes a Law: Congress Enacts Civil Rights Legislation.* Macmillan

De Grazia, Alfred (Ed.) *Congress: The First Branch of Government.* American Enterprise

Drury, Allen. *Advise and Consent.* Doubleday

Egger, R., and Harris, J. *The President and Congress.* McGraw-Hill

Green, Mark J.; Fallows, James M.; and Zwick, David R. *Who Runs Congress?* Bantam

Griffith, Ernest. *Congress: Its Contemporary Role.* NYU

Kennedy, John F. *Profiles in Courage.* Harper & Row

League of Women Voters. *The Federalist Papers Reexamined. Perspectives on Congress: Performance and Prospects.* Washington, DC

Liston, Robert. *We the People? Congressional Power.* McGraw-Hill

Percy, Charles. *I Want to Know About the United States Senate.* Doubleday

Polsby, Nelson. *Congress and the Presidency.* Prentice-Hall

Ralph Nader Congress Project. *Ruling Congress: How the House and Senate Rules Govern the Legislative Process.* Penguin

Switzer, Ellen. *There Ought to Be a Law: How Laws Are Made and Work.* Atheneum

Wright, Jim. *You and Your Congressman.* Coward, McCann and Geoghegan.

Unit Five

Bassett, Margaret. *Profiles and Portraits of American Presidents.* Bond Wheelwright

Binkley, Wilfred. *The Powers of the President: Problems of American Democracy.* Russell

Comay, Joan. *The UN in Action.* Macmillan

Corwin, Ernest. *Presidential Power and the Constitution.* Cornell

Coy, Harold. *First Book of Presidents.* Watts

Davis, James W. *National Party Conventions: Nominating Presidential Candidates.* Barron's

Durant, John and Alice. *Pictorial History of American Presidents.* A.S. Barnes & Co.

Durbin, Louise. *Inaugural Cavalcade.* Dodd, Mead

Egger, R., and Harris, J. *The President and Congress.* McGraw-Hill

Fincher, Ernest. *The Presidency: An American Invention.* Abelard-Schuman

Fincher, Ernest B. *The President of the United States.* Abelard-Schuman

Friendly, Henry J. *The Federal Administrative Agencies.* Harvard

Hoopes, Roy. *The Changing Vice-Presidency.* Crowell

Johnson, Gerald W. *The Cabinet.* Morrow

Johnson, Gerald W. *The Presidency.* Morrow

Kennedy, Robert F. *Thirteen Days.* Norton.

Michener, James A. *Presidential Lottery: The Reckless Gamble In Our Electoral System.* Random House

Neustadt, Richard. *Presidential Power: The Politics of Leadership with Reflections on Johnson and Nixon.* Wiley

Neuberger, Richard L. *Adventures in Politics.* Oxford

Polsby, Nelson. *Congress and the Presidency.* Prentice-Hall

Truman, Margaret. *Harry S. Truman.* Morrow

Weingast, David. *We Elect a President.* Messner

White, Theodore. *The Making of the President.* Bantam

Woodward, Bob, and Bernstein, Carl. *All the President's Men.* Simon & Schuster

Unit Six

Brindze, Ruth. *All About Courts and the Law.* Random House

Cox, Archibald. *The Role of the Supreme Court in American Government.* Oxford

Crabtree, A.P. *You and the Law.* Holt, Rinehart & Winston

Dorman, Michale. *Under Twenty-One: A Young People's Guide to Legal Rights.* Dell

Ernst, Morris L., and Schwartz, Alan U. *Lawyers and What They Do.* Watts.

Garraty, John A. (Ed.). *Quarrels that Have Shaped the Constitution.* Harper & Row.

Hanna, John Paul. *Teenagers and the Law.* Ginn

Hentoff, Nat. *The First Freedom: The Tumultuous History of Free Speech in America.* Dell

Johnson, Gerald W. *The Supreme Court.* Morrow.

Judson, Clara Ingram. *Mr. Justice Holmes. Follett*

League of Women Voters. *Federalist Papers Reexamined. The Growth of Judicial Power: Perspectives on the "Least Dangerous Branch".* Washington, DC

Lewis, Anthony. *Gideon's Trumpet.* Random House

Paulsen, M.G. *Equal Justice for the Poor Man.* Public Affairs Committee

Peterson, Helen S. *The Supreme Court in America's Story.* Garrard
Richards, Kenneth. *Story of the Supreme Court.* Childrens Press
Rosengart, Oliver. *The Rights of Suspects.* Dutton

Unit Seven

Beyer, B.K. and Penna, A.N. *Concepts in the Social Studies.* National Council for the Social Studies
Billington, Elizabeth T. *Understanding Ecology.* Warne
Carson, Rachel. *Silent Spring.* Houghton Mifflin
Congressional Reports, Editorial Research Reports, *Earth, Energy, and Environment.* Congressional Reports, Inc.
Earle, Alice. *Child Life in Colonial Days.* Macmillan
Elliott, Sarah M. *Our Dirty Air.* Messner
Halacy, D.S. *Fabulous Fireball: The Story of Solar Energy.* Macmillan
Hungerford, Harold R. *Ecology: The Circle of Life.* Childrens Press
Linquist, Harry (Ed.) *Education: Readings in the Process of Cultural Transmission.* Houghton Mifflin
Roosevelt, Eleanor. *You Learn By Living.* Harper & Row
Rondiere, Pierre. *Purity or Pollution: The Struggle for Water.* Watts
Rosenzweig, Linda W. (Ed.) *Developmental Perspectives on the Social Studies.* National Council for the Social Studies
Udall, Stewart. *The Quiet Crisis.* Holt Rinehart & Winston
Wade, Richard C. (Ed.) *Life in America Series.* Houghton Mifflin
Wynn, Richard, et al. *American Education.* McGraw-Hill

Unit Eight

Campbell, Persia. *The Consumer Interest: A Study in Consumer Economics.* (Social Problems and Social Policy Series). Arno
Faulkner, Harold U. *American Economic History.* Harper & Row
Gay, Kathlyn. *Be a Smart Shopper.* Messner
Park, Maud Wood. *Front Door Lobby.* Beacon
Grambs, Jean (Ed.) *Teaching About Women in the Social Studies.* National Council for the Social Studies
Hacker, Louis. *The Triumph of American Capitalism.* Columbia University Press
Malabre, Alfred, Jr. *Understanding the Economy: For People Who Can't Stand Economics.* New American Library.
McGough, Elizabeth. *Dollars & Sense.* Morrow
Meltzer, Milton. *Bread and Roses.* Random House
Roll, Eric. *A History of American Thought.* Irwin

LIST OF PUBLISHERS

Allyn & Bacon, Inc.
470 Atlantic Avenue
Boston, MA 02210

Atheneum Publishers
597 Fifth Ave.
New York, New York 10017

Delacorte Press
Div. of Dell Publishing Co. Inc.
One Dag Hammarskjold Plaza
New York, New York 10017

Doubleday & Co. Inc.
245 Park Ave.
New York, New York 10167

Harcourt Brace Jovanovich, Inc.
757 Third Avenue
New York, New York 10017

Holt, Rinehart, & Winston
CBS Educational & Professional Publishing
383 Madison Ave.
New York, New York 10017

Houghton Mifflin Co.
One Beacon St.
Boston, MA 02107

Macmillan Publishing Co., Inc.
866 Third Ave.
New York, New York 10022

McGraw-Hill, Inc.
1221 Ave. of the Americas
New York, New York 10020

William Morrow & Co.
105 Madison Ave.
New York, New York 10016

Penguin Books
Div. of Viking Penguin, Inc.
625 Madison Ave.
New York, New York 10016

Random House, Inc.
201 E. 50th St.
New York, New York 10022

Simon & Schuster, Inc.
1230 Ave. of the Americas
New York, New York 10020

Rand McNally & Co.
8255 Central Park Ave.
Skokie, Ill. 60076

SUGGESTED SOURCES FOR FURTHER STUDY

American's Creed
Articles of Confederation
Bill of Rights
Common Sense—Thomas Paine
Cross of Gold—William Jennings Bryan
Declaration of Independence
Emancipation Proclamation
English Bill of Rights
Federalist Papers
Fundamental Orders of Connecticut
Lincoln's Gettysburg Address
Magna Carta
Marbury vs. Madison
Maryland Act Concerning Religious Toleration
Mayflower Contract
Monroe Doctrine
Nathan Hale's Speech
Patrick Henry's Speech
Pledge of Allegiance
Star Spangled Banner
United States Constitution
Washington's Farewell Address

The complete text of the following documents is found within the pages of *We The People:*

	Page
Bill of Rights	575–576
Declaration of Independence	560–563
Emancipation Proclamation	585–586
Lincoln's Gettysburg Address	585
Mayflower Compact	584
Monroe Doctrine	584
Pledge of Allegiance	4
United States Constitution	565–583

The great documents that have shaped our nation's history provide the framework for the bulk of the material in this Civics book. Each chapter in *We The People* opens with a quote from the Constitution or another great document or address from our country's past, followed by a brief explanation of the document and its relation to the upcoming text.

The eight documents listed above are found in their entirety within the text and are also excerpted and quoted from at various points throughout the book. For example, the complete text of the Declaration of Independence is found on pages 560–563, but excerpts, quotes, and related art can also be found on pages 18, 31, 36, 74, 82, etc. The periodic mention of these documents throughout the text enables the student to see the relationship between the historical writing itself and its application to our present-day social and governmental system.

The Teacher's Annotations will help you in your teaching of the documents by serving as a valuable cross-referencing tool. They refer you from the text of a particular document in the Appendix to a pertinent explanation or excerpt in the chapter and vice-versa. The *We The People* program is based on the notable writings and addresses of our country's great historical figures in much the same way that our American way of government is based on these doctrines.

ANSWER KEY

This Answer Key provides a correct answer for every question that appears in the text, either in the activities within the chapter itself or in the "Building Skills in Civics" and "Chapter Test" sections at the end of each chapter. Answers to the Unit Tests also appear here.

In the case of activities that permit a variety of responses, the notation "Answers will vary" appears, along with at least one suggested response. Separate answers to the Chapter Pre-Test are not provided because these questions are answered by the "Focusing Ideas" statements at the beginning of the chapter.

The answers to the questions in the separate Test Book and in the Activity Book appear as Teacher's Annotations on the actual pages of those materials.

CHAPTER ONE: What Does it Mean to Be a Citizen? (p. 6) 1. A citizen is a person who lives in a particular country and gives his or her loyalty or allegiance to that country. 2. The Constitution pledges to protect the liberty of its citizens and to give them certain rights. 3. If the citizens did not accept their responsibilities, the nation could not function. 4. The United States government is a republic. **Who Were the Early Settlers of America? (p. 7)** 1. The Indians, Blacks, Spanish, French and English were the major early settlers. 2. The English colonies became dominant. 3. The Indians helped the early settlers to survive; Blacks contributed significantly to developing America; the Spanish built missions, cattle ranches and farms; the French contributed the Creole language and customs found in Louisiana; our official language, the law and our government came from the English. 4. They were brought here as slaves to work on the large Southern plantations. **What Were the Major Immigration Movements? (p. 9)** 1. In 1790 there were English, German, Dutch, French, Spanish, Swedish, Black and Native Americans. 2. The four major periods of immigration were from 1815 to 1860, 1865 to 1890, 1890 to 1924, and from World War II to the present. 3. English and German; northern Europeans; eastern and southern Europeans, Jews, Italians, people of Romania, Greece, Turkey, Albania, and Syria, Japanese, Filipinos, East Indians and Mexicans; refugees from Hungary, Cuba, Indochina and Haiti. 4. Congress passed laws from 1880 through the 1950's limiting the number of people who could enter the country, as well as the Immigration and Nationality Act of 1965 setting the yearly number of immigrants at 290,000. **How Do People Become Citizens? (p. 12)** 1. A citizen is a person born in this country or in a foreign country to parents who are U.S. citizens or who has been granted citizenship through the process of naturalization. 2. The only way to lose citizenship is to give it up by choice or have it taken away because of treason. 3. Give the court information about themselves and their families; show they can speak, read, and write English; bring two citizens to testify that they are honest; show they know something about U.S. history; understand our form of government. 4. Two values are the right to have rights in a particular country and to have those rights protected when in a foreign country.

Thinking Skills (p. 14) 1. By birth or naturalization. 2. Our official language, the law, and our form of government. 3. To regulate the flow of immigrants to the United States. 4. c. 5. b. **Vocabulary Skills (p. 14):** 1. True 2. True 3. allegiance. 4. Government. 5. republic. 6. True. 7. alien. 8. citizenship. **Study Skills—Using the Glossary (p. 15):** Answers will vary. *Suggestion:* immigrant. Both books give definitions of words. The dictionary gives many definitions for each word and the glossary gives the meaning as used in the text. Use the glossary to help you understand what you read in the book. Use the dictionary to help you choose how to use a word in a report. **Beyond The Book (p. 15):** Independent Projects. **Vocabulary Check (p. 16):** 1. allegiance 2. republic 3. government 4. aliens 5. citizenship 6. naturalization 7. treason 8. immigrants **Comprehension Check (p. 16):** 1. True 2. True 3. Freedom and opportunity and as refugees from oppression at home 4. True 5. A person may give up his or her citizenship by choice or by conviction for a serious crime. **Skill Builders—Graphs (p. 17):** 1. The graph illustrates the ethnic makeup of the U.S. population. 2. They clearly show the differences in numbers of each group of immigrants. 3. What country was the largest number of immigrants from? What country had the fewest? Does this graph show all the immigrants that came here during this period of time? 4. The graph shows the ethnic breakdown of the U.S. population around 1790. It is a circle graph, not a bar graph, and shows the population makeup for a different period. **Building Writing Skills (p. 17):** Answers will vary. *Suggestion:* 1a. Citizenship is gained by birth or by naturalization. A child born here or in another country to parents who are citizens of the U.S. are citizens by birth. An alien can become a citizen through naturalization by fulfilling certain requirements. Citizenship in a country grants the right to have rights in that country.

CHAPTER TWO: Why Is Government Necessary? (p. 24) 1. To provide protection, make rules for cooperative living and provide things the people cannot get for themselves. 2. When the laws are obeyed, officials are free to provide the common benefits of an organized society. 3. Rules for teamwork tell each person what he or she can and cannot do so that all are better off. 4. Another person, or society itself, might be harmed. **How Are All Governments Alike? (p. 26)** 1. Sovereignty, control of a particular land area or territory, and a national identity. 2. The state would not exist. 3. Common language, shared beliefs or ideals, and common customs or traditions. 4. National songs, a flag, a coat of arms, etc. **How Are Governments Different? (p. 28)** 1. In a direct democracy people meet and make their own laws; in a republic, representatives are elected. 2. Total power is in the hands of one person or one group of people in a totalitarian state. 3. By looking at the opposition party, if there is one. 4. To prevent their power being taken from them. **What Is Free Self-Government? (p. 31)** 1. Self government allows people to have a real choice in selecting their officials. 2. Government cannot take inherent rights away from people, so the people must govern themselves. 3. Elections provide leaders who are concerned with the rights and liberties of the people. 4. So that one party will not take all the power for itself.

Thinking Skills (p. 32): Answers will vary. *Suggestion:* 1. Governments provide protection, establish rules of teamwork, and provide common benefits. 2. A nation. 3. Democracy, republic, totalitarian, monarchy, constitutional monarchy, dictatorship. 4. a. **Vocabulary Skills (p. 32):** 1. civics 2. law 3. officer 4. totalitarian 5. democracy 6. monarchy 7. inherent right 8. dictatorship. **Study Skills—Using Facts To Support Generalizations (p. 33):** a, d, e. **Beyond The Book (p. 33):** Independent Projects. **Vocabulary Check (p. 34):** 1. True. 2. dictatorship 3. True. 4. True. 5. totalitarian 6. civics 7. monarchy 8. democracy **Comprehension Check (p. 34):** 1. c. 2. a. 3. b. **Skill Builders—Interpreting Maps (p. 35):** 1. The boundaries and size of its territory. 2. a. It's a map of the U.S. showing international boundaries, and state boundaries; it outlines the original thirteen states, shows state capitals and Washington, D.C., and has a scale of 150 miles to an inch. c. Texas is in the bottom center of the map bounded by New Mexico to the west, Oklahoma to the north, Arkansas and Louisiana to the east, and Mexico to the south. d. The states vary greatly in physical size. Questions will vary. **Building Writing Skills (p. 35):** Answers will vary. *Suggestions:* 1. In a democracy the officials are elected representatives of the people. 2. So that no one official or group of officials can concentrate too much power. 3. Because these services are expensive and are part of the common welfare. 4. This is a concise definition of democracy.

CHAPTER THREE: Who Are the People That Make Up Our Society? (p. 42) 1. Diversity in our nation protects the rights of individuals and minorities. 2. Italy, England, Germany, Mexico, and Poland. 3. Santa Fe, Los Angeles, New Orleans, and St. Louis. 4. Each ethnic group stands alone but together they make a whole. **Why Do Conflicts Arise? (p. 43)** 1. Living in a crowded area with people of differing customs; ways of earning a living and differences in living standards; and differences of opinion. 2. Intolerance, spoken conflict, and war. 3. It might threaten the unity of a nation. 4. It provides for progress because people can support what they believe to be right. **How Can We Compromise in Order To Keep Our Republic? (p. 47)** 1. Majority rule operates through the democratic process of respect for all involved. 2. To dissent or disagree with existing policies and thus modify or change government. 3. Differences are settled in a way that each side gives up something so that a middle-of-the-road solution is reached. 4. If too much power is given to the organized majority.

Thinking Skills (p. 48): 1. Because people of so many different ethnic groups live here in one country. "Salad bowl" emphasizes the uniqueness and individuality of each group that has not been lost. 2. Living closely together, different standards of living, different ways of earning a living, different opinions on national issues. 3. Rule according to the will of the majority of the people. 4. Answers will vary. 5. b. **Vocabulary Skills (p. 48):** 1. ethnic group 2. self government 3. modify 4. tolerance 5. compromise 6. minority 7. dissent. **Study Skills—Using The Index (p. 49):** 1. Democratic party. Political parties. 2. See index - Power, 23. 3. Italics is an illustration. Boldface is a vocabulary word. 4. To look up information on a subject for a report. **Beyond The Book (p. 49):** 1. a. Our population is a combination of many different cultures living together as one united nation. 2. Answers will vary. *Suggestions:* We trust in God. Liberty is very important. We honor our first President. The eagle symbolizes strength and courage. 3. Answers will vary. *Suggestions:* A small replica of our flag, the Declaration of Independence, the seal of the United States, a picture of Congress in session, a picture of the Justices of the Supreme Court, and of a President. **Vocabulary Check (p. 50):** 1. minority 2. dissent 3. compromise 4. tolerance 5. self government 6. modify 7. ethnic group **Comprehension Check (p. 50):** "Cause of Conflict" a, d, e, i, j, "Compromise" b, c, f, g, h **Skill Builders—Interpreting Illustrations (p. 51):** Answers will vary. *Suggestions:* 1. Twenty-six. 2. "The Issues": a. Re-zone or keep the town as it is. b. How re-zoning will affect senior citizens, small businessmen, conservation, farming. "The Events": a. debate and campaigning. b. voting. "The Results": The majority vote settles the issue. 3. The picture should show how a congressional representative is elected: how he files, his campaign techniques, issues involved, who is affected, voters voting, representative accepting victory. **Building Writing Skills (p. 51):** 1. Tolerance allows for differences in opinion, custom, habits, values, goals, lifestyles. Prejudice is a narrow-minded view of how things ought to be and how other people ought to act. 2. Answers will vary. 3. Answers will vary. *Suggestions:* Neighbors, classmates, TV, movies, books, magazines, theater, music, newspaper articles, architecture, clothes, food, sports figures, actors and actresses. Reports will vary.

CHAPTER FOUR: What Are The Duties of Citizenship? (p. 57) 1. Obey the laws; serve on a jury; defend our nation; pay taxes; receive an education; use resources carefully. 2. Education, law enforcement, and national defense. 3. It is the foundation of self government. 4. It prepares one to vote and make good decisions. **What Are the Responsibilities of Citizenship? (p. 61)** 1. Voting, accepting public office, being aware of governmental activities, supporting elected officials, being informed about public officials. 2. So that our freedoms are not lost. 3. One cannot be punished for failure to act on responsibilities as one can for neglecting a duty. 4. They can take over government and use it for their own interests. **How Do We Think as Responsible Citizens? (p. 67)** 1. Define the issue; state the facts; identify statements of opinion as opposed to statements of fact; avoid the use of prejudice, support claims with facts; recognize propaganda in your own statements and in those of others. 2. It may help or hurt an institution, person or cause by persuading people to accept an idea. 3. An editor's opinion on a certain issue or problem. 4. You discover what is opinion and what is fact in the articles.

Thinking Skills (p. 68): 1. So they can be responsible in their behavior and act in ways that insure the continuance of our freedoms and our way of life. 2. An opinion is what a person thinks is true but cannot prove. A fact is something that has been proven to be true. Answers will vary. 3. Answers will vary. *Suggestion:* Avoid the use of prejudice. It is often difficult to admit we are prejudiced in some area. We may not even be aware that we are. 4. "Duties" g, a, j, e, b, c. "Responsibilities" d, f, k, h, i. **Vocabulary Skills (p. 68):** 1. duty 2. True 3. True 4. True 5. public opinion 6. True 7. True **Study Skills—Using Forms (p. 69):** 1. Perjury is punishable by imprisonment in a state prison. 2. Name, residence and mailing addresses, date of birth, occupation. 3. Which party to choose. 4. Anyone 18 or over. 5. Request it from the County registrar of voters. **Beyond The Book (p. 69):** 1. Independent Projects. 2. a. Income from all sources, number of dependents, deductions, adjustments to income, taxes paid, addresses, social security number. You need to be able to organize your information, relate facts, and add and subtract. b. A W-2 form is a statement of wages earned and taxes paid by an employee provided by an employer for income tax purposes. **Vocabulary Check (p. 70):** 1. propaganda 2. duty 3. responsibilities 4. political machine 5. public opinion 6. rights 7. taxes **Comprehension Check (p. 70):** 1. True 2. True 3. Failure to act on our duties is punishable by law. It is up to each of us to carry out our responsibilities. 4. So we are not misled by what we read or hear. 5. True **Skill Builders—Interpreting Tables (p. 71):** 1. The table that compares prices. 2. The taxation table. 1. They compare costs or taxes in the present with those of the past. 2. Table A shows the growing costs of food every ten years. Table B shows tax increases for ten year periods. 3. 1960 - 20.3¢/unit; 1982 - 45¢/unit. 20¢/unit more. 4. The line will continue straight up. 5. Table A illustrates inflation; Table B shows tax increases. 6. They present factual information rather than opinion. Activity: Tables present factual information in an organized form that makes comparison and conclusions easier. **Building Writing Skills (p. 71):** 1. Answers will vary. 2. Answers will vary. *Suggestion:* Paying taxes is a very important duty. We have asked our government for a lot of goods and services and we must pay for them. The only way government can function is through tax revenue. 3. Answers will vary.

UNIT ONE TEST

A. 1. Civic irresponsibility. He broke a law.
   2. It shows how teamwork is a part of citizenship.
   3. Answers will vary. *Suggestion:* Yes, people remember things that make them laugh. *or* No, serious subjects shouldn't be treated lightly.
   4. Answers will vary.
   5. Answers will vary. *Suggestions:* Yes, people pay attention to humor. *or* No, it's not a funny subject.

B. Answers will vary.

C. Answers will vary.

Chapter Five: What Does European History Tell us About Free Government? (p. 78) 1. Athens, Greece and Europe. 2. Courts shall be held in fixed places, justice shall not be sold; free men accused of a crime shall be tried by their equals, not by the king's judges; taxes shall not be levied except by consent of those taxed. 3. They ensure that people will not forget about what has been agreed upon and will continue to live by these agreements. 4. The oldest son or daughter or a close relative became king or queen. **How Did English Ideas About Freedom Influence the United States? (p. 80)** 1. The rights of self government that were guaranteed in England. 2. The Mayflower Compact. 3. An elected assembly of representatives of the people. 4. The House of Burgesses. **How Did the Colonists Object to Living Under English Laws? (p. 84)** 1. Because the colonists had no representation in the English parliament they should not have to pay the taxes imposed by England. 2. He had imposed taxes without the consent of the people; he had deprived the people in many cases of trial by jury; he had brought prisoners to England to be tried; he had cut off American trade; he had quartered troops in the homes of the people. 3. The Stamp Act, Congress and the Continental Congress. 4. Thomas Jefferson. **How Did the New Government Change? (p. 86)** 1. To protect the rights that are inherent to people. 2. There was no president to enforce the laws, and many states did not pay attention to them. 3. The states were united under one strong central government. 4. They wanted the United States to continue as a free nation with a way of government that could live for all time.

Thinking Skills (p. 88): 1. Written documents and records exist long after people die or forget what has been agreed upon and insure that future generations will continue to live by what was written in the past. 2. Answers will vary. *Suggestions:* King John taxed people very heavily. His court judges accepted bribes, the government was dishonest and unjust. 3. c. **Vocabulary Skills (p. 88):** 1. g. 2. a. 3. b. 4. e. 5. c. 6. f. 7. d. **Study Skills—Using Documents (p. 89):** 1. Magna Carta 2. Declaration of Independence 3. Answers will vary. **Beyond The Book (p. 89):** Independent Projects. **Vocabulary Check (p. 90):** 1. True 2. True 3. True 4. True 5. Articles of Confederation. **Comprehension Check (p. 90):** 1. a. weakness b. advantage c. advantage d. weakness e. weakness 2. b. 3. True **Skill Builders—Interpreting Time Lines (p. 91):** 1. 1765, 1787. 2. The Stamp Act Congress and the writing of the Constitution. 3.

Creation of the Stamp Act Congress. 4. Continental Congress. 5. Declaration of Independence. 6. Answers will vary.

Building Writing Skills (p. 91): 1. Answers will vary. *Suggestions:* a. There are certain rights that are inherent to man and should not be violated. b. The colonists pledged their life to each other and supported these freedoms and rights. c. Patrick Henry was willing to fight to the death for his and others' freedom. 2. Answers will vary. *Suggestion:* People came to the new land to find freedom from tyranny. The Mayflower Compact listed laws for the general good. The Magna Carta served as a model for all the documents of freedom and government. The English colonies became the strongest because of their laws and customs and the other colonies followed their example. The Declaration of Independence listed the wrongs done by King John of England so the colonists would not forget his tyranny. The Declaration then re-established the freedoms that were initiated in the Magna Carta as inherent rights.

CHAPTER SIX: How Was The Constitution Created? (p. 95) 1. The Preamble, the Articles, and the Amendments. 2. How to divide the power between the national government and the states; how each state would be represented in Congress; privileges for different regions, and protection for individual freedoms. 3. They are the people who wrote our Constitution and set up our plan of government. 4. Federalists wanted a strong central government. **What Is In The Preamble? (p. 98)** 1. "To walk or go before." 2. "We the People." 3. To stress that the Constitution makes the people the source of government. 4. Establish justice, insure domestic Tranquility, provide for the common defense, promote the general Welfare, and secure the Blessings of liberty to ourselves and our posterity. **What Is In The Articles? (p. 101)** 1. The Legislative, Executive, and Judicial. 2. Over the number of representatives that should be elected to Congress from each state. 3. By creating a Congress with two houses. 4. George Washington. **Why Is The Constitution a Living Document? (p. 103)** 1. Because what will happen in the future is not known. 2. It is concerned only with what is necessary to the process of establishing a strong democratic government and defined clearly that government and the law of the land. 3. Change. 4. It was planned so that it could be changed, and leaves the question of how laws are to be applied to each generation.

Thinking Skills (p. 104): 1. To form a more perfect union, establish justice, ensure domestic tranquility, provide for the common defense, promote the general welfare and secure the blessings of liberty to ourselves and our posterity. 2. Executive, legislative, judicial. 3. It allows for the future, it contains only those things necessary to the process of establishing a strong government and it allows for change. 4. c. 5. Answers will vary. *Suggestions:* A sharp dispute arose over the number of representatives that should be elected from each state. The convention did make a compromise. Instead of one house with either equal membership from each state or membership by population, it adopted a plan for two houses of Congress: a House of Representatives and a Senate. 6. Answers will vary. 7. a. The Living Constitution. b. Answers will vary. *Suggestion:* But it leaves to each generation of Americans the task of applying the laws and administering the government which it has created. **Vocabulary Skills (p. 104):** 1. preamble 2. tranquility 3. articles 4. census 5. founding fathers 6. amendments 7. posterity. **Study Skills—Outlining (p. 105):** I. Branches of Government A. The Executive branch is the office of the President. B. The Legislative branch includes the House of Representatives and the Senate. C. The Judicial branch includes the Supreme Court and other federal courts. **Beyond The Book (p. 105):** Independent Projects. **Vocabulary Check (p. 106):** 1. c. 2. d. 3. f. 4 a. 5. e. 6. b. 7. g. **Comprehension Check (p. 106):** 1. a, b, d, e. **Skill Builders—Interpreting Charts (p. 107):** Activity 1. If you wanted to understand why we no longer use the Articles of Confederation. Activity 2: 1. What its weaknesses were. 2. Items 2, 4, and 5. 3. Items 2, 4, and 5. 4. It shows how they wanted to strengthen the weaknesses of the government. **Building Writing Skills (p. 107):** 1. Answers will vary. *Suggestions:* a. The Importance of the Preamble. 1. The Preamble comes before the articles of the Constitution. 2. It explains the purpose of the Constitution. 3. Stresses the fact that the people are the source of power in the government. 4. The Constitution seeks to form a more perfect union. 5. States that the Constitution is designed to establish justice and insure domestic tranquility. 2. Under the Articles, states had a number of votes proportional to their populations. In the Constitution a compromise was reached by creating two houses. 3. How was the debate solved over how states would be represented in the legislative branch?

CHAPTER SEVEN: How Does The Constitution Provide for Change? (p. 111) 1. Congress can propose an amendment with a two-thirds vote in both houses or two-thirds of the state's legislatures can request that Congress call a convention. 2. Three-fourths of the states must approve a proposed amendment either in the legislature or a special convention. 3. All amendments have been proposed by congress. 4. Amendments are concerned with the larger ideas of a free government and how it should work. **Why Did People Want a Bill of Rights? (p. 113)** 1. They had seen these rights being taken away before by powerful rulers. 2. Rules of the king's church had been imposed and people had been unjustly arrested and imprisoned for long periods without trial. 3. Freedom of religion, speech, assembly, and the press. 4. Tenth. **What Kind of Changes Did the Amendments Call For? (p. 115)** 1. The Prohibition amendment was passed and later repealed; senators were to be elected by direct vote in each state; the length of the term as President was limited. 2. When the 21st amendment repealed the 18th. 3. States were left free to settle their own disputes; ties in presidential elections were prevented by a change in the election procedure; an income tax was created; "lame duck" officials were prevented; and "succession" of the Presidency was established. 4. "Lame ducks" were members of Congress who were not reelected and who had little or no influence or effectiveness. **How Did the Amendments Extend Rights and Freedoms? (p. 117)** 1. Freedom, citizenship, and suffrage. 2. Slaves, women, residents of Washington D.C. and people between the ages of 18 and 21. 3. The Equal Rights Amendment and statehood for Washington D.C. 4. Because they have such an important influence on our lives.

Thinking Skills (p. 118): 1. Congress can propose an amendment with a two-thirds vote in both houses, or two-thirds of the states' legislatures can request that Congress call a convention to write an amendment and propose it. 21. Three-fourths of the states must approve a proposal for it to become an amendment. 3. Bill of Rights. 4. a. 18th, 21st, 17th, 22nd. b. 11th, 12th, 16th, 20th, 25th. c. 13th, 14th, 15th, 19th, 23rd, 26th, 24th. 5. Time lines will vary in construction. 6. Import and income taxes. 7. 16th. **Vocabulary Skills (p. 118):** 1. True 2. jurisdiction 3. True 4. suffrage 5. True 6. Bill of Rights 7. lame ducks. **Study Skills—Using The Appendix (p. 119):** a. 1. The appendix begins on page 557. 2. In the section called Facts About the States, page 592. 3. By reading the heading of each one and placing them on a timeline. b. By checking to see which year each Amendment was added to the Constitution. **Beyond The Book (p. 119):** Independent Projects. **Vocabulary Check (p. 120):** 1. ratification 2. prohibition 3. repeals 4. Bill of Rights 5. jurisdiction 6. suffrage 7. lame ducks. **Comprehension Check (p. 120):** 1. True 2. The 18th Amendment 3. True 4. True 5. The first 10. **Skill Builders—Interpreting Time Charts (p. 121):** 1. When each amendment was added, a description of each and the reasons each was passed. 2. a. The process of how the Constitution can be applied to the changes in and growth of government in the U.S. b. The description column shows how rights were granted to more people and the changes in thinking about how government should be run. 3. In a column in chronological order. 4. How many amendments there are and the years they were passed. 5. Cabinet growth; development of federal programs and independent agencies; changes in foreign policy. **Building Writing Skills (p. 121):** Answers will vary. *Suggestions:* 1. The rights and responsibilities guaranteed by the Bill of Rights included freedom of speech, religion, assembly, petition and press, those rights considered inherent to man, freedom from unjust acts by government and powers not specifically given to the government. 2. a. Propose is to suggest; ratify is to accept and approve. Ratification is approval; repeal is to take out of effect. Rights are privileges inherent to man; responsibilities are actions that must be taken to insure those rights. 3. Answers will vary. *Suggestion:* (Answers based on the Chart in Chapter Eight "How Governments Share Authority") authority, confederation, unitary, power, function, states.

CHAPTER EIGHT: How Are National Governments Organized? (p. 126) 1. Confederation, unitary state, federation. 2. In a confederation the states keep most of the power; in a unitary state the central government has complete legal control; and in a federation the power is divided between the central government and the self-governing states. 3. Federal government. 4. So that citizens might participate in their own government. **How Does Federalism Mean "From Many, One?" (p. 128)** 1. Delegated powers, reserved powers, and concurrent powers. 2. Delegated powers are given to the states by the federal government; reserved powers are for states alone; concurrent powers are held by both. 3. Judges and courts resolve conflicts over power. 4. The states are the "many" unified in "one" nation and the eagle symbolizes the freedom and strength of this union. **How Do The States Cooperate With Each Other? (p. 130)** 1. The legal acts and records of a state are recognized throughout the nation by every other state. 2. It recognizes birth certificates, marriages, and business contracts as legal in every state. 3. By living there and by right of national citizenship. 4. A governor may refuse to extradite a prisoner if unfair treatment is probable. **How Do the Federal and State Governments Cooperate? (p. 133)** 1. Self government and protection from invasion. 2. An advantage is access to money to spend on the general welfare of state residents and one disadvantage is that the states may have to comply with conditions imposed by the federal government in order for the state to receive the money. 3. The balance between federal and state powers. 4. It must be answered in a democratic fashion.

Thinking Skills (p. 134): Answers will vary. *Suggestions:* 1. a. The federal government's powers were granted to it by the states and the people. b. The legal acts and records of a state are recognized throughout the nation by every other state. c. "The Citizens of each State shall be entitled to all Privileges and Immunities of Citizens in several States." 2. a. confederation—states keep most of the power and give the central government only limited authority. b. unitary state—a single central government has complete legal control over all the territory within its borders c. federation—authority is divided between the central government and self governing states. 3. The Founding Fathers knew that a strong central government was needed to unify the country. 4. By rulings of the Supreme Court. 5. b. **Vocabulary Skills (p. 134):** 1. b. 2. c. 3. d. 4. g. 5. a. 6. e. 7. f. 8. h. **Study Skills—Using A Card Catalog (p. 135):** Library Practice. **Beyond The Book (p. 135):** Independent Projects. **Vocabulary Check (p. 136):** 1. True 2. unitary state 3. federation 4. centralization 5. extradition 6. True 7. True 8. reserved powers. **Comprehension Check (p. 136):** 1. c. 2. c. 3. c. **Skill Builders—Interpreting Graphs (p. 137):** 1. Compares the populations of the first thirteen states. 2. It shows how much larger the population of some states, like Virginia and Pennsylvania, were than others like Delaware and Rhode Island. The size of their representation in Congress. 3. Virginia, Pennsylvania, North Carolina, Massachusetts, New York. Read a more detailed account of the discussions of the Continental Congress in an encyclopedia. **Building Writing Skills (p. 137):** Answers will vary. *Suggestions:* 1. Centralization means more powers go to the federal government. Decentralization mean the states and local governments determine laws and actions. 2. The fact that certain rights are not listed in the Constitution does not take them away from the people. 3. There is a stronger central government with necessary executive powers.

CHAPTER NINE: How Is State Government Organized? (p. 141) 1. They have three branches. 2. Most have two houses. 3. Governor and Lieutenant Governor. 4. It has a unicameral legislature. **How Do People Participate in State and Local Government? (p. 143)** 1. Election by the people. 2. Electors actually elect the President and Vice President. 3. Initiative allows the people to present a bill directly to the lawmakers, while referendum puts a law to popular vote. 4. Recall is removal of an official from office by popular vote. **How Do the States Provide Local Self-Government? (p. 145)** 1. By charter. 2. Maintenance of roads and buildings, keeping of records, and providing welfare. 3. Louisiana and Alaska. 4. Louisiana has parishes, and Alaska has boroughs. **What Are the Types of Municipal Government? (p. 149)** 1. Mayor-Council, City Manager, Home Rule. 2. Mayor and City Manager. 3. They are created by popular vote to provide services with the authority of all three branches of government.

Thinking Skills (p. 150): 1. Legislative, executive, and judicial. 2. The governor, lieutenant governor, secretary of state, treasurer, attorney general, superintendent of education, state controller, representatives and senators to the state legislature, mayor, city council members and county board of supervisors. 3. Through the initiative process. The referendum process. 4. In a weak mayor system, the mayor lacks many powers and is severely limited in those he has. 5. Fire protection, streets and sewers, libraries and parks. 6. b. **Vocabulary Skills (p. 150):** 1. county board 2. referendum 3. home rule 4. district 5. ordinance 6. initiative 7. municipality 8. recall **Study Skills—Outlining (p. 151):** Answers will vary. *Suggestions:* I. Three Types of Municipal Government A. Mayor-Council 1. Mayor is the chief officer of the city 2. City council makes the laws for the city B. City commission 1. Commissioners are chosen from the city at large 2. The executive powers are shared by the commissioners. C. City manager 1. Commissioners select the city manager, pass ordinances, decide on policies of the city. 2. All executive authority is given to the city manager. **Beyond The Book (p. 151):** Independent Projects. **Vocabulary Check (p. 152):** 1. c. 2. b. 3. h. 4. g. 5. a. 6. f. 7. d 8. e. **Comprehension Check (p. 152):** Weak Mayor System: c. d. f. Strong Mayor System: a. b. c. e. f. 2. a. True b. True c. False d. True **Skill Builders—Interpreting Illustrations (p. 153):** 1. Services of state government: education, safety, transportation, conservation, health, business. 2. Items included in each service. 3. No. 4. Answers will vary. 5. Answers will vary. Activity: Independent Project. **Building Writing Skills (p. 153):** 1. Answers will vary. *Suggestion:* Almost everything in my life is influenced by government: the school we attend, the buses we ride on, the streets we drive on, permits for the houses we live in, taxes that pay for regulation enforcement, fire protection, water, electricity, food quality. 2. Initiative provides a petition process by which citizens can present a bill proposal directly to a legislative body. Referendum provides a petition process to submit a bill that has been passed to popular vote. 3. What are some examples of local governments?

UNIT TWO TEST

A. 1. Answers will vary. *Suggestions:* Favorable—they look educated and businesslike. *or* Unfavorable—they look wealthy and prejudiced.
   2. Answers will vary. *Suggestions:* Yes. *or* It's just a representative portrait.
   3. Answers will vary. *Suggestions:* Yes, it defines the picture. *or* No, it may not include them all.
   4. Answers will vary.
   5. Answers will vary.

B. Answers will vary.

C. People became lazy and expected government to do everything. Be informed and accept the duties and responsibilities of citizenship.

CHAPTER TEN: How Did Political Parties Develop In America? (p. 161) 1. People with similar political beliefs joined together to influence the government. 2. The major parties often incorporate the opinions of other parties. 3. A group of people who do not agree with the two major parties. 4. Bull Moose and Populist. **How Are Political Parties Organized? (p. 163)** 1. Precinct at local level; state central committee; national committee. 2. Plans the national convention, picks the city, and directs the party's presidential campaign. 3. They are party leaders. 4. The presidential candidates. **How Do The Parties Select Their Candidates? (p. 167)** 1. You agree with the party's ideas about government and are able to vote for the candidate in the primary elections. 2. Because of family and friends, personal interests and your educational background and philosophy. 3. It has increased. 4. Democrats. **How Are Citizens Involved In Elections? (p. 169)** 1. Seeing and hearing the candidates in person or on TV. 2. Issues. 3. Those who lose the election give their support to the leaders elected by the majority. 4. Unite voters, make choices simpler, help build interest in public affairs, simply holding winning candidates accountable.

Thinking Skills (p. 170): 1. Over how much authority the President should have. 2. It provides for the election of the President by a majority most of the time. 3. a. represents the precinct in the party organization. b. directs campaigns for state officials and for the members of Congress from that state. c. heads the permanent party organization in the country. 4. Majority Rule. **Vocabulary Skills (p. 170):** 1. True 2. True 3. majority 4. nominee 5. True 6. True 7. precinct. **Study Skills—Using An Encyclopedia (p. 171):** Answers will vary. *Suggestion:* 1. World Book Encyclopedia—Democratic Party. 2. a. 4½ pages. b. Most of the article is on the history; only a few paragraphs are on present activities. 3. a. Graphs showing parties of Presidents, political cartoons and a picture of a famous President. b. To show highlights of the history. 4. Dixiecrat Party, Liberty League,

Political Convention, Political Party, U.S. History of. 5. Barnburner, Copperheads, Dixiecrat Party, Loco-Foco, New Deal, Reconstruction, Tamanny Society. **Beyond The Book (p. 171):** Independent Projects. **Vocabulary Check (p. 172):** 1. majority 2. third 3. nominee 4. primary 5. plurality 6. run-off 7. precinct. **Comprehension Check (p. 172):** 1. True 2. About how much authority the President should have. 3. True 4. True **Skill Builders—Interpreting Graphs (p. 173):** 1. Party Affiliations 2. Each figure represents an amount of people. 3. 10 million 4. How many people are in each party 5. How has party size grown or changed? Which party is the largest? When did changes in party affiliation occur? 6. The Democratic party is the largest. More people are choosing to vote independently. The Republican party is the smallest. **Building Writing Skills (p. 173):** 1. So he or she isn't too influenced by personalities or propaganda. 2. Answers will vary.

CHAPTER ELEVEN: How Does A Person Become A Candidate? (p. 177) 1. Because his parents were Democrats. 2. He agreed with the Republican ideas because of his business. 3. A petition with 200 signatures or a $400 fee. 4. The petition, so he could use the $400 in his campaign. **How Is A Campaign Organized? (p. 180)** 1. To create the strategy and run the campaign. 2. The important things you do during the campaign. 3. His opponent is the incumbent, he is low on funds, and is not well known. 4. Get out and meet people in person and have fund raisers. **How Are Issues Involved In A Campaign? (p. 182)** 1. Liberals want society to change, want government to make change, have national government more centralized; conservatives want less change, less government spending, national government more decentralized. 2. Through government action; by a method that doesn't increase government spending. 3. There are too many issues and they can be very complicated. 4. He should stick to his stand on an issue. **What Is Involved In An Actual Campaign? (p. 185)** 1. Printed material, TV and radio time, postage, and rent. 2. Fund raisers, donations, loans, and party contributions. 3. Asked people to vote. 4. Personal contact with people.

Thinking Skills (p. 186): 1a. You pay a $400 fee or file a petition signed by 200 people. b. Answers will vary. 2. What advertising will be done on TV and radio, what posters and campaign literature will look like. To win anything you have to plan your strategy carefully. 3. Costs: a. b. e. Income: c. d. f. 4. a. Door to door tours, debates, public appearances, advertisements and commercials, fund raising dinners, campaign materials. b & c. TV and radio ads. e. door to door tours, public appearances. **Vocabulary Skills (p. 186):** 1. f. 2. b. 3. a. 4. e. 5. d. 6. c. 7. h. 8. g. **Study Skills—Recognizing Techniques Of Persuasion (p. 187):** 1. TV and radio, inexpensive advertisements and personal appearance tours. 2. Answers will vary. 3. Slogans, inexpensive ads, personal appearances. 4. Answers will vary. *Suggestion:* TV and radio, slogans, opinion polls, inexpensive ads, personal appearances. 5. All of them. **Beyond The Book (p. 187):** Independent Projects. **Vocabulary Check (p. 188):** 1. liberal 2. True 3. True 4. True 5. incumbent 6. petition 7. True 8. campaign manager **Comprehension Check (p. 188):** 1. a 2. a 3. False 4. True 5. False **Skill Builders: Analyzing An Advertisement (p. 189):** 1. William Howard Taft and James Schoolcraft Sherman. 2. Grand Old Party. 3. Answers will vary. 4. That Taft and Sherman will be as good a President and Vice President as these famous former Presidents. **Building Writing Skills (p. 189):** 1. Answers will vary. *Suggestion:* Issue: Bussing to Promote Integration of Our Schools. Pro: promotes interaction between classes and races; equalizes the quality of education available to all; allows students to participate in the solution to a national problem. Con: is expensive and wastes time and gasoline; creates resentments; makes an artificial situation. Pro is the better position. 2. Independent Project

CHAPTER TWELVE: What Is The Difference Between Voting And Influence? (p. 195) 1. The peoples' opinions get their representatives to think and act as they want them to. 2. Direct influence is in voting, indirect is in expressing opinions. 3. People do not take the time to study public questions and should let their representatives have control; it is the duty of representatives to do as the people desire. 4. He felt lawmakers should be above public influence. **How Do Political Parties Influence Government? (p. 196)** 1. To gain support for their programs and future candidates. 2. Influencing its members of Congress and contributions. 3. Veto, appointments and support of other candidates. 4. Deny the right to sit on important committees. **Which Interest Groups Influence Government? (p. 199)** 1. A group of people who share a common interest. 2. Economic, public, and ethnic. 3. Economic groups share a common financial interest, as labor unions; public groups have a common interest in government, as consumer groups; ethnic groups are concerned with the problems of that minority. 4. They often determine the direction of government actions. **What Is the Role of Lobbyists? (p. 201)** 1. People who work to influence government. 2. They are paid to do this as a career. 3. They are required to register and send in reports four times a year. 4. Public opinion.

Thinking Skills (p. 202): 1. The elected officials and representatives of the people. 2. Through influencing an official. 3. Persuasion, contributions and restriction on insurgents. 4. Economic, public and political. 5. b. **Vocabulary Skills (p. 202):** 1. influence 2. lobbyist 3. insurgent 4. interest group 5. opinion poll 6. indirect participation 7. opinion campaign. **Study Skills—Using The Newspaper (p. 203):** Answers will vary. *Suggestion:* 1a. New York Times b. daily c. 131 years 2. a. four parts b. Front page section, Science Times & Education (on Tuesday), Business Day, and Sports 3. Headlines, National news, Business Digest, Around the World, Around the Nation, Washington Talk, Notes on People, Supreme Court Roundup, editorials, education, music, sports world specials, sports news briefs, Question box, theater, the arts, movies, radio, TV, Washington Watch, Business People, Company News, Market Place, Commodities, Advertising. 4. a. Section A. at the end. b. On the editorial page. 5. Answers will vary. 6. The news story is easier to understand because it contains mostly facts. The editorial is more interesting because it contains opinions and analyzes issues. **Beyond The Book (p. 203):** Independent Projects. **Vocabulary Check (p. 204):** 1. c. 2. b. 3. d. 4. a. 5. g. 6. f. 7. e. **Comprehension Check (p. 204):** 1. True 2. True 3. False 4. True 5. True 6. False 7. True **Skill Builders—Interpreting Illustrations (p. 205):** Answers will vary. *Suggestions:* 1a. A lobbyist is trying to influence a lawmaker in front of a government building. b. It makes me feel that lobbyists are pushy and greedy. c. It exaggerates the negative aspects of lobbying. The lawmaker looks intimidated. Yes, aspects which show the positive side of lobbying. Yes, more objectively showing dialogue. 2. Lobbyists are the people who really run the country by pressuring our lawmakers.

Building Writing Skills (p. 205): 1. Answers will vary. *Suggestions:* a. We must be true to ourselves to have the ability to stand up and speak out on our opinions. b. If we stick to a high standard of honesty others will be encouraged to do likewise. 2. Answers will vary.

UNIT THREE TEST

A. 1. Declare his or her intent to run and file a petition or pay the fee.
  2. Printed materials, postage, TV and radio time, gasoline. Answers will vary.
  3. Meeting the people personally. No. They all introduce the candidate to the public.
  4. Answers will vary. *Suggestions:* Yes, it sounds exciting. *or* No, it's too much work.

B. Answers will vary.

CHAPTER THIRTEEN: Who Serves In Congress? (p. 213) 1. Members of Congress should live in the state that elects them, be at least twenty-five years old and a citizen for seven years to be a representative; and thirty to be a senator as well as being a citizen for a least nine years. 2. Member of the House of Representatives are elected for two-year terms and senators for six-year terms. 3. Boundaries of congressional districts must change to keep up with population changes so that the votes are evenly distributed. 4. They did not want major changes in our government every few years. **What Are The Rules of Congress? (p. 217)** 1. The Senate has 100 members; the House of Representatives has 435. 2. The Vice President of the United States is the President of the Senate; the Senate president pro tempore serves in absence of the President; the presiding officer of the House is the Speaker and each party has a leader called a whip. 3. They are privileged from arrest and cannot be taken to court for anything they say while in session. 4. Censure is official criticism and expulsion is loss of membership and privileges.

Thinking Skills (p. 218): 1. Citizenship in the state a person is elected to represent; be at least 25 years old, a senator 30; be a U.S. citizen for at least 7 years. 2. Senator 6 years, Representative 2 years. 3. Senate-100; House-435. 4. Speaker of the House, president pro tempore, party whips. 5. Privileged from arrest in all cases except for treason, felony and breach of peace and for anything they might say during session. 6. Answers will vary. *Suggestions:* a. The Constitution established requirements for serving in Congress. b. If Congress desires, it may set a uniform election date. c. Each house is the judge of the election of its own members. d. There can be only one representative for every 30,000 people. **Vocabulary Skills (p. 218):** 1. True 2. True 3. representatives-at-large 4. True 5. True 6. censure **Study Skills—Topic Outlining (p. 219):** I. Requirements for members A. Senate 1. Citizen of U.S. for at least 7 years 2. 30 years of age B. House 1. Citizen of U.S. for at least 7 years b. 25 years of age II. Choosing a Congress A. Election date 1. Uniform election date 2. First Tuesday after first Monday in November B. After the election 1. Certificates of election 2. Judge of election C. Election results in dispute 1. Claims by opposing candidate 2. Committee examination of results III. Length of term A. Senators 1. One third of Senators elected every 2 years 2. Terms of six years B. Representatives 1. Term of office 2 years 2. Reflect public opinion changes **Beyond The Book (p. 219):** Independent Projects **Vocabulary Check (p. 220):** 1. congressional districts 2. representatives-at-large 3. censure 4. president pro tempore 5. legislative 6. majority party 7. expel 8. whip **Comprehension Check (p. 220):** 1. True 2. False 3. True 4. True 5. False 6. True 7. False 8. True **Skill Builders—Interpreting Circle Graphs (p. 221):** 1. The total of all the members of Congress. 2. The size of the "pieces of pie." 3. The actual numbers were translated into percentage. 4. The professions. The numbers are different. **Building Writing Skills (p. 221):** 1. Answers will vary: *Suggestion:* Serving in Congress; a. A Representative is elected every two years and reflects public opinion more closely. 2. Some Representatives have served for 20 years or more. c. Senators are elected for six year terms. d. The leaders of the two houses are the Speaker and the Vice President of the U.S. e. Members of Congress are afforded certain privileges 2. So that they might be free to attend important sessions. 3. Answers will vary.

CHAPTER FOURTEEN: What Are The Powers Granted To Congress? (p. 228) 1. To make laws for the good of the country; to print money; to levy and collect taxes; to provide for the common defense; to regulate trade with foreign nations and between states; standards for naturalization; and to establish postal services. 2. Congress can make laws only in certain areas. 3. The House of Representatives accuses the person of misconduct, the Senate sits as a court with Vice President of the United States presiding unless it is a trial of the President. 4. Because the House is more directly involved with the people. **How Has Congress Gained Additional Powers? (p. 230)** 1. It is the authority of Congress to make other laws if they were necessary in carrying out its assigned powers. 2. Established a national bank; controlled railroads becaue they cross state lines; and spent money to pay for the Public Health Service. 3. It can cause questionable activities to stop or be changed before a law becomes necessary. 4. Jefferson maintained that Congress had only the powers granted in the Constitution. **What Are the Limits on Congress? (p. 233)** 1. Congress cannot suspend habeas corpus, vote punishment, pass ex post facto laws, create special groups, nor impose special taxes. 2. States may not enter into treaties with foreign governments nor set and collect taxes on imports. 3. A person cannot be held prisoner without accusation. 4. Because all persons are considered equal under the law.

Thinking Skills (p. 234): 1. a. Coining money. b. establish a uniform standard of weights and measures. c. levy and collect taxes to provide for defense and the general welfare. d. provide for the common defense and declare war. e. regulation of trade with foreign nations and between states. f. pass laws of naturalization. g. establish postal service. 2. c. e. g. 3. Each picture shows what is involved in each power. **Vocabulary Skills (p. 234):** 1. d. 2. e. 3. f. 4. c. 5. g. 6. b. 7. a. **Study Skills—The Almanac (p. 235):** Answers will vary. *Suggestion:* based on *Information Please Almanac 1982.* 1. Seven subheadings in the Almanac. 2. Page 686. 3. The same as anywhere in the country. 4. The Smithsonian Institute building is in Washington, D.C. It's open daily 10-5:30. Information Center and Smithson's tomb are in original building. **Beyond The Book (p. 235):** Independent Projects. **Vocabulary Check (p. 236):** 1. True 2. an ex post facto law 3. writ of habeas corpus 4. True 5. True 6. True 7. elastic clause. **Comprehension Check (p. 236):** 1. a. 2. c. 3. True **Skill Builders—Interpreting Flow Charts (p. 237):** 1. Answers will vary. 2. Answers will vary. *Suggestion:* (flow chart in art) **Building Writing Skills (p. 237):** 1. Answers will vary. *Suggestion:* a. Implied powers: Powers based on the Constitutional authority, "to make all laws which will be necessary and proper." Stated powers: Powers specified in the Constitution. 2. Answers will vary. *Suggestion:* Sweeping powers of Congress. a. This is the doctrine of implied powers. b. The laws passed with this authority must be in line with stated powers. c. This is an example of how our Constitution is a living document. d. The authors said Congress has power to regulate commerce, taxes, etc., but not how to do it. e. Congress has created agencies and laws to spend money for the general welfare.

CHAPTER FIFTEEN: Who Makes Laws? (p. 243) 1. Members of Congress and the President. 2. A veto tells Congress that the President does not favor a law. 3. A bill is signed into law by a two-thirds majority of each house without the President's signature. 4. Because of the large volume of bills that come before Congress, preliminary detail study is done in committee. **What Are The Stages Of A Bill? (p. 251)** 1. Most laws made by Congress may originate in either the House of Representatives or the Senate. After a bill is proposed in one house, it is sent to a committee for study. If the committee approves the bill, it is then presented to the entire house. After debate, the house will vote on the bill. If it receives a majority vote, it goes to the other house. The second house will also send the bill to a committee for study. If it is passed by this house, the bill goes to the White House for the President's signature. A bill signed by the President becomes law. A bill vetoed by the President can still become a law if a two-thirds majority in each house votes to override the President's veto. 2. So that bills are given careful consideration and are not passed quickly. 3. Committee hearings and investigations determine what recommendation will be given a bill by the committee to the house. 4. The Rules Committee can block it or clear it for debate before the entire house.

Thinking Skills (p. 252): 1. Members of Congress. 2. Through the need for a majority vote and the system of checks and balances. 3. Special interest groups, the President, and large groups of citizens. 4. After study and investigation, a committee may recommend a bill for a vote or kill it. 5. If it is passed over his or her veto by a two-thirds vote in each house or he or she leaves it unsigned. 6. d. **Vocabulary Skills (p. 252):** 1. veto 2. majority report 3. bill 4. filibuster 5. minimum wage 6. override 7. committee **Study Skills—Editing A First Draft (p. 253):** Eliminate sentences 3, 5, and 8. **Beyond The Book (p. 253):** Independent Projects. **Vocabulary Check (p. 254):** 1. override 2. minimum wage 3. bill 4. majority report 5. filibuster 6. veto 7. committee **Comprehension Check (p. 254):** 1. True 2. False 3. True 4. True 5. False 6. True 7. True 8. False **Skill Builders—Flow Charts (p. 255):** Charts will vary. **Building Writing Skills (p. 255):** 1. a. Answers will vary. *Suggestion:* The Rules Committee is a powerful committee. It decides whether or not a bill should come up for debate. A bill may pass committee investigations and hearings but not make it through the Rules Committee. 2. To insure that each proposal is subjected to careful consideration and is not passed quickly and without thought. 3. Answers will vary. *Suggestion:* The bill should have become law. Restrictions could have been included protecting a family head from losing his or her job to a lower wage earner. It was worth the time and effort because it keeps our elected representatives aware of the needs of the citizens and conditions in the country.

CHAPTER SIXTEEN: Who Are Our State Lawmakers? (p. 261) 1. The average term for state legislators is four years; they must live in the state and district they serve and be from 21 to 25 years of age; there are generally two houses in state legislatures. 2. It is smaller and more democratic with less political or peer pressure. 3. It provided equal representation for district. 4. An attempt by the party in power to reapportion districts to assure themselves a majority. **How Is A State Legislature Organized? (p. 262)** 1. Each House has a presiding officer—the elected Speaker in the lower house and the lieutenant governor in the Senate—who appoint committee chairs, some committee members, assign bills and schedule them for debate. 2. Because of his or her influence in running the legislature. 3. It gives members with the longest length of time in office certain privileges. 4. It is important because of the right to choose which committee a member will serve on. **What Are Some Of The Problems Of State Lawmakers? (p. 264)** 1. They are paid a salary and benefits. 2. Demands of time, low salaries and costs of campaigning. 3. Paying money to a lawmaker to influence them. 4. Financial reasons mainly. **How Do County Governments Work? (p. 266)** 1. The county is mainly an administrative arm of the state.

2. Strict control by state constitutions has made it difficult to handle emerging conditions such as water and environmental pollution and suburban development. 3. Law enforcement, judicial administration, road construction and maintenance, keeping of public records, welfare, and administration of schools in some cases. 4. County authority is limited in meeting the needs of its citizens and in its own internal administration. **How Do Our City Lawmakers Work? (p. 267)** 1. A charter incorporates a group of people into a city. 2. It establishes the rules for governing life in the city. 3. According to parliamentary procedure. 4. Lawmakers want to know what citizens think about matters of public interest.

Thinking Skills (p. 268): 1. Most meet annually. 2. Four years for Senators and two years for Representatives. 3. They must be citizens of the U.S. and live in the state district they serve. A senator must be at least 25 years of age and a representative or delegate 21. 4. 110 representatives. 5. How to Become Politically Informed. **Vocabulary Skills (p. 268):** 1. True 2. gerrymander 3. True 4. patronage 5. True 6. True 7. biennial 8. True **Study Skills—Making A Formal Outline (p. 269):** A.: 2. It acts much like the legislature does. 3. Other persons or departments carry out the rules. B.: 1. An ordinance is a ruling to be obeyed within the city limits. 2. Councils decide who the city will tax and how. 3. They decide how the city government's money is to be spent. III A. Concise members have an agenda. B. Citizen participation is essential. **Beyond The Book (p. 269):** Independent Projects. **Vocabulary Check (p. 270):** 1. reapportion 2. calendar 3. gerrymander 4. charter 5. seniority 6. agenda 7. patronage. 8. biennial **Comprehension Check (p. 270):** 1. True 2. True 3. Reapportion the areas so that the representation remains proportional. 4. Those with more seniority pick the committees they are on and determine where they have their offices, where they sit in session, and where they park their cars. 5. True. **Skill Builders—Interpreting An Atlas (p. 271):** Answers will vary. **Building Writing Skills (p. 271):** Answers will vary. *Suggestions:* 1. redistricting-a re-drawing of boundaries after each 10 year census to keep representation equal; gerrymandering-attempt by the party in power to draw district lines that would give them a political advantage. 2. It is good because other compensations for our lawmakers are insufficient.

UNIT FOUR TEST

A. 1. California has more people.
   2. The population grew.
   3. Answers will vary. *Suggestions:* Yes, representation is proportioned across the country. *or* No, state areas with smaller populations are not well represented.
   4. Districts are reapportioned to reflect population changes.

B. Answers will vary.

C. Answers will vary. *Suggestions:* Yes, lawmakers have a very responsible job and should be recognized for it. *or* No, we pay them too much already.

CHAPTER SEVENTEEN: Who Can Qualify To Be President? (p. 279) 1. A person must be at least 35 years old, a native born citizen and a resident of the United States for the past 14 years. 2. Forty. 3. Lawyers, soldiers, planters, educators, businessmen, a tailor, an author, a journalist, an editor, an engineer, and an actor. 4. The Vice President. **What Is The Electoral System? (p. 283)** 1. Electors are chosen as representatives of the people and are responsible for casting votes for the President and Vice President. 2. They wanted the President to be elected by representatives of the people. 3. No alternative has been found to take its place. 4. By the number of senators and representatives each state has in Congress. **What Are The Steps To Being Elected President? (p. 287)** 1. The candidate announces his or her intent, begins to campaign, participates in a primary election to win the nomination by individual states, seeks nomination by party at the national convention campaigns across the country and is selected or not at the national election in November of election year. 2. Candidates who win primary elections in the states have a better chance of being nominated by their party at the national convention. 3. In the general election the people vote directly for the candidates who have been nominated to run for President in the primaries. 4. When no candidate for President receives a majority of the electoral votes cast.

Thinking Skills (p. 288): 1. The candidates must be U.S. citizens by birth, at least 35 years of age and a resident of the U.S. for the past fourteen years. 2. A salary of $200,000, a tax-free allowance, use of the White House, a jet airplane for travel and a retreat area, Camp David. 3. If the

President dies or resigns, the Vice President takes over. If the Vice President dies or resigns the President nominates a person to be approved by a majority vote of both houses. 4. By the number of Senators and Representatives the state has. 5. Answers will vary. *Suggestions:* a. The delegates to the original Constitutional Convention did not forsee that the President would be as directly elected by the votes of the people as he or she is today. b. Today electors rarely exercise a choice in voting for President or Vice President. c. Even if more than a million voters in a state favor the Republican candidate for President, all the electoral votes in that state will go to the Democratic candidate if the plurality of the Presidential vote in the state goes Democratic at the polls. d. The system can elect a President even though a rival candidate receives a larger percentage of the popular vote. **Vocabulary Skills (p. 288):** 1. d. 2. e. 3. a. 4. f. 5. g. 6. c. 7. b. **Study Skills—Editing (p. 289):** 1. The last sentence of paragraph 1 doesn't belong. 2. Delete "After taking office" in the second sentence in paragraph. 2. Change the last sentence to read, "The Constitution states that the oath must be administered by a government official." **Beyond The Book (p. 289):** Independent Projects. **Vocabulary Check (p. 290):** 1. electoral college 2. executive 3. True 4. True 5. True 6. True 7. True **Comprehension Check (p. 290):** 1. c. 2. c. 3. c. 4. b. **Skill Builders—Interpreting Comic Strips (p. 291):** 1. the commuter train, his office, his home, the train. It changes to show the passage of time. 2. Figures are rounded, men have large noses. 3. a. Sitting and talking. b. Making excuses. c. Are you going to vote? 4. Answers will vary. 5. Answers will vary. **Building Writing Skills (p. 291):** Answers will vary. *Suggestion:* 1. a. The Kinds of Persons Who Have Been President. There have been 40 Presidents since 1789. By profession 23 have been lawyers. Nine did not attend college. There is nothing in the Constitution that specifies whether the President be a man or a woman. Four of our Presidents were soldiers first. There were two planters, two educators, and two businessmen. 2. What are the steps to being elected President?

CHAPTER EIGHTEEN: What Powers Are Given To The President By The Constitution? (p. 297) 1. Power and responsibility to enforce laws; power to say how wars will be fought; power of appointment and pardon; veto power; power to make treaties; power to call special sessions of Congress. 2. By giving only a short general definition of the areas in which a President has powers. 3. It means that the President has the power to say how wars will be fought. 4. So that such an important decision will not be left to a person or group in a less responsible situation. **How Did The President's Powers Grow? (p. 301)** 1. As the diversity and complexity of the country grew, more and more laws were needed and the President's power grew and grew through enforcing these laws. 2. A group of appointed government officials who assist the President in enforcing the decisions of the executive office. 3. Through a majority of his own political party in Congress and by persuading members of Congress to pass legislation he initiates. 4. "Chief of State" means the President is the principal representative of our country; chief executive refers to his management function. **What Are The Limits Of The President's Power? (p. 304)** 1. The checks and balances provided by the Constitution of Congressional and judicial branches of government. 2. The power to govern the country is spread to the three branches of government and are overlapping. 3. The Civil Service system is a nonpartisan way of selecting most of the civilian employees in the executive branch of government. 4. To eliminate the spoils system.

Thinking Skills (p. 306): 1. By giving only a short general definition of the powers to be interpreted by future generations. 2. The power to say how a war will be fought, to send troops and planes to foreign lands, to control the use of weapons. 3. A bureaucracy is a group of appointed officials that the President has chosen to assist him in the duties of the office. 4. There is a staff to prepare legislation; the President will use personal persuasion; there is a lot of influence as party leader. 5. Congress can limit Presidential power. **Vocabulary Skills (p. 306):** 1. checks and balances 2. spoils system 3. commander in chief 4. chief of state 5. civil service 6. bureaucracy 7. inherent power **Study Skills—Making A Sentence Outline (p. 307):** I. The Constitution grants the President specific powers. A. There is power and responsibility to enforce laws. B. The President can pardon people. C. He or she can call special sessions of Congress. D. It gives power to make treaties. E. The President is commander in chief of the Army and Navy. II. The Constitution places limits on the President's powers. A. The judicial branch of the government can declare the President's action unconstitutional. B. The President can make appointments only if two-thirds of the Senate approves. C. Congress must first approve of most Presidential decisions. D. The President cannot acquire powers beyond those defined in the Constitution. III. The Constitution provides for free election of the people. **Beyond The Book (p. 307):** Independent Projects. **Vocabulary Check (p. 308):** 1. commander-in-chief 2. checks and balances 3. bureaucracy 4. inherent power 5. spoils system 6. chief of state 7. civil service **Comprehension Check (p. 308):** 1. a. True b. False c. True d. False e. False 2. Chief Executive: a, c, d; Chief of State: b, e. **Skill Builders—Interpreting Postage Stamps (p. 309):** 1. a. Helen Keller and Anne Sullivan. b. Paul Laurence Dunbar. c. Sam Houston 2. a. rifle, a gas lamp 3. In the encyclopedia 4. They honor famous people 5. Answers will vary. **Building Writing Skills (p. 309):** Answers will vary. *Suggestion:* 1. inherent powers—powers which Presidents believe belong to them in times of great emergency; checks and balances—the system which limits the powers of the President. 2. "Limits to Presidential Power. The most important limit to Presidential power comes from the people. The people elect the President every four years. All the President's powers come from the citizens themselves. The system of checks and balances distributes the power of government over the three branches.

CHAPTER NINETEEN: What Is The Cabinet? (p. 315) 1. From the word referring to the room where the king met with his advisors. 2. Answers will vary among: Secretaries of: State, Treasury, Interior, Agriculture, Commerce, Labor, Defense, Health and Human Services, Housing and Urban Development, Transportation, Energy, Education; and Attorney General. 3. It keeps the President informed on matters in each department, gives information to Congress, and assists in writing a proposed bill. 4. They function with regulatory authority in their special fields with executive, legislative and judicial responsibility. **What Are The Duties Of The Executive Departments? (p. 321)** 1. Departments of: State, Treasury, Defense, Justice, Interior, Agriculture, Commerce, Labor, Housing and Urban Development, Transportation, Energy, Health and Human Services. 2. Foreign affairs; finances; national defense; legal matters regarding federal laws; public lands; agricultural experiments; business and industry; needs of workers; better housing; transportation problems; energy resource management; promote the health and welfare of Americans. 3. Department of Health and Human Services. 4. Department of Treasury; the Department of Justice. **What Are The Duties Of The Executive Office? (p. 323)** 1. To inform and advise the President on many matters; speak for the President and carry out various duties assigned. 2. The White House keeps the public informed on what the President thinks about current issues; the Office of Budget and Management figures the national budget; the National Security Council advises the President on ways to assure national security. 3. By carrying out all the duties involved in gathering information and facts on which the President can make decisions. 4. Because the duties required demand more time than is possible for one person to handle.

Thinking Skills (p. 324): See list on page 313. 2. The President sends a proposed cabinet office to Congress where it must be approved or vetoed within 60 days. 3. As the population grew and the needs of the country expanded, the services provided by the government needed to be organized and directed. 4. & 5. The Bureau of Printing and Engraving mints coins and prints money. The Internal Revenue Service collects taxes. The Secret Service protects the President and his family and those of past Presidents. 6. To regulate the business activities in special cases and to protect the interests of business, consumers, and society. 7. Secretary of Defense: in charge of Army, Navy and Air Force, direct the training of reserve officers and citizen soldiers of the National Guard. Secretary of State: deals with governments of foreign countries, coordinates our ambassadors and ministers who speak for the President. 8. p. 312, 316, 317. **Vocabulary Skills (p. 324):** 1. True 2. press secretary 3. Administer 4. True 5. True 6. True 7. True **Study Skills—Preparing A First Draft (p. 325):** 1. "The Department of Agriculture." Partly due to advances made in federal programs, each farm worker of today produces up to ten times the amount of food produced in 1940. Therefore, the Department of Agriculture helps farmers find better markets for their products. Through the price-support system, it guarantees them a minimum price for wheat and other crops. It also arranges for loans to farmers. 2. "The U.S. Coast Guard" The U.S. Coast Guard is a part of the Department of Defense and has many duties. The Coast Guard maintains buoys and other devices to warn ships of dangerous capes and lighthouses. It patrols the ocean to warn ships of icebergs, which are massive floating bodies of ice broken from a glacier. **Beyond The Book (p. 325):** Independent Projects. **Vocabulary Check (p. 326):** 1. ambassador 2. consul 3. administer 4. press secretary 5. cabinet 6. minister 7. regulatory authority **Comprehension Check (p. 326):** 1. True 2. True 3. The Secretary of Defense 4. There are 14 departments. 5. True **Skill Builders—Interpreting Photographs (p. 327):** Answers will vary. *Suggestions:* 1. Our President is an everyday citizen as well as chief of state. 2. The photograph presents an objective view of each role. 3. The people who support him in each role and the environment he works in. 4. The one of Ford in formal dress. **Building Writing Skills (p. 327).** a. & b.

CHAPTER TWENTY: What Is Our Foreign Policy? (p. 333) 1. All the goals and actions of one nation in relation to other nations. 2. Peace and security, international trade, and human rights and welfare. 3. It is not possible to remain isolated today because of close contact and great interaction with other countries. 4. To establish useful and beneficial relationships. **Who Makes Foreign Policy? (p. 336)** 1. The Department of State, the Congress, military leaders, businesses, and public opinion. 2. By advising the President on international affairs; by limiting the President's use of the armed services; by influencing our participation in military affairs; by doing business with other nations; by expressing our opinions. 3. We accept that country as a political equal in international affairs. 4. Programs in the form of goods, services or funds given to help other nations. **What Groups Of Nations Are Involved In Foreign Policy? (p. 338)** 1. NATO, SEATO, OAS, SALT, OPEC. 2. NATO—military alliance of free world; SEATO—safety of non-communist nations of Southeast Asia; OAS—closer non-military relations with Latin American countries; OPEC—we depend on them for raw materials. 3. A democratic form of government and an economic system of democratic socialism or free enterprise. 4. It is an organization of many countries working together for world peace.

Thinking Skills (p. 340): 1. Peace and security, international trade, and human rights. 2. Because we are in close contact with other nations through fast transportation, trade and communication. 3. To establish relationships that both sides can accept as useful and beneficial. 4. To strengthen our allies and help build the economies of developing countries. 5. The "Free World" refers to those groups of nations where democracy is the form of government and free enterprise or democratic socialism is the form of economy. 6. Answers will vary. *Suggestions:* The Free World nations have mutual defense treaties that pledge each member to defend any other who is attacked by nations outside the treaty. The Communist bloc countries are tied together by communist party rule. The Third World includes most of the nations and the majority of the people in the world. The U.S. and other Free World countries have entered into treaties and agreements with these countries in order to work for peace. **Vocabulary Skills (p. 340):** 1. g. 2. a. 3. b. 4. h. 5. d. 6. f. 7. e. 8. c. **Study Skills—*The Reader's Guide to Periodical Literature* (p. 341):** Independent activity. **Beyond The Book (p. 341):** Independent Projects. **Vocabulary Check (p. 342):** 1. recognize 2. detente 3. True 4. Diplomacy 5. True 6. True 7. foreign aid 8. True **Comprehension Check (p. 342):** 1. c. 2. False 3. False 4. True **Skill Builders—Interpreting Global Projections (p. 343):** 1. It is a polar map showing the air distances between continents. 2. It doesn't focus on any one area but shows the whole world. 3. a. It shows how close countries are to each other. b. It supports arguments against isolationism because of the nearness in time of countries. c. Answers will vary. 4. Other countries are our close neighbors. 5. Answers will vary. (These answers are based on the Polar Map of the World, page 1 of Rand McNally Premier Atlas.) **Building Writing Skills (p. 343):** Answers will vary. *Suggestions:* 1. diplomacy-the art of establishing relationships with countries that are useful and helpful to both sides; detente-an attempt to relax the tension in relations and increase peaceful negotiations of conflicts. 2. Free World countries have democratic forms of government. We are allies in the defense against communism. NATO and SEATO are two defense organizations of these countries. The economic systems are free enterprise or democratic socialism. Many allies are in Western Europe. 3. Foreign aid extends help to needy countries. It creates mutual benefits for both countries involved. Our policies are based on influencing countries towards democracy.

CHAPTER TWENTY-ONE: How Do State Executives Work? (p. 348) 1. Leading and directing the activities of a state. 2. Appointment, veto, power over the budget. 3. The body of administrators of a government or department. 4. A grievance commissioner should be elected or appointed to investigate citizens' complaints. **How Do County Executives Work? (p. 352)** 1. County Clerk, Sheriff, and County Attorney. 2. Clerk keeps the records of the county; the Sheriff maintains law and order, apprehends those who break the laws and collects evidence for the Attorney to prepare and present the case against the offender before the county court. 3. Maintain the physical buildings and properties of each county. 4. There is considerable cooperation with a trade-off of responsibilities. **How Do City Executives Work? (p. 355)** 1. The departments into which city administration is divided. 2. Manage the services of a city, hire the administrative department heads; administer the budget. 3. Perform executive functions in a limited area; avoid duplication of effort; not involved with politics. 4. They have little supervision or publicity, have large budgets and often perpetuate themselves after their usefulness has ended.

Thinking Skills (p. 356): 1. appointment, veto, budget 2. To prevent special boards from continuing on after their purpose is accomplished. 3. Each commissioner is responsible for the maintenance of buildings and properties within his or her precinct and for providing welfare for needy residents. 4. There is considerable trade-off between city and county such as maintenance of city-county hospitals and libraries. 5. It employs many people, operates on a budget, provides services to its residents and employees and establishes the rules and policies by which we live. 6. Special districts. **Vocabulary Skills (p. 356):** 1. sunset law 2. administrator 3. ombudsman 4. special district 5. executive 6. sheriff 7. city manager **Study Skills—Book Reports (p. 357):** Independent Project. **Beyond the Book (p. 357):** Independent Projects. **Vocabulary Check (p. 358):** 1. d. 2. b. 3. f. 4. a. 5. c. 6. e. 7. g. **Comprehension Check (p. 358):** 1. True 2. True 3. False 4. True 5. "Activities of the Governor:" b, d, e. **Skill Builders—Interpreting Diagrams (p. 359):** 1. The purpose of the diagram and the facts included. 2. Strong Mayor and Weak Mayor. 3. By the use of 3 separate columns. 4. How the governments are the same. 5. Diagrams will vary. *Suggestion:* **Building Writing Skills (p. 359):** Answers will vary. *Suggestions:* 1. What are some of the reasons for consolidating city and county governments? 2a. A special district performs limited functions. b. It collects its own taxes and runs its own business without the supervision of city or county government. c. They are called hidden governments because people are often unaware they exist. d. One district may cover several cities and is able to run its area more efficiently. e. The only control over a special district is by the vote. 3. City and county government often provide the same services, like schools, libraries, fire protection, road maintenance. By cooperating, they reduce costs and duplication of effort. Combining these duties and responsibilities cuts down on paperwork and waste of time and money.

UNIT FIVE TEST

A. 1. Carter, Sadat, Begin. It's an historical meeting. People who are aware of the government's activities.
   2. They appear friendly but formal and guarded.
   3. Answers will vary. *Suggestions:* Yes; it's part of his or her duty as chief of state. No; he or she should be more concerned with domestic issues.
   4. Yes. *or* No. Answers will vary. *Suggestions:* Yes; governments are made up of people. No; officials should set aside personal feelings as part of their responsible position.

B. Answers will vary.

C. Answers will vary.

CHAPTER TWENTY-TWO: How Did the Courts Develop? (p. 366) 1. First the states patterned state courts after those in England; then the Constitution established a federal court system in addition; both were independent branches of government. 2. It insures a fair trial by one's peers. 3. It prevents judges from being forced to decide without regard to justice. 4. To guarantee a fair and impartial trial. **How Does the Bill of Rights Protect Our Liberties? (p. 368)** 1. It guarantees the people their liberties and places limitations on government. 2. Freedom of religion, speech, assembly, petition, press, the right to keep and bear arms. 3. Yes—those reserved for the states or the people. 4. Prohibits unreasonable search, unjust trial or unusual punishment. **How Are Fair Trials Guaranteed? (p. 370)** 1. It forbids a trial to be held at a great distance from the crime, protects from unreasonable prosecution for treason, guarantees a trial by jury and the right to an attorney, protects against self incrimination, guarantees trial in an open court, limits to one trial for an offense. 2. Provides for a trial by peers rather than by a judge. 3. By providing for an attorney even if the accused cannot pay. 4. Testifying against oneself; being tried twice for the same crime. **How Does Government Provide Independent Courts? (p. 372)** 1. So that they may be free from influence and can see that everyone receives a fair hearing. 2. They are appointed for life and their salaries are fixed. 3. For life. 4. No federal official can threaten a judge with a decrease in salary or removal from office.

Thinking Skills (p. 374): The jury system developed over hundreds of years to insure fair trials for the common person. 2. By the freedom of judges from political influence. 3. Delete the third sentence. "A Guarantee of Fair Trials." **Vocabulary Skills (p. 374):** 1. True 2. True 3. self-incrimination 4. jeopardy 5. True 6. trial by ordeal 7. True **Study Skills—Watching Television News Shows (p. 375):** Independent Project **Beyond the Book (p. 375):** Independent Projects. **Vocabulary Check (p. 376):** 1. jury system 2. self-incrimination 3. jeopardy 4. justice 5. petition 6. trial by ordeal 7. cruel and unusual punishment **Comprehension Check (p. 376):** 1. True 2. True 3. Speech, religion, petition, press 4. True 5. By providing a trained person to speak for him in trial. **Skill Builders—Interpreting a Collage (p. 377):** Pictures, campaign buttons and memorabilia. Symbolic like the dove, eagle, scales, flag, star. 2. They all represent some important aspect of our history. 3. We are the history of our nation. 4. Answers will vary. 5. Presidents. **Building Writing Skills (p. 377):** Answers will vary. *Suggestions:* 1. With pictures and phrases showing the different methods of trials over the years. 2. If a person were assumed to be guilty there would be little efforrt made to establish his or her innocence. 3. "The Rights of an Accused Person" I. Right to an attorney A. Guaranteed by the Bill of Rights B. Counsel provided to those unable to pay II. Protection against self-incrimination A. Provided in the Fifth Amendment B. Cannot be used as evidence III. Right to face witnesses A. Trials are public hearings B. Evidence can be questioned IV. Jeopardy A. Danger of losing one's liberty B. Only one trial for an offense

CHAPTER TWENTY-THREE: What Kinds of Cases Appear In Court? (p. 382) 1. A criminal case is brought by the government to determine guilt and punishment of a person accused of a crime, and a civil case is a suit between people involving rights and privileges. 2. Different offenses involve laws on different levels, i.e., federal offenses are tried in federal courts. 3. To help clear the docket of many cases. 4. It doesn't involve a jury. **What Are the Duties of the United States Courts? (p. 384)** 1. District courts, courts of appeal and the Supreme Court. 2. It is the court of last appeal. 3. It decides whether or not an act of Congress is unconstitutional. 4. An act of Congress could not be enforced if it violated the constitutional rights of an individual. **What Are the Levels of State Courts? (p. 387)** 1. Justice of the Peace, district or circuit courts, and state supreme courts. 2. Misdemeanors are minor crimes, felonies are more serious crimes. 3. Because the district court is the chief trial court for cases involving state laws. 4. The state supreme court is a court of appeal to correct any error that may have occurred in a lower court; a police court tries persons charged with violation of city ordinances. **What Problems Face Our Courts? (p. 389)** 1. More and more people commit crimes and have differences that they take to court for settlement. 2. We don't want to interfere with the courts' protection of our rights. 3. They blame the courts for the ills of the country. 4. Those that don't require a jury.

Thinking Skills (p. 390): Answers will vary. *Suggestions:* 1. a. Suit between two people, disputes over property, disputes over payment. b. robbery, murder, kidnapping. 2. What laws are broken and which level of court has jurisdiction in the location of the crime or dispute. 3. delete sentence 3. "Problems Facing Our Courts." **Vocabulary Skills (p. 390):** 1. f. 2. b. 3. a. 4. d. 5. e. 6. c. 7. g. 8. h. **Study Skills—News Broadcasts (p. 391):** Independent Project **Beyond the Book (p. 391):** Independent Projects **Vocabulary Check (p. 392):** 1. appeal 2. True 3. True 4. False 5. True 6. misdemeanor 7. True 8. judicial review **Comprehension Check (p. 392):** 1. a and b 2. a **Skill Builders—Interpreting Photographs and Paintings (p. 393):** Independent Project. **Building Writing Skills (p. 393):** Answers will vary. *Suggestion:* 1. "Overworked Courts" There are many cases, such as divorce, traffic violations, adoptions, child custody, title research and auto accidents that could be handled by government agencies. These agencies could be created with the checks and balances that are inherent in our system of government and be subject to review every two years or so to prevent injustice. Where there is no dispute or crime involved there is no need for the broad expertise of a judge. There are paraprofessionals in many professions now. Paraprofessionals may be an answer to reducing the pressure on our vital judicial system. 2. The Supreme Court is a court of last appeal. It hears cases that are appealed from lower courts, both federal and state if a decision might have broad national impact. It must hear cases that involve disputes between states or cases involving the federal government. 3. a. In some cases the courts themselves have set limits on their actions to guarantee fair trials. b. Any person who is convicted of a violation of law is protected against excessive fines and cruel and unusual punishment. c. A person accused of a crime has the right to have a defense lawyer. d. In the U.S. a person is assumed to be innocent until proven guilty. e. If a person is convicted of a crime in one court and believes the court made a wrong decision, that person has the right to ask for a new trial in another court.

CHAPTER TWENTY-FOUR: How Does a Modern Law Enforcement Department Protect Us? (p. 398) 1. The evidence helps the jury to determine the guilt or innocence of a suspect. 2. It determines if there is enough evidence to justify bringing a suspect to trial. 3. It is a way to guarantee that a suspect will be available at the time of trial. 4. Sufficient evidence to issue a true bill of indictment. **What Does a Juvenile Officer Do? (p. 400)** 1. A juvenile is a boy who is between the ages of 10 and 17, or a girl age 10 to 18. 2. They are talked to and released to parents. 3. To help correct their behavior or pay for damages incurred by the juvenile. 4. In order to protect the young offender from influence of older law breakers. **How Does a Modern Law Enforcement Department Work? (p. 401)** 1. By providing complete background information on law violators. 2. Law enforcement officers must know more about law and civil liberties than the average citizen. 3. Two years of college training. 4. A complete physical description and a record of previous charges. **What Happens to a Juvenile in Court? (p. 404)** 1. The juvenile officer, probation officer, and prosecuting attorney meet to discuss the case and each tells what they know about the person and the home situation, then school records are gathered, witnesses located and evidence is prepared along with a social history of the child. 2. The child is provided with a lawyer if the parents can't afford one, evidence is heard to determine if the child is delinquent and correction is determined. 3. A felony is a serious crime such as burglary or murder. 4. The prosecutor must present enought evidence to tip the scales in his favor, to find the defendant guilty. **How Does a Lawyer Prepare a Defense for a Client? (p. 407)** 1. He is able to find all the evidence and information he needs to present his case. 2. A lawyer can't provide the best defense unless the client tells him the truth. 3. Power is not concentrated in any one area or official in the judicial process. 4. It would determine the depth of his involvement in the crime.

Thinking Skills (p. 408): 1. The briefing room where each shift is brought up to date on the activities; communications room where information is received; detectives, sergeants, lieutenants and district attorney who manage the department, research evidence, investigate leads and complete cases for trial. 2. Evidence is used to support the truth or falsity of the accusation. Interviews, search of the scene of the crime, collection of items of similarity in the actions of a suspect. 3. He interviews the juvenile and then the family and determines what course of action to take depending on the seriousness of the crime. 4. Only certified civilians and law enforcement officers. 5. Specialized training beyond the high school diploma. 6. "Independent Process" 7. "Lawyer's Preparation of a Good Defense" a. Does the defendant think he or she is guilty? b. What are the circumstances? c. Inform the person of their right. d. Is the charge a proper one? e. Was defendant told of their constitutional rights? f. Is he or she telling the truth to the lawyer? **Vocabulary Skills (p. 408):** 1. indictment 2. arraignment 3. juvenile 4. plaintiff 5. burden of proof 6. probation 7. bail 8. grand jury **Study Skills—Comparing Media Sources (p. 409):** Advantages: TV: immediate coverage and visual involvement. radio: immediate coverage Newspaper: more facts and analysis of events. weekly magazine: history of event and contributing factors. Disadvantages: TV: can't cover all events. radio: limited coverage. newspapers: opinion may affect facts. weekly magazine: may be biased. **Beyond The Book (p. 409):** Independent Projects. **Vocabulary Test (p. 410):** 1. f. 2. a. 3. b. 4. e. 5. c. 6. d. 7. h. 8. g. **Comprehension Check (p. 410):** 1. True 2. True 3. True 4. True 5. a, b, d, e **Skill Builders —Interpreting A Storyboard (p. 411):** Answers will vary. **Building Writing Skills (p. 411):** 1. Independent Project. 2. Answers will vary. *Suggestions:* Lawyers are trained professionals in the process of law. They use the process of inquiry to build their case. They know what the rights of the accused are. They can determine what is a proper charge. They are practiced at presenting a case in the best possible way.

CHAPTER TWENTY-FIVE: How Are Supreme Court Decisions Made? (p. 416) 1. Appeals reach the Supreme Court by way of a Writ of Mandamus from a lower court and is heard if it has important national implications. 2. Arguments are brought before the Court by the lawyers, and the Justices ask questions; they then meet in conference to present their opinions, a vote is taken with the majority deciding the case. 3. It has cut down on the paperwork involved in recording cases. 4. A dissenting opinion explains the minority decision; a concurring opinion that agrees with the majority but for different reasons. **What Are the Legal Rights of Individuals? (p. 417)** 1. Protection during search and seizure, the right to a speedy trial, the right to counsel, "Miranda" rights; the right to an impartial jury and judge; the right to call one's own witnesses and the right against self-incrimination. 2. States have included a Bill of Rights in their own constitutions. 3. They are relative and depend on the rights of others. 4. Extension of the legal rights in the Bill of Rights to the states. **What Are the Rights of Speech? (p. 420)** 1. It establishes the limit of tolerance for free speech and the danger it might create for the government. 2. The activities and literature of a group in opposition to the government can be as great a threat as actual speech. 3. If it does not constitute a threat to the government it is considered to be an expression of dissent only, one of the rights of free speech. 4. They wore their armbands only to express their opinion. **What Are the Rights Against Search and Seizure? (p. 422)** 1. It is based on the English law concept that a person's home is a castle. 2. It violates the basic human right of personal privacy. 3. It established the federal constitutional standards were the same for the states under the Fourteenth and Fifteenth Amendments. 4. Because the door was open. **What Are the Rights of Trial and Arrest? (p. 425)** 1. That the right of counsel is fundamental to the concept of justice. 2. It is part of the due process of law. 3. So that justice might be carried out. 4. A request to show just cause why and by what offense a person is being charged.

Thinking Skills (p. 426): 1. First Amendment: speech, religion, press, assembly, petition; Fourth Amendment: freedom from unreasonable search and seizure; Fifth Amendment: from self-incrimination. 2. Free Speech. I. First Amendment A. Not absolute rights B. Speech and assembly II. Clear and Present Danger A. *Schenck vs. U.S.* (1919) B. Immediate threat to country III. Silent or symbolic speech A. *Tinker vs. Des Moines School District* B. Expression of dissent in a peaceful manner IV. Court decisions A. *Dennis vs. U.S.* B. *Rochin vs. California* C. *Gideon vs. Wainwright* D. *Miranda vs. Arizona* 3. c. **Vocabulary Skills (p. 426):** 1. True 2. True 3. True 4. concurring opinion 5. True 6. due process 7. True **Study Skills—Using Different Sources of Information (p. 427):** Independent Projects **Beyond the Book (p. 427):** Independent projects. **Vocabulary Check (p. 428):** 1. original jurisdiction 2. appellate jurisdiction 3. Writ of Mandamus 4. concurring opinion 5. due process 6. procedural rights 7. dissenting opinion **Comprehension Check (p. 428):** 1. True 2. True 3. speech, assembly, due process of law 4. Arguments are heard and lawyers are questioned; justices prepare a decision; votes are cast at a weekly conference. 5. It is so stated in the Bill of Rights. **Skill Builders—Interpreting Cartoons (p. 429):** Answers will vary. **Building Writing Skills (p. 429):** Answers will vary. *Suggestions:* 1. A. Freedom of speech and assembly are relative and depend on the rights of others. b. Basis for the right of freedom from illegal search and seizure c. A citizen's right may be given up voluntarily, never taken away forcefully. 2. The Bill of Rights states our inherent rights and provides protection of them. The Magna Carta first set in writing certain inherent rights. The Mayflower Compact, Articles of Confederation, and the U.S. Constitution are built upon this heritage. 3. Answers will vary.

UNIT SIX TEST

A. 1. There are many different levels of law.
   2. Answers will vary. *Suggestions:* Yes, by removing certain types of cases from court hearings. No; all you could do is make more courts and judges.
   3. Answers will vary.
   4. Answers will vary. *Suggestions:* Yes, as much as is possible with their overload be-

cause of the freedom of judges from influence. No, people are not informed about the character of the judges that run for election.

B. Answers will vary.
C. Answers will vary.

CHAPTER TWENTY-SIX: What Is "Promoting the General Welfare"? (p. 436) 1. Every time we decide to do something good for the welfare of the public it will cost us something and restrict our freedom in one way or another. 2. It helps us to determine if the benefit is worth the cost and the loss of freedom. 3. We would be giving away all our freedoms. 4. Laws providing for the general welfare usually restrict our freedom. **How Have Other Governments Promoted the General Welfare? (p. 438):** 1. To prevent the strong from taking advantage of the weak. 2. The government takes complete responsibility for waying what is good for the citizens. 3. There may be a lot of security but no basis for individual ambition and pride in accomplishment. 4. It provides much security in benefits to the people as well as allowing personal freedoms and democratic procedures in government. **How Has the United States Promoted the General Welfare? (p. 441)** 1. Masses of people without jobs, income, food or shelter during the depression created more problems than the state and local governments could handle. 2. Social Security, Job Corps, food stamps, Headstart, Office of Economic Opportunity; Veterans benefits. 3. Because of the cost to taxpayers. 4. Training and opportunities for people who need to develop new or special skills. **What Resources Does Our Government Help to Conserve and Protect? (p. 445)** 1. Soil, water, nuclear resources, wildlife, air, and forests. 2. The Soil Conservation Service; Water Resources Board; Army Corps of Engineers; Nuclear Regulatory Commission; Fish and Wildlife Service; National Oceanic and Atmospheric Bureau; Forest Service; Energy Information Administration. 3. Wise use of natural resources is basic to promoting and maintaining the public welfare. 4. There is only a limited supply and industry is dependent upon them.

Thinking Skills (p. 446): 1. By providing services for people that they might not be able to get individually. 2. It becomes expensive, bureaucratic and bogged down with paperwork. 3. Answers will vary. *Suggestions:* a. Every time we decide to do something good for the welfare of the people it is going to cost us something in one way or another. b. Also once we decide how to do something we will usually restrict our freedoms in one way or another. c. So how much of a good thing can we do always comes down to the question of when we reach the point where the cost is greater than the good that is done. These programs were criticized because they greatly increased taxes. 4. "Wise Use of Our Environment." One important way our government protects us is by protecting our environment. The Soil Conservation Service teaches farmers to use the soil wisely. Other agencies work to protect our water supply, protect wildlife, and to regulate nuclear power plants. They also encourage the careful use of our natural resources. **Vocabulary Skills (p. 446):** 1. b. 2. c. 3. d. 4. a. 5. g. 6. e. 7. f. **Study Skills—Learning From News Shows (p. 447):** 1. a. They focus on discussing current issues. b. The format is different: debates present two sides of an issue, interviews and press conferences present one important person's viewpoint. 2. & 3. Answers will vary. **Beyond The Book (p. 447):** Independent Projects. **Vocabulary Check (p. 448):** 1. Medicare 2. True 3. Medicaid 4. general welfare 5. True 6. welfare state 7. True **Comprehension Check (p. 448):** 1. It is almost $59,000,000 higher. Answers will vary. *Suggestions:* 2. No, no department should be completely abolished. 3. It shows how the Constitution allows for an expansion of government into all areas to insure the public good. 4. Every time we decide to do something good for the welfare of people, it's going to cost us something one way or another. **Building Writing Skills (p. 449):** Answers will vary. *Suggestions:* 1. a. The Federal Nuclear Regulatory Commission makes and checks on safety standards for nuclear power plants. b. The Water Resources Board requires that cities and towns purify sewage before it is drained into any body of water. The Wildlife Service enforces laws passed by Congress to protect endangered species. The Forest Service works with lumber companies to help develop better ways of logging. 2. This is action taken by the government in providing goods and services or in passing laws that require people to help or not hurt each other. 3. "How do we do it" has been answered by various programs and services. "How much do we do" is a question that is constantly evaluated, every time a new program is proposed.

CHAPTER TWENTY-SEVEN: What Is Our Nation's Energy Problem? (p. 455) 1. The development of our industries depended upon machinery that needs oil to run. 2. Saudi Arabia, Iran, Venezuela, Kuwait, Iraq formed OPEC to control the price of oil on the world market. 3. Things that were formerly inexpensive became very expensive, and the OPEC countries became very important in our foreign affairs. 4. They began to hold back much of their oil to force prices higher. **What Can Be Done to Solve the Energy Problem? (p. 460)** 1. The conservation approach, the "large-scale" approach and the "small-scale" approach. 2. Conservation amounts to real savings in energy but would change our lifestyle; the "large-scale" approach is expensive and hard on the environment but makes the U.S. more self-sufficient in energy supply; the "small-scale" approach is not polluting but doesn't supply energy in sufficient quantity. 3. The balanced approach includes the advantages of each approach and reduces the advantages. 4. There was a radiation leak. **What Is the Role of Government in the Energy Problem? (p. 463)** 1. Determined where fuel oil could be used; assured available supplies to colder climates; established temperature controls; rationed gasoline; determined where fuel use was most important; provided money to help people pay heating bills. 2. Determine the price of natural gas and oil; increase the conservation of energy; find new ways to develop energy supplies. 3. Lowering highway speed limits, requiring cars to get better mileage. 4. It seeks new sources of energy without harming the environment.

Thinking Skills (p. 464): 1. a. To run automobiles, machinery, planes, trains, trucks, make plastics, drugs, and other petroleum based products. b. Oil and oil products were plentiful and cheap and we expanded the machinery of our industry on that basis. 2. We became dependent upon other countries for our oil supply and when it was cut back we were all forced to use less and pay more. 3. They are solutions to part of the problem because they can provide clean, simple and inexpensive energy on a small scale, for homes and small businesses. 4. b. **Vocabulary Skills (p. 464):** 1. conserve. 2. OPEC 3. energy 4. renewable resources 5. synfuel 6. solar power **Study Skills—Using the Yellow Pages (p. 465):** Independent Projects **Beyond the Book (p. 465): Independent Projects Vocabulary Check (p. 466):** 1. True 2. solar power 3. True 4. True 5. True 6. synfuel **Comprehension Check (p. 466):** 1. b 2. b 3. d 4. a 5. coal **Skill Builders—Interpreting Cartoons (p. 467):** 1. Answers will vary. *Suggestion:* a. Conservation and solar energy. b. It is the least harmful to the environment. c. Conservation. d. Nuclear. 2. Cartoons will vary. **Building Writing Skills (p. 467):** 1. The OPEC countries produce most of the world's fuel oil. If they wish to cut back on production and exports, we are left with an energy shortage and everything becomes more expensive. 2. Running farm equipment, trucks, food processing machinery became more expensive. Chemical fertilizers increased in price. 3. Answers will vary. *Suggestions:* Energy: The Conservation Approach. This approach should be used in cooperation with any other because it promotes clean environment, encourages us to value the resources we have and makes us aware of the limits of nature. 4. Increased need for energy from government lands may harm the wilderness environment.

CHAPTER TWENTY-EIGHT: What Is the History of Education In the United States? (p. 472) 1. Education began in the churches and by home tutoring and first became public in 1647 when a Massachusetts law stated that parents had to educate their children. 2. By teaching children information and values that Americans should hold in common, and standardized our language. 3. It provided for higher education in agriculture and technology. 4. Answers will vary. Educated citizens insure the continued success of our democracy. **How Is the Federal Government Involved In Education? (p. 475)** 1. Federal funds help to determine what is taught and has expanded our educational opportunities. 2. It established that segregated schools are unconstitutional. 3. State, local and private funds. 4. It distributes the funds approved by Congress for education. **How Are Educational Systems Organized? (p. 476)** 1. It works to establish and improve the quality of education throughout the country. 2. They set some standards for the local school systems and administer state school funds. 3. They make rules for the school system, hire teachers and administrators and control the amount of money given to schools. 4. High schools where trades are learned to prepare a student for work. **How Do Governments Support Higher Education? (p. 479)** 1. By giving financial aid to colleges and universities. 2. Mainly by state and local taxes. 3. By vote of the people, to provide vocational education, on the job training and a start on bachelor's degrees. 4. From grants for special projects, and state assistance for student tuition.

Thinking Skills (p. 480): 1. In homes and as apprentices or in England. 2. It required children of a certain age to attend school. Massachusetts in 1852. 3. To improve the quality of education throughout the country by giving aid and gathering new information. 4. b. **Vocabulary Skills (p. 480):** 1. b. 2. c. 3. d. 4. e. 5. f. 6. g. 7. a. **Study Skills—Using Different Sources of Information (p. 481):** Independent Projects. **Beyond the Book (p. 481):** Independent Projects. **Vocabulary Check (p. 482):** 1. public schools 2. compulsory 3. real tax 4. tutition 5. vocational 6. segregated 7. personal **Comprehension Check (p. 482):** 1. True 2. It gives us the power to determine through our elected officials how we want to resolve the issues. 3. Taxes on personal property other than real estate. 4. True 5. Establishes and maintains the quality of education across the country. **Skill Builders —Interpreting Tables (p. 483):** a. Business and management. Education and Social Science b. Military Science c. Law. Because of the increase in legal activity in our judical system. **Building Writing Skills (p. 483):** Answers will vary. *Suggestions:* 1. Segreated schools are unequal in the quality of education provided. The *Brown vs. Topeka* case stated that segrated schools violated the equal protection clause of the Fourteenth Amendment, and began the systematic desegregation of our schools and other institutions. 2. Real property taxes are taxes on real estate, housing, buildings and businesses; personal property taxes are taxes on any property other than real property.

CHAPTER TWENTY-NINE: What Is Freedom of Religion? (p. 487) 1. People may believe as they choose and may practice those beliefs as long as they do not violate the law. 2. By prohibiting religious practices that might break other laws. 3. If a leader gains enough control over the followers to threaten their welfare. 4. Answers will vary. **What Does the Separation of Church and State Mean? (p. 491)** 1. "Neither a state nor the federal government can set up a church or pass laws which aid one religion, aid all religions or prefer one religion to another." 2. Through out national motto, the oath of office public officials take, the prayers said before sessions of Congress and Supreme Court and national holidays. 3. Answers will vary. The Supreme Court has ruled which religious observations violate the First Amendment and what non-devotional study of religious ideas are legal and have extended public services to parochial study.

Thinking Skills (p. 492): 1. They were arrested, tortured or killed. 2. So they could worship as they pleased. No. They may have feared that they would once again be forced to worship another way and decided to prevent this. 3. Freedom to worship as one pleases as long as the belief does not violate the law. 4. A person may not break a law, hurt another, or disturb the peace in the name of a religious belief. Yes. Religion is a very emotional subject and the law is objective in its protection of rights of others. 5. No church is supported by the government and no taxes are collected to support a church. No laws are passed to control patricular churches. 6. b. **Vocabulary Skills (p. 492):** 1. evolution 2. state religion 3. True 4. True 5. True **Study Skills—Using Skimming Techniques (p. 493):** No answers required. **Beyond the Book (p. 493):** Independent Projects. **Vocabulary Check (p. 494):** 1. evolution 2. state religion 3. religious freedom 4. separation of church and state 5. parochial. **Comprehension Check (p. 494):** 1. False 2. True 3. True 4a. 1 & 4. b. 2 & 3. **Skill Builders—Interpreting Photographs (p. 495):** a. They still use horse and buggy. b. Can't tell from picture. c. The people show this. d. Can't tell from picture. e. They are in a country scene with no signs of city. f. They look like farm people from the 1800's when life was simpler. **Building Writing Skills (p. 495)** 1. Answers will vary. *Suggestion:* The Supreme Court has ruled that prayer, flag salute, and religious teaching cannot be done in public schools. Non-devotional use of the Bible and study of different religions is permissible. Parochial schools may receive government aid as do public schools. Evolution can be taught as established by the Scopes trial. 2. (c) The State of Tennesse passed a law prohibiting the teaching of theories contrary to the creationist beliefs that were stated in the Bible. They did this in 1925. (added) The theory of evolution was becoming acceptable at that time. (d) English scientist Charles Darwin theorized that man evolved over millions of years from lower forms of life. (b) John T. Scopes was tried and convicted for teaching evolution in the public schools. (a) The Supreme released Scopes on a technicality. 3. Why was freedom of religion included in the First Amendment? 4. Answers will vary. *Suggestion:* No. There are so many different beliefs that each should be taught separately, so no one is forced to accept what is contrary to their beliefs. Yes. A religious belief is a very important part of education.

UNIT SEVEN TEST

A. 1. It has expanded and there is much more to be taught. Answers will vary. *Suggestions:* Better; more money is put into and more time and research. Worse; our reading and math abilities are low.
2. Answers will vary.
3. Answers will vary.

B. Answers will vary.

CHAPTER THIRTY: Why Do Nations Need an Economic System? (p. 503): 1. There is less of something available than the people want or need. 2. Answers will vary. So that as many needs as possible can be filled. 3. We all want to be able to have the goods and services we need. 4. We can only use a natural resource for one thing at a time. **How Do Other Economic Systems Work? (p. 506):** 1. In a traditional economy what will be produced today is the same as what has always been produced so things change very little and the economy grows slowly. 2. Because the people are not allowed to participate in determining what good will be produced and who will receive them. 3. Answers will vary. 4. Societies were all originally tribal in organization. **How Does a Free Market Work? (p. 510):** 1. Free choice and private property. 2. Competitive markets provide people with the freedom to choose what will be produced. 3. Answers will vary. Because it is part of a free market economy. 4. Taxation and gas rationing. **What Problems Do All Economies Face? (p. 513):** 1. Recession and inflation. 2. A recession begins when people stop buying large numbers of goods and others will not be needed to produce those goods and will lose their jobs and their income. 3. Stopping inflation can cause a recession by causing people to spend less money and buy fewer goods. 4. Unemployment and lower production.

Thinking Skills (p. 514): 1. Because there is a limit to the ability to supply sufficient amounts of all goods everyone wants. 2. What goods will be produced and who gets the goods that are produced. 3. A traditional economy does things the way it always has. A planned economy is set up by a few people and is very controlled. 4. Because the questions of economic choice are answered by people free to choose what to buy and what to sell. 5. Private property is essential to free choice. If you do not own your business you can't decide what to sell. If you don't own your labor or skills you can't choose how you will use them. **Vocabulary Skills (p. 514):** 1. economic scarcity. 2. planned 3. private property 4. mixed practices 5. recession 6. inflation 7. competitive economy 8. free enterprise **Study Skills—Using Periodicals (p. 515):** Independent Project. **Beyond the Book (p. 515):** Independent Projects. **Vocabulary Check (p. 516):** 1. True 2. competitive market 3. economic scarcity 4. mixed practices 5. True 6. recession 7. True **Comprehension Check (p. 516):** 1. c 2. a **Skill Builders—Interpreting Tables (p. 517):** Answers will vary. **Building Writing Skills (p. 517):** Answers will vary. *Suggestion:* 1. c. A recession occurs when an economy fails to work in making jobs and incomes available to people. Many people are out of work, or unemployed. Then they are not able to buy the goods and services they need and want. Life becomes very difficult for those who are unemployed. 2. It is almost impossible to have a pure form of economy. Interactions between people lead to mixed practices. It is a good idea because everyone benefits from the opportunities and flexibility of a mixed economy. 3. Answers will vary.

CHAPTER THIRTY-ONE: What Is a Capitalist Economy? (p. 523) 1. Capitalism is a free economy and buildings, land and the things that produce goods and services are privately owned by citizens, while in communism these things are owned by the government. 2. About 95% goes to pay for costs and 5% goes to profit. 3. Profits make it possible and worthwhile for a person to stay in business. 4. By maintaining prices and wages near what they are worth all people and all businesses. **How Does Our Government Protect Competition? (p. 526):** 1. A large company or group of companies who control prices and selling practices to eliminate competition. Anti-trust laws require businesses to compete fairly. 2. It is easier and cheaper to have only one firm provide the service. 3. It encourages lower prices and better service. 4. It is being reduced by deregulation of the service and encouragement of competition in new ways of providing the service. **How Did Change Take Place In Our Economy? (p. 529):** 1. Answers will vary. Cars have replaced carriages, ships move without sails, airplanes fly, light and heat are made without fire, food and clothes are bought from huge stores. 2. The things we take for granted every day come from our ability to produce new and abundant goods. 3. Machines produce more, at a faster rate and with more control, thus increasing production. 4. Answers will vary. Knowledge creates new ways to use natural resources to promote economic growth. **How Does a Modern Economy Affect You? (p. 533):** 1. People are working fewer hours and producing more. 2. By use of machines that can produce more in less time. 3. The change from manufacturing to services and the increasing use of complicated machinery. 4. Paraprofessionals, such as dental assistants, work along with professionals.

Thinking Skills (p. 534): 1. The business process consists of people or businesses trying to sell something for more than what it costs so that they make a profit and can stay in business. 2. Competition encourages business to provide the best goods or services at the lowest price possible. 3. Electric companies, water, and telephone. They are basic to our way of life and we and the government depend upon them. 4. Economic conditions change because new ways to use our resources are discovered. 5. Oil, sugar, steel and many other products. Congress passed anti-trust laws. 6. Competition causes people to make their best effort. Competition in sports is often direct and physical, business is not. **Vocabulary Skills (p. 534):** 1. automation 2. capitalism 3. communist 4. profit 5. trust 6. public utility 7. monopoly 8. socialism. **Study Skills—Using the Encyclopedia (p. 535):** Independent Study. Answers will vary. **Beyond the Book (p. 535):** Independent Projects. **Vocabulary Check (p. 536):** 1. monopoly 2. automation 3. capitalism 4. public utility 5. socialism 6. communism 7. profit 8. monopoly **Comprehension Check (p. 536):** 1. True 2. The anti-trust laws were passed. 3. True 4. Nine-tenths of all Americans lived on farms. 5. Forty hours 6. True **Skill Builders—Interpreting Tables (p. 537):** 1. Yes 2. Mining and utilities 3. It's the hardest work. No. The free economy determines the salaries. **Building Writing Skills (p. 537):** Answers will vary. *Suggestions:* 1. The business process consists of people selling goods for more than it costs to make them. Competition insures the highest quality product at the lowest cost while still providing a profit for the businesses. 2. Companies got together and set prices. Monopolies and trusts were formed. They agree not to compete. There is no competition to control prices. To have only one seller is not good for the buyer who has no other choice. 3. Deregulation will return competition to areas of our economy and the value of goods and services rendered will increase along with the costs.

CHAPTER THIRTY-TWO: What Are a Consumer's Responsibilities? (p. 542): 1. We must make a choice between the many ways we can spend our money, and accept that when we buy one thing we can't buy another until we have more money. 2. Budgeting helps us to think before we spend money so we can make wise choices. 3. So we can be aware of how much we spend and what it is we buy, and avoid making mistakes in buying. 4. Buying without thinking about our need for the item. **How Does a Consumer Become Informed? (p. 546):** 1. It gives us information about what is for sale, what it looks like, how long it will last, where it's available and how much it costs. 2. Articles in newspapers and magazines, government pamphlets and consumer affairs publications. 3. Because it involves all of the other things we must buy after the first purchase. 4. When an advertiser claims an advantage for a product it does not have. **How Does a Consumer Prepare for the Future? (p. 548)** 1. By saving, by investing, with insurance and by buying durable goods. 2. Stock investments may pay higher dividends than the interest on a bank account but there is the risk that the company may lose money or go out of business. 3. Life insurance makes money available after a parent dies; auto insurance pays for the costs of an accident; health insurance pays for medical and hospital expenses. 4. A way of saving money for income after retirement. **What Should You Look for In a Contract? (p. 551):** 1. It is legally binding under the law and reminds each party of their part in the agreement. 2. As proof that he or she has agreed to pay the amount specified in the contract. 3. The court might order the person to pay all the money owned at once. 4. For non-payment of credit.

Thinking Skills (p. 552): Answers will vary. *Suggestions:* 1. Having money forces us to make a choice between the many ways we might use it. 2. So that you can make responsible choices, get the most value for your money, and not overspend. 3. By investments in securities, bonds, real estate and insurance. 4. So that the costs of an accident will be paid and the injured parties will not be financially hurt. By insuring that your expenses will be paid if you or your car are injured. 5. The items agreed to in a contract can be forgotten or changed if they are not written down. **Vocabulary Skills (p. 552):** 1. interest 2. True 3. garnisheed 4. True 5. warranty 6. consumers 7. True **Study Skills—Using the Glossary and Dictionary (p. 553):** Answers will vary. *Suggestion:* consumer: (dictionary) one that consumes (uses up, does away with completely, destroys); specifically one that utilizes economic goods; (glossary) A person who buys goods and services for his or her own use or that of his or her family. **Beyond the Book (p. 553):** Independent Projects. **Vocabulary Check (p. 554):** 1. principal 2. budget 3. warranty 4. consumer 5. impulse buying 6. contract 7. reposses 8. garnisheed **Comprehension Check (p. 554):** 1. True 2. It gives factual information about the product, how much it might cost, how to use it and benefits to use. 3. True 4. It allows the consumer to use money wisely within the limitation of its availability. 5. True **Skill Builders—Interpreting Charts (p. 555):** a. Education of people 25-34 years old. b. There are 8% fewer in 1970. c. Yes. Statistics prove this in the chart. d. Income varies according to level of education. e. Answers will vary. f. Yes. You can make more money if you have more education. **Building Writing Skills (p. 555):** Answers will vary. *Suggestion:* 1. Before buying a refrigerator, read unbiased opinions about different makes. Shop around for the best price. Find out where to borrow sufficient money at lowest interest. 2. Banks or savings and loans, stocks and bonds, real estate investments are various ways to save. Answers will vary. *Suggestion:* I favor real estate because the value of property is always increasing. 3. Being informed is being responsible for yourself. You can purchase exactly what you want when you have the facts about what you want. You will be aware of all the costs involved in buying something. You will be better prepared to spend within your limits. 4. A person must be advised of the process. Because of the Supreme Court ruling.

UNIT EIGHT TEST

A. 1. Not as many people will be able to buy the product.
   2. Lower
   3. Where the lines cross. The price allows for demand to equal supply.

B. Answers will vary.

C. Answers will vary.

We The People

We The People

CIVICS IN THE UNITED STATES

Robert A. Carter
Social Studies Coordinator
Midland Independent School District
Midland, Texas

John M. Richards
Corpus Christi State University
Corpus Christi, Texas

Coronado Publishers

San Diego • New York • Chicago • Dallas

Cover: We the People, collage on wood by Fred Otnes (American, 1926—). Coronado Publishers collection. Photographed for printing by Stephen McCarroll.

Printed in the United States of America ISBN 0-15-771000-9

Table of Contents

We the People is your textbook. You will find many references throughout the book to "you" as a student. We have made every effort to provide the information and activities you need to understand our American government and your place within it.

Tradition: This is an unusual book in that it is both old and new. On the one hand, *We the People* is one of the most enduring American textbooks. It has been in print for more than fifty years, and we are the second generation of authors that the book has had. On the other hand, this is an entirely new book, with a new format and page design, totally new artwork, and content that is either newly written or completely revised from the previous edition. As you will learn in the text, we believe that combining respect for tradition with an ability to adapt to the needs of the time is what gives the American system its strength.

Constitutional Theme: The theme of *We the People,* as the title indicates, is the United States Constitution. Each chapter begins with an excerpt from the Constitution, and the content of the chapter explains how a particular aspect of our government relates to, and is affected by, the words of this great document.

Consistent Format: Your book is arranged in a systematic way. There are eight Units and thirty-two Chapters. Each chapter has a two-page introduction. Then there is a Pre-Test and the "Building Vocabulary" section. At the end of the chapter, there is a Summary, followed by two pages of "Building Skills in Civics" and a two-page Test. Within the chapter, each section has three Objectives and four "Check for Understanding" activities.

Varied Design: We believe that Civics is an exciting subject, and we have attempted to convey this excitement to you. We've tried to express the great diversity within our nation by providing a wide variety of artwork in the book—historical photographs and paintings, original illustrations, cartoons, charts, diagrams, graphs, maps, and tables.

Patriotism: As you read *We the People* you will become aware that we, the authors, believe the American system of government to be the very best. We don't apologize for this belief. Through your use of this book, we hope you will reach this conclusion yourself. We have also emphasized that each of your rights carries a responsibility. It takes effort for a free people to remain free.

We hope that you will enjoy using this book, and also that you will remember what you have learned here as you carry out your role as an American citizen.

Unit One · Freedom Through Responsible Citizenship

*I*f someone said that you must have rules in order to be free, what would you say? A logical answer might be: "You're wrong. How can I be free if there are rules telling me what I can or can't do?"

But let's imagine what would happen if we did do whatever we wanted to. What if you decided that you were going to drive on the left side of the road instead of the right? The result would be that someone would get hurt. So, you can see that rules are necessary for our welfare. Without them, we really do not have freedom—only chaos and disorder. Such is the basis for our government.

Each unit begins with an illustration that depicts the theme of the unit itself. In this case, people are exercising responsible citizenship by obeying the traffic laws.

Have students identify two instances in the illustration where people are obeying the law. (Car is stopping; people are crossing at proper time.)

Chapter One · The American Citizen

Document: The Constitution of the United States (September 17, 1787)

"WE, the people of the United States . . . do ordain and establish this Constitution for the United States of America." (Preamble)

Section 1. All persons born or naturalized in the United States, and subject to the jurisdiction thereof, are citizens of the United States and of the State wherein they reside. No State shall make or enforce any law which shall abridge the privileges or immunities of citizens of the United States; nor shall any State deprive any person of life, liberty, or property, without due process of law; nor deny to any person within its jurisdiction the equal protection of the laws." (Amendment XIV—July 28, 1868)

The United States shall guarantee to every State in this Union a Republican Form of Government . . ." (Article IV, Section 4)

"To establish a uniform Rule of Naturalization (power granted to Congress) . . ." (Article 1, Section 8)

No Person except a natural born Citizen . . . shall be eligible to the Office of President; . . ." (Article II, Section 1)

Each chapter also begins with a thematic illustration. This one depicts the Constitutional Convention.

The entire text of the Constitution is printed in the Appendix, beginning on page 564.

WE, THE PEOPLE, as stated in the Preamble to the Constitution, means every man, woman, and child in the United States. The Constitution is for everyone. When the Fourteenth Amendment was added to the Constitution in 1868, it brought the full rights of citizenship to all the states. Your Constitution guarantees that you will live within a republic—a form of government that allows representation for all its citizens.

From the beginning of our nation, our citizens have come from all parts of the world. The Constitution provides that Congress can pass laws making these new persons citizens of our land. It is a privilege that has become the envy of people throughout the world.

FOCUSING IDEAS

- Being a citizen means living in a particular country and pledging loyalty to that country's government.
- The early settlers of America were the Indians, Spanish, Blacks, French, and English.
- The major immigration movements in America occurred between 1600–1860, 1865–1890, 1890–1924, and 1945 to the present.
- People become citizens of the U.S. either by birth or by choice.

"Focusing Ideas" appear at the end of each chapter introduction. They describe the central concepts that are presented in the chapter.

The illustration depicts immigrants arriving at New York Harbor in the late 1800's, during the peak period of immigration. Ask your students what they know about conditions in the countries these immigrants left.

PRE-TEST

1. What does it mean to be a citizen? What does citizenship involve?
2. Who were the early settlers of what became the United States of America?
3. What were the major immigration movements by which the United States was settled?
4. How does someone from another country become a citizen of the United States?

WHAT DOES IT MEAN TO BE A CITIZEN?

Objectives: After you have read this section, you will be able to:

- Describe what "citizenship" means.
- Explain why it is important for citizens to accept their responsibilities.
- Understand the role of the Constitution in defining the rights of a citizen.

You have probably heard the words "loyalty" and "allegiance" at some time in your life. Almost everyone in this country has said the Pledge of Allegiance to the flag. Americans feel great pride in their country as they recite:

"I pledge allegiance to the flag of the United States of America, and to the republic for which it stands, one nation under God, indivisible, with liberty and justice for all."

Do you know that if citizens did not give their loyalty or *allegiance* to their country, there would really be no country? Do you realize that if everyone refused to accept

This class begins each school day by reciting the Pledge of Allegiance. Does your class do this? Have you thought about what the words mean?

Building Vocabulary:
allegiance *(4)* • government *(5)* • republic *(5)* • citizenship *(6)* • immigrant *(8)* • alien *(11)* • naturalization *(11)* • treason *(12)*

Each chapter begins with a Pre-Test. The questions in the Pre-Test are identical to the subheadings within the chapter.

The Pledge summarizes the concept of American citizenship very eloquently in just thirty-one words. As you discuss its meaning, you may wish to break it down phrase by phrase.

The United States draws its strength from the fact that our society is made up of many different groups. We are unique in that our country was settled by people from all over the world.

Ask students to compare the text of the Pledge of Allegiance to that of the American's Creed, written in 1917 by William Tyler Page.

the responsibilities and duties of citizenship, this country and its states and towns could no longer function? Loyalty is a very necessary part of citizenship. In fact, one way to lose your citizenship is to be found guilty of trying to harm your own country or to help its enemies.

As a citizen, you live under a *government.* Government is the way people have organized to make rules or laws by which they can live together in peace. Your form of government in the United States is a *republic.* In a republic, the people govern themselves through elected representatives. Since you and other people—the citizens—make up the government, your acceptance of your responsibilities and duties is very important to the working of this nation.

This nation has pledged through a document called "The Constitution of the United States of America," that its citizens are protected by liberty and have certain rights. These rights exist to provide justice for everyone. The agreement works most effectively as a partnership. You accept your responsibilities, and the government protects your rights. In this way, government can be made to serve your needs as a citizen.

The United States is one nation made up of many different racial and ethnic groups. Throughout our history, it has been neces-

Discuss the concept of loyalty to one's country. Ask your students to name at least two people from your state, past or present, who have shown exceptional loyalty to our country.

Ask your students to do research on the word "republic" and discuss how this form of government developed.

sary for our citizens to work together to maintain national unity. When a country splits into individual groups and each one wants its own way, civil disorder usually occurs. Learning how to keep the United States as "one nation" (as the Pledge of Allegiance says) is a vital part of your citizenship education.

A *citizen* is a person who lives in a particular country and who pledges loyalty to the government of that country. Many millions of people have emigrated to these shores to obtain the prize of *citizenship.* At one time, more than a million persons each year came to our country. These were people who had known what it was to live without freedom and in poverty, and who had come to live where they might enjoy personal liberty and the opportunity to earn a living.

Check for Understanding: Now that you have completed this section, you should be able to answer these questions:

1. What is the meaning of the term "citizenship"?
2. What role does the Constitution have in determining the rights of an American citizen?
3. What can happen if people do not accept their responsibility as citizens?
4. What is the particular form of government that the United States has?

WHO WERE THE EARLY SETTLERS OF AMERICA?

Objectives: After you have read this section, you will be able to:

- List the major racial and ethnic groups to settle in America.
- Tell which ethnic group became the dominant one in America.
- Name one influence on the settlement of America of each of these groups—Indians, Spanish, Blacks, French, and English.

The first Americans

The first settlers of America were the Indians, or Native Americans. The name "Indian" was first used in 1492, when Christopher Columbus landed in the Americas with the mistaken belief that he had found a western route to India. Today, many members of this group refer to themselves as "Native Americans," because they were the first people to settle the Americas.

Many scientists believe the Indians originally came from Asia. They probably traveled in boats and came to America through Alaska and the Aleutian Islands. Some groups might have come by sled over the ice during the winter. The scientists say that these Asian peoples then moved southward through North and South America.

No one knows the exact number of Indians who lived in the Americas before the time of Columbus, but anthropologists have estimated the number to be between one and three million in what is now the United States. These Indians helped the Europeans to survive when they first arrived in the new land. Without such assistance, it is almost certain that the first European settlers would have perished.

Blacks in America

The first black people arrived in America in 1619 at the colony of Jamestown, Virginia. In the following years, hundreds of thousands of black slaves were brought from Africa and the West Indies. Most of them

Each section of the chapter begins with a list of three Objectives. (See above for an example.)

The American Indians (Native Americans) have contributed much to this country. How many contributions can your students list? (Foods, place names, new words in the language, etc.)

were sent to the southern colonies to work on the large plantations there. These blacks were not immigrants in the same way that the Europeans were. They were settlers, of course, but they did not choose to come to America. As they cleared the land and worked in the fields, they made a significant contribution to the development of America. Today, their descendants as free men and women continue to enrich American life with their cultural contributions.

The Spanish settlers

Columbus' voyages gave Spain a head start in settling the New World. In the 1500's Spain established a huge empire in the Americas. Eventually, large Spanish settlements were found in what is now Florida and California, and in Texas, New Mexico, and other parts of the American Southwest. The Spanish built missions, cattle ranches, and farms. In time, many of these Spanish settlers married Native Americans. Today, the descendants of the early settlers maintain the customs, traditions, food, and language of Spanish America.

The French settlers

The French established colonies in the New World at around the same time that the English did. Most French colonies were along the Great Lakes. French settlements could also be found along the Mississippi River, especially New Orleans, and in the state of Texas. These French settlers engaged mainly in fur trading and farming.

By working with the Indians, the French hoped to maintain control over much of North America. However, it was difficult to oversee such a vast territory, and a disagreement arose between the English and the French that led to war. In the French and Indian War, the French and their Indian allies were defeated by the English. Thus, the English colonies were able to establish their control over America. Today, French influence in the United States is best seen in the Creole language and the customs of the people of the state of Louisiana, whose ancestors originally came from France.

The English colonies

The original thirteen colonies that became the United States were settled mainly by immigrants from England. The first permanent English colony was established at Jamestown, Virginia in 1607. Early colonies were also established in parts of what is now New York, New Jersey, Pennsylvania, and Delaware by the Dutch and the Swedes. However, the English also settled in these areas, and eventually they took control of them.

The early colonies had many people with different languages and customs. At one time it seemed that the new land would have three languages—Spanish, French, and English. The English colonies were the strongest, and gradually the others began to follow English customs. The official language, the law, and the government of the United States are from the English tradition. However, each group of people added their own customs to the new land in which they lived.

Check for Understanding: Now that you have completed this section, you should be able to answer these questions.

1. What were the major racial or ethnic groups that settled in America in early times?
2. Which of these ethnic groups became the dominant one?
3. What is one influence on America of each of these groups?
4. How did the blacks come to America?

For what were the following people famous? Benjamin Banneker (helped design Washington, D.C.); Martin Luther King, Jr. (led the Civil Rights movement); George Washington Carver (widespread agricultural knowledge); Barbara Jordan (outstanding legislator). Ask your students to name three additional prominent black people and list their accomplishments.

WHAT WERE THE MAJOR IMMIGRATION MOVEMENTS TO THIS COUNTRY?

Objectives: After you have read this section, you will be able to:

- Describe the ethnic makeup of America in 1790.
- List the four major immigration movements and the ethnic makeup of each one.
- Explain how immigration has been limited at various times in history.

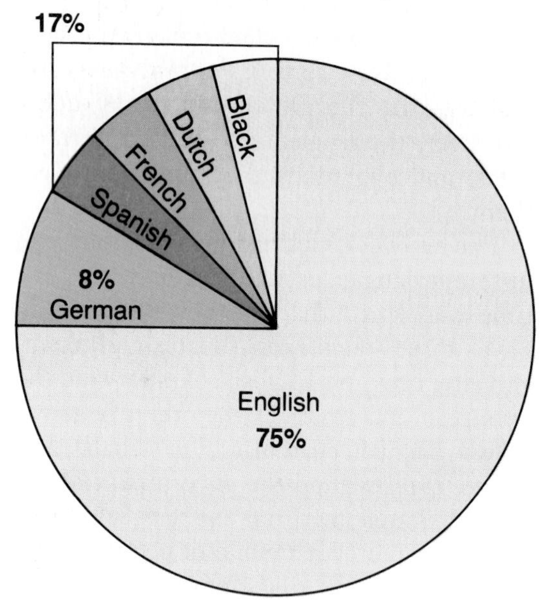

The graph shows the percentages of the different nationalities in America in 1790.

Immigration to 1790

America has been molded by millions of *immigrants*. These are people who came to live in America from other countries. In one sense, all the people who have ever lived in America were immigrants, even the Native Americans, because they had all come here from another place. But the word "immigrant" as we use it today means those persons who emigrated to the United States after the country was founded as a new nation in 1776.

In the first census, taken in 1790, there were nearly four million Americans. The census is the official counting of the people and is taken every ten years. At that time, 75 percent of the people were of English descent. German-Americans were eight percent of the population. Smaller groups of people were of Dutch, French, Spanish, and Swedish background. There were an additional 750,000 black people, living mostly in the South.

The first immigration movement

The English were the largest immigrant group in America from 1600 to 1800. From 1815 to 1860, the first large movement of immigration took place. Most of these immigrants were from western Europe. They came not only from England, but also from the other parts of the British Isles—Scotland, Wales, and Ireland—and from southwestern Germany as well. About seven and a half million people came at that time. A small number of Chinese came also. During the Civil War, immigration virtually stopped.

The second immigration movement

The second great wave of immigration began at the close of the Civil War in 1865. This movement lasted until about 1890. Some western Europeans still came, but now northern Europeans came, too. These newcomers were from Norway, Sweden, Denmark, and Finland. About eight million people made the journey to America during that time.

On a map of the U.S., show cities that reflect Spanish influence on our geography, such as San Antonio, Los Angeles, El Paso, Santa Fe, etc. Ask your students to write a paragraph or two showing Spanish contributions to America. Then have them do similar paragraphs for other ethnic groups.

The third immigration movement

The largest movement of immigrants came between 1890 and 1924. More than twenty million people arrived in America. People still came from western and northern Europe. Now, many came from eastern and southern Europe as well. Czechs, Slovaks, Hungarians, Serbs, Poles, Russians, and Ukranians came in large numbers.

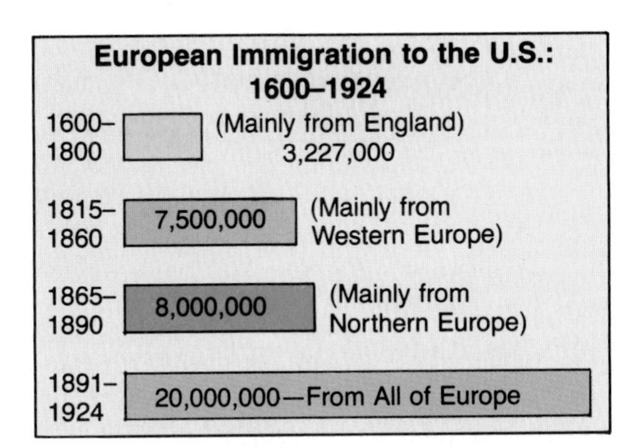

The four major immigration movements.

Nearly two million Jews from eastern Europe, and four million persons from Italy came to America also. Other countries from which immigrants came were Rumania, Greece, Turkey, Albania, and Syria. Japanese, Filipinos, East Indians, and Mexicans came to start new homes in the United States. By 1900, immigrants represented almost every country in the world.

The fourth immigration movement

The last great movement dates from the end of World War II, in 1945, to the present day. This movement is different from the others in that it includes a number of people who were forced to leave their countries as refugees. Many immigrants came to the U.S. in the years immediately after World War II from countries that had been involved in the war. In later years, there were more refugees from other countries affected by war or revolution—from Hungary in the 1950's, from Cuba from 1959 to the present, from Indo-China in the 1970's and 80's, and from Haiti in the 1980's.

Efforts to limit immigration

When a great many immigrants began arriving, some Americans became alarmed. They thought that the new people were coming more rapidly than we could train them in the ways of American citizenship. People were afraid that the immigrants would be willing to work for lower pay than American-born persons.

Beginning in the 1880's and continuing through the 1950's, Congress passed laws that limited the number of people who could enter our country from each foreign country. This limit is called a "quota." These laws have been changed from time to time because of changing world conditions. Current U.S. policy was established by the Immigration and Nationality Act of 1965, which states that no more than 290,000 immigrants may enter the United States each year—120,000 from the Western Hemisphere and 170,000 from the Eastern Hemisphere. As a result of this law, persons who want to come to the United States to gain citizenship may have to wait for years.

Check for Understanding: Now that you have completed this section, you should be able to answer these questions:

1. What was the ethnic makeup of America in 1790?
2. What were the four major immigration movements?
3. Which were the ethnic groups that made up each of these four movements?
4. What are some laws that have restricted immigration to the U.S.?

Issues in Civics: Should all immigration to the U.S. be completely stopped? Select four students to debate this question. Have the class vote after the debate.

Note that the three Objectives that appear at the beginning of each section are always followed by four "Check for Understanding" questions at the end of the section.

Major Changes in U.S. Immigration Policy

1798– Alien and Sedition Act requires newcomers to live 14 years in the U.S. before they can attain citizenship.

1802– Term of residency for aliens is reduced to five years. Congress bans the importing of slaves.

1882– Insane people, convicts, and people unable to support themselves prohibited from entering the U.S. Exclusion Act bars immigrants from China.

1907–1908 "Gentleman's Agreement" with the government of Japan keeps out Japanese laborers.

1917– Congress passes a law requiring adult immigrants to take a literacy test.

1921– Immigration Act of 1921 sets a limit on the number of newcomers from each country. Countries in northern and western Europe receive most of the quotas, and very few places are given to countries in southern and eastern Europe. Asians are barred completely.

1924– The Immigration Act of 1924 (Johnson Act) cuts the 1921 quotas in half.

1940– Aliens required to register with the government once a year.

1943– Chinese Exclusion Act of 1882 is repealed.

1948– Displaced Persons Act admits refugees from World War II.

1950– Internal Security Act denies admission to Communists and Fascists.

1952– McCarran-Walter Act confirms the 1921 quota system and adds severe new restrictions.

1965– New Immigration and Nationality Act eliminates quotas that favor one nation over another.

1976– Amendment to the 1965 Act extends system to nations of North and South America.

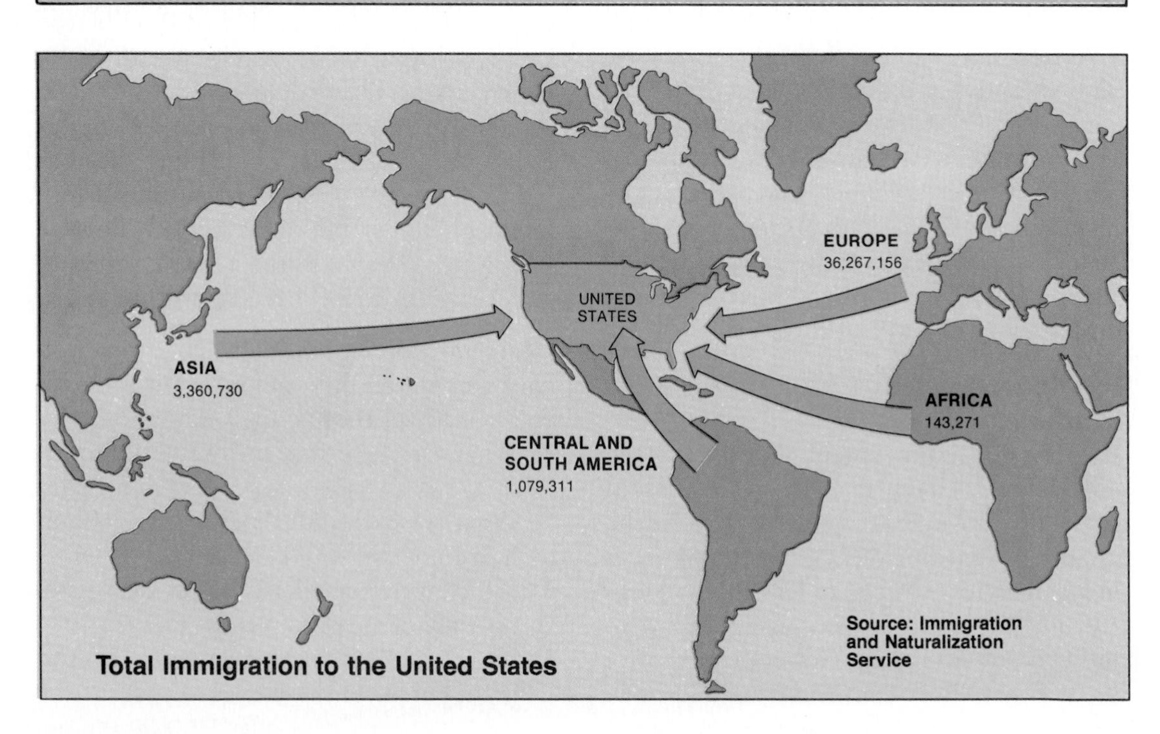

Total Immigration to the United States

Ask your students to discuss why there have been so many immigrants from Europe and relatively few from South America and Africa.

Issues in Civics: New immigrants from a particular ethnic group tend to work for lower pay and to live together in one area. What are the good and bad points of this?

HOW DO PEOPLE BECOME CITIZENS?

Objectives: After you have read this section, you should be able to:

- Distinguish the basic characteristics of citizenship.
- Explain how citizenship can be lost.
- Describe the value of citizenship.

Citizenship by birth

Citizenship in the United States is gained in two ways—by birth, or by choice. All persons born here are citizens of the United States and of the state in which they live. They enjoy all the benefits of American citizenship.

If a child whose parents are from the United States is born in a foreign land, he or she is a United States citizen because the parents are. Even a child born to foreign parents living in the United States is a citizen by birth; however, at the age of 18, the child must declare his citizenship either to this country or to the country of his parents' citizenship.

Aliens

Citizens of other countries who live in the United States are called *aliens*. Some aliens hope to become citizens of the United States eventually. Others are here to work or to go to school for a short time. Aliens must obey all the laws of the United States. They have full legal protection under the Bill of Rights. All aliens must report their address to the government once each year, in January. They may be deported—sent back to their home country—if they fail to report each year or to obey U.S. laws. All cases involving questions about whether a person can properly claim American citizenship are handled by the United States Department of Justice.

Citizenship by choice

Congress has the right to grant citizenship to people who have come from other countries. This process is called *naturalization*. When foreign-born people want to become citizens, they must first meet two requirements. They must be over eighteen years of age, and they must have lived in the United States for at least five years. They can then go to an office to file a request for naturalization.

Two new citizens of the U.S. recite the Oath of Allegiance. (See page 13 for the text of the Oath.)

Aliens filing for naturalization must give the court information about themselves and their families. They must show they can speak, read, and write English. They must bring two citizens to testify that they are honest. They must show that they know

Ask an interested student to find out how a citizen would be naturalized in your community and describe the process to the class.

Issues in Civics: "Do naturalized citizens make the best citizens?" This could be a question for debate or an essay paper with students taking a for or against position.

something about American history and that they understand our form of government.

When they have shown these things, the applicants then take an oath. In this oath, they give up their allegiance to the government or ruler of the land from which they came. They pledge allegiance to the United States and its government. They are then declared citizens.

New citizens have all the privileges of native-born citizens, except those of serving as President or Vice-President of the United States. They can, however, hold any other government office. For example, Henry Kissinger, former Secretary of State, was born in Germany; Senator S. I. Hayakawa of California was born in Canada. Children under twenty-one years of age become citizens of the United States when their parents are naturalized, if they are living in this country with their parents. A foreign-born person who has served in the armed forces of the United States for at least one year may become a citizen without having lived here for five years.

Loss of the rights of citizenship

In the case of *Afroyim v. Rush* (1967) the Supreme Court, by a five-to-four vote, decided that the only way citizens could lose their citizenship was to give it up by choice. However, this decision does not extend to cases of *treason*—attempting to overthrow the government or to otherwise harm this country or help its enemies. For such an act people may still lose their American citizenship. One can also lose certain rights of citizenship by being convicted of a serious crime.

People can choose to give up their citizenship by moving to another country. They can also give formal notice to the government that they intend to give up their citizenship. Justice Hugo Black, in writing the majority opinion in the Afroyim case, said, "In our country the people are sovereign, and the government cannot sever its relationship to the people by taking away their citizenship."

The value of citizenship

One way to look at the worth of citizenship is to think of what the loss of citizenship means. Former Chief Justice Earl Warren felt that taking away a person's citizenship was "cruel and unusual punishment," which is prohibited by the Sixth Amendment to the Constitution. Even though no physical harm might come to such a person, he or she would become stateless—a man or woman without a country. He or she would actually lose the right to have rights.

Another value of citizenship is that the United States protects the rights and interests of its citizens when they are in foreign countries. If citizens are treated badly or unjustly jailed when they are in a foreign land, our government will demand that amends be made or that they be released.

Many people value their citizenship highly because they came to this country at a great sacrifice. They saw the opportunity to realize their dreams in a land where freedom and justice are greatly valued.

Check for Understanding: Now that you have completed this section, you should be able to answer these questions:

1. What are the basic characteristics of citizenship?
2. What do people who are not citizens have to do to become naturalized?
3. How can someone lose United States citizenship?
4. What are two values of citizenship?

Ask an interested student to give a report on *The Man Without a Country*, by Edward Everett Hale, which describes a stateless person.

There are four "Check for Understanding" questions per section. Three evaluate mastery of the Objectives; the fourth is a "wild card" question testing a specific area of knowledge.

A poem by Emma Lazarus that is inscribed on the Statue of Liberty says, "Give us your tired, your poor, your huddled masses yearning to breathe free . . ." These immigrants came to America from Europe in 1902.

SUMMARY

You, as a citizen, owe your allegiance to your country. As a citizen, you have certain rights guaranteed to you in the Constitution. It is because of these rights that large numbers of people from other countries have emigrated to America from the beginning of our country to the present day.

The English system of government and the English language became the way of life in the United States after the French, Spanish, Dutch, and Swedish lost control of their colonies to England. However, every other group that came to America has left its influence on the nation.

A person gains citizenship by birth or by naturalization. An alien, or non-citizen, may go through a process of naturalization to become a citizen. A person may lose citizenship by committing an act of treason. The privileges of citizenship can be lost by being sent to prison for a serious crime.

The Oath of Allegiance

Every alien applying for American citizenship must, as the final step, take the following oath of allegiance to the United States:

"I hereby declare, on oath, that I absolutely and entirely renounce and abjure all allegiance and fidelity to any foreign prince, potentate, state, or sovereignty, of whom or which I have heretofore been a subject or citizen; that I will support and defend the Constitution and laws of the United States against all enemies, foreign and domestic; that I will bear true faith and allegiance to the same; that I will bear arms on behalf of the United States when required by the law; or that I will perform noncombatant service in the armed forces of the United States when required by the law; or that I will perform work of national importance under civilian direction when required by the law; and that I take this obligation freely without any mental reservation or purpose of evasion; so help me God."

The caption above refers to a poem by Emma Lazarus. Ask a student to obtain the entire text and read it to the class.

Discuss the text of the Oath of Citizenship. Explain the meaning of the various key phrases.

BUILDING SKILLS IN CIVICS

THINKING SKILLS

1. What ways can someone become a U.S. citizen?
2. What contributions did the original English settlers make to American culture?
3. Why do we have a quota system on immigration?
4. Which of the following is *not* a step to becoming a naturalized citizen?
   a. filing a petition for citizenship after living in the U.S.
   b. showing an ability to speak, read, and write in English.
   c. owning a home or business.
5. Choose the title below that you think best fits this paragraph.

   People come to America from many parts of the world in hopes of finding better jobs and greater personal freedom. They want to live in a place where people govern themselves.

   a. Changes in Immigration Laws
   b. Reasons for Coming to the U.S.
   c. The Four Great Immigrations

VOCABULARY SKILLS

Some of the underlined words in the sentences below are used correctly, but others are not. If the word is used correctly, write True. If it is not, replace it with the best choice from the list.

allegiance	government	treason	republic
naturalization	alien	citizenship	immigrant

1. One way to lose citizenship is to be found guilty of <u>treason</u>.
2. Through a process called <u>naturalization</u>, aliens can become citizens.
3. The final step in naturalization is to pledge an oath of <u>republic</u>.
4. <u>Citizenship</u> is the way people have organized to make rules and laws by which they can live together in peace.
5. In a <u>government</u>, people rule themselves through representatives.
6. <u>Aliens</u> are citizens of a country other than the one they live in.

The Teacher's Introduction at the front of the book provides a full description of these activities and gives recommendations for their use.

7. An immigrant can become a citizen by following certain steps.
8. The Constitution protects the rights of allegiance.

STUDY SKILLS—USING THE GLOSSARY

In the back of your book there is a *glossary*. It lists the important new words that are presented in the book and gives the meaning of each one as it is used in the text. A dictionary also gives the meaning of a word. However, since many words have more than one meaning and the dictionary gives them all, a glossary is often faster and easier to use. At the end of each definition in the Glossary for this book, there is a page number. This tells you where in the book the word, or entry, is used or explained. Activity: Choose one word from this chapter's vocabulary list. Find the word in the Glossary, then turn to the page where the word is used and reread the section it is in. Now, locate the same word in the dictionary you usually use. Compare the information given in the dictionary with that given in the Glossary. How are the two books alike? How are they different?

BEYOND THE BOOK

1. Interview a naturalized citizen to learn how and why he or she became a citizen. What was the hardest part of the process? What changes did being a citizen bring in his or her life?
2. As a class project, prepare a bulletin board that will show where you and your classmates originally came from. Put up a large map of the world. Then you and the others in your class can write your names on a flag and put it on the appropriate country or region that your family or ancestors emigrated from.
3. Read a biography of an immigrant. Prepare a report summarizing the person's reasons for coming to this country, the challenges the new life presented, and the contributions that he or she made to American life.
4. Make your own family heritage chart. Show when your family came to the U.S., where they came from, and where they first settled.

Answers to the Skill-Building Activities on these pages appear in the Answer Key in the front of the book.

CHAPTER ONE TEST

VOCABULARY CHECK

Fill in each blank with the word that best fits the sentence.

1. Citizens pledge ______ to their country. (allegiance - republic)
2. You live in a ______, which is a nation where people govern themselves through representatives. (republic - citizenship)
3. ______ is the way people have organized to make and enforce laws. (government - republic)
4. Persons who are citizens of another country are called ______. (allegiance - aliens)
5. Certain rights and responsibilities go with the right of ______ in this country. (allegiance - citizenship)
6. Congress has the right to grant citizenship to immigrants by a process called ______. (immigration - naturalization)
7. An act of ______ is an attempt to overthrow the government. (treason - naturalization)
8. The quota system places a limit on the number of ______ who can be admitted from another country. (immigrants - citizens)

COMPREHENSION CHECK

Write True if the question and answer match. If they do not, write an answer to the question.

1. Who were the first settlers of what is now the United States?—The first settlers of the U.S. were called Indians by Columbus and are now often referred to as Native Americans.
2. Historically, where have immigrants to America come from?—By 1900 immigrants to America represented about every country.
3. What are two reasons why people immigrated to the U.S.?—People thought the immigrants were coming too rapidly.
4. Which group of settlers did not come to America willingly?—Thousands of black people were brought as slaves.
5. How can U.S. citizenship be lost?—If aliens fail to obey our laws, they may be deported.

The format and teaching technique of the Chapter Tests are described in the Teacher's Introduction.

SKILL BUILDERS—INTERPRETING GRAPHS

A *graph* is a way of showing certain kinds of information visually. Complicated information is often easier to understand on a graph than it is in a written description. A graph can help you by saving time. It can also help you answer questions like: How many? How much? How often? How far?

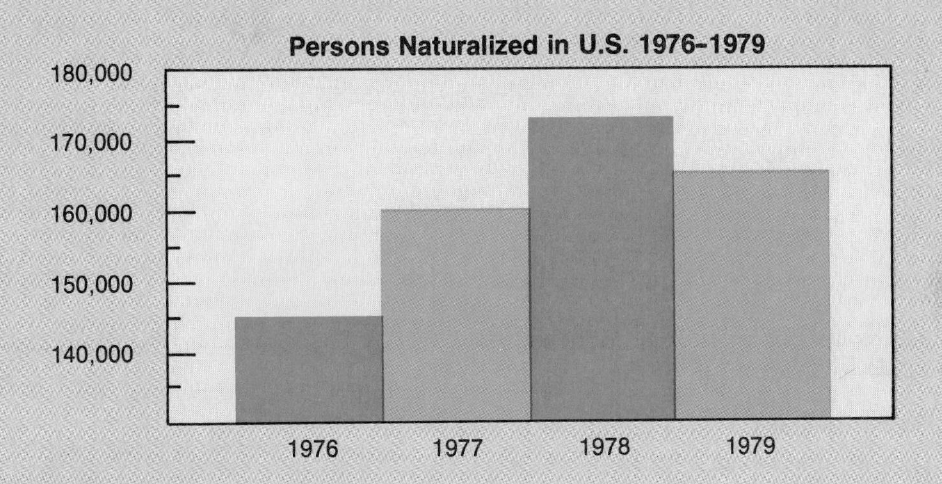

Activity: Look at this graph and practice your graph-reading skills.

1. What does the title tell you about the purpose of the graph?
2. How do the bars make it easy for you to compare information?
3. What does the longest bar tell you? The shortest?
4. Find another graph in Chapter One. Describe what it shows.

BUILDING WRITING SKILLS

Choose one of the titles below. Write five to eight sentences that would belong in a report with that title.

a. Gaining Citizenship
b. Early Settlers in America
c. Good Reasons for Immigration

Answers to the Chapter Tests appear in the Answer Key in the front of the book.

Chapter Two
Government of the People

Documents: Declaration of Independence (July 4, 1776)
The Constitution of the United States

"We hold these truths to be self-evident, that all men are created equal, that they are endowed by their Creator with certain unalienable Rights, that among these are Life, Liberty and the pursuit of Happiness. That to secure these rights, Governments are instituted among Men, deriving their just powers from the consent of the governed . . ." (Declaration of Independence)

"WE THE PEOPLE of the United States, in Order to form a more perfect union, establish Justice, insure domestic Tranquility, provide for the common defence, promote the general Welfare, and secure the Blessings of Liberty to ourselves and our Posterity, do ordain and establish this Constitution for the United States of America." (Preamble)

"The Congress shall have Power to lay and collect Taxes, Duties, Imposts and Excises, to pay the Debts and provide for the common Defence and general Welfare of the United States; . . . (Article I, Section 8)

When Thomas Jefferson wrote the words to the Declaration of Independence in 1776, a unique concept in government was being

The two portraits are of King George III at the time of the American Revolution, and of Thomas Jefferson in the act of signing the Declaration of Independence.

The complete text of the Declaration of Independence can be found in the Appendix on pages 560–563.

established—the concept of equality for all. This dream of equality is still a goal of our nation today as we strive for equality between the sexes and among all races, religions, and ethnic groups.

The Preamble to the Constitution aptly states the purposes of a free government as these: (1) Establish justice (2) Insure domestic tranquility (3) Provide for the common defense (4) Promote the general welfare (5) Secure liberty for all generations of our country. The Constitution gave Congress the power to collect taxes in order to provide for these aims.

The objectives stated in the Constitution are still applicable to our nation today and will always be worthy goals for a free people.

FOCUSING IDEAS

- Government is necessary to provide rights for citizens, to provide protection, to set rules, and to provide common benefits.
- All governments are alike in that they all have a territory, and the people within each develop an identification with their country.
- Governments differ in that there are varying degrees of power that are afforded to the people in different nations.
- A free self-government is one that is of, by, and for the people.

The Illustration depicts a crowd singing the "Star-Spangled Banner" at a World Series baseball game. Ask the students to identify symbols of the U.S. government in the picture (national anthem, flags, bunting, military honor guard, etc.)

PRE-TEST

1. What is government? Why is it necessary?
2. Can you name three ways in which all governments are alike?
3. What are three ways in which governments are different?
4. What are the characteristics of a free government? How does it differ from a totalitarian government?

WHY IS GOVERNMENT NECESSARY?

Objectives: After reading this section, you will be able to:
- State what government is.
- Give three reasons why government is necessary.
- Tell why it is important to obey the law.

"I should be able to drive as fast as I want, as long as I'm careful." "Government regulations are unnecessary—they just get in the way when you're trying to do something." "I don't understand why we have to pay taxes—we'd help the economy more by spending the money ourselves." "Why should I obey that law? Nobody else in this town does."

Have you ever heard anyone express any of these feelings? If you did, you know they were saying something about government. Each person had encountered a restraint that was placed upon them by government. Sometimes people feel that these restrictions should apply to others but not them.

Government is indeed a personal thing, because it affects our lives so much on a day-to-day basis. Yet, government is also more than our individual concerns, as important as these are. Organized life as we know it could not function without government. If each of the speakers above had his or her own way, another person, or even society itself, might be harmed.

Whenever people live together in the same place and in the same way, they need a government. As you know from Chapter One, "government" means the way that people have organized to make and enforce rules for a community, a state, or a nation. The rules made by government are called *laws*. The persons who are responsible for making and enforcing laws are known as government *officers* or *officials*.

The story of "Whiz Bang"

One way to demonstrate the need for an organized government is to look at the story of a new community known as "Whiz Bang." Whiz Bang grew up in the oil fields of the West in the 1920's. Following the discovery of oil, the town came into being almost overnight. The great majority of the people were willing to obey the law, but

---

Building Vocabulary:
law *(20)* • officer *(20)* • civics *(22)* • democracy *(26)* • totalitarian *(27)* • monarchy *(28)* • dictatorship *(28)* • inherent right *(31)*

Issues in Civics: Have your class debate the following statement. "It's wrong that you have to be 18 or over to play video games during school hours in this town." Is this a sensible law?

Each chapter begins with a "Building Vocabulary" section at the bottom of the page. The numbers indicate the page on which the word is presented.

The East Texas city of Kilgore grew very rapidly after a huge oil reserve was discovered near there in 1930. At one time there were more than 1000 oil derricks in the downtown section. The role of government is very important in such rapidly-growing communities.

because the town was so new, everybody was busy taking care of his own interests. Nobody took on the responsibility of forming a government for the new community. Criminals came to town. People were killed. When an oil driller and his family arrived, their children were sick with measles. Instead of keeping them at home, the parents permitted them to go wherever they pleased. Thus they exposed others to their germs. Since there was no public health officer, other people in the community had no way of protesting about the spread of the disease.

Conditions grew worse—until a committee of citizens called a mass meeting at which the people elected officers. The people agreed to help the officers in keeping law and order. Criminals who did not leave the city of their own accord were arrested and thrown into jail. Persons with contagious diseases were quarantined. Rules were made for the disposal of sewage and garbage. Through community organization, government came to Whiz Bang.

Responsibility through law

Lois Russell was hurrying to school because she was sure she was going to be late. Just as she came to the street corner, the traffic light turned red. As she waited for the light to change, she was afraid that having to stop would make her late for class. Soon the light turned green, and Lois was on her

Talk about a hypothetical baseball game between your school and another in which there are no umpires and no agreed-upon rules. What would happen?

Ask for examples of other situations like "Whiz Bang." Why else would a community grow very quickly? What problems does this cause?

way. She arrived at school just in time for the bell, still upset that the red light had almost made her late.

If she had taken time to think about it, that traffic light could have given her an example to use in her *civics* or American government class. The traffic light was placed on the corner by a local government. When Lois stopped, she was obeying one of the laws of government. Laws make demands on people. This is one way that governments work. People must obey the rules of their government, or they will be punished. The laws state those things that people must do. When you obey laws, you help make the government work.

Rights for people

The example of the traffic light shows why people are willing to accept the limits set by government. While Lois was waiting, others went through the intersection on a green light. These people had the right to proceed safely without having to worry about other cars and people.

Lois Russell was impatient because she was afraid that waiting for the light would make her late for school.

Providing protection

Government helps protect us from those who would rob or cheat. It protects us from other nations that would harm citizens of the United States. All governments have power, or the strength and force that gives them the ability to act. Governments force most people to obey the rules by using their power to catch and punish those who don't obey. Thus Lois was able to get to school safely under her government's protection.

Rules of teamwork

To use power to protect people from criminals, or even from other nations, is not the only reason that people form governments. Suppose there was no traffic light on that corner. Even if Lois and all the other people there were careful, something still could have gone wrong. If a number of cars going in different directions arrived at the intersection at the same time, there might have been a traffic jam that would have stopped everyone. There even could have been a collision in which cars were wrecked.

People living together in a city, state, or nation can cause many problems for themselves and others simply by going about their everyday activities. They can cause traffic jams, pollution, and other problems without intending to do wrong. Most of these problems can be avoided if people cooperate in living together. But how are people to know the best rules for cooperation? If many cars arrive at an intersection at the same time, who is to determine what should be done?

Relate school government to civil government by comparing teacher power and governmental power, or student body rules and regulations with local laws.

Lois, our hypothetical student, decided to obey the law in this situation. Ask your students what they would have done in the same situation.

Ask your students to discuss these various actions of government. Which is most important? Which costs the most? Which most affects them?

Ask students to list other services that government provides.

Governments are needed to set the rules of teamwork or cooperation. Then each citizen of the country knows what he or she can and cannot do, or should and should not do, in order that all citizens may be better off.

Providing common benefits

Governments do other things besides providing protection and making the rules for cooperative living. Lois Russell was walking to a public school, on a concrete sidewalk, next to a paved road. She was receiving the benefits of good sidewalks, roads, controlled traffic, and an education. Acting alone, she and her family, no matter how wealthy or hard-working they might be, would not have been able to provide any of these. Thus, an important reason why people form governments is to have a means of providing those things that they are not able to get for themselves by acting alone.

Check for Understanding: Now that you have completed this section, you should be able to answer these questions:

1. What are three reasons why government is necessary?
2. How does obeying the law help government to function properly?
3. Why can government be compared to "teamwork" or a "partnership"?
4. What might happen in this society if everyone acted on his or her own without regard for the law?

HOW ARE ALL GOVERNMENTS ALIKE?

Objectives: After reading this section, you will be able to:

- Define the characteristics that make up each kind of state in the world.
- Explain what might happen if one of these characteristics were removed.
- List the things that the people within a state have in common.

The "state" or nation

This book is about government in the United States, but each of the other countries in the world has a government, too. Within most of these countries, as in this one, there are political subdivisions, usually known as states, provinces, or regions. These different subdivisions of the central government have some form of government of their own. What things do all of the world's central governments have in common?

For one thing, each government must be free to rule or govern. This right to rule comes from the people of a nation and from the recognition given to a nation by other countries. As you look at the diagram on page 25, you will see the word "sovereign" along with the word "state." Sovereignty refers to the power to govern. Without sovereignty, no nation could long exist, because its government could not enforce its rules.

When rule originates with the people, or "populus" in Latin (from which our word "popular" comes), the term of "popular sovereignty" is often used. In the days when nations were ruled by kings or queens, these rulers were called "sovereigns" because the power of the state or nation resided in them. Louis XIV, king of France from 1638 to 1715, once said, "L'état, c'est moi" or "I am the state." Today, although the term "sovereign" is still used, in most countries that have a royal family the real power comes from the people.

Issues in Civics: Discuss the following question: If you had to eliminate one of the government services discussed in this chapter, because of tax cuts, which would you choose? Why?

Ask your students to draw a cartoon or make a poster from magazine pictures to illustrate one of the government services described in this chapter.

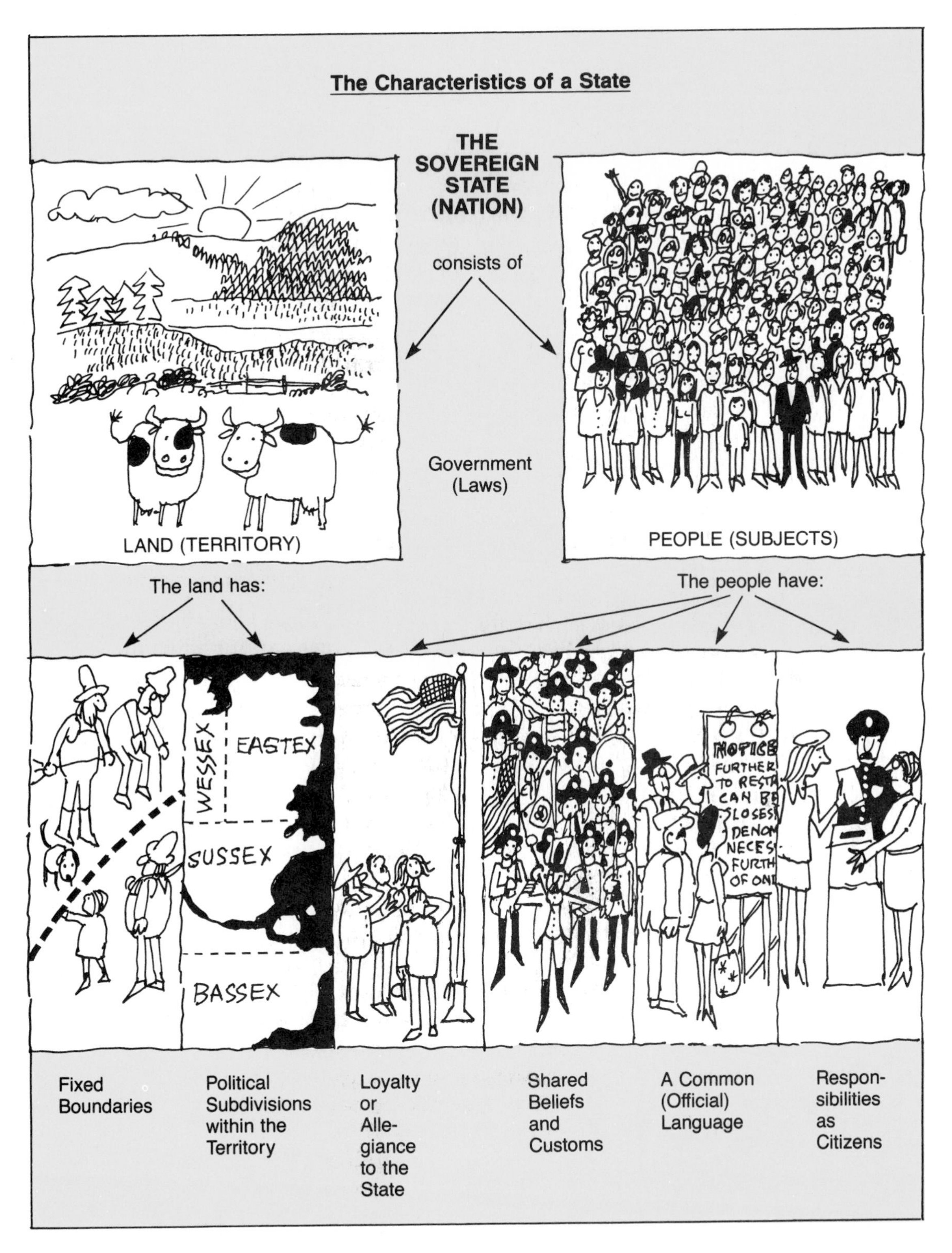

Ask students to give examples of "shared beliefs and customs" of the American state.

Discuss the question of why a single common language is important to a state. Ask for examples of nations where the lack of this can cause problems. (Canada, Belgium, India, Nigeria, etc.)

Territories

All governments have a territory, or land area, that is under their control. This territory is limited by a boundary or border, and all the land within it is under that government. The term "subject" is sometimes used to refer to people under the control of a government. This word was especially used in olden days to refer to people living under a king or queen.

As you can see in the diagram on page 25, there are political subdivisions within a territory. All countries have towns and cities. These separate subdivisions must have governments to enforce the rules of the town or city. Sometimes there is a strong tie between the central government and its separate towns and cities. In other situations, there is a very limited connection to the central government. The cities and towns within the United States are largely self-governing.

People or subjects

The people, or subjects, within a nation develop an identification with their country. This identification is usually expressed in some symbolic way, through such things as a national song, a flag, a coat-of-arms, and so on. The feeling arising from such identification is referred to as patriotism, loyalty, or nationalism.

Unity comes to the people of a particular nation when there exists a common language, shared beliefs or ideals, and common customs or traditions. For example, the American people adopted the English language, traditions, and beliefs because England was the dominant nation in the New World at the time when the colonies were settled.

Check for Understanding: Now that you have completed this section, you should be able to answer these questions:

1. What are the major characteristics of a state or nation?
2. What might happen if you removed one of these characteristics from the state?
3. What are three things that the people of a nation have in common?
4. What are the symbols by which people identify with their country?

HOW ARE GOVERNMENTS DIFFERENT?

Objectives: After reading this section, you will be able to:

- Explain the difference between the two forms of free government, a direct democracy and a republic.
- Describe the way in which democratic republics, totalitarian republics, and dictatorships differ.
- Explain how the use of power and the right to vote determine the freedom, or lack of freedom, that a particular group of people have.

Democracies and republics

One way that governments are different is the question of how much power the people have in selecting officials and making laws. In a democracy or a republic, people are supposed to have a great deal of voice in the selection process. The word *democracy* comes from two Greek words—"demos," or "people" and "kratia," or "rule." As early as 500 B.C., democracy was practiced in the Greek city-state of Athens. The people met and made their own laws. A

Have your students interview three adults to find out if they think your community is well run. Why? Is it better run than your state government? How would they improve it?

Issues in Civics: The role of nationalism—Ask your students to write a paragraph showing the good and bad effects of nationalism.

true democracy, then, is a government where the people themselves vote directly for laws that are to govern them. But today we often hear the word "democracy" used to describe any country in which people make their own laws, either directly or indirectly through representatives.

The word republic comes from two Latin words—"res publica" which literally mean "public thing" but in loose translation have come to mean "affairs of the people." Latin was the language of ancient Rome. In Rome, there was an indirect rather than a direct democracy. People elected senators as their representatives to meet and make laws for the nation. Since the United States has elected representatives, it can be said to be a republic in the same way that Rome was. The word "republic" is used in this book to refer to the United States, and it is also the word used in the Pledge (". . . and to the *republic* for which it stands . . .")

The complete text of the Pledge of Allegiance can be found on page 4.

These voters in Hungary have little doubt about the outcome of the election, because there is only one candidate for each office.

Totalitarian republics

If you look at a list of countries, you will see that most call themselves "republics." This list of republics includes not only the United States, Canada, and Mexico, but also many of the Communist countries, which call themselves "People's Republics." Therefore, it is important to know more than just the name of a country's government to determine how much freedom the people in that nation actually have in choosing their leaders.

In most Communist countries people do elect representatives to a lawmaking body. However, only the Communist party is allowed to list candidates for office. It lists only one person.

If there is no opposition party or parties, the people of a nation have no real choice. An opposition party lists candidates for office, presenting different points of view and often suggesting different laws. Without opposition, the real leader of a Communist country is usually the Chairman of the Communist Party. He may or may not share the control with other people in the party. But, in any case, the views and ideas of a few members of the party control the government. Governments that are controlled by only one authority or party, and which allow no opposition, are called *totalitarian*. This means that the total power is in the hands of one person or one group of people. Totalitarian governments often have little regard for the rights and freedom of average citizens.

Have a student give a short report on the government of ancient Athens.

Cite several "laws" at your school. Ask your students which ones they would insist on changing if they were making their own laws.

Other governments

There are other types of governments that have only one man or woman as the ruler. Among these is a *monarchy*. In a monarchy one person—the monarch—becomes head of the government by birth. This person may be a king, queen, emperor, empress, or sheik. If he or she dies or leaves office, the eldest son or daughter (or whoever is the closest living relative) inherits their power. In the past, many monarchs had total or absolute power. Today, however, there are only a few such rulers. Most absolute monarchs gave up their power long ago to representatives of the people. For example, England, Japan, and Sweden have elected representatives who are accepted by the monarchs as the policy-making bodies of the country. Such governments are called constitutional monarchies. They still have a monarch, but are governed much like republics.

Dictatorships

Dictatorships are another form of government by one person. In such a government, one person dictates or establishes and enforces all the laws. That person's word is law, and he or she is responsible to no one else. A dictator governs much like a sheik or king of old. Dictators, however, do no inherit power, but seize it from the people.

A lesson to learn from history is that many countries have lost their freedom when the people were afraid that their existing government could not work or that another nation might conquer them. Dictators have used these fears to take power from the country's elected representatives. They often used the threat of violence or imprisonment to discourage those who tried to take their power away from them. In order to rule, they must silence all possible opposition.

Check for Understanding: Now that you have completed this section, you should be able to answer these questions:

1. How does a direct democracy differ from a republic, which is an indirect or representative democracy?
2. What is one main difference among democracies, totalitarian states, and dictatorships?
3. If you knew who or which group had the power in a country, how could you predict the form of government?
4. Why do dictatorships want to silence their opposition?

WHAT IS FREE SELF-GOVERNMENT?

Objectives: After reading this section, you will be able to:

- Understand the major difference between a free self-government and all other kinds of government.
- Define inherent rights and know their meaning for freedom.
- Understand why free elections are essential to self-government.

What's in a name?

Things may seem confusing as to what makes up a free government. Some republics can be totalitarian and not be free. Many monarchies are now constitutional monarchies and provide free self-government. And any of these forms can be taken over by a dictator. The important thing, then, is not what a government is

Using a world map, ask your students to name the major countries that call themselves republics.

These pictures represent five basic types of government—the *direct democracy* of ancient Greece, the *republic* of Rome, the *monarchy* of medieval England, the *dictatorship* of Benito Mussolini in Italy, and the *totalitarian* government of the Soviet Union.

The complete text of the Gettysburg Address can be found in the Appendix on page 585.

called, or how it is organized. What is important is how it provides for the rights and liberties of its people.

Of, by, and for the people

A free government is one that not only is called a republic, but that allows people to have a real choice in selecting their officials. In his famous Gettysburg Address, Abraham Lincoln described the government of the United States as being "of the people, by the people, for the people." This is the best and simplest definition of a free government.

A government is "of the people" when few, if any, restrictions prevent someone from holding an office, when most of the people may vote for whom they wish, and when people may oppose those with whom they disagree.

A government is "by the people" when it is formed by the citizens who decide how it is to act, and when it acts only with their consent.

A government is "for the people" when it works to make the citizens' lives better and safer. A free government is assured when people have free choice in elections, and elected leaders are concerned with the people's rights and liberties.

Make a chart with examples of contemporary nations with totalitarian, monarchical, dictatorial, and democratic types of governments.

As the illustration indicates, monarchies are a historic form of government, but they are not common today. Discuss the reasons why this is so.

Discuss various forms of government in terms of who holds the power. Ask your students why the process of voting was chosen to illustrate the concept of a democratic republic.

Ask interested students to do research as to how several prominent modern dictators took power. What led up to their taking over? Why did the people accept it?

Protection of rights

The citizens of the United States believe that self-government is an *inherent*, or *unalienable, right* of human beings. The word "inherent" is taken from a Latin word "inhaerens" meaning "to stick." An inherent right is one that sticks to us; it cannot justly be taken away. You have an inherent right to live, to train your body or your mind, and to attempt to find happiness in life. "Unalienable" means "that cannot be separated or transferred."

The belief that certain rights are inherent, or unalienable, was stated in the Declaration of Independence:

"We hold these truths to be self-evident, that all men are created equal, that they are endowed by their Creator with certain unalienable Rights, that among these are Life, Liberty, and the pursuit of Happiness. That to secure these rights, Governments are instituted among Men, deriving their just powers from the consent of the governed . . ."

Under self-government, the will of the majority rules. But the majority must be fair to the minority. Every citizen has the right to vote, and the vote of one citizen counts as much as the vote of any other.

To insure our inherent rights, a government must meet these requirements:

1. It must be one where the people are the source of power.
2. Its officials must be elected for a limited time and their power restricted.
3. The rights of any opposition and minorities must be protected by laws.
4. Its laws must permit free exchange of ideas and opinions.
5. The government must be such that all individuals under it can earn a living.

Check for Understanding: Now that you have completed this section, you should be able to answer these questions:

1. What is one major difference between self-government and all other kinds?
2. How does the possession of inherent rights imply free self-government?
3. Why are elections so important to self-government?
4. Why is it necessary to protect the rights of the opposition?

SUMMARY

Living with others requires cooperation and rules. In a community, state, or nation, the agency that provides rules (laws) for living together is called government. Officers are those persons responsible for making and enforcing laws. The reason why we have governments is to provide those things that the people acting alone cannot get for themselves. For example, governments provide protection against criminals; control traffic; provide services such as fire protection, roads, education; and many others.

All governments need to be sovereign, have geographic boundaries, laws, and people who share common beliefs and traditions, and have a common language. Forms of government, however, may vary. In a democracy or republic there is some form of self-government. In a dictatorship, the people are ruled by one person. An absolute monarchy is like a dictatorship, except the ruler gains his or her position by birth. But in any government the real question is whether it provides for individual rights.

Using the dictators' careers that were researched earlier, ask your students to show how people can relinquish freedoms for the sake of government efficiency.

Discuss an inherent right of your students—one that is free from school regulations, parental restrictions, and legal boundaries.

BUILDING SKILLS IN CIVICS

THINKING SKILLS

1. What are three reasons why people need governments?
2. What do these sentences describe?
   a. It has a territory.
   b. It has power to control.
   c. It has laws and officials.
3. Review the meaning of the word *government* in the Glossary. Then read through the chapter quickly and make a list of the words in *italic* type that belong under the heading "Systems of Government."
4. Choose the title below that you think best fits this paragraph.

> Some governments are controlled by only one party. The party allows no opposition and usually works primarily for its own benefit, or for the benefit of a small group of people. Those in power often have little regard for the rights and freedom of average citizens.

   a. Totalitarian Governments
   b. Democratic Governments
   c. Constitutional Monarchies

VOCABULARY SKILLS

Match each term with the correct definition.

officer	monarchy	democracy	law
civics	inherent right	dictatorship	totalitarian

1. The study of government and of the duties, rights, and responsibilities of citizens.
2. A rule that a nation and its people follow.
3. A person who is responsible for making and enforcing laws.
4. A government in which a single group has all the power.
5. A form of government in which the people rule.
6. The head of this government is determined by birth.
7. An essential right belonging to the people.
8. One person rules in this form of government.

Each left-hand page of the "Building Skills in Civics" section contains the same two headings: "Thinking Skills" and "Vocabulary Skills".

STUDY SKILLS—USING FACTS TO SUPPORT GENERALIZATIONS

A *generalization* is not just a useful way of summarizing facts. It also can help you organize information. The general statement must not, however, contradict the details on which it is based.

Activity: Read the following generalization:

> Systems of government vary in how much power the people under them have in selecting their officials and in making laws.

Which of these specific statements below support the general statement above?

a. In a dictatorship one person establishes and enforces all laws.
b. In Communist countries only one party is allowed to list candidates.
c. Governments do many other things in addition to providing protection.
d. In a democracy the people make their own laws, either directly or indirectly through representatives.
e. In a constitutional monarchy there is a person selected by birth as the monarch, but the people are governed in much the same way as in a republic.

BEYOND THE BOOK

1. Using a world map, or a list of the countries in the world, make a list of those countries that have the word "republic" in their title. Then discuss the following questions. Do the citizens of all these countries have the same amount of personal freedom? Why do so many countries with different political systems call themselves "republics?"

2. Pick a topic from the list below. Find at least one picture from a magazine that illustrates the concept you have chosen. Show your picture to the rest of the class and explain to them why you chose it.

a. Government Services
b. Observing the Rules
c. Government Officials

Each right-hand page contains the two headings "Study Skills" and "Beyond the Book".

CHAPTER TWO TEST

VOCABULARY CHECK

Some of the underlined words in the sentences below are used correctly; others are not. If the sentence is correct, write True. If it is not, replace the word with the best choice from the list.

official	totalitarian	law
monarchy	dictatorship	inherent right
democracy	civics	

1. The laws state those things that people must do.
2. One unelected ruler is in control in a democracy.
3. The belief that we have certain inherent rights is stated in the "Declaration of Independence."
4. Officials are responsible for making and enforcing laws.
5. A civics government allows no opposition.
6. This totalitarian book describes our government and the rights, responsibilities, and duties of citizenship.
7. In a democracy, the head of the government gains his or her position by birth.
8. The people have the final word in a dictatorship.

COMPREHENSION CHECK

1. Which of these is *not* a reason why governments are needed?
   a. to provide protection.
   b. to provide a territory.
   c. to provide common beliefs.
2. All governments have:
   a. the power to make and enforce laws in their own territory.
   b. opposition parties.
   c. little regard for the rights of citizens.
3. Under self-government, the will of the majority rules, but the majority must:
   a. have inherent rights.
   b. respect the rights of the minority.
   c. have officers.

The first page of the Chapter Test consists of a Vocabulary Check and a Comprehension Check.

SKILL BUILDERS—INTERPRETING MAPS

1. Of the common features of all governments, which one can best be seen and learned about from a *map*?
2. Look at the map of the United States on pages 558-559. Build your map skills by developing the habit of using a map to learn about the location, size, and characteristics of an area.
   a. First read the title and the legend, which will tell you what the symbols on the map mean. In the map on pages 558-559, what information do the title and legend give?
   b. Think of the area you are looking at as though it were a globe. Ask yourself where it is in relation to the rest of the world.
   c. Some of the boundaries shown on a political map are imaginary ones. Others are natural features of the land. Give some examples of each of these boundaries from the map on pages 558-559. Choose one state and describe its location, borders and relationship to other states.
   d. What does this map tell you about the size of states? Write two questions about size that can be answered using this map.

BUILDING WRITING SKILLS

1. Explain one major difference between a totalitarian government and a democratic government.
2. Why do you think government officials in a republic are elected for a limited time?
3. What is the advantage of having government, rather than individuals, provide such services as fire and police protection, street maintenance, and traffic control?
4. Tell in your own words what is meant by Abraham Lincoln's phrase in the Gettysburg Address "of the people, by the people, for the people."

The second page always consists of two sections: "Skill Builders" and "Building Writing Skills".

Chapter Three • Our Republic Today

Documents: Declaration of Independence
The Constitution of the United States

"We hold these truths to be self-evident, that all men are created equal . . ." (Declaration of Independence)

"The United States shall guarantee to every State in this Union a Republican Form of Government . . ." (Article IV, Section 4)

"Congress shall make no law . . . abridging the freedom of speech . . ." (Amendment I, November 3, 1791)

"The right of citizens of the united States to vote shall not be denied or abridged by the united States or by any State on account of race, color, or previous condition of servitude." (Amendment XV, Section 1, March 30, 1870)

"The right of citizens of the United States to vote shall not be denied or abridged by the United States or by any States on account of sex . . . (Amendment XIX, August 26, 1920)

The writers of the Constitution knew that maintaining our republic was going to be a difficult task. They were aware that the colonies

This illustration depicts the ethnic variety of the United States. Ask students to discuss the question of why this variety is such an asset to our nation.

The complete text of the Constitution can be found in the Appendix, beginning on page 564.

had been founded by peoples from many countries, with many different customs and beliefs. It was inevitable that conflicts would arise out of such diversity. Their best hope in maintaining a free nation was to see that the Constitution reflected the democratic process—one with representation, checks and balances, protection for minorities, guaranteed freedoms, and majority rule.

Throughout the years, our Republic has survived because we, the people have been willing to extend the rights of citizens. With the addition of the Fifteenth and Nineteenth Amendments to the Constitution, the right to vote was extended, regardless of race, color, or sex. Many times over the course of our history we have had to take action to defend our republic and what it stands for.

FOCUSING IDEAS

- The American people come from every ethnic and cultural group.
- Conflicts arise in our society because the interests and lifestyles of our varied peoples clash.
- The democratic process enables Americans to compromise with each other in order to resolve the conflicts in our society.

Issues in Civics: "Ethnic groups should retain their traditional values." "No, we're all Americans, and they should adapt to the American mainstream." Discuss this issue with the class in the context of the Constitution.

PRE-TEST

1. Which ethnic groups make up the American society?
2. Why do conflicts arise within a society?
3. What is the importance of compromise within a nation of many peoples?

WHO ARE THE PEOPLE THAT MAKE UP OUR SOCIETY?

Objectives: After reading this section, you will be able to:

- Recognize the value in diversity of our people in the United States.
- List four cities that have unusual ethnic backgrounds.
- Identify the countries that have contributed the most immigrants to the U.S.

After the Constitutional Convention in 1787, Benjamin Franklin was asked whether the new country of the United States would be a monarchy or a republic. Franklin answered, "A republic, if you can keep it."

The United States has kept its republic for almost two hundred years. Through the years, responsible citizens have kept irre-

Building Vocabulary:
self-government *(39)* • ethnic group *(40)* • minority *(44)* • dissent *(47)* • modify *(47)* • tolerance *(47)* • compromise *(47)*

Make the class aware that, at Franklin's insistence, Jefferson deleted over 400 words about abolishing slavery in the Declaration of Independence. Why was this compromise necessary?

Note that the items that appear in the "Focusing Ideas" section always deal with the same concepts as the Pre-Test.

sponsible persons from destroying our republic. Some people might believe that there is only one way to think in order to be a good citizen. Actually, there must be diversity in thinking to keep the republic strong. James Madison, known as the "Father of the Constitution," argued in favor of this diversity in the "Federalist Papers," saying that as long as we make sure that our society is "broken into many parts, then the rights of individuals, or of the minority, will be in little danger from interested combinations of the majority."

You may one day live in a time when it will be difficult to maintain *self-government.* Someone is always eager to use power the wrong way. By learning about self-government, you can learn how to make sure power is used the right way.

Ask students to research some of the arguments set forth in The Federalist: No. X of 1787.

People from many backgrounds

As you learned in Chapter One, English colonists were in the majority when our republic was established. However, from the very beginning of the republic, people from many backgrounds have helped to establish our system of self-government.

Today there are about 230 million people in the United States. About half of these people are able to trace their origins back to some other part of the world. All parts of Europe, Africa, Asia, and Latin America are listed as places of origin. About eleven million of the people now living in the United States were born in a foreign country. Italy, England, Germany, Mexico, and Poland are the five countries contributing the greatest number of people to this nation over the years.

Many ethnic groups in the U.S. celebrate traditional holidays. These are four typical celebrations—Chinese New Year, an Irish St. Patrick's Day festival, Polish dancers on Pulaski Day, and a Basque parade in Nevada.

With a map of the world, have the students locate each country that has contributed heavily to our population.

You could then have the students make a graph showing the percentage of each country's immigration to the U.S.

An American salad bowl

The United States is often known as a "melting pot," meaning the people from every *ethnic group* came together to form one kind of person—the American. However, this isn't really accurate, because there isn't just one kind of American. People from different ethnic, or national, groups retain the ideas and customs of those groups. Actually, a better comparison is to a giant salad bowl. Each ingredient of a salad stands alone, but together they make a whole. This has been true of the various national groups in America. Each individual ethnic or cultural group has contributed its ideas and customs to the whole country. The nation would suffer a great loss if any group had their language and culture destroyed.

A map of the country shows these many influences. State names such as Texas and Massachusetts are American Indian in origin. Cities such as Santa Fe and Los Angeles show our Mexican and Spanish heritage. New Orleans and St. Louis have a French background.

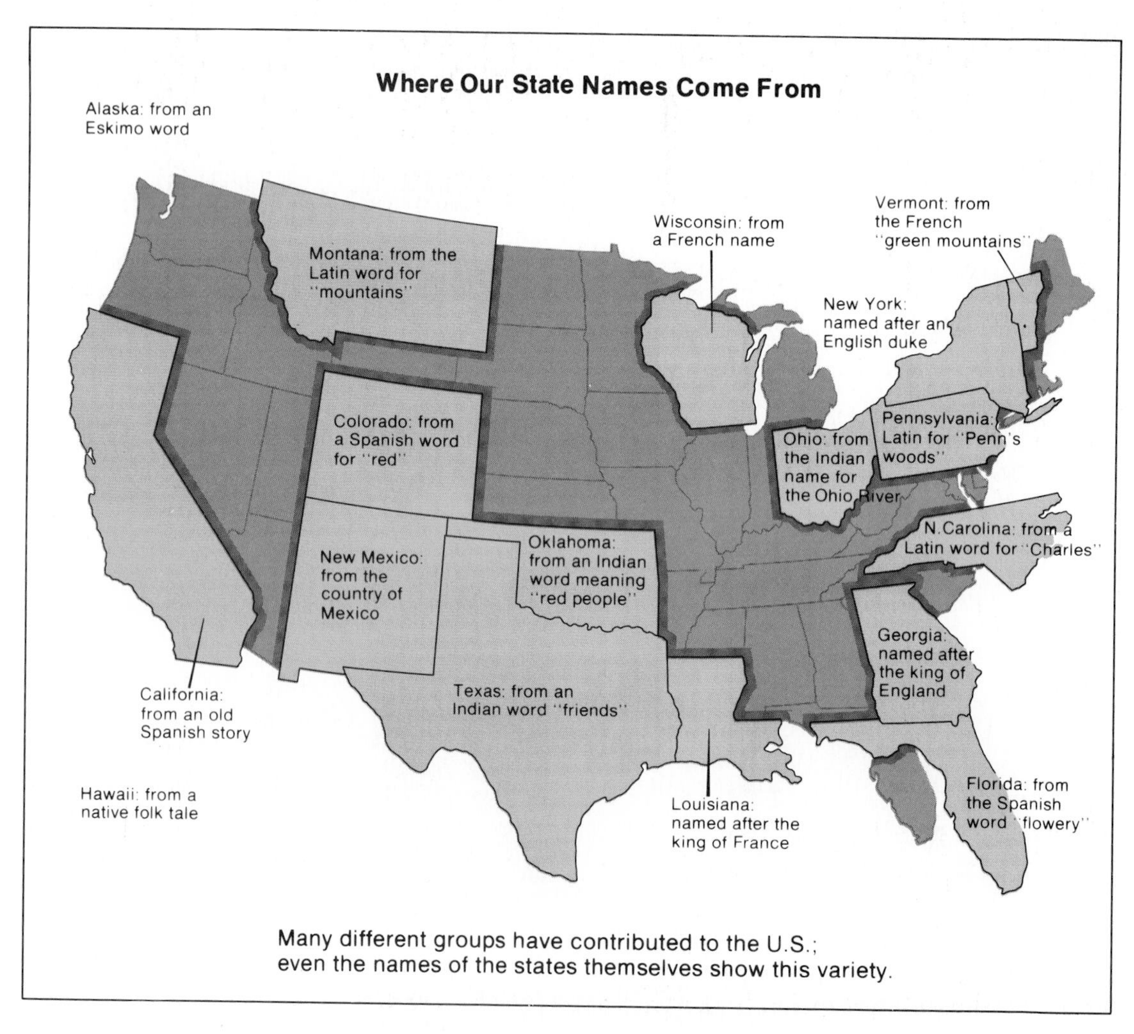

Many different groups have contributed to the U.S.; even the names of the states themselves show this variety.

Have your students name at least five major cities in your state and do research into the origin of each city's name.

Have the students make a bulletin board showing the contributions of various ethnic groups to the U.S.

America's political leaders came from many different ethnic backgrounds. Top row, left to right: Jane Byrne, mayor of Chicago; Peter McDonnell, Navajo tribal chairman; Ella Grasso, former governor of Connecticut; bottom row: Henry Cisneros, mayor of San Antonio; Congresswoman Shirley Chisolm; Hawaii's governor, George Ariyoshi.

Many people enjoy such "ethnic" foods as pizza, enchiladas, tacos, and sausage. If you are one of them, you share in the customs of the Italian, Mexican, and German peoples. Some of the things that Americans most enjoy were introduced into this country by other cultures. Like a bowl of salad, the nation grows better as each culture contributes its own flavor to the whole.

Large cities serving as examples

America's cities serve as examples of how many people and ideas make up our republic. Large cities often have more people of one national origin than do the large cities of their former homeland. For example, at one time more Irish people lived in New York City than in any city in Ireland, including Dublin.

Urban areas with over 100,000 population continue to grow. Three out of every four people live in one of these areas. While our urban areas continue to serve as examples of how people live together and exchange ideas and customs, this concentration of people can lead to conflicts.

Ask your students to identify various other "ethnic" political leaders in addition to those pictured above.

Check for Understanding: Now that you have completed this section, you should be able to answer these questions:

1. What is the value of our nation being very diverse?
2. Which countries have contributed the most people to our population?
3. What are four U.S. cities that have unique cultural backgrounds?
4. Why is it a better reference to say that America is a "salad bowl" rather than a "melting pot"?

WHY DO CONFLICTS ARISE?

Objectives: After reading this section, you will be able to:

- List three reasons why conflicts arise.
- Identify at least three different kinds of conflicts.
- Tell why conflict can be harmful to the nation.

People living close together

When the United States was a very young country, people were spread over a wide area. People who earned their living in different ways or came from different places might never see each other. But this changed. By 1900, Americans were moving to cities in greater numbers. As jobs became more plentiful in the cities, more people left the farms. During World War II, many people sought work in different parts of the country. Statistics now show that the average American moves to a new home once every six years. Americans, as they move within the country, find themselves living with many different kinds of people.

This way of life causes occasional conflicts. Things our neighbors do may bother us. If they make noise, burn trash, or if their yards become dirty, this may annoy us. If they speak a foreign tongue or go to a church we don't understand, our differences may increase. It takes patience and tolerance to live in a crowded area without conflicts.

Reasons for conflict

There are many reasons why conflicts arise. Some people have been left behind by the general increase in the standard of living. As these people seek equal treatment and opportunity, their desires sometimes conflict with those of other people who may feel that their own position in the society will be threatened by change.

The way people earn their living may create differences. Organized labor, working men and women who belong to a union, and management, those who own and operate businesses, disagree sometimes about wages and working conditions. Adults and young people, or people of different cultures or races often disagree. These differences are usually resolved in a peaceful manner.

Once in our nation's history, citizens from different sections of the country allowed their differences to turn into war. This conflict was called the Civil War, or the War Between the States. War did not solve the problems that caused it. Today people seek other ways to solve disagreements.

Everyone will not always agree

Our nation has made great progress because men and women have spoken and fought for what they believed to be right. This kind of conflict can be good if it is not

Urban Crowding

Prejudice

Political Differences

Disagreement Over Individual Rights

destructive. Indeed, the laws of our country protect freedom of speech. But this freedom carries a responsibility not to harm others. As Chief Justice Oliver Wendell Holmes said, "free speech would not protect a man shouting 'Fire' in a theater and causing a panic."

The important problem facing any organization or government is to find a way to settle differences of opinion before the unity of the group or nation is threatened. If we are able to solve this problem, we will be able to keep our republic and enjoy the freedom it holds for us.

Check for Understanding: Now that you have completed this section, you should be able to answer these questions:

1. What are three reasons why conflicts arise?
2. What are three different kinds of conflict?
3. What is bad about conflict?
4. What is one way in which conflict can be helpful to the nation?

Have students select an instance of conflict from the illustrations and suggest a way of solving it.

HOW CAN WE COMPROMISE IN ORDER TO KEEP OUR REPUBLIC?

Objectives: After reading this section, you will be able to:

- Explain how majority rule operates in a republic.
- Describe the role of the minority in the American system.
- Realize the value of compromise and tolerance in a republic.

Majority rule

Let's use an example to see how we can have differences of opinion and still keep our republic. Suppose your class has just raised $200 by washing people's cars on Saturdays. Some class members want to spend the money to buy books for the school library. You, and some others, think that the money should be spent on a trip for your class alone.

Your class holds a meeting. You say that the money comes from your hard work, and the class should have the right to spend it on themselves instead of on the whole school. Finally a vote is taken. Your side loses, sixteen votes to twelve. The money will go to the library, rather than for the trip.

You are told that if you are a good citizen, you will accept the will of the majority. But why accept this decision, when you are convinced it is wrong?

Democratic process

You accept the decision not because it is necessarily right or because the majority voted for it, but because it was decided through a democratic procedure. Democratic procedure has many parts besides the actual vote itself. To keep self-government, each part must be respected.

This class at Watson High School raised money for the track team by running a car wash.

Free speech and debate

The class held open debate and allowed free speech. Everyone was allowed to express an opinion. As students expressed different ideas, some persons changed their minds. A very important part of the democratic process is to permit all ideas and opinions to be presented. Even the *minority* —those who are opposed to the majority— have the opportunity to give their reasons and ideas. The purpose of free speech and debate is to help people make up their minds in an atmosphere of fairness.

Ask your students to think of a similar situation in their own experience. How was the issue resolved?

Respect for the minority

As differences are debated, there is respect for the minority and their opinions. The democratic process provides equal treatment for all sides in debate and in voting. Those who disagree are not ignored, shouted down, or otherwise kept silent.

Protection for the individual

Each person feels free to express an opinion and to vote the way he or she wishes. No individual may be punished for using the right to speak or vote as he or she thinks proper.

Free elections

When the time comes for a final decision, it is made by all who are eligible to vote, or by their representatives. No individual is excluded from voting because he or she disagrees with the majority. Even though the minority lost the election, what they said is still important. Their arguments allowed both sides of the question to be presented. The split of the votes shows the extent to which there was disagreement within the group.

Some members of the class disagreed. They thought the money should go to the class itself, not the library.

Correcting mistakes and changing opinion

The real advantage of the democratic process is that it allows for changes that correct mistakes or account for shifts in opinion. Your class may have made a mistake. Your arguments, and the number of persons who supported you, may cause your class to change its use of money in the future. In the same way, our republican government has made many changes.

Suppose a country or group did away with all opposition. Such a country or group could not change to react to changing times and conditions. This is one of the problems in a dictatorship. Under that form of government, those who oppose the leader may be threatened or punished. If the leader makes a mistake, there is no one to point it out.

A free republic can listen to the opposition and may change its ways. There have been times in our nation's history when this has been the case. Slavery, prohibition, women's right to vote, segregated schools, and the voting age have been decided one way at a certain point in our history but then changed at a later date.

Minority opinions in action

Most such changes occur because the minority continues to work within the democratic process. When someone does not have his or her opinion accepted and with-

Ask students to choose one of the situations where opinion changed—women's suffrage, for example—and do research into the events that caused this change.

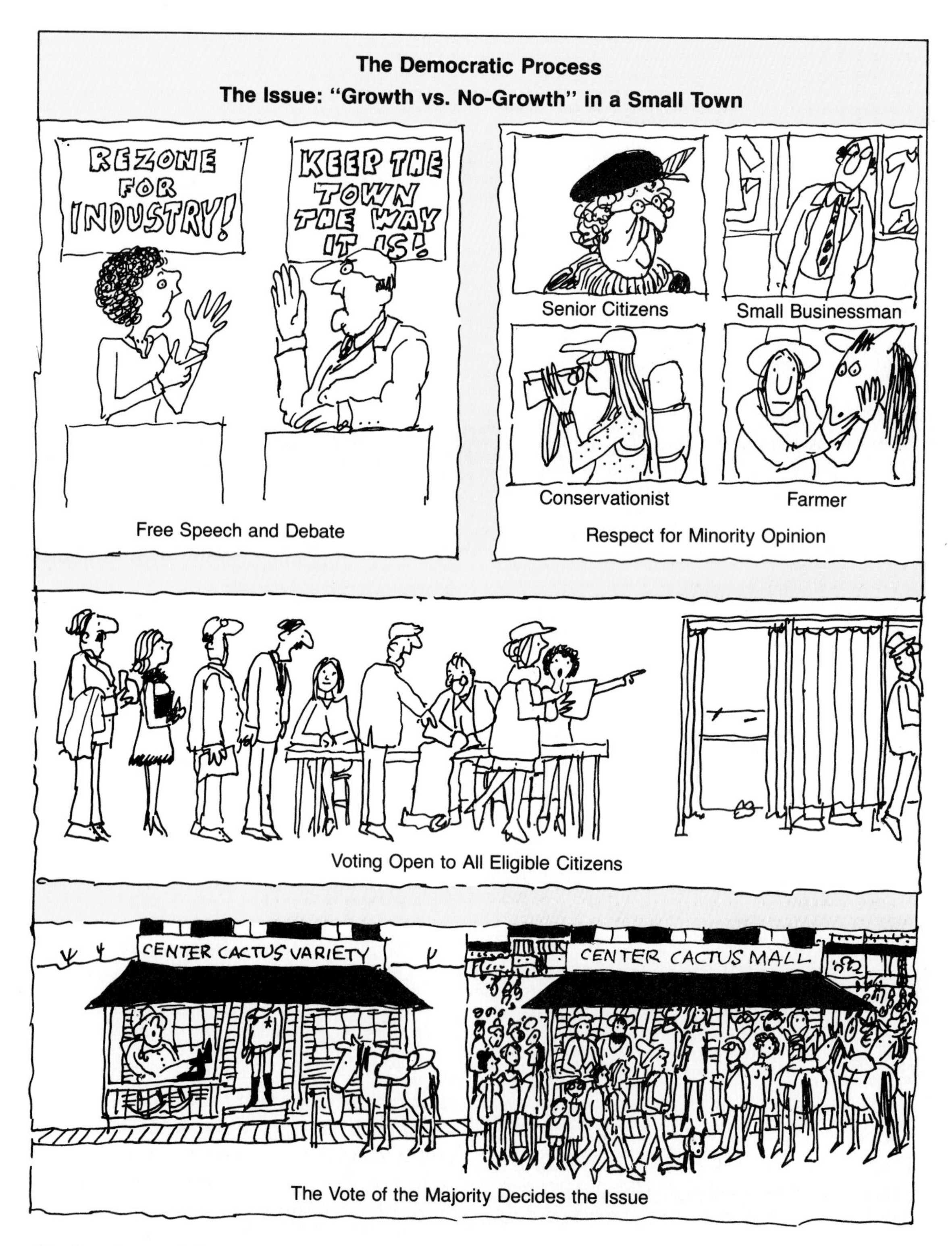

Has there been a similar "growth" controversy in your community lately? Discuss how the issue was resolved.

draws from participation in government, the nation loses a source of correction. Therefore, a free government does not destroy minority opposition. *Dissent*, or having an opinion that disagrees with existing policy, will often have an effect on government. Even if dissent doesn't win in the long run, it may still cause the nation to *modify* or change its policies.

People's differences can be settled in a way that is fair and democratic. This idea is important to a free government. In order to give all the people the right to their beliefs, we must have tolerance. *Tolerance* means that we must allow people to express beliefs with which we disagree. A famous saying, attributed to the French philosopher Voltaire, puts it this way: "I may disapprove of what you say, but I will defend to the death your right to say it."

Within the political process, one way to settle differences is through compromise. *Compromise* means settling differences in such a way that each side makes concessions or gives up something. One of the most damaging conditions in a republic is for one side to insist that it alone has moral truth. This form of argument leaves the opposition in a position of either condemning what has been said and appearing to be against the truth, or agreeing because they fear the political and social consequences of disagreement. Realistic self-government provides a middle-of-the-road solution for problems that arise from conflicts among different groups.

Compromise keeps a nation from extremes, either in solutions or in ideals. It says there is a balance between liberty and authority, between the self-expression of the free individual and the necessary power of the majority, and between the right of conscience and the power of organized moral authority. Without compromise, the organized majority can become the master of the nation, instead of the servant of the people. If this ever happened, the republic would be lost.

Check for Understanding: Now that you have completed this section, you should be able to answer these questions:

1. How does majority rule operate in a republic?
2. What is the role of the minority?
3. What is the value of tolerance and compromise in a republic?
4. How can a republic be lost?

SUMMARY

You live in a republic—a nation where the people govern themselves through persons elected to represent them. Our nation is made up of people from many different backgrounds. Large, concentrated cities serve as an example of how people can live together without destructive conflict.

The democratic process also helps people live together. It includes free speech, open debate, and free elections. You must understand and participate in this process to help keep our republic and protect your individual rights. Respect for the minority—people who dissent from the opinion of the majority—allows for both sides of a problem to be heard. In time, support of what is good and just in the ideas of the minority can cause policies to be modified.

Compromise and tolerance are a necessary part of the democratic process. Without them, a majority can become the master of a nation instead of its servant.

Have the class collect letters to the editor showing a dissenting opinion. Then show why they agree or disagree by collecting background information.

BUILDING SKILLS IN CIVICS

THINKING SKILLS

1. Why is the population of the United States often called "a melting pot?" Why does this book refer to it as a "salad bowl?"
2. What are four things that can cause conflict in American life?
3. What is meant by "majority rule?"
4. Find four sentences in this chapter that support this generalization:
   "Our nation draws its strength from many races and many nationalities."
5. Choose the title below that you think best fits this paragraph.
   Within the political process, one way to settle conflicts that arise is through compromise. Each side makes concessions or gives up something in order to find a middle-of-the-road solution that both sides can agree on.
   a. Tolerance b. Compromise c. Free Speech

VOCABULARY SKILLS

Fill in each blank with the word that best fits the sentence.

self-government	minority	ethnic group	modify
tolerance	dissent	compromise	

1. Each ______ that has come to the United States has contributed ideas and customs to the whole country.
2. In a ______ people govern themselves through elected representatives.
3. Dissent can often cause a nation to change its policies, or to ______ them.
4. Without ______ it isn't possible for people with different religions and political beliefs to live together successfully.
5. One way to settle differences is for each side to ______.
6. Respect for the ______, or those who disagree with the opinion of the majority, is essential in a democracy.
7. A free society has to allow for ______, for people to think differently from the majority, or it cannot remain free.

Each of the vocabulary words presented in the chapter appears in the "Vocabulary Skills" activity.

STUDY SKILLS—USING AN INDEX

The *index* of a book is an alphabetical list of the important words or concepts in that book. Each entry in an index is followed by the page number showing you where in the book that idea is discussed. In some cases, subtopics are also listed after the main entry. For example, in the Index of this book you will find:

District, **149,** *260,*
  congressional, 211
  special, 353

This tells you that the idea of a "district" is discussed on pages 149 and 260. However, if you want to know specifically about congressional districts, you should look on page 211.

Activity: Practice your skills by looking through the Index for the answers to the following questions:

1. Which two topics could you look under to find out about the Democratic Party?
2. What powers are taught about in this text?
3. What does it mean when a page number is in italics? bold face?
4. When are Index skills important for a student?

BEYOND THE BOOK

1. Look on the back of a quarter, or any other U.S. coin, and you will see both English words and Latin words. These Latin words "E pluribus unum" are the motto of the U.S.A. They mean "from many, one." Why is this an excellent motto for our country?
2. Scientists use objects and tools and coins to learn about people. Imagine that the only thing the scientists of the future had from our country were its coins. What could they tell about the United States?
3. Collect five items or pictures of items that you would include in a time capsule to tell people in the future about our government.

CHAPTER THREE TEST

VOCABULARY CHECK

Match each term with its definition.

a. dissent
b. tolerance
c. minority
d. compromise
e. ethnic group
f. self-government
g. modify

1. A group within a society that differs from most members of that society; a group that is not in power.
2. To have thoughts or opinions that are different from the views of the majority.
3. One way to settle a conflict.
4. The attitude that others' have a right to their ideas and beliefs no matter how different they are from one's own.
5. A government ruled by the people through elected representatives.
6. To change or to reduce in strength.
7. People united by such ties as national origin, religion, race, or language.

COMPREHENSION CHECK

Write "Cause of Conflict" and "Compromise" on your paper. Put each of these ideas under the correct heading:

a. People living more closely together in cities.
b. Making concessions or giving up something.
c. A political process.
d. Differences in cultural backgrounds.
e. Having different opinions about wages and working conditions.
f. A "give-and-take" method.
g. A way of keeping people from extremes.
h. A solution for a problem.
i. The different ways other people do things.
j. Differences in standard of living.

Each vocabulary word also appears in the Vocabulary Test.

SKILL BUILDERS—INTERPRETING ILLUSTRATIONS

The old saying "One picture is worth a thousand words" is true, *if* you can understand the language of pictures. Each chapter of this book includes ways to help you do that by teaching you how to see, to organize and to express the idea in an *illustration*. Follow these steps:

1. SEE EVERYTHING—The first step in using a picture is to look at it carefully. Start with the picture on page 46. Make sure you see every detail. Count how many different things you see, then look again to make sure you've seen everything.
2. ORGANIZE THE DATA—Next you organize your information. Write these headings on your paper, "The Issue," "The Events," and "The Result." Under each heading write the information you have gathered from the picture that goes with that heading.
3. EXPRESS IN WORDS—The next step is to make sure you understand what you are seeing. Imagine that you have never seen this picture. You want to find an illustration that shows the idea of "the democratic process." Write a description for someone to help you find what you are looking for. In your description, identify the main idea that the picture will help teach.

Now practice the three steps, SEEING, ORGANIZING, and EXPRESSING, with other pictures.

BUILDING WRITING SKILLS

1. Explain the difference between *tolerance* and *prejudice.*
2. Select another picture in one of the first three chapters. Describe it, making sure to express the idea of tolerance or prejudice. Give your paper to another class member who will then try to identify your picture. Notice which clues help identify the picture.
3. Make a list of all the ways you come into contact with other cultures in your daily life. After you compare your list to another student's, write a short paper with details from your list. You will have to include some general statements.

Chapter Four • Our Duties and Responsibilities as Citizens

Documents: The Constitution of the United States
Laws of the United States: Draft Registration (1980)

"The Congress shall have Power to lay and collect Taxes, Duties, Imposts and Excises, to pay the Debts and provide for the common Defence and general Welfare of the United States . . . To provide for organizing, arming, and disciplining, the Militia . . ." (Article I, Section 8)

"In all criminal prosecutions, the accused shall enjoy the right to a speedy and public trial, by an impartial jury of the State and district wherein the crime shall have been committed . . ." (Amendment VI, November 3, 1791)

All eighteen-year-old males are required upon the instance of their eighteenth birthday to register for the draft. Failure to comply with this law carries with it a penalty.

National pride is a key ingredient in an individual's willingness to accept certain civic responsibilities. Although no one can force a citizen to believe in his or her country, the law can require citizens to accept certain duties or pay penalties for non-compliance, as in the case of mandatory jury duty or draft registration. Civic responsibility is crucial to the survival of any nation if it is to flourish. A free people

The illustrations depict a colonial militia and men signing up for the draft in World War II. They thus exemplify citizens' duty to defend their country. Why is the power to support an army contained in the Constitution?

should regard the duties and responsibilities of citizenship as investments in their nation's future. Theodore Roosevelt once said, "The first requisite of a good citizen in this Republic of ours is that he shall be able and willing to pull his weight." With this statement he was emphasizing the importance of giving to the society in which we live, in return for all the benefits we derive from living in such a democracy.

FOCUSING IDEAS

- The duties of citizenship include obeying laws, serving on a jury, defending the nation, paying taxes, getting an education and protecting the environment.
- The responsibilities that Americans accept as part of citizenship include voting, accepting public office, being aware of the affairs of government, supporting public officials, being informed, and preserving the self-government.
- Public opinion, as expressed through radio, TV, newspapers, and interpersonal communication, helps responsible citizens to think clearly. By writing letters to elected officials, we can influence their thinking, and by recognizing propaganda in our own statements as well as others, we can reach accurate conclusions on the issues based on facts, not biased opinions.

The illustration depicts one of a citizen's central responsibilities: keeping informed about government.

Issues in Civics: What is meant by Roosevelt's statement about a citizen pulling his or her weight? What are certain things required of a citizen?

PRE-TEST

1. What are the duties that a citizen must perform in our republic?
2. What are a citizen's responsibilities?
3. How can a responsible citizen make up his or her mind about the issues?

WHAT ARE THE DUTIES OF CITIZENSHIP?

Objectives: After reading this section, you will be able to:

- List the duties of citizenship.
- Explain how taxation provides services for the nation.
- Understand why jury duty is so important in the democratic process.

Citizens have duties

United States citizenship, as you learned in Chapter One, is a matter of birthright—a privilege of being born in this country. But this privilege carries with it certain duties. These *duties* are the things that people "must" do. In other words, these duties are prescribed by law and cannot be escaped without a penalty being imposed.

One of the first duties of any citizen is to obey the laws. As you have already learned, failure to obey the laws causes problems within a society. We, as citizens, must help the law-enforcement authorities to protect us from harmful acts. This means it is your duty to report anything unlawful to which you are a witness. It is also your duty to testify in court if you have evidence to present.

Serving on a jury

Another of the duties of a citizen is jury service. The idea of a trial by jury is enshrined in several guarantees of the Constitution. As you will learn in another chapter, a jury trial is fundamental to our justice system in the United States. It is also the foundation of popular sovereignty. Indeed, an early observer of American government, Alexis de Tocqueville, had this to say about jury duty: "The jury, which is the most energetic means of making the people rule, is also the most effective means of teaching it to rule."

In most states, the system of drawing juries is so arranged that no person is drawn for such service more often than once every two to five years. Some people may never serve. Even though the service is not often required and is not a great burden, many seek to escape the duty. Although jury duty can be frustrating and inconvenient, it is the most rewarding civic duty that average citizens get a chance to perform, far more so than voting or paying taxes. It is the acting out of the democratic ideal with your neighbors. However, jury trials can be no better

---

Building Vocabulary:
duty *(54)* • tax *(56)* • right *(57)* • responsibility *(58)* • political machine *(59)* • public opinion *(63)* • propaganda *(64)*

There are either seven or eight different vocabulary items presented in each chapter.

If possible, interview someone who has served on a jury. Report on jury duty to the class. Should everyone have to serve on a jury?

Ask your students to list other duties of citizens. Have them interview adults in their neighborhoods and see what they think their duties are. Then have them compare the two lists.

ITEM	UNIT	1890	1900	1910	1920	1930	1940	1950	1960	1970	1982
Round steak*	¢/ unit shown	12.3	13.2	17.4	39.5	42.6	36.4	93.6	105.5	130.2	175
Bread*	¢/ unit shown				11.5	8.6	8.0	14.3	20.3	24.3	45
Butter*	¢/ unit shown	25.5	26.1	35.9	70.1	46.4	36.0	72.9	74.9	86.6	185
Potatoes**	¢/ unit shown	16.0	14.0	17.0	63.0	36.0	23.9	46.1	71.8	89.7	100
Sugar***	¢/ unit shown	34.5	30.5	30.0	97.0	30.5	26.0	48.7	58.2	64.8	125

* = 1 lb. ** = 10 lbs. *** = 5 lbs.

The chart indicates the average price of five common Good items from 1890 to 1982. The price of each item is at least four times what it was before World War II.

than those selected to serve on the jury. If citizens evade such duties, then we may expect to find injustice in our courts.

Defending our nation

United States citizens may be called upon to help defend the nation by serving in the armed forces. When our nation is attacked, or when world conditions are such that the possibility of war exists, Congress passes draft laws. These laws require that persons of a certain age who meet mental and physical qualifications be drafted into the armed forces. There is now a law requiring all males to register for the draft on their eighteenth birthday, although there are at present no plans to implement the draft. Failure to register is an unlawful act and carries a penalty. Persons who object to armed service for conscientious reasons, either religious or moral, may serve in a noncombat position. While service in the armed forces can interrupt one's career and personal life, it is nevertheless a duty of citizens, if called, to protect the nation.

Paying taxes

The expenses of government are met by money collected through taxation. People must pay for the services they expect from their government. These services range from defense costs to welfare costs. Every unit of government, from the local to the national level, collects some kind of *taxes*.

Government today costs more than it did ten years ago. One reason is that people have come to expect more and more services from the government. Another is that inflation, or higher costs for goods and services, takes more money. To get more for our money, we must ask our government officials to spend tax dollars wisely. Also, we as citizens must not ask government to do things that we can do ourselves.

Let us examine some areas in which more government services today mean higher costs. Years ago many students did not go far in school. But today, most students now stay in school at least through high school. Many go on to state colleges and universities. These schools may have well-trained teaching staffs and new equipment. The costs are paid by taxpayers.

Many inventions have made new demands on government. The use of automobiles, for example, has required new laws to control traffic. Special police officers are needed to enforce these laws. And new roads are needed to carry the traffic.

The changing world has made greater demands on government, too. The total

Issue in Civics: Debate the question: "Should women have to register for the draft?"

Ask your students to note how much prices have increased. Why has the greatest rate of increase taken place in recent years?

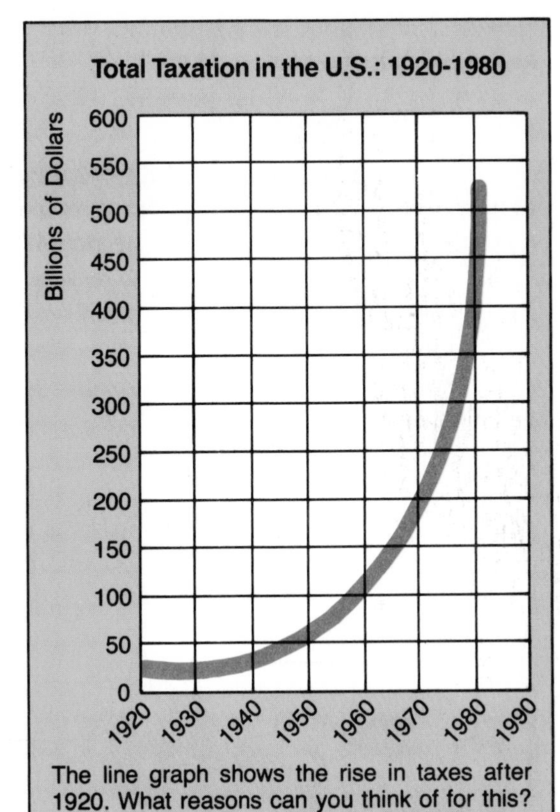

The line graph shows the rise in taxes after 1920. What reasons can you think of for this? The 1980 level was approximately $520 billion. How do you think the graph will look if it is brought up to date ten years from now? Explain your answer.

cost of keeping a strong national defense is much greater today than even in the days of World War II. The government is helping more people through welfare aid. It is also helping some foreign countries with aid. The cost of cleaning up the environment means higher expenses.

Receiving an education

People must be well informed if they are to "keep the republic," in Franklin's words. Laws require young people to go to school. If people get a good basic education, they will be prepared to vote and make good decisions as citizens.

Protecting the environment

Laws have been passed to bring about more careful use of the environment. But each citizen can take some personal responsibility for a clean environment. We can prevent litter from polluting the ground and smog or noise from polluting the air.

Check for Understanding: Now that you have completed this section, you should be able to answer these questions:

1. What are the various duties that are required of a citizen?
2. What are three services of government provided by taxation?
3. Why is jury duty important to a democracy?
4. How can education help a person to be a good citizen?

WHAT ARE THE RESPONSIBILITIES OF CITIZENSHIP?

Objectives: After reading this section, you will be able to:

- List the responsibilities of citizenship.
- Tell why it is important to exercise these responsibilities.
- Explain the difference between a duty and a responsibility.

Citizenship

Your American citizenship gives you many *rights*. One of these rights is freedom from arrest without cause. Another is the right to live and to seek happiness. And it is also your right to say that you do not agree with what the government does and says. But in

Ask students to find out how their state compares with others in rate of taxation.

Issue in Civics: "Guns vs. Butter" Should a greater portion of our federal tax money be devoted to "the common Defense" or to "the general Welfare"?

return for these rights, citizenship gives you responsibilities.

These citizenship *responsibilities* are the things that one "ought" to do. They differ from one's duties as a citizen in that one cannot be punished by law for failure to do them. Nevertheless, most American citizens accept their responsibilities, because they realize government would not function effectively if they did not.

Voting

We must never forget that the responsibility for our government rests with the people. Voting is the chief way in which the people of the United States choose what their

A Political Machine

One Unelected Boss Controls Everything

Voters Vote for the Same Party Regardless of Candidates or Issues

Friends of the 'Machine' Get Special Favors

The General Public Is Often Not Well Served

Ask students to do research on well-known political machines—the Tweed Ring, Tammany Hall, Huey Long, Boss Pendergast, etc.

government will do. Lincoln once said that people in a republic deserve the government they get. He meant that citizens have the power to change their government by voting, and that if they do not bother to vote for good candidates, they deserve the poor service they get from bad candidates. They are not forced to vote, but it is their most important responsibility to exercise in order to have good government. The following story illustrates what can happen if citizens do not accept their responsibility to vote.

A man was able to make himself a city's boss by getting a group of people to form a political machine. A *political machine* is an organized bloc of voters who vote the way they are told to vote. The boss and his machine ran candidates for all city offices. Few honest people were willing to run against them. Many citizens did not even bother to vote.

The dishonest mayor and council won the election. They began to give contracts for street paving to the friends of the boss. The city paid more for these projects than they were worth. When a new fire truck was needed, the officials paid a higher price than the truck was worth. Then the man who sold the truck could pay money to the political boss as a reward for giving him the business. (This is called a "kickback.")

This situation lasted for many years. Decent citizens lost interest in city elections. Some said that all politicians were crooked and refused to vote. Some thought it was too much trouble to vote. But the people who had made deals with the machine voted every time. The machine stayed in power until concerned citizens began to meet their responsibilities. They started to speak out against the boss. Honest candidates opposed the machine in elections. The machine lost its control when enough citizens voted for the honest candidates. By making use of the vote, people brought back free government.

Accepting public office

In a republic, qualified citizens should be ready to accept office if the good of the country demands it. John Tyler, after leaving the Presidency, was elected as a road overseer of a small road district in the farming community where he lived in Virginia. The office carried no honor for a man who had been President, yet he served so well that his district became famous for having the best roads in Virginia.

John Tyler, President of the U.S. from 1841 to 1845, was also willing to serve the public in a much lower office.

Issues in Civics: Declining Voter Turnout. What are the reasons? What are its effects?

Ask students how they feel about Tyler's service. Is it demeaning for an ex-President to serve in such a minor role?

Electing people to office

Whenever citizens go to the trouble of persuading capable and honest persons to become candidates for office and then work for their election, they can have good public officials. Government in a republic such as ours is never better than its citizens make it. The voters can work for a political party of their own choosing. They can begin at the precinct level by watching the polls to prevent election fraud. They can participate in other ways as well. By being involved, citizens can act to insure better government.

Watching government expenses

Since we, the people, are the government, it is our responsibility to be interested in governmental activities. We have a right to demand that the people we elect to local, state, and national governments manage each branch of government efficiently.

Andrew Jackson, when President, managed the United States government so well that he was able to pay off the national debt

Andrew Jackson paid off the final installment of the national debt in 1835. He was the only President ever to do this.

Since World War II, the federal government has found it very difficult to balance the budget because expenses have grown much faster than revenues.

Issue in Civics: Virtually every recent President has taken office with a promise to balance the budget, yet the deficit continues to grow. Why is this so? What can be done about it?

for the only time in our history. Jackson was able to do that because he believed that a nation, like a thrifty family, should live within its means. Once, in a message to Congress, Jackson wrote, "There is, perhaps, no one of the powers of the federal government so liable to abuse as the taxing power."

Today the goal is to balance the federal budget. At every level, citizens want their governments to live within its means. In watching how governments spend money, a good citizen must do more than complain. A person must be aware of the fact that many benefits are received from the government—benefits that cannot be furnished free. We cannot expect good police and fire protection, good highways, and good schools unless we are willing to pay for them. It is necessary for a citizen to know the value of the things received, as well as the value of the taxes paid, and to weigh what one gets against what one pays out.

Supporting public officials

All citizens should support the necessary work of the federal, state, and local governments. When we elect capable persons to office, it is important to continue to help them. Without our support, selfish persons may try to capture the interests of lawmakers and public officials. Sometimes the character of public officials is unfairly attacked by people who would damage their effectiveness.

Being informed

With every right there are one or more responsibilities that go along with it. The right to vote, for example, goes along with the responsibility to be informed.

In the complex field of local and national politics where many candidates are running for offices, it may be difficult for the average voter to be fully informed about the best person for each office. In this case, it is wise to check the candidate by listings prepared by the League of Women Voters, a non-partisan organization dedicated to helping preserve good government. There are several civic organizations that print information about political candidates. However, it is best for you, the citizen, to master the six steps to clear thinking presented in the next section. With these steps in mind, you will be able to inform yourself on the issues and candidates running for public office.

The responsibility of liberty

You may think that it is certain that America will always have good government and will always be free, since it has been free since the nation began. But you have also learned that dictators and political machines can take over a government. People can lose freedom when they forget their duties and responsibilities. The republic of Rome and the democracy of Athens are two such examples of a people who fell prey to dictators and tyrants. They did not bear in mind the words of the patriot Thomas Paine in his pamphlet *The American Crisis:* "What we obtain too cheaply, we esteem too lightly." In other words, they did not care enough to preserve their self-government.

Check for Understanding: Now that you have completed this section, you should be able to answer these questions:

1. What are the responsibilities of citizenship?
2. Why is it important to exercise these responsibilities?
3. How do citizens' duties differ from their responsibilities?
4. Why are political bosses and machines not good for a democratic republic?

Issue in Civics: Jackson also said that the federal government should "shower its favors alike on the high and the low, the rich and the poor". Discuss this statement—does the government do this today? Should it?

Note that thematic illustrations such as this relate directly to the text, in that the items they depict—"vote in elections" "accept public office" and so on—are the same as the headings of the text itself, in this case, pp. 58-61.

HOW DO WE THINK AS RESPONSIBLE CITIZENS?

Objectives: After reading this section, you will be able to:
- List the six steps to clear thinking.
- Explain propaganda and its effects on people.
- Make an analysis of the editorial page of a newspaper.

Forming opinions

You probably get your opinions from a number of sources. The media, or news sources such as radio, TV, and newspapers, help you form opinions. So do friends, neighbors, parents and other family members, religious leaders, and teachers. All of these make up what is known as *public opinion.*

Elected officials react to public opinion. They recognize that the people are the source of their power. Writing letters to government officials can influence their thinking, because a politician knows that if the voters are unhappy he or she will not stay in office. Former Speaker of the House Sam Rayburn once said, "If a man sends me a penciled note on tablet paper, he's usually an angry voter. I'll answer his letter right away."

Clear thinking

Have you ever heard these statements? "Say that again, but leave out your opinion." "I think there is a bit of prejudice in what you've said." "Do you have any evidence for that charge?" If you have, you know someone was trying to focus your thoughts more clearly on the problem. To help you see the steps involved in learning to think clearly, two documents, or papers, will be presented. You will be looking in each document for evidence of clear and unclear ways of thinking.

The first document is an editorial from a fictitious high school newspaper, the James High *Echo*. An editorial is the editor's opinion on a certain issue or problem. An opinion is what the editor thinks is true, but cannot prove. A fact is something that has been proven to be true. As you read the editorial, think about the following things:
1. What is the issue?
2. What words should be defined?
3. What are the facts in this editorial?
4. What are the opinions in this editorial?

New Group
at James High

A new student group has been formed at James High. These students are known on campus as the "Future Ones" or "Wayouts." They have had a lot of attention in recent weeks.

The "Future Ones" have been interested in putting up candidates for the student council. These candidates don't discuss and debate the important issues as the better-known candidates from the major students groups do. They also hold their meetings at oddly scattered places around campus.

A new student group at James High is not a bad idea. However, a group that discusses real issues would serve the needs of the whole student body better. Introducing such issues as a two-hour lunch period, snacks in the library, and staggered school hours is not a contribution to progress.

There are changes each of us would like to see at James High. But these changes will come about by facing the important issues that the major student groups have raised. Unimportant or foolish issues have no place in a meaningful campaign, and a group that stands for such unimportant issues is a group going nowhere.

—Bob Dalton, Editor

The editor sees the issue as a new student group that raises its own issues. Why these students felt the need to form a group is not discussed. This might be viewed as

Sam Rayburn's policy is similar to that of Charles Revson, a well-known business executive, who always refused to answer phone calls personally—except when an angry customer was on the line. Then he himself would deal with the person immediately. Discuss this concept of the effect of public opinion on individuals in power.

the main issue by others. The spreading of ideas by individuals or groups trying to persuade people to accept those ideas is called *propaganda*. Propaganda may be used to help or hurt an institution, person, or cause.

The editor used a propaganda method known as "name-calling" to sway student opinion. Referring to these students as "wayouts" or "future ones" makes their ideas seem less serious. These negative words show prejudice on the part of the editor. Prejudice is reaching a conclusion based on opinions, not facts. The editor hopes to influence readers against the ideas of the group in this way.

The editor also tries to convince the reader that everybody else agrees with his stated position. This is another propaganda method. It puts pressure on the reader to agree with the majority. In this case, the editor claims that the new student group's goals are not important. This is because they are not the issues raised by the so-called "major" candidates. The editor suggests another way in which the new group goes against the majority. They hold their meetings in unusual places. The choice of the words "oddly scattered places" gives the reader this idea.

Propaganda may also use words which are general in nature. Words such as "major," "important," "minor," "meaningful," and "progress" invite certain questions. "Meaningful" or "important" to whom? "Major" or "minor" by what standards? What is "progress"? The readers only know the editor's opinions. He does not think that the "Future Ones" have important or meaningful ideas.

The "Future Ones" were a new group of students at James High who wanted to raise different issues for student government to consider.

Issues in Civics: "Propaganda is always harmful because it distorts the issues." Debate this statement.

Ask interested students to bring in examples of propaganda, either historic or contemporary.

The facts in this editorial seem to be:
1. There is a new student group at James High.
2. The new group has raised some new issues.

Some opinions in the editorial are:
1. A group that considers issues raised by the major candidates would serve the needs of the student body best.
2. Introducing new issues is often an obstacle to progress.
3. The places where a group meets are important in judging how worthwhile the group is.

A letter-to-the-editor document

The next document is a reply from one of the students at James High to the editor. This reply is known as a "letter to the editor." As you read it, think about these things:
1. Does the writer of the letter understand the issue?
2. Does the writer state only the facts and avoid opinions?
3. Does the writer use any form of propaganda?

Dear Editor:

This letter is written to answer your editorial in the November issue of the James High Echo.

In the editorial you state "a group that discusses real issues would serve the needs of the whole student body better." This type of generalization is unfair. Any student with an issue related to school life should be able to raise the issue for discussion in the campaign. the editorial also states that the "Future Ones" do not debate the major issues with other candidates, but instead hold their own meetings.

If the only issues debated at meetings are the ones the better-known candidates raise, then it is understandable that the "Future Ones" hold their own meetings. Small-minded people who believe that the only important issues are the ones that interest them are the ones who do not contribute to progress. They are the ones who are going nowhere.

Cindy Trout

The writer of the letter seems to understand the problem. She thinks that any issue related to student life should be discussed. Such open discussion of issues would get students more involved. The writer expresses another opinion in the last paragraph of her letter. She suggests that the editor favors discussion of only the issues that interest him. Uses of propaganda are also found in the letter to the editor. An example of name-calling is the use of the term, "small-minded." The general term "progress" is used, too. Both terms are quoted from the original editorial to make fun of it.

Steps to clear thinking

Read the six steps to clear thinking that are listed below. They can help you to think, speak, and write more clearly.

---

1. Define the issue.
2. State the facts.
3. Identify statements of opinion as opposed to statements of fact.
4. Avoid the use of prejudice.
5. Support your claims with facts.
6. Recognize propaganda in your own statements and in the statements of others.

Check for Understanding: Now that you have finished this section, you should be able to answer these questions:
1. What are the six important steps to clear thinking?
2. What is propaganda, and what are its effects?
3. What is an editorial?
4. How can an analysis of the editorial page of a newspaper help you to understand the newspaper's position on certain issues?

Ask the class to find examples of editorials and letters to the editor from the school newspaper. Have them apply the criteria that are listed in this chapter.

Ask students to state their personal opinions about the fictitious issue of the "Future Ones." Were they a responsible group? Why were they criticized?

Examples of Propaganda

Mass Appeal

"All across the U.S.A., people drink Bubble-O to feel refreshed!"

Popular Symbols

"Congressman Cypher is a great family man"

Prestige by Association

"Leo Zilch is a leader in the tradition of Thomas Jefferson."

Testimonials

"Todd Trendy brushes his teeth with Star-Brite"

Scare Tactics

"This town will die if we don't build the new shopping center."

Stereotyping

"Today's students have it easy compared to the old days."

Have students give actual examples of each of these types of propaganda. Ask them why they think these techniques are widely used. Which do they think is the most effective?

How People Get Information Under Different Types of Government

Free	Controlled
Newspapers are owned privately. They are free to print any views. They may be sued for slander, however, if they print harmful opinions that cannot be proven.	Only *newspapers* favorable to the government are allowed. All articles are examined for approval by the government.
TV and radio stations and networks are owned privately. They may discuss any news and any opinions. The federal government does regulate decency and public service information.	*TV and radio* stations are owned and operated by the government. Programs praising government policy are featured.
The right to assemble is guaranteed in the Bill of Rights. People may gather to hear or exchange ideas. Such gatherings may be stopped only if they threaten the peace.	The *right to assemble* is not guaranteed. People are not allowed to gather to hear unapproved speakers or to make their own voices heard.

SUMMARY

All citizens have responsibilities to their government. We cannot take our freedom for granted, or we may lose it. Citizens in some countries have lost their free governments. We can act as responsible citizens by obeying laws, by voting, by serving on juries, and by protecting our nation and its environment.

Citizens are responsible for paying for government in taxes. They need to realize what their government provides and the cost of these things.

People need to think as citizens. They need to understand how to act responsibly in order to keep free government.

Each citizen needs to be well-informed. People need information so they can influence government to do the things they want done. They can do this through public opinion and through the vote. Clear thinking is important to every concerned citizen of the United States. Some basic steps for thinking clearly have been suggested in this chapter.

Have an interested student research the provisions in *The Fundamental Orders of Connecticut,* a 17th century document that stressed the welfare of the community.

BUILDING SKILLS IN CIVICS

THINKING SKILLS

1. Why is it important that citizens be well informed?
2. What is the difference between a fact and an opinion? Give an example of a fact and an opinion about your school.
3. Reread the six "steps to clear thinking." Which do you think is the hardest step? Why?
4. Write the headings "Duties" and "Responsibilities" on your paper and classify the following items under them.
   a. Report unlawful acts
   b. Serve in the armed forces
   c. Pay taxes
   d. Vote
   e. Serve on a jury
   f. Accept public office
   g. Obey the laws
   h. Be interested in governmental activities
   i. Be informed
   j. Testify in court
   k. Support public officials

VOCABULARY SKILLS

Some of the underlined words in the sentences below are used correctly, but others are not. If the sentence is correct, write True. If it is not, replace the word with the best choice from the list.

right	public opinion	political machine	duty
tax	propaganda	responsibility	

1. It is your <u>responsibility</u> to report any unlawful act you witness and to testify in court if you have evidence.
2. <u>Taxes</u> are required to help pay the costs of government.
3. <u>Propaganda</u> is used in an effort to influence the way people think.
4. American citizenship gives you many <u>rights</u>, as well as many responsibilities.
5. The views, attitudes, and opinions of the citizens is their <u>duty</u>.
6. The <u>political machine</u> lost its control when enough citizens began to meet their responsibilities and voted for honest candidates.
7. A <u>duty</u> is something that a person ought to do to have better government.

STUDY SKILLS—USING FORMS

Forms are used to simplify and standardize the process of getting information. They can be used as a source of information for you as well as for others. You probably filled out a form when you applied for a library card or took a standardized test.

Activity: Look at the form below and answer these questions: What three things are included in the "Warning and Statement"? What personal information is asked for? What decisions does the person registering have to make? Who is eligible to vote? How can you acquire an absentee ballot?

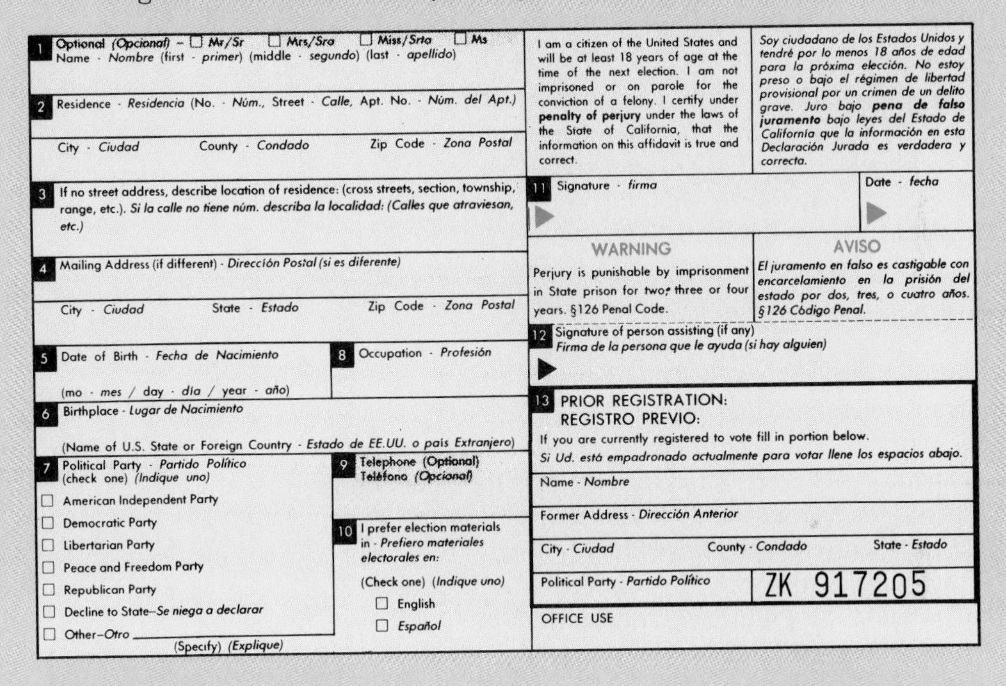

1 Optional *(Opcional)* – ☐ Mr/Sr ☐ Mrs/Sra ☐ Miss/Srta ☐ Ms
Name - *Nombre* (first - *primer*) (middle - *segundo*) (last - *apellido*)

2 Residence - *Residencia* (No. - *Núm.*, Street - *Calle*, Apt. No. - *Núm. del Apt.*)
City - *Ciudad* County - *Condado* Zip Code - *Zona Postal*

3 If no street address, describe location of residence: (cross streets, section, township, range, etc.). *Si la calle no tiene núm. describa la localidad: (Calles que atraviesan, etc.)*

4 Mailing Address (if different) - *Dirección Postal (si es diferente)*
City - *Ciudad* State - *Estado* Zip Code - *Zona Postal*

5 Date of Birth - *Fecha de Nacimiento*
(mo - *mes* / day - *día* / year - *año*)

8 Occupation - *Profesión*

6 Birthplace - *Lugar de Nacimiento*
(Name of U.S. State or Foreign Country - *Estado de EE.UU. o país Extranjero*)

7 Political Party - *Partido Político* (check one) *(Indique uno)*
☐ American Independent Party
☐ Democratic Party
☐ Libertarian Party
☐ Peace and Freedom Party
☐ Republican Party
☐ Decline to State—*Se niega a declarar*
☐ Other—*Otro* ________ (Specify) *(Explique)*

9 Telephone (Optional) *Teléfono (Opcional)*

10 I prefer election materials in - *Prefiero materiales electorales en:*
(Check one) *(Indique uno)*
☐ English
☐ *Español*

I am a citizen of the United States and will be at least 18 years of age at the time of the next election. I am not imprisoned or on parole for the conviction of a felony. I certify under **penalty of perjury** under the laws of the State of California, that the information on this affidavit is true and correct.

Soy ciudadano de los Estados Unidos y tendré por lo menos 18 años de edad para la próxima elección. No estoy preso o bajo el régimen de libertad provisional por un crimen de un delito grave. Juro bajo ***pena de falso juramento*** *bajo leyes del Estado de California que la información en esta Declaración Jurada es verdadera y correcta.*

11 Signature - *firma* ▶ Date - *fecha* ▶

WARNING
Perjury is punishable by imprisonment in State prison for two, three or four years. §126 Penal Code.

AVISO
El juramento en falso es castigable con encarcelamiento en la prisión del estado por dos, tres, o cuatro años. §126 Código Penal.

12 Signature of person assisting (if any)
Firma de la persona que le ayuda (si hay alguien) ▶

13 PRIOR REGISTRATION:
REGISTRO PREVIO:
If you are currently registered to vote fill in portion below.
Si Ud. está empadronado actualmente para votar llene los espacios abajo.
Name - *Nombre*
Former Address - *Dirección Anterior*
City - *Ciudad* County - *Condado* State - *Estado*
Political Party - *Partido Político* ZK 917205

OFFICE USE

BEYOND THE BOOK

1. Create a bulletin board display using the different kinds of forms that people fill out in your shcool and your community.
2. Examine a federal income tax form. Identify the kind of information that is asked for and the skills needed to complete the form. Find out what a "W-2" form is, how it is used, and where it is obtained.

CHAPTER FOUR TEST

VOCABULARY CHECK

Fill in each blank with the word that best completes the sentence.

1. Ideas, facts, and rumors which exist to influence our political thinking are called ______. (public opinion - propaganda)
2. It is a citizen's ______ to obey the laws. (duty - responsibility)
3. In return for your rights, American citizenship gives you ______. (responsibilities - public opinion)
4. A ______ can be successful if citizens do not bother to vote. (republic - political machine)
5. Sometimes public groups change their actions because ______ is against them. (public opinion - inflation)
6. One of the ______ of American citizens is freedom of arrest without cause. (duties - rights)
7. ______ pay for the building and maintenance of streets and highways. (propaganda - taxes)

COMPREHENSION CHECK

Write True if the question and answer match. If they do not, write an answer to the question.

1. What is the effect of strong public opinion on government policy?—Elected officials react to public opinion because they recognize that voters are the source of their power.
2. How can propaganda be used?—Propaganda may be used to try to help or to hurt an institution, person or cause.
3. What is the difference between duties and responsibilities? —You are learning how citizens fulfill their duties and responsibilities and why both are necessary.
4. Why is it important to be able to tell the difference between a fact and an opinion?—People need information so they can influence government. They can do this through public opinion and with the vote.
5. Why is it important to be informed?—A person needs to be well-informed in order to help select qualified people for offices and to influence government officials.

SKILL BUILDERS—INTERPRETING TABLES

Tables like the ones you see on pages 56 and 57 of Chapter Four are a means of arranging certain kinds of statistics or data in columns or rows on the page. This makes the information easy to read and to use. When you read a table, begin by reading the title. It will quickly tell you the purpose of the table.

Activity: Which of the tables would you use:

1. To help explain why you need a larger allowance than people your age received twenty years ago.
2. To understand why people take home a smaller percentage of their paycheck then they did twenty years ago.

Activity: Answer the following questions about these tables:

1. How are the two tables alike?
2. What do the columns show in Table A? Table B?
3. What is the difference in the cost of bread in 1960 and 1982? If these predictions were accurate, how much more will bread cost in 1990 than in 1982?
4. What do you think will happen to the rate of taxation in 1990?
5. Which topic in this chapter does Table A help you know more about? Table B?
6. How do these exact figures help you know more about each topic?

Activity: Look for some tables in your local newspaper. Explain why these tables help make information easier to understand.

BUILDING WRITING SKILLS

1. To show you understand the difference between facts and opinions, choose one of the topics below. Write one paragraph about your topic that contains only facts. Write a second one that contains only opinions.
   a. School Rules   b. Television   c. Sports
2. Identify one duty that a citizen has and tell why it is important.
3. Describe two television commercials you have recently seen. Say what the purpose of each was and how each one tried to achieve that goal. Then explain why a television commercial is an example of propaganda.

UNIT ONE TEST

"Well, it doesn't say I can't run!"

A. Look at the cartoon above. Then answer the following questions:

1. Does the cartoon show civic responsibility, or civic irresponsibility? Why do you think so?
2. How does this cartoon relate to the information presented in Unit One?
3. Do you think the cartoonist was successful in getting his or her viewpoint across? Why or why not?
4. If you were going to draw a cartoon on this subject, how would you do it differently? What would *your* caption read?
5. Do you think that making a statement through the use of humor is effective? Explain your opinion.

B. President John F. Kennedy said in his inaugural speech, "Ask not what your country can do for you—ask what you can do for your country." What can each citizen of the United States *do* for this country? Make a list of at least eight different ways that a citizen can contribute. Which citizen actions do *you* take part in? What do you think you could do for your country that you don't do now?

C. Using information from Unit One and your own opinions, write a speech called "The American Salad Bowl." Make sure you have facts to back up any opinions that you express in the speech.

Unit Two
Our American Government

The Constitution was written by the founders of our country to ensure basic freedoms for their own generation and for all generations to come. As a citizen of the United States, you are protected each day of your life by the laws set forth in the original document, as well as by the Amendments that have been added since the Constitution was signed. Because the Constitution established a framework for our democratic government while also providing for the future, it is known as a "living document"—one that is constructed in such a way that it can continue to adapt to the needs of changing times.

The complete text of the Constitution can be found in the Appendix, beginning on page 564.

Chapter Five · Our Government Before the Constitution

Document: The Declaration of Independence

"When in the Course of human events, it becomes necessary for one people to dissolve the political bands which have connected them with another, and to assume among the Powers of the earth, the separate and equal station to which the laws of Nature and of Nature's God entitle them, a decent respect to the opinions of mankind, requires that they should declare the causes which impel them to the separation . . .

"In every stage of these Oppressions We Have Petitioned for Redress in the most humble terms: Our repeated Petitions have been answered only by repeated injury. A Prince, whose character is thus marked by every act which may define a Tyrant, is unfit to be ruler of a free people . . .

"We, therefore, the Representatives of the United States of America, in General Congress, Assembled, appealing to the Supreme Judge of the world for the rectitude of our intentions, do, in the Name, and by Authority of the good People of these Colonies, solemnly publish and declare, That these United Colonies are, and of Right ought to be Free and Independent States; that they are Absolved from all Allegiance to the British Crown, and that all political connection between them and the State of Great Britain, is and ought to be totally dissolved; . . ."

The complete text of the Declaration of Independence can be found in the Appendix on pages 560–563.

Did you ever stop to consider that the Founding Fathers of our country were revolutionaries? That they were people who wished to overthrow one form of government and start a completely new one? Yet, this *was* the intention of the writers of the Declaration of Independence. They wrote that it had become necessary to break away from England, or "Dissolve the political bonds which have connected them" with England. They would then create a new government.

These were bold, inflammatory words; in essence, a justification to the rest of the world for the American Revolution. The drafters of the Declaration listed the specific grievances and injustices that made this break from England necessary, and in doing so, created one of the great political documents in history. Historian Samuel Eliot Morison said of the Declaration: "These words are more revolutionary than anything written by Robespierre, Marx, or Lenin, more explosive than the atom, a continual challenge to ourselves as well as an inspiration to the oppressed of all the world."

FOCUSING IDEAS

- European history tells us that free government can be lost.
- The English people brought many democratic ideals to the New World that have influenced the United States to this day.
- Objection to English rule led to the Declaration of Independence.
- The Constitutional Convention delegates wrote a strong Constitution that strengthened the central government.

PRE-TEST

1. What does European history tell us about free government?
2. How did English ideas about freedom influence the United States?
3. In what ways did the American colonists show their dissatisfaction with English rule?
4. How did the American government change in the early days of the country?

WHAT DOES EUROPEAN HISTORY TELL US ABOUT FREE GOVERNMENT?

Objectives: After reading this section, you will be able to:

- Describe how countries in the past have lost their freedom.
- List four rights that were provided for in the Magna Carta.
- Explain why written documents are important to keeping freedom.

By now you know that being a citizen of the United States, or living in this country, requires many duties and responsibilities. It also offers many rights and freedoms. Sometimes, it is easy for those of us who have always lived in a free country to forget how important freedom really is.

Freedom can be lost

The complete story of the growth of freedom is too long to tell in any one book. But if you could read the whole story, you would find that many countries gained freedom, only to lose it later. The government of the ancient Greek city of Athens gave rise to the word "democracy." But the

The emperor Nero was one of the dictators who ruled ancient Rome.

Building vocabulary:
tyrant *(77)* • Magna Carta *(77)* • House of Burgesses *(79)* • Mayflower Compact *(79)* • Stamp Act Congress *(81)* • Continental Congress *(81)* • Articles of Confederation *(85)*

Pre-Test questions do not have to be answered immediately, but rather are intended to stimulate students' thinking about the concepts to be developed in the chapter.

Ask interested students to research the history of the republic of Rome. Why did the people lose power to the emperors?

people of Athens lost their free self-government in a war. The people of Rome established one of the first republics, but later they became careless, and the Caesars became dictators over the Roman people.

Europe lost freedom

The people of Europe had government long before they could read or write. The earliest form of government was that of the tribe. Tribes were small groups of people who lived in a small area. The chiefs or leaders of the tribes were chosen for their talent for the hunt, for war, or for wise decision-making. As the numbers of people increased in Europe, more land was needed. Tribes fought over the right to hunt or to farm on certain land. Some tribes united to fight others. Their chiefs chose one of themselves to rule the united tribes. This ruler of many people in a large area became a king or queen.

At first, European kings and queens were chosen by the people. Later, when a king or queen died, it was the custom for the oldest son to come to the throne without an election. If there was no son, the oldest daughter became queen. If the king or queen had no children, some other close relative became the ruler. The kings and queens often wanted to increase their power by adding to their kingdoms. Other tribes were conquered and more people lost their freedom. Eventually most people in Europe were under the firm control of kings and queens. After that, the struggle to regain freedom for the people took more than 1,000 years.

The kings and queens were powerful and had strong armies. No group of citizens could act against them. Some European rulers were good and ruled for the people, but other rulers were *tyrants*. They were cruel and ruled for their own benefit.

King John of England was forced to set his seal on the Magna Carta at Runnymede on June 15, 1215.

King John and the Magna Carta

King John taxed the people very heavily. His court judges decided cases in favor of whoever paid the most money. The government was dishonest and unjust; many of the officials could be bribed. This misuse of the power of government was too much for many people, so they decided to act. A group of clergymen, nobles, and landowners, headed by Stephen Langton, Archbishop of Canterbury, demanded that King John sign the *Magna Carta*. Magna Carta is a Latin term meaning "great charter." The Magna Carta provided several important rights:

1. Courts shall be held in fixed places.
2. Justice shall not be sold.
3. Freemen accused of a crime shall be tried by their equals, not by the king's judges.
4. Taxes shall not be levied except by consent of those taxed.

Issues in Civics: "A monarchy is the best form of government—*if* you have a good king." Discuss the strengths and weaknesses of the monarchical system.

The four rights listed above still exist today as principles of the United States. Ask the class to analyze the influence of the Magna Carta on our government.

At first, the Magna Carta did not provide these rights for all English people. It was only a single step in limiting the power of kings. It was intended to apply to the upper classes rather than the general population. A long way remained to go in English society before every person would gain political freedom.

Documents are important to freedom

The Magna Carta was a written and signed document. A document is something written or printed that gives information or proof of some fact. The Magna Carta listed certain limitations on the power of government and guaranteed certain rights to the people. Because written records exist long after people die or forget what has been agreed upon, documents help ensure that future generations will continue to live by what was written in the past.

Check for Understanding: Now that you have completed this section, you should be able to answer these questions:

1. What are two countries or areas that have lost their freedom?
2. What were four rights contained in the Magna Carta?
3. Why are documents important to keeping freedom?
4. In ancient Europe, how was a new king chosen if the king or queen died?

The original document of the Magna Carta, handwritten in Latin, contained 63 clauses restricting the powers of the King.

HOW DID ENGLISH IDEAS ABOUT FREEDOM INFLUENCE THE UNITED STATES?

Objectives: After reading this section, you will be able to:

- Explain the source of the early colonists' ideas about self-government.
- Name the first important document written in the English colonial period.
- Describe what the colonies had in common in terms of government.

People of many cultures contributed to the development of the United States. The American Indians were here first. Their civilization had been developing for hundreds of years before the Europeans arrived. The Spaniards were the first Europeans to explore and settle in Florida and the Southwest.

Although the world in general has a greater degree of freedom today than in the past, the path of history has been an "up-and-down" process rather than a steady improvement. Cite recent examples of nations that have suffered setbacks in terms of free government, such as Hungary in 1956, Czechoslovakia in 1968, Poland in 1982.

The Mayflower Compact was so called because the Pilgrims signed it on board their ship, the *Mayflower,* just before landing in the New World.

Many other groups, including the Dutch, French, Germans, and Swedes, settled in North America. Each group contributed ideas of government. However, most ideas for the new government along the Atlantic seacoast came from the English colonists. Some rights of self-government were guaranteed in England, and thus it was not a new idea to the colonists.

It was about four hundred years after the signing of the Magna Carta when English people began to cross the Atlantic Ocean to make homes in America. In their hard struggle to establish themselves in a new world, these people brought many democratic ideals with them.

The complete text of the Mayflower Compact can be found in the Appendix on page 584.

The first Virginia Assembly

The first assembly in any of the colonies was elected by the property owners of Virginia at the request of Governor George Yeardley. The members of the assembly called themselves Burgesses. The *House of Burgesses* was the first body of lawmakers to be elected in the English way anywhere in the New World.

The Mayflower Compact

When the first English settlers arrived in Massachusetts in 1620, they drew up an agreement known as the *Mayflower Compact.* In the Compact, the settlers agreed to make laws for the general good.

Only seven countries in the world have not had their system of government change since 1914, and five of these follow the English tradition (Great Britain, U.S., Canada, Australia, New Zealand—the others are Sweden and Switzerland). Why is this so—is it the English system itself, the nature of these countries, or what?

Colonial governments

The English colonists were proud to call themselves English. Often they named their children for English kings and queens. Over a period of 150 years, the English colonists established a total of thirteen colonies along the Atlantic coast.

The various English colonies had different forms of government, but all of them included an elected assembly of representatives of the people. Most of the colonies also had governors who were appointed by the king. In Maryland, Pennsylvania, and Delaware the governors were appointed by favorites of the king to whom he had given the colonies. In Rhode Island and Connecticut, the people elected their own governors. Regardless of the way the governor was chosen, each colony also had an elected assembly. The colonists had a large degree of self-government, and they were determined not to lose it.

Check for Understanding: Now that you have completed this section, you should be able to answer these questions:

1. What nation was the main source of the early colonists' ideas about self-government?
2. What was the first important document of the colonial period?
3. What did the English colonies have in common in terms of government?
4. What was the first law-making body?

HOW DID THE COLONISTS OBJECT TO LIVING UNDER ENGLISH LAWS?

Objectives: After reading this section, you will be able to:

- Explain in your own words the meaning of "No taxation without representation."
- List five ways that the Declaration of Independence accused King George II of misusing power.
- List two of the early Congresses started by the colonists.

Although the colonists had a voice in colonial government through elected assemblies, they were also subject to laws passed in Great Britain. Both the American colonists and the British people were taxed and governed by Parliament. But the colonists were not allowed to elect representatives to Parliament as the British did. The colonists argued that if they were to be subject to the laws of Parliament, they should be able to elect representatives to Parliament. If this was not the case, then the colonies should have more powers for their own assemblies. This argument came to a head in 1765 with the Stamp Act.

The Stamp Act Congress

King George III caused Parliament to pass a law requiring people to pay a new tax. People had to buy stamps to be put on all legal documents. These included deeds, mortgages, marriage licenses, and even newspapers. The law applied to both Great Britain and the colonies. The colonists protested saying again that if they had no representation in Parliament, they should be taxed only by their own assemblies. Their cry of protest was: "No taxation without representation." In the Virginia assembly, Patrick Henry introduced this resolution, which was passed: "Resolved, that the general assembly of this colony has the only and sole right and power to lay

The Stamp Act was passed to help finance the French and Indian War. The French presence in the New World was a threat to the English colonists, and most colonists supported the war. Was King George justified in asking the colonists to give financial support to a war that was seen as providing protection to them?

taxes and imposts upon the inhabitants of this colony."

Similar resolutions were adopted in other colonies. However, each colony was acting alone. Teamwork was needed to show King George III and Parliament that the colonies meant what they said. Nine of the colonies sent delegates to what became known as the *Stamp Act Congress*. It met in New York City in the year 1765. The protests of the Stamp Act Congress caused the repeal of the Stamp Act.

The Continental Congress

In England Parliament continued to pass tax laws. In 1774 twelve colonies sent representatives to Philadelphia to protest these new taxes. This meeting was called the *Continental Congress*. The Congress asked Parliament for the repeal of eleven tax laws that hampered colonial trade. The Congress voted to meet the next year to consider any answer that King George III and Parliament might send.

Resistance with arms

King George III answered the Continental Congress by sending troops to enforce the collection of the tax. Many Americans were concerned, because Great Britain was one of the most powerful nations in the world. But other people insisted upon resistance. Their views were expressed by Patrick Henry before the Virginia assembly, "Is life

The fighting at Lexington, Massachusetts, in the first battle of the American colonists' war for independence from Britain. From a contemporary engraving by Amos Doolittle.

Issues in Civics: The two European nations who were England's main rivals in the New World—Spain and France, had much less of a tradition of democracy and individual rights than England. Would our system have been different if either of these countries had been the primary influence on the U.S.? Why?/Why not?

so dear or peace so sweet as to be purchased at the price of chains and slavery? Forbid it, Almighty God! I know not what course others may take, but as for me, give me liberty or give me death!"

Three weeks later, British troops fired on American minutemen (volunteers who were ready to fight at a minute's notice) at Lexington. War had begun. At first, each state raised troops and fought alone. One month after the Battle of Lexington, the Continental Congress voted to raise an army. George Washington was named Commander-in-Chief of the combined colonial forces.

The Declaration of Independence

The colonists' anger and resentment toward England grew. On July 4, 1776, the Continental Congress issued the Declaration of Independence. A committee was formed to write the Declaration that included Benjamin Franklin, John Adams, Thomas Jefferson, Robert R. Livingston, and Roger Sherman. The others asked Jefferson to write the document. Franklin and John Adams made a few changes in the final version, but essentially the words are Jefferson's. There was much disagreement about whether or not the Congress should issue the declara-

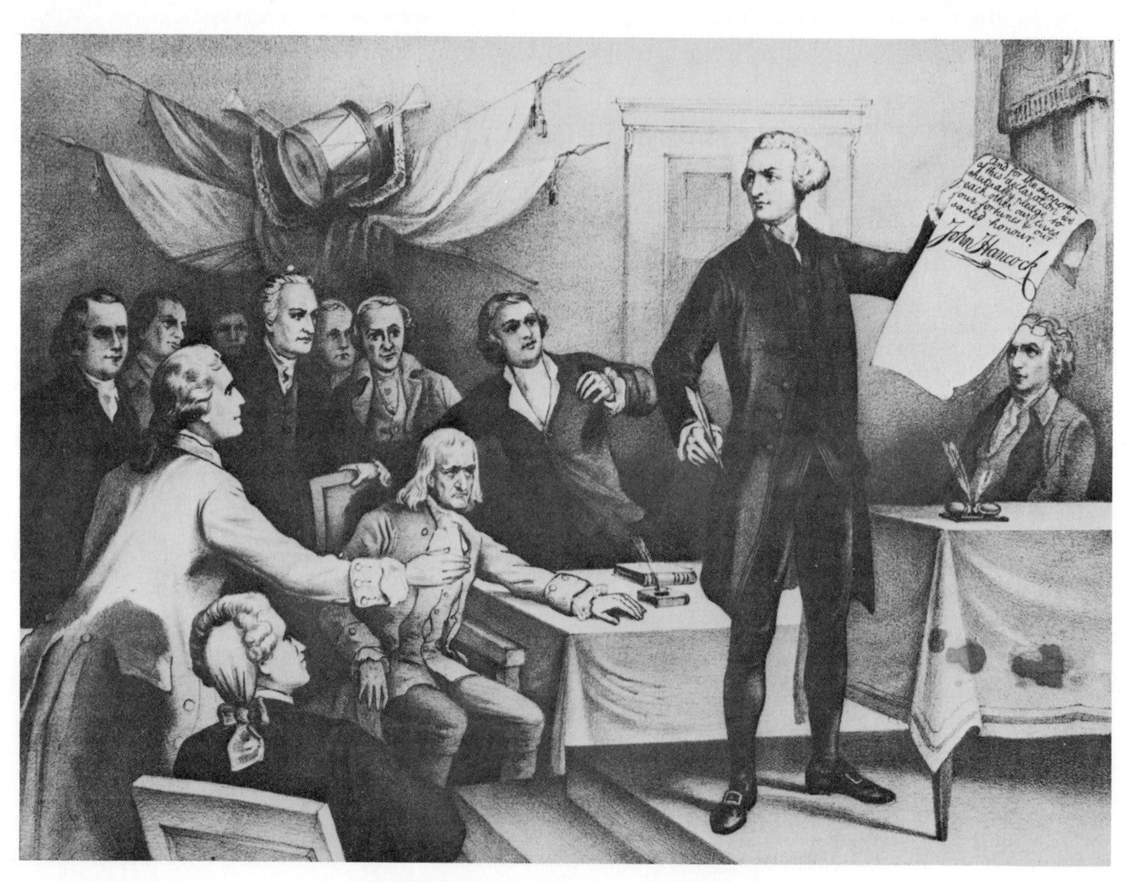

John Hancock was president of the Continental Congress. He said that he made his signature very large "so that King George could read it without his spectacles."

Issues in Civics: Men who rank among the most famous and most honored figures in American history —Washington, Franklin, Jefferson, Adams, Hamilton, et al,—might have been jailed or even executed had the colonies lost the war. Were their actions justified? How do these men compare with revolutionaries in other countries today?

Declaration of Independence.

Fac-simile of the original document in the hand-writing of Thomas Jefferson.

[Copied by permission from the MS. in the Department of State, at Washington.]

A Declaration by the Representatives of the UNITED STATES OF AMERICA, in General Congress assembled.

When in the course of human events it becomes necessary for ~~a~~ one people to dissolve the political bands which have connected them with ~~another~~ another, and to [~~advance from that subordination in which they have hitherto remained, & to~~] assume among the powers of the earth the ~~equal & independant~~ separate and equal station to which the laws of nature & of nature's god entitle them, a decent respect to the opinions of mankind requires that they should declare the causes which impel them to ~~the change~~ the separation.

We hold these truths to be ~~sacred & undeniable~~ self-evident; that all men are created equal ~~& independant~~; that ~~from that equal creation they derive~~ they are endowed by their creator with ~~equal rights some of which are~~ certain [inherent &] inalienable rights; that among ~~which~~ these are ~~the preservation of~~ life ~~&~~ liberty, & the pursuit of happiness; that to secure these ~~ends~~ rights, go-vernments are instituted among men, deriving their just powers from the consent of the governed; that whenever any form of government ~~shall~~ becomes destructive of these ends, it is the right of the people to alter or to abolish it, & to institute new government, laying it's foundation on such principles & organising it's powers in such form, as to them shall seem most likely to effect their safety & happiness. prudence indeed will dictate that governments long established should not be changed for light & transient causes: and accordingly all experience hath shewn that mankind are more disposed to suffer while evils are sufferable, than to right themselves by abolishing the forms to which they are accustomed. but

The complete text of the Declaration of Independence can be found in the Appendix on pages 560–563.

This original version of the Declaration of Independence, including Jefferson's actual editing, is presented here to stress the concept of the Declaration as a personal, living document.

tion. Many members hoped to settle things peacefully and remain a part of England. They pointed out that even some members of Parliament thought the colonies were being treated unjustly. Finally a vote was taken. The Declaration passed.

The Declaration of Independence listed the things King George III had done that misused power and ignored the rights of people:

> He had imposed taxes without the consent of the people.
> He had deprived the people in many cases of trial by jury.
> He had transported prisoners to England to be tried.
> He had made judges dependent upon his will.
> He had cut off American trade.
> He had suspended sessions of the colonial legislatures.
> He had quartered troops in the homes of the people.

After listing the abuses the writers said, "A prince, whose character is thus marked by every act which may define a Tyrant, is unfit to be the ruler of a free people."

Near the conclusion of the Declaration are these words, ". . . these United Colonies are, and of Right ought to be Free and Independent States." The final sentence reads, "And for the support of this Declaration, with a firm reliance on the Protection of Divine Providence, we mutually pledge to each other our Lives, our Fortunes and our sacred Honor."

Check for Understanding: Now that you have completed this section, you should be able to answer these questions:

1. What does the phrase "no taxation without representation" mean?
2. What were five ways that King George III was accused of misusing power?
3. What were two early Congresses started by the colonists?
4. Who was the principal author of the Declaration of Independence?

HOW DID THE NEW GOVERNMENT CHANGE?

Objectives: After completing this section, you will be able to:

- Identify the purpose of government, according to the Declaration of Independence.
- Explain the problems between the national government and the states, under the Articles of Confederation.
- Identify the new idea of government set forth in the Ordinance of 1787.

Elections and laws

The Declaration of Independence sets forth many strong ideas about governments and people. It states that people are created equal, with certain rights. Governments should be established only to protect these rights. Since governments are established for and by the people, the people have the right and duty to change any government that is no longer protecting their rights.

The Declaration says that people have the right to overthrow the government if it is not protecting their rights and will not change. Under an absolute ruler, then as now, people have few means of controlling government. Under democratic government, people do not need to revolt when

You may wish to explain and discuss the list of charges against King George that are presented above.

The term "prince," as used above, is a general term for "monarch," rather than a literal use of the word.

they think government is not protecting their rights. First, they try to persuade their representatives to change the government's policies. If that does not work, they can elect new representatives. In this way people with free elections need never use revolution to change government. Although they were still at war with England, the people of the new America were to change their government in several important ways without having to resort to violence among themselves.

The Articles of Confederation

Before the War for Independence ended, all thirteen colonies had set up state governments. The legislatures and governors were elected. At that time, not all persons could vote. In most states voting rights were given only to men who owned property. So that the states might work together for the good of all, the Continental Congress drew up a Constitution, the *Articles of Confederation*. It provided for a congress to be elected by the legislatures of the states. There was no president to enforce the laws.

The Articles were adopted by the thirteen states in 1781. Some of the states paid little attention to them. Each state could coin or print money, and many kinds of money were in circulation. Congress could not tax people. It could ask for soldiers for the army, but it could not force the states to provide them. It was supposed to regulate trade, but the states did as they pleased. Some states collected taxes on imports from other states.

Under the Articles of Confederation the central government was not strong enough. However, it did manage to build an army and fight the War for Independence. It also established relationships with other countries. In many cases it gained their support for the new United States. It set up the beginnings of what are now the Departments of State, Treasury, and Defense.

The Ordinance of 1787

The Continental Congress passed the Ordinance of 1787, an important plan for government of the Northwest Territory. This territory was all of the land from Pennsylvania on the east to the Mississippi River on the west, and north of the Ohio River to Canada. Virginia, Massachusetts, Connecticut, and New York all had claims on the land. The states agreed to give them up to the national government to govern as territories.

Congress divided the land into territories that could become states as soon as they had enough settlers. This was a new idea in government. It gave territories the right to become self-governing states.

The Constitutional Convention

The leaders of the Continental Congress realized that if the United States were to continue as a nation, it had to have a stronger central government. Congress called a convention for May 1787, to discuss revising and reviewing the Articles of Confederation.

The people who wrote the new Constitution wanted a way of government that could live for all time. They had to compromise on differences of opinion. The Constitution they wrote was probably better as a result of this give and take.

When the Constitution was submitted to the people, many sincere persons opposed it. Patrick Henry, among others, felt that it gave too much power to the central government. It was finally adopted by all thirteen states. A strong nation had been formed with all the states under one government.

Issues in Civics: Patrick Henry, who is generally regarded as the epitome of an American patriot, opposed the Constitution. He feared that it gave too much power to the central government and would eventually lead to excessive governmental influence. Were his fears justified? What might Henry's role be if he were alive today?

A contemporary engraving showing George Washington serving as President of the Constitutional Convention in Philadelphia in 1787.

Check for Understanding: Now that you have completed this section, you should be able to answer these questions:

1. According to the Declaration of Independence, what is the reason for establishing a government?
2. What was the problem in the relation between the states and the national government under the Articles of Confederation?
3. What was the new idea of government that was established by the Ordinance of 1787?
4. What did the leaders of Congress hope to accomplish by creating a new Constitution?

Washington was the obvious choice to lead the Convention, as he had been the obvious choice to lead the Continental Army, as he would be the obvious choice to lead the new country. How might these times have been different had Washington not lived? How might today's nation be different?

SUMMARY

History tells us that gaining self-government has been a long struggle. In early times, people in Europe lost the freedom to choose their rulers and had to struggle to regain freedom. A major step toward self-government was made in 1215 when King John of England was forced to sign the Magna Carta. This charter restored certain rights to the English people.

Most English colonies in America governed themselves by elected assemblies. The colonists protested when England taxed them without consent. They united to protest taxes at the Stamp Act Congress and the First Continental Congress. England then sent troops who fired on the minutemen at Lexington. This began a war, and the colonies soon issued the Declaration of Independence.

State governments worked together during the War of Independence, under the Articles of Confederation. The Second Continental Congress was able to carry on the war and win the friendship of other countries. It passed the Ordinance of 1787. The ordinance established the idea that new territories could also become states.

The central government created by the Articles of Confederation was not strong enough. This was corrected by the Constitutional Convention in 1787. The delegates wrote a strong Constitution. It strengthened the central government and brought the states closer together.

The purpose of the illustration is to point out that the Constitution developed as part of a sequence of events that progressed toward freedom.

Each chapter concludes with a Summary that states in concise fashion the principal facts of the chapter.

BUILDING SKILLS IN CIVICS

THINKING SKILLS

1. How do written documents help ensure that freedoms won by one generation will be extended to the next?
2. Read through the chapter and find items to fit the topic "Complaints About the King."
3. Choose the title that you think best tells the main idea of this paragraph.

   The national government lacked important powers. There was no office of President, and the national government could not collect taxes to pay its expenses. Each state regulated its own trade and had the right to issue its own money.

   a. "No Taxation Without Representation"
   b. Reasons for the Repeal of the Stamp Act
   c. Weaknesses of the Articles of Confederation

VOCABULARY SKILLS

Match each term with its definition.

a. tyrant
b. Magna Carta
c. House of Burgesses
d. Mayflower Compact
e. Stamp Act Congress
f. Continental Congress
g. Articles of Confederation

1. Drawn up by the Continental Congress, this document created a weak central government and strong state governments.
2. Any absolute ruler who rules in a cruel and unjust manner.
3. A written document that put limitations on the power of King John and restored rights to the English people.
4. Representatives of nine colonies who met to protest the King's requirement that stamps appear on all legal documents.
5. This was the first body of lawmakers in North America.
6. Representatives of the thirteen colonies who met and signed the Declaration of Independence on July 4, 1776.
7. An agreement to make laws for the general good of the people that was drawn up by the first English settlers in Massachusetts.

STUDY SKILLS—USING DOCUMENTS

Look at the picture on page 73. These people are in Washington, D.C., looking at the original copy of the Constitution. This and other original *documents* that provide the basis for our governmental system, such as the Declaration of Independence, are protected by glass so that you and future generations can see them.

It is important when you are studying civics and government to read these documents. They give you the basis for all the comments that are made about them. At the beginning of each chapter in this book you will find excerpts from these papers. These excerpts, or parts, give you the original on which all the interpretation is based. In this book they also tell you the theme of the chapter. The entire document is reprinted in the Appendix.

Activity: Which document does this chapter begin with? Which one is included in the chapter? Why do you think it is important to read documents in their original form rather than just read about them?

BEYOND THE BOOK

1. Help yourself build a clearer image of life in the 1700's by reading a biography of one of the colonists. Give a report that tells how life in that era was different from your own, that shows the challenges your subject faced, and that describes the contributions he or she made to our nation.
2. Compare colonial times to the present either through pictures that you find or by giving an oral report on one of the following topics:

   a. Voters c. Source of new states
   b. Taxes d. Printing money

3. As you read the original documents from the past you may see that some things about the American English language, including spelling, have changed. Analyze the "Mayflower Compact" and identify three words or phrases that show how the language has changed. Look through letters, diaries, or newspapers from the 1700's and identify other changes in the way English was used then and now.

"Beyond the Book" activities are intended to provide students with a means of applying the civics lessons they have learned in the chapter to the world outside the classroom.

CHAPTER FIVE TEST

VOCABULARY CHECK

Some of the underlined words in the sentences below are used correctly, but others are not. If the sentence is correct, write True. If it is not, replace the word with the best choice from the list.

Articles of Confederation	tyrant
Continental Congress	House of Burgesses
Stamp Act Congress	Magna Carta
Mayflower Compact	

1. A major step toward self-government was made when the tyrant, King John, was forced to sign the Magna Carta.
2. Land-owning colonists elected lawmakers to serve in the House of Burgesses.
3. In the Mayflower Compact the first English settlers agreed to make laws for the general good of the people.
4. The teamwork of the colonies in forming the Stamp Act Congress and the Continental Congress showed King George III the colonies meant what they said.
5. Under the Magna Carta the national government lacked important powers and there was no office of President.

COMPREHENSION CHECK

1. Identify each of the following items as either an advantage or a weakness of the Articles of Confederation.
   a. Central government lacked powers
   b. Built an army to fight for independence
   c. No office of President
   d. Many kinds of money coined
   e. Provided for a congress to be elected by state legislatures
2. The Constitutional Convention was called to discuss revising and reviewing the:
   a. Declaration of Independence
   b. Articles of Confederation
   c. Mayflower Compact
3. True or False: American colonists wanted to elect their own representatives to the Parliament that made their laws.

SKILL BUILDERS—INTERPRETING TIME LINES

By helping you picture the sequence of events, *time lines* make it easier for you to connect events, to remember them and to understand how one event is related to another one. In this chapter you learned about several historically important events that defined the need for a Constitution of the United States.

1765	Stamp Act Congress
1774	Continental Congress Convened
1776	Signing of Declaration of Independence
1781	Articles of Confederation
1787	Constitution

Activity: Look at the time line above. What is the first date? the last date? All the events happened between which two events? Which event in the following list should be point 'A' on the line?

—Signing of the Declaration of Independence
—Writing of the Articles of Confederation
—Creation of the Stamp Act Congress

Which should be point 'B'? Point 'C'?
Pictures also help you visualize or remember events. Make another time line using these same five events. For at least two of the events, include a picture that would help you remember.

BUILDING WRITING SKILLS

1. Tell in your own words what each of these excerpts means:
   a. "We hold these truths to be self-evident . . ."
   b. "And for the support of the Declaration, with a firm reliance on the Protection of Divine Providence, we mutually pledge to each other our lives, our fortunes and our sacred honor."
   c. "I know not what course others might take, but as for me, give me liberty or give me death."
2. Write at least six sentences you would include in a report called "Why Self-Government Developed in the American Colonies."

"Skill Builders" involve the use of an illustration, either one that appears for the first time on the test page or one that appears in the chapter itself.

Chapter Six • Our Living Constitution

Document: The Constitution of the United States

Preamble: WE THE PEOPLE of the United States, in Order to form a more perfect Union, establish Justice, insure domestic Tranquility, provide for the common defence, promote the general Welfare, and secure the Blessings of Liberty to ourselves and our Posterity, do ordain and establish this Constitution for the United States of America.

Although the Preamble to the Constitution is very brief—only 52 words—it is very important in that it describes the source of the powers conferred by the rest of the Constitution in the three words "WE THE PEOPLE," and states the purpose of the document.

One of the statements of purpose, "to promote the general welfare," has been of great importance in the 20th century as it has helped to uphold many vital acts of social legislation that were not specifically listed as powers of Congress.

The brevity of the Preamble mirrors the concise embodiment of the Constitution as a whole. Because it is concise, yet states general statements of principle, the Constitution has allowed for the

The people in the illustration are reading the Preamble to the Constitution, at the time it was actually written. Ask students if they realize that the Founding Fathers made provisions for future generations as well as for the era of the people shown in the picture. Which line in the Preamble refers to this idea?

extension of meaning and purpose, enabling it to be applicable to all generations.

This thought was voiced by Henry Clay in 1850 when he said, "The Constitution of the United States was made not merely for the generation that then existed, but for posterity—unlimited, undefined, endless, perpetual posterity."

FOCUSING IDEAS

- The Constitution was created by the "Founding Fathers" to insure freedom and justice for the new country and to meet the interests and needs of all citizens.
- The Preamble was written to explain the purpose of the Constitution and to define the main premise of American democracy.
- The Articles of the Constitution establish the basic structure of American government and defines the relationship between the states and the federal government.
- The Constitution is a living document because it establishes a general framework for our democratic government but allows for the needs of changing times.

The students in the picture are reading from this very civics book, *We the People.* Ask your class if they know why civics is taught in school and why its study can promote a better appreciation of one's country.

PRE-TEST

1. How was the Constitution created?
2. What is contained in the Preamble of the Constitution?
3. What is contained in the Articles of the Constitution?
4. Why is the Constitution a living document?

HOW WAS THE CONSTITUTION CREATED?

Objectives: After you have read this section, you will be able to:

- List the three parts of the Constitution.
- Explain three disagreements that arose during the Constitutional Convention.
- Explain the term "Founding Fathers."

In this chapter you will read about the Constitution of the United States. This is the most important of our country's great documents. It is still in effect two centuries after it was written. It sets the limits of government. The duties of citizens are stated in it. It states the rights of the people. It also gives rise to our responsibilities and freedoms. The government of our nation still runs well based upon what a few men wrote almost 200 years ago.

James Madison of Virginia, often called the "Father of the Constitution."

It was written by the Founding Fathers

The people who wrote our Constitution are the nation's founders. These people, who are known as the *founding fathers* of this nation, faced the problem of setting up a sound plan of government. They wanted to divide power between the central government and the states. They also wanted to protect the liberties of the people. They planned and wrote the Constitution to insure freedom and justice for the new country. However, before they reached this goal, there were bitter debates that sometimes threatened to break up the Constitutional Convention.

Building vocabulary:
founding fathers *(94)* • preamble *(96)* • tranquility *(97)* • posterity *(98)* • article *(98)* • census *(100)* • amendment *(102)*

Vocabulary items are italicized as they appear in the text. (See *founding fathers* above.)

Ask an interested student to do research to learn why Madison is referred to as the "Father of the Constitution."

Alexander Hamilton of New York, Benjamin Franklin of Pennsylvania, and George Washington of Virginia were among the delegates who played leading roles in the creation of the Constitution.

There were many disagreements

There were many issues that caused arguments at the convention. The major one was the question of how much power to give the national government and how much power to give the states. The group called the federalists supported a strong central government. The group known as the anti-federalists wanted strong state governments.

Small and large states could not agree on how to be represented in Congress. The small states wanted all states to have an equal vote in Congress. The large states objected. They wanted size to determine voting power.

Conflicts arose between different regions of the country, especially between the North and South. The North wanted laws that would give it some of the South's sea trade. The South wanted laws that would let them keep certain trade areas.

A bill of rights to protect individual freedoms was hotly disputed. No provision was made for this in the Articles of the Constitution. Many delegates felt a bill of rights was necessary and proper.

The delegates reached compromises on all of these issues. The interests and needs of all thirteen colonies were taken into account when the delegates planned the new government.

The Constitution which our nation's founders wrote consists of three parts: the Preamble, the Articles, and the Amendments. The first amendments were added four years after the original Constitution was written.

Check for Understanding: Now that you have completed this section, you should be able to answer these questions:

1. What are the three parts of the Constitution?
2. What were three disagreements during the Constitutional Convention?
3. What is the meaning of the term "Founding Fathers"?
4. What was the difference between the federalists and the anti-federalists?

Have interested students select one individual among the founders and explain what his role was at the Convention.

Answers to the "Check for Understanding" questions appear in the Answer Key at the front of your book.

WHAT IS IN THE PREAMBLE?

Objectives: After you have read this section, you should be able to:

- Define and explain the word "Preamble."
- List five reasons given in the Preamble for establishing the Constitution.
- Explain, why the words "We the People" appear in larger letters.

"We the People"

The first three words of the Preamble, "We the People," are written in large letters. This stresses the fact that the United States Constitution makes the people the source of power in government. When the constitution was written in 1787, very few people in the world ruled themselves. Our national founders believed that the Constitution should be written by and for the people. All laws should stem from the people.

The words "We the People" begin the Constitution, and they also serve as the title of this book, in honor of their use in the Constitution.

The purpose of the Preamble

The delegates to the Convention wrote a statement introducing the Constitution. It is called the Preamble. *Preamble* is taken from a Latin word meaning "to walk or go before." The Preamble comes before the Articles of the Constitution. It was written to explain the purpose of the Constitution.

It is short, but very important.

> "We the People of the United States, in Order to form a more perfect Union, establish justice, insure domestic Tranquility, provide for the common defense, promote the general Welfare, and secure the Blessings of Liberty to ourselves and our Posterity, do ordain and establish this Constitution for the United States of America."

"A more perfect Union"

The Preamble states that the people of the United States seek "to form a more perfect Union." The union of states under the Articles of Confederation had been far from perfect. The new Constitution created a stronger central government. It was also more democratic than many other charters of government that had been written before. The Constitution is so sound that since 1787 it has served as a model for many new republics in other parts of the world.

"Justice" and "tranquility"

The Preamble next says that the Constitution is designed to "establish justice" and

Have students discuss the content of the Articles of Confederation to determine why the Founding Fathers felt that a new document had to be created to replace that original set of laws.

"insure domestic *tranquility.*" Tranquility means "peacefulness" or "quiet." In the 1780's, relations among the individual states were not completely tranquil. There were no courts with authority to settle the states' differences. The Constitution established ways to settle disputes among the states.

"The common defense"

The third point of the Preamble is that the federal government should "provide for the common defense." The Constitution enables the union of states to raise an army and build a navy to protect its people, so that the citizens may be secure against foreign aggression.

What the Preamble Says

"We the People"

"A More Perfect Union"

"Justice" and "Tranquility"

"The Common Defense"

"The General Welfare"

"Ourselves and Our Posterity"

Several leading figures of the time did not sign the Constitution, for various reasons—Thomas Jefferson, John Jay, John and Samuel Adams, Patrick Henry, George Mason, Edmund Randolph. Ask an interested student to research the reasons for this.

"The general welfare"

The fourth purpose stated in the Preamble is to "promote the general Welfare." The Constitution includes laws that provide for the health, education, and well-being of the people. The nation's founders believed that this was the duty of a sound government.

"Ourselves and our posterity"

The men who wrote the Constitution were students of history. They knew that the democracy of Athens and the republic of Rome had failed. They realized that constant watchfulness is the price of liberty. They wished to make America a free country. They wanted this not only for themselves, but for all the generations to come. The word *posterity* means "future generations." The writers wanted to build a democracy that would last. With this goal in mind, the nation's founders structured the Constitution to create a long-lasting democracy in America.

Check for Understanding: Now that you have completed this section, you should be able to answer these questions:

1. What does the word "Preamble" mean?
2. What are the first three words of the Preamble?
3. Why are these words in larger letters?
4. According to the words of the Preamble, what are five reasons for establishing the Constitution?

WHAT IS IN THE ARTICLES?

Objectives: After you have finished reading this section, you will be able to:

- List the three branches of government.
- Explain the disagreement between the states as to their representation.
- Describe how the Congress represented a compromise.

Three branches of government

Seven articles follow the Preamble. These *Articles* establish the basic structure of American government. They also create the relationship between the many states and the national government.

The nation's founders worked through the summer of 1787 at the Constitutional Convention in Philadelphia. They tried to create an enduring and lasting government. Many conflicts arose. But the solutions they found helped to make the Constitution a sound structure of democracy.

The Constitution provides that the government of the United States is divided into three branches. Each branch has separate duties. The Legislative Branch is responsible for making laws. It passes laws to meet the changing needs of the people and to protect them. The Executive Branch is headed by the President. It is responsible for enforcing the laws. The executive branch must make the decisions to put the laws passed by the legislative branch into effect. The Judicial Branch is composed of federal courts. The highest court of the land is the Supreme Court. There are also federal courts in each of the states. These courts are responsible for deciding conflicts under the law.

The Founding Fathers structured the Constitution so that power is divided among the three branches. Actions by one branch can be checked and balanced by the others.

Issues in Civics: Do students think that the three branches that our government is divided into are sufficient to make, enforce, and judge the laws of our country? Why?/Why not?

The Articles and the Constitution

Weaknesses in the Articles of Confederation:	How the Constitution corrected these weaknesses:
All states, large and small, had one vote.	States are represented according to population in the House and equally in the Senate.
Congress did not have the power to make and collect taxes.	Congress was given the power to make and collect taxes.
Congress could not control trade between the states and with foreign nations.	Congress was given the power to control trade between the states and with foreign nations.
There was no President to enforce the acts of Congress.	The President enforces the acts of Congress.
There was no national court system.	There is a national system of courts headed by a Supreme Court.
All states had to agree to any change made to the Articles of Confederation.	Two-thirds vote of both Houses of Congress and approval by three-fourths of states is necessary to change the Constitution.
Two-thirds majority was needed to pass ordinary laws.	Simple majority is required.

Ask a student to read through the full text of the Articles of Confederation and report on the ways in which the Constitution improved upon its provisions.

Which branch of government would students most like to be involved in if they were going to undertake a government career? Why?

Two legislative houses

Article I, section 1 of the Constitution reads: "All legislative Powers herein granted shall be vested in a Congress of the United States, which shall consist of a Senate and House of Representatives."

This first section contains only twenty-five words. However, it required a month for the Constitutional Convention to write them. A sharp dispute arose over the number of representatives that should be elected from each state. The small and large states could not agree.

Virginia was the state with the most people at that time. The Virginia delegates presented a plan under which the states with large populations would have more representatives than the states with small populations. For instance, Virginia had sixteen times as many people as the state of Delaware. The Virginians argued that they therefore ought to have sixteen times as many representatives as the smaller state would have.

States with many people, such as New York, Massachusetts, and Pennsylvania, agreed with the Virginia plan. But the more lightly populated states objected for obvious reasons. The debate became bitter. Some delegates feared that the country might even go to war over the issue. The doors to the Convention were closed, and no outsiders were admitted. When the delegates first met on May 14, 1787, they had expected to have their work completed in a few days. But there were so many serious issues to be resolved that the session continued until September 17th.

Under the Articles of Confederation, a small state had the same vote as any other state. The small states wanted to continue this way. New Jersey proposed that the small states should have as many votes as the more populated states. This proposal made James Madison of Virginia exclaim, "It will not be just to Virginia, which is sixteen times as large as Delaware!"

At this William Paterson, a delegate from New Jersey, flung back, "Shall I submit the welfare of New Jersey with five votes when Virginia has sixteen? I will never consent."

Many days passed with no signs of agreement. Some of the delegates suggested that a compromise be made. This sounded promising to Benjamin Franklin of Pennsylvania. He stated, "When a joiner wishes to fit two boards, he sometimes pares off a bit from both."

The result of the compromise

The convention did make a compromise. Instead of one house with either equal membership from each state or membership by population, it adopted a plan for two houses of Congress: a House of Representatives and a Senate. The number of representatives allowed to each state in the House depends on the population of that state. In the Senate, however, each state is represented equally. The largest state in the nation has two senators. The smallest also has two.

As the population of a state changes, the number of representatives also changes. Article I, section 3 of the Constitution provides that all the people in each state be counted every ten years. Such a count of the population is called a *census*, from the Latin word "censere" meaning "to tax"—in ancient Rome a count of the population was made for the purpose of collecting taxes. On the basis of the census figures, each state is allowed a certain number of representatives. The Constitution provides that every state shall have at least one representative.

Ask students to do research to see if their own congressional district gained or lost any representatives as a result of the most recent census.

The House of Representatives is often called simply the House. A representative is also called a member of Congress, or a Congressman or Congresswoman. The term Congress is used to mean both representatives and senators. The House of Representatives is sometimes called the Lower House and the Senate the Upper House. With only a few differences, they have equal powers.

Other departments

In Article II the Constitution establishes the executive department. It states the manner in which the President is to be elected. Powers which the President holds are also listed. Article III describes how federal court judges shall be selected and their role in the government of the United States.

Articles IV-VII

Article IV of the Constitution establishes the relation of the states to each other. Article V provides ways by which the Constitution can be amended. Article VI states the supremacy of federal government laws over state government laws. All federal and state officials must regard the Constitution as supreme law. Article VII deals with the ratification or approval of the Constitution by the states.

A signed document

The delegates agreed upon the final writing of the Constitution. They signed their names to the finished document on September 17, 1787. George Washington signed first as President of the Convention and Deputy of Virginia. The delegates then signed their names as representatives of their states.

Check for Understanding: Now that you have completed this section, you should be able to answer these questions:

1. What are the three branches of the government?
2. How did the states disagree about representation?
3. How did Congress arrive at a compromise?
4. Who was the first person to sign the finished Constitution? Why did he sign first?

WHY IS THE CONSTITUTION A LIVING DOCUMENT?

Objectives: After you have read this section, you will be able to:

- Describe the difficulties in writing a document that has to apply to the future.
- Give two reasons why the Constitution still is effective after two hundred years.
- Define the term "amendment."

It allows for the future

Suppose your class had to write a constitution that would govern your school for the next two hundred years. You might say that this would be impossible. You would be writing rules for a school you could only guess about. There might be ten times as many students in the school or only one-tenth as many. Teachers might appear on a television screen instead of being in the room. Computers might replace textbooks. Students might learn at home rather than in school. How could you write rules for a place you wouldn't know about? Wouldn't many problems arise between then and now? Wouldn't changes have to be made?

Issues in Civics: Do students think that the Constitution will continue to be the foundation for our country's government 200 years from now? Why?/Why not?

Planning for the Future

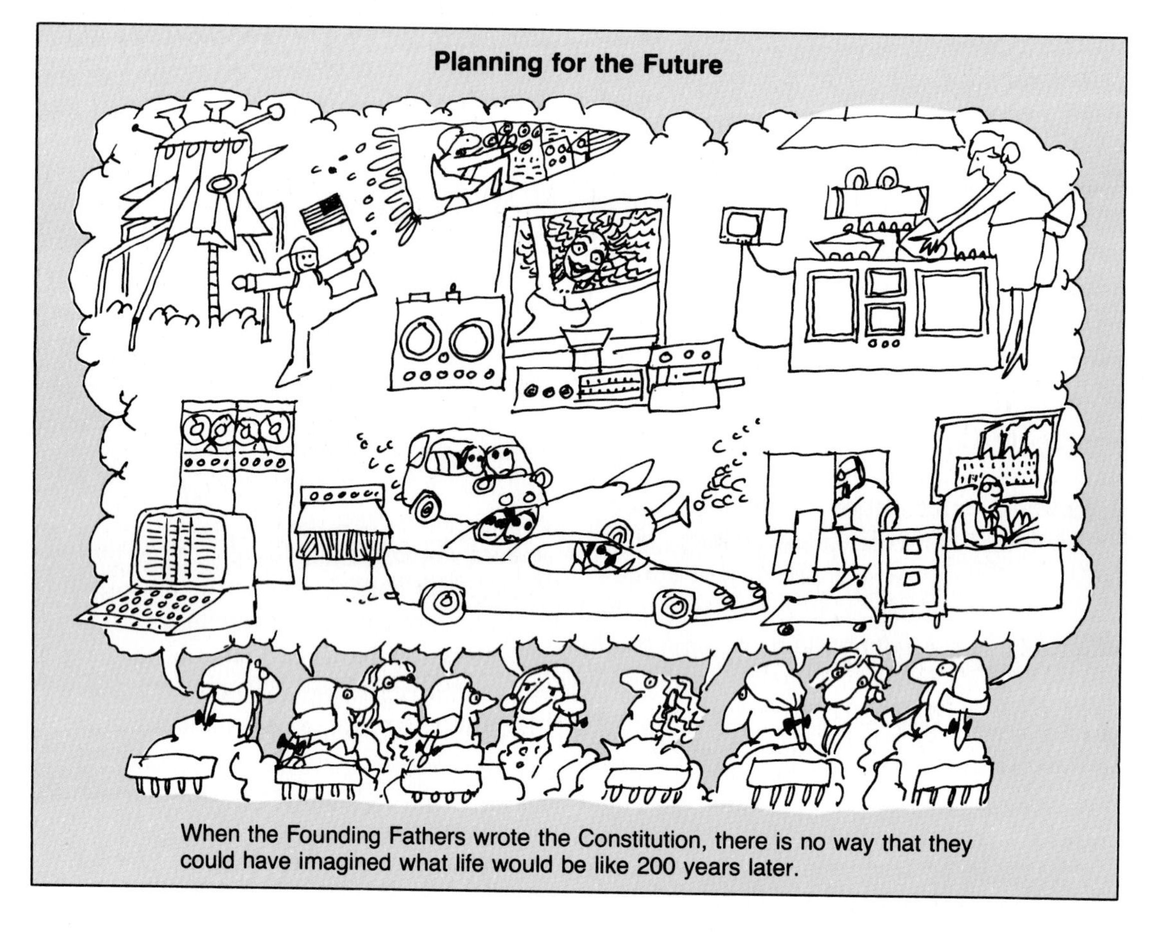

When the Founding Fathers wrote the Constitution, there is no way that they could have imagined what life would be like 200 years later.

The Founding Fathers of our country faced a similar problem. Yet they wrote a living document. How could these people have written such a document without knowing what was to happen in the future?

It contains only important things

There are several reasons why the Constitution is a living document. Its authors were concerned only with things that were necessary to the process of establishing a strong democratic government. The structure of government and the law of the land were clearly defined. How the constitutional laws should be applied or the government administered were not included. For example, the Constitution gave Congress the control of trade between states. If it had limited the control to goods that traveled by oxen or by boat—the most common forms of transportation in the 1780's—the Constitution would have had to be changed each time a new means of transportation was invented.

It allows for change

In addition, the authors planned for the Constitution to be amended, or changed. Shortly after the Constitution was adopted, ten *amendments*, or additions, were attached to it. These ten amendments listed certain basic rights of people. They also prohibited the government from denying people these rights. The first ten amendments are called the Bill of Rights.

Discuss with your students the importance of the amendment process and how it allows the Constitution to remain a living document.

The complete text of the Bill of Rights can be found in the Appendix on pages 575–76.

Methods of transportation have changed greatly from the time of the Constitution to the present day.

Check for Understanding: Now that you have completed this section, you should be able to answer these questions:

1. Why is it difficult to write a document that has to apply for many years in the future?
2. What are two reasons why the Constitution has remained effective?
3. What is the meaning of the term "amendment"?
4. Why is the Constitution referred to as a "living document"?

SUMMARY

The Constitution was written by a group often called the Founding Fathers. They faced a great many disagreements as to what should be in the document. The final Constitution consisted of the Preamble, the Articles, and the Amendments.

The Preamble introduces the Constitution. It defines the main premise of American democracy, that government's power comes from the power of the people.

The Articles establish a separation of power among the legislative, executive, and judicial branches. Each has powers that check and balance the others. Delegates to the Constitutional Convention argued about how states should be represented. A compromise was reached by establishing a Congress of two houses.

The Constitution is a living document. It establishes a framework and basic laws for our democratic government. But it leaves to each generation of Americans the task of applying the laws and administering the government which it has created. This quality has allowed the Constitution to meet the needs of people in different times. For this reason, we still have a strong democratic government in the United States.

The amendment process that is part of the Constitution allows new ideas and needed changes to be made peacefully. This provision for orderly change in the government has made the United States Constitution one of the greatest documents in the world.

Ask students to think of amendments that *they* think should be added to the Constitution. Why do they think as they do?

BUILDING SKILLS IN CIVICS

THINKING SKILLS

1. What reasons does the Preamble give for establishing the Constitution?
2. What are the three branches of the government?
3. Explain why the Constitution is called a "living document."
4. Which of the following did not cause arguments at the Constitutional convention between the large and small states?
   a. Small states wanted all states to have an equal vote in Congress.
   b. Large states wanted voting power to be determined by population.
   c. Southern states wanted laws made which would let them keep certain trade areas.
5. Find three statements in the chapter that support this sentence: The convention made a compromise in order to settle the arguments between large and small states.
6. Turn to the chapter pre-test (page 94). Write the number of the answers you can answer correctly now.
7. Write the chapter title, and give one sentence that relates to its meaning.

VOCABULARY SKILLS

Fill in each blank in the sentences below with the word from the list that best completes that sentence.

preamble	tranquility	founding fathers	posterity
articles	census	amendment	

1. The ______ explains the purpose of the Constitution.
2. The Constitution is designed to insure domestic ______ by establishing ways for states to settle disputes among themselves.
3. The ______ of the Constitution establish a separation of power among the three branches of government.
4. The number of representatives a state has is determined by the ______ figures.

5. The people who wrote our Constitution are known as the ______.
6. There are ten ______ in the Bill of Rights.
7. The nation's founders wanted America to be free for their own generation and also for ______.

STUDY SKILLS—OUTLINING

Outlining is essential in good report writing. A good outline helps to sequence ideas, summarize information, and show relationships between main ideas; it also helps us to write clearly and to the point.

An outline shows how information is logically organized into categories and sub-categories. Here is an example of an outline for the topic "How to make a simple outline using roman numerals, capital letters, and indenting."

I. Use Roman numerals for the main points.
   A. Use capital letter 'A' for the first subtopic, and indent.
   B. Use capital letter 'B' for the next subtopic.
   C. Use succeeding capital letters for the other subtopics.

List three subtopics about the topic "Branches of Government" in a simple outline form. Use your book for information.

BEYOND THE BOOK

1. Collect pictures that illustrate the important points in the Preamble to the Constitution. Tell why you chose each picture.
2. Arrange the pictures you collected in their order of importance. Interview several people, and see if they agree or disagree with your order.
3. Have your classmates tell how each of your pictures illustrates the Preamble.

CHAPTER SIX TEST

VOCABULARY CHECK

Match each term with its definition.

a. preamble b. article c. tranquility g. founding fathers
d. census e. posterity f. amendment

1. Peacefulness or quiet.
2. A count of the population.
3. A change in a bill or law.
4. The first part of the Constitution.
5. Generations to come.
6. The part of the Constitution that establishes the basic structure of American government.
7. The people who wrote our Constitution.

COMPREHENSION CHECK

1. Identify which of the following points belong in a paper called "Disagreements During the Constitutional Convention"
   a. Small states wanted all states to have an equal vote.
   b. Large states wanted population to determine the number of votes.
   c. The word "Preamble" means "to walk before"
   d. The North wanted some of the South's sea trade.
   e. The South wanted to keep some areas of trade.
   f. Some of the delegates suggested a compromise.
   g. The convention adopted a plan for two houses of Congress.
   h. The Constitution is the most important of our country's documents.
2. True or False: The Preamble is the introduction to the Constitution.
3. True or False: The Constitution has lasted for over 200 years because it goes into great detail about government.
4. True or False: The number of representatives a state has depends on its population.
5. True or False: The three branches of our government are the legislative, executive, and judicial.

6. The first ten amendments to the Constitution are called the Preamble.
7. The amendment process allows for changes in the Constitution to be made peacefully.

SKILL BUILDERS—INTERPRETING CHARTS

A *chart* is a way of arranging words and/or pictures to convey information quickly and easily. Like graphs and maps, the title tells what the main purpose of the chart is.

Activity: Look at the chart on page 99. Which of these reasons would you use this chart for?

1. If you wanted to understand why we no longer use the Articles of Confederation.
2. If you wanted to understand the idea of three separate branches of government.

Activity: Answer the following questions about the chart.

1. What does the title tell you about the Articles of Confederation?
2. Which items tell you that the Constitution affects all three branches of the government?
3. Which items tell you the Articles did not affect all three branches?
4. How does this chart help you to know what the Founding Fathers were thinking at the Convention?

BUILDING WRITING SKILLS

1. Choose one of the titles below and write five or six factual statements that support the subject.
   a. The Importance of the Preamble
   b. The Constitution—A Living Document
   c. Debate at the Convention
2. Explain the difference between the number of votes a state had under the Articles of Confederation and the number it has under the Constitution.
3. Write a question which the following statement answers.
   Answer: A compromise was reached by establishing a Congress of two houses.

Chapter Seven
Amending the Constitution

Document: The Constitution of the United States

Article V: "The Congress, whenever two thirds of both Houses shall deem it necessary shall propose Amendments to this Constitution, or, on the Application of the legislatures of two-thirds of the several States, shall call a convention for proposing Amendments, which, in either Case, shall be valid to all intents and Purposes, as Part of this Constitution, when ratified by the Legislatures of three fourths thereof, as the one or the other Mode of Ratification may be proposed by the Congress; Provided . . . that no State, without its Consent, shall be deprived of its equal Suffrage in the Senate.

What would the state of our government be if the Founding Fathers had not made provisions for amendments to the Constitution? Without this provision, whenever people wanted to make changes in government, they would have had to do away with the original Constitution and create a new document. This would have been an impractical way of running a government.

Even with the provision for amending the Constitution, only twenty-six amendments have ever been ratified in our history. The framers of the Constitution purposely made it difficult to put through an amendment so as not to disrupt the original purposes set forth in it.

The illustration shows how blacks, long denied the right to vote, progressed in just over one hundred years of political involvement to the point where some of our leading political figures are black (in this case Tom Bradley, mayor of Los Angeles).

Although the Constitution sets no time limit during which the states must ratify a proposed amendment, the courts have held that amendments must be ratified within a reasonable time—a time that Congress decides upon. Since the early 1900's, most proposed amendments have included a rule that necessary ratification should occur within seven years.

FOCUSING IDEAS

- The Constitution provides for peaceful change through the amendment process. Amendments must first be proposed by Congress or at a convention called for by two-thirds of the state's legislatures. Amendments must be ratified by three-fourths of the states.
- People wanted a Bill of Rights because they wanted the Constitution to set forth in writing the basic rights of free people.
- Amendments called for changes in tax and liquor laws, senate and Presidential elections, Presidential terms, and suits against states, among others.
- The amendments extended rights and responsibilities to citizens by abolishing slavery, and by extending citizenship and suffrage (the right to vote).

Women also gained the vote through a Constitutional amendment, and as the illustration shows they are now also included in the ranks of prominent leaders (in this case Ella Grasso, late governor of Connecticut).

PRE-TEST

1. How does the Constitution provide for change?
2. Why did the people want a bill of rights added?
3. What kind of changes did the amendments call for?
4. How have freedom and responsibility been extended by the amendments?

HOW DOES THE CONSTITUTION PROVIDE FOR CHANGE?

Objectives: After you have read this section, you will be able to:

- Identify the two ways that the Constitution may be amended.
- Tell which one of these has been used more often.
- Explain why there have been so few amendments.

You have seen how the Constitution was completed. The authors were generally content with their work, but they knew that some things might have been left out and that changes might have to be made in the future. Therefore, they provided for the Constitution to be changed.

The authors of the Constitution were concerned that most governments were changed only by violence. They thought government should change peacefully. They believed it was better for changes in government to be made after careful study and planning.

Under the Constitution, the states gave up many powers to the federal government. Therefore, the states could change the Constitution if a majority of them favored the change. The only restriction was that a change could not deny a state its representation in the Senate without that state's consent.

Proposing an amendment

New amendments to the Constitution can be proposed in two ways. Congress can propose an amendment with a two-thirds vote in both houses. Or, two-thirds of the state's legislatures can request that Congress call a convention. Then the convention will write and propose the amendment.

Ratifying an amendment

Once an amendment is proposed it is sent to the states for *ratification*, or approval. Three-fourths of the states must approve the proposal for it to become an amendment. Each state legislature can vote on the proposal, or a state convention can be called to vote. The first set of amendments, the Bill of Rights, was proposed by Congress and ratified by the state legislatures. All other amendments that followed have also been proposed by Congress. All but the twenty-first amendment have been ratified by the state legislatures.

Building vocabulary:
ratification *(110)* • Bill of Rights *(112)* • Prohibition *(113)* • repeal *(113)* • jurisdiction *(115)* • revenue *(115)* • lame duck *(115)* • suffrage *(116)*

Have your students write a report on one of the amendments that particularly interests them. Have them report on its background and how it came to be passed.

The complete text of the Bill of Rights can be found in the Appendix on pages 575–76.

Chronological Chart Of Constitutional Amendments

Amendment No.	Date	Description	Reason
1–10	1791	The Bill of Rights	To protect rights
11	1795	Suits against States	To solve a problem
12	1804	Separate election of President and Vice-President	To solve a problem
13	1865	Forbids slavery	To extend rights
14	1868	Citizenship and protection for all persons in the U.S.	To extend rights
15	1870	The right to vote for all races	To extend rights
16	1913	Income tax	To solve a problem
17	1913	Direct election of Senators	To solve a problem
18	1919	Prohibition	To reflect changing ideas
19	1920	Voting rights for women	To extend rights
20	1932	New date for taking office	To solve a problem
21	1933	Repeal of prohibition	To reflect changing ideas
22	1951	Two-term Presidential limit	To enforce tradition
23	1961	Voting rights in the District of Columbia	To extend rights
24	1964	Poll tax forbidden	To protect rights
25	1967	Presidential succession	To solve a problem
26	1971	Voting rights for 18-year-olds	To extend rights

Concern with basic rights

The Founding Fathers were concerned most of all with safeguarding a free republic. They wanted to limit the powers of government and protect the rights of individuals. They were not so much concerned with detail as they were with larger ideas and the ways that a free government should work. Our Constitution states important rules of government in a small number of words. The amendments follow this practice also. For example, the eighth amendment, in just sixteen words, sets important limits on the power of government. Even though our way of life is not the same as it was 200 years ago, our thinking about government is much the same. As a result, we have had few changes in our Constitution and in our freedoms.

> Excessive bail shall not be required, nor excessive fines imposed, nor cruel and unusual punishments inflicted.

Check for Understanding: Now that you have completed this section, you should be able to answer these questions:

1. What are two different ways that an amendment to the Constitution can be proposed?
2. What are two different ways that a proposed Constitutional amendment can be ratified?
3. Which of these has been used more often?
4. Why have the amendments been written with a small number of words?

The eighth amendment is a good example of the great influence that can be exerted by just a few words in the Constitution. The phrase "cruel and unusual punishments" was cited by the Supreme Court in ruling the death penalty unconstitutional because it violated this clause.

WHY DID THE PEOPLE WANT A BILL OF RIGHTS?

Objectives: After you have read this section, you will be able to:

- Explain why the people wanted a written guarantee of their rights.
- Give two examples of people's rights having been lost in the past.
- List four different freedoms that are guaranteed by the first amendment.

Human rights were not listed in the original Constitution. The first ten amendments to the Constitution are called the *Bill of Rights.* How the Bill of Rights came about is an important part of our history. The original Constitution only described the new government and listed its powers. These powers were very limited, and it would have been difficult for the government to legally violate the basic rights of its citizens. But the colonists wanted even more protection. They wanted the new Constitution to set in writing the basic rights of free people.

Rights had been promised before

The colonists looked back on a history in which people had won many rights from kings. As far back as 1628, the King of England told the people that they could not be arrested and jailed without just cause. The people of England had been given the right to carry arms for their safety. The American people also knew that these rights had been taken away by unjust, powerful rulers. They had seen kings attempt to impose the rules of the king's church. People had been unjustly arrested and imprisioned for long periods without trial. As these promises were broken, many people fled to the colonies.

Even in the American colonies, many promised rights had been lost. In 1733, a New York newspaper publisher, John Zenger, was thrown into prison because he printed the truth about a dishonest royal governor. English soldiers were being stationed in people's homes. Citizens were arrested for crimes and thrown into prison for long periods of time. The people wanted to be sure that these things would not happen in the new United States, but the new Constitution had nothing in it to guarantee this.

The first ten amendments protect freedom

The first amendment to the Constitution guarantees certain freedoms to individuals. Among these are freedom of religion, speech, assembly, petition, and the press.

King Charles I soon broke his promise to grant civil rights to the English people.

Discuss with students the events in our nation's early history that led to people's demand for a Bill of Rights.

English soldiers burn copies of John Peter Zenger's newspaper because he criticized the colonial governor.

Others of the first ten amendments also protect people from unjust actions by government. People are protected from housing soldiers, unreasonable search and arrest, unfair or unjust trials, excessive violence or cruel punishment. Under the tenth amendment, the powers that are not specifically given to the federal government by the Constitution are reserved to the states. The Bill of Rights is a basic document that protects our civil rights. It is so important that you will spend an entire chapter on these first ten amendments.

Check for Understanding: Now that you have completed this section, you should be able to answer these questions:

1. Why did the American people want a written guarantee of their rights?
2. What were two examples of people's rights having been lost in the past?
3. What are four different freedoms guaranteed by the first amendment?
4. Which amendment reserves power to the states?

WHAT KIND OF CHANGES DID THE AMENDMENTS CALL FOR?

Objectives: After you have read this section, you will be able to:

- List four situations in which a change in the people's thinking about government brought about an amendment to the Constitution.
- Describe the only situation in our history in which an amendment was passed but was later repealed by another amendment.
- List five problems of government that were solved by the passage of an amendment.

Prohibition tried and repealed

In 1919, the passage of the eighteenth amendment established *Prohibition.* This amendment prohibited the sale, manufacture or transportation of any kind of alcoholic beverage. This is often called the "Great Experiment." Since Prohibition was imposed by a Constitutional amendment, another amendment was needed to *repeal* it. Prohibition was repealed in 1933, when people changed their thinking about this issue. The twenty-first is the only amendment that repealed a previous amendment.

Issues in Civics: Ask students if they think Prohibition was a practical idea or a foolish one. Why do they think as they do? What are the chances of new "dry laws" being introduced?

Barrels of beer being destroyed by Federal agents after Prohibition went into effect.

A group of citizens petition Congress to change the law which created prohibition.

It is also the only one that was ratified by state conventions rather than by the state legislatures.

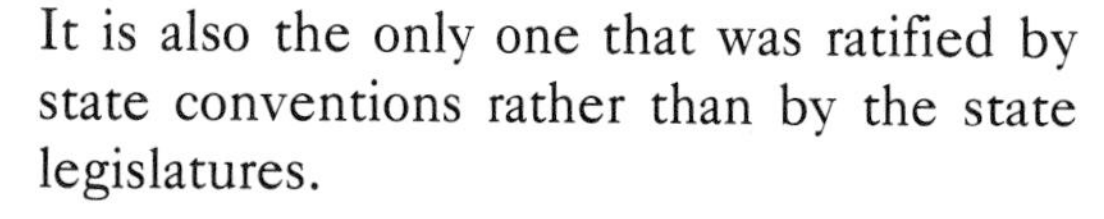

A change in the election of senators

Up until 1913 the members of the senate were selected by various ways among the states. For the most part, senators were selected by the legislatures of the state and were not voted upon by all the people. The seventeenth amendment stated that all senators in all states would be elected by the direct vote of the people.

A tradition enforced

The original Constitution did not state how long the President was permitted to remain in office. After serving for eight years, or two terms, George Washington left the presidency. This tradition continued throughout most of our history. No other President served more than two terms until Franklin D. Roosevelt. Roosevelt was elected for four terms, in 1932, 1936, 1940, and 1944. The people decided to enforce the tradition of two terms in 1951. The twenty-second amendment now limits the time a person may serve as President to no more than two elected terms, or one elected term plus two years of an unelected term.

Suits against states

In the history of the United States, there were only five governmental problems that have required amendments. Many problems have faced our government, but most have been solved in some way other than amending the Constitution.

Issues in Civics: Do students think that Presidents should be permitted to serve for more than two terms, or do they think that the present system works for the best?

After the Constitution was adopted, a citizen tried to use the federal courts to sue a state, in the case of *Chisolm vs. Georgia*. The state of Georgia refused to respond to the suit, and the Supreme Court ruled in favor of Chisolm. People became concerned, because to allow this practice would have given the federal courts *jurisdiction* (the power to apply the law) over the states. The eleventh amendment prohibited the practice in 1795, leaving each state free to settle its own internal disputes.

Ties in presidential elections

The presidential election of 1800 resulted in a tie. The twelfth amendment changed the election procedure in 1804 and determined the ways that ties in the voting for President would be broken.

A source of new revenue

For years the United States depended upon import taxes for most of its *revenue*, or income. As the government grew and needed new taxes for greater revenue an income tax was proposed—a tax on the earnings of businesses and individuals. To do this, it was necessary to change the Constitution. The income tax was added to the Constitution by the sixteenth amendment in 1913.

"Lame Ducks" avoided

Under the original Constitution, a newly elected President and Congress did not take office until March 4th. With elections being held in November, four months passed before the newly elected officials took office. Those members of Congress who were leaving office were called "*lame ducks*" because they had little influence or effectiveness during those four months. This was changed with the twentieth amendment in 1933. Now members of Congress take office on January 3rd. The President takes office on January 20th. This amendment also set up a rule in case the newly elected President dies, by which the Vice-President-elect assumes the office.

Presidential succession

An important issue facing our government is the question of what would happen if the President of the United States were to die or become ill and be unable to serve. This question was finally answered in 1967 by the twenty-fifth amendment. It outlines the rules that are followed if either death or disability should come to the President.

Check for Understanding: Now that you have completed this section, you should be able to answer these questions:

1. What were four situations in which a change in thinking brought about an amendment?
2. What was the only time when an amendment was repealed?
3. What were five problems to government that were solved by amendments?
4. Who were the 'lame ducks," and why were they called this?

HOW DID THE AMENDMENTS EXTEND RIGHTS AND FREEDOMS?

Objectives: After you have read this section, you will be able to:

- List three freedoms provided to former slaves by amendments.
- Name four groups who have received the right to vote through amendments.
- Describe two amendments that have been proposed but not yet ratified.

The year that the "lame duck" practice ended, 1933, was one in which Congress was more active than at any point in its history. Have an interested student research the period known as the "First Hundred Days."

Abolishing slavery

Most of the amendments to the Constitution have been adopted to extend freedom and responsibility to citizens. One of the most important of these was the thirteenth amendment, which was adopted in 1865. This amendment outlawed slavery. Up to then it had been legal in many states.

Extending citizenship

The fourteenth amendment was passed in 1868. It established the rules of citizenship for the United States government and for the states. The important part of this amendment was that it made all of the recently freed slaves full citizens.

Extending suffrage

To extend *suffrage* means to extend the right to vote. Four amendments have assured new groups of people the right and responsibility of voting. In 1870, the fifteenth amendment stated that the right to vote could not be denied on account of "race, color or previous condition of servitude." This meant that no former slave could be denied the right to vote. Up until 1920 many states would not allow women to vote. This restriction was removed with the adoption of the nineteenth amendment, which is often called the Women's Suffrage Amendment. However, there was still one place where citizens were unable to vote for the Presidency. This was the capital city of Washington, which is legally known as the District of Columbia. The twenty-third amendment, passed in 1961, gave the residents of Washington, D.C., the right to vote in Presidential elections. In 1971, the twenty-sixth amendment prohibited any state from denying the vote to people between the ages of 18 and 21. This amendment thus provided people the right to vote after their eighteenth birthday.

Thousands of proposed amendments

Many thousands of new amendments have been suggested over the years. Many prospective amendments are introduced in each session of Congress. These suggested amendments deal with many parts of government and people's lives. But very few of these are ever actually proposed by Congress, because amendments are so important and can have so much influence on our lives.

Two amendments have been recently proposed by Congress. As of now, they have not been ratified by the necessary number of states. One of these would treat the District of Columbia as if it were a state. The other proposed amendment, known as the "Equal Rights Amendment" (ERA), would prohibit rights to be denied to either women or men on the basis of sex. Such proposed amendments would be added to the Constitution if ratified by three-fourths of the states within a certain period of time.

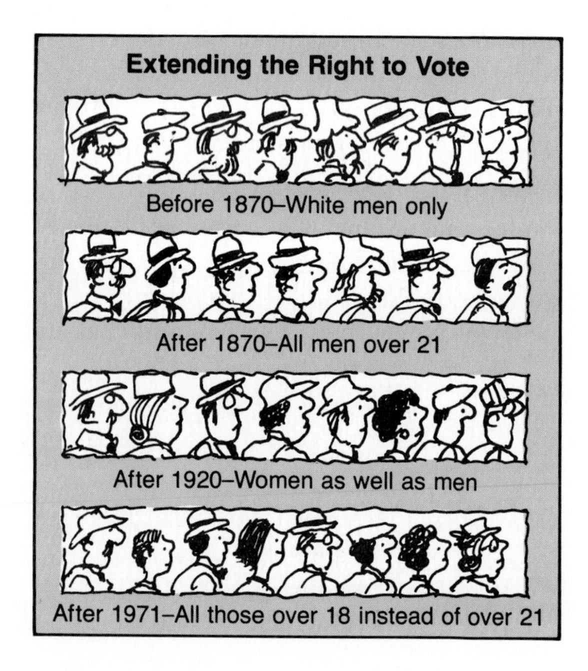

Discuss with your students the early struggles of the suffragettes to obtain voting rights.

The complete text of the Emancipation Proclamation can be found in the Appendix on pages 585–86.

Check for Understanding: Now that you have completed this section, you should be able to answer these questions:

1. What were three rights extended to former slaves by amendments?
2. What were four groups whose right to vote came about through amendments?
3. Which two amendments have been proposed by Congress but not ratified by the states?
4. Why are so few of the suggested amendments actually proposed by Congress?

SUMMARY

The Constitution provides for peaceful change in the nation's government. Amendments must first be proposed by the Congress or at a convention called for by two-thirds of the state's legislatures. All amendments must be ratified by three-fourths of the states.

There have been few amendments to the Constitution to express limits on government and the way a free government will work. The amendments, like the Constitution itself, use only a few, clear words to set down important ideas.

The early colonists were not content with a document that would simply list the powers of the new government. They also wanted a special list of the rights of free citizens. This list became the first ten amendments to the Constitution, or the Bill of Rights. They provide a written guarantee of freedom.

Four amendments were brought about because of changes in people's thinking about government. They were the two Prohibition amendments, the direct election of senators, and the limit on the term of office of the President.

Five amendments were necessary to solve problems of government. One prevented states from being sued. One prevented Presidential elections ending in a tie. The remaining three approved the income tax, avoided "lame duck" officials, and decided who succeeds the President in case of death or disability.

Amendments are used to extend rights and responsibilities to participate in government to many people. This was done by freeing the slaves and making them citizens as well as by extending suffrage to them. Over the years, women, residents of the District of Columbia, and people between the ages of eighteen and twenty-one have also been given the right and responsibility to vote.

Every year there are many hundreds of proposed amendments introduced in Congress. Few of these are ever proposed by Congress because amendments are so important. At the present time, two amendments have been proposed but not yet ratified by the necessary number of states.

Beginning on page 575, there is a list of all the amendments to the Constitution, showing the year in which they were adopted. Look at this list to determine which amendments increased your freedoms, rights, and responsibilities. Such amendments would include the first ten, or Bill of Rights. They would also include those that would provide the rights and responsibilities of people to become citizens and to vote in establishing their government. Sixteen of the twenty-four—three-fourths of all the amendments—extend freedom and responsibility to the people.

Have an interested student compare the provisions in the 1689 English Bill of Rights, which stood as a legal guarantee of English liberty, with that of our country's Bill of Rights.

If the Bill of Rights is so crucial to our system of government, why was it omitted from the original Constitution? Ask interested students to research this question.

BUILDING SKILLS IN CIVICS

THINKING SKILLS

1. What two ways can an amendment to the Constitution be proposed?
2. How is an amendment ratified?
3. What document do the following points describe?
   a. Provides a written guarantee of freedom.
   b. Lists the rights of free citizens.
   c. Makes up part of the Constitution.
4. Which amendments were ratified to:
   —allow for changes in thought.
   —solve government problems.
   —extend rights and responsibilities.
5. Make a time line showing the dates each of the twenty-six amendments were ratified. Vary the space between the points to show how much time passed between each event.
6. What two different kinds of revenue are collected by the federal government?
7. Which amendment deals exclusively with raising revenue?

VOCABULARY SKILLS

Some of the underlined words in the sentences below are used correctly, but others are not. If the sentence is correct, write True. If it is not, replace the word with the best choice from the list.

ratification	prohibition	jurisdiction	lame duck
suffrage	Bill of Rights	repeal	

1. In 1919 the passage of the eighteenth amendment established the <u>prohibition</u> of the making, sale, or transportation of alcoholic beverages.
2. <u>Suffrage</u> is the authority to apply the law to someone.
3. The eighteenth amendment established Prohibition; the twenty-first amendment <u>repealed</u> it.
4. Extending <u>jurisdiction</u> means giving more people the right to vote.

5. A proposed amendment is sent for ratification to the states.
6. The first ten amendments to the Constitution are called the ratification.
7. Members of Congress were called repeals because they were leaving office and had little power during their final months.

STUDY SKILLS—USING AN APPENDIX

The *appendix* is a section of the textbook that provides supplementary information. This special section is an excellent reference tool. It contains, among other things, a map of the U.S., information about the Presidents and about each state in the U.S., and the complete text of important documents.

Since you are often referred to the Appendix, it is important to know how to use it. First, check the back of your book to find which page the Appendix begins on.

Next, use the Table of Contents to find out exactly what is contained in the Appendix. Where in the Appendix could you locate statistics about your state? How could you use the Appendix to make a time line showing the date each of the amendments were ratified?

BEYOND THE BOOK

1. Prepare a bulletin board showing how most of the amendments to the Constitution have been adopted to extend American's rights and responsibilities.
2. Interview a naturalized citizen in order to find out how his or her rights and responsibilities were different under previous government as compared with the United States government. How do you account for the differences?
3. Play a game of "Password" using the vocabulary words from the chapter. The student who is "It" and sits with his or her back to the chalkboard. Without letting this person see another student, write a vocabulary word on the board. The person calls on individual students seated in the room to give a one-word clue to the word. This continues until "It" guesses correctly, or until five clues have been given.

Encourage your students to browse through the Appendix independently, because there is a great variety of information there, including the unique feature "Thoughts on Free Government."

CHAPTER SEVEN TEST

VOCABULARY CHECK

Fill in each blank with the word that best completes the sentence.

1. If an amendment is proposed, it is sent to the states for ______. (jurisdiction - ratification)
2. The eighteenth amendment established the ______ of alcoholic beverages. (prohibition - ratification)
3. The twenty-first is the only amendment that seems to ______ a previous amendment. (repeal, revenue)
4. The first ten amendments to the Constitution are called the ______. (Magna Carta - Bill of Rights)
5. Under the eleventh amendment, federal courts are not allowed ______ over the states. (revenue - jurisdiction)
6. A state is prohibited from denying ______ to people between the ages of eighteen and twenty-one. (prohibition - suffrage)
7. Members of Congress were called ______ because they had little effectiveness during their final months in office. (lame ducks - amendments)

COMPREHENSION CHECK

Write True if the question and answer match. If they do not, write an answer to the question.

1. How may Congress propose an amendment?—Congress may propose an amendment with a two-thirds vote in both houses.
2. Which amendment established prohibition of alcoholic beverages?—The thirteenth amendment stated that no one in our country could be a slave.
3. Why did the people want a Bill of Rights added to the Constitution?—The people wanted a Bill of Rights to guarantee in writing their rights as free citizens.
4. How do the states ratify a proposed amendment?—Three-fourths of the states must approve the proposal in order for it to become an amendment.
5. Which amendments make up the Bill of Rights?—A person may serve as President for no more than two terms.

SKILL BUILDERS—INTERPRETING TIME CHARTS

A *time chart* is designed to show you a sequence of activities, or the steps in a process or a plan.

Reading a time chart is like reading any other graph, map, or chart. Start with the title, and then ask questions about the information.

Constitutional Amendments

Bill of Rights	11th	12th	13th	14th	15th	16th and 17th	18th
1791	1798	1804	1865	1868	1870	1913	1919

19th	20th and 21st	22nd	23rd	24th	25th	26th
1920	1933	1951	1961	1964	1967	1971

1. What information does the time chart above show?
2. What process is being analyzed? How does the time chart show the various steps of this process?
3. How does the time chart indicate the reasons for this process?
4. What are two other kinds of information this chart provides?
5. What other topics in this unit could be shown on a time chart?

BUILDING WRITING SKILLS

1. Write a paragraph that summarizes the rights and responsibilities guaranteed by the Bill of Rights.
2. Explain the difference between these pairs of words:
   propose - ratify
   ratification - repeal
   rights - responsibilities
3. Look at a chart or graph from the last three chapters. Write one-word clues that describe that chart. Say each clue then call on a member of the class to guess which visual you are describing. Continue until someone correctly gives you the page number and title of the chart, or until you run out of clues.

The "Skill Builders" section always involves the interpretation of some kind of visual device.

Chapter Eight
Federal and State Government

Document: The Constitution of the United States

Article VI: This Constitution, and the Laws of the United States which shall be made in Pursuance thereof; and all Treaties made, or which shall be made, under the Authority of the United States, shall be the supreme Law of the Land; and the Judges in every State shall be bound thereby, any Thing in the Constitution or Laws of any State to the Contrary notwithstanding.

Amendment X: The powers not delegated to the United States by the Constitution, nor prohibited by it to the States, are reserved to the States respectively, or to the people.

You can see that many problems could arise regarding the division of power between the local, state, and federal levels of government. The question of "Which government has the power to do what?" can lead to confusion.

Acticle VI means that when state laws conflict with the laws of the nation, the national laws are superior. However, Amendment X was adopted to confirm that the states or the people retain all powers not given to the national government. The Constitution says that the

The picture shows the skyline of the political capital of our country. Have students name as many buildings and monuments in Washington, D.C. as they can. Have they ever visited any of them?

federal government can make any "necessary and proper" laws to carry out its specific powers.

In general, the federal government is supreme when it has the power to act, but in all other cases, the states have power. Confusion often results because it is hard to determine the precise rights that the states possess.

FOCUSING IDEAS

- National governments can be organized as confederations, unitary states, or federations.
- It can be said that Federalism means "From many, one" because many individual states cooperate together as one nation.
- The states cooperate with each other by honoring each other's acts and by passing laws that are basically uniform throughout the nation.
- The federal and state governments cooperate through the creation of new states, respect for federal property, guarantees of self-government, protection of the states by the federal government, and through federal grants-in-aid.

Ask students if they know their *own* state's nickname, and if so, how it got its name. Discuss the ways in which each state has managed to keep its identity while functioning as a part of the country as a whole.

PRE-TEST

1. What are the different ways in which a national government can be organized? Which one is used in this country, and why?
2. What is the meaning of the federal motto "E pluribus unum," or "From Many, One"?
3. Under our system of federalism, how do the states cooperate with each other?
4. How do the federal government and the various states cooperate?

HOW ARE NATIONAL GOVERNMENTS ORGANIZED?

Objectives: After you have read this section, you will be able to:

- Describe three types of national government.
- Explain the role of the central government in each type.
- Tell which type is used in the U.S.

You live as a citizen of more than one government. You live in a town with its government, and the town is within a county, a state, and, of course, the United States. These governments all work together and share power to rule. The relationship between the states and the federal government is spelled out in the Constitution. Knowing how this relationship began and how other governments are organized helps us to understand our government today.

A confederation

When the Constitutional Convention met, the delegates knew there was a need for a strong central government. At that time the United States was a confederation of the thirteen states. A *confederation* exists when the states keep most of the power and give the central government only limited authority to deal with a small number of matters. The states hold the real power. They do not feel that they have to abide by all the rules of the central government.

The national government under the Articles of Confederation had not been able to meet and solve many of the young nation's problems. It could not collect taxes and pay off the national debt. It had no power to regulate trade. Each state was almost an independent nation. The confederation was not working.

A unitary state

A second type of government is called a unitary state. In a *unitary state* there is a single central government that has complete legal control over all the territory

---

Building vocabulary:
confederation *(124)* • unitary state *(124)* • federalism *(125)* • delegated, reserved, and concurrent powers *(127)* • extradition *(130)* • uniform laws *(130)* • grant-in-aid *(132)* • centralization/decentralization *(132)*

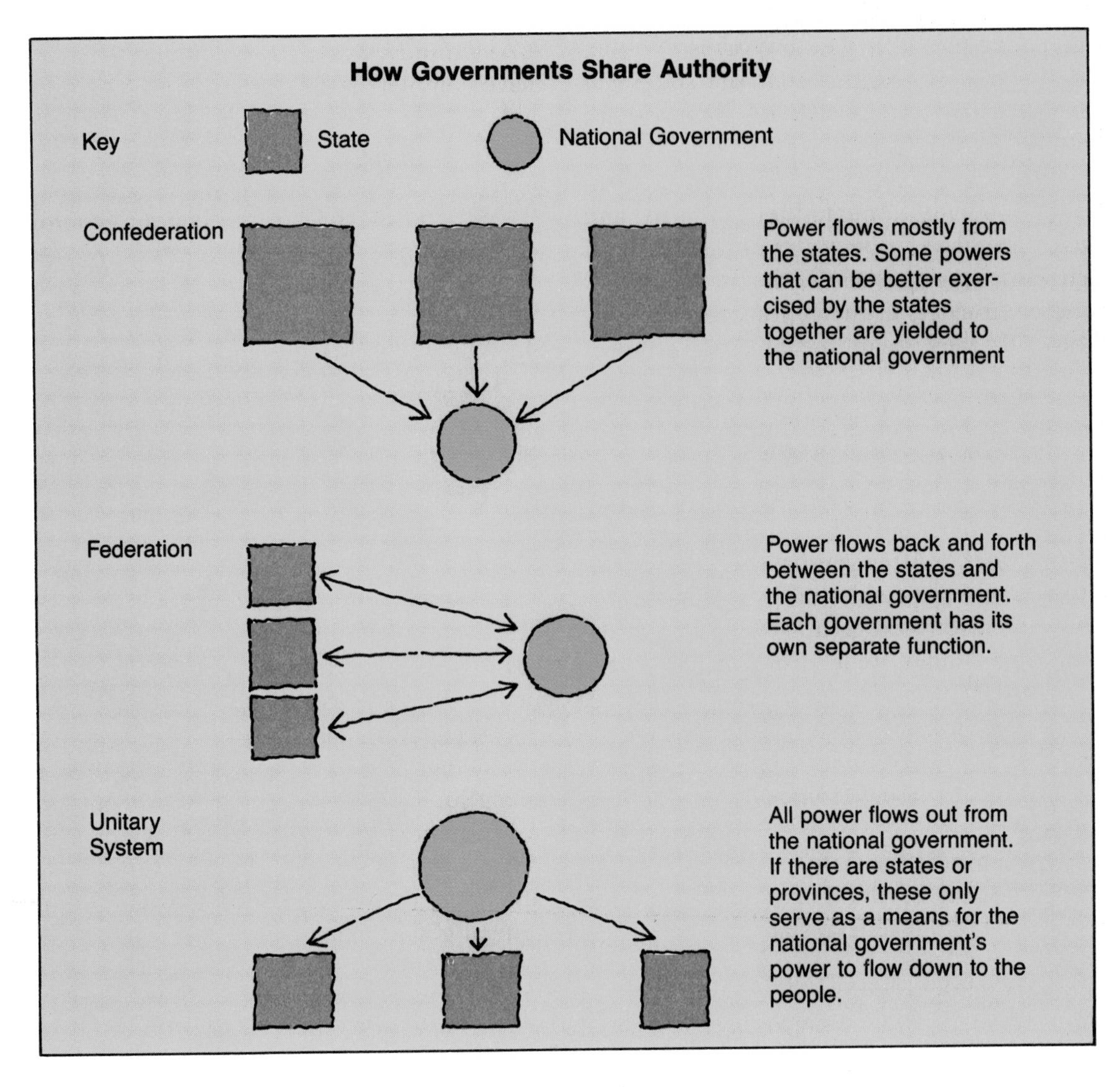

within its borders. There may be local governments in the cities and provinces, but their authority comes from the central government and they are under its control. The primary purpose of these local governments is to carry out the laws of the strong, central government. The delegates to the Constitutional Convention rejected a unitary government. They had experienced many problems with the king of England, and therefore they distrusted a central government that was too strong. They believed that a unitary government did not allow the states enough power.

A federation

In place of a confederation or a unitary government, the Constitutional Convention decided on a federation of governments. This form of government is called *federalism*. A government is a federation if authority is divided between the central govern-

Ask students to think of examples that show that the federal government shares its powers with the state governments.

ment and the self-governing states. Neither the central government nor the states get their power from each other. Both receive their powers from the same source—the Constitution. Also, both levels of government operate through their officials and exercise power directly over the lives of citizens. In other words, the states are not merely districts of the central government. Instead, they share the governing power with it.

Check for Understanding: Now that you have completed this section, you should be able to answer these questions:

1. What are the three types of national government?
2. What is the role of the central government in each type?
3. Which type is used in the United States today?
4. Why was this type chosen by the Founding Fathers?

HOW DOES FEDERALISM MEAN "FROM MANY, ONE"?

Objectives: After you have read this section, you will be able to:

- Name the three groups of powers established under federalism and explain which branch of government has each of these powers.
- Explain how conflicts over governmental powers are resolved under the Constitution.
- Explain how the national motto and the Great Seal of the United States are a symbol of our federalism.

The states shared powers

The states were in existence first. They called the Constitutional Convention into session. They expressed the will of the people through the delegates they chose. They had the final choice of ratifying or approving the new government, or not doing so. The federal government's powers were granted to it by the states and the people. Also, the states kept for themselves all rights that they did not grant to the federal government.

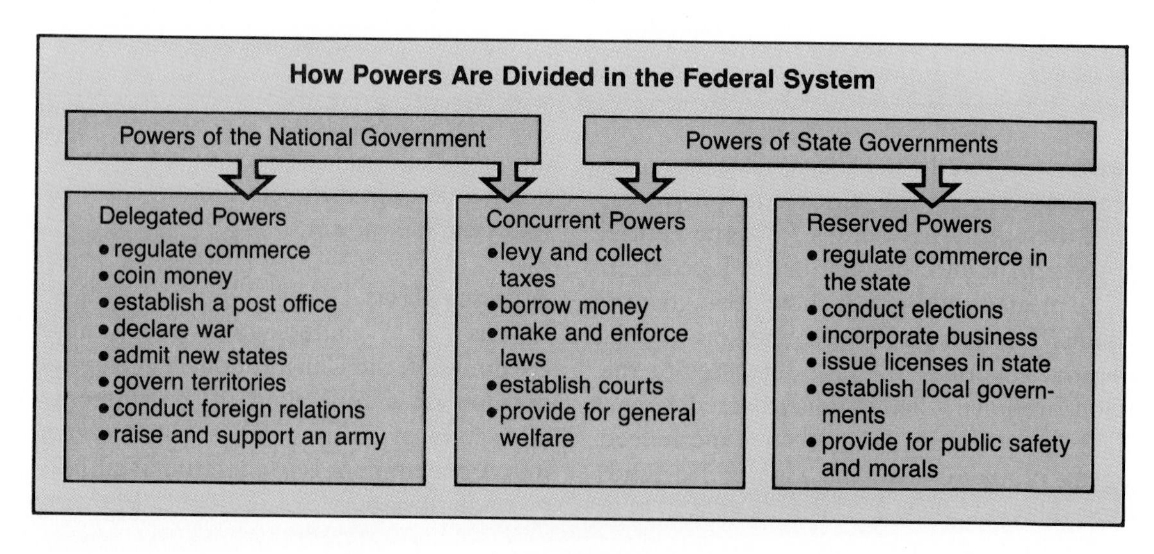

Federalism means three groups of powers

The states didn't just give powers to the federal government. Rather, they gave certain powers to each branch of government. Article I of the Constitution lists many powers given to Congress. Article II lists the powers of the President and Article III lists the powers of the federal courts. Finally, Article VI establishes the importance of all of these powers. This article states that federal powers are "The Supreme Law of the Land." This means that when the federal government has the power to do something, this power has authority over the power of particular areas of government. The Constitution thus gives many powers only to the Federal government.

The Constitution lists much of what government can do. The Bill of Rights is concerned with what government cannot do. Amendment X of the Bill of Rights says that powers not given to the federal government are reserved for the states. Thus, the states have certain powers that the federal government cannot have.

This means that there are three kinds of governmental authority in the United States. There are the *delegated powers*. These are delegated, or given, by the states to the federal government. There are also the *reserved powers*. These are reserved, or held back by the states for them alone. Finally, there are *concurrent powers*. These are powers that are held by both the states and the federal government. These three groups of powers demonstrate the way federalism works in the United States.

Resolving conflicts

These who planned the Constitution knew that federalism could lead to conflicts. Arguments could arise as to whether a certain power was delegated or reserved, or about which government might have the controlling influence when there was a conflict over concurrent powers.

Article VI says: "This Constitution, and the Laws of the United States which shall be made in Pursuance thereof; and all Treaties made, or which shall be made, under the Authority of the United States, shall be the Supreme Law of the Land; and the Judges in every State shall be bound thereby, anything in the Constitution or Laws of any State to the Contrary notwithstanding."

This means that the judges and courts are to determine when there are conflicts in federalism. It is up to them to determine if both the federal and state governments are staying within their own powers. There are still many conflicts over power. But the Constitution says that federal powers are supreme. It also charges the judges and courts to abide by this.

The national motto

Even before the Constitution was written, the Congress under the Articles of Confederation adopted a national motto. It is *E Pluribus Unum*. This is a Latin phrase meaning "from many, one." (It was the custom at that time for mottoes to be expressed in Latin because it was an international language of government and learning.) Congress placed this motto upon the Great Seal, which appears on all important government papers. You will find it printed on the back of every dollar bill. On the left side of the bill you will see the reverse side of the Great Seal. Its central figure is a pyramid with thirteen steps, each step representing one of the original states. On the right side you will see the front of the seal, the main figure of which is an eagle. The eagle was

The complete text of the Constitution can be found in the Appendix, beginning on page 564. The complete text of the Bill of Rights can be found in the Appendix on pages 575–76.

Discuss the motto, *"E Pluribus Unum"* with your students. Ask them if they think this is a fitting phrase for our nation.

The Great Seal of the United States. The olive branch in the right claw stands for a desire for peace; the arrows in the left stand for the ability to wage war if necessary.

chosen as the national symbol of the United States because it represents freedom and strength. In the eagle's bill is a ribbon bearing the national motto. The thirteen stars that appear just above the eagle and the thirteen stripes on its shield represent the thirteen original states. The Great Seal shows that many states became one nation, the United States.

Check for Understanding: Now that you have completed this section, you should be able to answer these questions:

1. What are the three kinds of power established under federalism?
2. Which branch of government has each of these powers?
3. How are conflicts over power resolved under the Constitution?
4. How do the national motto and the Great Seal symbolize federalism?

HOW DO THE STATES COOPERATE WITH EACH OTHER?

Objectives: After you have read this section, you will be able to:

- Explain the meaning of "Full Faith and Credit."
- Give three examples of how Article IV of the Constitution has affected, or might affect, your life.
- Explain how a person becomes a citizen of a state.

Through the Constitution

During your life you have probably visited another state at some time. This means you went from the control of one state government to the control of another. But very likely you didn't notice a difference. You are able to move around as a free citizen because the Constitution provides a system by which the states will cooperate. Articles IV and VI of the Constitution deal with the relationships of states to each other. Without these provisions, it would be difficult for the United States to exist as one nation in the way that it does.

Each state honors the acts of others

Article IV begins, "Full Faith and Credit shall be given in each State to the public Acts, Records, and judicial Proceedings of every other State." In other words, the legal acts and records of a state are recognized throughout the nation by every other state.

Discuss the importance of cooperation among the individual states with your students. What examples can they think of that show this cooperation?

In this country people may travel freely from one state to another without concern that their rights will be effected.

Because of this statement, your birth certificate is good in all the states and not just in the state where you were born. If a man and woman are married in one state, the marriage holds good in all other states. If two persons make a business contract in one state, it is good in other states. If you owe a person a debt in one state, you will still owe it if you move to another state. Rulings of a judge in one state are binding on a person in all states, as are all other public acts and records. At times the Supreme Court has made an exception to this rule. Sometimes in divorce cases, for example, a person might take up residence in another state to take advantage of different laws there.

Rights of state citizenship

The Constitution provides that all states cooperate with each other in a way that is very important to us today. Most Americans will move to a different state at least once in their lives. With modern highways and jet airplanes, they may even be in several different states in a single day when traveling as visitors or on business. What happens to your rights as an American citizen when you move or travel away from home?

The Fourteenth Amendment says that each citizen of the United States is also a citizen of the state in which he or she lives. As a citizen you may move and live in any other state and be a citizen of that new state. A state may require you to live there for a certain period of time before you can vote in an election or do certain other things. The purpose of this policy is to be sure that you do intend to make this place your home.

The Constitution also provides for people who visit or have business in a state other than their home state. Article IV states, "The Citizens of each State shall be enti-

Why do students think that some states require a person to live in a state for a certain amount of time before taking advantage of certain privileges? Do they think this is fair?

tled to all Privileges and Immunities of Citizens in several States." This sentence means that as a visitor, you will be protected by federal and state laws. You may work, buy property, or conduct other business. Of course, you also have the responsibilities of citizenship as a visitor. You must continue to obey the laws of the federal government as well as those of the state you are visiting.

Other cooperation between states

States cooperate in many ways other than those states in the Constitution. If a person accused of a crime in one state escapes to another, the officers of this second state will arrest the person. The suspect will be held in jail until officers come from the state where the crime was committed and take the person back for trial.

The governor of a state may ask the governor of another state to send back an accused criminal who has fled. This practice is called *extradition*. If the governor fears that the prisoner will not have a fair trial in the other state, he or she may refuse to return the prisoner. But ordinarily the states help each other in arresting persons accused of crime.

Uniform codes or laws

States cooperate in passing laws that are *uniform*, or the same. These laws are written by lawyers or representatives from all states. Each state will then pass them in their legislatures with only a few changes. There are still many laws that are different in each state. However, most important laws are the same from one state to another.

Check for Understanding: Now that you have completed this section, you should be able to answer these questions:

1. What is the meaning of the phrase "Full Faith and Credit"?
2. What are three ways in which Article IV can affect your life?
3. How does one become a citizen of a new state?
4. What is one exception to the policy that the laws of one state are binding on the other states?

HOW DO THE FEDERAL AND STATE GOVERNMENTS COOPERATE?

Objectives: After you have read this section, you will be able to:

- List two things that the national government must guarantee or provide to the states.
- Explain one advantage and one disadvantage of the grant-in-aid policy.
- Describe the issue of centralization versus decentralization.

Creating new states

Article IV also provides that new states may be admitted to the Union by an act of Congress. After a state is admitted, it has all the rights of other states. None of its boundaries may be changed, either to add or to take away territory, without its own consent. Congress, too, must agree to any changes of state borders.

Respecting federal property

The states must respect the property of the United States that lies within their borders. Congress has full authority over such property as forts, arsenals, national parks, and public lands.

Ask students to name the different states they have lived in. Can they think of any laws that were not uniform among these states?

Anson Jones, President of the Republic of Texas, officially declares Texas a state of the Union on February 19, 1846.

Guarantees of self-government

No state may be ruled by a king or a dictator. On this matter Article IV says, "The United States shall guarantee to every State in this Union a Republican Form of Government . . ." As we have learned, a republic is a country where the people govern themselves through their elected representatives. If an elected governor should attempt to seize control of the state government as a dictator, it would be the duty of the United States to remove the person from power and to restore freedom. Thus the Constitution gives the federal government the right to protect the people of a state whenever their inherent rights and freedoms as citizens are threatened by a dictator.

Have an interested student report on the events that led up to the Republic of Texas joining the United States in 1846.

Providing protection

Article IV also requires that the United States government send armed forces to protect any state from invasion. If disorders occur within a state and the state government is unable to restore order, the legislature of the state may ask the United States government for help. If the legislature is not meeting at the time, the governor of the state may ask the federal government for help.

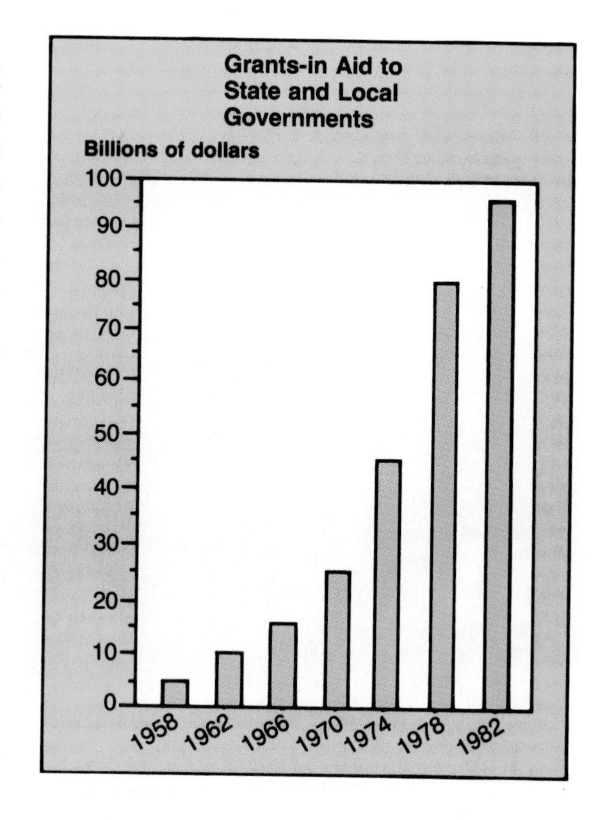

Federal grants-in-aid

The Constitution says Congress may spend money for the general welfare. One way this is done is through federal *grants-in-aid.* These are grants of funds to the states to be used in certain ways. Each year the federal government gives billions of dollars to the states under these grants.

As these grants increase in size, the importance and power of the federal government also increases. The state governments that get federal grants must spend these funds only for certain services. Some of the grants go for education and welfare. Others help build highways and maintain the National Guard. Without these grants, many states would be unable to provide certain services.

Some people are critical of grants-in-aid. In order to receive the money, states must meet certain conditions. They must do things in a specific way. There is much paperwork involved. Because of these conditions, some persons oppose giving these grants to the states. They say they should either be given without conditions, or not given at all.

A democratic process

You have probably decided that federalism is not a simple type of government. The federal government has certain powers, and the fifty states have other powers. Also, the federal government may use grants-in-aid to get state and local governments to do things in a certain way. This brings up the issue of centralization versus decentralization.

Centralization means that more power goes to the federal government. It uses full powers and provides many grants-in-aid. Centralization calls for government actions that are essentially the same across the entire country.

Decentralization means that more power goes to the individual states. The federal government uses few powers and provides less money in the form of grants-in-aid. Decentralization calls for laws and actions to be determined more by states and local governments. Governments may be different, but these differences are set by local citizens.

How much centralization or decentralization we should have will always be a serious question in a federal system of government. It is most important, however, that this question be answered in a democratic fashion. As citizens we should study this issue. We should elect leaders who will follow our wishes. In this way the form of cooperation between states and the federal government, and the amount and kind of power that each has, will be set in a peaceful, legal way.

Check for Understanding: Now that you have completed this section, you should be able to answer these questions:

1. What are two things that national government must or provide to the states?
2. What is one advantage—and one disadvantage—of grants-in-aid?
3. What is the issue of centralization versus decentralization?
4. What is the most important thing to do in dealing with this issue?

SUMMARY

There are three ways that national governments may be organized. A confederation has strong state governments giving limited power to the national government. A unitary state has a strong national government. In a federation, both state and national governments share power.

Federalism in the United States started with the states giving up power to the federal government in the Constitution. In the Bill of Rights the states reserved for themselves all powers not given to the federal government. This means that we have three groups of powers: (1) delegated powers of the federal government, (2) reserved powers of the states, and (3) concurrent powers held by both the states and federal government. Conflicts over these powers are resolved in the courts. This idea of federalism is symbolized in the national motto, and it is also represented on the Great Seal of the United States of "E Pluribus Unum,"

The Constitution provides a system for all states to cooperate together as one nation. All legal judgments, documents, contracts, and other laws binding in one state are to be honored by all other states. The rights of a citizen in one state are also honored by all other states. The way that states cooperate and work together help make the United States one nation.

The states and the federal government cooperate in many ways. The Constitution says that the United States will guarantee states self-government and provide them protection. The states must also respect federal property. The federal government also uses grants-in-aid to get the states to take certain actions.

This brings up the question of centralization versus decentralization. This important question must be answered by the democratic process if the fifty state governments and the federal government are to cooperate successfully.

Issues in Civics: Ask students whether they are generally more in favor of centralization or decentralization.

BUILDING SKILLS IN CIVICS

THINKING SKILLS

1. Copy three sentences from this chapter containing facts that support this generalization:
   States cooperate together in order to help make one nation.
2. What is meant by:
   a. confederation b. unitary state c. federation
3. Why did federalism replace the confederation?
4. When conflicts over power arise in our federal system, how are they resolved?
5. Choose the title below that fits this paragraph best.
   Citizens decide how they want their government to run. Local and state governments determine the laws and policies instead of a federal government.
   a. Federalism b. Decentralization c. Welfare

VOCABULARY SKILLS

Match each term with its definition.

a. confederation
b. unitary state
c. federalism
d. concurrent powers
e. uniform laws
f. grants-in-aid
g. extradition
h. centralization

1. A single central government that has complete legal control over all the territory within its borders.
2. In this system of government authority is divided between the central government and the self-governing states.
3. Unlike delegated and reserved powers, these are held jointly by the federal government and the states.
4. The practice of the governor of a state that an accused criminal has left asking the governor of the state the criminal has gone to send the accused person back.
5. In this system of government, the states keep most of the power and give the central government limited authority only.
6. Important laws that are almost the same from state to state.

7. Federal funds given to states, as long as the states meet certain conditions, and do things in a certain way.
8. This means that more power goes to the federal government, as opposed to decentralization, where more power goes to the individual states.

STUDY SKILLS—USING A CARD CATALOG

The *card catalog* is the most complete source of information about books that a library has. It consists of index cards that describe each book in the library. Each card gives the author, the title, and a brief description of the book and tells you how to find it. These cards are put in drawers and arranged in alphabetical order. Each drawer is labeled. To make it easier to find a book each one is classified in three ways, by author, last name first, (Smith, J.); by title, (How to Write a Report); and by subject (report writing). Usually, but not always, the card catalog is alphabetized according to this system so all the author cards are in the same section, the title cards in another section and the subject cards in yet another.

Each book in a library is identified by a call number. You will see this number in the upper left-hand corner of the card and on the spine of the book.

Activity: Look in the subject section of your library's card catalogue. Select any three cards on Citizenship. Copy each call number, author's name, and title. See if you can locate the books in the library. How many other books on Citizenship do you see in the same section of the library?

BEYOND THE BOOK

1. Construct a chart that shows the three ways national governments may be organized.
2. Read the biography of one of the Founding Fathers and prepare a report summarizing his stand on decentralization.
3. Choose a topic from the list and make a collage. To do this, cut out pictures and words from newspapers and magazines and arrange them so that they illustrate your topic.

CHAPTER EIGHT TEST

VOCABULARY CHECK

Some of the underlined words in the sentences below are used correctly, but others are not. If the sentence is correct, write True. If it is not, replace the word with the best choice from the list.

confederation	federation	extradition
unitary state	centralization	grants-in-aid
uniform laws	concurrent powers	

1. A confederation exists when states give the central government limited authority only.
2. When the central government has complete control over all the territory within its borders, it is known as a federation.
3. Uniform laws are a form of government in which authority is divided between the central government and the states.
4. Federation means that more power goes to the federal government.
5. The practice of the governor of one state asking the governor of another state to send back an accused criminal who has fled is called grants-in-aid.
6. States cooperate by passing uniform laws.
7. In order to receive grants-in-aid, states must follow certain practices.
8. Concurrent powers are those that are held back by the states and the federal government.

COMPREHENSION CHECK

1. ______ is *not* a way governments are organized?
   a. confederation
   b. unitary state
   c. uniform laws
2. Which of these is a feature of a centralized government?
   a. The federal government uses less power.
   b. States pass uniform laws.
   c. More power goes to the federal government.

3. Federalism can lead to conflicts because ______.
   a. the federal government has all the power.
   b. the federal judges have all the power.
   c. it is not always clear which powers are delegated and which are reserved.

SKILL BUILDERS—INTERPRETING GRAPHS

Look at the picture below. This is a *population graph*. Like other graphs, it shows the relative size of various items.

Populations of the Thirteen Original States

Key: = 100,000

Virginia
Pennsylvania
North Carolina
Massachusetts
New York
Maryland
South Carolina
Connecticut
New Jersey
New Hampshire
Georgia
Rhode Island
Delaware

Activity: Study the graph and answer these questions.

1. What information do the title and the caption give you?
2. How does the graph help you understand why some states wanted each state to have an equal vote in Congress, while others wanted population to determine representation?
3. Which states do you think favored having their voting power in Congress determined by their population? How can you check your answers?

BUILDING WRITING SKILLS

1. Explain the difference between centralization and decentralization.
2. Tell in your own words the meaning of the Tenth Amendment.
3. What are some of the advantages of a federation of states, as compared to a confederation of states?

Chapter Nine
State and Local Government

Document: The Constitution of the United States

Article IV, Section 3: New States may be admitted by the Congress into this Union; but no new States shall be formed or erected within the Jurisdiction of any other State; nor any State be formed by the Junction of two or more States, or Parts of States, without the Consent of the Legislatures of the States concerned as well as of the Congress . . .

Article IV, Section 4: The United States shall guarantee to every State in this Union a Republican Form of Government, and shall protect each of them against Invasion; and on Application of the legislature, or of the Executive (when the legislature cannot be convened) against domestic Violence.

Did you ever think what might happen if every state could choose its own kind of government or have the jurisdiction to form states within states at will? One state might have a king, another a dictator, while others might have a governor and a legislature. The result would be that our United States would not be united at all.

Article IV, Section 3 of the Constitution prevents this conflict by saying that new states can't be formed by dividing already existing states without the consent of Congress and the state legislatures.

As shown in the picture, a governor, as the chief executive of his or her state, is privileged to live in an often luxurious residence, owned by the state. What other privileges do politicians at this level of government enjoy? Discuss with your students.

Article IV, Section 4 protects the citizens of individual states even more by requiring the federal government to make sure that every state has a republican form of government, that is, a government in which the people elect representatives who govern them.

Many states have established governments that are structured much like that of the federal government. This is also somewhat true of local governments. This must mean that the structure of the federal government seemed like a worthy role model for other levels of government to follow.

FOCUSING IDEAS

- People participate in state or local government through direct elections, the adoption of state constitutions, direct lawmaking, and through the power of the impeachment or recall process.
- The states provide local self-government by dividing its legislatures into smaller units and allowing them to set forth certain laws. Some of these local governments are county and city governments and school districts that have the power to make laws, collect taxes, and provide services. However, state laws place limits on what these governments can do.
- The types of municipal government are the mayor-council plan, the city commission form, and the city manager plan.

The complete text of the Constitution can be found in the Appendix, beginning on page 564.

PRE-TEST

1. How is the organization of state government different from that of the federal government? How is it similar?
2. How do people participate directly in state government?
3. How do the states provide for local self-government?
4. What are the different types of municipal government?

HOW ARE STATE GOVERNMENTS ORGANIZED?

Objectives: After you have read this section, you will be able to:

- Explain how state governments are similar to the national government.
- Describe the way in which state legislatures are organized.
- Provide the titles that are equivalent to President and Vice President in state government.

When someone speaks of the "government," you probably think of the federal government in Washington, D.C. Actually, there are thousands of governments in the United States.

There are fifty state governments, thousands of county governments, and thousands more city governments in the United States. There are also districts and authorities that perform specific services. In a certain city the citizens might live under eight different kinds of governmental authority. The laws these various governments pass, and the services they provide, are very important in the daily lives of all citizens.

State governments are similar in form to the federal government. Each state government has legislative, executive, and judicial branches. But while all states are organized with three branches, they all have many different rules. When you study state and local governments, you will need special information to find out the organization, rules, and powers in your own state and city or county.

Legislative branches

The lawmaking branch of the state government is called the legislature. Except in Nebraska, all legislatures have two houses. The names of the two houses vary among the states. Some states call one the House of Representatives or the Assembly and the other the Senate. In Nebraska the legislature has only one house, the Senate. A lawmaking body of this kind is called a "unicameral" legislature. Unicameral is a Latin word meaning "one house or chamber." Other states have bicameral, or two houses, legislatures. The various states have different rules as to when the legislature meets. In most states there is one session each year.

Building vocabulary:
initiative *(142)* • referendum *(143)* • recall *(143)* • county board *(144)* • municipality *(146)* • ordinance *(146)* • home rule *(147)* • district *(149)*

Ask students if they know of the different kinds of governmental authority that they live under in their city.

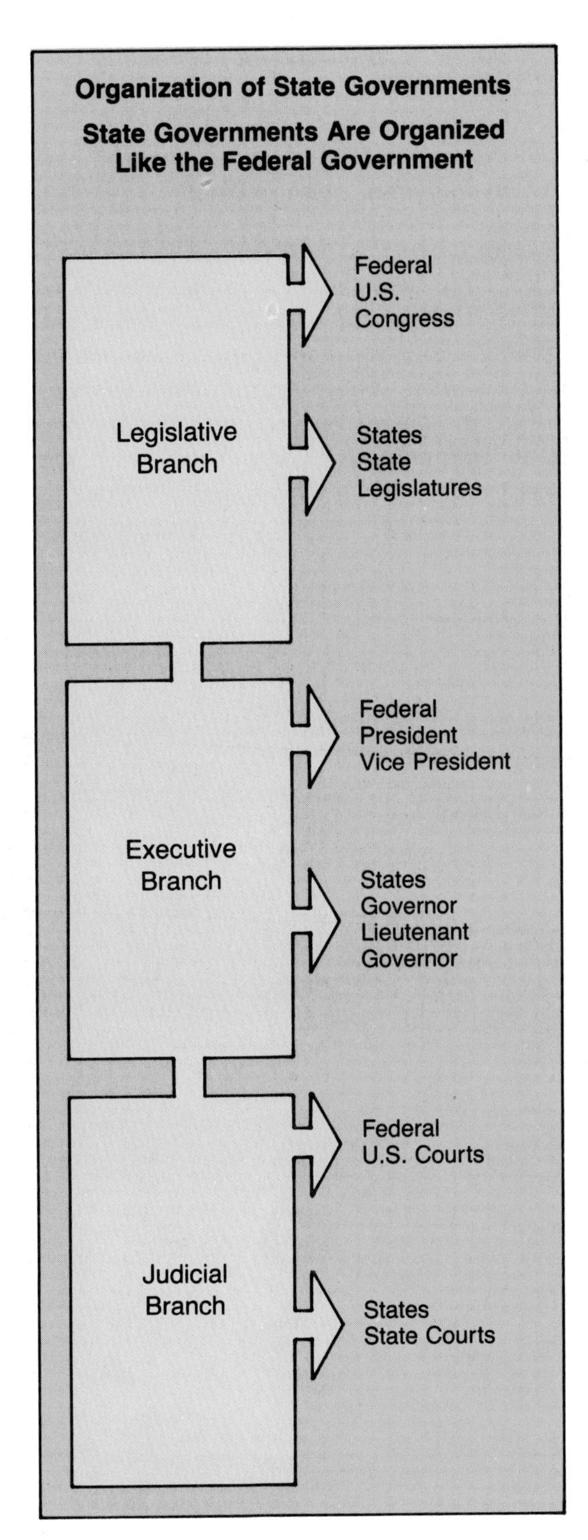

The state legislatures pass more laws than Congress. These laws affect our daily lives very closely. The state lawmakers regulate traffic. They set aside funds to build highways and bridges. They provide for public education. They affect our lives in many other ways.

Executive officers

The chief executive officer of each state is called the governor. He or she manages most of the state's institutions and may veto bills passed by the legislature. In case of the governor's death, disability, or removal from office, the lieutenant governor becomes governor. States have other officers as well. There is a secretary of state to keep the records. A treasurer keeps financial accounts for the state. An attorney general oversees the enforcement of laws. And a superintendent of education directs the educational program of the state.

In most states, the lieutenant governor, the secretary of state, the treasurer, and other officers are not appointed by the governor. They are elected separately in the same election in which the governor is chosen. Each state also has a number of boards or commissions. Usually the governor of the state appoints the members of these boards. Such appointments may be subject to approval by the upper chamber of the legislature.

Check for Understanding: Now that you have completed this section, you should be able to answer these questions:

1. How are state governments similar to the national government?
2. How are state legislatures organized?
3. What is the equivalent of the President and Vice President at the state level?
4. In what way is Nebraska different from all other states?

Ask an interested student to compare your state's constitution with the U.S. Constitution and note the similarities and differences between the two documents.

HOW DO PEOPLE PARTICIPATE IN STATE OR LOCAL GOVERNMENT?

Objectives: After you have read this section, you will be able to:

- Explain what a direct election is.
- Define the terms "initiative" and "referendum."
- Explain how these terms differ from "recall."

Direct election

In your earlier studies, you learned that the states created the federal government by giving it certain powers. The states elect the President and amend the Constitution. However, the people have more direct control over their state and local governments. They elect the governor and other officers directly. They elect their state and local representatives. People have other direct powers in state and local government, which vary from place to place.

State constitutions

Each state has a constitution that was adopted by the people of the state. Since the people adopt the constitution, the people can change it. The constitution of the states differ in some respects, but all have the same general pattern. You should study the constitution of your own state in order to fully understand your state's government.

Direct lawmaking

Several states have plans whereby the people may have a direct part in making laws. One part of this plan is known as the *initiative*. The initiative is an extension of

Local Self-Government

State Constitutions | Direct Election | Initiative and Referendum | Recall

Issues in Civics: Have a student research the effects of Proposition 13, an initiative that had far-reaching effects in the state of California.

the right of petition which is guaranteed by the U.S. Constitution. It allows the people to bring bills before a lawmaking body for consideration. A certain percentage of voters must sign a petition requesting passage of a bill. Then the legislators debate it. If they fail to pass the bill, it often must be put to a popular vote within a specified time period. If a majority of the voters favor the bill, it then becomes a law. The governor cannot veto such a bill.

In some states there is a provision that when a bill is defeated by a vote of the people, it cannot again be brought before the people through this process for a certain number of years. This is to prevent a particular lawmaker or group from bringing the same or a similar bill before each new session of the legislature.

Most states that have a provision for the initiative also have the *referendum*, a vote by which a majority opinion is determined. One kind of referendum provides that approved bills must wait ninety days before becoming law. If a certain percentage of the voters sign a petition during this period, the measure must be put to a popular vote. The bill becomes law if a majority of the voters favor it. A majority vote against the bill may also defeat it. The governor has no veto power in such cases. Only the voters can repeal such a law.

Removing an officer

The legislature may remove an officer by an impeachment process similar to that used by Congress. In most states the governor may remove from office any of his appointees. Some state constitutions also have a *recall* provision for removing an officer. Under this plan a portion of the voters, usually 25 percent, may demand an election for an officer's removal. When the petition is presented, the governor must call an election, even if the issue to be voted on is his or her own removal. In the election that follows the people may replace the officer, or they may vote to keep him or her in office.

Check for Understanding: Now that you have completed this section, you should be able to answer these questions:

1. What is a direct election?
2. How does this differ from an election at the national level?
3. What is the meaning of the terms "initiative" and "referendum?"
4. How do these differ from a "recall?"

HOW DO THE STATES PROVIDE LOCAL SELF-GOVERNMENT?

Objectives: After you have read this section, you will be able to:

- Explain how states create local governments.
- List four services provided by county governments.
- Describe the system of government that is used in those states that do not have counties.

States create local governments

The state government has the power to make laws for the people of the state. Most states give the people the right to govern themselves in local matters. State constitutions and laws provide for local governments to be formed. Some of these local governments are county and city governments and school districts.

Do students know of any referendums that have been proposed in their area? Were they approved?

Each of these governments can make laws, collect taxes, and provide services. State laws place limits on what these governments can do. For instance, each state sets its own rules for public schools. The states, in turn, may give each school district the right to hire its own teachers, as long as these teachers meet the state requirements. Each local school district decides for itself such matters as whether or not to build a new school.

Counties and townships

Each state in the United States, except Louisiana and Alaska, is divided by its legislature into small units called counties. Alaska has units known as boroughs and Louisiana has parishes, but these function very much like counties. Counties are in turn divided by state law into townships. Counties and townships are a heritage from colonial days. In colonial New England, the unit of local government was the town. In the South, it was the county. Later the two systems of county and township government were combined.

County government is similar in most states. The legislative body of the county may be called the *county board* or the county court. When it is called the county court, the body does not act as a judicial court, but it is the legislative body of the county. The members of the county board are called county commissioners. Members of the county court are called county judges.

Counties are among the few governmental bodies in the United States that have no administrative head. In most counties the chief elected officials are all legislators. There is no county executive officer, such

Ask students why they think these services are customarily provided by state governments rather than the national government.

as the state's governor or the nation's President. The responsibility for carrying out the laws made by the county commissioners is assigned separately to various other officers. Some of these are the county clerk, the county treasurer, and the sheriff. These officers are also elected by the people. Only in rare cases is there a county manager or other chief executive.

The responsibilities of county government are many. It plays a small but important part in the daily lives of the citizens. The county keeps many records of individuals, from birth certificates to death certificates. Most of the roads, outside of the city streets and the main highways, are built and maintained by the county government. The sheriff is responsible for law enforcement throughout the entire county. The county is also responsible for much of the work in taking care of the poor and providing them with food, clothing, and medicine. County governments also perform many other duties that concern the county alone. In some states the county board, in agreement with state laws, divides the county into townships and names each township. In these states the township officers assign taxes and perform duties that have to do with the township. The township officers are elected by the people of the township.

In some parts of New England, the chief unit of local government is the town. A New England town would be called a township in most other parts of the nation. It includes both rural and city areas. In New England the people of each town gather once a year at the town meeting to set tax rates and make rules. In a small town this is a fine example of democracy at work. In a large town only a small percentage of the voters attend such meetings. Thus a minority makes laws for all people in the town.

A typical New England town meeting in Manchester, New Hampshire.

Each state determines by law or by its constitution what the duties of the county and the township officers shall be. Since these duties vary in different states, you should study the system in your own state to see how it works.

Check for Understanding: Now that you have completed this section, you should be able to answer these questions:

1. How are local governments created by the states?
2. What are four services provided by county governments?
3. Which states do not have counties?
4. What is the local unit of government in these states?

Ask students if town meetings take place in their city. If not, do they think that these meetings *should* take place in order to allow citizens to voice their opinions?

WHAT ARE THE TYPES OF MUNICIPAL GOVERNMENT?

Objectives: After you have read this section, you will be able to:

- List the three types of municipal government.
- Name the executive in each type of municipal government.
- Explain how districts and authorities function as units of government.

The government of a village, town, or city is called a municipal government. These local governmental units are needed because special problems must be solved at the community level. A self-governing town or city is called a *municipality*. The state laws determine the form of government for municipalities. The state grants the city a charter that defines the city's authority to govern itself.

Mayor-Council

Three kinds of government are common among the cities of the United States. These are the mayor-council plan, the commission plan, and the city manager plan. The mayor-council plan of government is the oldest and most common form. The mayor is the chief officer of a city and can be compared to the governor of the state. Under the mayor-council plan, laws for a city are made by a city council. Laws passed by the council are called *ordinances* to distinguish them from laws made by Congress or by state legislatures. Under the mayor-council plan the city may be divided into sections called wards. Each of these wards elects one or more councilmen or councilwomen to represent it. Other cities elect councilmen-at-large. Everybody in

The city council of Minneapolis, Minnesota conducting a meeting.

Ask an interested student to attend a city council meeting and report back to the class.

the city has an opportunity to vote for every candidate for the city council. In some cities members of the council are called aldermen or alderwomen. Ordinances that are passed by the city council must be signed by the mayor before they can become law.

Cities using the mayor-council type of government may have a strong mayor or a weak mayor. Under a weak mayor system, the mayor has little authority. He or she may not veto ordinances. The mayor is limited in making appointments. The council exercises most of the power. Under a strong mayor government, the mayor is more powerful. He or she has veto power, although the council can pass ordinances over a veto. He or she also has the authority to administer the laws and to appoint various officials.

City commission

The commission form of government was first used in this country in Galveston, Texas. This city suffered severely from a hurricane in 1900. Some citizens thought they could best work together to rebuild the city if they changed their form of government. They decided to do away with the mayor-council system and replace it with what became known as the commision form of government.

Five commissioners were chosen to replace the council and mayor. Instead of representing wards, the commissioners were chosen from the city at large by all the voters. One of the five commissioners bore the title of mayor. But this office offered no real power. The mayor's only executive duty was to preside at the meetings of the commission. The executive power was now shared by four other commissioners, each of whom headed a department of the city government. The mayor could vote with the other commissioners but had no veto power.

Commission government has spread from Galveston to many cities, towns, and villages over the United States. Since a commissioner represents the whole city instead of a single ward, he or she is interested in the welfare of the entire city. The commission plan usually provides for the election of commissioners or a non-partisan ticket. This means that candidates do not run on any party ticket.

City manager

The city manager plan of government grew out of the commission government. Only a few cities adopted it at first. Then a great flood brought disaster to Dayton, Ohio in 1913. There was loss of life and great property damage. The city manager took charge of the affairs of Dayton. He managed the city government so well that many other cities adopted the plan.

Under the city manager plan, commissioners are usually elected from the city at large. They are chosen on a nonpartisan ticket. The commissioners select the city manager, pass the ordinances, and decide all the policies of the city. But unlike the commission plan, the commissioners have no executive authority. All executive authority is turned over to the city manager. The city manager is employed for as long as her or his services give satisfaction. The city manager is very much like the manager of a business. In a business, a group of directors set the policy, while leaving management to a single chief executive officer. So it is with the city manager system.

Home rule

Many people believe that states should grant cities *home rule*. Under home rule the

Ask students what they know about the form of government in their city. Do they have a mayor-council type of government or another kind? How efficient do they think their city's government is?

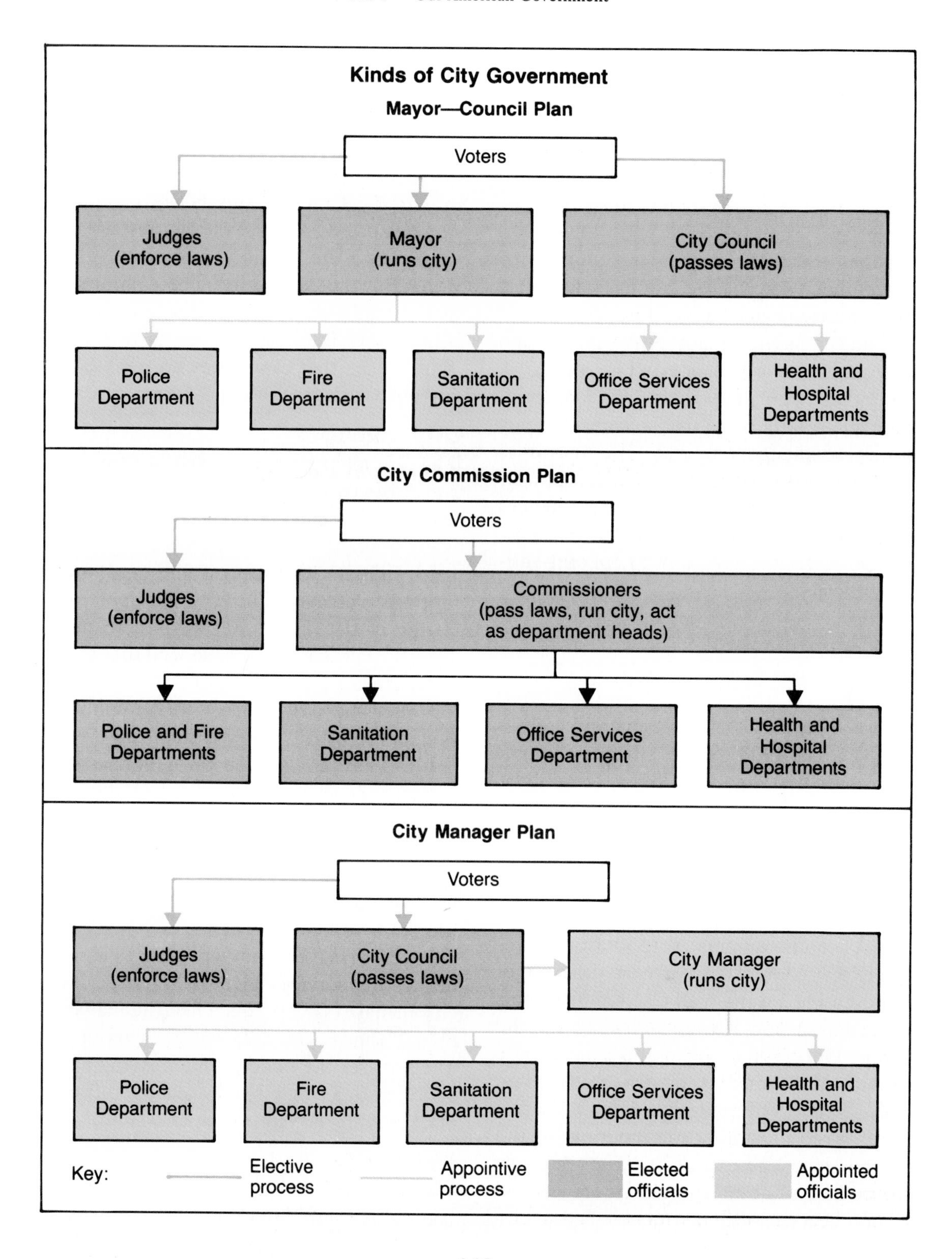
Kinds of City Government
Mayor—Council Plan
Voters
Judges (enforce laws)
Mayor (runs city)
City Council (passes laws)
Police Department
Fire Department
Sanitation Department
Office Services Department
Health and Hospital Departments
City Commission Plan
Voters
Judges (enforce laws)
Commissioners (pass laws, run city, act as department heads)
Police and Fire Departments
Sanitation Department
Office Services Department
Health and Hospital Departments
City Manager Plan
Voters
Judges (enforce laws)
City Council (passes laws)
City Manager (runs city)
Police Department
Fire Department
Sanitation Department
Office Services Department
Health and Hospital Departments
Key:
Elective process
Appointive process
Elected officials
Appointed officials

citizens of the city have much more to say as to how their city should be governed. Each city can make up its own charter and choose the kind of government that suits it best. Under such a plan, city governments have much more freedom. They can pass the kinds of laws that the citizens need and want. In those states where home rule does not exist, the legislature may pass a law to give home rule to a city.

The city government provides police and fire protection. It builds sidewalks, streets, and public buildings. It maintains parks. It regulates utilities such as telephone, electric, gas, and water companies. The city also regulates private transportation companies. Some cities, however, prefer to own and operate transportation services themselves.

Districts and authorities

There are many times when the people of an area need special services. One community may need a hospital. Another city may lie near the ocean or a large river and need to develop a port. Many states allow the people to create special *districts* or authorities to provide such needed services. These districts are examples of how people cooperate together through government to provide new services as new needs arise.

School districts

Each state provides for local governments of school districts. The school district is governed by a board of education. Such boards are selected in different ways and have different forms in various states. Usually the board of education is elected on a non-partisan basis and is a unicameral body. The board makes the regulations for the schools in its district and hires the teachers and other employees. The number of members on the board varies. The chief executive officer of the board is a superintendent. It is that person's responsibility to manage the schools in agreement with the policies set by the board.

Check for Understanding: Now that you have completed this section, you should be able to answer these questions:

1. What are the three types of municipal government?
2. Which is the most common?
3. Who is the chief executive in each type?
4. How do districts and authorities function as units of government?

SUMMARY

States are organized much like the federal government. All states have a governor, a legislature, and courts. They also have other officers. But states differ as to the rules of their government and the ways that officers are elected or appointed.

Each state is a republic in form and has a constitution that was adopted by the people of the state. The state legislature is the lawmaking body for the citizens of a state. State executive officers include the governor, lieutenant governor, secretary of state, treasurer, attorney general, and superintendent of education.

People live under many different governments and under many different kinds of laws, ordinances, and regulations. The people in rural communities live under federal, state, county, and township governments. The people in cities, towns and villages live under these governments and under municipal government also.

Issues in Civics: Have your students discuss the changes they would institute if they were members of the board of education in their school district. Are they satisfied with the way their district is run *now*?

BUILDING SKILLS IN CIVICS

THINKING SKILLS

1. What are the three branches into which state government is organized?
2. Which state and local officials do people elect directly?
3. How do some states give their citizens a direct part in making laws? In defeating proposed laws?
4. What are the differences in the weak mayor system of government and the strong mayor system of government?
5. What are five services that city governments provide?
6. Which of the following is *not* an example of the city manager plan:
   a. Commissioners are usually elected.
   b. Commissioners have executive authority.
   c. Commissioners employ a city manager.

VOCABULARY SKILLS

Fill in each blank with the word that best completes the sentence.

initiative	county board	home rule	recall
referendum	ordinance	district	municipality

1. The legislative branch of the county is often called the ______.
2. One kind of ______ provides that laws approved by the legislature can be put to a popular vote if enough voters sign a petition to that effect within ninety days.
3. Under ______, each city can make up its own charter and choose its own kind of government.
4. A ______ authority can provide special types of services that are important to a particular area.
5. An ______ is made and passed by a city government.
6. The ______ procedure allows people to propose new bills.
7. A city which is self-governing is called a ______.
8. A ______ provision allows voters to petition for an election to determine an officer's removal.

STUDY SKILLS—OUTLINING

An *outline* is a way of organizing information so that the minor points are systematically arranged under the major ones. Outlines help you to organize information systematically, so that you can keep focused on what you are doing.

In a formal outline major headings are indicated by Roman numerals, subheadings by capital letters, and supporting facts by numbers. Here is a format for a formal outline:

I. ______________________
  A. ______________________
    1. ______________________
    2. ______________________
  B. ______________________
    1. ______________________
    2. ______________________
  C. ______________________
    1. ______________________
    2. ______________________
II. (and so on)

Use this form to organize a formal outline that has the major heading "Three Types of Municipal Governments."

BEYOND THE BOOK

1. Construct a chart that shows which city and county offices provide services for you or your family. To find the proper information, you may need to consult resources such as the telephone book, the library, and people who are well informed on the subject.
2. Collect letters to the editor from local newpapers that have comments about city and county services. Organize these letters according to the types of services they are about. Which services are mentioned most often? Why do you suppose this is so? Are the comments mostly negative or positive? Why?
3. Prepare an oral report on one of the activities suggested above. Write key words on the chalkboard to show your main points and the supporting details.

CHAPTER NINE TEST

VOCABULARY CHECK

Match each term with its definition.

a. initiative
b. referendum
c. county board
d. recall
e. ordinance
f. municipality
g. home rule
h. district

1. The law-making body of a county.
2. The provision that people can petition to have a bill put to a popular vote.
3. Authorities that provide special services to citizens living in certain areas.
4. The principal that allows a city to determine its own kind of government.
5. A provision that allows any citizen to bring bills before the legislature for consideration.
6. A self-governing town or city.
7. A procedure that provides for removing an officer in a lawful and orderly manner.
8. Regulations passed by a city government.

COMPREHENSION CHECK

1. Write Weak Mayor System and Strong Mayor System on your paper. Identify the points from the list below that belong under each heading.
   a. The mayor may appoint various officials.
   b. The mayor has the authority to administer the law.
   c. The city council makes laws for the city.
   d. There are limits on the appointments a mayor can make.
   e. The city council can pass ordinances over a mayor's veto.
2. Indicate whether the following statements are true or false.
   a. There are thousands of governments in the United States.
   b. Each state has a legislative, an executive, and a judicial branch of government.
   c. The chief executive officer of each state is called the commissioner.
   d. The state government has the power to make laws for all the people who live in that state.

SKILL BUILDERS—INTERPRETING ILLUSTRATIONS

Look at the illustrated chart on page 144. Study it in terms of the *illustration* skills you learned in Chapter Three. Then answer the following questions:

1. Name the six services of state government that are shown in the chart.
2. What additional information is given with each illustration?
3. Does the chart tell *all* of the services of state government?
4. Which of the services of state government do you think are the most important? Least important? Why do you think so?
5. Can you think of other services of state government? What are they?
6. Do you think that presenting the information in this chart through the use of illustrations is an effective way of getting the point across? Why or why not? If you were going to present this same information in a different way, how would you do it? Through the use of photos? Tables? Graphs? Explain.

Activity: Write a letter to your state representative asking him or her what the major issues affecting the state are. What does he or she think should be done about the problems? Do you agree? Why or why not? Use facts to support your opinions.

BUILDING WRITING SKILLS

1. Give examples of how your life is directly influenced by federal, state, and local governments.
2. Explain the difference between the terms *initiative* and *referendum*.
3. Write a question that the following statement will answer.
   State constitutions and laws provide for this. Some examples are county and city governments, and school districts.

UNIT TWO TEST

A. Study the painting above of the Founding Fathers. Then answer the following questions:

1. Did the artist portray the men in the painting in a favorable or unfavorable light? What makes you say so?
2. Was the artist trying to get a certain point across, or just drawing a representative portrait?
3. Do you think the painting corresponds well to the chapter? Why or why not?
4. Give this painting a title of your own. Explain why you make your particular choice.
5. Is there anything you particularly like or dislike about the painting? Explain your answer.

B. If you could go back in time and speak to the members of the Constitutional Convention, what questions would you want to ask them? What questions do you think they would want to ask *you* about the world you live in and the things that affect you? Would you advise them to change the Constitution in any way, based on events that have happened since colonial days? Is there anything else you would like to express to them? Explain.

C. Some societies in the past have lost their freedoms. Why did this happen? How can we prevent *our* freedoms from being lost?

Unit Tests use an illustration to lead into an evaluation of the general theme of the unit.

Unit Three • People and Their Government

Government has a major influence on your life every day, and you, in turn, play a vital role in influencing your government. All the laws that are passed and enforced by the various levels of government, and all the services that the government provides, are initiated by people—people who are affected by your opinions, your actions, and your voting decisions.

By taking advantage of your rights, and by living up to your responsibilities, *you* determine who will run your government and in what manner your government will be run.

The woman in the illustration is speaking out on an issue at a local town meeting. This unit deals with the structure of our government and the way in which individual citizens fit into this structure.

Chapter Ten
People and Political Parties

Document: NONE

Notice that the document section above is blank. In all other chapter openers, there are quotations from the Constitution or other great documents of the United States.

There is no quote above because when the Founding Fathers met in Philadelphia in 1787 to draw up the Constitution, they included no mention of political parties in it. George Washington, who presided over the Constitutional Convention, opposed the development of political parties, as did many other early political leaders.

However, as time went on, common political, social, and economic interests united certain groups of people and caused the formation of political organizations. One group called the Federalists supported a strong national government, while their opposition, the Anti-Federalists (later called the Democratic-Republican party) supported a weak central government.

The Federalists, led by Alexander Hamilton, and the Democratic-Republicans, led by Thomas Jefferson, both split after the 1816 presidential election. One of the Democratic-Republican groups came under Andrew Jackson's leadership and eventually came to be known as the Democratic Party.

The people in the picture are helping to choose their party's Presidential nominee. Ask students if they know any of the steps that led up to this point in the political process.

The Republican Party started as a series of antislavery meetings in the midwest in 1854. At that time, the Whig Party, who opposed the extention of slavery, was breaking up and joined with the Republican Party, who also represented this viewpoint. The Republican Party gained followers rapidly. Its policies appealed to many people, including merchants, industrialists, and farmers.

FOCUSING IDEAS

- Political parties in the United States developed in Washington's time with the Federalists and Anti-Federalists gaining support from opposing sides.
- Each political party has an organization on the local, state, and national levels. The voters of each party participate in the nomination of party candidates for office.
- The political parties select their candidates through primary elections and national conventions.
- Citizens become involved in elections by listening to the candidates through the various forms of the media, by studying the issues, and by then voting for the party of their choice. Some people also become involved by working in campaigns for a certain candidate or by working for a specific political party.

This picture shows the opposing major party working to choose *their* Presidential nominee. Ask students if they can see anything different about the two parties' conventions.

PRE-TEST

1. How did American political parties develop?
2. How are political parties organized?
3. How do political parties select their candidates?
4. How are citizens involved in elections?

HOW DID POLITICAL PARTIES DEVELOP IN AMERICA?

Objectives: After completing this section, you will be able to:

- Explain how political parties started in the United States.
- Give two reasons why the U.S. has had only two major parties.
- Give two examples of a third party.

A political party is a group of people who have joined together in order to influence the government. There is more than one way to look at a political party. A party means the people from that party who serve in high places in government. It also means the group of party leaders who run the party's business. Then there are the party workers at the local level. These people work hard for the party and get out the vote. And finally there are the voters who identify with the party and vote for the party's candidates.

The Constitution of the United States makes no arrangements for political parties. They are mentioned in only a few of the laws that govern the nation. American history shows that the Democrats were the major party from the founding of the country until the War Between the States. From then until the early 1900's, the Republicans were mostly in charge. After 1930, the Democrats were in power more often. Since 1952, the two parties have shared control of the national government. Today more and more people are calling themselves "independents." But most voters still refer to themselves as either a Republican or a Democrat.

Since parties are not mentioned anywhere in the Constitution, they are sometimes called "extra-legal", meaning that they are organizations that developed in addition to the law. But there have been many laws passed to control them, because they are the usual way in which people carry on the business of government at local, state, and national levels.

Political parties are not new

The writers of the Constitution knew about political parties in England and other countries. People with the same political beliefs had been working together to influence the affairs of their government. At the time the Constitution was written, the American people did not completely agree about the kind of government they should have and

Building vocabulary:
majority *(160)* • plurality *(160)* • third party *(160)* • precinct *(162)* • primary *(164)* • nominee *(164)* • runoff *(164)* • platform *(166)*

Ask students to imagine that they are of voting age. What political party would they choose to be affiliated with? Do their opinions have anything to do with the party that their parents belong to?

The complete text of the Constitution can be found in the Appendix, beginning on page 564.

Political Parties Since 1868

Year	Democratic Party	Republican Party	Major Third Party(s)
1868		■	
1872		■	
1876		■	Greenback
1880		■	Greenback
1884	■		
1888		■	
1892	■		Populist
1896		■	
1900		■	Socialist
1904		■	Socialist
1908		■	Socialist
1912	■		Progressive Socialist
1916	■		Socialist
1920		■	Socialist
1924		■	Progressive
1928		■	Socialist
1932	■		Socialist
1936	■		Socialist Union
1940	■		Socialist
1944	■		Socialist
1948	■		States' Rights Socialist Progressive
1952		■	
1956		■	
1960	■		
1964	■		
1968		■	American
1972		■	American
1976	■		
1980		■	Independent

■ Party holding the Presidency

what it should do. These differences of opinion would later cause political interests to form into political parties. The great service of the first President, George Washington, was to give the new nation a sense of unity and to rise above party factions. Even during Washington's presidency, however, some members of his cabinet began to show differences of opinion. Thomas Jefferson, who was Secretary of State, feared that Washington was taking on too much authority. Alexander Hamilton, the Secretary of the Treasury, urged Washington to take even greater authority. Two parties began to form, with these men as their leaders. Hamilton's party was known as the Federalist party, and Jefferson's as the Anti-Federalist, or Democratic-Republican party. Members of Congress and other citizens began to take sides and to support the opinions of one of these parties. This was the beginning of the two-party system in the United States.

The United States as a two-party country

A very important fact emerges when one studies the nation's two major political parties. They are both well over one hundred years old. They seem to be among the more permanent and unchanging features of American politics. Most threats to the two-party system have been short-lived.

Why do we have only two major political parties in the United States? One reason is the fact that the English political system was a two-party system. Many of the early inhabitants of our country were born in England and carried this tradition to the United States. A more important reason is that under our system of presidential elections, each party puts up a single candidate for the office of President. The one with

Have students research the principles Washington stated in his Farewell Address of 1796.

Have an interested student do further research on the differences between Thomas Jefferson and Alexander Hamilton that led to the creation of the two-party system.

The Tory Party was one of England's two major parties. It was led by King George III.

The leader of the opposition Whig Party was the prime minister, Sir Robert Walpole.

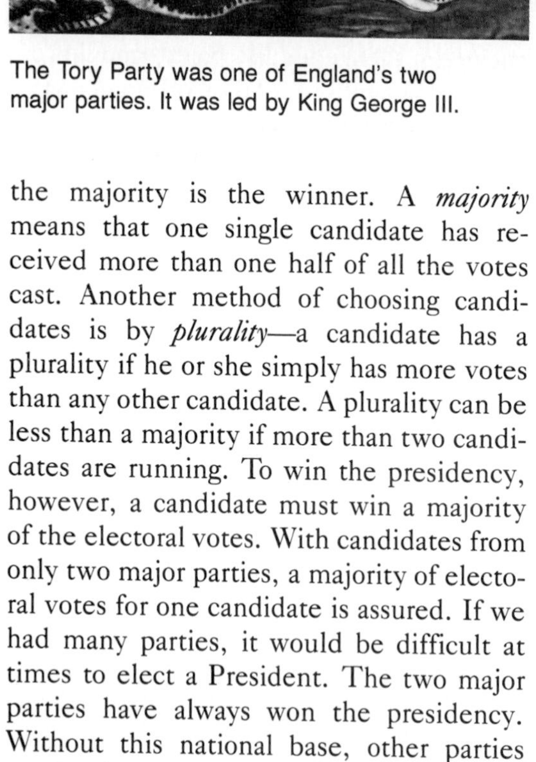

the majority is the winner. A *majority* means that one single candidate has received more than one half of all the votes cast. Another method of choosing candidates is by *plurality*—a candidate has a plurality if he or she simply has more votes than any other candidate. A plurality can be less than a majority if more than two candidates are running. To win the presidency, however, a candidate must win a majority of the electoral votes. With candidates from only two major parties, a majority of electoral votes for one candidate is assured. If we had many parties, it would be difficult at times to elect a President. The two major parties have always won the presidency. Without this national base, other parties tend to lose strength and wither away.

Third parties

A group of people who do not agree with the positions of the two major political parties will sometimes form another party. Such a party is called a *third party*, or a minor party. Some third parties gain large numbers of members and threaten the major parties' control. In 1912, former President Theodore Roosevelt left the Republican party to form the Progressive or "Bull Moose" party. Roosevelt came in second in the election for President by winning more votes than the Republican candidate. In 1968 Governor George Wallace of Alabama formed the American Independent party. This party won the most votes in five states and received more popular votes than any other third party in history.

No third party has ever won the presidency. Since 1860 there have been only four presidential elections (1892, 1912, 1924, and 1968) in which all third parties together polled more than 10% of the vote. If a third party wins a large number of votes, it is likely that some of the ideas that it supports will be taken over by one or both of the major parties. The major parties hope

Issues in Civics: Third parties can influence elections by drawing voters away from the major party candidates. Do students think that third parties help or hurt the political process by doing this?

Have students do further research on the Tory and Whig parties in England. Have them find out what each party stood for.

to win back the support of the voters who left them for the third party because of strong opinions on a certain issue or issues. For example, the Populist party favored the use of the secret ballot in elections. This idea won many votes for the Populist candidates. Later the secret ballot was favored by both the Republican and Democratic parties; and it eventually became the accepted method voting.

Check for Understanding: Now that you have completed this section, you should be able to answer these questions:

1. How did political parties develop in the United States?
2. What are two reasons why the U.S. has had only two major parties?
3. What is a third party?
4. What are two examples of important third parties in our history?

Among the important third-party candidates for President have been Theodore Roosevelt (top left), Robert M. LaFollette (top right), Norman Thomas (lower left), and John Anderson (lower right).

HOW ARE POLITICAL PARTIES ORGANIZED?

Objectives: After you have read this section, you will be able to:

- Describe how parties are organized on the state and local levels.
- List three duties of a party's national committee.
- Explain how candidates are involved in party organizations.

Parties on the local level

Each major party has a local, state, and national organization. At the local level, the basic unit of party organization is the precinct. A *precinct* is the smallest voting district. Each precinct has one voting place and usually contains from five hundred to a thousand voters. The precinct captain or committee member represents the precinct in the party organization.

Parties on the state level

Each major party also has a state central committee for each state. The party sets up its own rules for choosing committee members. They may be chosen by legislative districts, counties, or at some other level. The job of the state committee is to direct the campaigns for state officials and for the members of Congress from that state. The state central committee also supervises the party's presidential campaign in that state.

Parties on the national level

One man and one woman from each state and territory are also members of the national committee of the party. The national committee heads the permanent party organization in the country. This committee is controlled by the national chairperson, who

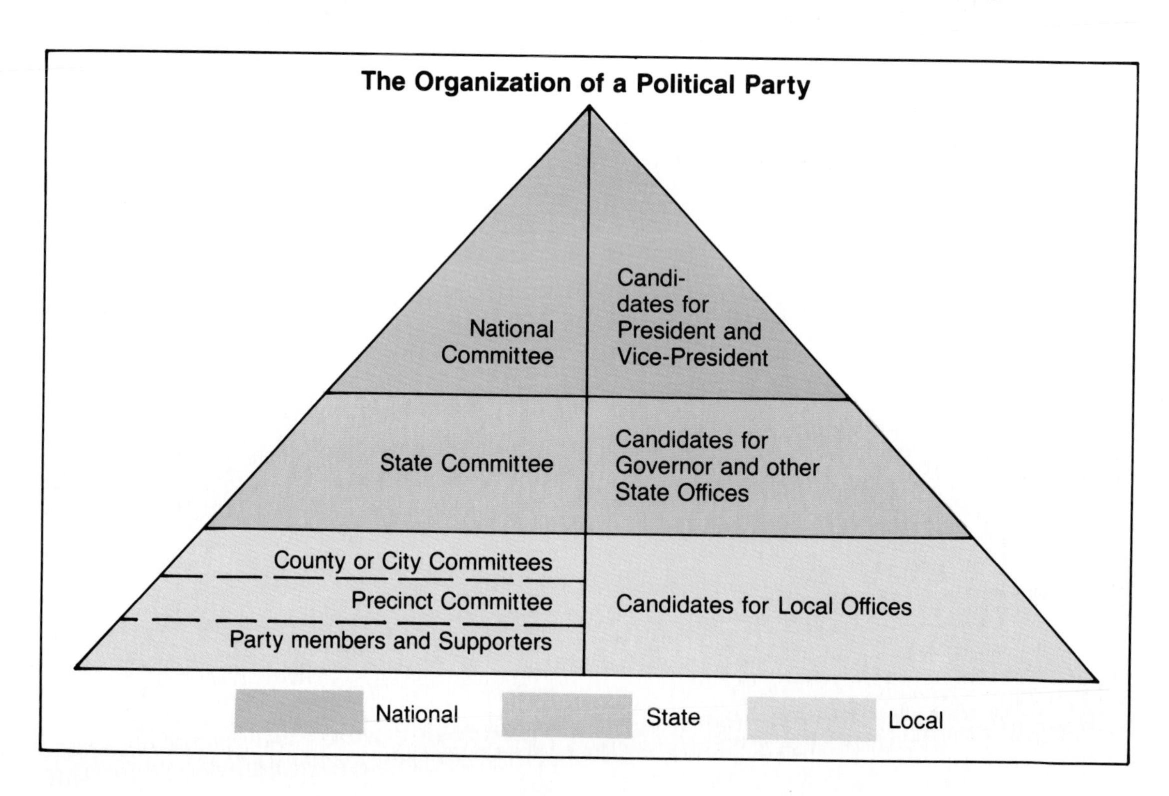

The members of a local political party meet to discuss the issues in an upcoming city election.

has been appointed by the party's last presidential nominee. The national committee is responsible for planning the next national convention of the party. It also chooses the convention city. But the most important work of the national committee is to direct the party's presidential campaign.

Candidates and the party

People who run for office are also important in a political party. Often they have more influence than the party officers. For example, the President is the national head of his or her party. The person who was defeated for President in the last election is usually the official leader of the other party. In the same way, governors, senators, legislators, mayors, and all other elected candidates have influence within the party. Of course, candidates who win elections are more important in the party than those who lose. But even losing candidates, although they may not have any official jobs, still have much influence.

Check for Understanding: Now that you have completed this section, you should be able to answer these questions:

1. How are political parties organized at the state and local levels?
2. What are three duties of a party's national committee?
3. How are candidates involved in party organizations?
4. Who are the national leaders of the two major parties?

Ask students to think of ways that a party's losing candidates can still have influence within their parties. Do students think that losing candidates *should* have such influence?

HOW DO THE PARTIES SELECT THEIR CANDIDATES?

Objectives: After you have read this section, you will be able to:
- Define the term "primary election."
- Explain the main function of the national convention.
- Give three reasons why people join political parties.

Primary elections

The major parties want to do one thing above all else—win elections. Only if its candidates are elected to office can a party really influence government. Many people within a party may want to be the party's candidate for election. But the party can select only one person as its candidate for each office.

For a long time all candidates were nominated at state conventions of their parties. The state convention is still used in some states. In most other states, however, the voters of each party vote by ballot to nominate their party's candidates. This method is called a *primary* election. Primary means "first," and the primary elections must come before the general election, which is usually held in November. Primary elections are very much like regular elections. But in a primary, the voters of most states are allowed to choose only among candidates of their own party.

In general, the candidate who receives a plurality of the votes becomes the *nominee*, or person who is nominated for office. In a few states a majority vote is needed for nomination. In those states, it is sometimes necessary to hold a *runoff* election after the primary, if no candidate has received a majority. This election is held to choose between the two candidates who have won the highest number of votes. The winner of this runoff election becomes the party's nominee for the office.

Bill Brock of Tennessee, chairman of the Republican National Committee.

National convention

Both the Democratic and Republican parties choose their candidates for President and Vice-President in a national convention. Months before the conventions are held, leaders of each party discuss persons who might be considered as candidates for nomination. Usually the party thinks of people who have already had high-level government experience of some kind, perhaps as a governor or senator. In the last hundred years, fifteen of the eighteen Presidents previously served as either governor or senator. On occasion, however, the parties have nominated a war hero. George Washington, Zachary Taylor, Ulysses S. Grant, and Dwight Eisenhower are all generals who won the presidency without having held a previous political office.

Point out the locations of the last three Democratic and Republican national conventions on a map. Ask students if they can think of any reasons why these cities were chosen for the conventions.

The longest national convention in history was the 1924 Democratic Convention. It took 102 ballots before John W. Davis was nominated as a compromise candidate.

Anyone can seek a party's nomination for President. Support of the party leaders isn't always needed. Jimmy Carter won the Democratic nomination for President in 1976 as an "outsider" by proving his ability to win votes in the presidential primary elections.

Reasons for joining a party

You may already think of yourself as a Democrat or Republican even though you have never done anything to actually join the party. You are able to do this because you don't belong to a political party as you do to a club or other organization. People associate themselves with a party by simply saying that they support the party and its candidates. But very few people really sign up as a party member and receive a membership card. Being a part of a political party is important to many people, but they do not have any written proof of membership. It is just a matter of how they usually vote and which candidates for office they usually support.

Do you consider yourself to be either a Republican or a Democrat? If so, have you thought about the reason why? It could be

Have interested students research the political leanings of the fifty states. Which are predominantly Republican or Democratic? Do they have any ideas on why this is true?

The Democratic Convention of 1980, in which Jimmy Carter was nominated for re-election.

The Republicans nominated Ronald Reagan at their 1980 National Convention.

because your family or your friends also support the party. Or it could be because you admire one of the leaders of that party, either a person from its history or someone who is in office now.

Many people join a particular party because they agree with that party's *platform*—its ideas about what government should do. They believe that the candidates of one party are more likely to act according to these ideas if they are elected. You already have such ideas about government, or you may develop these ideas later. You at some point may decide to join a different party, or even not to belong to any party. Among recent Presidents, Ronald Reagan, elected as a Republican, was a Democrat for much of his life, and Dwight Eisenhower did not formally join a political party until he began to campaign for President. Your education may give you ideas about governments and parties. It may be that your religion, your ethnic group, the place you live, or the people you associate with will determine your choice of a party. Throughout our history many people have made their choice for one or more of these reasons. But as you form ideas about what you want government to do, you will also form your selection of a political party.

Many people belong to political parties because of personal interests. Someday, you may hold a job or own a business that will be better off if one party's candidates are elected. You may want a particular government program or law that would help you. If this does happen to you, then you would support a party because of your personal interests.

Independent voters

Many people remain independent. They do not belong to or support either the Demo-

Poll the students to see which party they would identify the following professions with: medicine, factory work, education, construction, law. Why do they think as they do?

crat or Republican party. They choose to support different candidates in different elections.

In recent years, more and more people have been calling themselves independent. Today, there are even more independents than there are Republicans. But even though there are more Democrats than anything else, Republicans have still elected presidents recently—in fact they have won five of the last eight elections. This means that although people consider themselves members of a certain party, they may not always vote for the candidate of that party in a national election, but do so only in local elections.

Check for Understanding: Now that you have read this section, you should be able to answer these questions:

1. What is the meaning of the term "primary election"?
2. What is the main function of the national convention?
3. What are three reasons why people join a particular political party?
4. Are there more Democrats or more Republicans in the U.S. at this time?

HOW ARE CITIZENS INVOLVED IN ELECTIONS?

Objectives: After you have read this section, you should be able to:

- Describe the events in a typical election campaign.
- Explain what is the most important factor in a campaign.
- Define the phrase "accepting majority rule."

Campaign techniques in a Presidential election include banners, songs, posters, and promotional items such as bumper stickers, shopping bags, and balloons.

Ask students if they have ever worked on a political campaign or if they think they ever would. Why or why not?

Campaign buttons have been a popular device for many years in Presidential elections.

Listening to the candidates

Party candidates are selected in primary elections or conventions. Then the campaign for the general election begins. Candidates for President will run for office across the nation. Governors will travel across the states. All candidates for office will try to see and talk to the people that may vote for them. The purpose of the campaign is to bring the candidates and the issues before the people. The nominees make many speeches. Often the members of their families travel around making speeches as well. Every voter has an opportunity to hear the candidates, in person or over the radio or television, and to read about their speeches in the newspapers. Today television is the main way in which the candidates are brought before the people. The media and opinion polls greatly influence people in modern elections. In a presidential election millions of dollars will be spent placing a candidate in office.

Studying the issues

An election campaign involves many things. You will see TV commercials, speeches, posters, and bumper stickers. These are used to get people to vote for candidates. But the most important part of a campaign is the issues—what each candidate thinks about government. Issues also mean what the candidate will do if elected to office—what do they promise to do or not do. These issues should be studied by voters. This is the reason you should support one candidate over the other. If you think about it, you will see that bumper stickers and posters are not good reasons to vote for any candidate.

A presidential campaign is one of the most exciting events in our government. But soon it is over. The party has done all it can do. It is now time for the people to vote and to select their President. Citizens watch TV and listen to the radio to find out the election results. They are observing the historic act of a free people selecting their government.

Accepting majority rule

In some countries the losing parties refuse to accept defeat. They try to gain power by using military force. In the United States the people accept the results of an election. The entire country accepts the will of the majority. The successful candidates are sworn into the various offices, from that of President of the United States to the lowest city or county elective office.

The value of political parties

The major parties help to unite the voters. They bring together people who share some of the same beliefs. To gain votes, parties

Issues in Civics: An election campaign often costs a lot of money. Do students think it's fair that a candidate with a lot of money can do more TV spots, etc., than a candidate with less money?

Party Affiliation				
Year	Democratic	Republican	Independent	President's Party
1952	42%	34%	24%	Republican
1956	47%	33%	20%	Republican
1960	48%	30%	22%	Democratic
1964	50%	27%	23%	Democratic
1968	45%	28%	27%	Republican
1972	43%	28%	29%	Republican
1976	41%	21%	38%	Democratic
1980	50%	20%	30%	Republican

make the choices simpler. Parties also help to build an interest in public affairs. Thousands of people go to work in campaigns for the candidates of their choice. Jobs may be given to those who work hard to elect a candidate. Also, people from minority groups have been able to move upward through their work in political parties. The things we believe in as a people have been emphasized through the political process. We make public decisions about what we want when we vote for a political candidate. Finally, parties make it easier to hold the winning candidates accountable to the public for their actions while in office. The "outs" see to it that the "ins" do not forget their promises.

Check for Understanding: Now that you have completed this section, you should be able to answer these questions:

1. What is the most important form of communication in a typical election campaign?
2. What should be the most important factor in a campaign?
3. What is meant by the phrase "accepting majority rule"?
4. What are four things that political parties contribute to our nation?

SUMMARY

The United States has always been primarily a two-party country. Its two major political parties play a very important role in our government. Though third parties have existed, they have won very few elections. However, they help win acceptance for new ideas and practices. Each political party has an organization on the local, state, and national levels. The voters of each party participate in the nomination of party candidates for office through primary elections which are held in many states. The party candidates for President and Vice-President are nominated at the national conventions. The party's platform, or statement of principles, is also written at the convention. Political parties serve to unify the voters by offering them choices.

Ask students if they think that political parties can actually make a winning candidate keep his or her campaign promises. Why or why not?

BUILDING SKILLS IN CIVICS

THINKING SKILLS

1. What disagreement about Washington's presidency gave rise to the two-party system?
2. What advantage does a two-party system have over a multi-party system?
3. What is the major function of each of these party offices?
   precinct captain
   state central committee
   national committee
4. Choose the title that you think best fits the paragraph:
   In the United States the people accept the results of an election as final. The defeated party does not try to force its way into power when the successful candidates are sworn into the various offices.

   Plurality   Runoff   Majority Rule

VOCABULARY SKILLS

Some of the underlined words in the sentences below are used correctly, others are not. If the sentence is correct, write True. If it is not, replace the word with the best choice from the list.

precinct	plurality	primary	nominee
majority	third party	runoff	

1. A majority is more than one half of the votes.
2. People who differ with the two major parties have the right to form a third party.
3. A candidate with more votes than any other candidate, even though the number is not a majority, has a runoff.
4. The party's choice to run in an election is called the third party.
5. In a primary election, the voters cast ballots to nominate a candidate for their own party.
6. If no candidate has received a majority, a runoff election is held.
7. The most basic unit of party organization is the nominee.

STUDY SKILLS—USING AN ENCYCLOPEDIA

An *encyclopedia* is a reference work that provides basic information about either general subjects, in which case it covers all fields, or about a specific subject, in which case it covers every part of one subject. Although information in most encyclopedias is arranged in straight alphabetical order, the best way to start using one is by looking at the index, which tells you how the information in that set is arranged. If the set you are using is in straight alphabetical order, look at the spine of each volume until you find the one that includes the first letter of your topic. For example, if you are doing research on the Democratic party, look for the volume that starts before 'De-' and ends after it. In some encyclopedias each letter has its own volume, so you would simply look in the volume labeled 'D.' However, others do not end a volume at the end of a letter. In one leading encyclopedia you would have to look in the volume "Deccan - Electron," in another "Conifer - Diseases."

Activities:

1. Choose an encyclopedia to look up either the subject "Republican Party" or "Democratic Party."
2. How many pages of information are there? How much space is devoted to the history of the party? How much to its current activities?
3. What illustrations are used? Why were they chosen?
4. What are the cross-references to other subjects?
5. According to the index, where else is the subject discussed in the encyclopedia?

BEYOND THE BOOK

1. Use the card catalog to find books about American elections. What words did you look up in order to find your information? Did the catalog give cross-references? How did they help you?
2. Interview someone who has worked for a political party at the local level. Find out what his or her responsibilities were. How did these local responsibilities relate to the larger party?
3. Write a letter to the editor of your school or local newspaper that will convince people to become actively involved in an upcoming election.

CHAPTER TEN TEST

VOCABULARY CHECK

Fill in each blank with the word that best completes the sentence.

1. A ______ is more than half of the votes cast. (plurality - majority)
2. People who don't agree with the two major parties may join a/an ______ party (extra-legal - third)
3. A ______ is the party's choice to be its candidate for a certain office. (platform - nominee)
4. Members of a party hold ______ elections to select a nominee for an office. (precincts - primary)
5. A ______ means that a candidate received more votes than any other candidate. (plurality - majority)
6. In some elections, when no candidate receives a majority of votes, a ______ is held between the two highest vote-getters. (runoff - precinct)
7. The smallest voting district is called a ______. (precinct - platform)

COMPREHENSION CHECK

Write True if the question and answer match. If they do not, write a statement that answers the question.

1. What does the Constitution say about political parties? —The Constitution does not have any mention of political parties at all.
2. What debate about Washington's use of power started the two-party system in America? —Washington gave the new nation a sense of unity, and helped people rise above party factions.
3. How could the existence of several major political parties make electing a president difficult? —A president must win by a majority of electoral votes, and this could be difficult if we had many major parties.
4. How can you become a member of a political party? —Anyone can become a member of a political party by supporting the party and its candidates.

SKILL BUILDERS—INTERPRETING GRAPHS

Pictoral *graphs* such as the one below are especially effective for showing relationships and making comparisons.

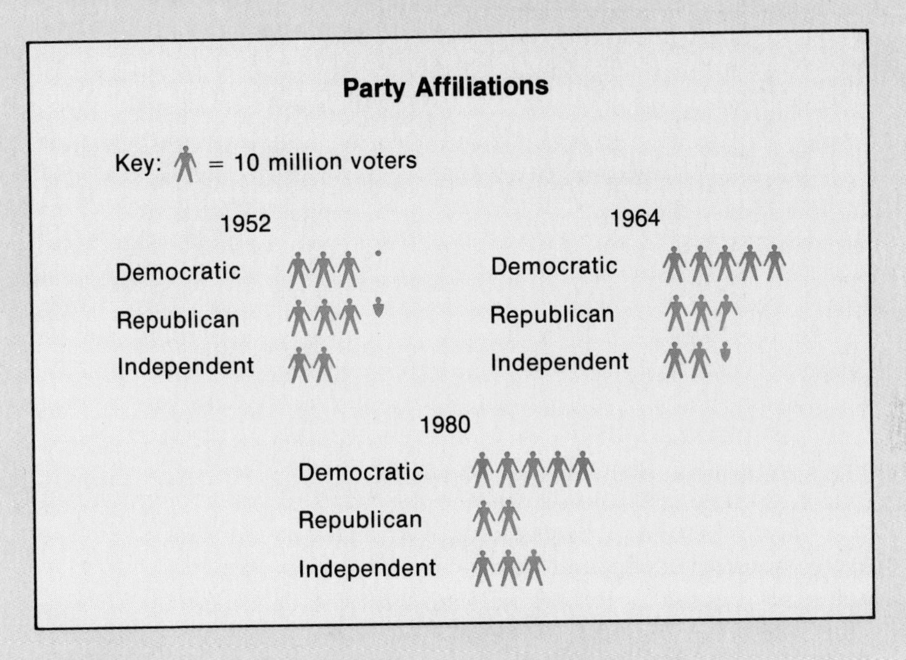

Activity: Answer the following questions about this graph.

1. What does the title tell us?
2. What is the purpose of the figures of people?
3. How many voters does each figure stand for?
4. What does each row of figures show?
5. What are three questions that the graph could help us answer?
6. What generalizations can you make from the data in this graph?

BUILDING WRITING SKILLS

1. Why do you think it is important for a citizen to study the issues before casting a vote?
2. What issues would you consider important if you were running for school office?

Chapter Eleven
Running in an Election

Document: The Constitution of the United States

Article I, Section 2: The House of Representatives shall be composed of Members chosen every second Year by the People of the several States, and the Electors in each State shall have the Qualifications requisite for Electors of the most numerous Branch of the State Legislature.

No person shall be a Representative who shall not have attained to the Age of twenty five Years, and been seven Years a Citizen of the United States, and who shall not, when elected, be an Inhabitant of that State in which he shall be chosen.

Article I, Section 3: The Senate of the United States shall be composed of two Senators from each State, chosen . . . for six Years; and each Senator shall have one Vote.

No person shall be a Senator who shall not have attained to the Age of thirty Years, and been nine Years a Citizen of the United States, and who shall not, when elected, be an Inhabitant of that State for which he shall be chosen.

Article I, Section 4: The Times, Places and Manner of holding Elections for Senators and Representatives, shall be prescribed in each State by the Legislature thereof; but the Congress may at any time by Law make or alter such Regulations, . . .

The picture shows several politicians from our nation's history campaigning for the highest office in the land. Ask students if they are aware of the time and expense involved in a Presidential campaign and the months of planning that precede one.

In a democracy such as the United States, voters elect national, state, county, and local officials. As you can see, there are laws regarding eligibility requirements for candidates as well as laws pertaining to the method and manner of holding elections.

Running for office has changed over the years as a result of the many legal and technological changes in our society. The various forms of the broadcast media allow a candidate to be seen and heard by thousands of people, and air travel allows candidates to visit many different regions of the country in one day. Legal changes have also led to changing campaign practices. During the 1970's, many states enacted strict regulation of campaign funds, requiring campaign organizations to keep accurate records of contributions and expenses.

FOCUSING IDEAS

- In many states, a person who wants to be a candidate for office must file by petition or pay a filing fee.
- A person can organize a successful campaign by using careful strategy and by enlisting the help of a competent campaign manager.
- Issues are important to a campaign because they often inspire a person to run for office, and, in turn, influence voters' decisions.
- A campaign is a time-consuming and expensive undertaking involving public contact, fundraising, and the enlistment of volunteers.

The complete text of the Constitution can be found in the Appendix, beginning on page 564.

Issues in Civics: Discuss with your students the ways in which technological changes have affected political campaigns over the years.

PRE-TEST

1. How does a person become a candidate for office?
2. How is an election campaign organized?
3. How are issues involved in a campaign?
4. What is involved in an actual campaign?

HOW DOES A PERSON BECOME A CANDIDATE?

Objectives: After you have read this section, you will be able to:

- Describe how one typical candidate chose his political party.
- Explain the candidate's reason for changing parties.
- List two ways a candidate can file for office.

Elections are probably the most exciting part of government. They are also the most important part of government. All governments say that they govern for the people, but this can only be true if officials come into office by free elections, where citizens have a choice to vote for whom they please among the candidates. Since elections are so important, the following story is also an important part of your understanding of citizenship and government.

Mary Gentry was taking a civics class at Clinton High School. A general election campaign was going on, and while the class was talking about elections, they realized there were a lot of things they didn't know. Mary said, "A friend of my family is a candidate for the state legislature. His name is Kermit Ross. He's the Republican candidate. If he would let me talk to him and spend some time with him during the campaign, I could report back to the class about what I found out."

Mary volunteered to interview a local candidate for office as a project for her Civics class.

Building vocabulary:
petition *(177)* • campaign manager *(178)* • strategy *(179)* • incumbent *(179)* • push card *(179)* • liberal *(181)* • conservative *(181)* • donor *(183)*

Ask students to think of a time when they voted in a school election. On what basis did they make their voting choices? Do they regret the choices they made?

Choosing a political party

The teacher and the rest of the class agreed, so the next day after school, Mary and her friend Sam Elliott met with Mr. Ross. One of the first questions they asked was why he decided to run for the state legislature. Mr. Ross replied, "It started a long time before this election, when I first became interested in government and politics. I grew up as a Democrat, because of my father. He was a factory worker and always voted Democratic. He still does today, and he always thought I'd end up as a Democrat too."

Mr. Ross continued: "After I got out of college, I went into business with my older brother. I still considered myself to be a Democrat, but as I began to get more interested in politics, I decided to become a Republican. As a small businessman, I agree more with the way Republicans think about government and the things they want to do. Of course, I don't always agree with all their policies. But I do agree enough of the time that I decided to join the Republican party, even before I decided to run for office myself."

Filing for office

"But how do you run for the legislature?" asked Sam. "Do you just tell the party you want to be their candidate?"

"Actually, no," Ross replied, "You have to follow a procedure to become a candidate. In our state you file in one of two ways. Either you pay a filing fee of $400, or you file by *petition*. To file by petition, you have to have 200 or more registered voters sign the petition for you as a candidate. I decided to file by petition, because I didn't want to spend $400 that I could use in my campaign instead. That's the way I became a candidate."

Mary meets with Kermit Ross at the school.

"So that's the way you first became a candidate," said Sam. "You're wrong again," said Mr. Ross. "I ran for the legislature four years ago. I lost to the Democratic candidate. That's why I decided to run my campaign in a different way this time. Come back tomorrow and we'll talk about that."

Check for Understanding: Now that you have completed this section, you should be able to answer these questions:

1. How did Kermit Ross choose his first political party?
2. Why did he change parties later?
3. What are two ways a candidate can file for office?
4. Which did Mr. Ross choose, and why?

Issues in Civics: Certain political figures in our nation's history have changed political parties during their careers. Can students understand what might cause a politician to do this?

HOW IS A CAMPAIGN ORGANIZED?

Objectives: When you have read this section, you will be able to:

- Describe the role of a campaign manager.
- Explain the meaning of the term "campaign strategy."
- Outline the major issues in one candidate's strategy.

A candidate's strategy

The next day Sam and Mary met again with Mr. Ross to learn about his campaign experience. "Well," said Mr. Ross, "Four years ago, I ran the campaign myself. I decided everything that would be done—what my posters would look like, where I would make speeches, and what would be on radio and TV. Maybe that's why I lost," he said, and laughed. "Many candidates run their own campaign," he continued. "But they have to know a lot about politics and elections. I was new and inexperienced, so I guess I didn't do a good job. Anyway, this time I decided to do it differently. I decided to go out and hire a professional manager."

The campaign manager

"Sometime you'll meet the man I'm talking about, Bob Kane. He's my *campaign manager*," said Mr. Ross. "He's running three campaigns for three different candidates this time, and he spends two days a week with me."

Mary asked, "What do you mean when you say you 'hired' Mr. Kane?"

"I signed two agreements," replied Mr. Ross. "One was a contract. It says that I'll pay him to manage the campaign. I told you I didn't have much money. So Mr. Kane agreed to have me owe him the money and pay him over time. The other was a management agreement. It says what each of us is to do during the campaign. I decide what I'm going to say about all the issues. Bob Kane won't give his own opinion on these issues, or try to influence my thinking. In this way, I'm my own person."

Mr. Ross continued: "The agreement does say, however, that Bob Kane will tell me when to use each issue. He'll tell me to speak about one issue or another. He'll also tell me which issues to emphasize and which to make less important. The agreement also says that Bob Kane will design all my campaign materials—all my cards, posters, bumper stickers, as well as my radio and TV commercials. It also calls for me to do everything he says to do throughout the election. He's in complete charge of me during the campaign."

"He really is in charge of everything. But why does he want so much control?" asked Mary.

"You can ask him that two days from now," said Mr. Ross, "He'll be in town, and you can ask him questions."

Selecting a strategy

The next time Sam and Mary went to see Mr. Ross, they got to meet Bob Kane, and they found out how he was managing the campaign.

"I know a lot about elections," said Mr. Kane. "I've run campaigns for both Democrats and Republicans. Issues are important to me, but what's more important is a candidate that I like—one that I think will do a good job in office. I've won more elections than I've lost, because I do a good job of figuring out what makes people decide to vote for a certain candidate. I like to believe that I always know the right strategy to use."

Have an interested student interview a local campaign manager or other campaign worker to find out the nature of his or her duties.

Sam visited the headquarters of another candidate, Jim Bates.

"What do you mean by strategy?" asked Mary.

"*Strategy*," said Mr. Kane, "means the important things you're trying to do all through the campaign. It means the way you plan the campaign in order to win. In this campaign Kermit Ross has three big problems. First, he's not very well known. Few people knew him before he decided to run. Second, his opponent, Bill Hancock, is an *incumbent*. Incumbent means that Mr. Hancock is already in office—he was elected to the legislature in the last election. Finally, the third thing is that we have very little money to spend. Kermit can't buy much radio and TV time, because it's very expensive. Those are the things we have to look at," said Bob Kane.

"It sounds really gloomy for Mr. Ross," said Sam. "How do you win an election when people don't know him but do know his incumbent opponent and you don't have much money to spend?

Bob Kane laughed. "Well, it certainly isn't going to be easy," he said. "But we have our strategy—something to deal with each of those three problems. First, we're running a door-to-door campaign. Every evening Mr. Ross walks from house to house. He knocks on the door and introduces himself. He talks to the people at home and asks them to vote for him. In this way people will get to know him."

"And of course," said Mary, "that doesn't cost much money."

"That's right," replied Mr. Kane, "You remembered that one important thing is that we don't have much money. And it doesn't cost money for Mr. Ross to walk the streets. We only spend a little money on push cards."

"Push cards," asked Sam, "What are those?"

"Those are little calling cards. They have Mr. Ross' name and picture on them. Mr. Ross hands them out when he calls on people at home and whenever he talks to anyone. We call them *push cards* because he is always pushing them into someone's hands. That is another way of getting people to see the name of Kermit Ross."

"I see now how you are getting Mr. Ross' name to be known and without spending too much money," said Mary. "But what are you doing about the fact that Mr. Hancock is an incumbent? That's also part of your strategy."

"Let's save that one for later," said Mr. Kane. "Why don't you come with me tomorrow while our candidate makes some speeches?"

Have students discuss the strategy that *they* would use if they were directing the campaign of a candidate for office. Would they use the same methods mentioned here?

Check for Understanding: Now that you have completed this section, you should be able to answer these questions:

1. What is the role of a campaign manager?
2. What is campaign strategy?
3. What are the three main problems that face Kermit Ross in his campaign for election?
4. How has Bob Kane decided to deal with one of these problems?

HOW ARE ISSUES INVOLVED IN A CAMPAIGN?

Objectives: When you have read this section, you will be able to:

- Define the terms "conservative" and "liberal."
- Explain the difference between conservative and liberal thinking on a particular issue.
- Give two reasons why candidates in an election often talk only a little about each issue.

The next day, Sam and Mary were excused from school to spend the whole day with Mr. Ross. Early in the morning they went to a breakfast group where Mr. Ross talked for about fifteen minutes. Then they went to a recording studio. Mr. Ross recorded a campaign commercial to be used on the radio. It was very short. It would run for less than a minute. At noon, Mr. Ross talked before another group. His opponent, Mr. Hancock, was also there. Each man talked for ten minutes. Finally, they went to a neighborhood meeting in the afternoon. One of Mr. Ross' friends had invited some neighbors in to listen to him. Again Mr. Ross talked for only a few minutes.

Then it was almost time for Mr. Ross to go out on his door-to-door walking tour. But before he left, he asked, "Do you have any questions about today?"

"Yes," said Mary, "In class we're always told that issues are the most important thing in an election. Today you talked about the

Kermit Ross and his opponent Bill Hancock held a televised debate at a local studio.

Have students discuss the issues that are important to them in their community. Are these issues being dealt with to their satisfaction? Why or why not?

state's problems—about taxes, schools, highways, water, and other things. But, you didn't say that much about what you would do about these issues. And Mr. Hancock didn't say what he would do, either. Why don't candidates talk more about the issues?"

"You have a point," said Mr. Ross. "I'm sure you knew that this is one of the main things people criticize us for during the campaign. But there are good reasons for this. For one, we have only a little time to talk at each place. There are many issues, and only a few minutes to speak about them. This means we can't spend too much time on any one thing."

"Also," continued Mr. Ross, "some issues are very difficult to deal with in a short time. They're just too complicated. Finally, some people are very concerned about one problem or issue. Others may be mainly interested in another issue. And all these people are in the same audience. You can't talk about all the things that are important to all the people in just a few minutes."

"I understand," said Sam, "You mention an issue. Then you say a little bit about it."

"That's right," continued Mr. Ross. "People listen to find out if candidates know about issues. They also want to have some idea about how candidates feel about them. That's about all you can do in a short time."

Using a general approach

"Mr. Ross," said Mary, "When you talked about your opponent, you called Mr. Hancock your 'liberal opponent'. What do you mean by that?"

Mr. Ross replied, "When people think about government, their attitude can generally be described in one of two ways—liberal or conservative."

"*Liberals* generally want society to change, and they want the government to act to bring about this change. Often liberals want a larger role for government, a more centralized national government, and more government spending. *Conservatives*, on the other hand, generally want less change in society than liberals do, and they believe that if change is to take place, it should not be by government action, but by other means. Conservatives often want a smaller role for government, a more decentralized national government, and less government spending."

"Of course," Mr. Ross continued, "these are simple definitions, and life—and politics—aren't always that simple. But generally, the people who consider themselves to be conservatives will think in the same way on a certain issue. In the same way, liberals usually think in the same way about issues."

"Oh, I understand," said Sam, "when you call Mr. Hancock your 'liberal opponent' you're talking about his general attitude about all the issues."

"That's right, in a way," said Mr. Ross. "It means that he will usually agree with one group of people on an issue. They will usually try to solve a problem through a new government program. That is generally the liberal approach. I will usually agree with the other group. I will generally try to solve that same problem by some method that does not increase the government's power and does not cost more tax money. This is generally the conservative approach."

The importance of issues

"All right, I understand that saying a candidate is a liberal or a conservative is a way of talking about all the issues at once," said

Do your students consider themselves to be liberals or conservatives, or neither? Have them explain the labels they apply to themselves.

Sam. "Still, I'm not really convinced that issues are important in a campaign."

"I can see why you might think that way," said Mr. Ross. "Candidates don't mention specific issues that much on radio, TV, or posters. But still, they are very important to us. For example, it was my concern over the issues that made me decide to become a candidate. I'm concerned about the problems in our state, and I want to see them solved in certain ways. That's why I'm a candidate today."

Mr. Ross continued: "When I meet people who ask me about an issue, I give them all of the time I have to tell them what I think. I don't have much time in speeches, but if people want to talk about an issue face to face, I'll do it. A hard part of being a candidate is to talk with a group that disagrees with you. The other day I met with a group of workers in a plant. They want a certain law to be passed because they think it will provide more jobs. But I'm against that law—I think it will hurt business instead of helping it. If I said I agreed with them, I might win some votes. Anyway, I told them I didn't agree with them, but asked them to vote for me anyway. A candidate can't keep changing his position on the issues just to please the people he happens to be talking to at the time."

Check for Understanding: Now that you have completed this section, you should be able to answer these questions:

1. What are three main differences between conservatives and liberals in their attitude toward the role of government in society?
2. How do liberals usually think change should take place in society? What about conservatives?
3. What are two reasons why candidates don't give a lot of time to a particular issue?
4. According to Mr. Ross, how should the issues influence a candidate as he talks to the voters?

WHAT IS INVOLVED IN AN ACTUAL CAMPAIGN?

Objectives: After you have read this section, you will be able to:

- List four ways that money is spent during a campaign.
- List four ways that candidates can raise money.
- Describe the final stages of a campaign.

Sam and Mary decided to stay and help Mr. Ross with his campaign. Sam's job was to put letters about Mr. Ross into envelopes. Mary's job was to address the envelopes. She copied names and addresses from a list of voters. The two students started to talk.

"You know," said Sam, "It obviously takes a lot of money for a campaign. These letters had to be printed; then there's the cost of the envelopes and postage. And think of all the posters and the bumper stickers. And I haven't mentioned the really expensive things—radio and TV commercials. They'll cost hundreds of dollars, even though they're only a few seconds long on the air."

"That's right," said Mary. "And then there are other costs. There's the rent on this headquarters office. And we can't forget the payment to Mr. Kane. Mr. Ross will owe that, even if he isn't paying it now."

Issues in Civics: Some politicians have been accused of "waffling" on the issues—that is, changing one's opinions on an issue depending on who one is talking to. What do students think of this?

Sam said, "And even with all of this money being spent, he may not win the election. I wonder where it all comes from. Let's see if we can ask someone."

The students were lucky. Mrs. Sutton was in the office; she was Mr. Ross' campaign treasurer. The treasurer is responsible for keeping track of how money is received and spent during a campaign. She talked with Sam and Mary: "We raised the money in many ways. In the beginning, Mr. Ross borrowed some money from a bank. He'll have to pay that back at some point. After that we sent out letters to friends of Mr. Ross and to many Republicans. We asked them to give a donation. This brought in a little money. But we still needed more for the campaign.

"Then," Mrs. Sutton continued, "Mr. Ross and I went to some big *donors*. These are wealthy people who usually support conservative or Republican candidates. These people know the state laws on campaign contributions. If they give more than fifty dollars, we must report it. Everyone can find out how much they give. People may even read about it in the newspaper. Still, many of them supported Mr. Ross' ideas. Some of them gave large amounts of money. We also went to the state Republican Committee," said Mrs. Sutton. "They raise money from all over the state. They use some of it to support certain candidates. The committee gave some money to our campaign."

"Finally, we held a fund raising dinner. A nationally important Republican Congressman volunteered to come to town. He has many supporters and friends; in fact, he might even become the Republican candidate for President some day. The charge was 150 dollars for each plate. Of course, most of the money went for Mr. Ross' campaign and not for food. But people came to show their support for Mr. Ross and the Congressman. They also wanted to meet the Congressman. This raised more money for the campaign. In these ways, we raised quite a bit of money," finished Mrs. Sutton. "But there will still be a debt left over after the campaign. It takes a lot of money to run for political office in this country."

Sam and Mary were very excited. Today was election day! They had spent time with Mr. Ross. They had worked as volunteers. Soon they would know the result of the election. The students spent the day with Mr. Ross. They went to all the polls, or voting places. They traveled in a car that was covered with "Ross for Legislature" poster and bumper stickers.

Mr. Ross shook many hands. He asked people to vote for him. Sam and Mary

Running a campaign calls for many different kinds of expenses.

Why do students think that some newspapers print the names of donors and the amounts that they contribute to certain political candidates?

Methods of Campaigning

Door–to–Door Tours

Debates

Public Appearances

Advertisements and Commercials

Fund-Raising Dinners

Campaign Materials

Which of the methods of campaigning shown on this page do students think is the least effective? Most effective? Why do they think as they do?

handed out "push cards." They said, "Please vote for Kermit Ross." This went on all day. At seven o'clock, the polls closed. Then they all went back to the headquarters to watch the results on TV.

The TV news reported the results of many elections, including that for President. But the people at Ross headquarters wanted most to know about the Ross-Hancock election.

At nine o'clock, Mr. Hancock was ahead by about 500 votes. But Bob Kane wasn't worried. "The precincts that will go for us haven't all reported yet," he said. Finally, by ten-thirty in the evening, the final results were in. The vote was:

Kermit Ross—16,839
Bill Hancock—15,587

Kermit Ross had won the election by 1,252 votes. He had defeated his incumbent opponent. Kermit Ross was the new Republican representative in the state legislature.

Check for Understanding: Now that you have completed this section, you should be able to answer these questions:

1. What are four different things that candidates spend money on during an election campaign?
2. What are four ways that candidates can raise money?
3. What did Mr. Ross do on the last day of the campaign?
4. Do you think that Bob Kane's strategy was the main reason why Mr. Ross won the election?

SUMMARY

Individuals in the U.S. often change from one political party to another. As people grow older and their lives change they find their interests are no longer best served by the party they preferred when they were younger, or the party their parents preferred.

There are certain procedures that must be followed for an individual to run for public office. These procedures differ from state to state.

Although many candidates for public office run their own campaign, others have a campaign manager. The job of the campaign manager is to help the candidate plan an effective campaign strategy that will make it possible for the office seeker to overcome weaknesses. It is not the job of the campaign manager to control the candidate. This relationship is usually agreed to in a contract.

In general, people who follow conservative political thinking tend to resist change and to believe that if change is to take place, it should not be through government action. They prefer limited government, are against centralization, and resist spending government money. Liberal politicians tend to want a larger role for government, a more centralized national government, and increased government spending. They believe that government can act to cause change for the better.

Expenses for a campaign for public office include such things as postage, bumper stickers, radio or TV commercials, office space, and the services of advisers. In order to meet these expenses a candidate must raise money, such as by borrowing, by getting contributions from wealthy donors or from the political party; or by having large fund-raising events.

Ask students if they know how votes are cast in their towns' elections—by written ballot, by voting machines, etc.?

BUILDING SKILLS IN CIVICS

THINKING SKILLS

1. What are the two ways to file for office? Name one advantage and one disadvantage of each method.
2. What is a campaign strategy? Why is strategy essential to a successful campaign?
3. What are the two main points the following items describe? Which items belong with which point?
   a. cost of postage and printing
   b. campaign manager's salary
   c. donations and contributions
   d. special dinner where the cost of a plate far exceeds the price of food
   e. TV and radio commercials
   f. state committee's fund
4. Make a list of the campaign activities you can identify in the illustration on page 184. Which ones are the most expensive? Which ones reach a large group? Which ones depend on individual contact?

VOCABULARY SKILLS

Match each term with its definition. If you need help, use the Glossary.

a. strategy	b. conservative	c. liberal	d. incumbent
e. campaign manager	f. push card	g. petition	h. donor

1. An inexpensive calling card that candidates for public office give to voters.
2. A person who is generally against a large, centralized government and who believes that social change should not come from government action.
3. The way a campaign is planned in order to win.
4. The candidate's campaign planner.
5. An office holder.

6. A person who is generally in favor of social change through government action and who wants to increase the authority of the central government.
7. Wealthy people who support candidates.
8. To file in this way, a candidate must get a certain number of voters to sign for him or her.

STUDY SKILLS—RECOGNIZING TECHNIQUES OF PERSUASION

During a campaign, many *techniques of persuasion* are used to influence a citizen to vote for a particular candidate. Which of the following were included in this chapter. Which have you seen used? Which would you select to use if you were a candidate for a school office? Which are most likely to be used in a local election? For the election of the President?

1. Television and Radio
2. Newspaper and Magazines
3. Songs and Slogans
4. Inexpensive Advertisements
5. Opinion Polls
6. Personal Appearance Tours

BEYOND THE BOOK

1. Call the League of Women Voters to get information on the work they do. Give an oral report about it.
2. Call or write local radio and TV stations and newspapers to find out how much political advertising costs. Prepare a chart comparing radio and TV rates per minute with the newspaper rate per page.
3. Interview, or read an article about, someone who works in the advertising business. Find out what can be done to get a reader's attention. Find ads that use these techniques in newspapers and magazines. Show these to your classmates and find out which techniques they feel are the most effective. Use one of the techniques to create a poster for a candidate for school office.

CHAPTER ELEVEN TEST

VOCABULARY CHECK

Some of the underlined words in the sentences below are used correctly; others are not. If the sentence is correct, write True. If it is not, replace the word with the best choice from the list.

strategy	conservative	liberal	push cards
incumbent	petition	donor	campaign manager

1. The conservative position generally wants government to change society, and to be bigger and to spend more money.
2. Candidates give people push cards as a reminder of their campaign.
3. The conservative position is generally in favor of a decentralized federal government that spends less money.
4. A campaign strategy defines the key issues a candidate will stress and how he or she will work to win.
5. A liberal candidate is one that was elected to the office in the previous election and is already known by the voters.
6. One way to become a candidate for office is to file by strategy.
7. Sometimes, wealthy donors support political candidates.
8. A donor is the person who runs a candidate's campaign.

COMPREHENSION CHECK

1. Article VI of the Constitution says that an official will ______.
   a. be bound by oath to support the Constitution.
   b. be a member of an established political party.
2. Which of the following is *not* a way to become a candidate?
   a. complete a management agreement
   b. pay a filing fee
   c. file a signed petition
3. True or False: In most of his speeches, Mr. Ross spent a long time explaining the issues.
4. True or False: By law, the source of large amounts of money must be public information.
5. True or False: The candidate that spends the most money always wins the election.

SKILL BUILDERS—ANALYZING AN ADVERTISEMENT

Political *advertising* uses many of the same techniques used in commercial advertising. One of these is "prestige by association." The advertisement tries to persuade you to buy a product because it is associated with someone you like, admire, or respect.

Activity: This is a campaign poster from the 1908 Presidential election. Use it to answer these questions:

1. Who is running for President and for Vice President?
2. What do the initials G.O.P. stand for?
3. Which of the names around the picture do you recognize?
4. What association is the voter supposed to make?

BUILDING WRITING SKILLS

Make a list of some issues you would want a future President to take a stand on. Choose one issue, describe both sides of it, and indicate which position you think is the better one.

Chapter Twelve
People Influence Their Government

Document: The Constitution of the United States

Amendment XIX, Section 1. The right of citizens of the United States to vote shall not be denied or abridged by the United States or by any States on account of sex.

Amendment XV, Section 1. The right of citizens of the United States to vote shall not be denied or abridged by the United States or by any State on account of race, color, or previous condition of servitude.

Amendment XXIV, Section 1. The right of citizens of the United States to vote in any primary or other election for President or Vice-President, for electors for Vice-President or President, or for Senator or Representative in Congress, shall not be denied or abridged by the United States or any State by reason of failure to pay any poll tax or other tax.

Amendment XXVI, Section 1. The right of citizens of the United States, who are eighteen years of age or older, to vote shall not be denied or abridged by the United States or by any State on account of age.

Voting is a direct act of participation in government and one of the most important rights that American citizens possess. Amendments

The picture shows one of the ways in which people can influence their government. Ask students if they can think of any other means of influence.

The complete text of the Constitution can be found in the Appendix, beginning on page 564.

that have been added to the Constitution broaden the rights of citizens by preventing voting discrimination due to sex, race, or age. The Constitution allows each state to set qualifications for voting as long as these qualifications do not violate the Constitution.

Voting is one of the best ways for people to participate in government because it allows them to choose who will govern, and so, have an affect on the laws that are proposed or rejected. Unfortunately, many eligible voters in the United States rarely vote or only vote if they have something to gain from a particular election. To derive maximum benefits from our voting rights, *all* citizens should partake in elections of public officials.

FOCUSING IDEAS

- Voting differs from influence in that it is a direct act of government participation rather than an indirect one.
- Political parties influence government through the use of persuasion, contributions, and through the denial of certain privileges.
- Economic, public, and single interest groups influence government.
- Lobbyists try to influence government officials by providing them with information and by organizing public opinion campaigns.

The picture shows a possible result of citizen participation in government—a speech being given by a politician on the issues brought up by her constituents. Ask students if they were aware of the influence each citizen can have on government.

PRE-TEST

1. What is the difference between voting for officials and influencing those officials?
2. How do political parties influence government?
3. Which special-interest groups have an influence on government?
4. What is the role of lobbyists in our government?

WHAT IS THE DIFFERENCE BETWEEN VOTING AND INFLUENCE?

Objectives: After you have read this section, you will be able to:
- Define the term "influence."
- Distinguish between direct participation in government and indirect participation.
- Understand the arguments for and against influence in government.

You have been reading and studying about ways that people participate directly in their government. They do this by belonging to a political party, by voting, and by being candidates for office. Campaigns and elections decide who will become the officials in government. And people make this decision by voting.

After the election is over, how do people continue to participate in government?

Do people have anything to say about how officials will act and what they will do once they have been elected?

Do people have anything to say about which laws are passed and how these laws are enforced once they have elected their officials?

These are important questions concerning your government, and they are what you will read about in this chapter.

Voting as direct participation

When you use your right as a citizen to vote, you are participating directly in government. Once you have voted, you have little other direct participation in government. You obey laws, exercise your rights, and meet your responsibilities, but you cannot say directly which laws are made and you cannot say directly how they should be enforced.

Once officials have been elected, they become representatives of the people. You have read that our government is called a representative republic. Those elected to office are to represent you and all citizens in making laws and enforcing them.

Influencing as indirect participation

Many citizens still have *indirect participation* in government. They do this by influencing elected officials. To *influence* means

---

Building vocabulary:
indirect participation *(192)* • influence *(192)* • insurgent *(195)* • interest group *(196)* • lobbyist *(199)* • opinion campaign *(200)* • opinion poll *(201)*

Issues in Civics: Should a representative of the people vote according to the wishes of his or her constituents or according to his or her own beliefs? Discuss this issue with your students.

to get somebody to think as you do or act as you think they should act. People try to get elected officers to think as they do and to pass laws that they would like to see passed. They cannot directly vote for the laws but they can influence, or persuade, officials how to vote.

The role of influence

Before you read about those who use influence, put yourself in the role of a member of Congress. Imagine that you represent a district in the House of Representatives. It is almost time to vote on an important bill to help control pollution. You are convinced it is a good bill that will benefit most of the people of the country as a whole.

However, you know that the majority of the people in your own district are not in favor of this bill. These are the people you represent. They elected you to the House. You will ask them to re-elect you next year. When the time comes to vote on this bill, should you do what you think is right? Or, as a representative of the people, should you vote as they want you to?

The argument against influence

The Founding Fathers were opposed to public influence on government. They believed the people would elect the best person from their district to act for them. They wanted a true representative republic —a government in which those elected were expected to devote their full time to a study of the country's needs, without consulting the people about specific bills. The authors of the Constitution believed that most people were too busy with their own affairs to be able to study public questions as well as their representatives could. They did not want elected representatives to be influenced by outside opinions, which might or might not be well-informed.

Farmers gather in Washington, D.C. in 1981 to demonstrate against government agricultural policies.

This view was clearly expressed by George Washington. While presiding over the Constitutional Convention, he said in reference to the preparation of the Constitution, "If, to please the people, we offer what we ourselves disapprove, how can we afterward defend our work? Let us raise a standard to which the wise and honest can repair."

The argument for influence

Many people believe that it is the duty of elected representatives to do what the people think is desirable. The argument is that only in this way do the people's wishes really become law. Some officials even mail out opinion polls to the people. The polls help them to better understand what the

Have an interested student write to his or her representative in Congress to find out if there was ever a time when letters from constituents influenced the representative's views.

Which of the methods of influence shown on this page do students think is most effective? Least effective?

people want from their government and how they should vote.

No matter how you feel on the subject of influence, someone will disagree with you. The question will never be answered in a republic. Today some lawmakers make their decisions independently and will not change them. Others will always seek what the voters want. Regardless of how they feel, all elected officials will be subject to some form of influence.

Check for Understanding: Now that you have finished this section, you should be able to answer these questions:

1. What does the term "influence" mean in government?
2. What is the difference between direct and indirect influence in government?
3. What are the arguments for and against influence?
4. What were George Washington's views on influence?

HOW DO POLITICAL PARTIES INFLUENCE GOVERNMENT?

Objectives: After you have read this section, you will be able to:

- Explain why political parties try to influence the government between elections.
- Describe two ways in which the party uses its influence.
- List three ways that the President and the state governors influence lawmakers.

The party organization

Political parties are primarily interested in winning elections. But they continue to remain organized between elections. A party will try to influence members of Congress and legislatures how to vote. They will try to persuade them to vote for laws that will help the party win other elections. On very important questions, the party leadership will try to get every member of the party to vote the same way on a question. In this way, the political party's organization continues to influence government between elections.

Members of the same party often disagree. Sometimes those members who refuse to vote for the party on a particular issue are called *insurgents*. Often the party tries to punish insurgents in the hope of forcing them to be loyal. One severe punishment is to deny insurgents the right to sit on important committees or to appoint people to important offices.

Party contributions

Political parties also influence officials through the use of money. Each year the party receives money from its supporters to help its members be re-elected. The party leaders say how much will be given to each party member to spend on campaigning. They may decide not to give money to party members who do not vote according to party policy.

The influence of the President or the governors

The President of the United States, and most state governors, have three ways to influence lawmakers. The first of these is the *veto* power, or the power to refuse to sign a bill into law. By threatening to use the veto, the President or a governor may influence lawmakers to change the content of a bill or to defeat it. A second way of influencing government is through the appointment power. The President of the United States, and most governors, are able

Issues in Civics: Do students think that it's fair for party members to punish insurgents? Why or why not?

President Carter meets with Thomas Murphy (left) of General Motors and Douglas Frazier of the United Auto Workers.

to appoint people to office. Many people seek these appointments and many other people want their friends and supporters to be appointed. The President and governors can influence how laws are enforced by seeing that those who are appointed think and act as they do. They can also influence other officials who want certain people appointed. Through careful use of the appointment power, the President and governors have great influence over the way that government will work.

The President is not only head of the nation, but also head of his or her political party. In the same way, the governor is head of the state government and also head of the state's political party. The President and most governors work closely with members of their party. They can usually persuade others to follow their lead. Whenever they give speeches or hold press conferences, their words are listened to and their views are considered important. In this way the leaders of government constantly have an influence on the government.

Check for Understanding: Now that you have completed this section, you should be able to answer these questions:

1. Why do political parties try to influence the government between elections?
2. In what ways do they carry out this influence?
3. What are three ways in which the President and state governors influence lawmakers?
4. What is one way that a party reacts to its "insurgent" members?

WHICH INTEREST GROUPS INFLUENCE GOVERNMENT?

Objectives: After you have read this section, you will be able to:

- Define the term "interest group."
- List three types of interest groups
- Identify the differences between these three groups.

Economic interest groups

Few people are powerful enough to be able to influence government just by themselves. Therefore, most people influence government by belonging to or supporting *interest groups*. These are groups of people who share a common interest. They will use persuasion and arguments to see that laws are passed that favor their interest. Whatever it is they believe in or want to happen, they will do their best to see that members of Congress or legislatures support it. Economic interest groups are made up of people who earn their income in the same way. They may be labor unions repre-

Have students brainstorm to think of issues that the people in the photo might have been discussing. Do students think it's wise for a President to meet regularly with interest groups?

senting workers in many jobs. They may also be small business people who seek to try to influence government to support small business. Doctors, dentists, lawyers, and other professional people also form interest groups.

Economic interest groups often seek laws which will increase their profits, wages, and incomes. But most economic interest groups use influence in ways other than just to affect their members' incomes. Doctors, for example, will try to influence legislation concerning medicine, not only to help themselves but because they are knowledgeable about medicine and how it should be used. Labor unions support laws that they believe will help all working people. In this way, most economic interest groups believe they are working for many people, not just for their members. It is up to the elected officials to determine which of these claims are right and just, and which may be selfish.

Public, or political interest groups

Public, or political interest groups are made up of many people who have a common interest in their government. They will influence officials to support those issues that their members believe in. Public interest groups are generally different from economic groups in two ways. First, their members may be in many types of work. But they still share common thoughts about government. Second, economic interest groups such as labor unions provide many other services for their members, but most

A convention of the Anti-Slavery Society in 1840. William Lloyd Garrison was the leader of this single-issue interest group.

Have an interested student do further research on William Lloyd Garrison and the Anti-Slavery Society.

public interest groups do very little else other than try to influence government, because this is the group's main reason for existing.

Many ethnic minority groups belong to a political interest group that is concerned with the problems of that minority. Other political groups share the same general thoughts about government. They may be liberals who generally support changing government to their way of thinking. Other interest groups are conservative. They try to influence government to seek conservative answers to problems. There are many reasons why people will join public or political interest groups. But they are all trying to influence government to do those things that they believe are in the public interest, or what they believe is the best for all people. An important job for elected officials and all citizens is trying to decide if the claims of public interest groups are right and correct.

Single interest groups

Single interest groups have members who are for or against one particular issue. They will try to influence government to enforce or to pass a particular law. Single interest groups have been very important in our

Have each student choose an issue that is of particular interest to him or her and make a poster to influence people to vote according to the student's own beliefs.

nation's history. Abolitionist groups helped outlaw slavery. The women's suffrage movement made it possible for women to vote. Often a single interest group that exists to gain support for a new law will disappear if that law is passed. Other single interest groups will continue to exist over a long period of time. This is particularly true of those that are concerned with protecting a particular right. Single interest groups are different from all other interest groups in tht other groups will be concerned with many laws and many issues. Single interest groups, however, have only one issue that concerns them. They try to influence government only when that particular issue is concerned.

Check for Understanding: Now that you have completed this section, you should be able to answer these questions:

1. What is an "interest group"?
2. What are three types of interest groups?
3. What is the difference between these groups?
4. What are two ways in which interest groups have had an important influence in our history?

WHAT IS THE ROLE OF LOBBYISTS?

Objectives: After you have read this section, you will be able to:

- Explain how lobbyists are different from other citizens in influence.
- Describe how lobbyists work to influence government.
- Describe how lobbyists are controlled by law.

Lobbyists are people whose work is to try to influence government. The term comes from the fact that these people often wait in the *lobby* of a capitol building to talk to lawmakers. Lobbyists are different from other citizens who try to influence government because it is a full-time job for lobbyists. Many organizations pay lobbyists to live in Washington and in state capitals. An interest group may provide lobbyists with handsomely furnished offices and may pay them salaries greater than those of members of Congress. They are given these things because the group considers the work of the lobbyists to be very important.

Lobbyists spend much of their time talking to many officials in government. They

A lobbyist presents her organization's point of view on an upcoming legislative issue.

Ask students if they were aware that there were people who had full-time jobs as lobbyists. Does this fact surprise them? Would *they* ever want to lobby for a living?

try to provide them with information about how issues will affect members of the interest group they represent. They help officials understand what people think about the issues. Lobbyists also spend much time with their own members to help them understand the problems facing government. Sometimes lobbyists will try to influence their own members by suggesting which candidates members should vote for to protect their interests. Providing information in this way is an important part of a lobbyist's job.

Richard Viguerie and an aide go over printouts in his computerized mailing center. Viguerie mails 100 million letters a year to lawmakers on behalf of conservative interest groups.

Opinion campaigns

A lobbyist usually tries to make it appear that he or she represents many people. To do this, they often try to organize public *opinion campaigns.* They will write to members of the lobbying organization, asking them to send their representatives letters and telegrams for or against a certain bill. The organization members persuade their friends, neighbors, and employees to send more letters and telegrams. The impact of receiving thousands of letters or telegrams supporting or opposing an issue will certainly have an effect on a lawmaker's thoughts about the issue. Lobbyists buy advertising space to urge the people to write their congressmen and congresswomen. Some people feel that many lobbists really do represent public opinion. They feel their efforts can provide an effective means for making the wishes of the people known to their representatives. Others feel that an organized lobby campaign does not measure true public opinion but is an attempt to put unfair pressure on lawmakers to vote in a certain way.

Lobbyists of the national government are required by law to register and turn in reports to Congress four times a year. Most state governments have similar laws controlling lobbyists within the state. Most lobbyists must tell what money they have received and what money they have spent. In Congress, they must also report what bills they are interested in. In this way, people are aware of what lobbyists do and how honest they are in influencing government.

Public opinion

Public opinion, or what the majority of ordinary citizens believe, has the greatest influence of all, more than any lobbyist or any interest group. When the citizens become united on a subject, their government must listen. This united opinion is shown in many ways. *Opinion polls* (interviews with a number of people), letters to Congress, public speakers, sermons in churches, television, and radio and newspapers make public opinion known. When the majority of people thought eighteen-year-old citizens should vote, it did not take long for this to become the law of the land. The public opinion of united citizens will often cause national and state officials to act.

Social movements and pressure groups help form public opinion. The President of the United States tries to form public opinion to support what he thinks are good measures. Some of the President's appointees do the same. Candidates who are campaigning for election also try to form public opinion.

Check for Understanding: Now that you have completed this section, you should be able to answer these questions:

1. What is a lobbyist? How do lobbyists work?
2. How do lobbyists differ from others who are trying to influence government?
3. How are lobbyists controlled by law?
4. What kind of influence is stronger than lobbying or special interest groups?

SUMMARY

Other than voting, the only way for average citizens to participate in government is by trying to get elected representatives to pass laws they want passed. This is called influence. The role of influence is an important question facing a republic. Some people, including the Founding Fathers, thought elected representatives should make their own decisions, independent of the people who voted for them. Others believe the duty of representatives is to carry out the wishes of the people in their districts, regardless of their own opinions.

Political parties want to influence lawmakers in order to keep the party strong. They can do this because the party helps candidates with money and other support, and senior members can deny insurgents certain priviledges of the party.

One of the strongest ways the President and the state governors have of influencing lawmakers is the power of appointment. Those who vote with the President or the governor might either be considered for an appointed office or have the opportunity to suggest someone for it.

Groups can be formed on the basis of common economic interests, common public or political interests, or on a single interest. These groups work to persuade lawmakers to vote in the ways they want them to.

People who work for organizations full time to influence the decisions of government are called lobbyists. Through such things as opinion polls, lobbyists often try to convince congressmen that the things they want for their special groups are really wanted by the majority of the people. National lobbyists are required to register and to report to Congress the laws they are interested in. According to many people, the most effective kind of political influence is public opinion, as shown by opinion polls, letters, public speakers, sermons, and so on.

Have students ever been asked questions as part of a public opinion campaign? Do they think that such campaigns can have a major influence on lawmakers?

BUILDING SKILLS IN CIVICS

THINKING SKILLS

1. Outside of elections, who participates directly in government?
2. How can the average citizen participate indirectly in government decisions?
3. What ways can political parties influence government?
4. Name three types of interest groups.
5. Which of the following did the founders of our government *not* believe in?
   a. They believed in a true representative government.
   b. They believed that elected representatives could study public questions better than most other people.
   c. They believed that elected representatives should be influenced by outside opinions.

VOCABULARY SKILLS

Fill in each blank with the word form the list that best completes the sentence.

influence	interest group	indirect participation
lobbyist	insurgent	opinion campaign
		opinion poll

1. To cause people to think as you do, or to act as you would is to ______ them.
2. A person who is hired by an interest group to influence public officials is called a ______
3. Members of a party who refuse to vote for the party on a certain issue are called ______.
4. A group of people who join together to promote a common concern is called an ______.
5. A lobbyist tries to make it appear that he or she represents many people by organizing public ______.
6. Citizens have ______ in government by influencing elected officials.
7. ______, radio reports, and letters to Congress are just some of the ways that public opinion is made known.

STUDY SKILLS—USING A NEWSPAPER

Newspapers are an excellent source of information about world, national, and local events. Using a newspaper as a study tool is not difficult once you are familiar with the way the paper is organized.

All newspapers have a masthead, which tells you the title, the date of publication, who owns the paper, and either the number of years it has been published or the number of issues it has published. Newspapers are divided into sections. There is an abbreviated index to tell you where to find these sections and the regular features.

Activity: Answer the following questions about your local or city newspaper.

1. What is the name? How often is it published? How long has it been in existence?
2. How many parts does it have? What is each one called?
3. What features does your newspaper include?
4. Where is the editorial page? The letters to the editor?
5. Who are the regular featured columnists?
6. Read one news story about politics and one political editorial. Which one is easier for you to understand? Which one is more interesting? Explain your answers.

BEYOND THE BOOK

1. Read the editorials, columns, and letters to the editor on the editorial page of your newspaper. Divide them into two groups, according to whether or not you agree with the opinions expressed.
2. Read a biography or a biographical article of a recent President of the United States. In what ways did he use his status and power to influence members of government?
3. Editorial pages often use political cartoons as a means of commentary on public events. Read the political cartoons in your local newspaper every day for several days.
4. Choose an amendment from the Bill of Rights. Pretend that it is being proposed as a law today. Prepare a short argument that might influence lawmakers to vote for it.

CHAPTER TWELVE TEST

VOCABULARY CHECK

Match each term with its definition.

a. influence
b. opinion poll
c. indirect participation
d. opinion campaign
e. insurgent
f. interest group
g. lobbyist

1. Participating in government by influencing officials.
2. A way that public opinion is made known.
3. Lobbyists organize them so people think that the lobbyists represent many citizens.
4. To be able to get somebody to think as you do, or act as you want them to.
5. People paid by interest groups to influence government.
6. A group of people who organize to promote a common interest.
7. A party member who doesn't vote with his or her party on a certain issue.

COMPREHENSION CHECK

Indicate whether these statements are true or false.

1. Lobbyists help officials understand what other people think about the issues.
2. Economic interest groups are made of people who earn their income in the same way.
3. Once you have voted, you have many opportunities for direct participation in government.
4. Political parties can punish insurgents in their party in the hope of forcing them to be loyal.
5. Single interest groups try to influence government to defeat or pass one particular law.
6. Public interest groups try to influence officials to vote without considering outside influence.
7. The President can influence lawmakers by using his or her influence as head of state.

SKILL BUILDERS—INTERPRETING ILLUSTRATIONS

The *illustrations* in this book have been chosen for a variety of reasons—to stir feelings, to give information about historic events, and to make certain kinds of information easier to understand. It is important to be aware of what is being communicated by an illustration. As we have seen in other chapters, we can do this by looking at a picture critically.

Lobbyist: Without us, you legislators wouldn't know *anything* about what the people want!

Activities:

1. How does the illustration make its point? What parts are exaggerated? What details are included that might influence our opinions? Are there parts of the picture left out that could have been included? Could this same scene have been shown in a different way?
2. Make a general statement that summarizes the message of the picture.

BUILDING WRITING SKILLS

1. Tell in your own words what each of the following quotations mean:

   "If, to please the people, we offer what we ourselves disapprove, how can we afterward defend our work?"

   "Let us raise a standard to which the wise and honest can repair."
2. Write a paragraph that tells your opinion about how important outside influence should be in governmental affairs.

UNIT THREE TEST

A Political Campaign: John Smith for U.S. Senate

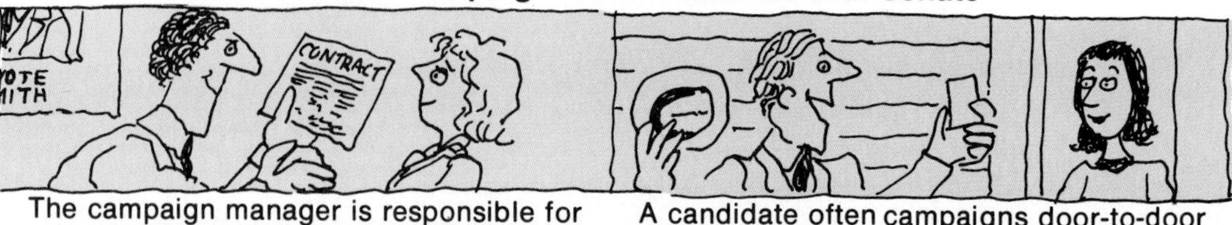

The campaign manager is responsible for running all aspects of the campaign.

A candidate often campaigns door-to-door to ask people to vote for him.

A lot of money can be raised for a campaign at a fund-raising dinner.

Traveling and making speeches take up a lot of a candidate's time.

A. Study the diagram above. Then answer the following questions:

1. What is the first step a person must make in preparation for a political campaign?
2. Why do you think a political campaign is often so expensive? What information from the diagram makes you think so?
3. Are there any steps that a candidate takes that you think are absolutely necessary to success? Any that you think are not helpful? Explain your answer.
4. Now that you have seen how complicated a political campaign can be, do you think that *you* would ever want to be a candidate or a campaign manager? Why/Why not?

B. Select one of the following topics as the focus for a letter to the editor of your daily newspaper:

Third parties	Interest groups	Political platforms
Lobbyists	Indirect participation	Primary elections

Choose a particular slant for your letter. Your topic sentence should clearly show the way you feel on the subject. To help you organize your ideas, make a list of several facts or opinions you wish to include in your letter. Do you balance all your opinions with facts? Do the facts you include effectively support your opinions?

Unit Four
Our Nation's Lawmakers

Examples of the presence of law in our lives are countless, because government is around us every day. But do you know how laws are made? And by whom they are made?

We are represented on the federal, state, and local levels, and each level has specific responsibilities that affect us in different ways. Sometimes, the responsibility for a problem has shifted back and forth between the levels, but it is through cooperation between all three levels of government that we can best govern ourselves as a free people.

The illustration shows a view of the Texas state capitol building. Ask students if they know the names of any state lawmakers who work there and the duties they perform.

Chapter Thirteen
Congress: Our National Lawmakers

Document: The Constitution of the United States

Article I, Section 1. All legislative Powers herein granted shall be vested in a Congress of the United States, which shall consist of a Senate and House of Representatives.

Article I, Section 4. The Congress shall assemble at least once in every Year, (and such Meeting shall be on the first Monday in December, unless they shall by Law appoint a different Day).

Article I, Section 5. Each House shall be the Judge of the Elections, Returns and Qualifications of its own Members, and a Majority of each shall constitute a Quorum to do Business; but a smaller Number may adjourn from day to day, and may be authorized to compel the Attendance of absent Members, in such Manner, and under such Penalties as each House may provide.

Each House may determine the Rules of its Proceedings, punish its Members for disorderly Behaviour, and with the Concurrence of two thirds, expel a Member. . . .

Neither House, during the Session of Congress, shall, without the Consent of the other, adjourn for more than three days, nor to any other Place than that in which the two Houses shall be sitting.

The picture shows the arena for our nation's lawmakers. Ask students if they know who makes up Congress and how this body works in relation to the President.

The complete text of the Constitution can be found in the Appendix, beginning on page 564.

The delegates to the Constitutional Convention set forth specific laws regarding the business of Congress so that the injustices of the past would not be repeated. In the Declaration of Independence, the king of Great Britain was cited for "refusing to pass laws for the accommodation of large districts of people," calling together "legislative bodies at places unusual . . . for the sole purpose of fatiguing them into compliance with his measures," and for dissolving "Representative Houses repeatedly . . ." The laws of the Constitution, calling for equal representation for all states and a pre-determined schedule for Congressional sessions, prevent the recurrence of such abuses by our national lawmakers.

FOCUSING IDEAS

- Senators and representatives who are elected by popular vote serve in Congress.
- The rules of Congress are concerned with limitations on membership size, meeting time regulations, and officer elections.
- Congressional members may not be arrested during attendance at either House nor on their way to and from Congress, and they may not be taken to court for anything they say in Congress.

Issues in Civics: In the Declaration of Independence, King George was cited for dissolving "Representative Houses repeatedly . . ." Ask your students if they think the President could ever have the power to dissolve *our* House of Representatives.

PRE-TEST

1. Who are the actual members of Congress?
2. Whom do these representatives serve?
3. What rules are involved in the workings of Congress?
4. What are the privileges of members of Congress?

WHO SERVES IN CONGRESS?

Objectives: After you have read this section, you will be able to:

- List the requirements for serving in Congress.
- State the length of service for members.
- Describe the principle of "one man, one vote."

The designers of the Constitution gave Congress all *legislative* powers. This means that all federal laws are passed by our senators and representatives. Many of the things we do every day are controlled in some way by these laws. This gives Congress, and the people who are elected to represent us there, a great deal of power and importance in our lives.

Requirements for serving

The Constitution established requirements for serving in Congress. Almost any citizen, however, is eligible to try to become a member. Members of Congress should live or have residence in the state that elects them. A representative must be at least twenty-five years old, and a senator must be thirty. A representative must have been a citizen of the U.S. for at least seven years. A senator has a nine-year requirement.

Choosing a Congress

The Constitution says that if Congress desires, it may set a uniform election date. Congress set the election date for the first Tuesday after the first Monday in November in years that can be divided evenly by two, such as 1984, 1986, and so on.

Since senators represent the state, the Constitution originally provided for their election by the state legislatures. However, the Constitution was amended. Senators are now elected by the people of the state on a national election day.

Each house is the judge of the election of its own members. After the election, an officer of each state gives certificates of election to those who received the most votes. The certificates of election are carried to Washington and shown to an officer of the body concerned, either the Senate or the House. Generally, the certificates are received without question. Occasionally, another candidate claims to have been elected. When this happens, a committee is appointed to examine the evidence. Committee members may have to recount the vote. After they have done everything to find the facts, the entire body votes.

Building vocabulary:
legislative *(210)* • congressional district *(212)* • representative-at-large *(212)* • president pro tempore *(215)* • majority/minority party *(215)* • whip *(216)* • censure *(217)* • expel *(217)*

Why do students think that there are minimum age requirements for serving in Congress? Do students think these requirements are valid? Why or why not?

Professions of Members of 96th* Congress					
Senate		**House of Representatives**			
Lawyer	65	Lawyer	205	Funeral Director	1
Business Executive	12	Business Executive	52	Boxer	1
Farmer	5	Educator	48	Civic Volunteer	1
Professor	5	Public Official	26	Coach	1
Astronaut	2	Farmer	20	Engineer	1
Editor	2	Broker	13	Labor Executive	1
Journalist	2	TV, Radio, Newspapers	12	Pro-Football Player	1
Airline Co-Pilot	1	Clergyman, Social Worker	8	Other	17
Author	1	Tradesman	8		
Broadcast Executive	1	Medicine	7		
Management Consultant	1	Publishing	6		
Pricing Analyst	1	Banker	4		
Real Estate Developer	1				
Veterinarian	1				

*Each Congress is numbered. The first Congress was elected in 1788 and met from 1789 to 1791. Each Congress lasts for two years. The 96th Congress began meeting in 1979; the 97th, in 1981, and so on.

Length of service

Members of the House are elected for terms of two years. Senators are elected for six years. The terms of one-third of the senators expire every two years. Thus, in any election, at least two-thirds of the senators stay in office.

The representatives' two-year term was set for a reason. The people can have new representatives every two years as public opinion shifts. Senators serve a term of six years, so they are more independent.

The founders did not want major changes in our government every few years. They felt the country would be served best by close study of each change. If the people were influenced by a new idea, they could react to this by electing representatives to the House who agreed with their views. If the idea should prove to be unsound, however, the Senate, the body that is less sensitive to the public, would act to slow the people's desire for change.

John McCormack of Massachusetts was elected to twenty-one consecutive two-year terms in Congress, from 1928 to 1971.

Issues in Civics: Presidents are only allowed to serve in that office for two terms. Do students think it's fair that a Congressional representative is able to serve as long as John McCormack did?

In many cases, representatives do not get voted out of office as easily as you might think. In districts where one party is very strong, a representative is almost certain to be re-elected. As a result, many representatives remain in Congress for twenty years or longer. Emanuel Cellar, Democrat from New York, served in the House for 50 years, or 25 two-year terms, and John McCormack, Democrat from Massachusetts and long-time speaker of the House, served for 42 years.

Whom do the representatives serve?

Since 1842 the law has required that each state be divided into *congressional districts.* The boundaries are set by the state legislature. Each district sends one member to the House. Some districts cover many square miles of farmland or open country. Others may be but one part of a big city. In recent years more and more people have left rural areas and moved to the cities. As people move to urban areas, these cities should gain more representatives. But some states have not changed their districts to give the rural areas fewer representatives and the cities more. As a result, the number of people living in a congressional district in one recent year varied from 177,000 to 951,000. Both of these districts, despite this difference in population, elected one representative to the House.

Many people have attacked this system as unfair because it makes the votes of people in small districts worth more than those of people in large districts. Often minority groups feel that they do not have enough representation because they live in urban areas with a large number of people in each district. Some people argue that the state legislatures should do their best to see that each district contains about the same number of voters.

In 1964, the Supreme Court ruled that state legislatures must change the boundaries of congressional districts to keep up with changes in the population. Some have called this the "one man, one vote" rule. In recent years, this rule has been made to apply to some state and local districts. A number of state legislatures have changed the boundary lines of their districts so that the population is spread more equally among them.

A state may also gain or lose representatives when its population changes. As people move from place to place, a state may see its population grow rapidly, grow slowly, or even become smaller. The number of representatives is limited to 435. After each census, each state is assigned its proper share of representatives. Thus, a state may gain or lose representatives every ten years. If its representation does change because of population gain or loss, the state legislature must then draw new boundaries for its congressional districts.

Sometimes a legislature fails to divide a state into a sufficient number of districts. There are not enough to elect the number of representatives apportioned to that state. The extra representatives are then elected by all of the people of that state. A representative that is so chosen is called a *representative-at-large.* At the present time, Alaska, Delaware, Nevada, North Dakota, Vermont, and Wyoming each have only one representative. These representatives also run at large. In addition to representatives from the states, Washington, D.C. and the territory of Puerto Rico each elect one non-voting member to the House of Representative.

How do students feel about the "one man, one vote" rule? Were they aware that districts with a greater population didn't always have a proportionate number of representatives?

Have an interested student do background research on a representative he or she is familiar with. Approximately how many constituents does this representative have in his or her district?

The largest and smallest Congressional districts, each represented in the House by one person, are the state of Alaska, which is 566,432 square miles, and the "Silk Stocking District" of Manhattan, which is only 6 square miles.

Check for Understanding: Now that you have finished this section, you should be able to answer these questions:

1. What are the requirements for serving in Congress?
2. What is the length of service for members of Congress?
3. What is meant by the phrase "one man, one vote"?
4. Why did the founders of our nation want a term in the Senate to be longer than one in the House?

WHAT ARE THE RULES OF CONGRESS?

Objectives: After reading this section, you will be able to:

- Name the number of members in each body of Congress.
- List the titles of the principal leaders of Congress.
- Describe the privileges of the members of Congress.

The size of Congress

The number of members in the Senate is set down in Article I of the Constitution—two from each state. The first Senate had 26 members, two from each of the original thirteen states. The Senate has grown in membership as new states have been added to the union. It reached its present size of 100 members in 1961, when senators from the new states of Hawaii and Alaska joined the body. Before that, the Senate had consisted of 96 members for the previous 48 years, since the time when New Mexico and Arizona joined the union. Because of the system of having two Senators per state, the Senate will always have an even number of members and thus ties in voting will always be possible. This is why the Vice President is given the power to cast a tie-breaking vote in case this should happen.

Number of State Representatives in Congress*

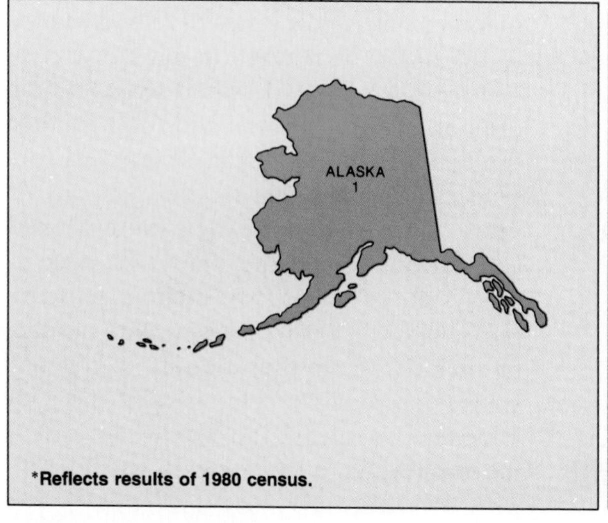

***Reflects results of 1980 census.**

The number of members in the House of Representatives is not specifically set down in the Constitution. It only states that there should not be more than one representative for every thirty thousand people. The original House consisted of 65 members, distributed among the states according to a formula described in the Constitution. The number has varied since then according to changes in the population. In 1913, the same year that the Senate increased its membership to 96, the House reached its present level of 435 members. Unlike the Senate, the House did not add new seats when Hawaii and Alaska became states.

When Congress meets

Congress meets in Washington, D.C. on January 3rd of each year. When January 3rd falls on a Sunday, it is the custom to postpone the meeting until the next day.

In nations ruled by dictators, the dictator calls meetings of the legislative body only if he or she wants to. The same was true in the days when monarchs had absolute power. One of England's kings failed to call a meeting of Parliament for eleven years. For 175 years, the kings of France did not call their national assembly into session.

The founders, therefore, wrote into the Constitution that Congress must meet at least once a year. If the need arises, the President may also call on the Congress to meet in extra sessions. President Franklin D. Roosevelt called Congress into session the day after Pearl Harbor was attacked so that a declaration of war could be issued.

Officers of Congress

Each house elects its own officers. The only exception is the Vice President of the United States, who is President of the Senate. Since the Vice President is not a senator, he or she votes only in case of a tie. In this way, the Vice President occasionally decides important questions. The Senate also chooses a *president pro tempore.* The phrase "pro tempore" comes from Latin and literally means "for a time." He or she serves as President of the Senate if the Vice President is absent or becomes President of the United States.

The House of Representatives elects a presiding officer called the Speaker. The Speaker is a member of the House and may vote on all matters. The positions of the Vice President as President of the Senate, the president pro tempore, and the Speaker of the House are all described in the Constitution. As time went on, most members of Congress were elected as members of one political party or another. The party with the most members in each house is called the *majority party*. The other party is called the *minority party.* It has become the practice for the majority of the Senate to select the president pro tempore. The majority party in the House selects the Speaker from the membership of their party.

Howard Baker, Senate majority leader, with Republican Congressional leaders.

Have an interested student do research to find out the names of the people who currently hold these positions in our nation: Speaker of the House, Majority leader, Minority leader.

In addition, each party in each house selects a majority leader or a minority leader. Each of these leaders also has an assistant known as a *whip*. The whip is responsible for seeing that the members of his or her party are present when a vote takes place. These eight people are merely leaders of their party and not officers of Congress.

What privileges do members have?

The Constitution says senators and representatives:

shall in all Cases, except Treason, Felony, and Breach of the Peace, be privileged from Arrest during their Attendance at the Session of their respective Houses, and in going to and returning from the same.

They also may not be taken to court for anything they say while Congress is in session.

This exemption for members of Congress is to prevent them from being arrested on false charges. There is the chance someone would do that to keep a member from attending an important meeting of Congress. It also permits them to say what they please in a speech or debate on the floor of the House or Senate.

Senator Harrison Williams announcing his resignation in 1982, after having been criticized by the Senate for misconduct.

Leadership in Congress

Senate		House	
Vice-President President Pro Tempore		Speaker	
Majority Leader	Minority Leader	Majority Leader	Minority Leader
Majority Whip	Minority Whip	Majority Whip	Minority Whip

Have an interested student do research on the "Abscam" investigation that led to the censure of certain Congressional members in the early 1980's.

The complete text of the Constitution can be found in the Appendix, beginning on page 564.

Punishing a member

No court can punish a member of Congress for what he or she says on the floor. However, the other members may do so. Each body makes its own rules for its proceedings. If a member is considered to have been guilty of some kind of misconduct or wrongdoing, the other members of that body may vote a punishment. Ordinarily, this punishment is in the form of a *censure.* A censure is an official criticism, but a person who is censured does not lose his or her membership or the privileges that go with it. In extreme cases, a body may *expel,* or remove from membership, a person by a two-thirds vote. Only a few members have ever been expelled in our history, and none since the Civil War.

When Congress ends a session

When both houses have finished their work for the session, they may adjourn. This means they stop business. One house cannot adjourn without the consent of the other.

Check for Understanding: Now that you have completed this section, you should be able to answer these questions:

1. How many members does each body of Congress have?
2. What are the titles of the leaders of Congress?
3. What are the privileges of a member of Congress?
4. What is the difference between being censured and being expelled?

SUMMARY

The Constitution set certain qualifications for membership in Congress and made rules for its organization. Senators must be at least thirty years old and citizens of the United States for nine years. Representatives must be at least twenty-five years old and citizens for seven years. Representatives are elected for two years. Each state has two senators elected for six years. Each representative has a congressional district. As its population changes, a state may gain or lose congressional districts. According to the "one man, one vote" decision of the Supreme Court, each district should have about the same number of people living in it.

The number of senators, two per state, is set down in the Constitution. There are presently 100 senators. Because this is an even number, there is always a possibility of a tie, so the Vice President has the power to cast a tie-breaking vote. The number of representatives is not determined by the Constitution.

Congress starts on January 3rd of each year. Members of Congress are protected by law from being arrested for political reasons. They cannot be arrested while in the Congress, nor on their way to or from the Congress. Neither can they be taken to court for things they say in the House or the Senate.

The Senate and the House of Representatives can punish one of their members if they find him or her guilty of misconduct or wrongdoing. This is usually done by censure, but expulsion is also possible. Expulsion requires a two-thirds vote.

Congress adjourns when it has finished its work for that session. One house cannot adjourn without the consent of the other house.

BUILDING SKILLS IN CIVICS

THINKING SKILLS

1. What are the requirements for serving in Congress?
2. How long are the terms a senator and a representative?
3. How many members are there in each house of Congress?
4. What are the principal positions of leadership in Congress?
5. What privileges are given to senators and representatives by the Constitution?
6. Read through the chapter and write four factual sentences that support this statement: "The Constitution is specific in regard to many things about the business of Congress."

VOCABULARY SKILLS

Some of the underlined words in the sentences below are used correctly, but others are not. If the sentence is correct, write True. If it is not, replace the word with the best choice from the list.

legislative	president pro tempore	censure
congressional districts	majority party	expel
representative-at-large	whip	

1. Congressional districts are areas within a state with boundaries set by a state legislature.
2. Legislative means having to do with laws, or the power to make laws.
3. If a state does not yet have enough districts to elect its full number of representatives, the extra representatives are elected by all the people of the state, and are called congressional districts.
4. The party with the most members in each house is the majority party.
5. The president pro tempore serves as President of the Senate if the Vice-President is absent or becomes President of the United States.
6. When members of Congress decide to whip another member, it amounts to an official criticism.

STUDY SKILLS—TOPIC OUTLINING

In a formal outline Roman numerals, capital letters, and Arabic numerals show headings, subheadings, and supporting facts. Each type of letter and number should be lined up, one under the other.

In a *topic outline* short phrases rather than sentences are used to describe each category.

Activity: Complete the following outline using information from the chapter. Have a partner check your work.

Theme: The Constitution is specific in regard to many things about the business of Congress.

I. Requirements for members
   A. Senate
      1.
      2.
   B. House
      1.
      2.
II. Choosing a Congress
   A. Election date
      1.
      2.
   B. After the election
      1.
      2.
   C. Election results in dispute
      1.
      2.
III. Length of term
   A. Senators
      1.
      2.
   B. Representatives
      1.
      2.

BEYOND THE BOOK

1. Create a bulletin board display that shows why the "One man, one vote" rule was enacted.
2. Look for newspaper or magazine pictures that show members of Congress. Study each of the pictures in order to determine its point of view. Classify the pictures into three categories: "Positive Point of View," "Negative Point of View," and "Mixed or Neutral Point of View."
3. Prepare an oral report using your pictures. Describe the questions you asked yourself as you classified the pictures.

CHAPTER THIRTEEN TEST

VOCABULARY CHECK

Match each term with its definition.

legislative	president pro tempore	censure
congressional districts	majority party	expel
representative-at-large	whip	

1. An area within a state, the boundaries of which are set by a state legislature, from which one member of the House of Representatives is elected.
2. A representative elected by all the people of a state.
3. An official criticism by one's Congressional colleagues.
4. A senator elected by his or her fellow senators to serve as President of the Senate if the Vice-President is absent or becomes President of the United States.
5. Having to do with laws, or the power to make laws.
6. The party with the most members in each house.
7. When a member of Congress is removed by a two-thirds vote.
8. The person responsible for seeing that members of his or her party are present when a vote takes place.

COMPREHENSION CHECK

Indicate whether these statements are true or false.

1. Members of Congress must have residence in the state that elects them.
2. Senators are now elected by their state legislatures.
3. In any election year, at least two-thirds of the senators stay in office.
4. Some representative stay in Congress for twenty years or longer.
5. Each congressional district sends two members to the House.
6. A state may lose representatives if the census shows that it has lost population.
7. The party with the most members in each house is called the Privileged Party.
8. One reason members of Congress have special privileges is so that they can't be kept from attending important meetings.

SKILL BUILDERS—INTERPRETING CIRCLE GRAPHS

When you want to show relationships of parts to the whole, such as fractional parts, percents, or proportions, a *circle* or *pie graph* is often your best visual tool. See how the information from the chart on page 218 is transferred to a circle graph.

Professions of Congressional Members

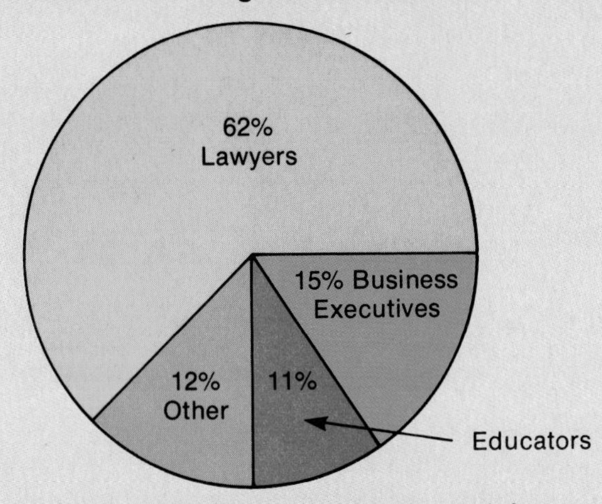

1. Read the title. What is shown by the whole circle?
2. What features of this graph make it easy to compare parts?
3. What had to be done to the information on the original chart in order to translate it into the graphs?
4. Compare the graphs to the chart. What information is the same? What is different?

BUILDING WRITING SKILLS

1. Choose one of the titles below. Write five factual sentences that belong in a report with that title.
   a. Serving in Congress
   b. One Man, One Vote
   c. Leadership in Congress
2. Why is it important for members of Congress to have certain privileges?
3. Choose any picture in this unit. Use the picture-reading skills you have learned to determine how the artist or photographer is making a personal comment.

Chapter Fourteen • The Powers and Limits of Congress

Document: The Constitution of the United States

Section 8. The Congress shall have Power to lay and collect Taxes, Duties, Imposts and Excises, to pay the Debts and provide for the common Defence and general Welfare of the United States . . . To borrow Money on the credit of the United States . . . To regulate Commerce with foreign Nations . . . To establish a uniform Rule of Naturalization . . . To coin money . . . To provide for the Punishment of counterfeiting . . . To establish Post Offices and post Roads . . . To promote the Progress of Science and useful Arts . . . To declare War . . . To raise and support Armies . . . To provide and maintain a Navy . . . To make Rules for the Government and Regulation of the land and naval Forces . . . To make all Laws which shall be necessary and proper for carrying into Execution the foregoing Powers, and all other Powers vested by this Constitution in the Government of the United States, or in a Department or Officer thereof.

The powers stated above are just *some* of the ways in which Congress uses its lawmaking authority. Although the most important task of Congress is to make laws, Congress also plays an important role in amending the Constitution, conducting investigations, and reviewing the work of the other branches of the federal government.

Ask students to name the powers of Congress that are depicted in the picture. Are they surprised that some of these powers come under Congressional authority?

The complete text of the Constitution can be found in the Appendix, beginning on page 564.

Although the Constitution gives Congress all the lawmaking powers of the federal government, it does not give all these powers in the same way. Article I, Section 8 of the Constitution lists the *expressed powers* of Congress, but the *implied powers* are not listed anywhere in the document. However, Article I, Section 8 does say that Congress can pass all laws that are "necessary and proper" for carrying out the expressed powers.

FOCUSING IDEAS

- Congress has the power to coin money, establish a weights and measures system, levy taxes, provide for the common defense, regulate trade, set naturalization laws, and establish postal services, among other powers.
- The doctrine of implied powers gave Congress additional powers that are not listed in the Constitution.
- The powers of Congress are limited in that it cannot suspend the privilege of habeas corpus, pass a bill of attainder or an ex post facto law, nor treat people differently through the tax laws.

Issues in Civics: Ask students how public opinion can limit the powers of Congress. Have they ever written to a Congressman or Congresswoman?

PRE-TEST

1. What are the powers that are granted to Congress by the Constitution?
2. Which one of these powers is very general, rather than specific?
3. How has Congress gained power beyond what is in the Constitution?
4. What limits does the Constitution place on the power of Congress?

WHAT ARE THE POWERS GRANTED TO CONGRESS?

Objectives: After reading this section, you will be able to:
- List the major powers of Congress.
- Explain the restrictions on these powers.
- Describe the impeachment process.

Almost every evening, the television and radio news reports and the newspapers inform us about what has happened in Congress that day. Even if Congress is not in session, the news reports may still tell us what certain senators or representatives have done or said. The activities of Congress are of great interest to the people. As you read about the powers granted to Congress by the Constitution, you may be surprised at how few actual powers there are. You may wonder how Congress can be so important when it has so few powers.

The people, through the Constitution, gave Congress the power to make laws for the good of the whole country. Each state legislature has the powers to make the laws for the people of that state.

There may be conflicts between a state law and a law made by the Congress. In that case the national law would prevail. But Congress does not have complete power. The Constitution gives Congress the power to make laws only in the areas discussed on the following pages.

Coining money

Congress makes the laws for providing money. States cannot print it, nor can individuals. Since Congress alone has the authority over money, a dollar is worth the same amount in any state or territory.

Weights and measures

Congress establishes a uniform system of weights and measures for all states. You can order a hundred pounds of sugar, a gallon of milk, or a yard of cloth and be sure of receiving the same amount anywhere in the United States. Recently, Congress passed a law indicating that the country will replace this traditional system of measurement with the international metric system.

Building Vocabulary:
impeachment *(227)* • doctrine of implied powers *(229)* • elastic clause *(229)* • investigative committee *(230)* • writ of habeas corpus *(232)* • bill of attainder *(232)* • ex post facto *(232)*

Were students aware that the U.S. is one of the few countries in the world that has not yet fully converted to the metric system? Do students think it is wise for our country to switch to this system?

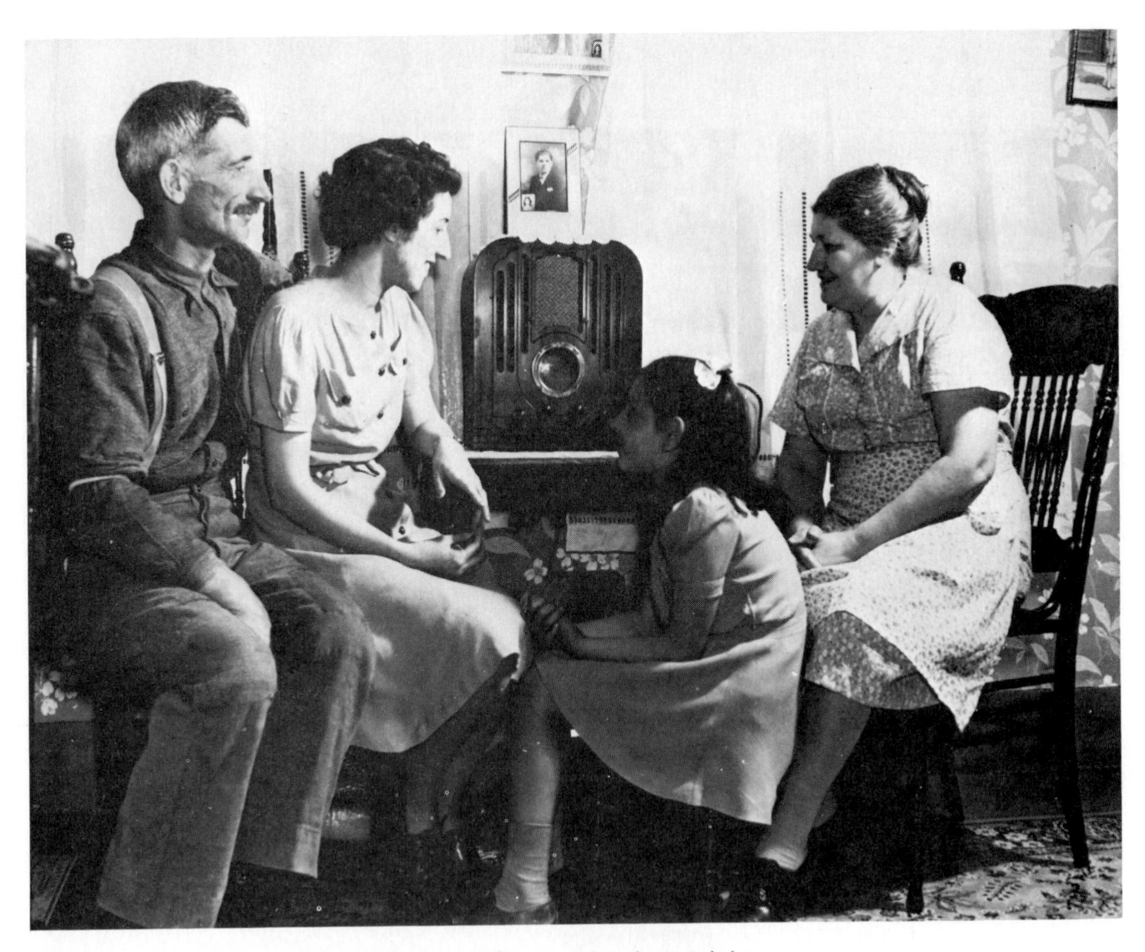

A family in Provincetown, Mass. listens to a Congressional speech in 1942. News broadcasts like this one keep people informed about events in Congress.

Taxes and spending

Congress may levy and collect taxes to provide for defense and general welfare. We have to pay for everything we get, whether it be food, clothing, or shelter. So it is with government services. The people of the United States tax themselves through their representatives. Only Congress can act in the name of the government to borrow money, pay debts, and spend money from the Treasury. Even the President may not draw money from the Treasury until permission is voted by Congress.

In matters of taxation, the House and the Senate do not have equal power. The bills must originate or start in the House. The Senate may only change the bills. Those bills that are changed are then sent back to the House to be voted on again. The power to originate tax bills is given to the House and not the Senate for good reason. The people pay taxes, and the House is more directly involved with the people because its members must face re-election every two years instead of every six as do the members of the Senate.

Powers of Congress
Delegated in Article I, Section 8

Coin Money

Impeach Officials

Establish System of Weights and Measures

Collect Taxes

Create Federal Courts

Make Laws for Naturalization

Borrow Money

Insure Patents and Copyrights

Establish a Postal System

Regulate Trade

Provide for Defense and Declare War

Have Authority over Forts and Federal Buildings

Implied Powers

To make all laws that are "necessary and proper" to carry out the delegated powers

To "provide for the general welfare" of the U.S.

Discuss with students the ways in which the powers of Congress shown here affect their daily lives.

Providing for defense and declaring war

Congress has the duty of providing for the common defense, and only Congress can declare war. The President may ask Congress to declare war, but he cannot do it. While Congress has the power to raise and support an army, navy, air force, or national guard, it cannot make an allowance of money for the armed services for more than two years at a time. This prevents the buildup of a great military force without a careful review by Congress at least once every two years. Congress also has the power to make rules for the organization and control of the various branches of the armed services.

Regulating trade

Congress passes laws to regulate trade with foreign nations and between states. This includes the regulation of airlines, railroads, and truck routes; radio and television companies; telephone and telegraph companies; power and utility companies, and many others.

Laws for naturalization

Many people have become citizens because Congress has passed many laws that enable persons born of foreign parents outside of the United States to take out United States citizenship.

Establishing postal services

For many years, Congress provided the money for post offices, hired postal employees, and arranged for the carrying of mail. In 1970 Congress created the United States Postal Service. This service is still a part of the government, but it now acts with greater independence, much like a private business.

Other powers

Congress can allow patents to be issued to inventors, and copyrights to be issued to artists and writers so that they may have exclusive right to profit from their work for a certain period of time. It also creates federal courts lower than the Supreme Court, provides punishment for piracy or other crimes on the high seas, makes laws for the District of Columbia, and has full authority over all forts, arsenals, navy yards, and other federal buildings. Congress also has the general authority to make laws to provide for the public welfare and to carry out the other powers granted in the Constitution.

Impeachment trials

If it is believed that an official of the United States is guilty of wrongdoing while in office, the House of Representatives alone has the power to accuse that person of misconduct and to demand that the person be removed from his or her government position. Such an accusation by the House is called an *impeachment*, a word that comes from the French language and means "impede," or "prevent from doing something."

When the House impeaches an official, the Senate sits as a court and hears the evidence. If two-thirds of the senators believe that the official is guilty, they may remove him or her from office. A verdict of guilty disqualifies an official from ever holding another office in the United States government. The Vice President presides over the Senate in all impeachment trials, except when the President is tried. Since the Vice President would become President if a vote of guilty were returned, he or she is considered to be an interested party and not qualified to preside over the impeachment

Have students debate the issue of whether President Nixon should have been impeached during the latter part of his term in office. Make sure students use facts to back up opinions.

trial of the President. The Chief Justice of the Supreme Court presides over the Senate in such cases.

Though the penalty imposed by the Senate for a convicted official cannot be more than the loss of his or her office and the loss of the right to ever hold another United States government office, he or she may still be tried in regular courts for the same offense.

Check for Understanding: Now that you have completed this section, you should be able to answer these questions:

1. What are the major powers of Congress?
2. What restrictions are placed on those powers by the Constitution?
3. How does the impeachment process work?
4. Why do tax bills originate in the House rather than in the Senate?

HOW HAS CONGRESS GAINED ADDITIONAL POWERS?

Objectives: After you have read this section, you will be able to:

- Explain the idea of "implied powers."
- Give examples of such powers.
- State the purpose of an investigative committee.

Look over the powers given to Congress in the Constitution (page 567). Do you see any power to establish a national banking system, to send people into space, or to spend money on public health? Yet, Congress has done all of these things and more. How it gained this authority is an interesting part of our government's development.

Implied powers

In 1790 Alexander Hamilton was Secretary of the Treasury. He proposed a national bank. Thomas Jefferson, who was the Secretary of State, opposed this plan. Jefferson argued that Congress could not do this, since the power was not granted in the Constitution.

Hamilton and his followers replied that Congress was granted the power to coin and regulate the value of money. In addition, Article I, Section 8 of the Constitution

Congress has authorized programs to send people into space, even though the Constitution could not possibly have anticipated this power.

Issues in Civics: Some people have criticized Congress for authorizing funds for programs that are not necessarily important, such as the space program. Do students think that such programs are frivolous?

granted the authority "to make all laws which will be necessary and proper" to carry out the powers that were listed. Thus, they argued, Congress could establish a national bank if it was necessary and proper in order to regulate the value of money.

The argument went on, and Congress finally passed the bank act. The argument was taken to the Supreme Court in the case of *McCulloch vs. Maryland* (1819). The court agreed with Hamilton. Chief Justice John Marshall said that Congress did have the authority to make other laws if they were "necessary and proper" to carrying out its assigned powers. This has been called the *doctrine of implied powers*. Article I, Section 8 has come to be known as the *elastic clause* because this clause stretches like elastic, to allow Congress to have such powers as are necessary to carry out the original powers in the Constitution. Congress can pass many laws, but only if they are necessary to execute the Constitution.

Sweeping powers

By using the doctrine of implied powers, Congress has done much that is not listed in the Constitution. However, such laws have been in line with stated powers. Congress can control trade between states. Thus, it was able to control railroads that cross state lines. Congress can spend money for the general welfare. Thus, it was able to spend it for the Public Health Service. Through this doctrine Congress has sweeping powers to pass laws on many things.

A 1951 Senate investigating committee chaired by Estes Kefauver (right) hears testimony from New Orleans mayor DeLesseps Morrison (left) about organized crime in his city.

The doctrine of implied powers is an example of how the Constitution remains a living document. Since the authors did not go into detail, they only said, for example, that Congress could regulate the value of money. They did not say how it is to be regulated. They left this and many other decisions about our government to be made as the need arose.

Investigative powers

Congress has still other powers that are not directly related to lawmaking. Congress may set up an *investigative* or study committee to see how laws are being enforced or where new laws are needed. Sometimes there are over one hundred such investigations going on while Congress is in session. These committees have the power to hear witnesses and gather information. The information that the committees gather is made available to the public. Much of the news you hear or see about Congress is from such investigative committees. Discovering the truth about illegal activities or troublesome situations gives Congress more power. These investigations can cause questionable activities to stop or be changed even without any new laws being passed.

Check for Understanding: Now that you have completed this section, you should be able to answer these questions:

1. What is meant by "implied powers" of Congress?
2. What are three examples of powers Congress has taken which were not stated in the Constitution?
3. How can the investigative process provide for change without passing a new law?
4. What was the dispute about implied powers between Thomas Jefferson and Alexander Hamilton?

WHAT ARE THE LIMITS ON CONGRESS?

Objectives: After you read this section, you will be able to:

- Name at least five restrictions on the powers of Congress.
- Describe restrictions placed on the states by the Constitution.
- Explain the importance of the rule of habeas corpus.

You have read how Congress gained power that was implied but not stated in the Constitution. If Congress has these sweeping powers, it is very important that there be limits. Of course, final control lies with the people who elect the members of Congress.

If the people are to be free to choose, they must be free from fear. They must know that Congress cannot bribe them to gain support or punish them for any opposition. The authors of the Constitution knew this. They listed certain things that Congress cannot do. As you read about these limitations, you will notice that most of them protect individual rights.

Cannot suspend habeas corpus

In some countries, people may be put in jail on the mere suspicion of having done wrong. They can be kept in jail for long periods without being accused of a crime or taken to trial. Dictators and other unelected leaders have often used the practice of imprisonment without trial as a way of punishing those people who disagree with their politics.

Have an interested student do research on the findings of a Congressional committee, such as the one that recently re-investigated John Kennedy's assassination, or committees that have looked into the organized crime problem.

What Congress *Cannot* Do

Vote to Punish Someone

Tax Different States at Different Rates

Accept Gifts from a Foreign Country

Enforce an "Ex Post Facto" Law

Take Money from the Treasury Except by Law

Suspend *Habeas Corpus*

What do students think would happen if Congress were permitted to tax the individuals of different states at different rates?

In the United States, if you are held in jail without accusation, your attorney may go before a judge and obtain an order bringing you into open court. Unless a warrant is issued charging you with a definite offense, you will be released at once. The judge's order is called a *writ of habeas corpus*. In Latin it literally means "You shall have the body." However, in usage, this has come to mean "bring the prisoner to court or before the judge for trial."

This right to habeas corpus and a free hearing cannot be denied to anybody in the United States. The only exception is in the case of invasion of the country by a foreign enemy or the outbreak of a civil war. Even then, only persons suspected of aiding the enemy may be jailed.

Cannot vote punishment

When the Constitution was written, it was a common practice in nearly all of the nations of the world for the lawmaking bodies to pass a *bill of attainder* against certain persons who were considered to be opponents of the state. Such a bill convicted these people of crime without a trial. In the United States, Congress cannot pass such a law. No person can be found guilty except after a trial in court.

Even in an impeachment trial, if the Senate finds an official of the United States guilty, it can only remove the official from office. Only the courts can fine or imprison the guilty person for wrongdoing.

Ex post facto laws

Ex post facto is a phrase from Latin meaning "done after the fact," or "done after something else happens." You cannot be punished for an act committed before there was a law against it, because the law was passed "after the fact" of your committing the act. For example, there was a time when anyone who wished to do so could build and operate a radio station without the government's permission. Then Congress passed a law requiring that permission to operate a station must first be obtained from the federal government, or a penalty would follow. However, the law could not provide punishment for those who began operation of their radio stations before the law was passed. For those station operators, the law would have been *ex post facto* or "after the fact."

All are equal

All people, cities, and states must be taxed on an equal basis. No one person or group of people can be threatened with a special tax or be forced to pay more than a fair share.

In the United States all persons are considered equal before the law. The founders were opposed to the European system of nobility, in which people with the title of king, prince, duke, count, and so on were considered to be more important than the average person. Therefore, the government cannot grant a title of nobility to any person. Also, no official of the United States can accept money, gifts, offices, titles, or other rewards from a foreign nation. When a foreign nation does present gifts to our country these gifts become the property of the nation as a whole, rather than of the official who receives them. This rule exists so that foreign countries will not be able to influence our officials by giving them presents.

Restrictions on the states

When the people adopted the Constitution, they gave to the federal government authority over certain matters. In these matters the United States has more power than the states as a group. The United States may

Issues in Civics: Ex post facto laws prevent someone from being punished for an act committed before there was a law against it. Do students think that people who were convicted of committing a crime that *later* became a legal activity should be released from jail, or otherwise cleared of the charge?

make treaties with foreign governments, but the states may not. Only the federal government may set and collect taxes on imports.

States may enter into agreements or contracts with each other. However, permission must first be obtained from Congress. An example of this is the Colorado Basin Compact. The Colorado River drains all or parts of seven states. Six of these states, after obtaining permission from Congress, entered into an agreement for the division of the water of that river and the electric power generated at Hoover Dam.

Check for Understanding: Now that you have completed this section, you should be able to answer these questions:

1. What are five restrictions on the powers of Congress?
2. What are two restrictions on the powers of states?
3. What is the importance to the individual of the writ of habeas corpus?
4. Why does the Constitution forbid Congress to give someone a title?

Hoover dam, on the Arizona-Nevada border, was built by the Federal government to provide water power for several states.

SUMMARY

Congress can make laws only within the limits specified in the Constitution. Congress can coin money, establish a uniform system of weights and measures, levy and collect taxes with bills that originate in the House, provide for the nation's defense, regulate trade between the states and with foreign nations, determine naturalization laws, impeach government officials, and provide a postal service.

Congress gained increased control through the doctrine of implied powers. It may pass laws about things not listed in the Constitution if these laws are connected to a given power. This gives Congress sweeping powers to do many things. Congress also holds investigations which have power to change the way laws are enforced. States must obtain permission from Congress to enter agreements with each other.

Most limits on the power of Congress protect individual rights. Congress cannot suspend the privilege of habeas corpus, pass a bill of attainder or an ex post facto law, nor treat people differently through the tax laws.

BUILDING SKILLS IN CIVICS

THINKING SKILLS

1. What are the major powers given to Congress?
2. Which of the following items are not powers of Congress?
   a. makes rules for the organization of the armed forces.
   b. creates federal courts lower than the Supreme Court.
   c. makes allowances of money for the armed forces for an indefinite period of time.
   d. regulates airlines, railroads, and truck routes.
   e. gives states the right to coin money.
   f. establishes a uniform system of weights and measures.
   g. asks the states to vote for a declaration of war.
3. How does the chart on "Powers of Congress' on page 226 show each of the powers the Constitution gives to Congress?

VOCABULARY SKILLS

Match each term with its definition.

a. elastic clause
b. investigative committee
c. bill of attainder
d. impeachment
e. writ of habeas corpus
f. ex post facto
g. doctrine of implied powers

1. A group of legislators that hears witnesses and gathers information.
2. A judge's order stating that a prisoner must either be accused of a crime or released from imprisonment.
3. A bill passed by a lawmaking body that convicts a person of a crime without the benefit of a trial.
4. The powers Congress has that are suggested rather than actually listed by the Constitution.
5. A Latin phrase that means "done after something else happens".
6. An accusation by the House of Representatives that an official of the United States government is guilty of wrongdoing.
7. The section of the Constitution that allows the powers of the Constitution to expand to meet new problems.

STUDY SKILLS—USING AN ALMANAC

Choosing the right source of information can save you hours of searching. When you have a question that requires a short answer, the librarian is often your best source. If your are looking for up-to-date information contained in a single volume, a general *almanac* is especially useful.

An almanac is published once a year. It contains current facts about countries, states, cities, business, political parties, population, major events, and many other subjects.

There are also specialized almanacs which contain facts about a more specific range of topics, such as economics. Get to know these information books. They are an important study tool as you practice finding information books. They are an important study tool as you practice finding information by yourself.

Activities:

1. Find "Washington, D.C." in the index and an almanac. How many sub-headings are there?
2. What page would you turn to in order to find out about the population of Washington D.C.?
3. What are the qualifications for voting in Washington D.C.?
4. Choose one other subheading. Write three factual statements that you find in the almanac that belong under the subheading.

BEYOND THE BOOK

1. Use graph paper to create a word search game. Include vocabulary words from the last two chapters. Trade with a partner.
2. Find pictures that match one of the topics below. Display your pictures and tell why you selected each one.
   a. Powers of Congress
   b. Restrictions on the Powers of Congress
   c. The Impeachment Process
3. Find five articles from newspapers or magazines that discuss laws passed by Congress. Classify these laws according to the categories of *Constitutional Powers of Congress* or *Implied Powers of Congress*.

CHAPTER FOURTEEN TEST

VOCABULARY CHECK

Some of the underlined words in the sentences below are used correctly, others are not. If the sentence is correct, write True. If it is not, replace the word with the best choice from the list.

impeachment	doctrine of implied powers	elastic clause
investigative	writ of habeas corpus	
bill of attainder	ex post facto	

1. The House has the power of impeachment if it believes that an official is guilty of wrongdoing.
2. A writ of habeas corpus states that you cannot be punished for an act committed before there was a law against it.
3. An order to bring the prisoner to court either for trial or for release from unlawful restraint is called a bill of attainder.
4. The doctrine of implied powers means that the Constitution gives Congress powers other than those listed.
5. A bill of attainder is a bill passed by a lawmaking body which convicts a person without a trial.
6. Congress may set up an investigative committee to see how laws are being enforced or where new laws are needed.
7. The part of the U.S. Constitution that gives Congress its implied powers is ex post facto.

COMPREHENSION CHECK

1. In matters of taxation,
   a. bills must originate in the House.
   b. bills may be changed by the House.
   c. the Senate and House have equal power.
2. In matters of defense,
   a. only the President can declare war.
   b. the Congress must ask the President to declare war.
   c. only Congress can declare war.
3. True or False: States must obtain permission from Congress before entering into agreements with each other.

SKILL BUILDERS—INTERPRETING FLOW CHARTS

A *flow chart* show a sequence of activities. A flow chart can also record cause-and-effect relationships, and show alternative steps. This simple flow chart shows the steps in a Congressional decision.

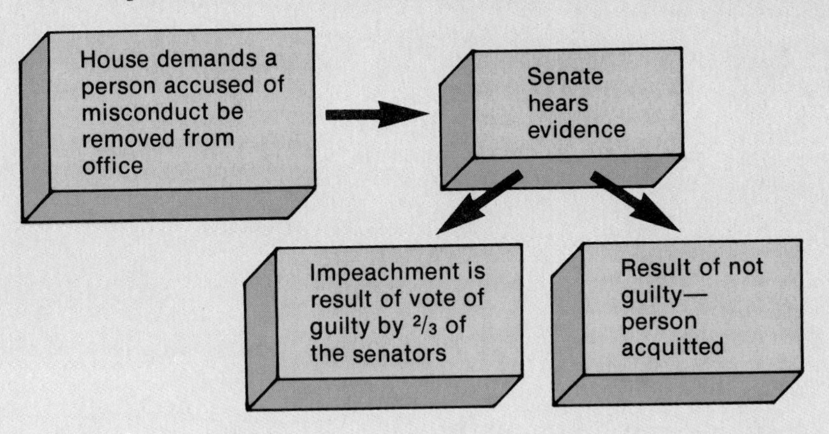

This chart shows that alternative outcomes are possible.

Activities:

1. Construct a simple flow chart showing the sequence of something you do at school.
2. Construct a flow chart showing the steps in the Presidential impeachment process.

BUILDING WRITING SKILLS

1. Choose one of the pairs of words below. Write sentences explaining the differences between the terms.
   implied powers - stated powers
   investigative committee - impeachment
   ex post facto - habeas corpus
2. Choose one topic from the list below. Discuss it with a partner, then write at least five sentences about your topic.
   a. Restrictions on Congressional Power
   b. Restrictions on States' Power
   c. Sweeping Powers of Congress

Chapter Fifteen • How Our National Laws Are Made

Document: The Constitution of the United States

Article I, Section 7. All Bills for raising Revenue shall originate in the House of Representatives; but the Senate may propose or concur with Amendments as on other Bills.

Every Bill which shall have passed the House of Representatives and the Senate, shall, before it becomes a Law, be presented to the President of the United States; if he approves he shall sign it, but if not he shall return it, with his Objections to that House in which it shall have originated, who shall enter the Objections at large on their Journal, and proceed to reconsider it. If after such Reconsideration two thirds of the House shall agree to pass the Bill, it shall be sent together with the Objections, to the other House, by which it shall likewise be reconsidered, and if approved by two thirds of that House, it shall become a Law. But in all such Cases the Votes of both Houses shall be determined by yeas and Nays, and the Names of the Persons voting for and against the Bill shall be entered on the Journal of each House respectively. If any Bill shall not be returned by the President within ten Days (Sundays excepted) after it shall have been presented to him, the Same shall be a Law, in like Manner as if he had signed it, unless the Congress by their Adjournment prevent its Return, in which Case it shall not be a Law.

Every Order, Resolution, or Vote . . . shall be presented to the President of the United States; and before the Same shall take Effect, shall be approved by him, or being disapproved by him, shall be repassed by two thirds of the Senate and House . . .

The pictures on these two pages show just a few of the steps involved in the passage of a law. Ask students if they were aware that the law-making process was so complicated.

The complete text of the Constitution can be found in the Appendix, beginning on page 564.

Article I, Section 7, of the Constitution specifies the manner in which a bill eventually becomes a federal law. The lawmaking process is lengthy and complicated due to the scrutiny that each proposed bill undergoes by both Houses of Congress and the President. However, this process is the best way of assuring citizens that the laws that govern them have been carefully considered and will serve the most people in the most efficient way.

Some people believe that the practice of requiring a bill to pass through both Houses is costly and unnecessary. Thomas Jefferson once posed the question of why we have two Houses to George Washington. Washington's reply was, "You have observed that to cool coffee, you can pour it into a saucer. So, it is with Congress. We pour the legislation from one House into the other to cool it off."

FOCUSING IDEAS

- The responsibility for making laws is shared by the President and members of both Houses of Congress.
- There are many stages involved in the passage of a bill into law. It must be proposed in one House, sent to a committee for study, presented to the Houses as a whole, sent to the other House, and sent to the President. If the President signs the bill, it becomes law; if it's vetoed by the President, it can still become law if a two-thirds majority in each House votes to override the veto.

Issues in Civics: George Washington's quote from this page explains why two Houses are needed in Congress. What did he mean when he said that legislation is poured from one House to the other to "cool it off"? Discuss with students.

PRE-TEST

1. Who makes the laws in our country?
2. What is the role of the President in lawmaking?
3. What are the stages that a bill must go through to become a law?
4. Why is it a good thing that there are so many different stages?

WHO MAKES LAWS?

Objectives: After you have read this section, you will be able to:

- Name the persons involved in making laws.
- Explain what a "veto" is.
- Explain the role of the committee system in lawmaking.

How does a law come into being? You know that the Constitution gives Congress certain powers to make laws. This great responsibility relates to the lives of everyone in the United States. A good law can have many benefits, and a poor law can do a lot of harm. How can Congress be sure that only good laws are passed?

Suppose a club in your school has a problem. It isn't working very well and the members are losing interest. One member has a plan to make the club run more smoothly. She presents the plan at a meeting. It is moved that the club adopt the plan. If a majority votes for the motion, the plan will go into effect.

The action taken by your club in adopting a new plan is much like the passing of a new law by Congress. However, there are some differences. The Constitution has established a system of checks and balances that delays the passage of a law until it has been thoroughly considered.

The role of Congress

Ideas for laws come from many sources. Special interest groups recommend legislation to members of Congress. As you have read in Chapter 14, investigative committees of Congress may want a particular law passed. The President may urge the passage of special laws. Also, large groups of citizens may press for a certain law. But only a member of Congress may introduce a law at the national level of government.

If a member of Congress sees a need, he or she may write a proposed law made to meet that need. Such a proposed law is called a *bill.* He or she presents the bill to the house of which he or she is a member. Even if a majority votes for it, however, the bill does not become a law at once. It must go to the other house of Congress. That house may vote against it. In that case the

Building Vocabulary:
bill *(240)* • veto *(241)* • override *(241)* • committee *(241)* • minimum wage *(246)* • majority/minority report *(248)* • filibuster *(249)*

These students are talking about the need for a new set of rules for their after-school club.

bill dies. Or, perhaps the second house wishes to change the wording of the bill. Then the newly-worded version of the bill is returned to the house for more consideration. Even if the second house should pass the original bill, it still does not become a law at once.

The role of the President

The bill then goes to the President. If the President does not favor the bill, he or she sends it back to the house where it originated with a message explaining why it is being returned. This is called a *veto*. "Veto" is from a Latin word meaning "I forbid." After reading the veto message, the house may vote on the bill again. If fewer than two-thirds of the members favor it, the bill dies. If two-thirds or more favor it, it is then sent to the second house. There, if two-thirds of those members vote for it, the bill becomes a law without the President's signature. This is called *overriding* the President's veto.

The Constitution provides this system to discourage the passage of bills harmful to the nation as a whole. If the House and Senate present a bill that the President considers to be a mistake, he or she is given an opportunity to forbid its passage through the veto. It cannot then become a law unless a definite majority of representatives and senators vote for it over the President's objections.

Study by committees

So many bills come before Congress that no representative or senator has time to give them all full consideration. The preliminary, detailed work is done by *committees*. The Constitution does not mention committees, but it does say, "Each House may determine the Rules of Its Proceedings. . . ." (Article I, Section 5, page 566). Except when immediate legislative action is needed in an emergency, bills are studied by committees before they are considered by the whole house.

How many Congressional committees can students think of that they've heard about on TV or in the newspaper? Do they know the purpose of these committees?

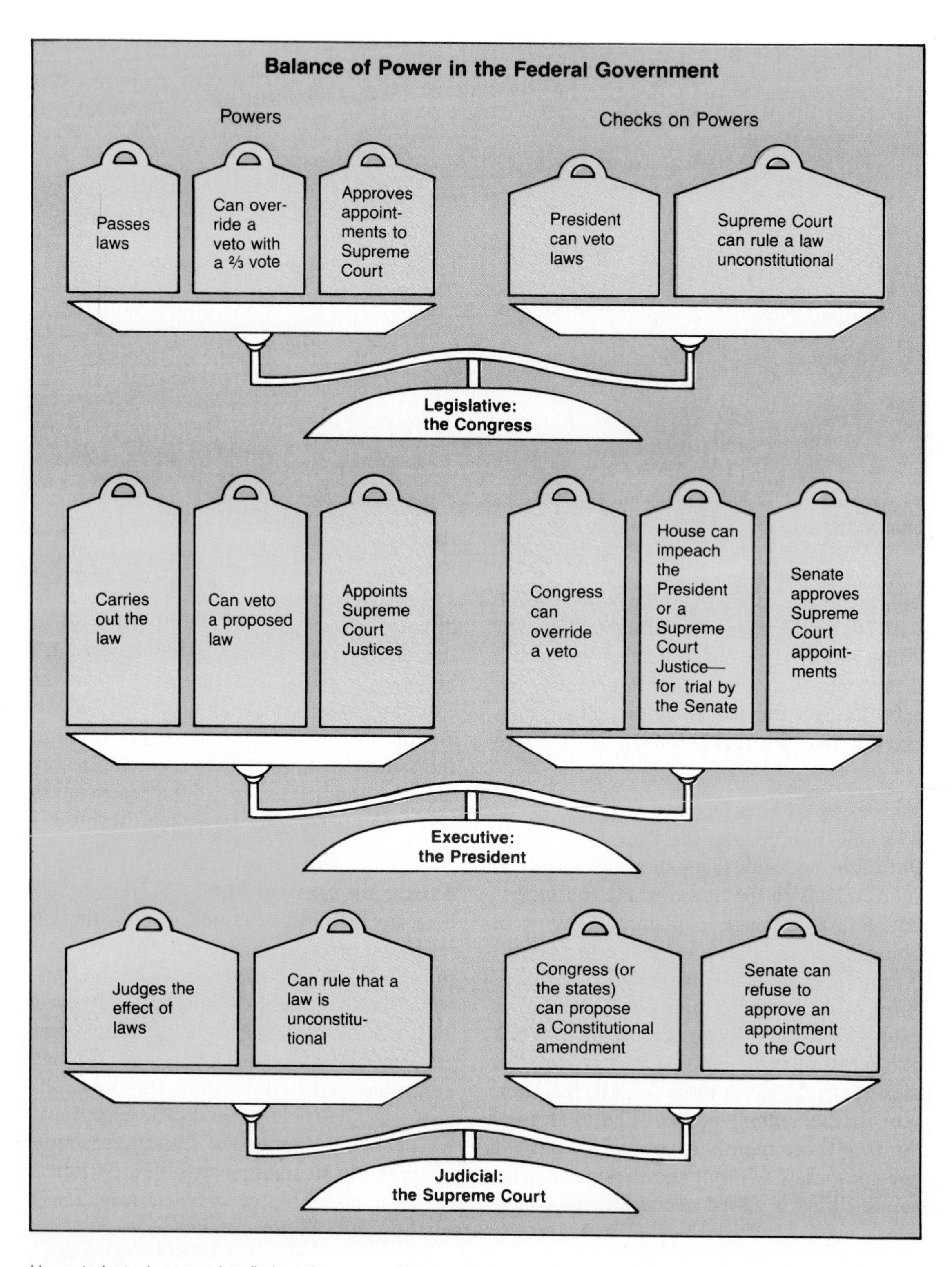

Have students do research to find out the names of the Presidents who appointed the current Supreme Court justices.

Check for Understanding: Now that you have completed this section, you should be able to answer these questions:

1. Who are the persons who are directly involved in making laws?
2. What is a "veto"?
3. What does it mean to "override" a veto?
4. How does the committee system help Congress do its work?

WHAT ARE THE STAGES OF A BILL?

Objectives: After you have read this section, you will be able to:

- Understand the steps involved in the passage of a bill.
- Explain why so many steps are necessary.
- Explain why the committee is so important to passing a bill.

Many bills are introduced

A bill has a life of its own. The following story of an imaginary bill shows this. The bill is not real, but it is about a problem that has often been considered by Congress. All of the steps in the struggle for the passage of this bill are typical of many bills.

Some bills are presented to Congress and become laws within a few weeks or even a few days. Some bills take years before they become laws. However, most bills that are introduced never become laws at all. In a recent year, there were 6,927 bills introduced in Congress. Only 309 became laws. Some of those that were introduced were combined into other bills that were passed. Some were kept in a committee and never brought to a vote.

Congresswoman Janet Barlow talked to a group of students who were looking for after-school jobs.

The steps to a law

Our story describes how an imaginary member of Congress, Congresswoman Janet Barlow, becomes concerned with a problem faced by the youth of her district and the nation. It will tell how Congress, the President, and other people react to this bill to solve the problem. In this case fifteen steps are taken after the problem is studied by our imaginary representative. As you read the story, identify each of the fifteen steps.

1. Most bills can be introduced into either house. In this example, the bill is introduced in the House of Representatives. The bill is given a number by the Clerk of the House, its title is read and it is ordered printed. Then, the Speaker of the House sends it to the appropriate committee.
2. The committee holds public hearings on the bill.

3. The full committee meets to consider the facts. It may kill the bill or put it aside, or, if it agrees with the bill, it may approve it with or without amendments. It can also rewrite it or draft a completely new bill.
4. The committee may recommend the bill for passage. If so, it is then listed on the House calendar and sent to the Rules Committee.
5. The Rules Committee is one of the most powerful committees in the House of Representatives. After the bill has been recommended for passage from the committee to which it was referred, the Rules Committee can block it or clear it for debate before the entire House.
6. The bill comes up for debate in the House and is given its second reading. The bill may be amended, or returned to the committee for revision, or approved by the House. Before the final vote is taken, the bill is given its third reading.
7. If the bill passes, it goes to the Senate for action. There it is given a number, its title read, and it is ordered to be printed. The presiding officer of the Senate sends it to the proper committee.
8. Hearings may be held. (The action here is similar to the House of Representatives.)
9. The Senate committee may reject the bill, prepare a new one, or accept the bill with or without amendments.
10. The Senate committee may recommend the bill for passage. It is listed on the calendar.
11. The bill is debated and voted on.
12. If the bill contains differences, either house may request a conference committee to iron out the differences. The conference committee meets and returns the revised bill to both houses for approval.
13. The House and Senate consider the revised bill. If both houses pass the bill, the Speaker of the House signs the bill for the House of Representatives and the President of the Senate signs it for that body. The bill is then sent to the President of the United States.
14. The President signs or vetoes the bill, or allows it to become law without his signature.
15. Congress may again pass the bill over the President's veto by a two-thirds vote of both houses.

Noticing a problem

Representative Barlow was in her home district while Congress was out of session. She gave a talk to the freshman class at Riverside High School. After the talk, some of the students came to her to discuss a problem they were having. Many of them could not find jobs for the summer and after school. There were not enough jobs available for teenagers.

Representative Barlow explained that there was little that she could do directly. She said that the students could not expect the government to provide jobs for them if there was no work to do. She also mentioned that their complaint reminded her of a problem that she and others had talked about. She would talk to people and see if she could do something in order to let the youths help themselves.

A problem to study

After her talk with the pupils of Riverside High, Representative Barlow talked to teachers and parents in her district. She found that most of them were concerned

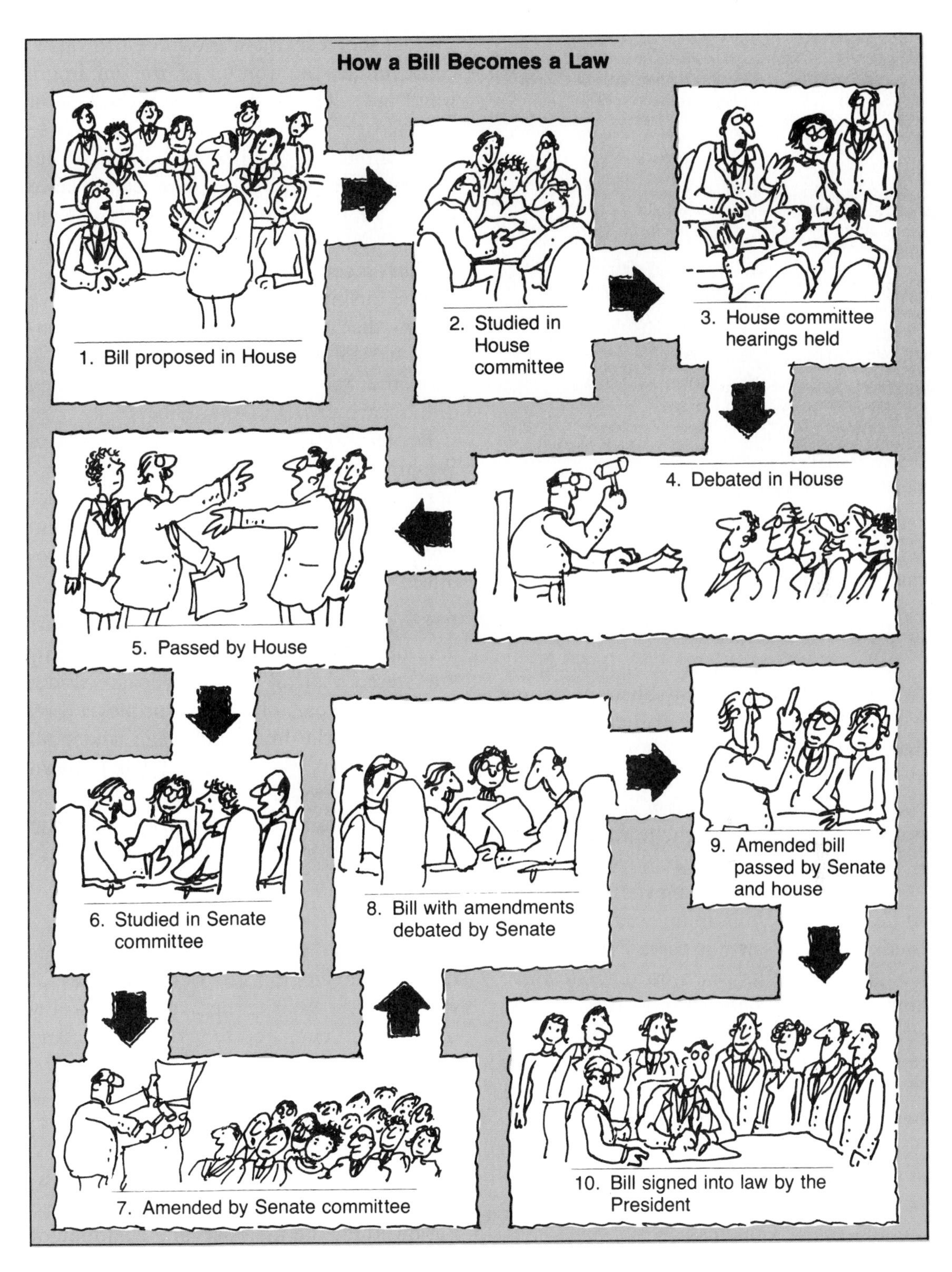

Have students pick an issue, "draft a bill" and role-play the steps in its passage through both houses.

Representative Barlow talked to local business people about the bill she was going to introduce.

that the students could not find jobs. They hoped that Representative Barlow could help solve the problem.

Following these discussions, Representative Barlow talked to many business people within her district. Many of them said they had both summer and after-school jobs available. But hiring teenagers at the regular wage would not be profitable for them; they wanted to pay less than the minimum hourly rate allowed by law.

The problem was that most of these firms came under the minimum wage law. The minimum wage law was passed years ago by Congress under its power to regulate trade among states. Congress was interested in seeing that every working man and woman received a fair day's pay. So a law was passed stating that all firms that sell goods between the states or manufacture goods to be sold between the states have to pay a *minimum wage* to their workers. They cannot pay their workers any less than the amount set by Congress.

Over the years more and more firms have come under the control of the minimum wage law. The law applies regardless of how old or young the workers are. While some firms are not involved in trade between states, many separate states have passed minimum wage laws of their own. Thus, most firms are forced to pay all workers a certain amount.

The business people told Representative Barlow that they didn't believe these teenagers could do valuable enough work to earn the minimum wage, because they didn't have enough experience.

Representative Barlow then returned to Washington. She talked with other members of Congress and many other people. After reading and studying the minimum wage law, Representative Barlow introduced a new bill.

Introducing a bill

The bill introduced by Representative Barlow stated that all people who are under twenty-one years of age and employeed by firms under the minimum wage law could legally receive less than the minimum wage. They would be paid at a rate agreed upon by them and their employeer—a rate which might or might not equal the minimum wage.

The bill in committee

After it was introduced, the bill was referred to a committee of the House for special study. Representative Barlow knew that her bill could be sent to one of many committees. It might go to the Labor and Public Welfare Committee because it would affect labor and wages. It might go to the Interstate and Foreign Commerce Committee because it would change a law concerning interstate trade. Representative Barlow knew the members and chairmen of

Ask students if they know what the minimum wage law is in their state. Do they think this wage is sufficient to support an individual?

both committees, and she thought those in the Interstate and Foreign Commerce Committee would be more in favor of her law. She talked to the Speaker of the House and convinced him to send it to that committee.

Representative Barlow knew that this committee would play an important role in the effort to get her bill passed. The committee chairman has a lot to say about whether or not the members of a committee consider the bill. It is his or her job to determine which matters come before the committee. If this committee chairman opposed Representative Barlow's bill, he or she could put off consideration. Other members of the committee might not even see the bill. Representative Barlow knew that she had to convince the chairman of the importance of considering the bill. She talked to the committee chairman. She argued that this bill should be brought before the committee for discussion and study. She said she hoped that the committee would bring the bill before the present session of Congress.

Ms. Barlow telephoned the committee chairman to try to get him to support her bill.

Public hearing

The chairman of the committee called for a public hearing on the bill. At the hearing, they heard witnesses testify for and against the bill. Afterwards, the committee met to study all the evidence.

Most businesses favored the bill. They pointed out that they had many jobs which needed to be done and which youths could do if they could be paid less than the minimum wage. They also said they could hire students at lower wages and increase their pay as they became more experienced. Eventually they might become full-time workers.

Many educators and parents also testified. They talked about the advantages to teenagers of being able to hold jobs. They repeated many things that Representative Barlow had heard before about learning on the job, gaining experience, and earning money.

Not all of the business people and educators were convinced that the bill was good. Some said that a few selfish businesses might hire students at very low pay for hard jobs when they could really afford to pay more. Some educators pointed out that if teenagers got summer jobs they might not choose to return to school. This would be throwing away their chance to complete their education and get better jobs in the future.

Many people representing labor appeared before the committee. Most of them opposed the law. They pointed out that the purpose of the minimum wage law is to protect the income of working people. They argued that these students would take good jobs away from people who support families. They felt that some firms would fire experienced workers in order to hire a student. Some of those representing labor did say that they would support the bill if they could be assured that it would only make jobs possible for teenagers and not take jobs away from adults. These were all good arguments and they impressed Representative Barlow and the members of the committee.

The committee meets

In addition to the public hearing, the members of the committee heard from people in their districts, they read reports, and they received many letters and other written opinions. They studied all this material carefully before they decided how to vote on the bill.

Committee reports

Having completed its work, the committee, by a majority vote, recommended to the House that the bill be passed. This recommendation by the majority is called a *majority report.* A smaller group of committee members were opposed to the bill. They recommended to the House that the bill not be passed. This recommendation is called the *minority report.*

The bill is sent to the Rules Committee for its approval. If the members of the Rules Committee oppose the bill, it will not be sent to the House for debate. However, the Rules Committee liked this bill, and sent it on to the House floor for debate.

Passing the bill

The bill was given its second reading in the House. Finally, it was ready for the third reading and the final vote. The House passed the bill by a majority vote and it went to the Senate.

The bill in the Senate

The bill was given a number, its title was read, and it was ordered to be printed. The presiding officer sent the bill on to the appropriate committee for study. Here the bill went through the same procedure as it did in the House of Representatives. A public hearing was held, the committee studied the bill, and finally made its recommendation to the Senate for debate. The bill was listed on the calendar. In the Senate, a bill does not go through a Rules Committee before action is taken on the floor. The Senate debated the question for several days.

Starting a filibuster

Two senators came from a state where there were a large number of working people. These senators had received many letters and had talked with many people from their state who were opposed to the bill. The two senators remembered the advice that is said to have been given by one of the Founding Fathers: "When in the majority, vote; when in the minority, talk." They decided to talk the bill to death. When the motion was made for its passage, one of the two senators rose to speak against it. The speech began at eleven in the morning and lasted until three in the afternoon. Then the other senator from that state spoke from then until the Senate adjourned that night. The next day they continued to speak against the bill, each taking turns so that the other might rest.

Have an interested student do research to find out the longest amount of time that a filibuster has lasted in our nation's history.

The Frank Capra film "Mr. Smith Goes to Washington" (1939) starred James Stewart as a Senator who single-handedly carries on a filibuster for several days.

In the House the time for debate is limited. When a bill comes before the House, it is agreed on what the limit will be. Then it is agreed who shall speak and how much time each speaker shall have. In the Senate anyone may speak for as long as is wished until a two-thirds vote of the senators ends debate. In this case a two-thirds vote could not be obtained. The senators let it be known that they would speak for months, if necessary, to kill the bill. Such a proceeding is called a *filibuster*. Some people say the filibuster is an unfair practice. Realizing that the two senators were determined to keep on talking, and that no business could be taken care of until they yielded the floor, some of the other senators offered to make a compromise.

Amending and passing the bill

The opponents agreed that they would stop their filibuster if an amendment were added. The amendment would make the bill apply only to people under eighteen who are full-time students in a high school or college and not doing any kind of "adult" work. After this amendment was introduced and passed, the Senate passed the entire bill.

When a change is made in a bill, it must be sent back to the other house. The House of Representatives did not agree with all of the changes. They wanted the bill to apply to all people who were under the age of eighteen and not just to full-time students, and to all kinds of work and not just to "non-adult" work.

Conference committee

Each house appointed a conference committee. The purpose of the conference committee was to agree upon a compromise between the houses. The committee met together behind closed doors. They did not listen to witnesses. They finally agreed that the bill would apply to those under the age of eighteen. They agreed with the House that the bill should not be limited by the type of work that the youths might do. But they also agreed with the Senate that the bill should apply only to students.

Public opinion

The revised bill passed both houses. It was then sent to the White House for the President's signature. Even after the compromise, many people who had opposed the bill were still against it. They set out to organize opposition to the bill. They had their followers send letters and telegrams to the President. They began to print leaflets and advertisements stating their opposition. They talked about the evils of child labor. They argued that children would be forced to work long hours for low wages as had happened in this country in the past.

Presidential veto

All of this opposition impressed the President. He vetoed the bill and gave his reasons in a message to Congress. He was in sympathy with the importance of getting jobs for the youth of the nation. But he did not feel that the country could run the risk of having people lose their jobs when families depend on them. He said, "The time for the teenagers to work will come, but children of all ages and the parents who support them must come first." He sent the vetoed bill back to the House of Representatives for further consideration.

The fate of the bill

When the veto message was received in the House, Representative Barlow moved for the passage of the bill over the President's veto. She felt that the President's fears were exaggerated and that the bill was important to youth. The House engaged in more debate. At last the House agreed with Representative Barlow and passed the bill with more than a two-thirds vote. It was then sent to the Senate.

In the Senate, debate was held again. An effort was made to have every senator present when the vote was taken. Finally, the time came for a vote. Five senators were absent. Sixty voted for the bill, but thirty-five voted against it. This was less than the necessary two-thirds majority, which is 67 votes. The Senate did not pass the bill over the President's veto.

A fair hearing

In this way Representative Barlow's amended bill failed to become a law. For months members of Congress had given a great deal of time and study to the matter. Public opinion was heard. It had influenced the Congress and the President. Each house acted as a check on the ideas of the other. The President played a major part. But in the end the bill did not become a law.

Preventing quick action

Representative Barlow was disappointed, but she knew that her ideas had been given a fair hearing. She realized that some people might think it would be better to have just one house that could pass bills quickly. But she agreed with the writers of the Constitution that a great deal of time should be given to consideration of a bill and that the President should have a voice in the decision.

Do students think that too much time is spent debating the issues involved in each bill that is proposed to Congress? Why do they think as they do?

Check for Understanding: Now that you have completed this section, you should be able to answer these questions:

1. What are the different steps involved in the passage of a bill?
2. Why are so many steps necessary for the passage of a bill?
3. How does what takes place during committee hearings influence the voting on a bill?
4. What is the importance to the House of Representatives of the Rules Committee? What happens if the Rules Committee approves a bill?

Standing Committees of Congress	
House of Representatives	**Senate**
House Administration	Rules and Administration
Interstate and Foreign Commerce	Commerce
Ways and Means	District of Columbia
Public Lands	Finance
Post Office and Civil Service	Foreign Relations
District of Columbia	Judiciary
Judiciary	Armed Services
Veterans' Affairs	Post Office and Civil Service
Government Operations	Interior and Insular Affairs
Agriculture	Agriculture and Forestry
International Relations	Public Works
Armed Services	Government Operations
Public Buildings and Grounds	Appropriations
Appropriations	Labor and Public Welfare
Banking and Currency	Banking, Housing, and Urban Affairs
Education and Labor	Aeronautical and Space Science
Rules	Veterans' Affairs
Merchant Marine and Fisheries	Budget
Small Business	
Science and Technology	
Standards of Official Conduct	
Budget	

SUMMARY

Most laws made by Congress may originate in either the House of Representatives or the Senate. After a bill is proposed in one house, it is sent to a committee for study. If the committee approves the bill, it is then presented to the entire house. After debate, the house will vote on the bill. If it receives a majority vote, it goes to the other house. The second house will also send the bill to a committee for study. If it is passed by this house, the bill goes to the White House for the President's signature. A bill signed by the President becomes law. A bill vetoed by the President can still become a law if a two-thirds majority in each house votes to override the President's veto.

Which of the committees listed here were students already familiar with? Do they think that any of the committees could be abolished? Any that could be added?

BUILDING SKILLS IN CIVICS

THINKING SKILLS

1. Which persons are involved in making laws?
2. How does the Constitution discourage the passage of bills that are harmful to the nation as a whole?
3. What are three sources of ideas for a bill?
4. How many committee hearings influence the vote?
5. How can a bill vetoed by the President still become a law?
6. Which of the following are *not* true about the steps involved in the passage of a bill?
   a. Except in an emergency, bills are studied by committees before they are considered by the whole house.
   b. The President may introduce a bill before Congress.
   c. Most bills can be introduced into either house.
   d. The President must sign the bill in order for it to become law.

VOCABULARY SKILLS

Fill in each blank with the word from the list that best completes the sentence.

committee bill	override	minimum wage
veto	majority report	filibuster

1. If the President does not favor a bill, he or she sends it back to the house where it originated without his or her signature.
2. When more than half of the members of a Congressional committee agree with a recommendation they issue a ______.
3. A plan or proposal for a law is called ______.
4. One or more senators can start a ______ in order to block the passage of a bill.
5. The law that says that certain firms must pay workers at least a certain amount of money is called ______.
6. Congress can ______ a President's veto.
7. Because so many bills come before Congress, the preliminary, detailed work is done by ______.

STUDY SKILLS—EDITING A FIRST DRAFT

When you work hard on a report, you record more information than you can possibly use. Your notes probably have been arranged and re-arranged. You know your subject, and are ready to write all your ideas on paper in a logical order. This is called the *first draft.* It allows you to see the strengths of your report, and also lets you correct your errors as you prepare the final version. This entire process of going from rough notes to finished copy is called *editing.* These are some of the questions to consider when you edit your first draft:

Does it follow the outline? Does it stay on the topic?

Do the headings, subheadings, and supporting facts flow smoothly and logically from one idea to the next?

Activity: Rewrite the following paragraph. Eliminate the sentences that do not relate to the main idea, and which are therefore irrelevant.

Ideas for laws come from many sources. Special interest groups recommend legislation to members of Congress. Our city has many laws. Some investigative committees of Congress may want a particular law passed. Citizens should know the issues before they vote. Some large groups of citizens press for laws. The President may urge the passage of special laws. The President may serve for only two terms.

BEYOND THE BOOK

1. Make a bulletin board showing that ideas from many sources can influence a member of Congress to propose a law.
2. Use an almanac to find information about the last session of Congress. Make a list showing the number of bills proposed, the number passed, the number vetoed, and the number overriden by Congress.
3. Collect letters to the editor that comment on proposed bills now in Congress. See if you can find political cartoons to match the opinions given in the letters.
4. Prepare an oral report which traces the process of an actual bill from its introduction to the final outcome.

CHAPTER FIFTEEN TEST

VOCABULARY CHECK

Match each term with its definition.

bill	override	committee	minimum wage
veto	majority report	filibuster	

1. Two-thirds of the votes in each house that make into law a bill previously vetoed by the President.
2. The least amount of money that can be paid to employees of certain firms.
3. A proposal or a plan for a law.
4. A report to the house by members of a Congressional committee who agree with the majority's recommendations.
5. Long speeches by a Senator or a group of Senators that block the passage of a bill.
6. The refusal of the President to sign a bill and the message that explains why.
7. A congressional group that does preliminary work on a bill.

COMPREHENSION CHECK

Indicate whether the following statements are true or false.

1. After a bill is introduced in Congress, it is sent to a committee.
2. The committee chairman must place the proposed bill before the committee for immediate consideration.
3. If the committee recommends the bill for passage, it is sent to the Rules Committee.
4. The Rules Committee can block the passage of the bill or clear it for debate before the entire House.
5. If the bill passes the House vote, it is sent to the President for signature.
6. The Senate may reject the bill, prepare a new one, amend the bill, or accept it.
7. Both houses must pass the bill before it is sent to the President.
8. A Presidential veto of a bill means that it can never become a law.

SKILL BUILDERS—INTERPRETING FLOW CHARTS

Make a *flow chart* with the heading "Steps in the Passage of a Bill". Use boxes, arrows, and key words as you did in Chapter 14. The information you will need is in this chapter. Show each step of the process, including the possibilities of the bill being rejected or amended. Use the chart below as a model.

Passage of a Bill

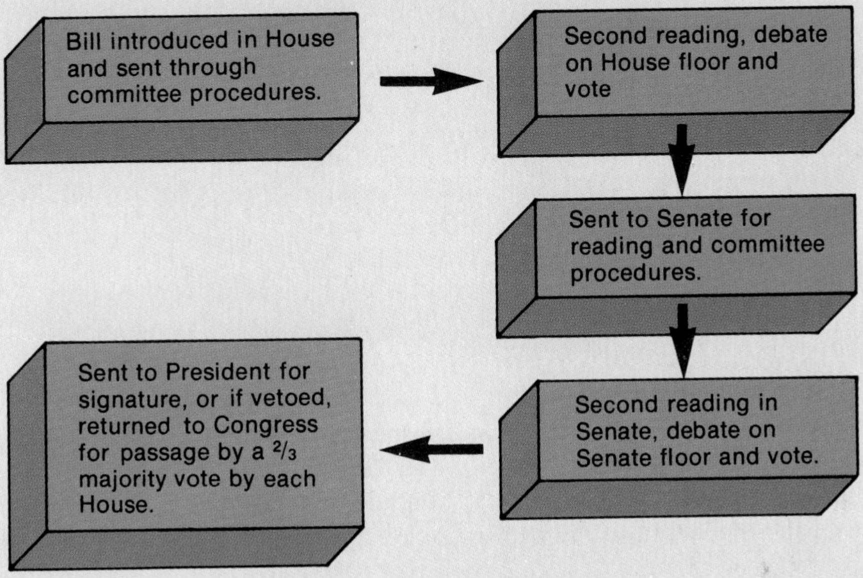

Bill introduced in House and sent through committee procedures. →

Second reading, debate on House floor and vote ↓

Sent to Senate for reading and committee procedures. ↓

Second reading in Senate, debate on Senate floor and vote. ←

Sent to President for signature, or if vetoed, returned to Congress for passage by a 2/3 majority vote by each House.

BUILDING WRITING SKILLS

1. Choose one of the titles below. Write factual statements that belong in a report with that title.
   a. The Rules Committee
   b. Persons Who Make Laws
   c. Importance of the Committee System
2. Why are so many steps necessary for the passage of a bill?
3. Write a paragraph that tells your feelings about the fate of Representative Barlow's bill. Was it worth all the time and effort? Did any good come out of what happened?

Chapter Sixteen
Our State and Local Lawmakers

Document: The Constitution of the United States

Amendment X: The powers not delegated to the United States by the Constitution, nor prohibited by it to the States, are reserved to the States respectively, or to the people.

Article I, Section 10. No State shall enter into any Treaty, Alliance, or Confederation; grant Letters of Marque and Reprisal; coin Money; emit Bills of Credit; make any Thing but gold and silver Coin a Tender in Payment of Debts; pass any Bill of Attainder, ex post facto Law, or Law impairing the Obligation of Contracts, or grant any Title of Nobility.

No State shall, without the Consent of the Congress, lay any Imposts or Duties on Imports or Exports, except what may be absolutely necessary for executing its inspection Laws: and the net Produce of all Duties and Imposts, laid by any State on Imports or Exports, shall be for the Use of the Treasury of the United States; and all such Laws shall be subject to the Revision and Controul of the Congress.

No State shall, without the Consent of Congress, lay any Duty of Tonnage, keep Troops, or Ships of War in time of Peace, enter into any Agreement or Compact with another State, or with a foreign Power, or engage in War, unless actually invaded . . .

Although it may seem that the states can do very little on their own without the consent of Congress, our state and local lawmakers actual-

The picture shows a state lawmaker dealing with his constituents' grievances. Ask students if they have ever had occasion to talk to a state or local lawmaker about a particular issue.

The complete text of the Constitution can be found in the Appendix, beginning on page 564.

ly have many powers and duties. State lawmakers are responsible for enforcing criminal law, protecting property rights, supervising public education, operating public welfare programs, maintaining highways, operating state parks and regulating state-owned land.

Local lawmakers help provide safety, health, and welfare services, provide public education, keep official records, collect taxes, and cooperate with other levels of lawmakers to provide public housing for low-income families, among other responsibilities. Although each state government has legal control over all local governments in the state, many American are in favor of local governments dealing with their problems. They believe that smaller, local governments are more responsive to their wishes than the higher levels.

FOCUSING IDEAS

- Our state lawmakers are the senators and representatives who comprise the state legislatures.
- The major officers in a state legislature are the lieutenant governor, speaker, speaker pro tempore, and president pro tempore.
- Many state lawmakers have problems dealing with bribery, time pressures, and the cost of campaigning.
- City councils are the most common policymaking body for cities.
- County governments often assume the duties once performed by overburdened municipal governments.

As the picture shows, local lawmakers are heavily involved in the workings of their city or town. Ask students what duties the mayor of *their* town performs.

PRE-TEST

1. Who are the people who make the laws in our states?
2. In what way is a state legislature organized?
3. What are some of the problems that state lawmakers face?
4. What is involved in the workings of county governments?
5. What is involved in the workings of city governments?

WHO ARE OUR STATE LAWMAKERS?

Objectives: After you have read this section, you will be able to:

- Name the term, qualifications, and number of houses for state legislatures.
- Describe a typical attitude of legislators toward service in the legislature.
- Explain the term "gerrymandering."

Many citizens find that their closest contact with state government comes through their local representative to the state legislature. These representatives live in the immediate area and are available to the citizens. Most of them work at other jobs or own a business within the community because the salary for a legislator is not sufficient to support them. People call on their legislators for all kinds of information, even when it is a federal problem and not a state one.

As the states were empowered by the United States Constitution to govern their respective areas, so each state by its own constitution was able to set up county governments. The setting up of governments at the local level brings state government

The state capitol in Raleigh, North Carolina, has a monument honoring three famous citizens of the state—Presidents Andrew Jackson, James K. Polk, and Andrew Johnson.

Building Vocabulary:
biennial *(259)* • reapportion *(260)* • gerrymander *(261)* • calendar *(262)* • seniority *(262)* • patronage *(262)* • charter *(266)* • agenda *(267)*

Are there any monuments in students' cities that honor famous citizens? If so, who do the monuments honor and what did the people do to deserve it?

closer to the people. As people collected into larger communities, it became necessary to provide more services and law enforcement. This was done by a charter granted by the state legislature to the city or town. Both the county and city or town govern by consent of the people.

Where and when state lawmakers work

State lawmakers work at their respective state capitals where the legislature is located, and at offices within their home districts. As you learned in chapter 9, all states except Nebraska, which is unicameral ("one chamber") elect representatives to a bicameral ("two chamber") legislature. The upper house is known as the Senate, and the lower house is most often called the House of Representatives. Five states name their lower house the Assembly, and three call it the House of Delegates.

Tennessee state representatives meet in the capitol building.

As recently as 1961, a majority of state legislatures met only on a biennial basis, or every other year. *Biennial* is made from two Latin words, "bi," ("two") and "annus" ("year"). Today only seven states retain biennial sessions; the rest have annual sessions. However, the governor usually may call a special session at any time. In Texas, one of the states still holding biennial sessions, the matter of having an annual session has come up several times, and been voted down each time. The attitude among some citizens in these remaining biennial states seems to be: "If the legislators aren't meeting, they can't do you any harm." But in the states with annual sessions, especially the larger ones, the lawmakers usually stay in session almost as long as the Congress because they have a large amount of work to do.

Terms for state lawmakers

The state senate generally has fewer members serving for longer terms than the house does. For example, Minnesota has 67 senators, while Alaska and Nevada each have 20. The average number in the upper house for all states is 39. Only twelve states have senators serving a two-year term instead of the more common four-year term.

The representatives or delegates are elected for a two-year term in all states except Alabama, Louisiana, Mississippi, and Maryland, where they serve for four years. This practice of running for election every two years keeps the representatives in closer touch with the people, just as it does at the national level. The size of the lower house varies from 400 members in New Hampshire, the largest number, to 40 in Alaska, the smallest number. The average is 110. Michigan with 38 senators and 110 representatives is typical.

Discuss with students the number of state senators that your state has and whether this number is adequate to serve your state's needs.

In all states the members of the legislature can run for reelection and may serve any number of terms.

Qualifications and service

The qualifications for senator, representative, or delegate vary from state to state. As is true at the national level, all legislators who wish to serve must be citizens of the United States. They also must live in the state and district in which they serve. In most states, a senator must be at least 25 years of age, and a representative or delegate must be at least 21 years of age. Some states have lowered the age for a senator to 21 and that of a representative to 18. In Texas, for example, a senator must be at least 26 years old and a representative must be 21.

Tom Craddick, a Republican, is a member of the Texas state legislature from the 50th District.

How do senators and representatives feel about service in the legislature?

These comments from two legislators probably reflect the typical attitude about service. State Representative Tom Craddick of Midland, Texas, a Republican, had this to say about his service in the house: "I wanted to be a member of the house of representatives ever since I was young. I still like being a member after fourteen years. I've chosen to remain in the House rather than running for state senator or for the national Congress, or being appointed as secretary of state by our governor."

On the other hand, Senator Pete Snelson, a Democrat from the 25th senatorial district with sixteen years service, had this to say. "I much prefer the senate. It is smaller; my personal impact is greater; and it is more democratic with more individual freedom. And there is less pressure from the political party or from one's peers. It is more deliberative and more flexible. The two houses act as a check-and-balance of each other. Each house has its weak and strong points."

Lawmakers serve in districts

Each state divides its land into smaller areas known as districts, from which representatives and senators are elected. The combining of several representative districts makes up a senatorial district, which is the larger because there are fewer senators than representatives in all fifty states. Districts were affected in the 1960's when the "one man-one vote" rule was put into effect. It took several Supreme Court decisions to make the necessary redistricting mandatory. To comply with this one man-one vote law, districts must be *reapportioned* after each ten-year census, so that there are approximately the same number of people in each.

Have an interested student contact one of his or her state representatives to find out how this politician feels about his or her service in the state.

This is not as simple as it sounds. It is not done by laying a ruler on a map and marking off squares containing a certain number of persons. Each group involved, particularly the two major political parties, maneuver for an advantage. The party in power in a state tries to draw a district in any shape that will give them a small majority in as many districts as possible, and concentrate all the voting strength of the opposing party in as few districts as possible. This is called *gerrymandering.* It is named after Elbridge Gerry, an early governor of Massachusetts, whose party redistricted the state in 1812. People thought some of the districts were shaped like a salamander, and Gerry's name was combined with (sala)mander to form the word "gerrymander" to describe this procedure.

Check for Understanding: Now that you have completed this section, you should be able to answer these questions:

1. What are the average terms, qualifications, and number of houses for state legislatures?
2. Why do some state senators prefer the senate to the house?
3. How did "one man-one vote" affect state legislatures?
4. What is meant by "gerrymandering"?

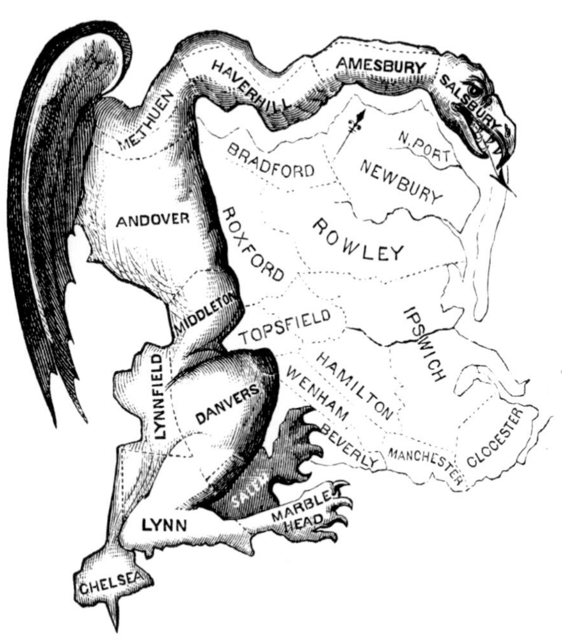

The original cartoon that created the word "gerrymander" in 1812. The body of the creature is made up of election districts created by the Jeffersonian Party.

HOW IS A STATE LEGISLATURE ORGANIZED?

Objectives: After you have read this section, you will be able to:

- Describe how a state legislature is organized.
- Explain why the Speaker of the House is a powerful position.
- Describe the privileges of seniority and explain why they are important.

Presiding officers and their duties

The presiding officer of the senate in most states is the lieutenant governor. In all states, the members of the house of representatives elect a speaker who presides over the sessions. When the presiding officer is absent, the speaker appoints a speaker pro tempore, a word from the Latin *pro tempore* meaning "for the time," and in the senate the lieutenant governor appoints a president pro tempore.

These presiding officers have positions of great power. They appoint the chairman, vice chairman, and about half of the members of each of the standing committees.

Have a student find out the salary of the legislators in your state. Does the student think that this compensation is too low, too high, or fitting for the job?

They recognize members who wish to speak and can favor those who support their own views on the legislation under consideration. They assign bills to the committees of their choice for study and report, and schedule them on the *calendar* for debate and voting. The calendar is the order of business appearing before the legislative session. The speaker of the house is considered by many to be the most powerful person in the state, next to the governor. In the senate the lieutenant governor has the same power, but in deference to the governor he or she usually keeps a low profile before the general public.

The seniority system

In both houses *seniority*, or consecutive length of time in office, is very important. Those who have more seniority get to choose the committees on which they serve, rather than being appointed to them by the presiding officer. Seniority also determines where legislators have their offices, where they sit in the chamber, and even where they park their cars. Some proponents for legislative improvements would like to do away with, or at least decrease, seniority privileges, but others think it encourages experienced legislators to stay in office for a longer time.

Check for Understanding: Now that you have completed this section, you should be able to answer these questions:

1. How is a state legislature organized?
2. Why is the Speaker of the House a powerful position?
3. How does the seniority system work?
4. Why is seniority important?

WHAT ARE SOME OF THE PROBLEMS OF STATE LAWMAKERS?

Objectives: After you have read this section, you will be able to:

- Explain how state lawmakers are compensated.
- List at least three problems facing a state lawmaker.
- Be aware of the problem of bribery.

Compensation for state lawmakers

The compensation, or salary and benefits, paid to members of the legislature varies widely in the fifty states. California, New York, and Illinois pay the most: $53,490, $43,000, and $40,408 respectively. New Hampshire pays the least, with $200 for a two-year term. Many states provide a *per diem*, a Latin term meaning "per day," of a stated sum to help pay the legislator's expenses while he or she is away from home. They also receive traveling expenses to and from their home to the state capital. In addition, at least in most of the states, the members of both houses receive a specified sum for office expenses, including stamps, stationery, and office help—the services of a secretary at the very least. Most of them will have at least one aide, to help them by doing research and by making various studies needed to understand the bills that are introduced and to vote intelligently on them.

Some legislators will hire a member of their own family and thus add to the family income. Others will manage to get family members and relatives on the *patronage* list, to be appointed as clerks, or to some other post, oftentimes with little or nothing to do. Patronage is the distribution of jobs or favors on a political basis.

Bribery

Especially where salaries are low, special interests may carry their efforts to extremes. When money is paid to a lawmaker or administrator, it is called *bribery* and is a felony, or against the law. This practice occurs at any level of government. And since it is always done in secret, the public is seldom aware of how widespread bribery can be. It was once discovered by federal authorities that most of the counties in one state had received "bribe money" on county purchases of road and bridge-building equipment. Newspapers, television, and other media often help to bring such corruption or dishonesty of public officials into the light.

More subtle ways of influencing public officials are by entertaining them at meals, with free tickets to entertainment, gifts, promises of future employment, and expensive trips. The ways to influence public officials are endless. Every lawmaker must be alert to persons who want to influence him or her by "free gifts," whatever the kind.

Being a lawmaker requires a great deal of time, even when the legislature is not in session. Representative Craddick once reported: "Last Sunday I had 26 different calls from people needing help of one kind or another." Senator Snelson estimated that he spent one-half to three-fourths of his time on government business, even when the legislature was not in session.

Not every legislator is willing to devote this much time to public service. The heavy turnover of members of state legislatures is a problem. On the average, half of the legislators in the United States serve only one term, or about two years, whereas it is generally felt that a legislator does not become truly effective until he or she has served at least three sessions. Many of these "one-timers" feel that for financial reasons they cannot afford to stay in the legislature. Others leave for different reasons, such as to take up another office, or because they do not like being in office. Some serve a short time to achieve one particular goal and leave after that is done.

Another problem facing legislators is the cost of campaigning. This is a major area for reform, although there is disagreement about what reforms would be best. There is a trend toward public financing, as is now done in presidential campaigns, but there is considerable opposition to this measure. Some persons think that at least there should be a strict limit, with a careful accounting of the money spent on each campaign, as well as a shortening of the campaign period.

This new state legislator faces a typical problem, in that his legislative salary is far less than he earned as a lawyer.

Can students think of any legislation that *they* would like to have passed in their state? Would they consider writing to their state legislators to propose these laws?

Check for Understanding: Now that you have completed this section, you should be able to answer these questions:

1. How are state legislators compensated for their service?
2. What are three problems facing state lawmakers?
3. What is bribery?
4. Why do many legislators serve only one term?

HOW DO COUNTY GOVERNMENTS WORK?

Objectives: After you have read this section, you will be able to:

- Explain the place the county has as a government in our system of government.
- List at least two problems with the use of the country as a government.
- Give examples of a county government functioning in different ways.

Historical background

The county as a unit of government originated in Great Britain, and its roots can be traced back to the Saxon settlements of the 5th century. The title "count" was given to the most important citizen of the county. English colonists brought the idea of a county as a unit of government with them to the New World.

In the United States today there are over 3,000 counties. It is our largest division of local government. Connecticut and Rhode Island do not have any kind of subdivision like a county. The differences in size range from 20,131 square miles in San Bernardino County, California, to 24 square miles in Arlington County, Virginia. Loving County, Texas, has a population of fewer than two hundred persons, while Los Angeles County, California has more than seven million people.

County size is tailored to allow people living in the county to be able to reach the county seat without too much difficulty. In the wide open spaces of the West, a person in frontier times was supposed to be able to ride on horseback to the county seat in a single day. Often the county seat would be the only city or town in the county. However, there are counties that are full of cities and towns, with little agricultural area. The county is no longer just a rural arm of the state government, but an important governmental unit in itself.

The traditional functions of counties have been law enforcement, judicial administration, road construction and maintenance, the keeping of public records, welfare, and, in some cases, administration of schools. But counties today, particularly in

The county courthouse of Tarrant County, in Fort Worth, Texas, as shown in an engraving made in 1879.

Issues in Civics: Do students think that the county government has come to assume too many duties? Are county governments now as overburdened as some city ones are?

urban areas, also have assumed duties once performed mainly by overburdened municipal governments.

The policymaking function

Because the county is mainly an administrative arm of the state, it does not have a constitution of its own, nor a charter as a city does. The organization and functions of the county are specified by the state constitution, and limited to those functions permitted. A former county judge in Texas explained the distinction: "The county cannot do anything unless it is expressly allowed by the state, whereas the city can do anything that is not specifically denied it by the state."

The principle of separation of powers was ignored whenever counties were created. Thus they do a little bit of everything. Sometimes they act as a legislative branch, then judicial, and also executive. There is no real executive in charge of the affairs of most counties, although some counties now hire a manager or a personnel director.

Problems with county government

Strict control by state constitutions has made it difficult over the years to handle emerging conditions, such as water and environmental pollution. It also hinders the control of development around a recreational area for the benefit of the people living there. It takes considerable time to get special permission to handle this kind of problem. For instance, if there are people living on the shore of a lake who are littering the area and polluting the water, the county must get special permission from the state to correct this situation. It may take several months, or even longer, to get this permission.

The two main criticisms of county government are that it needs more authority to meet the needs of the citizenship and that it requires more centralized administrative authority. This latter criticism is being dealt with in some places through the use of professional administrators. Today sixteen percent of the counties in the United States are now operating with an administrator appointed by the board, and five percent elect an administrator along with the board. Some counties are working up to the use of such an administrator gradually by hiring a personnel manager and a county engineer.

The county of San Diego, California, is among those that now employ the services of a professional chief administrator.

Check for Understanding: Now that you have completed this section, you should be able to answer these questions:

1. What is the place of county government in our system of government?
2. What are two problems with the county as a unit of government?
3. What are the different roles a county government can have?
4. What are two criticisms of counties?

HOW DO CITY LAWMAKERS WORK?

Objectives: After you have read this section, you will be able to:

- Explain what a charter is.
- Describe a city council and explain what it does.
- Recognize the need for citizen participation at the local level.

Historical background

The city is our oldest governmental unit, going back in time to the oldest known civilizations, such as ancient Egypt, Babylonia, and Mesopotamia. Democracy was born in the city-states of early Greece, even though it extended only to the male, free-born citizens of the city and surrounding territories. The city is the governmental unit that most closely touches the life of the citizen. We are very well aware when water doesn't run from our faucets, or there are potholes in our streets, or when crime is threatening our lives and property.

A city is an area, within a county, that has its own local government, though it is also subject to the laws of the nation, state and county. When a group of people wish to incorporate into a city, they petition for, and receive, a *charter* from the state government. This charter sets out the boundaries, governmental powers and functions, and method of finance, of the city, as well as the election and appointment of officials.

From Chapter 9 you will recall that there are three main forms of city government. The mayor-council form is used by all the cities in the United States with over a million population, and 75% of those between a half million and a million. Over half the cities under 10,000 population also prefer the mayor-council form. Over the United States, 4% of the cities use the commission form, and 35% use the council-manager form. Over half of the cities from 25,000 to 500,000 in population prefer the council-manager plan.

The ancient city-state of Babylonia was one of the world's earliest organized units of government.

Have an interested student obtain a copy of your city's charter and then discuss the powers and functions that your city has with other class members.

City councils

The city council, which is the most common form of policymaking body for cities, acts much like a legislature does. It is concerned with establishing the rules for governing life in the city or town. There are usually other persons or departments that carry out these rules.

City councils vary in size

Chicago's fifty-member council is the nation's largest. Several small towns have councils with only two members. The average is somewhere between seven to nine members. Terms of office differ from city to city as well; however, four-year terms are the most common.

Councils pass ordinances within the legal limits of their charters. As you recall from Chapter 9, an ordinance is a ruling to be obeyed within the city limits. For example, there are usually ordinances in most cities about pets running loose, fireworks, and traffic signals, just to name a few. Two of the most important lawmaking duties that councils perform have to do with taxation and spending. Councils decide who is to be taxed by the city and how. And they also decide how the city government's money is to be spent.

A council meeting is conducted according to parliamentary procedure. Council members have an *agenda*, which is a list of matters to be acted upon, and work with motions, which are sometimes voted on directly and sometimes passed to a committee for further study. Special groups, if they are recognized as such, often can be of use in the decision process. Citizen participation is essential for a well-run government. At all levels from the federal government to the local school board, lawmakers welcome the thoughts of the people; indeed, they want to know what the citizens think about matters of public interest.

Check for Understanding: Now that you have completed this section, you should be able to answer these questions:

1. What is a charter?
2. What is the work of the city council?
3. How are council meetings conducted?
4. Why is citizen participation important in city government?

SUMMARY

There is a chain of legislative command. The state is empowered by the United States Constitution; the county is under the state constitution; and the city is chartered by the state legislature. Each entity has its place in the governing of the nation, and each has a governing body resembling that of the other, but also differing in some ways.

Each unit of local government requires work and cooperation from its citizens. Some state and local lawmakers receive a salary, but many work on a volunteer basis. And at the state level salaries are so low that lawmakers must have additional jobs. Influence and bribery can be problems where salaries are so low.

There are problems involved in all levels of government. And solutions are numerous, and probably none of them perfect. The citizens need to be active in their state and local governments if these problems are to be solved to the best advantage of all groups.

Ask students to name any ordinances that they know of that are in effect in their city. Do they think these ordinances are beneficial, or detrimental to their city?

BUILDING SKILLS IN CIVICS

THINKING SKILLS

1. How often do the majority of state legislatures meet?
2. What are the lengths of the terms most senators and representatives serve?
3. What are the qualifications for a senator or representative in most states?
4. What is the average size of the lower house for state legislatures?
5. Write an appropriate title for the following paragraph:
   "You should take courses in Government and Civics, as well as History. You should become involved in student government, civic groups, and other organizations. Also, you should follow the news of the day and sit in on political party meetings."

VOCABULARY CHECK

Some of the underlined words in the sentences below are used correctly, others are not. If the sentence is correct, write True. If it is not, replace the word with the best choice from the list.

biennial	reapportion	seniority	charter
gerrymander	calender	agenda	patronage

1. Districts must be <u>reapportioned</u> after every ten-year census.
2. <u>Patronage</u> means that the party in power in a state tries to give itself a small majority in as many districts as possible.
3. The <u>calendar</u> is the order of business appearing before the legislative session.
4. <u>Seniority</u> is the distribution of jobs or favors on a political basis.
5. When a group of people wish to incorporate into a city, they petition for a <u>charter</u> from the state government.
6. An <u>agenda</u> is a list of matters to be acted upon.
7. Today, only seven states retain <u>calendar</u> sessions; the rest have annual sessions.
8. Consecutive length of time in office is called <u>seniority</u>.

STUDY SKILLS—MAKING A FORMAL OUTLINE

An informal outline can be a list of questions or topics you plan to cover that will help you keep track of your work. Later, as you use the formal outline, you organize ideas in a traditional pattern.

The rules for a *formal outline* are the same as those for a topic outline, except that the headings, subheadings, and supporting facts are written as complete sentences rather than as short phrases.

Activity: Copy the sentence outline below. Find information in the chapter to fill in the missing points.

Theme: The City Council acts much like the legislature does.

I. The city is our oldest form of governmental unit.
  A. It goes back in time to the civilization of Egypt.
  B. Democracy of a limited sort was born in the ancient Greek city-states.
II. The city is an area, within a country, which has its own local government.
  A. The city council is the most common form of policymaking.
    1. It establishes rules for governing life in the city.
    2.
    3.
  B. Councils pass ordinances within the legal limits of their charters.
    1.
    2.
    3.

BEYOND THE BOOK

1. Arrange a display of books and magazines that tell about lawmakers. Next to each, write two questions that can be answered by that source.

2. Collect local newspapers for several days. Identify the news stories according to those that are mainly local news, state news, national news, and world news. What conclusions can you make from your work?

CHAPTER SIXTEEN TEST

VOCABULARY CHECK

Fill in each blank with the word in parentheses that best completes the sentence. Use the correct tense of the word.

1. The law requires a state to ______ its congressional districts after every ten-year census. (reapportion - district)
2. The ______ is the order of business appearing before the legislative session. (calendar - agenda)
3. ______ means that the party in power in a state tries to give themselves a small majority in as many districts as possible. (seniority - gerrymander)
4. People must petition for a ______ from the state government when they wish to incorporate into a city. (charter - agenda)
5. Consecutive length of time in an office is called ______. (patronage - seniority)
6. An ______ is a list of matters to be acted upon. (charter - agenda)
7. ______ is the distribution of jobs or favors on a political basis. (patronage - biennial)
8. Most states retain annual sessions, not ______ ones. (biennial - calendar)

COMPREHENSION CHECK

Write True if the question and answer go together. If they do not, write a new answer that fits the question.

1. What is the average term for state legislators? —The average term is four years for senators and two years for representatives.
2. What are the average age qualifications for legislators? —In most states, a senator must be at least 25 years old, and a representative must be at least 21 years old.
3. What does each district have to do after each national census to comply with the "one man-one vote" rule? —Presiding officers appoint the chairman, vice chairman, and many committee members.

4. What are some of the privileges enjoyed by representatives with seniority? —The committee divides the work among the members and allows experts and interested people to present their viewpoints.
5. What happens if a bill passes both houses, but is amended so that both versions do not agree? —The bill goes back to a conference committee composed of members of both houses.

SKILL BUILDERS—INTERPRETING AN ATLAS

An *atlas* is a collection of maps showing different kinds of information about an area—political boundaries, physical features, population, economic activity, and so on. The index makes it easy for you to find the information you are looking for by giving you the page number and the grid square where the entry appears.

Activity: Use an atlas to find a map that shows you the physical features of an area, or a *topographic map*. What information does the key give you? Make up three questions that could be answered by using this map. What are some generalizations you can make from this information? Use the atlas to locate another topographic map, this time of a state of the United States. Describe what the map tells you.

BUILDING WRITING SKILLS

1. Write sentences to explain the differences between one of these pairs of words.
   redistricting - gerrymandering
   lieutenant Governor - speaker
   district - county
2. Choose one of the sentences below and write a short argument in favor of it.
   a. The seniority system is good because it encourages experienced lawmakers to stay in office.
   b. The seniority system is bad because it gives people privileges just for being re-elected.

UNIT FOUR TEST

TEXAS: Congressional Districts

Texas: 1980 Census - 14,228,383
1970 Census - 11,198,655
House seats - 27
Seats gained or lost - (+3)

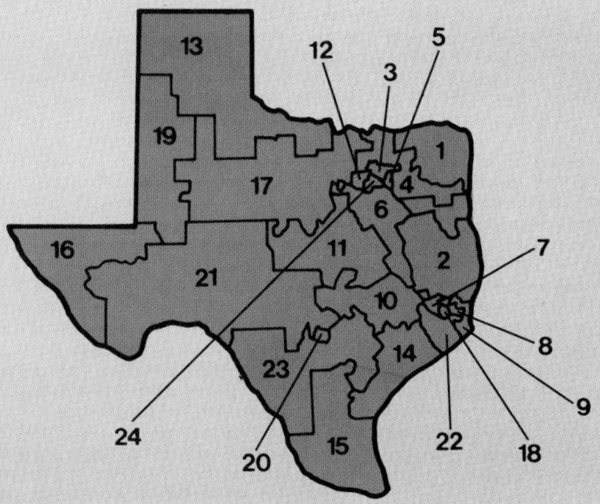

A. Look at the map above and the facts that pertain to it. Then answer these questions:

1. Although Texas is the largest state in the continental U.S., California has 18 more house seats. Why is this so?
2. Why did Texas gain three house seats since the 1970 census?
3. Does it look like Texas is fairly represented? Why? Why not?
4. How does the term "reapportionment" apply to the map and facts above?

B. Choose one of the following generalizations. Then write at least five factual sentences that apply to it.

1. Our national lawmakers serve to see that our needs are met.
2. The people, through the Constitution, gave Congress the power to make laws for the good of the country.
3. Citizens need to be active in their state and local governments in order to exercise their rights and responsibilities.

C. Chapter 13 details some of the privileges that members of Congress have. Do you think these privileges are deserved? Why? Why not? If *you* were a member of Congress, are there any other privileges you would want?

You may want to apply Activity 'A' above to your own state as well.

Unit Five
Our Nation's Executives

*H*ave you ever wondered what it would be like to be a chief executive of a nation, state, or city? You would be in a position of power and would also be afforded many privileges. However, you would also be responsible for overseeing the execution of laws that would affect thousands, or even millions of people.

Few of our nation's executives consider their jobs to be "fun." Rather, they are acutely aware of the grave responsibilities that their jobs involve and they do their best to live up to the expectations of their constituents.

The illustration depicts Truman's 1948 election campaign. Truman's famous desk-top sign "The buck stops here" is a fitting description of the role of our nation's chief executives at the national, state, and local levels.

Chapter Seventeen
The President

Document: The Constitution of the United States

Article II, Section 1. The executive Power shall be vested in a President of the United States of America. He shall hold his Office during the Term of four Years, and, together with the Vice-President, chosen for the same Term, be elected, as follows

No Person except a natural born Citizen, . . . shall be eligible to the Office of President; neither shall any Person be eligible to that Office who shall not have attained to the Age of thirty five Years, and been fourteen Years a Resident within the United States.

In Case of the Removal of the President from Office, or of his Death, Resignation, or Inability to discharge the Powers and Duties of the said Office, the Same shall devolve on the Vice President, and the Congress may by Law provide for the Case of Removal, Death, Resignation or Inability, both of the President and Vice President, declaring what Officer shall then act as President, and such Officer shall act accordingly, until the Disability be removed, or a President shall be elected.

The President shall, at stated Times, receive for his Services, a Compensation, which shall neither be increased nor diminished during the Period for which he shall have been elected, and he shall not receive within that Period any other Emolument . . .

The illustration symbolizes the office of the Presidency. Ask your students which of these things they feel is most central to the office of President. Which is less essential?

The complete text of the Constitution can be found in the Appendix, beginning on page 564.

The President of the United States is the nation's chief executive and the most powerful elected official in the country. Ever since the Founding Fathers established the office of the Presidency, the responsibilities and powers of our chief executive have expanded tremendously. This is due partly to the dynamic personalities of certain Presidents, but is also a result of circumstance. The President's power may decline during peacetime, but may increase during wartime or periods of economic hardship.

FOCUSING IDEAS

- A person must meet certain requirements in order to be eligible for the office of President.
- The electoral college elects the President and Vice President. It is composed of electors from every state who vote for the Presidential candidate who got the most votes in their state.
- The steps to being elected President involve announcing one's bid for office, running in primaries, nomination by one's party, campaigning, winning the popular vote, and winning a majority of electoral votes.

Issues in Civics: Over the years the power of the President has grown tremendously. Ask students if they think this power should be curtailed or if it should be allowed to increase.

PRE-TEST

1. What are the qualifications that a person must have to be President?
2. What happens to the Presidency if the President dies?
3. What is the electoral system?
4. What are the steps to being elected President?

WHO CAN QUALIFY TO BE PRESIDENT?

Objectives: After you have read this section, you will be able to:

- State the qualifications for the office of President.
- Describe the kind of persons who have been President.
- Explain what happens to the Presidency if the President dies.

Laws alone are not sufficient to govern a country. There must be officers with *executive* power to enforce or carry out these laws. The Constitution determines who shall have this power when it says, "The executive power shall be vested in a President of the United States of America." This means that one person, the President, has the power to carry out the national laws. This one sentence has made the President the most powerful person in the United States, if not the world. It makes selecting the President one of the most important decisions made by the people of the United States. It makes the Presidential election the most exciting one in the nation, because every U.S. citizen is affected by its outcome.

The President conducts daily business from this room in the White House, known as the Oval Office.

Building Vocabulary:
executive *(276)* • inauguration *(278)* • elector *(280)* • electoral college *(280)* • popular vote *(281)* • platform *(285)* • minority President *(286)* •

All Presidents have had to make difficult decisions. Have an interested student choose one President and write a report on a difficult decision that this Chief Executive had to make.

Those who have served

George Washington was the first President of the United States, in 1789. He has been followed by thirty-nine others. By profession twenty-three have been lawyers, and four were soldiers. There were two each of these—planters, educators, and businessmen. There was one each of these—tailor, author, journalist, editor, engineer, and actor. Some have been wealthy; others have been poor. Nine did not attend college; however, of this number several were among the most outstanding ever to be President. Some men made good Presidents; others did not.

To date, there has not been a woman President or Vice President. Although the Constitution sets forth certain qualifications for the office, it does not specify whether the person should be a man or woman. Therefore the American voters may choose either a man or woman, as they desire. In the future, then, it is entirely possible that a woman candidate may be elected President. Great Britain, the nation whose political tradition is closest to our own, elected a woman, Margaret Thatcher, as the head of its government in 1979.

All those who have served were known to the public before they were elected. Some were better known than others. Yet, each had a following. Also, each one was backed by a major political party. Each one had to fight a long, hard political battle to gain the office of President. Obtaining the Office of the President is not an easy task.

Margaret Thatcher of the Conservative Party became the first woman to be elected as head of a Western democracy when she was chosen as Prime Minister of Great Britain in 1979.

Issues in Civics: Ask students if they think there will ever be a woman President. Why do they think as they do?

Have students do library research to see if they can find a rating on the Presidents that has been compiled by historians. Ask them if they agree with the material they find.

Qualifications for President

The Constitution sets forth the qualifications that a President must have. To be eligible for President, a person must be at least thirty-five years old and a native-born citizen. He or she must also have been a resident within the United States for at least the past fourteen years.

Term of office

The President is elected for a four-year term and is eligible for a second term of four years. As you read in Chapter Seven, the original Constitution did not put any limit on the number of terms a President could serve. But the twenty-second amendment, ratified in 1951, sets a limit of two terms. The Constitution does not state how much the President should be paid. It simply says that he "shall receive for his services, a compensation." At the present time the President is paid a salary of $200,000 a year. In addition, the President receives a tax-free allowance, plus a taxable office expense allowance. The President also has the White House as a residence and the use of a jet airplane, Air Force One, for travel. There is also a large estate available for weekend or vacation uses—Camp David, in the mountains of Maryland.

The President and Vice President take office on January 20 or the following day if that day falls on Sunday. Before taking office, the President takes an oath. The text is written in the Constitution:

"I do solemnly swear (or affirm) that I will faithfully execute the Office of President of the United States, and will to the best of my ability, preserve, protect and defend the Constitution of the United States."

The *inauguration* of the President is a solemn ceremony. Millions of people now hear it on radio or see it on television. The Chief Justice of the Supreme Court reads the words of the oath, and the President-elect repeats them.

It is merely a custom for the Chief Justice to administer the oath to the President. The Constitution does not state specifically who should do this. Any judge, clerk, notary public, or other officer empowered to give an oath to a citizen may perform this service for the President of the United States.

How to prepare for the Presidency

There is no particular course of study that will prepare a person to be the President of the United States. Each has to find the way that best works for him or her. When he was asked about this, John F. Kennedy, our thirty-fifth President, replied: "You would be well advised to practice stern discipline and vigorous effort. High qualities and great achievements are not merely matters of chance or birth. They are the produce of long and disciplined toil."

Presidents who have known and worked with all kinds of people, who know the different parts of the country, and who have knowledge of other countries and their people, seem to be better prepared for the office. Those who have understood and accepted their own strengths and weaknesses have made better Presidents. Yet, the Presidency is a peculiar office that is shaped by the individual who holds it, and in turn Presidents themselves often have risen to greatness shaped by the office—and the time in which they lived.

The Vice President is next in line

The Constitution provides that if a President dies, or is unable to serve, the Vice President shall take his or her place. If a

Have a student choose one President that he or she feels was a particularly good or poor President and write a speech supporting his or her opinion.

The President serves in a dual role, as both the official leader of the U.S. government and as the unofficial "first citizen" of the country.

person is elected President but dies before taking office, the Vice President-elect then becomes President.

The twenty-fifth amendment to the Constitution says that if there is a vacancy in the Vice Presidency, the President will nominate a person to that office. This person must receive a majority vote of both houses of Congress in order to take office. When Spiro Agnew resigned as Vice President in 1973, President Richard Nixon nominated Gerald Ford to become Vice President. Nixon's choice was confirmed by Congress. In 1974, when Nixon himself resigned as President, Gerald Ford then became President and served until 1976. This is the only time in our history when the Presidency was held by someone who was not elected as either President or Vice President.

These amendments and laws are important because they provide for a smooth continuation of power. In cases of death, assassination, or resignation, the office of President has been filled according to the laws. There have been no tragic periods of uncertainty, struggle, or revolution, as has often been the case in other countries when a leader died or left office unexpectedly.

Check for Understanding: Now that you have completed this section, you should be able to answer these questions:

1. What are the qualifications for President?
2. How many Presidents have we had?
3. What kind of people have served as President?
4. Who succeeds the President in case of death or disability?

Ask students if they think it's important for there to be a smooth transition between Presidential administrations. Why do they think so?

WHAT IS THE ELECTORAL SYSTEM?

Objectives: After you have read this section, you will be able to:
- Describe the electoral system.
- Explain the intention of the Founding Fathers in establishing it.
- Tell why the system still is in operation today.

A system adopted in the Constitution

The delegates to the original Constitutional Convention did not foresee that the President would be as directly elected by the votes of the people as he or she is today. When the Constitution was written, most nations were ruled by kings and queens who had inherited their offices. The people were not accustomed to electing national officials. The members of the Constitutional Convention, however, wanted the President to be chosen by representatives of the people. Some thought that the Congress should elect the President. Others thought that either the governors or the state legislators should do the choosing. Other plans were considered, but most of them involved different ways that the representatives of the people would select a President.

A compromise plan

After a long debate, the Constitutional Convention compromised by adopting an electoral system:

"Each State shall appoint, in such manner as the Legislature thereof may direct, a Number of Electors equal to the whole number of Senators and Representatives to which the State may be entitled in Congress; but no Senator or Representative, or Person holding an Office or Trust or Profit under the United States, Shall be appointed an Elector."

For example, in a state that has eight representatives and two senators in Congress, add eight and two, and the total of ten members of Congress equals the number of electors to be chosen by the voters in that state. The entire group of *electors* chosen from all states to select the President is called the *electoral college.* The word "college" in this sense does not have its usual meaning of "a place of higher education," but has the older meaning of "a group of a people who are organized to perform a certain duty."

Election by electors

The electoral college has only one duty. They elect the President and the Vice President. The writers of the Constitution expected that each state would select as its electors persons of great wisdom, character, and patriotism. They hoped that the electors would take time to study the fitness of people for office, and they would choose the best possible citizens for President and Vice President. That is exactly what the electors did in the first two elections for President.

Free choice by electors

Under the system originally provided by the Constitution, each elector voted for two persons. The one receiving the highest number of votes was declared President. Every elector voted for George Washington, and he was declared President. Not all voted for John Adams, but he received the second largest number of votes and was declared Vice President. Though the electors were unanimous in choosing Washington as President, they had been free to vote as they pleased, without any commitment to a political party or candidate.

Issues in Civics: Ask students if they think the electoral college should be abolished? Why or why not?

An 1877 woodcut shows the deadlock in the electoral college over the Hayes-Tilden election. The empty chair represents disputed votes from Florida. A special committee ruled the votes should go to Hayes.

Choices made by the party

This early system is totally different from the way a President is selected now. Today the electors rarely exercise a choice in voting for President and Vice President. As political parties were formed, party representatives nominated candidates for President and Vice President. They also nominated the electors. As a result, the chosen electors are expected to vote for the person their parties have nominated. They usually do so, though sometimes a party is surprised when one of its electors does not vote for the party candidate. This happened most recently in 1976. Gerald Ford was the Republican nominee, but one Republican elector from the state of Washington voted for Ronald Reagan, the candidate whom Ford had defeated for the Republican nomination.

Election by the people

Each state legislature can decide how the electors shall be chosen. In the early years of our nation, the legislators in the various states chose the electors. After about twenty years the legislatures began to pass laws providing that the people should vote for electors. Today the people in each state vote for that state's electors. Since the electors will usually vote for their party's candidate for President, the people are almost voting directly for the President.

Popular vote vs. electoral vote

Two sets of electors are nominated in each state, one by the Democratic party and one by the Republican party. If a plurality of the *popular vote* in the state (the vote of the people themselves), is cast for the Democratic electors, then they are all elected.

Electoral Votes by State

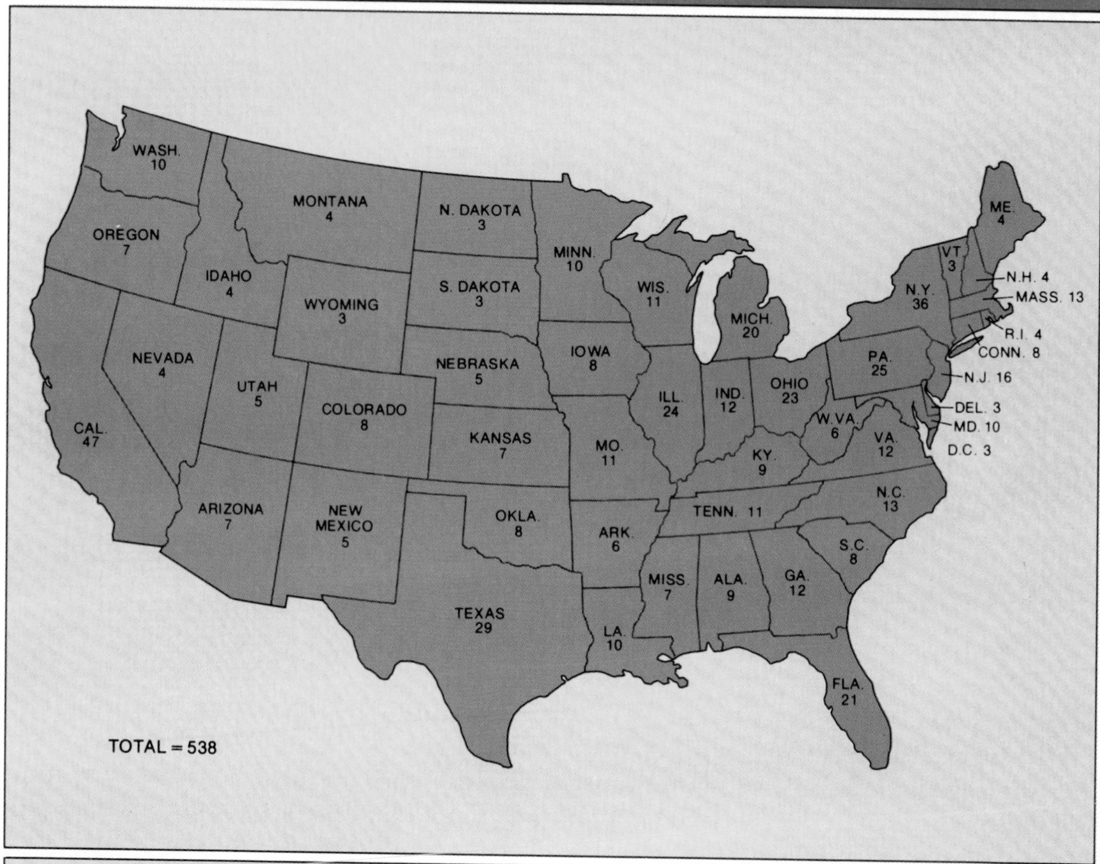

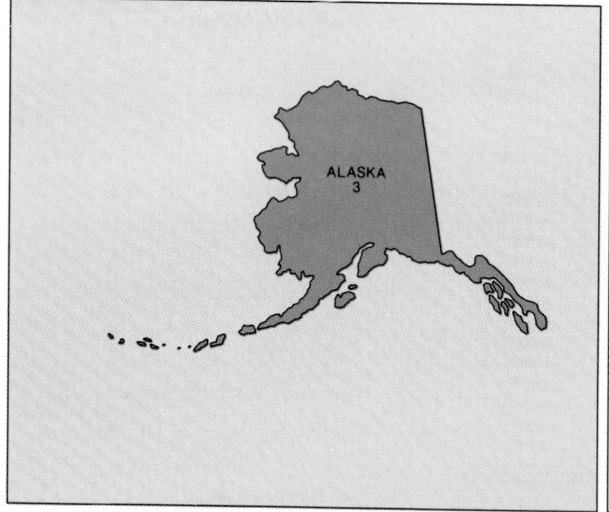

Even if more than a million voters in a state favor the Republican candidate for President, all the electoral votes in that state will go to the Democratic candidate if the plurality of the Presidential vote in the state goes Democratic at the polls.

A winner in the popular vote can lose the election

Many people believe that the electoral system should be changed. They say the system can elect a President even though a rival candidate receives a larger percentage of the popular vote. In the election of 1888, Grover Cleveland received the majority of the popular vote. However, Benjamin Harrison received a majority of the electoral vote and became President.

Other plans suggested

Critics of the electoral system have suggested a number of other systems. One is to elect the President and Vice President directly by vote of the people. Another is to change to a "weighted" system, so that each state can split its electoral votes according to the way the popular vote is split in that state. This would avoid the "all or nothing" system of the electoral college. For example, in the 1976 Presidential election the states of Georgia and Virginia each had twelve electoral votes. Jimmy Carter won Georgia by a plurality of about 500,000 votes. Gerald Ford won Virginia by a plurality of about 20,000 votes. Thus each received the equal total of twelve electoral votes, although the difference in the popular vote in the two states was about 480,000. Under the weighted system, if a state has ten electoral votes, a candidate with sixty percent of the popular vote would get six electoral votes, not ten. An opponent with forty percent of the popular vote would get four votes, instead of zero.

Small states are protected

The states with small populations will not readily agree to the direct election of the President. Under the present system the small states have much more power in the choice of the President than they would under a system of popular election.

We can observe this by comparing New York and Nevada. The state of New York has nearly sixty times as many people as Nevada. In the electoral college New York's advantage is reduced. New York has forty-one electoral votes, while Nevada has three. New York has only about fourteen times as much power in choosing a President as Nevada, though it is about sixty times Nevada's population.

The electoral system works

Defenders of the electoral system say that using only popular votes would force elections into the House of Representatives. Third parties would increase their strength. They argue that since this system has served us well since the nation began, there is no need to change it. Whenever a Presidential election is approaching, the debate on whether or not to change the electoral college system begins again. A candidate with great support in the most populous states might want to change it.

Check for Understanding: Now that you have completed this section, you should be able to answer these questions:

1. How does the electoral process work?
2. What was the original intention of the Founding Fathers in establishing the electoral system?
3. Why is the electoral system still retained today?
4. How is it determined how many electors a state will have?

Issues in Civics: Do students think that it's fair that a winner in the popular vote can lose a Presidential election if he or she does not win the electoral vote?

Steps to the Presidency

1. Announcement of Candidacy
2. Primary Campaigns
3. National Convention
4. Presidential campaign
5. General Election
6. Electoral Vote
7. Electoral results to Congress
8. The Presidency

WHAT ARE THE STEPS TO BEING ELECTED PRESIDENT?

Objectives: After you have read this section, you will be able to:

- List the steps involved in being elected to the Presidency.
- Describe what happens in primary and general elections.
- Tell how an election might be decided in the House of Representatives.

When our country began, the electoral college alone had the power of electing the President. But in recent times the power to elect the President has been divided. Political parties and the popular vote, as well as the electoral college, all hold power in electing a President. The way this process works can be seen by following the steps that a person goes through to be elected.

The announcement

Usually the candidate announces, or tells newspaper and TV reporters, that he will try to become the President. This announcement is made many months before the election. The candidate will campaign —make speeches and appearances—to try to win the nomination of his party. After one person has announced, the nation waits to see who else will enter the race. Some candidates enter the race early, while others wait until later.

The Presidential primary

Most announced candidates will enter some or all of the state Presidential primary elections. If they win one or more of the primaries, their chances of winning their party's nomination are much greater.

In a recent election, thirty-one of the fifty states held primary elections. The rules of the primary elections may differ from one state to another. Some states allow voters to vote for the candidate they prefer. Other primaries select delegates, who may or may not be required to support certain candidates. When all of the primary elections are over, some candidates will have dropped out. Those who have won some primaries will still be in the running. They will go to their parties' conventions with a certain number of delegates pledged to support them, based on the votes they received in the primaries.

The national convention

The remaining candidates then seek the nomination of their parties at the national convention. Each party's delegates from all of the states gather together at their convention. They adopt a *platform*—the stands that the party wants to take on major issues. Finally they select the party's nominees for President and Vice President. Sometimes the results of the primaries have clearly determined who will be nominated. In other cases, the selection is not known until the final ballot is cast by the delegates. The delegates could, if they wished, select a person who had not even announced or won any primaries, but this is unlikely. At most national conventions, the parties nominate candidates who are well-known party leaders. After the delegates in each party have selected their choice for President and Vice President, the campaign begins.

The campaign

The final campaign for election takes place for two or three months before the election. The final candidates go around the country making speeches and appearing on TV. In some campaigns the two major party candidates have appeared together in a televised debate. All of these efforts are to try to win votes on the actual day of the election.

Ask students if they were aware that there were so many steps involved in running for the Presidency. Would they ever want to run for this office?

The general election

The people finally go to the polls to select their President on the first Tuesday after the first Monday in November of the election year. When voters go to the polls, they see the candidates' names printed on the ballots or voting machines in every state. The voters cast their ballots for one Presidential candidate, but actually they are voting for the electors of that candidate's party. In some states the electors' names are on the ballots. In other states they are not. For example, when voters in 1980 indicated their choices either for Jimmy Carter or Ronald Reagan, in some states they were really voting for electors of the candidates' political parties.

The electoral vote

In the final result, it is the electoral vote that elects the President. The electors from each state meet in their state capitals on the first Monday after the second Wednesday following the election. There they vote for President and Vice President. While electors traditionally vote for the party nominee, they do not have to do so. They can vote as they please.

Counting the vote

Three records are made of the electoral vote. One is carried personally by an elector to the President of the Senate. In the House of Representatives on the following January 6th, the representatives and senators each choose two tellers. These four persons count the ballots in the presence of the members of both houses. Of course, except in unusual cases, the results of the election are known as soon as the votes are counted in November. However, the election is not official until tellers announce the result to Congress.

An electoral majority needed to win

The candidates receiving the highest number of electoral votes for President and Vice President are declared elected, provided they have received a majority of the electoral votes to be elected.

A winning candidate who does not receive a majority of the popular vote has sometimes been called a *minority President.* This refers only to a minority of the popular vote. It cannot mean a minority of the electoral votes, because the candidate cannot be elected President without a majority of electoral votes.

A frequent reason for a winning President to receive less than half of the popular votes has been the presence of a third party. Minority presidents have not been uncommon in our history. There have been fifteen, including in recent times Harry Truman in 1948, John F. Kennedy in 1960, and Richard Nixon in 1968.

Election of the President by the House

If no candidate for President receives a majority of the electoral votes cast, the House of Representatives elects the President. When the Presidential election takes place in the House, each state has only one vote. In the election of 1800 the Constitution provided that each elector vote for two persons. Thomas Jefferson was the Presidential choice of the Democratic-Republican party. Aaron Burr was its choice for Vice President. All the electors of this party voted for both Jefferson and Burr. Both men thus received the same number of votes, but neither received a majority. The House of Representatives then voted, and they elected Thomas Jefferson to the Presidency.

Have an interested student do a report on a minority President and tell whether this President's administration was a successful one.

After that election the Constitution was changed to provide that each elector cast one vote for President and one vote for Vice President. That plan is still in use today.

Another failure of the electors to choose a President occurred in 1824, when none of four leading candidates, Andrew Jackson, John Quincy Adams, William H. Crawford, and Henry Clay, received a majority of the electoral votes. In choosing a President, the House of Representatives could vote for any of the top three candidates. Andrew Jackson had received the most electoral votes with 99, but he did not have a majority. John Quincy Adams received the next highest number, 84. The representatives used the authority to elect any one of the top three and chose Adams, who became President with just 32% of the electoral vote and 30% of the popular vote.

Election of the Vice President by the Senate

If the electors fail to give a majority to any candidate for Vice President, the Senate will vote. In 1836 no candidate received a majority in the electoral college. The vote was then given over to the Senate to decide. Richard M. Johnson, who had the most electoral votes, was elected.

Check for Understanding: Now that you have completed this section, you should be able to answer these questions:

1. What are the steps involved in being elected President?
2. What happens in a primary election?
3. How does the general election in November differ from the primary election?
4. Under what circumstances could an election be decided in the House?

SUMMARY

The Constitution set forth the qualifications a person must have to become President or Vice President of the United States. That person must be thirty-five, a native-born citizen and have lived in the U.S. for at least the past 14 years. Other than that, anyone, man or woman, is eligible to be President.

The number of terms a President can serve was limited to two by the twenty-second amendment, passed in 1951. A term is four years. The President takes office on January 20, or the day after, in the year following his election.

If the President dies or cannot serve, the Vice President replaces him or her. If the office of Vice President becomes vacant, the President appoints a replacement.

The electoral college is composed of electors from every state. Each state chooses as many electors as it has members of Congress. Although not bound to do so by law, these electors vote for the candidate who got the most votes in their state. Some people believe the electoral college should be reformed, perhaps by using a "weighted" system.

The steps to becoming President involve announcing, running in primaries, getting the nomination of the party at the national convention, campaigning, winning the popular vote, winning a majority of electoral votes. If no candidate for President receives a majority in the electoral college, the election is decided in the House of Representatives. In the case of the electoral college not giving a majority to a Vice Presidential candidate, the Senate votes.

Have students do research to find out which Vice Presidents went on to become the Chief Executive of our nation.

BUILDING SKILLS IN CIVICS

THINKING SKILLS

1. What are the qualifications for the office of President according to the Constitution?
2. What are some of the compensations a President receives for his or her service?
3. How does the Constitution provide for a smooth continuation of power in case the President or Vice-President dies or resigns?
4. How are the number of electoral votes for each state determined?
5. Find four factual statements in the chapter that support this generalization:

   The power to elect the President has been divided in recent times.

VOCABULARY SKILLS

Match each term with its definition.

a. executive
b. elector
c. platform
d. electoral college
e. minority President
f. inauguration
g. popular vote

1. The entire group of electors that meets to vote for the President of the United States.
2. A President elected without a majority of the popular vote, because there were more than two candidates, or because the electoral college did not reflect the popular vote.
3. The person who has the authority and duty of managing the affairs of a nation, or a state, and of putting its laws into effect.
4. The ceremony in which the President-elect is sworn into office.
5. The votes actually cast by the people in an election, as opposed to the electoral votes.
6. A party's position on important issues.
7. A person chosen by the voters in each state to formally select the President and the Vice-President of the United States.

STUDY SKILLS—EDITING

The first version of a report is called a first draft. This is a rough version that probably needs a lot of editing. As you read over the first draft, be as objective as possible, and consider the following three questions:

1. Does the paper stay on the point?
2. Does it contain the correct information?
3. Does it follow a logical sequence?

If the answer to any of these questions is "No", then it is necessary for you to *edit* your first draft.

Activity: Each paragraph below needs editing. First, identify the problem. Next, edit and rewrite each one. Then, write a title that gives the main idea of each paragraph.

> "The Constitution set forth the qualifications a person must have to become President of the United States. That person must be thirty-five, a native-born citizen, and lived in the U.S. for at least the past ten years. Some people believe the electoral college should be reformed."
>
> "The inauguration of the President usually takes place on January 20. After taking office, the Chief Justice reads the words of an oath, and the President-elect repeats them. Millions of people now witness the event on radio or television. The Constitution states that the oath must be administered by a member of Congress."

BEYOND THE BOOK

1. Construct a chart that shows the reasons for and against reforming the electoral system. Use the chart as the basis for a bulletin board. Have other class members contribute information that is relevant to the topic.
2. Use the school library to find information about the twenty-second amendment. What events led to its passage? Who was opposed to its passage?
3. Interview people who remember the events leading up to the twenty-second amendment. Find out what they think of the amendment and of the reasons for passing it.

CHAPTER SEVENTEEN TEST

VOCABULARY CHECK

Some of the underlined words in the sentences below are used correctly; others are not. If the sentence is correct, write True. If it is not, replace the word with the best choice from the list.

inauguration	minority president	elector	executive
popular vote	electoral college	platform	

1. The entire group of electors chosen from all the states to select the President is called the platform.
2. In order to carry out laws, there must be officers with elector powers.
3. The presence of a popular third party candidate is a common reason for the election of a minority president.
4. Today the people in each state vote for that state's electors.
5. A political party's platform is its position on important issues.
6. The inauguration is when the President and Vice-President are sworn into office.
7. Even if a candidate receives a majority of the popular vote, he or she may not be elected.

COMPREHENSION CHECK

1. If the President dies, or is unable to serve,
   a. the Senate meets to vote on a successor.
   b. a general election is called.
   c. the Vice-President assumes the office.
2. Delegates gather at the national convention to:
   a. wait and see who will enter the Presidential race.
   b. hold primary elections.
   c. select the party's nominees for President and Vice-President.
3. A Vice-President could be elected by the Senate if:
   a. electors fail to give a majority to any candidate.
   b. enough citizens sign a petition.
   c. the Vice-President resigns.

SKILL BUILDERS—INTERPRETING COMIC STRIPS

Comic strips, like cartoons, use simplified pictures, symbols, exaggeration of details, and humor to present a point of view. The comic strip also tells a story in sequence, and uses dialogue. An effective comic strip can present a point of view with great force.

1. What is the setting of each frame? Does it change? Explain.
2. What physical characteristics does the artist give the figures?
3. What are the figures doing? What are they saying? What do you think the man asked them?
4. What symbols has the cartoonist used? How do they help communicate the artist's point of view?
5. What generalizations can you make about this comic strip?

BUILDING WRITING SKILLS

1. Choose one of the titles below and write five or six factual statements that belong in a report with that title.
   a. The Kinds of Persons Who Have Been Presidents
   b. Primary and General Elections
   c. Problems in Presidential Elections
2. Write a question that the following statement answers.
   Some involve announcing, running in primaries, campaigning, winning the popular and electoral votes, and taking the Oath of Office.

Chapter Eighteen • The Powers and Limits of the Presidency

Document: Constitution of the United States

Article II, Section 2. The President shall be Commander in Chief of the Army and Navy of the United States, and of the militia of the several States, when called into the actual Service of the United States; he may require the Opinion, in writing, of the principal Officer in each of the executive Departments, upon any Subject relating to the Duties of their respective Offices, and he shall have Power to grant Reprieves and Pardons for Offences against the United States, except in Cases of Impeachment.

He shall have Power, by and with the Advice and Consent of the Senate, to make Treaties, provided two thirds of the Senators present concur; and he shall nominate, and by and with the Advice and Consent of the Senate, shall appoint Ambassadors, other public Ministers and Consuls, Judges of the Supreme Court, and all other officers of the United States, whose Appointments are not herein otherwise provided for, and which shall be established by law . . .

Article II, Section 4. The President, Vice President and all civil Officers of the United States, shall be removed from Office on Impeachment for, and Conviction of, Treason, Bribery, or other high Crimes and Misdemeanors.

The pictures on these two pages show various Presidents of the past and present. Ask students if they can name these men and describe any major events that occurred in their administrations.

The complete text of the Constitution can be found in the Appendix, beginning on page 564.

The Constitution gives the President of the United States many powers that enable him or her to shape and determine national policy, provided that the President, to the best of his or her ability, will "faithfully execute the Office . . ." and will "preserve, protect and defend the Constitution of the United States." The original framers of the Constitution realized that the powers of the President would need to be modified in years to come and, so, defined the President's role in a broad fashion.

In much the same way that Congress is limited in the way it uses its powers, the President is limited by checks by Congress and the Supreme Court. For example, the Constitution requires that the Senate must approve all treaties made by the President and give its advice and consent when the President appoints government officials.

FOCUSING IDEAS

- The Constitution gives the President broad powers, enabling him or her to shape and determine national policy.
- The President's powers grew as a result of the growth of America and the need for more federal laws.
- The President's power is limited by the Constitution, the Congress, the court system, and by the people who elected him or her.

Issues in Civics: In the past two decades several Presidents have been criticized for lack of strength in dealing with the issues. Based on what they know of U.S. history, ask students how they think modern Presidents compare to those of the 1800's and early 1900's.

PRE-TEST

1. What powers does the Constitution grant the President?
2. How did the role of the President develop over time?
3. What limits does the Constitution place on the office of the President?
4. What role does Congress play in the limitation of presidential power?

WHAT POWERS ARE GIVEN TO THE PRESIDENT BY THE CONSTITUTION?

Objectives: After you have read this section, you will be able to:

- List the powers of the President.
- Tell how the Constitution allows for change in these powers.
- Explain the title "commander-in-chief."

The President of the United States is a very important person. As head of the executive department, he or she has great responsibilities. Among other duties, the President carries out federal laws, helps to shape foreign policy, is in charge of national defense, and helps to form his or her party's stand on various current issues.

Many of the President's powers come from the provisions of the Constitution. These powers are used by consent of the majority of the people. The President performs duties to serve and protect the people. Because the United States plays a major role in world affairs, the President's actions also affect people in many foreign countries.

The Constitution and the people also limit the President's powers. The other branches of the government have the power through the Constitution to check some of the President's powers when he or she assumes too much control of the government. Public opinion and the public's vote limit the President's actions, too.

The powers given to the President by the Constitution seem very few. They are much like the powers that the Constitution gives to Congress. In 1787 the writers of the Constitution knew that the President's duties would change over a period of time. So, in Article II they gave only a short, general definition of the areas in which the President has power. The Constitution gives each President the duty of applying the powers of the office to serve and protect the people. This enables each President to meet the needs of the time rather than being restricted by specific rules. The Constitution makes the office of the President practical and flexible.

Building vocabulary:
commander-in-chief *(296)* • bureaucracy *(299)* • chief of state *(301)* • inherent power *(301)* • checks and balances *(303)* • spoils system *(303)* • civil service *(303)*

Discuss with students the importance of the flexibility that the Constitution gave the office of the President.

Powers of the President

Approves or Vetoes Bills

Commands the Armed Forces

Appoints Ambassadors and Other Federal Officials

Proposes Laws and Programs to Congress

Conducts Foreign Policy

May Pardon People Guilty of Federal Crimes

Which of the powers of the President do students think is the least important? Most important?

The President can declare a "disaster area" and order emergency federal aid after an event such as this flood in Indiana.

The power and responsibility to enforce laws

Article II, section 1 of the Constitution states, "The executive power shall be vested in a President of the United States." This means that the President is given the executive power to carry out the laws that are made by Congress. The President is the chief executive or head law enforcer of the country.

Commander-in-chief

In Article II, section 2 the Constitution says that the President is the "*commander-in-chief* of the Army and Navy of the United States." This simple statement gives the President much power. It has given the president what Abraham Lincoln called the "war powers." Only Congress, however, can actually decide that we will go to war. The President then has the power to say how the war will be fought. The leaders of the armed forces must carry out these plans. The President can also send our troops, planes, and ships to foreign lands to protect citizens of the United States or our national interests.

The President controls the use of weapons. This is a great responsibility in our times. Modern nuclear weapons are very powerful, powerful enough to cause great destruction. The President must make the decision as to whether or not these weapons are to be used.

Have an interested student research a time when a President ordered troops into a foreign country when there was no war.

The power of appointment and pardon

The Constitution gives the President the power to appoint many officials in the United States. The President can do this only "with the advice and consent of the Senate." This means that the Senate must approve the President's appointment by a two-thirds vote. The President also directs the work of government employees. This is an important responsibility today because there are so many government employees.

The President also has the power to pardon people who have been convicted of federal crimes. President Ford used this power in 1974 to pardon Richard Nixon of crimes that he might have committed while he was President. President Carter used it in 1977 to pardon draft evaders of the Vietnam war.

President Ford signs the order granting a pardon to former President Nixon.

Veto power

The Constitution gives the President the power to veto or reject any bills passed by Congress. This gives the President some control over laws that Congress makes. Congress can override a presidential veto, but this is difficult. The bill must win a vote of a two-thirds majority in both houses to be passed and made into law.

The power to make treaties

The Constitution states that the President "shall have the power, by and with the advise and consent of the Senate, to make treaties." The President must have a treaty approved by a two-thirds majority vote of the Senate. Then the treaty can be put into effect. The President also appoints United States ambassadors, ministers, and consuls to foreign countries. Foreign ambassadors in the United States are received by the President and by members of the Department of State.

The power to call special sessions of Congress

The Constitution grants the President the power to call special sessions of Congress. This power also gives the President some control over Congress. Special sessions are usually called in a national emergency, such as threat of war, or other grave circumstance. They are also convened or assembled when the President wants to influence Congress to pass a bill that the President favors.

Check for Understanding: Now that you have completed this section, you should be able to answer these questions:

1. What are the powers of the President?
2. How did the writers of the Constitution allow for changes in the role of the President?
3. What is meant by the title "commander-in-chief"?
4. Why does the United States give the authority to decide on the use of nuclear weapons to the President?

Do students think that the office of the Presidency is too much for one person to handle? What alternatives can they think of?

Issues in Civics: Do students think that President Ford should have pardoned Richard Nixon? Why?/Why not?

HOW DID THE PRESIDENT'S POWERS GROW?

Objectives: After you have read this section, you will be able to:

- Describe how the powers of the Presidency grew.
- Explain which of those powers have taken on greater importance.
- Explain what a "bureaucracy" is.

By America's growth

When the Constitution first established the Office of President, America was a small country. Most people were farmers and had the same needs. The duties of the President were fewer. Over the years, the number of people in America increased. Many new industries developed. The number of people in cities grew. America became involved in world affairs. The United States expanded on many frontiers. More and more federal laws were made to serve the people's needs as our country grew.

The President's job of enforcing these new laws grew and grew. Now the office of the President must make many rules and decisions to see that the laws are carried out. It is the duty of the President to decide when and how the laws of the land should be executed.

The President's first concern when enforcing a law is to serve fairly the needs of Americans. Because America is a nation of many needs, its laws are complicated. Most laws passed by Congress call for things to be built, services to be provided, or actions to be controlled. And the President must decide how to apply the Federal laws to fit the needs of many businesses and people.

The bureaucracy

The President cannot attend to all these duties personally. Many cabinet positions, government agencies, bureaus, and departments have been established to aid the President. All of these groups help to enforce the decisions of the executive office. The President and all the individuals and

The President represents his or her country as the head of the state and as the leader of the government.

Do students think that there is too much bureaucracy in our government? What makes them think as they do?

groups who work for the President are called the executive branch of the government. The President appoints most of the people to various posts in this branch. When people refer to the executive branch, they often use the word *bureaucracy*. This word means a group of non-elective, or appointed, government officials. As the President's duties have grown, the size of the bureaucracy has also grown.

Leadership in foreign affairs

The President's role as our country's leader in foreign affairs has increased in importance as the United States has grown. The Constitution makes the President the Commander-in-Chief of the armed forces. It also grants the President the power to make treaties. These powers enable the President to direct the United States in foreign affairs. The President can order the armed forces into foreign countries. This action can persuade other governments to act differently. With the approval of the Senate, the President makes treaties with other countries. This enables her or him to establish our relationships with the rest of the nations of the world.

Leadership of the party

The President has another power besides the powers stated in the Constitution. The chief executive has much influence as the leader of his or her political party. Power over a particular party gives the President power over that party's members of Congress. If the President's party holds a majority of seats in Congress, the President usually will have an easy time getting favored laws passed.

The President provides the leadership for legislation. He or she has a staff to prepare legislation. The President begins by laying out legislative matters to members of his or her own political party. Then, staff members from the President's Office meet with members of Congress to influence them to vote for the President's legislation. Often, the President will invite Congressional members to the White House to influence them to vote his or her way on a bill. This kind of persuasion is very powerful because most members of Congress are reluctant to oppose the President openly, especially if the legislation concerns national defense or a reduction in taxes.

Yet, it must be realized that many times the Presidency is an office of uncertain power in domestic affairs. For example, successive presidents in recent years have wrestled unsuccessfully with trying to establish an energy policy, reform the tax system, balance the budget, and coordinate our national welfare system.

Chief of state

The Constitution invests the President with the power to be the Chief Executive, but does not specifically describe the duties of being a head of the nation or state. The framers of the Constitution assumed the functions of managing the state and representing the state would be tied into one. However, this idea was unique in the world, even though by 1787, when the Constitution was written, Great Britain assigned the management function to a prime minister and the representation function to the king.

This dual role has always presented problems to American presidents. They must on the one hand engage in "rough-and-tumble" politics to obtain the Presidency and on the other hand, once the office has been granted, rise above partisanship to represent all the people of the country. The ability to do this has depended, of course,

Discuss with students the importance of the President's influence over his or her political party.

Privileges of the Presidency

Presidential Seal

Theme Song: "Hail to the Chief"

Presidential Aircraft

Honor Guard

Access to the Media

White House

Can students think of any other privileges that the President has that aren't mentioned here? What are they?

on the person occupying the Presidency. Some have been very successful at this, largely due to personality. Others, either because of lack of popularity or events like an unpopular war, have found it difficult to function as head of state and at the same time manage the affairs of government. However, the successful use of the role of *chief of state* can increase the power of any President, because this role allows him or her to rally the nation to a particular cause or course of action.

Check for Understanding: Now that you have completed this section, you should be able to answer these questions:

1. How did the powers of the Presidency grow?
2. Which of these powers have taken on greater importance?
3. What is a bureaucracy, and how does it work?
4. What is meant by the term "chief of state"? How does this differ from chief executive?

WHAT ARE THE LIMITS OF THE PRESIDENT'S POWER?

Objectives: After you have read this section, you will be able to:

- Describe the system of checks and balances.
- Explain the limits on the President's powers.
- Describe the work of the Civil Service.

There are also limits to the President's powers. Many of the kings of long ago were absolute rulers. They could issue orders that had the force of law. Dictators can issue such orders today. However, the President is not such a ruler. The President faces limitations that are defined by the Constitution. The President must work within these prescribed limits.

Constitutional limits

The Constitution limits the President's powers. The President cannot acquire powers beyond those defined. Some Presidents have claimed that they have *inherent powers*. These are powers which Presidents believe belong to them in times of great emergency. Such an emergency arose in 1952. Workers in the steel mills went on strike. Steel was needed to build war materials for our armed forces fighting in Korea, so production needed to be continued. Prompt action was necessary. President Truman asked the Attorney General for advice. The Attorney General said that the President could exercise inherent powers in times of emergency.

President Truman took control of the steel mills. The steel companies then appealed to the courts. The courts said that the Constitution gave the President no such power. Also, Congress had not granted the President this power. The Supreme Court ruled that the President has no inherent powers, not even in an emergency. The Supreme Court ordered the control of the mills returned to the owners. This decision showed that the President is limited to the powers defined in the Constitution. The two houses of Congress and the court system also help to control the President's powers.

Have an interested student write a report on a President who used inherent powers to deal with a great emergency.

Sewell Avery, chairman of Montgomery Ward & Co., was evicted from his own office by military police after failing to comply with a Presidential order during World War II.

The laws of Congress

The President makes many rules and decisions in enforcing laws. Most of these decisions can be carried out only as long as Congress approves them. If Congress dislikes the way the President is doing something, it can limit or check presidential powers in certain areas. For example, suppose Congress has passed a bill giving the President power to spend money on a particular disaster relief program. If Congress does not like the way that the President is spending the money, it will refuse to permit any more money to be spent until the program is changed. Congress can also limit how the President enforces a law by stating exactly how the President should carry out the law or prohibiting certain things from being done when the law is put into effect.

Often Congress will pass a law for a particular period of time. At the end of that time, Congress will review the rules that the President has made in enforcing the law. They can change these rules if they

Issues in Civics: Discuss with students the role of Congress in our system of checks and balances. Do students think this system is a good one?

wish to do so. Congress can then stop the President from acting in one way, or it can direct the President to act in another way.

The judicial branch

The court system or the judicial branch of the government can also limit the President's power. It can declare the President's action unconstitutional.

The President's powers are limited by both the judicial and legislative branches of the government. The President can, in turn, limit the powers of both these branches. Each branch of government can check and balance the powers of the other two. This system of *checks and balances* ensures that no one branch will gain too much power. Each branch acts to check the actions of the other two should they overstep the powers granted by the Constitution.

The Supreme Court checked Franklin D. Roosevelt's power by declaring the NRA, a federal agency, unconstitutional.

Limits on appointment power

The President's power to make appointments is also limited. The Constitution provides that the President shall name persons for office "with the advice and consent of the Senate." Most appointments must be submitted to the Senate. They do not become effective unless two-thirds of the Senate approves. If the Senate rejects an appointment, the President must select another person. The new appointment must be submitted to the Senate for approval by a two-thirds majority.

The Civil Service system

Early Presidents selected the best persons they could find for positions in the government. New Presidents who came into office would retain nearly all the old employees as long as they served well.

This method was changed after the election of 1828. In that year many federal employees worked to re-elect President John Quincy Adams. After Andrew Jackson won the election, he fired those who had opposed him. They were replaced with persons belonging to Jackson's party. The practice of firing old employees and appointing political supporters to office came to be called the *spoils system*. Presidents who came after Andrew Jackson also appointed loyal party members to office under the spoils system.

The spoils system became such an accepted practice that political supporters expected to get jobs when their candidates won. One disappointed office seeker, angry at not receiving an appointment, shot and killed President James A. Garfield in 1881. Shocked by the tragedy, Congress enacted the *Civil Service* Act of 1883. This act provided for a Civil Service Commission. This commission is now called the Office of

Issues in Civics: Ask students what they know of the civil service system and what the strong and/or weak points of this system are.

The assasination of President Garfield by Charles Giteau, who had hoped to be appointed to a government job, brought about the passage of the Civil Service Act.

Personnel Management. This office does the work of selecting most of the civilian employees in the executive branch of the government. Those who want government positions must take an examination. Jobs are given to applicants who score well.

When people receive an appointment to a government office from the Office of Personnel Management, they cannot be fired merely because a new President takes over. However, there may be a need to discontinue some jobs when they are no longer needed.

The servant of the people

The most important limit upon the President is the part of the Constitution that provides for free election of the President by the people. This makes him or her the servant of the people. Each President receives the powers of office from the people. To be re-elected to office, the President must keep the support of the people.

Check for Understanding: Now that you have completed this section, you should be able to answer these questions:

1. What are the limits on the President's powers?
2. How does the check and balance system work?
3. What is the Civil Service system?
4. Why was Civil Service created?

Almost all Presidents try to do what is best for the country even if everyone does not agree with his or her actions. Can students think of a time when they did not agree with a President's policies?

Civil Service jobs are awarded on the basis of competitive examinations.

SUMMARY

The Constitution gives the President many powers. It makes the President head of the executive department. In this office the President has the power to enforce laws that Congress makes. The President is Commander-in-Chief of the armed forces. The President can also pardon people for many offenses. The power to veto bills and to call special sessions of Congress are given to the President. As chief executive, the President can appoint people to many government offices and can make treaties with foreign countries. These actions must first have the approval of the Senate.

As the United States has grown, the President's duties have grown. Congress has passed many new laws to serve and protect the people. The President must make many decisions and rules to carry out these laws. The President cannot take care of all the duties of the office personally. A bureaucracy has grown to help the President perform all the duties. The President's power as head of his or her political party has grown as political parties have gained more influence in government.

The President is limited to the powers specifically granted in the Constitution. The President does not have inherent powers. Both Congress and the Supreme Court can check and balance the President's power. Congress can limit the President's ability to carry out a law. The Senate can refuse to approve the President's appointments to government offices. The Supreme Court can declare any of the President's actions unconstitutional.

The most important limit to Presidential power, however, comes from the people. The President is elected by the people. All the President's powers are obtained from the citizens themselves.

BUILDING SKILLS IN CIVICS

THINKING SKILLS

1. How does the Constitution provide for a practical and flexible office of the President?
2. What powers does the President have as commander-in-chief?
3. Why do people often use the word "bureaucracy" when referring to the executive branch?
4. How does the chief executive provide the leadership for legislation?
5. Write a title which you think best fits the main idea of the following paragraph.

   President Truman took control of the steel mills. The courts said that the Constitution gave him no such power. Also, Congress had not granted this power. The Supreme Court ruled that control of the mills be returned to the owners.

VOCABULARY SKILLS

Fill in each blank with the word that best completes the sentence.

commander-in-chief	inherent power	chief of state	checks and balances
civil service	spoils system	bureaucracy	

1. The system of ______ prevents one branch of the government from gaining too much power.
2. The practice of firing old employees and appointing political supporters to office is known as the ______.
3. The Constitution makes the President the ______ of the Army and Navy of the United States.
4. The President is the ______ of the United States.
5. The civilian employees of the executive branch of the government make up the ______.
6. A group of non-elective, or appointed, government officials is often called a ______.
7. Some presidents have claimed that they have ______ in times of great emergency.

STUDY SKILLS—MAKING A SENTENCE OUTLINE

In a *sentence outline* all the headings, the subheadings, and the supporting facts are written in sentence form.

Activity: Arrange the following notes in a sentence outline form. Some of the notes are written in sentences and others are not. Make those phrases into sentences.

1. Power and responsibility to enforce laws.
2. Provides for free election of the President.
3. The Constitution grants the President specific powers.
4. The judicial branch of the government can declare the President's action unconstitutional.
5. Cannot acquire powers beyond those defined in the Constitution.
6. Can pardon people.
7. The Constitution places limits on the President's powers.
8. Can make appointments only if two-thirds of the Senate approves.
9. Commander-in-chief of Army and Navy.
10. Congress must first approve of most Presidential decisions.
11. Can call special sessions of Congress.
12. Power to make treaties.

BEYOND THE BOOK

1. Construct a flow chart that shows the limits placed by the Constitution on the President's power to make appointments. Explain how this system differs from the orders given by an absolute ruler.
2. Use the card catalog to find sources of information about three United States Presidents that held office before the twentieth century. Using these sources, prepare a report about how the power of the Presidency grew under each President.
3. Pick a topic from the list below. Collect pictures that go with the topic you chose. Show the pictures to the class.
   a. Bureaucracy
   b. The Chief of State
   c. Checks and Balances

CHAPTER EIGHTEEN TEST

VOCABULARY CHECK

Match each term with its definition.

commander-in-chief	inherent power	bureaucracy	checks and balances
civil service	spoils system	chief of state	

1. The commander of all the armed forces of a nation.
2. The system that prevents one branch of the government from gaining too much power.
3. A group of government officials that are appointed, rather than elected.
4. Powers which some Presidents have claimed in times of great emergency.
5. The practice of firing old employees and appointing political supporters to office.
6. The person who is the administrative head of a nation.
7. The civilian employees of the executive branch.

COMPREHENSION CHECK

1. Indicate whether the following statements are true or false.
   a. The Constitution and the people limit the President's power.
   b. The President has the power to actually decide that we will go to war.
   c. The President appoints United States ambassadors.
   d. As the President's duties have grown, the size of the bureaucracy has decreased.
   e. An example of inherent power is the President's veto power.
2. Write *Chief Executive* and *Chief of State* on your paper. Identify the items in the list that belong under each topic.
   a. The President has the power to enforce laws.
   b. The President can rally the nation to a particular cause.
   c. The President has the power to pardon people who have been accused of federal crimes.
   d. The President is the representative of the entire nation.

SKILL BUILDERS—INTERPRETING POSTAGE STAMPS

United States Stamps and Stories is a valuable reference tool that tells the stories behind the pictures and designs on the *postage stamps* we use. It is published annually and is available at every post office in the U.S. We can use postage stamps to learn about people, events and causes in American history.

Activities:

1. Who are the people in each stamp?
2. What other objects are in each stamp?
3. What generalization can you make for each stamp?
4. Compare and contrast the various stamps.

BUILDING WRITING SKILLS

1. Write sentences that explain the difference between the words in one of the pairs below.
   pardon - veto
   chief executive - chief of state
   inherent power - checks and balances
2. Edit the paragraph and rewrite it correctly. Then give it a title.
   "The most important limit to Presidential power comes from the people. The President is appointed by the people. All the President's inherent powers are obtained from the citizens themselves. Some Presidents have found it difficult to function as head of state and at the same time manage the affairs of government."

Chapter Nineteen · How the President Administers the Laws

Document: The Constitution of the United States

Article II, Section 3. He shall from time to time give to the Congress Information of the State of the Union, and recommend to their Consideration such Measures as he shall judge necessary and expedient; he may, on extraordinary Occasions, convene both Houses, or either of them, and in case of Disagreement between them, with Respect to the Time of Adjournment, he may adjourn them to such Time as he shall think proper; he shall receive Ambassadors and other public Ministers; he shall take Care that the Laws be faithfully executed, and shall Commission all the Officers of the united States.

The Constitution provides that the President "shall take care that the laws be faithfully executed." But every government head needs advisers to help him or her administer the laws. Although the Constitution did not mention a "Cabinet" per se, it does state that the President "may require the opinion, in writing, of the principal officer in each of the executive departments, upon any subject relating to the duties of their respective offices . . ." These offices constitute "the Cabinet."

As the head of the executive departments, the Cabinet members are legal officers of the federal government and are responsible for carry-

The picture shows a U.S. President presiding over a Cabinet meeting. Are students surprised that the President is surrounded by so many advisors? Do students think a President should rely on his or her own judgment for the most part?

ing out government policies. The role of the Cabinet varies with different Presidents, but the final decision on an issue is always the President's. As our second President, John Adams, once said, "In all great and essential measures, the President is bound by honor and his conscience . . . to use his own mature and unbiased judgment." Our thirty-third President Harry Truman voiced a similar sentiment when he said, "The buck stops here."

FOCUSING IDEAS

- The term "cabinet" refers to the heads of the executive departments who meet with the President to discuss affairs of state.
- The duties of the executive departments include dealing with foreign affairs, managing the country's finances, running the armed forces, enforcing federal laws, taking care of the public lands, working on agricultural concerns, collecting business information, promoting better working conditions, dealing with urban development, working on transportation problems, managing energy resources, and promoting the general welfare.
- The independent agencies are responsible for protecting the interests of business, consumers, and society. They combine some of the legislative, executive, and judicial powers of government.

The complete text of the Constitution can be found in the Appendix, beginning on page 564.

Issues in Civics: Ask students if they think the federal government has grown too big and has entered too many aspects of people's lives. Why do students think as they do?

PRE-TEST

1. What role does the Cabinet have in helping the President run the nation?
2. What duties do the executive departments perform?
3. What are the primary duties of the Executive Office?
4. What are the duties and responsibilities of the independent agencies?

WHAT IS THE CABINET?

Objectives: After you have read this section, you will be able to:

- Define the term "cabinet" and tell where the word comes from.
- Name the major departments of the present cabinet.
- Tell how the cabinet helps the President to administer the laws.

President Abraham Lincoln meets with the members of his cabinet to discuss strategy during the War Between the States.

Building Vocabulary:
administer *(313)* • cabinet *(313)* • ambassador *(315)* • minister *(315)* • consul *(315)* • press secretary *(322)* • regulatory authority *(323)*

Bring up Truman's "The buck stops here" statement again. What did he mean by this? (That the President can't "pass the buck" to anyone else, but must make the final decision.)

The complete text of Lincoln's Emancipation Proclamation can be found in the Appendix on pages 585–86.

The President is the chief executive of the country. He or she must manage the government so that laws passed by Congress are enforced. *Administering* the laws today is a very complex job and requires the services of many administrators whose titles differ throughout the government. Most of these chief administrators report ultimately to the President as the chief executive.

As the President's duties have expanded over the years, the number of people who help the President has also grown. When George Washington was President in 1790, there were 350 civilian employees of the government—government employees who were not in the armed forces. There were 49,200 civilians employed by the government in 1861 when Abraham Lincoln was President. Today there are about three million civilians working for the government. The civilian employees are organized into three groups: the thirteen executive departments, the Executive Office of the President, and the independent agencies.

The heads of the executive departments

Among the principal officers appointed by the President, with the approval of the Senate, are the heads of the executive departments. These people are called the *cabinet*. The term "cabinet" used to mean a kind of room, rather than a piece of furniture. The word was used to refer to the room where a king met with his close advisors. The cabinet offices and the years in which they were established are:

Secretary of State (1789)
Secretary of Treasury (1789)
Attorney General (1789)
Secretary of Interior (1849)
Secretary of Agriculture (1889)
Secretary of Commerce (1913)
Secretary of Labor (1913)
Secretary of Defense (1949)
Secretary of Health and Human Services (1953)
Secretary of Housing and Urban Development (1966)
Secretary of Transportation (1966)
Secretary of Energy (1977)
Secretary of Education (1980)

There have not always been thirteen members of the cabinet, and the members have not always had the same titles. George Washington had only four people in his cabinet. The members of his cabinet included the Secretaries of State, Treasury, and War, and the Attorney General.

The cabinet reflects our history

Over the years the President's cabinet has grown and changed. It has adapted to the needs of the United States. For example, the Department of Interior was established in 1849. A new department was needed to manage the newly acquired land in the West. The Secretary of Agriculture was added as we became an important agicultural country. The Secretaries of Commerce and Labor were added as transportation and industry grew. When the Air Force became a separate branch of the military services, the different branches needed more coordination. Also, people felt that the title "Secretary of War" did not properly reflect the emphasis on peace in the world after World War II ended. Thus the old title of Secretary of War was changed in 1949 to Secretary of Defense to reflect current needs.

Through the years more and more people moved into the cities. The government became concerned with education, welfare, housing, and transportation in the cities. As

Have an interested student do research on women who have served in the cabinet. What role did they play? How effective were they?

Growth of the President's Cabinet

	George Washington	Ronald Reagan
Secretary of State	Thomas Jefferson 1789 Edmund Randolph 1794 Timothy Pickering 1795	Alexander M. Haig, Jr. 1981
Secretary of the Treasury	Alexander Hamilton 1789 Oliver Wolcott, Jr. 1795	Donald T. Regan 1981
Secretary of War	Henry Knox 1789 Timothy Pickering 1795 James McHenry 1796	
Attorney General	Edmund Randolph 1789 William Bradford 1794 Charles Lee 1795	William French Smith 1981
Secretary of Defense		Caspar W. Weinberger 1981
Secretary of the Interior		James G. Watt 1981
Secretary of Agriculture		John R. Block 1981
Secretary of Commerce		Malcolm Baldrige 1981
Secretary of Labor		Raymond J. Donovan 1981
Secretary of Health and Human Services		Richard S. Schweiker 1981
Secretary of Housing and Urban Development		Samuel R. Pierce, Jr. 1981
Secretary of Transportation		Andrew L. Lewis, Jr. 1981
Secretary of Energy		James B. Edwards 1981
Secretary of Education		T.H. Bell 1981

a result, the Departments of Health, Education, and Welfare, of Housing and Urban Development, and of Transportation were added to the President's cabinet.

In 1970 the Postmaster General was removed from the cabinet. It was decided that this job could best be carried on outside the executive departments. Our country is now confronted with problems of a shortage in energy resources. In 1977 the Department of Energy was created to cope with the energy problems that our nation faces. In 1980 the Secretary of Education was added to the cabinet and the function of education was removed from the Department of Health, Education, and Welfare, which then became the Department of Health and Human Services. The ways that

Have students clip newspaper articles that refer to one of the departments of the cabinet. Is one department mentioned a lot more than another? Why do students think this is so?

the cabinet has changed show the past and present needs of the United States.

Our founders realized that the country's needs would change over time. Therefore, there is no mention in the Constitution of the cabinet or of the executive branch in general. Instead, Congress allows the President to reorder or change some parts of the executive branch. Names and duties of the department heads or cabinet members can be changed. New cabinet offices can be created, too. The President must first send the suggested changes to Congress for approval. Congress has sixty days to veto or reject the changes. If Congress approves the plan, the suggested changes then go into effect.

Today the President usually holds meetings of the cabinet every week. The meetings take place in the Cabinet Room of the White House. Some Presidents include officials in the executive branch along with the members of the cabinet.

Cabinet members have two jobs. Each one is head of an executive department. All members also meet with the President to discuss matters of public importance. The President calls a meeting of the cabinet members whenever he or she wishes to discuss affairs of state with them. Members of the cabinet often help the President by giving information to members of Congress. A cabinet member is also able to assist the President in writing a proposed bill.

Check for Understanding: Now that you have completed this section, you should be able to answer these questions:

1. Where does the term "cabinet" come from?
2. What are the major departments of the cabinet?
3. How does the cabinet help the President to administer the laws?
4. Why were the cabinet positions not written into the Constitution?

WHAT ARE THE DUTIES OF THE EXECUTIVE DEPARTMENTS?

Objectives: After you have read this section, you will be able to:

- List at least five executive departments.
- Describe the duties of each one.
- Identify which executive department has the largest budget.

The State Department

The State Department deals with foreign affairs. The Secretary of State, under the direction of the President, is chiefly responsible for dealing with governments of other nations.

In order that nations can communicate and live together well, a plan has been worked out over many years. Under this plan the ruler or chief executive of a nation appoints persons to represent the nation at the capitals and major cities of other countries. A representative of high rank is called an *ambassador*. A representative of a lesser rank is called a *minister*. There also are *consuls* who look after the business interests of their nation abroad. Consuls live in important business centers of foreign countries. Ambassadors and ministers live in the capitals and the important cities of the nations.

The United States Constitution provides that the President shall receive foreign ambassadors and ministers. Many times the President has other responsibilities of great-

Have an interested student do a report on ex-Secretary of State Henry Kissinger. What did he accomplish when he was in office? Why was he controversial?

George C. Marshall served as both Secretary of State and Secretary of Defense.

er importance. When this happens, this duty is assigned to the Secretary of State.

The Constitution states that, with the approval of the Senate, the President can appoint ambassadors and ministers to the countries with which we have formal relationships. These are countries that send ambassadors and ministers to the United States. We also trade and have exchange programs with these countries.

The Secretary of State instructs our foreign ambassadors regarding what actions they shall take in foreign affairs. If the United States has a major matter to take up with a foreign government, the Secretary of State gives the ambassador a message to deliver to that government. The message informs the country that we wish to speak to them about certain concerns. Our ambassadors, ministers, and consuls deal with officials of other nations on many matters that concern the United States. They make frequent reports to Washington. Their reports deal with developments in the countries where they are stationed.

The Treasury Department

This department, headed by the Secretary of the Treasury, manages the finances of the country. The department directs the collection of the nation's taxes and the payment of debts. It advises members of Congress on finances. The Treasury directs the minting of coins and the engraving and printing of paper money. The Secretary of Treasury's signature appears on every piece of paper money issued by the Bureau of Printing and Engraving.

The Internal Revenue Service, often called the IRS, is a branch of the Treasury. It is the work of the IRS to collect all federal taxes in the United States. This includes taxes from almost every family in the country. The service has offices that are located in many cities and towns.

The Secret Service is also part of the Treasury Department. It was founded during the War Between the States to deal with people who printed illegal money. It finds and arrests persons who avoid paying federal taxes. After President McKinley was killed, Congress gave the Secret Service the task of protecting the President. Today the Secret Service protects the President, the Vice President, and former Presidents and their families. It will also protect other important members of the government, including candidates for President and Vice President, if required to do so by the President. Once again in 1981, with the attempted assassination of President Reagan, the nation was reminded of how important the job of protecting the President is.

What is your students' reaction when you mention the Internal Revenue Service? Ask them if they think most people are honest when filling out tax returns. Why do they think so?

Ivy Baker Priest, former U.S. Treasurer, providing the official signature for paper money.

The Defense Department

In the past, the Defense Department was called the War Department. It was one of the first departments organized by Congress in 1789. A few years later it was divided into the War Department and the Navy Department. The War Department had charge of the Army. The Navy Department had charge of the Navy. In 1949, Congress united all branches of the military service into one department and named it the Defense Department.

The President is Commander-in-Chief of the armed forces. This provision was written into the Constitution so that the military would not be independent of civilian control. This provision helps to prevent an ambitious general or admiral from using the armed forces to seize control of the government of our country.

The Secretary of Defense, like the President, is a civilian. He or she is in charge of the Army, Navy, and Air Force. Undersecretaries direct each of the three branches of the armed forces. They report to the secretary. The Secretary of Defense and staff also direct the training of reserve officers and of citizen soldiers who belong to the National Guard of the various states. Today the Defense Department is one of the largest departments in the government. It has over a million civilian employees. It is responsible for over two million members of the armed forces.

The Department of Justice

The Attorney General is head of this department. He or she helps the President enforce federal laws and advises the President on legal matters. The Attorney General has many assistants throughout the United States. Some of these are United States district attorneys. District attorneys are responsible in court for trying people accused of breaking federal laws. Other assistants are the United States marshals and their deputies. They are responsible for enforcing federal laws. On a federal level they are like police officers who enforce local laws.

The Department of Justice has charge of all federal prisons. It also grants citizenship to foreigners. The Federal Bureau of Investigation, often called the FBI, is also controlled by the Department of Justice. The work of the Justice Department has grown as transportation systems have improved. Jet airplanes and interstate highways help

Issues in Civics: Do students think that the Defense Department budget should be increased or decreased? Why?

Ask students if they think our prison system is an effective one. Can they think of any ways to improve the system?

people move quickly across the country. This easy movement makes it hard for state authorities to deal with criminals such as sky-jackers, kidnappers, and automobile thieves who move from one state to another. Today most criminals who cross state lines violate federal laws and will be hunted by special agents of the FBI.

Public lands like Yosemite National Park in California are supervised by the Department of Interior.

The Department of the Interior

This department, headed by the Secretary of the Interior, takes care of the public lands of the United States. An early, important duty of this office was helping people who wished to buy public lands. Today there is very little public land available for sale or for homesteading in the United States. One of the major duties of the Department of the Interior is to provide and protect public lands for the use of people of the United States. Another important duty of this department is to try to protect our environment and to conserve our national resources. An important section of the department is the Bureau of Indian Affairs, or BIA. This section takes care of government programs for Indians (Native Americans). BIA offices are located in most major cities and on some Indian reservations.

The Department of Agriculture

The Secretary of Agriculture heads this department. The department works with state agricultural colleges and experimental stations to improve the quality of livestock and field crops. The Soil Conservation Service and Forest Service are part of the Department of Agriculture. The Department of Agriculture helps farmers find better markets for their products. Through the price-support program, it guarantees them a minimum price for wheat and other crops. This department also arranges for loans to farmers who want to buy land or farm equipment. Partly due to advances made in federal programs, each farm worker of today produces, depending on the crop, anywhere from four to ten times the amount of food per man-hour that was produced in 1940.

The Department of Commerce

The Secretary of Commerce heads this department, which collects business infor-

Have an interested student do a report on President Teddy Roosevelt and his Secretary of the Interior. What effect did they have on our public lands?

mation. This helps business people sell the products of our industries. The department also informs them where they can buy the products they need. The National Weather Service is a section of the Department of Commerce. Most of the weather reports for our country are issued from the Weather Service.

The Bureau of the Census is a branch of the Department of Commerce. It takes a census or survey of the people every ten years. It states how many people there are in the country. It also shows much more than numbers. The recent census contains figures on age, income, sex, race, and kinds of work. Many other useful facts about people who live in the United States are also stated.

The Patent Office records all patents and trademarks on products. Its records protect the interests of inventors and manufacturers. The National Bureau of Standards keeps standards of weights and measures for the nation. It also conducts major research, which mainly deals with the testing of materials.

The Department of Labor

Congress created the Department of Labor in 1913 to promote better working conditions for those who work for wages. The Secretary of Labor heads this department. He or she advises the President and members of Congress on the needs of working men and women. The department collects labor statistics or records and establishes

The National Weather Service issues weather reports and monitors unusual weather conditions, such as this hurricane in Florida.

Do students think that it's important for inventors and manufacturers to patent their products? Why do they think so?

labor standards. It enforces federal laws on aid programs for workers. This department directs private pension programs and welfare plans. It also manages the public employment service. The Wage and Hour section of the department sees that all workers are paid according to the minimum wage law. Other divisions establish standards for women workers and apprentices. The Department of Labor is also responsible for the safety and health of workers on the job. This is one of the most important services that this department performs.

The Department of Housing and Urban Development

The Department of Housing and Urban Development (HUD) is responsible for solving many of the problems caused by the rapid growth of our cities. One goal of this department is to see that all citizens are able to find good housing at prices they can afford to pay. The department has attempted to do this by providing public housing. It also makes money available to individuals and builders who want to build better housing in our cities.

The Department of Housing and Urban Development has many sections. Many of its branches deal with housing and neighborhood development. Others manage federal disaster aid and flood and crime insurance. All sections of HUD help citizens who live in cities with their housing and urban problems.

The Department of Transportation

The Department of Transportation works to find solutions to transportation problems in the United States. One of its most important responsibilities is the problem of safety. One of its sections does research to make cars and highways safer for our use. This department also makes rules for the airlines.

The Urban Mass Transportation Administration, a section of the department, works on the problem of how to move many people from place to place in large cities. This is a growing problem. Cities need mass transportation. Gasoline which powers vehicles is becoming scarce. Fuel-powered vehicles pollute the air. The administration must figure out ways to deal with these problems.

The U.S. Coast Guard is in the Department of Transportation, too. The Coast Guard has many duties. It patrols the oceans to warn ships of icebergs. The Coast Guard maintains lighthouses, buoys, and other devices to warn ships of dangerous capes and rocks. Another part of its job is to enforce federal laws and safety regulations on the seas.

The Department of Energy

This department was established in 1977. It helps manage the nation's scarce energy resources. Among the rules made by this department are those which determine the bulk prices of natural gas and oil. When the country has very cold winters, the fuel needed to heat homes often become scarce in certain parts of the country. The department then has the duty to shift gas and oil supplies from one part of the country to another. This department is also involved in developing new energy sources, such as safe nuclear plants, solar energy systems, and others.

The Department of Health and Human Services

Upon the inauguration of this department in 1980, President Carter said: "the reorganization of the former Department of Health, Education, and Welfare brings a

Issues in Civics: Discuss this issues with your students: Should nuclear power plants be used as an energy source in this country, or should they be abolished?

new focus and also will bring new energies to our struggle against poverty, disease, and inequality." And he felt the new seal of the Department of Health and Human Services (HHS) was fitting because it showed "the wings of an eagle: aggressive, confident, proud, sheltering those who are young, the aged, the disadvantaged, and the poor."

The budget of HHS is the third-largest budget in the world, second only to the United States budget as a whole and that of the Soviet Union. These billions reflect a belief that the federal government has a major role in promoting the health and welfare of all Americans. However, as the budget grows, this belief is being challenged. Many people think that private citizens, as well as local and state governments, should assume more responsibilities for health and welfare. Hundreds of agencies are used in the administration of these services.

The primary agency of the Department of Health and Human Services is the Social Security Administration. Wage earners and employers contribute the large sums that support this benefit program. The federal Social Security system works with state governments in many related areas, including unemployment compensation, aid to dependent children, and vocational rehabilitation.

This department also enforces the Pure Food and Drug Acts. For example, a recent ruling of the Food and Drug Administration requires that labels on food packages include a list of the product's nutritional values. There is also a Public Health Service that enforces quarantines, examines immigrants, and provides hospital care for Coast Guard personnel and a few other federal employees. Much of the work of the Public Health Service is administering federal health care grants to state and local governments.

The Department of Education

On May 7, 1980, the Department of Education became the thirteenth government department. The first Secretary of Education, Shirley Hufstedler, in speaking of the new department said: "It will be a department that sees its role as a helping, supportive friend of education, as a simplifier and a streamliner of regulations and paperwork, and not as the holder of the federal purse and not as a power beyond the reach of local decisions." The legislation that created the Department of Education contained checks on its future growth; each annual appropriation act includes a personnel ceiling for the department. There are over 150 programs for which the department has responsibility.

The Department of Education administers federal scholarships, loans, grants, and direct aid to state departments of education. Special funds aid gifted students, the mentally and physically handicapped, library development, and vocational education. The department supports educational research, compiles studies on education, and plans international teacher exchanges. It also runs schools for overseas dependents and migrant workers, and administers science education and college housing loan programs.

Check for Understanding: Now that you have completed this section, you should be able to answer these questions:

1. What are the five of the thirteen departments of the executive branch?
2. What are the duties of each one?
3. Which of these departments has the largest budget?
4. Which one contains the Secret Service?

Do students think it's important for food packages to include a list of the product's ingredients and nutritional value? Why or why not?

WHAT ARE THE DUTIES OF THE EXECUTIVE OFFICE?

Objectives: After you have read this section, you will be able to:

- Describe the duties of the Executive Office.
- List the three main offices in which this Office is divided.
- Explain the role of independent federal agencies.

The executive departments are the largest departments in the executive branch of the government. However, there are other important agencies. Chief among these is the Executive Office of the President. The duties of the President have grown a great deal. It would be impossible for one person to do all of the things that are necessary. The Executive Office employs people who work closely with the President. They advise him or her on many matters. They often speak for the President or carry out various duties that the President assigns them.

James Hagerty served as Press Secretary to President Eisenhower.

The White House Office

This office is a section of the Executive Office. It is headed by the Assistant to the President, who often attends cabinet meetings. Other members of the White House are special advisors and secretaries who work closely with the President. The President's *press secretary* holds press conferences for television and newspaper reporters. The press secretary is the person who lets people know what the President thinks about current domestic and international issues.

The Office of Budget and Management

This office is headed by a director who is appointed by the President. The director's duty is to figure out the national government's budget for the coming year. The budget is presented to Congress for approval. After approval, no department may spend more than the Director of the Budget provided for it, except in an emergency. The growth in the size of the budget has made the director's job extremely difficult, because it seems that no one can comprehend all the complexities involved in spending billions of dollars annually. Ever since World War II, the goal of a balanced budget has become difficult to attain because expenditures have consistently exceeded the income from taxes.

National Security Council

This is a council composed of important civilians and military officers of the United States. Their most important role is to advise the President in an emergency. They also advise the President on ways to make the United States more secure.

Ask students if they know the names of the current President's press secretary and Director of the Budget. What duties do these people perform in the Executive Office?

The independent agencies

The independent agencies were begun in the late 1800's to protect the interests of business, consumers, and society. Since the Constitution made no specific reference to the organization of the executive branch, successive Presidents and Congresses have had to deal with this problem. It became apparent in the late 1880's that the growth of the economic system required some kind of regulatory bodies. While cabinet officers had administrative authority, they often lacked the power to enforce the law.

Congress used its power to regulate interstate commerce to create more than fifty independent, specialized agencies with wide *regulatory authority* in their special fields. These agencies have come to operate almost as a "fourth branch" of the federal government, combining some of the legislative, executive, and judicial powers of the other three branches. For instance, the Federal Communications Commission (FCC) has a legislative function when it sets down the rules for broadcasting power for radio stations. The FCC has an executive function whenever it enforces its own regulations. This is the case if the FCC tells a radio station that it has violated one of its regulations by using an improper broadcast frequency. The FCC is using a judicial function if it holds hearings for accused violators and hands out fines or suspensions. A radio station that broadcast consistently on the wrong frequency would probably be warned first, then fined, and eventually suspended from operations if it did not comply with the Federal Communications Commission.

The names of the agencies vary, although most are known as boards, commissions, or administrations. Unlike other administrators in government, the members usually serve long terms, approximately seven years. They can be removed from office only "for cause."

Check for Understanding: Now that you have completed this section, you should be able to answer these questions:

1. What are the duties of the Executive Office?
2. What are the functions of the three main branches of this Office?
3. How does the Executive Office work to assist the President?
4. What is the responsibility of the independent agencies?

SUMMARY

The President's cabinet consists of the secretaries of the thirteen executive departments. State, Treasury, Defense, Justice, Interior, Agriculture, Commerce, Labor, Health and Human Services, Housing and Urban Development, Transportation, Energy, and Education.

To meet new conditions and new demands made upon the President, the various branches of the Executive Office have been established. These branches make reports and give advice to the President. Chief among the branches of the Executive Office is the White House Office. This office works closely with the President.

The independent agencies were created to help enforce the law. They are named "independent" because they do not report to any executive department and the members serve long terms, approximately seven years. There are over fifty of these independent agencies.

Ask students if they know the names of any independent agencies other than the FCC. What function do these agencies serve?

BUILDINGS SKILLS IN CIVICS

THINKING SKILLS

1. What are the offices in the President's cabinet?
2. How are new cabinet offices created?
3. How does the creation of new cabinet offices reflect our history?
4. What are the branches of the Treasury Department?
5. What is the function of each branch?
6. Why did independent agencies come into existence?
7. Compare the duties of the Secretary of Defense to those of the Secretary of State.
8. Find three pictures of cabinet members in the book. Write the page number for each one.

VOCABULARY SKILLS

Some of the underlined words in the sentences below are used correctly, others are not. If the sentence is correct, write True. If it is not, replace it with the best choice from the list.

administer	regulatory	cabinet	ambassador
minister	authority	consul	press secretary

1. An ambassador is the highest ranking representative of the nation to other countries.
2. The President's minister holds press conferences for television and newspaper reporters.
3. It is a very complex job to consul the nation today, and requires the services of many administrators.
4. A minister is a representative of the United States to a foreign country who is of lower rank than ambassador.
5. A consul looks after the business interests of the United States abroad.
6. Congress has used its power to create independent specialized agencies with wide regulatory authority.
7. The cabinet is made up of the heads of the national executive departments.

STUDY SKILLS—PREPARING A FIRST DRAFT

When you write a report, you choose a topic and use the library to locate reference materials. As you read, you take notes and list questions you hope to answer in your report. You make an informal outline of these notes, and then arrange them in a formal outline.

Writing the *first draft* lets you get your ideas on paper, and lets you view the work as a whole.

The following three problems are typical of a first draft:

1. It doesn't stay on the topic.
2. It contains incorrect information or uses wrong terms.
3. It is not arranged in the correct sequence.

Activity: The following paragraphs are first drafts and need editing. Identify the problem; edit and rewrite each; write a title that tells the main idea of each paragraph.

Through the price-support program, it guarantees them a minimum price for wheat and other crops. Partly due to advances made in federal programs, each farm worker of today produces up to ten times the amount of food produced in 1940. Therefore, the Department of Agriculture helps farmers find better markets for their products. It also arranges for loans to farmers.

The U.S. Coast Guard is a part of the Department of Defense. The Coast Guard has many duties. It patrols the ocean to warn ships of icebergs. These are massive floating bodies of ice broken from a glacier. They are especially dangerous because most of the surface is below the water. The Coast Guard maintains buoys and other devices to warn ships of dangerous capes and lighthouses.

BEYOND THE BOOK

1. Write the first draft of a paragraph about any topic you choose. Exchange it with a partner. Each of you will edit, rewrite, and give a title to your partner's paragraph.
2. Use magazines and newspapers to locate current information about members of the cabinet and their responsibilities.

CHAPTER NINETEEN TEST

VOCABULARY CHECK

Fill in the blank with the word that best completes the sentence.

1. It is the duty of the (ambassador - press secretary) to represent the nation in other countries.
2. A (consul - minister) is appointed to look after business interests in foreign countries.
3. It is a very complex job, and it requires the services of many administrators to (minister - administer) the laws today.
4. The (ambassador - press secretary) lets reporters know what the President thinks about current issues.
5. The heads of the executive departments are called the (cabinet - regulatory authority).
6. Representatives to foreign countries of a lesser rank than ambassadors are called (ministers - cabinet).
7. Congress created independent agencies with wide (consul - regulatory authority).

COMPREHENSION CHECK

Write True if the question and answer match. If not, write an answer that goes with the question.

1. What is the main duty of the State Department? —Its main duty is to deal with foreign affairs.
2. What does the Secretary of the Treasury do? —He or she manages the finances of the country.
3. Who is in charge of the Army, Navy, and the Air Force? —The Secretary of Labor advises the President and members of Congress on the needs of working men and women.
4. How many departments are there in the executive branch? —The names of the some fifty agencies vary, although most are known as boards, commissions, or administrators.
5. What are the duties of the Executive Office? —The Executive Office advises the President, often speaks for the President, and carries out various duties.

SKILL BUILDERS—INTERPRETING PHOTOGRAPHS

Photographs are full of information. They often show a point of view. We have to ask ourselves whether the photograph is objective in reporting a subject, or showing only one side of an issue.

Activity: Here are two different photographs from this book. They both show Gerald Ford as President. Answer these questions.

1. What is the message contained in each photograph?
2. Is the photograph being objective, or making a point?
3. Each photograph is only a part of the total subject of Gerald Ford as President. What parts have been left out?
4. Which photograph would better illustrate a report on the President as chief of state?

BUILDING WRITING SKILLS

Which of the sentences below support this generalization?

"The Executive Office helps the President meet new conditions and new demands brought about by changing times."

a. The Office of Budget and Management figures out the national government's budget for the coming year.
b. The National Security Council advises the President in an emergency.
c. The Constitution provides that the President shall receive foreign ambassadors and ministers.

Chapter Twenty · Setting a Foreign Policy

Documents: Truman's Statement of Foreign Policy (Oct. 27, 1945)
The Constitution of the United States

Truman's Statement:

" . . . We have no objective which need clash with the peaceful aims of any other nation . . .

We believe that all peoples who are prepared for self-government should be permitted to choose their own form of government . . .

We believe that full economic collaboration between all nations, great and small, is essential to the improvement of living conditions all over the world . . .

Article I, Section 8. . . . The Congress shall have Power to declare War, grant Letters of Marque and Reprisal, and make Rules concerning Captures on Land and Water . . . To provide for calling forth the Militia to execute the Laws of the union, suppress Insurrections and repel Invasions

Article II, Section 2. (The President) shall have Power, by and with the Advice and Consent of the Senate, to make Treaties . . .

The President and the Congress share the responsibility of setting the foreign policy of our nation. The Constitution gives the President the

The picture depicts some of the great moments in U.S. foreign policy. Ask students if they can name any other events, speeches, or meetings that had a major effect on foreign relations.

The complete text of the Constitution can be found in the Appendix, beginning on page 564.

power to make treaties; make executive agreements with other countries; and appoint ambassadors and ministers, subject to Senate approval. The Chief Executive is also responsible for proposing foreign aid legislation, taking part in international conferences, and receiving foreign diplomats. The President's chief adviser in the area of foreign relations is the Secretary of State.

A nation's ability to uphold a foreign policy depends on its resources, military strength, and the loyalty of its people—coupled with the cooperation it receives from other nations. Changing economic and political conditions make the shaping of U.S. foreign policy a continually complex process.

FOCUSING IDEAS

- U.S. foreign policy is guided by a concern for its own citizens and their land, their political sovereignty among the nations of the world, and by a concern for the human rights of other peoples.
- U.S. foreign policy is influenced by the President, the State Department, Congress, national military leaders, and by the people.
- Our foreign policy often deals with members of the Free World, the Communist bloc, and the Third World.

Issues in Civics: The United States has often been criticized for being overly involved in the affairs of foreign nations. Ask students if they think this is the case, and if so, why?

PRE-TEST

1. What is involved in making the foreign policy of the U.S.?
2. Who is responsible for making U.S. foreign policy?
3. What groups of nations are involved in foreign policy?
4. What is the role of the United Nations?

WHAT IS OUR FOREIGN POLICY?

Objectives: After you have read this section, you will be able to:

- Explain the meaning of the term "foreign policy."
- List three aims of United States foreign policy.
- Describe how our foreign policy has changed over the years.

One of the most important tasks facing the President is dealing with other nations. The United States must maintain friendship with other nations, in order to trade and maintain peace. It must also be prepared to defend itself in case of war.

Our actions toward other nations

All of the goals and actions of one nation in relation to other nations are called its foreign policy. Every nation is guided in its foreign policy by many interests. Nations need to protect their citizens, their land, and their political sovereignty among the nations of the world. There are always times when the interests of two or more nations come into conflict. Often, the result of this conflict has been war. There are other ways to resolve conflicts, however, and nations try to find balanced compromises or to work together to reach common goals. This art of establishing relationships that both sides can accept as useful and beneficial is called *diplomacy*. A person who engages in activities to establish these relationships is known as a diplomat. Nations with peaceful foreign policies try to resolve conflicts by negotiation and agreement rather than by war. In the age of nuclear weapons with their tremendous powers of destruction, an unlimited global war would mean certain disaster for much of the world.

The national seal of the United States shows an eagle that carries in one claw an olive branch, the symbol of peace. In the other claw the eagle carries arrows, a symbol of war. This seal is a symbol of our national foreign policy. At the same time that we strive for peace, we must be prepared to defend ourselves in case of war.

A changing policy

When George Washington left the Presidency, he gave a farewell address. He said we should not be "interweaving our destiny with that of any part of Europe . . ." For

Building Vocabulary:
diplomacy *(330)* • isolationism *(331)* • detente *(332)* • embargo *(333)* • treaty *(333)* • recognize *(334)* • summit conference *(334)* • foreign aid *(335)* • Free World *(337)* • Monroe Doctrine *(337)* • Third World *(338)*

Issues in Civics: Do students think that any aspects of our nation's foreign policy should be changed? Have them explain their answers.

Washington's Farewell Address set forth important principles regarding American foreign policy. Have students report on the text of his Address and how it affected the century that followed.

years afterward the United States tried to follow his advice to live alone in peace. This policy is called *isolationism.* It means to be isolated, or involved as little as possible with other nations. Whether or not we agree with Washington's attitude, a policy like this is no longer possible today. In our world millions of people are in touch with other nations every day. Fast transportation and communication and the role of trade constantly increase international involvement. Food, raw materials, and manufactured goods move from one country to another in great quantities. American companies have branches and investments overseas. Other countries are investing more and more in the United States. Today it is not possible for any large industrial nation to be isolated from other countries.

A shrinking world

Sometimes you will hear the expression "our shrinking world," which means that today we can travel, send messages, and ship goods around the world in a faster, easier manner. This also means that our day-to-day lives are more involved with the people and government of other nations than ever before. The actions of our military and private citizens, our President, our State Department, and other public officials can effect changes in international relationships very rapidly.

Peace and security

During our early history the United States was fairly safe from attack by other countries. At that time military attacks could not be carried out from long distance. A nation

Nuclear weapons pose a great threat to U.S. security, as was shown in the Cuban Missile Crisis of 1962, when Soviet nuclear missile installations were erected in Cuba.

Have an interested student do a detailed report on the causes and effects of the Cuban Missile Crisis of 1962.

could be attacked only by being invaded by another country. With large oceans at our eastern and western borders, we could be rapidly invaded only from Mexico or Canada. In modern times, the inventions of airplanes, long-range missiles, and nuclear warheads have changed all that. Now the United States could be rapidly attacked by many other nations. If a major war breaks out anywhere in the world, it can quickly involve our country. We must be constantly in communication with the rest of the world to maintain our own peace and security. Increased communication also increases our understanding of other nations, and can lead to more responsible foreign policies on all sides.

Our security became a very serious problem during the Cold War, when the Soviet Union with its Communist satellite countries and the free republics of the Western world opposed one another. This was called a "cold war" because the two sides were openly hostile to each other but did not actually engage in a full-scale war. Following the defeat of Nazi Germany in World War II, the Soviet Union controlled many eastern European countries. Communist control increased in Asia as well. Eventually it led to American involvement in war in Korea and Vietnam. Following the Vietnam War, the Soviet Union and the United States gradually entered into a diplomatic relationship known as *detente*, or peaceful competition. Detente is an attempt to relax relations between the Soviet Union and the United States. Its goal is increased peaceful negotiation of conflicts. Supporters of detente say that this policy is necessary to avoid the possibility of nuclear war with the Soviet Union. Critics of detente, on the other hand, say that this policy will allow the Soviet Union to expand its influence in the world. These critics argue that the Soviet Union is not committed to peaceful co-existence and must be opposed by strong military force.

International trade

For many years the United States bought and sold only a few goods and services overseas. Today many companies sell more goods to other countries than they sell in the United States. Food products, airplanes, and machine parts are the most important things that we sell to other nations. In turn, we buy clothing, automobiles, television sets, electronic parts, and many other goods from overseas. Recently, over half of all the petroleum, or oil, that we used was imported from overseas, mainly through the Organization of Petroleum Exporting Countries (OPEC). Our depen-

The U.S. carries out extensive trade with foreign nations.

Issues in Civics: Do students think that the detente with the Soviet Union is reasonable and practical, or do they think this policy will allow that nation to expand its world influence?

dence upon overseas trade was shown in 1973–1974, following the Arab-Israeli war of 1973, when the Arab nations set up an oil embargo against the United States and other nations that had supported Israel. Under this *embargo*, the Arab countries refused to sell oil to those nations. The result in the United States was a severe shortage of gasoline and oil. This oil crisis emphasized why a major part of foreign policy is devoted to keeping trade open with other nations. It also showed a need for the United States to find new sources of energy and energy fuels, so that losing one source would not cause such a severe shortage.

Human rights and foreign policy

Our foreign policy is also concerned with human lives and human rights. A part of our foreign policy is to send emergency aid to nations suffering hardship after crop failures, floods, earthquakes, or other disasters. We also try to help people whose human rights are violated by talking to their government about changing its policies and sometimes by stopping trade or aid programs with the government.

Check for Understanding: Now that you have completed this section, you should be able to answer these questions:

1. What is the meaning of the term "foreign policy"?
2. What are three aims of United States foreign policy?
3. Why did the United States change from its original foreign policy of "isolationism"?
4. What is the main purpose of diplomacy?

WHO MAKES FOREIGN POLICY?

Objectives: After reading this section, you will be able to:

- Identify at least five groups that influence foreign policy in this country.
- Describe the various roles of each of these groups.
- Explain the purpose of foreign aid.

The President

Our Constitution gives the President primary responsibility for foreign policy. As Commander-in-Chief, the President can order the Army or Navy into areas of the world where peace is threatened. The President is responsible for treaties and executive agreements with other countries. A *treaty* is a contract signed by representatives of the nations making the agreement. Treaties have been used to pledge help if other nations are attacked, to limit armaments,

President Carter signing the Panama Canal treaty in 1977.

and to reach other important agreements. Executive agreements are minor agreements between nations. Usually these agreements set up trade, aid programs, or other such business relationships between nations.

Our President can also recognize other nations. To *recognize* a nation means that we accept its government as the sovereign or just government of its people, and we accept the nation as a political equal in international affairs. We then exchange ambassadors and have an open relationship with that country for trade, tourism, and political discussions. The President may refuse to recognize a country because it is believed that the government is not being responsible or just to its people or that it is not a stable government in some other way. For years the United States did not recognize or exchange ambassadors with Communist China (the People's Republic of China), which took control of the government of China in 1949, following a civil war. President Nixon visited China in 1972 without having recognized that nation. When President Carter extended recognition in 1979, it meant the United States would work with China in international cooperation.

It is always an important event when the President holds a *summit conference*, or meets directly with the top leaders of other nations. International press and television coverage keep the world informed of most of the summit conferences even while they are going on. During the cold war our Presidents met with leaders of Russia and other Communist countries to seek to maintain peace. President Carter, Secretary of State Cyrus Vance, and others met with the leaders of Egypt and Israel to help work out a peace agreement of 1979 between those nations.

Department of State

The Secretary of State ranks as the foremost presidential advisor on international affairs. How the President uses this advice depends on the personalities of the two people involved. Some Presidents prefer to make decisions on their own, leaving the Secretary of State to carry out policy rather than share in its formation. The President also has within the Executive Office persons who advise her or him on foreign policy, and in some cases these people also have a strong influence on the President's decisions. In several recent administrations the head of the National Security Council (NSC) has been an important force in shaping our foreign policy. The final approval of any policy is of course always the President's responsibility. The Department of State, under the direction of the Secretary of State, is responsible for the day-to-day work of foreign policy. This department has over 30,000 people working for it. About 20,000 work overseas. These people gather information about what is going on in other countries and report back to the United States. They help American citizens who are visiting and doing business abroad. They do much of the work that results in treaties or agreements. The Secretary of State and members of the State Department are full-time foreign affairs workers.

The Congress

Congress is also involved in foreign policy. Article VI of the Constitution says ". . . all treaties . . . made, under the Authority of the United States, shall be the supreme Law of the Land . . ." Because all of the states and their laws are bound and limited by treaties, the Senate must give its consent by a two-thirds vote before a treaty can go into effect. If the President negotiates a

Issues in Civics: Do students think it was wise of President Carter to extend recognition of China in 1979? Why? Why not?

President Carter at a summit conference with the leaders of West Germany, France, and Great Britain. (From left: Helmut Schmidt, Giscard d'Estaing, James Callaghan.)

treaty and the Senate fails to approve it by a two-thirds vote, then the treaty is not binding on the states.

Because the Constitution states that only Congress and not the President can actually declare war on another country, Congress can limit the President's use of the armed services when they have been sent into combat by Presidential order. An example of this occurred during the Vietnam War in 1973, when Congress voted to deny funds to continue the bombing of Cambodia that had been ordered by President Nixon. Congress must also approve *foreign aid* programs, in the form of goods, services, or funds given to help other nations. Since World War II, foreign aid has been an important part of foreign policy. We have provided emergency relief, money, and advisers to strengthen our allies and help build up the economy in poor countries.

Other groups

National military leaders help set foreign policy by pointing out which countries are increasing their defense, and where we are weak and strong. They also influence our participation in defense treaties and decisions on providing military aid. The Defense Department also sends thousands of citizens abroad as members of the armed forces. Most of them are soldiers; many are

Have students do research to determine which countries the U.S. has given emergency aid to in recent years. What do they think of this practice by our country?

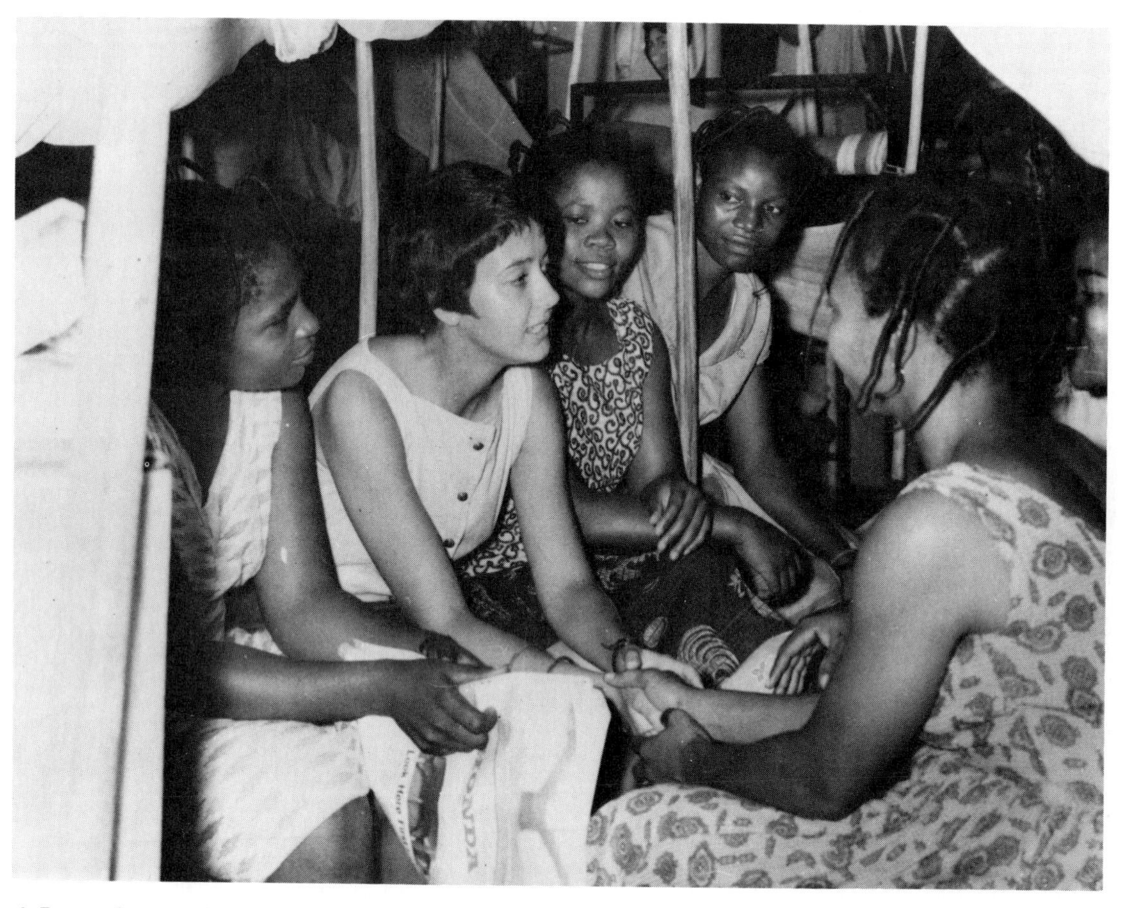

A Peace Corps volunteer with a group of students from her English as a second language in Benin City, Nigeria.

clerks, typists, translators, technicians, and teachers. All of these persons, including thousands of tourists who go abroad each year, are "unofficial ambassadors" of the United States and influence what nations think of us.

Business with offices or factories in other nations are also important in foreign policy-making. Nations are tied closer together when United States businesses do work overseas, or when foreign companies open plants or offices in our country. These actions increase international trade and affect foreign relations.

The will of the people is also strong influence. If public opinion is expressed about decisions that concern foreign relations, the President, the State Department, and the Congress will respond.

Check for Understanding: Now that you have completed this section, you should be able to answer these questions:

1. What groups help set foreign policy?
2. In what way does each group do this?
3. What happens when the President recognizes a country?
4. What is the purpose of foreign aid?

Have an interested student do research on the Peace Corps and its work around the world. How does this group affect foreign relations?

WHAT GROUPS OF NATIONS ARE INVOLVED IN FOREIGN POLICY?

Objectives: After you have read this section, you will be able to:

- Identify the major groups of nations with which the United States has relationships.
- Tell what kind of relationships exist between the United States and these groups.
- Describe the role of the United Nations in foreign policy.

By examining our foreign policy toward different nations, it is possible to identify certain groups. Usually these groups are determined by alliances among various nations or by the kinds of governments the nations have.

The Free World

The term "Free World" refers to those groups of nations where democracy is the form of government and free enterprise or democratic socialism is the form of economy that is used. Included in this group are Great Britain, France, the Netherlands, Italy, Belgium, Denmark, Norway, Sweden, Switzerland, West Germany, and other nations in Western Europe. Non-European countries considered to be in this group are the United States, Canada, Japan, Australia, and New Zealand. Most of these nations are opposed to communism and the totalitarian rule imposed on people by communist governments. The Free World nations have mutual defense treaties that pledge each member to defend any other who is attacked by nations outside the treaty. The North Atlantic Treaty Organization (NATO) is the primary American military alliance in the Free World. Its purpose is to provide for the mutual defense of Europe, particularly against the communist bloc. The Southeast Asia Treaty Organization (SEATO) composed of the countries of Great Britain, France, Australia, New Zealand, Thailand, the Philippines, and the United States, attempts to secure the safety of non-communist nations in Southeast Asia. Since the Vietnam War, communist governments have taken power in Vietnam, Laos, and Cambodia, so the military picture is complicated in this region of the world.

Latin America

United States policy toward Latin America, which includes the countries of Central and South America plus Mexico and the lands of the Caribbean, has for many years been one of protection. President James Monroe in the early 1820's was fearful that foreign governments might try to destroy the newly formed United States by establishing hostile governments in the Western Hemisphere. He declared in a statement, which became known as the Monroe Doctrine, that foreign powers were not to establish colonies in the Western Hemisphere or to interfere in the affairs of the countries in the Americas. Many Latin American nations came to believe that the United States used the Monroe Doctrine not to protect the Western Hemisphere, but to control affairs in their own countries. This is a belief that still exists today in the minds of some Latin Americans.

The presence of a communist government in Cuba and its efforts to extend its form of government to other Latin America countries has created a constant threat in the Western Hemisphere. The United

The complete text of the Monroe Doctrine can be found in the Appendix on page 584.

Have students indicate the Free World and Communist bloc nations on a map. Have they visited any of these nations?

States has sought to contain communism within Cuba. Some Latin American countries do not have democratic governments. At one time in the 1960's the United States, through the Alliance for Progress, which was an aid program to assist Latin American nations in fighting poverty, sought to encourage the growth of democratic governments. However, this has been a policy which has met with little success. Sometimes, the United States has supported non-democratic governments in the Western Hemisphere because of a belief that it is necessary to do this in order to contain communism.

President Franklin D. Roosevelt sought in the 1930's to improve relations with Latin America by establishing the Good Neighbor Policy. This policy aimed at ending the former "protection attitude" of the U.S. and replacing it with one of partnership with Latin American countries. One result was the formation of the Organization of American States (OAS). The OAS maintains programs designed to bring about closer political, cultural, and economic relations among its members. An older organization, the Pan American Union, with headquarters in Washington, D.C., now serves as the secretariat of the OAS.

The Communist bloc

The Communist bloc countries are tied together by communist party rule. The Communist bloc is headed by the Soviet Union, or Russia, and includes East Germany, Poland, Hungary, Yugoslavia, Rumania, Czechoslovakia, and other communist nations in Eastern Europe. These nations also have a mutual defense treaty similar to NATO, the Warsaw Pact.

The United States and other Free World countries have entered into treaties and agreements with these countries in order to work for peace. The Moscow Treaty pledged all the signers to stop aboveground nuclear testing. The United States and Russia have also engaged in a series of Strategic Arms Limitations Talks (SALT). Their goal is to limit the world's nuclear weapons.

The Third World

The "Third World" is a term used to describe the nations of the world that are non-aligned, or not directly associated, with either the "first world"—the United States and other Free World nations, or the "second world"—the Soviet Union and other members of the Communist Bloc. The Third World includes most of the nations and the majority of the people in the world. Many of these are newly developing nations. They are not yet major military powers, but they are powerful in world trade and have great potential for the future.

The role of the United Nations

The present international organization for world peace is the United Nations, or U.N. It was formed by fifty nations after World War II. Its headquarters are in New York City. The U.N. is composed of several important bodies. Of these, the United Nations Security Council and the United Nations General Assembly are most directly concerned with the settlement of world disputes. The U.S. supports the U.N. because it is an organization working for the same goal as our nation—world peace.

The Security Council

The Security Council consists of eleven members. Five of these—the United States, Great Britain, the Soviet Union, France, and the People's Republic of China

Issues in Civics: Do students think that the SALT talks can effectively limit the world's nuclear weapons? Why? Why not?

—are permanent members. Security Council actions must be supported by seven members, including all the permanent members. The Council investigates troubled areas and may order an end to any violence. U.N. troops from member nations can then be sent to the area to enforce the order.

The General Assembly

The General Assembly is composed of delegates from each member of the U.N. After discussion of an international problem, the Assembly issues a recommendation. U.N. recommendations are not backed by military force, but they do carry the weight of world opinion. The U.S. appoints an Ambassador and staff to be at the United Nations at all times.

A world forum

In ancient Rome, the Forum was a public place where questions of public interest were discussed. Today, questions of interest to all nations are brought to the United Nations. The U.N. is a forum because it is a place where nations can work for world peace.

U.N. welfare and service programs

The U.N. also engages in programs to promote better living for people all over the world. United Nations agencies such as the Food and Agriculture Organization, UNESCO (United Nations Emergency Services Commission) and the World Health Organization are helping many nations to fight poverty, hunger, and disease.

Check for Understanding: Now that you have completed this section, you should be able to answer these questions:

1. What are the major groups of nations with which the United States has relationships?
2. What kind of relationship exists with each group?
3. What do the nations that make up the Free World have in common?
4. What is the role of the United Nations in foreign policy?

SUMMARY

A nation's foreign policy is made up of all the actions it takes toward other nations. United States foreign policy is based upon peaceful cooperation, but we are also prepared for defense.

Most important goals of foreign policy today are work for peace and security, promotion of world trade, and concern for basic human rights for all people. Foreign policy is largely determined by the President. The Department of State, Congress, and other groups, including the general public, are also important.

Our foreign policy often deals with nations as members of three groups: the Free World, the Communist Bloc, and the Third World. Each group has different interests and different forms of government. Our foreign policy works with each group in different ways.

Along with most of the nations of the world, the United States takes part in the United Nations. As the only world forum, the United Nations is one of the strongest instruments for peace among nations of the world today.

Have students do research on a controversy between two countries that the U.N. has helped to settle.

BUILDING SKILLS IN CIVICS

THINKING SKILLS

1. What are three aims of United States foreign policy?
2. Why is it no longer possible for the United States to follow the policy of isolationism?
3. What is the main purpose of diplomacy?
4. What is the purpose of foreign aid?
5. What do "Free World" nations have in common?
6. Read through the chapter and find four factual statements that would support this generalization:
   Our foreign policy often deals with nations of three groups: the Free World, the Communist bloc, and the Third World.

VOCABULARY SKILLS

Match each term with its definition. Use the Glossary if you need help.

a. detente	c. isolationism	e. treaty	g. embargo
b. recognize	d. summit conference	f. foreign aid	h. diplomacy

1. A refusal by one nation, or a group of nations to trade products with other countries.
2. An attempt to relax relations and to increase peaceful negotiations of conflicts.
3. To officially accept a government as the true government of a nation.
4. The act of establishing relationships that both sides can accept as useful and beneficial.
5. A meeting of the chiefs-of-state of major powers.
6. Goods, services, or funds approved by Congress to be given to other countries.
7. A contract signed by representatives of different nations.
8. The policy of not becoming involved with issues outside your own country.

STUDY SKILLS—USING THE *READERS' GUIDE TO PERIODICAL LITERATURE*

Magazine articles are an excellent source of current information. To find an index of magazine articles, consult your public library for a copy of the *Readers' Guide to Periodical Literature.* This is an index to magazines, and is one of the most valuable study tools in the library. Use the *Readers' Guide* like the card catalog. Locate your topic by Title, Subject, or Author. A typical entry in the Reader's Guide looks like this:

DUE process of law
Due process in discipline. C.E. Alberti
bibl Clearing H. 51:12–14 S '77

This tells us important information:

Subject: Due Process of Law
Title of Article: Due Process in Discipline
Author: C.E. Alberti
bibl: The article has a bibliography.
Volume: 51
Pages: 12–14
Date of Publication: September, 1977

Activity: Find information about a topic from this chapter in the Readers' Guide.

BEYOND THE BOOK

1. Construct a chart showing the major groups of nations the United States has relationships with and identify the types of relationships it has.
2. Use the *Readers' Guide to Periodical Literature* to locate articles about the United Nations. How many references did you find? What is the main theme of each article?
3. Collect maps that show nations currently receiving foreign aid from the United States. Tell where you found your information.

CHAPTER TWENTY TEST

VOCABULARY CHECK

Some of the underlined words in the sentences below are used correctly, others are not. If the sentence is correct, write True. If it is not, replace the word with the best choice from the list.

detente	treaty	recognize	foreign aid
isolationism	embargo	summit conference	diplomacy

1. The act of establishing relationships between nations is called a treaty.
2. Foreign aid is the attempt to relax relations between the Soviet Union and the United States.
3. The Arab nations set up an oil embargo against those countries that supported Israel in the Arab-Israeli war of 1973–1974.
4. Detente is the art of establishing relations between countries that are satisfactory to both.
5. Isolationism means to be involved as little as possible with other nations.
6. The President may refuse to recognize the government of another country if for any reason it is not considered legitimate.
7. Diplomacy is money given to help other nations.
8. It is an important event when the President holds a summit conference with the chiefs of state of other world powers.

COMPREHENSION CHECK

1. Which of these are not aims of United States foreign policy?
   a. Peace and security
   b. International trade
   c. Isolationism
   d. Human rights
2. True or False: National military leaders help set foreign policy by pointing out where we are weak and where we are strong.
3. True or False: The Third World powers are major military powers.
4. True or False: The Security Council investigates troubled areas of the world, and may order an end to any violence.

SKILL BUILDERS—INTERPRETING GLOBAL PROJECTIONS

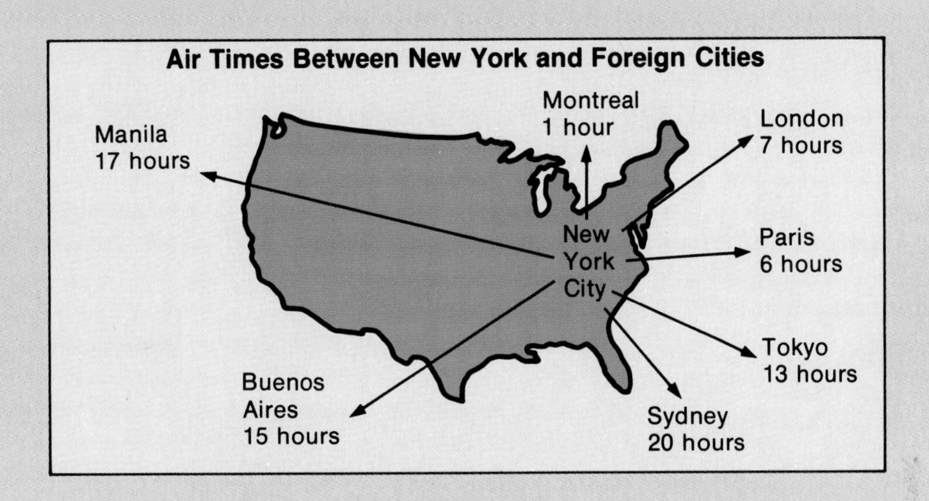

1. What information can you get from reading the title and the legend of the map?
2. What areas does this map focus on? What part of the world is not shown?
3. How could you use this map in a discussion about isolationism? What arguments *for* or *against* does the map help support? How could this map show relationships between various parts of "a shrinking world?"
4. What generalizations can you make from this map?

BUILDING WRITING SKILLS

1. Write sentences to explain the differences between the words in one of the pairs below.
   diplomacy - detente
   Monroe Doctrine - isolationism
   Security council - General Assembly
2. Discuss the topic "Free World Countries." Then write five sentences about the topic.
3. Write a paragraph that summarizes the purpose of foreign aid.

Chapter Twenty-One
Our State and Local Executives

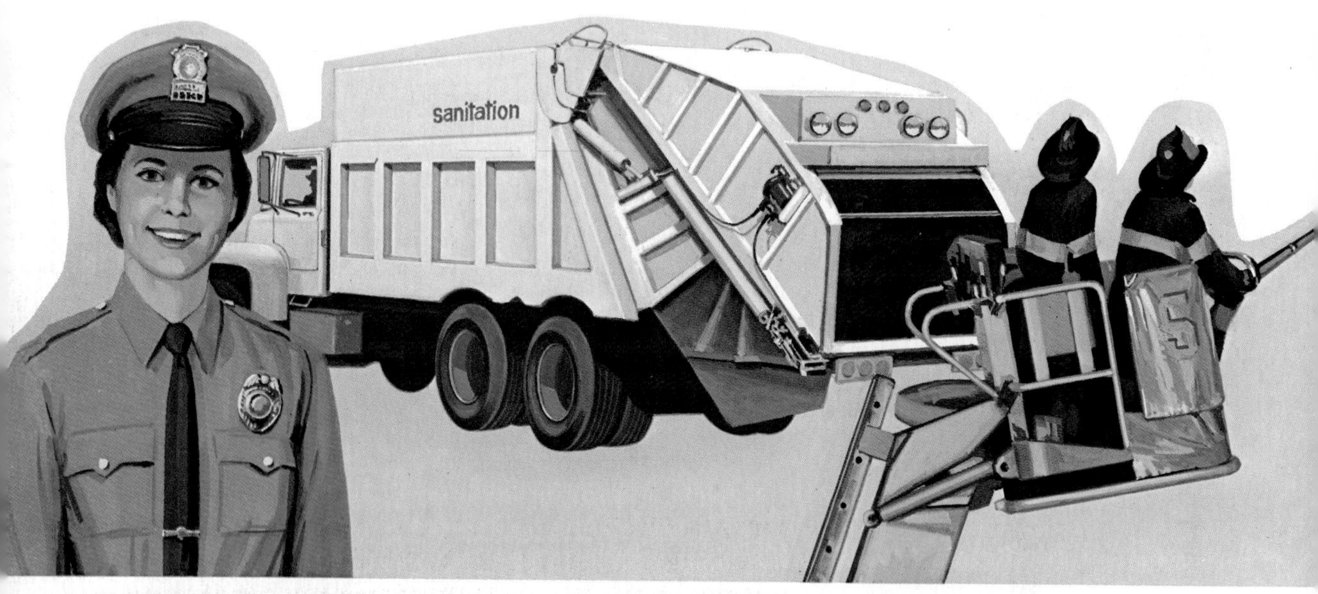

Document: The Constitution of the United States

Article IV, Section 1. Full Faith and Credit shall be given in each State to the Public Acts, Records, and judicial Proceedings of every other State. And the Congress may by general Laws prescribe the Manner in which such Acts, Records and Proceedings shall be proved, and the Effect thereof.

Article I, Section 2. The Citizens of each State shall be entitled to all Privileges and Immunities of Citizens in the several States.

Article VI. The Senators and Representatives . . . and the Members of the several State Legislatures, and all executive and judicial Officers, both of the United States and of the several States, shall be bound by Oath or Affirmation, to support this Constitution . . .

The executives at the state and local levels exert a tremendous amount of influence on our daily lives. The governor, the chief executive of each state, has the power to appoint and direct state officials or to remove them from office; and the constitution of each state authorizes the governor to see that the laws of the state are faithfully executed. The governor is also responsible for directing the preparation of the state budget, granting pardons, and commanding the state militia.

Ask your students if they are aware of all the services shown here that are provided by local government. Which do they feel are most important? Can they think of other services that are not pictured here?

The complete text of the Constitution can be found in the Appendix, beginning on page 564.

The governor is also the leader of his or her political party. Most states also elect other executive officials who include a lieutenant governor, secretary of state, treasurer, attorney general, and auditor.

The mayor or city manager is the executive at the city level, while several different people administer the laws at the county level. Both the state and local governments share the responsibility of dealing with matters of finance, welfare, and education.

FOCUSING IDEAS

- The governor is the chief executive of each state with the power of appointment, veto, and power over the budget through control of the bureaucracy.
- Counties are run by county commissioners and are divided into precincts, with one commissioner elected from each precinct. The county attorney and the sheriff are the main legal officers of the county, and the county clerk is responsible for keeping all records.
- Cities are run by mayors or by city managers. Each city administration department has an administrative head who is hired by the city manager, but who is subject to approval by the city council.

Issues in Civics: Are these services too expensive for the benefits they provide? Are there other ways they could be provided?

PRE-TEST

1. What function does a state executive perform?
2. What are the usual duties and responsibilities of a county executive?
3. What role does a city executive play in our government?

The finest laws in the world are of little value if they are not enforced. So we look to executives and administrators to carry out the will of our legislators. The two words, executive and administrator, are generally used interchangeably. However, there is a fine distinction between them. The *executive* might be called the "top boss", and the *administrator* the one who carries out his orders.

HOW DO STATE EXECUTIVES WORK?

Objectives: After you have read this section, you will be able to:
- Describe the work of the governor.
- Name three powers of the governor.
- Describe the state bureaucracy.

From the time people first began living in groups, someone had to be the leader and direct the activities of the group. From before the time of historical records, this leader made the rules and then enforced them. Much of the time this ruler was called a "governor."

One dictionary definition of governor is "the chief executive of a dependent or component unit in a political system." Before the thirteen colonies were formed into the United States, Great Britain sent governors to administer the affairs of the various states. Much of the colonial resentment and friction was caused by, and directed toward, these governors. This resentment and the frictions of the Civil War have been carried over into the constitutions of the states. The framers of the state constitutions chose to keep the power in the hands of the lawmakers rather than put it in the hands of the governor.

Miriam "Ma" Ferguson served two terms as governor of the state of Texas.

Building Vocabulary:
executive *(346)* • administrator *(346)* • sunset law *(348)* • ombudsman *(348)* • sheriff *(350)* • city manager *(352)* • special district *(353)*

All vocabulary items are defined in alphabetical order in the Glossary, beginning on page 598 of the Appendix.

Although the power of the governor is constitutionally weak, it is modified by his or her personality. A strong person can have power and influence through the force of personality, but a weak person will have little effect on the state government. Many governors have been strong leaders who went on to become presidents of the United States, and others have left a long and lasting imprint on their state and the whole country.

The salary of the governor ranges from $10,000 in Arkansas to $85,000 in New York, with most states paying in the mid-range. Almost all the states have four-year terms. Approximately one fourth forbid a second term, and one half limit the governor to two consecutive terms. Most, if not all states provide the governor with a "mansion" as a residence and a fund for expense items.

The three main powers residing in the governship are (1) appointment; (2) veto; (3) power over the budget through control of the bureaucracy.

Although all states elect some of the department heads of the state, many of them elect only a few officials, among them the attorney general, lieutenant governor, state treasurer, secretary of state, state auditor, and superintendent of education. The rest are appointed by the governor, usually with the approval of the senate, and within the limitations of the civil service merit system.

The governor's power over the budget is a strong control on the bureaucracy (the body of administrators of a government or government department). He does not have to veto the entire appropriations bill to make his wants known. He can veto one item without affecting the rest of the items on the bill. In this way the governor can say,

Richard Snelling, governor of Vermont, is an example of a governor whose strong personality enabled him to use the office effectively.

"Do what I want if you wish to be paid and have money to operate."

The veto power extends beyond the power to veto items in the budget. After a bill has been passed by both the house and senate, it goes to the governor to be signed, vetoed, or become a law without his signature. If a bill is vetoed, the legislature has the power to make the bill into a law over the veto by passing it again with (usually) a two-thirds majority.

Under the governor are ranks and files of elected officials, appointed officials, boards, commissions, and agencies. At one time California had over 360 boards, commissions and agencies, ranging from Board of Guide Dogs for the Blind to the Yacht and Ship Brokers' Commission. These boards and commissions have grown in an uncontrolled fashion in all the states, often to give employment to preferred people. Of

Assign students to collect newspaper articles, cartoons, and editorials about their state's governor. From the material they have compiled, do they think public opinion is for or against him or her?

course, there need to be officers and agencies to handle the vast amount of business of the state, but there should be also some control over this expansion.

Sunset laws are a relatively recent attempt to control the bureaucracy. They require that all boards, commissions, agencies, and departments be reviewed every twelve years to see if they are still necessary. Until a few years ago there was still a Confederate Veterans' Authority in Texas; there is also an egg marketing board and a film commission advisory board, among many others. Usually there is a paid chairman (who is frequently an ex-legislator), and volunteer members (often those most involved in the matter).

A current suggestion is that of an *ombudsman*—a watchdog or grievance commissioner—to be elected or appointed to investigate citizens' complaints. The idea originated in Sweden in 1809 and has since been adopted by a number of countries as an intermediary between the citizens and the governmental bureaucracy. The ombudsman is usually independent, impartial, universally accessible, and empowered only to recommend action.

Reformers are generally of the opinion that the governor should be given more authority over the administrative staff, with the elimination of most elective administrators and the extension of the governor's appointive power to include all department heads. This would, in practice, be more like the federal system of a cabinet working under and with the executive head of the government. They feel it is not fair to expect the governors to administer the laws of the state without giving them authority over those working under them.

Check for Understanding: Now that you have completed this section, you should be able to answer these questions:

1. What does the work of the governor consist of?
2. What are the governor's three main powers?
3. What is the state bureaucracy?
4. What is one major reform suggested for state administrative government?

An ombudsman meets with a group of concerned citizens to discuss their grievances.

Do students think that "sunset laws" really help to control the bureaucracy? Why? Why not?

Duties of a Governor
Recommends Laws
Enforces Laws
Oversees Budget
Appoints People to Office
Serves as Official Head of State
Leads His or Her Party in the State

HOW DO COUNTY EXECUTIVES WORK?

Objectives: After reading this section, you should be able to:

- Name the administrative officers of the county.
- Tell what the duties of the county commissioners are.
- Describe how county and city government cooperate.

The county board is the administrative agency as well as the policy-making body of the county. Actually, the county is the administrative arm of the state. Citizens cannot be expected to travel to the capital to conduct whatever business they have with the state. So the state comes to the citizens through the county government. This is much like a large company having a branch office in every city in which it does business.

The county commissioners are charged with maintaining the county courthouse, the jail, and other buildings in the city and county (the city is part of the county) that are provided or owned by the county. These might include a youth home, a museum, a library, a hospital, historical sites, or other buildings that the commissioners and the citizens of the county might have. The commissioners oversee the county cemetery, the county roads, bridges and ferries. They provide for the welfare of residents of the county who cannot provide for themselves.

Counties are divided into precincts, with one commissioner elected from each precinct. The commissioner from a particular precinct is responsible for the things required in that precinct, particularly for roads and bridges. The presiding officer of the county commissioners' court may be elected by the people, or chosen by the commissioners from one of their number. In many states the presiding officer is the county judge, and must be a lawyer or have a working knowledge of the law process. In other states the county judge is an officer separate from the presiding officer of the commission. The commissioners have stated times for meeting, and conduct their business according to parliamentary procedure with motions and formal votes. The proceedings are recorded by the county court.

The county attorney and the *sheriff* are generally considered the main legal officers of the county. The sheriff and his deputies maintain law and order and apprehend those who break the law. They are charged with the responsibility of collecting evidence within the limits of the civil rights of the offender. The evidence is then turned over to the county attorney, who prepares and presents the case against the offender before the county court.

The county clerk keeps all the records of the county, including those of the meetings of the county board, the justice of the peace courts, the juvenile court, the court of common law, the county court of law, the probate court, and the petit jury. All vital statistics (births, weddings, divorces, adoptions, and deaths), and all transactions pertaining to property (deeds, mortgages, liens, and contracts) are kept on file in this office. The county clerk also supervises the elections for the state. The district clerk keeps the records for all district courts in the county. The tax assessor or tax collector maintains his functions, and the treasurer keeps and disburses the money of the county.

In their opinion, which county officer do students think performs the most important service? Why do they think so?

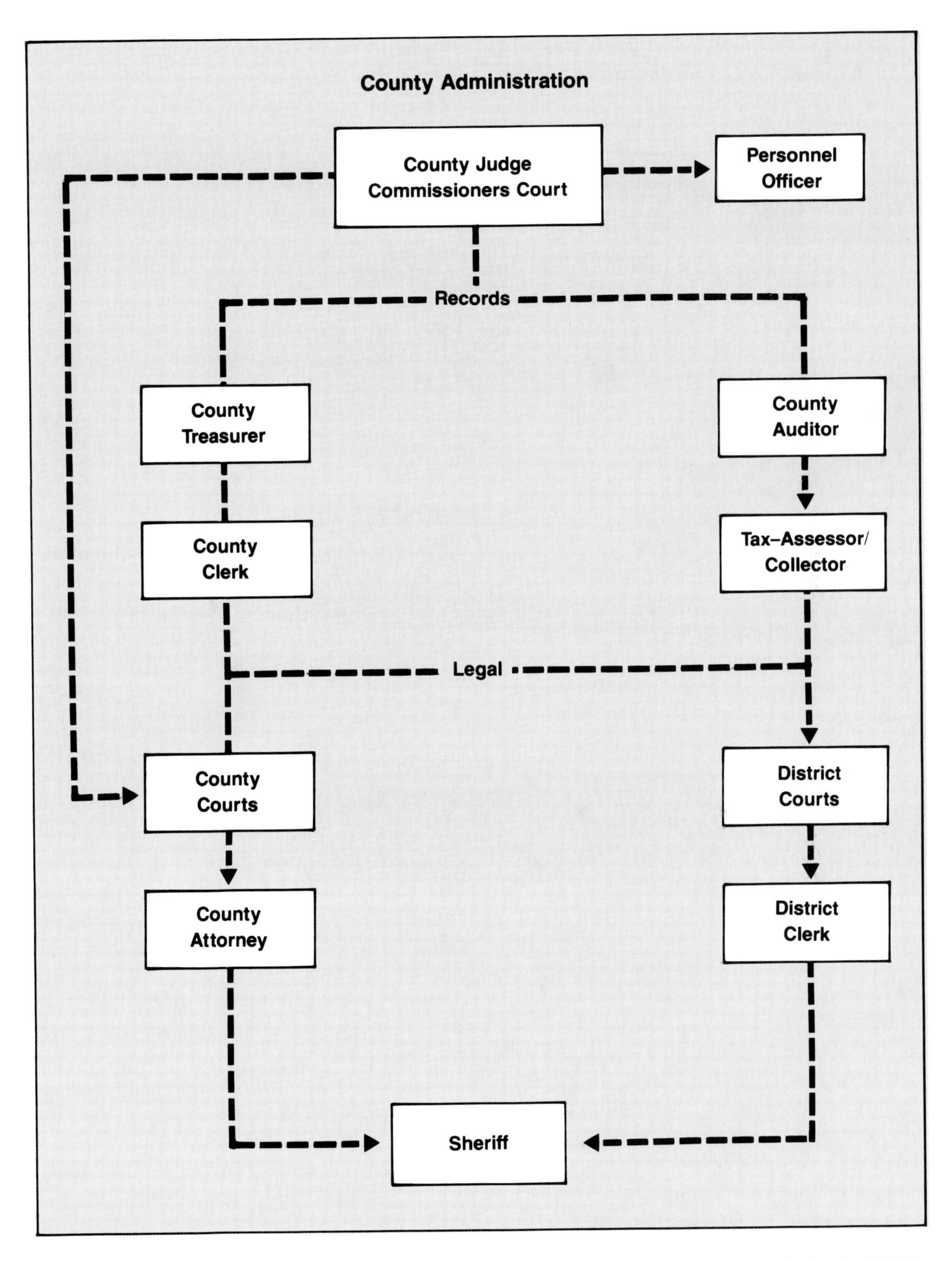

Issues in Civics: Do students think that the high tax rates throughout the country are adequately represented by the services we receive in our cities and counties?

All of these officers hire their own staffs, though in many counties a personnel officer presents to them a list of possible employees who have been screened. Otherwise, the selection of the employees must be approved by the commissioners' board. There is no specific place where an aspiring candidate for county office can receive training. Frequently candidates for election to these posts have worked in the department for a number of years and thus have received "on the job" training.

There is a slight trend toward developing a county manager system. Without such a manager, the county commissioners are expected to personally supervise all the business of the county. There usually is considerable cooperation between county and city, and a trade-off of responsibilities. Thus, the city fire department may fight fires in the county, and the county will supervise a city-county hospital or library. This eliminates considerable duplication of effort, and makes for efficiency of operation as well as saving in costs.

Even more desirable, in the opinion of many people, would be the consolidation of the city and county governments, especially where a county is sparsely settled with only one sizeable city or town. There has also been some movement for the consolidation of two or more counties into one, with a consequent saving in money spent.

There are associations to help the commissioners keep abreast of bills before the state legislature, news, and trends which would have an impact on the counties. Also, in most states there are one or more boards that coordinate the business of the counties, such as the Workman's Compensation Board.

Check for Understanding: Now that you have completed this section, you should be able to answer these questions:

1. Who are three county officers?
2. What are the duties of these officers?
3. What kind of things do county commissioners do?
4. How do the city and county cooperate?

HOW DO CITY EXECUTIVES WORK?

Objectives: After you have read this section, you should be able to:

- Realize the size of the city's administration.
- Explain how a city is operated like a business.
- Describe a "special district."

It is at the city level that most citizens keep in touch with their government. The city is the basic unit of government. It was the first form that government took in the earliest days of human history. The very word "citizen" is derived from the same word as "city." Everywhere we turn we are aware of the services of the city; the water from our faucets, the streets on which we ride or walk, the lights along the streets at night, the police patrolling to give us protection. All of this takes management, either by a mayor or by a *city manager* hired to run the city.

Running even a medium-sized city is big business. A city of approximately 100,000 population will have around 11,000 employees, and operate on a budget of $40 to $50 million dollars. Approximately half of this budget will come from taxes, direct and

Ask students to think of a time when their city government failed to provide a service. How did this situation affect them?

indirect, levied on the people living in the city, and from state and federal grants. The other half of the budget will be earned by water and sewer charges, which should be enough to support the operation of those departments, and other operations such as airports, hospitals, golf courses, and other services of the city for which a fee is collected.

Of course, the city manager also has to answer to the city council, and justify his actions. He or she must act within the lines of policy and the objectives outlined by the city council, for the council has the final authority in setting policy.

Each of the sixteen departments (which can be more or less in different cities) into which the city administration is divided has an administrative head. These are hired by the city manager but are subject to approval by the council. The personnel director screens prospective employees, but department heads are free to choose from this group without further approval being necessary. The department is also expected to stay within its budget, even though material is drawn from the central purchasing warehouse.

Just as a company must have clerical help in its offices, so the city has bookkeepers, accountants, secretaries, clerks, computer programmers and technicians, as well as many other types of employees. These are not only in the city manager's office, but in each department administrator's office as well.

Special districts, sometimes called "hidden governments" have a powerful impact on our cities, as well as counties and states. The most numerous and best known special district is the school district, though it cannot be really called a hidden government because it is in daily contact with the lives of most of the citizens. It is a "special district" because it collects its own taxes and runs its own business without any help or supervision by the city or county government. It answers only to the people, through citizen input and through the ballot box.

A special district is a unit of local government created by an act of the legislature to

When city government fails to provide services, the result is immediately obvious to everyone.

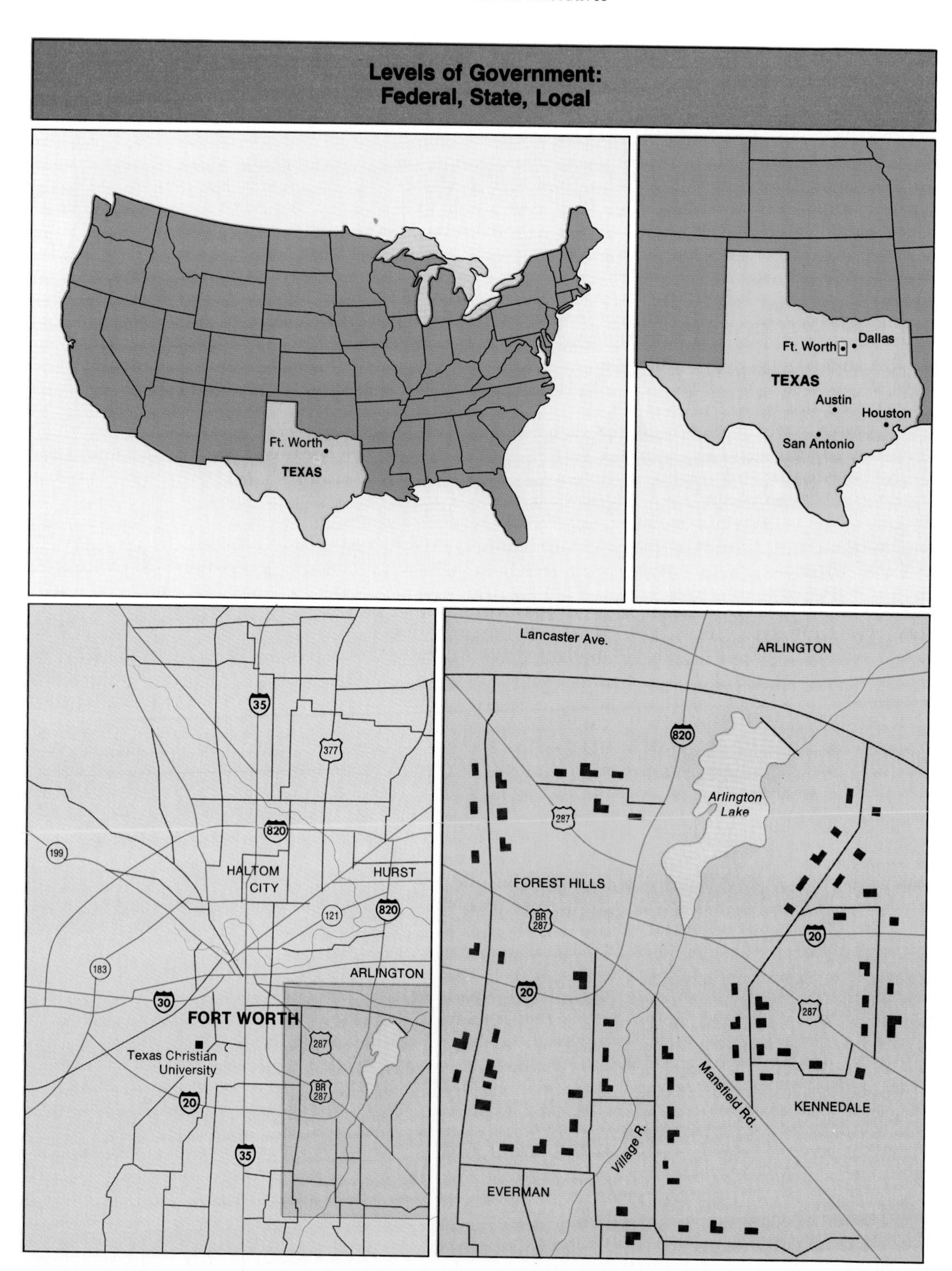

The maps above demonstrate how one locale, Fort Worth, exists as a part of various levels of government. It is a part of the nation of the U.S. and the State of Texas. It also has its own city government, which is divided into local districts. You might want to make a similar breakdown of levels of government for your own local area.

perform limited functions. Besides schools, they frequently are concerned with water conservation, hospital operation, sanitation, navigation, highways, weed and pest control, or any other resource or nuisance that needs more than the normal city or county operation or control. There are several reasons for the growth of special districts. Oftentimes the district covers several city or county units, such as for flood control, so that a unified approach makes for more efficient operation. Sometimes the city or county has already reached its bond limit and cannot finance a hospital or water district. And a unit with only one project is easier to manage than a city with sixteen "companies". These districts frequently have technical problems which are handled easier when not involved with politics.

The main problem with special districts is that they often are indeed "hidden governments". There is very little supervision of them either by the state or the local governments. They receive little publicity, and the average citizen is generally unaware of what is being done or how much it is costing in taxes. One researcher has found that the special districts in the United States collect and spend twice as much as the counties, almost as much as the cities, and half as much as the states. It is also possible that they perpetuate themselves after their usefulness has ended, unless they are terminated by a sunset law or by the vigilance of the citizens of the area.

A local school board meets to consider the issue of cutting the school budget.

Check for Understanding: Now that you have completed this section, you should be able to answer these questions:

1. What are the "companies" making up a city's operation?
2. What are two duties of the city manager or mayor?
3. What is a "special district"?
4. Why are special districts called "hidden governments?"

SUMMARY

After laws are made they must be enforced. This falls on the governor at the state level, and on the mayor or city manager at the city level. On the county level there is not one individual at the head of the administration except in the few counties that have gone to the manager plan. In other counties the law is administered by a number of different people who have been elected to their various positions.

The city is where the citizen is most aware of the government, because it is so obvious when services break down. City management is big business, and running a modern city is very much like running a modern corporation.

BUILDING SKILLS IN CIVICS

THINKING SKILLS

1. What three powers do state governors have?
2. What are the reasons that the sunset law was enacted?
3. What are the duties of the county commissioners?
4. How do the city and county cooperate?
5. In what ways is a city operated like a business?
6. Write a title that fits the following paragraph:

    Special districts are "hidden governments." There is very little supervision of them. They receive little publicity, and the average citizen is generally unaware of what is being done, or how much it is costing. They may also perpetuate themselves after their usefulness is ended.

VOCABULARY SKILLS

Fill in each blank with the word from the list that best completes the sentence.

executive	ombudsman	administrator	sheriff
sunset law	city manager	special district	

1. The ______ requires all boards, commissioners, agencies, and departments to be reviewed every twelve years to see if they are still necessary.
2. An ______ is in charge of carrying out the orders of the executive.
3. The ______ is usually independent, impartial, available to everyone, and can only recommend action.
4. A ______ is a unit of local government created by an act of the legislature to perform limited functions.
5. An ______ has the authority to manage the affairs of a nation or of a state.
6. The ______ is the main legal officer in a county who maintains law and order.
7. The ______ is the person who runs the affairs of the city.

STUDY SKILLS—PREPARING A BOOK REPORT

Book reports are a way of sharing information. This information can be presented informally—for instance, as a part of a classroom discussion—or it can be presented as a formal report.

You can give a formal book report orally, with visual aids that illustrate the main ideas or show relationships. These aids may include pictures from the book, charts, or diagrams. One of the most effective ways to illustrate important information is to write key words and abbreviations that emphasize main ideas on the chalkboard. Be sure to erase the old information before writing any new information. An oral book report follows the same format as a formal outline. In fact, you can even use index cards with key words or phrases to help you as you speak.

Activity: Choose a topic that interests you from this chapter or from the unit. Then, use the card catalog to locate several books on the topic. Choose a book you like. Read it, ask questions, take notes, arrange the notes in outline form, and indicate on your outline where your visuals will be used.

BEYOND THE BOOK

1. With the help of your classmates, construct an illustration that has for its main theme "A City Is Operated Much Like a Business."
2. Use the *Reader's Guide* to locate information on problems of American cities. Categorize these according to the type of problem, and the solutions suggested. Share your information with the class.
3. Collect and analyze old maps of your city. How have the centers of population and business changed over the years? Can you find out why this happened?
4. Prepare an oral report telling about the illustration described above, or about another illustration you made which shows one of the main points of this chapter.

CHAPTER TWENTY-ONE TEST

VOCABULARY CHECK

Match each term with its definition.

a. executive
b. administrator
c. sunset law
d. ombudsman
e. special district
f. sheriff
g. city manager

1. A person who works for the state to investigate complaints and recommend action.
2. This person carries out decisions that have been made regarding the management of government.
3. The main law enforcement officer of a county.
4. This person might be called the "top boss" in managing the affairs of a government, and in putting its laws into effect.
5. It requires that all agencies departments be reviewed every few years to see if they are still necessary.
6. A unit of local government created by the legislature to perform limited functions.
7. A person who is appointed to run the affairs of a city.

COMPREHENSION CHECK

1. True or False: Citizens can conduct business with the state through the county government.
2. True or False: The commissioner from a particular precinct is responsible for the things required in that district.
3. True or False: The main legal officer in the county is the district clerk.
4. True or False: The most common and best-known special district is the school district.
5. Write "Activities of the Governor" on your paper. Identify the points below that belong under that topic.
   a. Supervises the state elections.
   b. Apprehends those who break the law.
   c. Can veto all or part of a bill.
   d. Has power over the budget.

SKILL BUILDERS—INTERPRETING DIAGRAMS

A *Venn Diagram* can be used to classify information according to similarities and differences.

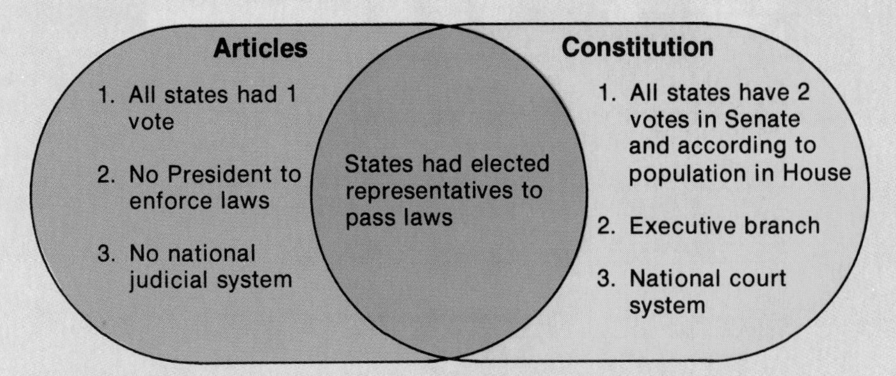

Activity: Look at the diagram and answer these questions.

1. What information is given in the title?
2. What kinds of city government are being compared?
3. How does the diagram show the things that are different?
4. What information is shown in the area where the circles overlap?
5. Construct Venn Diagrams to show similarities and differences between:
   the Articles of Confederation and the Constitution
   state executives and county executives

BUILDING WRITING SKILLS

1. Write a question that this paragraph could logically answer.

   Many people think that it would be desirable to consolidate the city and county governments, especially where a county has a small population. There has been some movement for the consolidation of two or more counties into one county, with a consequent saving in money spent.
2. Discuss the topic "Special Districts." Then write at least five sentences that support the topic.
3. Write a paragraph that describes the ways in which the city and the county governments cooperate.

UNIT FIVE TEST

A. Look at the photo above. Then answer the following questions:

1. Who are the people in the photo above? Why do you think the photographer took the picture? Who do you think this picture would be of interest to?
2. Can you tell anything about the feelings that the people in the photo have towards one another based on body language or facial expression?
3. Do you think it's important for a President to meet regularly with foreign dignitaries? Why or why not?
4. Do you think that personal feelings between officials of different countries can affect foreign policy? Do you think it *should?* Why or why not?

B. Former President Harry S. Truman once said, "No one who has not had the responsibility can really understand what it is like to be President, not even his closest aides or members of his immediate family. There is no end to the chain of responsibility that binds him . . ." Based on what you know about Presidential responsibility, do you agree with Truman's statement? Do *you* think you have an idea of what the job really entails? Would you ever want to hold this office? Why or why not?

C. Write a paragraph describing how U.S. foreign policy has changed over the years. Do you think the changes have been for the best? Explain your answer.

The photograph shows President Carter meeting with the leaders of Israel and Egypt, Menachem Begin and Anwar Sadat.

Unit Six
Justice Under the Law

The Bill of Rights was created to guarantee basic freedoms for American citizens, and it is the job of the courts to see that these rights are protected. In the pursuit of justice, our system seeks to protect the rights of the individual. In order to achieve this goal, both the rights of the accused and the accuser must be upheld and kept in balance. Justice, then, is the protection of the innocent, as well as punishment for the guilty. Seeing that this system of justice is maintained is up to all of us.

The complete text of the Bill of Rights can be found in the Appendix on pages 575–76.

The illustration depicts the functioning of the U.S. court system. Ask students if they know the names of the people depicted (judge, witness, attorney) and the function that each performs in court.

Chapter Twenty-Two
Safeguarding Our Liberties

Document: The Constitution of the United States

Article III, Section 1. The judicial Power of the United States, shall be vested in one supreme Court, and in such inferior Courts as the Congress may from time to time ordain and establish. The Judges, both of the supreme and inferior Courts, shall hold their Offices during good Behaviour, and shall, at stated Times, receive for their Services, a Compensation, which shall not be diminished during their Continuance in Office.

Article III, Section 2. . . . The Trial of all Crimes, except in Cases of Impeachment, shall be by Jury; and such Trial shall be held in the State where the said Crimes shall have been committed; but when not committed within any State, the Trial shall be at such Place or Places as the Congress may by Law have directed.

Amendment IX. The numeration in the Constitution, of certain rights, shall not be construed to deny or disparage others retained by the people.

The Bill of Rights guarantees certain basic freedoms for the citizens of the United States, but is the job of the courts to see that these liberties are safeguarded. When the Constitution was first adopted in

Discuss with your students where prison camps like this might be found today, with prisoners held for political reasons. What does this camp, and the attitude of the policemen, tell you about the type of government in that country?

1789, it contained few personal guarantees, and some states refused to ratify it unless a specific bill of rights was included. James Madison and Thomas Jefferson fought for the adoption of certain fundamental freedoms, and so, the Bill of Rights was created—assuring all citizens of the right to "life, liberty, and the pursuit of happiness." The courts in our country uphold these basic rights by interpreting the law, and by settling disputes between individuals and organizations.

FOCUSING IDEAS

- After the Revolutionary War, the Constitution established a court system in the U.S. modeled after the court system in England.
- The Bill of Rights protects our liberties by guaranteeing freedom of religion, speech, assembly, petition, the press, and by giving us the right to bear arms. People are also protected from unreasonable search and arrest, unfair trials, and excessive fines or cruel punishment, among other freedoms.
- Provisions are made in the Constitution guaranteeing fair trials for all American citizens.
- The Constitution ensures independent courts by having judges appointed by the President, with the approval of the Senate.

Where else would students see this scene of people marching outside the White House grounds? How does this scene contrast with the one on the opposite page?

What does this contrast tell you about the attitude of our government toward this type of activity?

PRE-TEST

1. How did the court system develop in the U.S.?
2. How does the Bill of Rights serve to protect our liberties?
3. How is the right to a fair trial guaranteed?
4. In what way does our government ensure an independent court system?

HOW DID THE COURTS DEVELOP?

Objectives: After you have read this section, you should be able to:

- Describe the stages in the development of the court system.
- Tell why the jury system is important to the idea of justice.
- See how a fair court system works to maintain justice.

Most things having to do with courts give an impression of dignity and wisdom. The Supreme Court Building in Washington, D.C. and most courthouses are impressive and solemn sights. Unlike the President, members of Congress, or a governor, most judges wear traditional black robes while they are at work. Such robes have been worn by judges for hundreds of years. These symbols are used to remind people who come to court, and those who work there, of the need for good conduct and wisdom. Both of these traits are necessary in the important job of our courts. The Bill of Rights is an important safeguard of our liberties. The courts have the important job of seeing that these inherent rights are protected.

Judges have worn black robes in court for centuries, as shown in this courtroom scene in Europe in the Middle Ages.

Providing justice

The job of the courts is to provide *justice*, or a fair hearing before the law. Wherever people live together, disputes and differences will arise. In order to settle these problems, governments have set down laws or rules. It is the job of the courts to see that questions about the laws are settled by just hearings.

Building Vocabulary:
justice *(364)* • trial by ordeal *(365)* • jury system *(366)* • petition *(367)* • cruel and unusual punishment *(368)* • self-incrimination *(370)* • jeopardy *(370)*

The complete text of the Bill of Rights can be found in the Appendix on pages 575–76.

Have an interested student compare the provisions in the 1689 English Bill of Rights, which stood as a legal guarantee of English liberty, with that of our country's Bill of Rights.

Rules and judges as a part of life

Rules, and the people who interpret them in a fair manner, are a part of everyday life. Most games and contests have rules that all must follow. When two teams meet in a game, there will usually be a referee or an umpire who belongs to neither team. This person is the one who makes decisions concerning the rules or the conduct of the players involved. A good umpire must know the rules, be impartial, and honest. In the same way, a judge must know the law and be fair to both sides.

Early judges

The world has had judges as long as people have lived together. In the early tribes the chief was the judge of the people. In a kingdom the king first acted as a judge. The place where the king lived was often called the king's court. This term was first used because of the king's role as a judge. Later, kings appointed others to represent them as judges in the courts of the land.

Unfair trials

In the past, people sometimes used unfair or strange methods to decide the guilt or innocence of persons charged with a crime. During the Middle Ages some rulers used "trial by water," "trial by combat," or "trial by fire." In a trial by water the accused was thrown into a lake or stream. If the person sank, he or she was considered guilty. If the person floated or swam, he or she was thought to be innocent. In a trial by combat the accused was given a sword with which to fight a knight or warrior. It was believed that an innocent person would defeat the knight. If the person lost, he was found guilty. In a trial by fire, a person had to put his hand in a fire or hold something hot. If he was not burned or if his burns healed quickly, he was declared innocent.

A baseball umpire must make decisions honestly and impartially, without favoring either side.

The demand for fair judgment

As time went on, people no longer would accept these methods of determining guilt or innocence at a *trial by ordeal.* They knew that whether a person could swim or could win in battle had little to do with being guilty or innocent. Proof of guilt or innocence became important. People began to demand that these important decisions be made with dignity and wisdom.

The people turned from unfair trials to the use of a court where a person could come before a judge. Each person could tell his or her side of the story. The person could bring witnesses to prove the points made. In the end the judge would decide.

The system worked well as long as the judges were chosen for their wisdom and were allowed to arrive at their own decisions. But sometimes the judges would decide the cases as the king wished. They were forced by others to decide without regard to justice. Because of this, many people did not get a fair trial.

Have a student research the Salem Witch Trials, then report. How many people were tried? What began the incident? What evidence was presented? Who presided over the trials? How many were executed?

Have a student (or group) research the Magna Carta. What was it? Who signed it? What was its purpose? When was it signed?

The court of King Henry VI of England in the 1400's.

The use of a jury

In order to insure a fair trial, the English people turned to the *jury system.* A jury is a group of people who are chosen to hear evidence in a case. It was felt that a group of people would be wiser than one person. If a juror was found to be a close friend of someone in the case, that person was removed from the jury. Under this system, the judge is in charge at the trial but does not decide the case. The judge explains the laws to the jurors, and the jury arrives at the verdict. This system of jury trials began in England long ago and was brought to America by the colonists.

America develops fair and independent courts

After the Revolutionary War, each state developed its own system of courts that were patterned after those in England. Under this system there were no federal courts, and the Articles of Confederation did not provide for federal courts. When the Constitution established a strong central government, it also established a federal court system.

In forming state and federal courts the colonists sought to guarantee a fair and impartial trial in court. They also established courts as independent branches in the federal and state governments. They are not subject to either threats or force by the legislative or the executive branch.

Many of the laws that provide for our courts were written into the Constitution. Others came about through amendments to the Constitution. In some cases the courts themselves have set limits on their actions in order to guarantee fair trials. These limitations demonstrate the constant concern of Americans, including many judges, to provide free courts that will safeguard our liberties.

Check for Understanding: Now that you have completed this section, you should be able to answer these questions:

1. What were the stages in the development of the U.S. court system?
2. Why is the jury system important to the idea of justice?
3. How does a fair court system work to maintain justice?
4. Why were state and federal courts formed?

Have students interview parents, neighbors, or other adults who have served on juries. Find out: 1. How they were notified. 2. How they were selected for a jury. 3. How long their duties were. 4. What type of trials did they serve on.

A trial in the mid-1800's in the "Old Bailey," the criminal court of London. The court building was built in 1550.

HOW DOES THE BILL OF RIGHTS PROTECT OUR LIBERTIES?

Objectives: After reading this section, you will be able to:

- Tell how the Bill of Rights protects your liberties.
- Explain the basic freedoms that the Bill of Rights provides for.
- Understand that we have other rights that are not listed in the Constitution.

The Constitution

The Constitution is the highest law in the nation. When the Constitution was amended in 1791, the Bill of Rights was added as the first ten amendments, as you read in Chapter 8. These amendments became a written guarantee that the federal government would protect the rights of citizens.

Basic freedoms for people

The Bill of Rights gives people basic privileges and protections. These are needed so that all can be free. All citizens of this country have freedom of religion. There is not a national church chosen by the government. There is freedom of speech, assembly, and *petition*. This means one may criti-

The complete text of the Bill of Rights can be found in the Appendix on pages 575–76.

On the board, have students list the Bill of Rights in their own words.

cize government, meet with others for peaceful action and talk, and write requests to all officials. There is freedom of the press. This means that papers, radios, and television may criticize things officials do. All may feel free to write such criticism.

People also have the right to keep and bear arms. States may register and control guns, but the federal government cannot stop people from having them. Without the guarantee of these basic freedoms, any of these things might be against the law here as they are in many nations.

Protection from governments

In addition to giving the people their liberties, the Bill of Rights also places limitations upon government. People are free from having soldiers stationed in their homes during peace. It may be done in a legal way only during time of war. They are protected from unreasonable search and arrest. Property and people may be searched and a person arrested only with proper cause and with written warrants.

Protection against an unfair or unjust trial is a part of the Bill of Rights. Any person who is convicted of a violation of a law is protected against excessive fines and *cruel and unusual punishment.* The punishment may fit the crime, but a person cannot be given a heavy punishment for a minor violation.

Other rights protected

The last two amendments of the Bill of Rights provide an even stronger guarantee of liberty. They say that listing certain rights of the people does not mean that other rights shall be denied. A free people have rights other than those listed in the Constitution. All powers that are not given to the United States government are reserved for the states or for the people.

Check for Understanding: Now that you have completed this section, you should be able to answer these questions:

1. How does the Bill of Rights protect our liberties?
2. What basic freedoms are provided for in the Bill of Rights?
3. Do we have other rights that are not in the Constitution?
4. What limitation does the Bill of Rights place on government?

HOW ARE FAIR TRIALS GUARANTEED?

Objectives: After you have read this section, you will be able to:

- Tell how the Constitution protects the individual from unreasonable court action.
- Explain how our jury system ensures a defendant a fair trial.
- Understand why it is important for an accused person to have an attorney.

No distant place for trial

The Constitution protects the individual in that it forbids a trial to be held at a great distance from the scene of the crime. The reason for this was to enable the accused to contact witnesses easily and to remain at home and close to his or her family. Unless the accused person asks for a trial in another judicial district, the trial cannot be removed from the community where the crime was alleged to have been committed.

No treason trial for politics

The people in the United States are free from unreasonable prosecution for treason. In a dictator-ruled country the dictator can

On a bulletin board have students paraphrase (or explain) each of the first examples of rights provided by each amendment.

An engraving of the colonial period shows the harsh feelings of the Americans toward having British soldiers quartered in their homes. The third amendment to the Constitution was a reaction against this unpopular practice.

charge opponents with treason if they do not agree with him or her. At times dictators have ordered large numbers of people to be put to death without trial. Our Constitution prevents the bringing of a charge of treason merely for political purposes by this provision: "Treason against the United States shall consist only in levying War against them, or in adhering to their Enemies giving Aid and Comfort."

Citizens of the United States cannot be convicted of treason without positive proof. The Constitution provides that no person can be convicted of treason without at least two witnesses to the same treasonable act, or unless the person confesses in open court.

A trial by jury

The original Constitution did not guarantee a trial by jury to all persons accused of federal crimes. But people thought this freedom so important that it was added as an amendment to the Constitution. Today any person who is accused of a serious crime has a right to a trial by jury. If the accused wishes, this right may be waived, or given up. However, it cannot be taken away.

Have your students research recent cases of treason. Ask them how they feel about the penalties. Were they severe enough? Too severe?

The right to an attorney

The right of an accused person to have an attorney for defense was also provided as an amendment to the Constitution. It has been the practice in federal courts and most states to provide an attorney for an accused person if that person is unable to pay for one. In 1966 the courts themselves made it an even stronger right. The courts said that arresting officers must inform a person accused of a crime of the right to an attorney. The police must also tell an accused person that he or she may remain silent until an attorney is present. In this way a person accused of a crime has the right to have a defense lawyer.

Protection against self-incrimination

In many dictatorships people are often forced to plead guilty and confess their crimes in the courts so that they can be found guilty. This behavior is prevented in the United States by the Fifth Amendment, which protects a person from *self-incrimination*, or being proven guilty by testifying against oneself. An accused person is not even required to speak in court if he or she feels it could be harmful. In the United States a person is assumed to be innocent until proven guilty. It is the duty of the prosecuting attorney to show that the person accused is guilty of a crime.

The right to face witnesses

Still another of the amendments says that trials must be held in an open court, where the defendant can face the accusers. The court compels all witnesses to testify.

No double jeopardy

The person who is on trial for a crime is in *jeopardy*. To be put in jeopardy is to be in danger of losing one's liberty. The amended Constitution says that no person shall "for the same offense be twice put in jeopardy of life and limb." This statement means a person cannot be placed in *double jeopardy*, or tried twice for the same crime. If a person is found innocent of a crime, the government cannot have that person brought to trial again for the same crime. This fact holds true even if new evidence is discovered later to prove the person guilty.

Check for Understanding. Now that you have completed this section, you should be able to answer these questions:

1. How does the Constitution protect an individual from unreasonable court action?
2. How does the jury system ensure a fair trial for a defendant?
3. How does the right to an attorney protect an accused person?
4. What is meant by "self-incrimination" and "double jeopardy"?

HOW DO GOVERNMENTS PROVIDE INDEPENDENT COURTS?

Objectives: After you have read this section, you will be able to:

- Understand why it is important for judges to act independently.
- Explain the provisions in our Constitution that prevent undue influence of judges.
- Describe the process involved in the selection of federal and state judges.

The Constitution and the courts have acted together to guarantee fair trials. But it is up to the judges to see that everyone

Issues in Civics: Are the rights of an accused person more protected than those of the victim?

Guarantees of a Fair Trial

No Distant Trial

Right to an Attorney

Trial by Jury in an Open Court

No Self-Incrimination

No Conviction for Treason Without Proof

No Double Jeopardy

Have students ever attended or been involved in a trial? Do they think the process was fair?

receives a fair hearing. In order to do this, the judges must be free of influence so that they can act independently. The Constitution and the states ensure independent courts.

Removal for federal judges

The authors of the Constitution did not wish to give people the responsibility of selecting the federal judges. They felt that these judges should be appointed by the President. How, then, could they make the judges of the federal court independent of the President?

The writers of the Constitution determined to do this by having the judges appointed for life or for the time of their good behavior. The President makes the judicial appointments with the approval of the majority of the Senators. Once the judges have been appointed, they cannot be removed except by impeachment. A federal judge cannot be impeached for the decisions he or she makes, but the judge is subject to the laws of the land just as other citizens are.

Salaries of federal judges

Salaries of federal judges are fixed by a law passed by Congress and signed by the President. The salary cannot be decreased as long as the judge is in office, but it can be increased. In this way the federal judges are independent of the President and of Congress after they are appointed. Because of these provisions in our Constitution, no federal official can threaten to decrease a judge's salary or to remove one from office to influence one of the court's decisions.

State judges

Most state judges are elected by the people. Another plan is to have them chosen by the governor on the recommendation of state associations of lawyers. Those who support this second plan say that the people are not competent to know the legal ability of those who seek to be a judge. The governor, through consultation with lawyers, can better know who is qualified to preside over a court.

Check for Understanding. Now that you have completed this section, you should be able to answer these questions:

1. Why is it important for judges to act independently?
2. How do our Constitutional provisions prevent a federal official from influencing a judge?
3. How are federal and state judges chosen for office?
4. Why is it important for the salaries of federal judges to be fixed?

A federal judge studies the facts of a case in preparation for an upcoming trial.

Have a student research the following: 1. How many Supreme Court Justices are there? 2. Who are they? 3. By which President was each appointed?

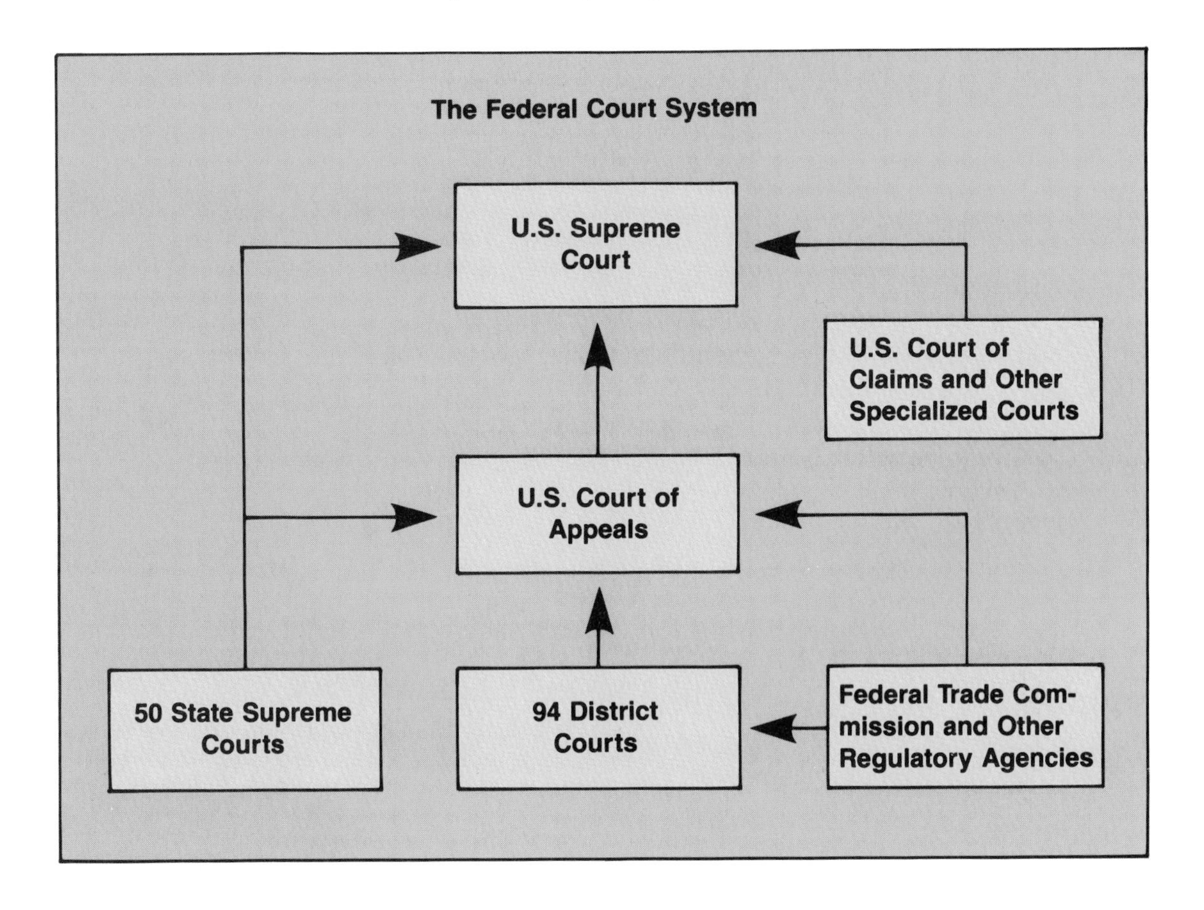

SUMMARY

The courts have worked together to provide the United States with a free and independent system of courts. A citizen may not be sent to a distant place for a trial nor be accused of treason for anything other than specifically named acts. All accused persons have a right to a trial by jury, to be represented by an attorney, to not testify against themselves, to face their witnesses, and to not be placed in double jeopardy.

The Bill of Rights is a group of amendments which guarantee freedoms for the people. Among these are freedom of religion, speech, assembly, petition, the press, and the right to bear arms. These laws also protect the people from unjust action by the government. People are protected from unreasonable search and arrest, unfair or unjust trials, and excessive fines or cruel punishment. In addition, people are given many rights other than those listed in the Bill of Rights.

The Constitution ensures that the judges will be an independent branch of government by having them appointed by the President, with the approval of the Senate, to serve for life. The salary of judges cannot be decreased and they can be removed from office only by impeachment. Most judges of state courts are elected by the people.

Issues in Civics: How are the judges in your state selected? Do students feel they should be appointed by the Governor or elected by the people?

BUILDING SKILLS IN CIVICS

THINKING SKILLS

1. How did the jury system develop?
2. How is a fair trial guaranteed?
3. Read and edit the paragraph below. Then write a title.

   The Constitution and the courts have acted together to guarantee fair trials. It is up to the judges to see that everyone receives a fair hearing. The Supreme Court Building is in Washington, D.C., and is a most impressive sight. In order to do this, the judges must be free of influence so they can act independently.

VOCABULARY SKILLS

Some of the underlined words in the sentences below are used correctly, others are not. If the sentence is correct, write True. If it is not, replace the word with the best choice from the list.

justice	self-incrimination	petition	trial by ordeal
jury system	jeopardy	cruel and unusual punishment	

1. In a jury system, the judge is in charge at the trial, but does not decide the case.
2. The job of the courts is to do justice, by providing a fair hearing before the law.
3. In many dictatorships people are forced to give evidence against themselves; this is prevented in the United States by the fifth amendment, which protects a person from jeopardy.
4. A person cannot be tried twice for the same crime. This would be double petition.
5. A petition is a written request to a public official.
6. A jury system is a barbaric method of determining guilt or innocence.
7. Cruel and unusual punishment is punishment that is too strong for the crime it is given for.

STUDY SKILLS—WATCHING TELEVISION NEWS SHOWS

Television can teach, inform, and entertain you. An excellent way to learn about current events is by watching TV news programs. These programs include news reports, editorials, feature stories, sports, reviews, helpful hints, consumer and business information, and advertisements. A news story is about an event that is important today. These stories always answer six basic questions that journalists call the "5 W's and 1 H." 1. Who is the story about? 2. What happened? 3. Where did it happen? 4. When did it happen? 5. Why did it happen? 6. How did it happen?

Activity: Fill in a copy of the chart below as you watch at least three different news reports.

Questions	Story #1	#2	#3
Did the reporter tell: 1. Who?			
2. What?			
3. Where?			
4. When?			
5. Why?			
6. How?			

BEYOND THE BOOK

1. Find out how people are selected for jury duty in your community. Interview someone who has recently served on a jury to learn more about the jury system.
2. As you watch the news on television or read it in a newspaper, make a list of events that show how the freedoms of the people are protected.
3. Use the "5 W's and 1 H" question system to analyze news stories in the newspaper.
4. Create a bulletin board that shows pictures of the freedoms protected by the Bill of Rights.

CHAPTER TWENTY-TWO TEST

VOCABULARY CHECK

Fill in each blank with the word from the list that best completes the sentence.

justice	jury system	self-incrimination	trial by ordeal
jeopardy	petition	cruel and unusual punishment	

1. In order to insure a fair trial, the English people began a ______.
2. The Fifth Amendment protects a person from ______.
3. To be put in ______ is to be placed in danger of losing one's liberties.
4. To guarantee ______ we have accepted the idea that a person is innocent until proven guilty.
5. A ______ is a written request to a public official.
6. A ______ is a harsh and unfair means to prove guilt or innocence.
7. ______ means that the punishment doesn't fit the crime because it is too severe.

COMPREHENSION CHECK

Write True if the question and answer go together. If they do not, write an answer that fits the question.

1. Historically, how did a fair trial system develop? —People turned from unfair methods of determining guilt or innocence like a "trial by combat" to the use of courts with a judge, and then with a jury.
2. Why did the founders of our nation form a state and federal court system? —In forming the state and federal courts, the founders sought to guarantee a fair and impartial trial in a court.
3. What are four basic freedoms provided for in the Bill of Rights? —The Bill of Rights gives people basic privileges and protections. These are needed so all can be free.
4. Did the original Constitution guarantee a trial by jury? —The original Constitution did not guarantee a trial by jury to all

persons accused of federal crimes, but the people thought this freedom was so important that it was added as an amendment.

5. How does the right to an attorney protect an accused person? —Today any person who is accused of a serious crime has a right to a trial by jury. This right cannot be taken away from a person.

SKILL BUILDERS—INTERPRETING A COLLAGE

Close your book and look carefully at the cover. This cover is a photograph of a three-dimensional collage by the American artist Fred Otnes, entitled *We the People*. A *collage* is a work of art consisting of a collection of different kinds of items. This collage was made by putting photographs and other items together into a new work.

Activity: Examine the cover carefully and then answer these questions.

1. What different kinds of objects did the artist use?
2. How do they fit together?
3. Why is the title *We the People* appropriate for the illustration?
4. What other title might also be appropriate?
5. Who are the people who appear on the cover? How many of them can you recognize?

BUILDING WRITING SKILLS

1. Describe how you would design a collage called "Trials: Past and Present."
2. Why is it important in our system of justice that a person be considered "innocent until proven guilty"?
3. Write an outline for a paper called "The Rights of an Accused Person." Use the following headings:
   a. Right to an Attorney
   b. Protection Against Self-Incrimination
   c. Right to Face Witnesses
   d. Jeopardy

Document: The Constitution of the United States

Article III, Section 2. The judicial Power shall extend to all Cases, in Law and Equity, arising under this Constitution, the Laws of the United States, and Treaties made, or which shall be made, under their Authority;—to all Cases affecting Ambassadors, other public Ministers and Consuls;—to all Cases of Admiralty and maritime Jurisdiction;—to Controversies to which the United States shall be a Party;—to Controversies between two or more States; (—between a State and Citizens of another State;)—between Citizens of different States, —between Citizens of the same State claiming Lands under Grants of different States, and between a State, or the Citizens thereof, and foreign States, (Citizens or Subjects).

Amendment VI. In all criminal prosecutions, the accused shall enjoy the right to a speedy and public trial, by an impartial jury of the State and district wherein the crime shall have been committed, which district shall have been previously ascertained by law, and to be informed of the nature and cause of the accusation; to be confronted with the witnesses against him; to have compulsory process for obtaining witnesses in his favor, and to have the Assistance of Counsel for his defence.

This scene shows the Supreme Court in session. Discuss with your students the power of the court to comment on the spirit of the laws as well as their content.

The court system in the United States is comprised of two systems—one run by the states, and the other by the federal government. The Constitution provided for a federal court system in order to interpret its laws, to settle disputes that go beyond the limits of any one state and also to settle disputes among the states.

The state courts in our country started as courts of the original colonies, and then became state courts when the colonies became states. They handle the bulk of the civil and criminal cases in the United States.

FOCUSING IDEAS

- The two kinds of cases that appear in court are criminal cases and civil cases.
- The duties of the United States courts include trying cases, handling appeals, determining the constitutionality of laws, and interpreting the law.
- The three levels of state courts are the justice-of-the-peace courts, district or circuit courts, and appellate or state supreme courts.
- Two problems that face our courts are overworked dockets, and attempts to limit the court's power to decide certain cases.

This is a local judge wearing the traditional black robes. How have pictures such as this contributed to the attitudes of citizens toward our court system?

PRE-TEST

1. What are some of the different kinds of cases that appear in U.S. courts?
2. What are the duties and responsibilities of the U.S. courts?
3. What are the levels and functions of the state courts?
4. What duties do the city courts perform in the U.S.?
5. What are some of the problems that face modern U.S. courts?

WHAT KINDS OF CASES APPEAR IN COURT?

Objectives: After reading this section, you will be able to:

- Distinguish between the two kinds of cases that are tried in our courts.
- Understand why different offenses are tried in different courts.
- See why plea bargaining is so prevalent in state courts.

When a person violates a law, he or she may end up in court. But which court will it be? The answer depends on whether a federal, state, or local law was violated. Just as we have many governments with separate laws, so we have separate court systems. We have one system of federal courts. We have fifty systems of state courts, and many more city courts. Each of these systems may be a little different from the others. However, they all seek to give fair hearings in order to protect our rights.

Criminal cases

Two kinds of cases are tried in our courts—criminal cases and civil cases. A *criminal case* is a case brought by the government to determine guilt and punishment of a person accused of a crime. Robbery, murder, and kidnapping are examples of such crimes. When a person is called to trial for this type of crime, it is called a criminal trial.

Civil cases

A *civil case* is a suit between people, brought to court by an individual involving rights and privileges. These cases usually involve disputes over property or agreements. Some property cases involve a question of who is the real owner of something, as for example when two people claim ownership of the same piece of land. A civil case may also arise when two people involved in a payment cannot agree that the payment was correct. The question of whether or not the payment is due to the other person may then come before a court.

Lawsuits in state courts

Most of our lawsuits are tried in state courts, because most of our legal dealings with each other come under state law. However, a person can be tried in a federal, state,

---

Building Vocabulary:
criminal/civil case *(380)* • plea bargaining *(381)* • appeal *(383)* • unconstitutional *(383)* • judicial review *(383)* • misdemeanor *(385)* • felony *(385)* • circuit court *(386)*.

If possible, find examples of criminal cases in the newspaper. Decorate a bulletin board with the articles. Try to show the various steps of a trial, selection of a jury, arguments, and decisions.

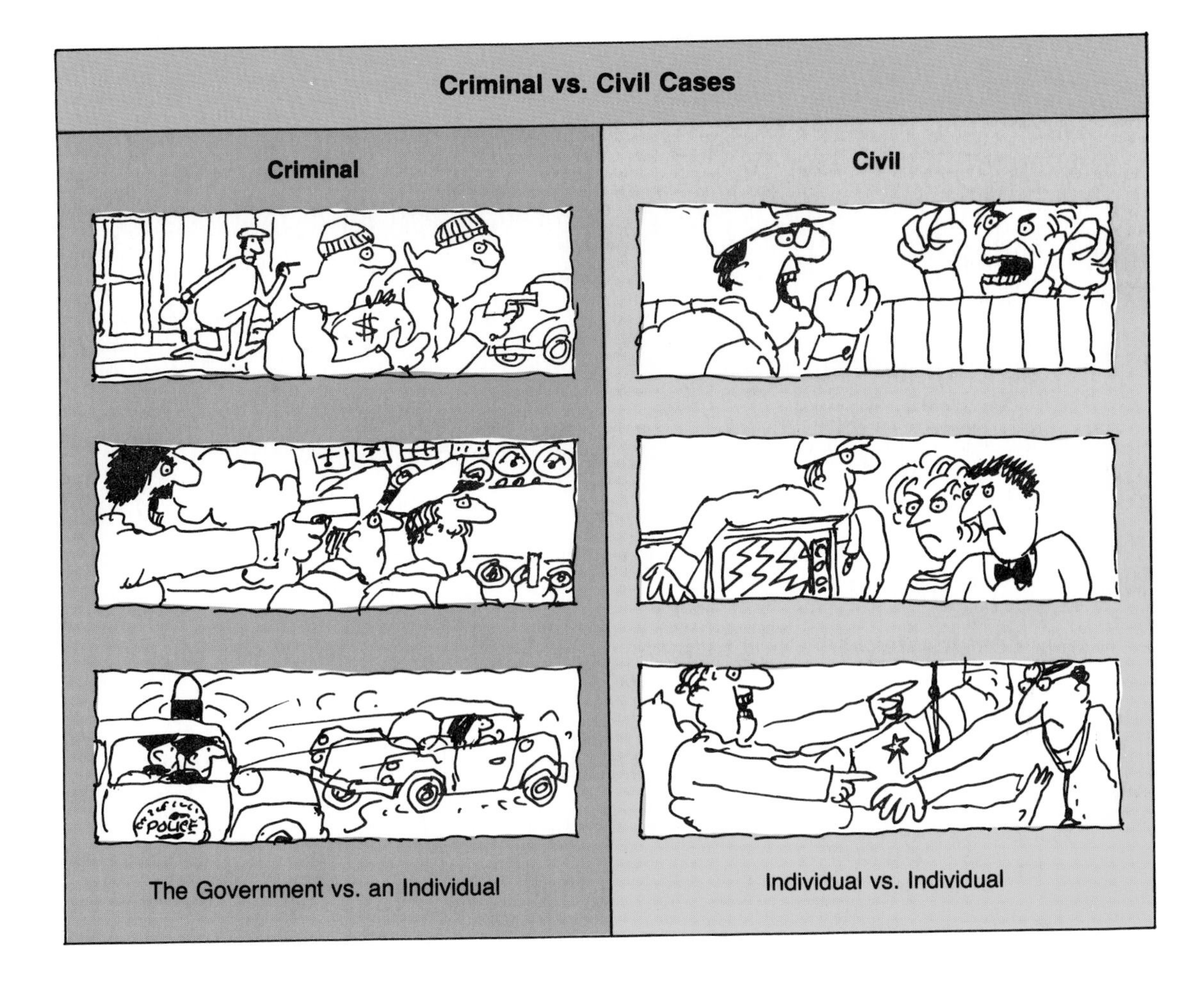

county, or city court for different offenses, though these offenses may seem to be parts of a single crime. Let us suppose a person steals a car in Georgia and drives to Alabama. While in Birmingham, Alabama, he drives through an intersection on a red light. He has violated three laws and can be tried three times, once for each separate offense. He can be tried in Birmingham city police court for driving through the red light. He can be tried for theft in the county in Georgia where he stole the automobile, and he can be tried in federal court for transporting a stolen car from one state to another.

Plea bargaining

In state courts, most criminal cases (in fact 90 percent)—are settled by *plea bargaining.* In plea bargaining, the prosecutor, the defense lawyer, and the police work out an agreement. In many courts, the judge is also a part of the process. Usually, the judge, in return for a guilty plea to a lesser charge, will reduce the sentence of the defendant. In this manner, courts are able to clear their dockets of dozens of cases. Although this practice might seem unfair because the judge and jury do not decide the case, the Supreme Court has ruled that plea bargaining is constitutional.

Issues in Civics: Is plea bargaining unfair? Does it allow lawyers to be lazy, and permit the guilty to get off with a "slap on the wrist"?

The district attorney and the defense lawyer meet with the judge to work out a plea bargaining agreement.

Check for Understanding: Now that you have completed this section, you should be able to answer these questions:

1. What is the principal difference between a civil and a criminal case?
2. Why are different offenses tried in different courts?
3. Why is plea bargaining so prevalent in state courts?
4. Why might plea bargaining seem unfair to some people?

WHAT ARE THE DUTIES OF THE UNITED STATES COURTS?

Objectives: After reading this section, you will be able to:

- Tell what three courts comprise the federal court system.
- Understand why the Supreme Court plays such an important role in the federal court system.
- Explain how judicial review differs from interpretation of a law by the Supreme Court.

Trying cases

The first trial before a federal court will most likely be conducted in a federal district court. This is the lowest trial court in the federal system. There is at least one district court in each state, and most states have two or more. District courts handle criminal cases when a person is accused of a crime that violates the laws of the United States. Civil cases, arising from disputes, will also be handled if a federal law is involved. Such cases may involve copyrights, patents, trademarks, or any of the other protections provided by federal laws. If two citizens who live in different states are involved in a dispute, the trial will be held in the federal courts rather than either state court of the states in which they live.

Handling appeals

Federal courts handle many appeals. An *appeal* is a request to have a case heard again before a higher court. If a person is convicted of a crime in one court and believes the court made a wrong decision, that person has the right to ask for a new trial in another court. The prosecuter, however, does not have the right of appeal under any circumstances. As you learned in Chapter 22, a person who is found innocent can never be tried again for that crime. A citizen may appeal from a federal district court to a United States federal court of appeals. Such a court is called an appellate court, which means it only reviews cases and is not a trial court. These are sometimes called circuit courts, and there are eleven of them, including one in the District of Columbia.

As a last resort the citizen may appeal to the Supreme Court of the United States. Nearly all cases before the Supreme Court are brought there on appeal from the lower federal courts. An appeal may come from a state supreme court when the case involves a federal law or the Constitution. The Constitution is the highest law of the land. The Supreme Court, as the highest of interpreters of the Constitution, plays an important role in the federal court system. The United States Supreme Court is composed of one Chief Justice and eight Associate Justices. The number of justices is determined by law and cannot be changed.

Determining constitutionality

The United States courts have one power that was first given to courts in this country. This is the power to decide whether a law agrees with the Constitution. If it does not agree, it can be declared *unconstitutional.* This power is called *judicial review*. Judicial review is not granted to the courts by the Constitution, but developed from an important decision made by Chief Justice John Marshall in 1803. In the case of *Marbury* vs. *Madison*, the Supreme Court ruled that an act of Congress could not be enforced if it violated the Constitutional rights of an individual. If the Supreme Court rules that an act of Congress is unconstitutional, then it is declared null and void and can no longer be enforced.

Chief Justice Marshall's ruling in *Marbury vs. Madison* established judicial review.

Deciding what the law means

The Supreme Court performs another valuable service. Some laws are very difficult to understand, and disputes may often arise over their meaning. Sometimes an officer of the government may think that the Constitution or other laws give the authority to take certain action. Other people may

Have an interested student report on Franklin D. Roosevelt's attempt to change the make-up of the Supreme Court.

question the right to do so. When such cases are brought before the Supreme Court, the court interprets the law. For example, in 1974 President Nixon took the position that the Constitution authorized him to withhold certain documents from a Senate committee. The Supreme Court ruled that he did not have this authority. Interpretation of the law is not the same thing as judicial review, for it does not mean that the Supreme Court rules on whether a law is unconstitutional. The Court merely says that an official may or may not engage in certain activities, or that a law should be interpreted in a certain way.

Check for Understanding: Now that you have completed this section, you should be able to answer these questions:

1. What three courts comprise the federal court system?
2. Why does the Supreme Court play such an important role in this system?
3. How is judicial review different from mere interpretation of a law?
4. What did the Supreme Court rule in the case of *Marbury vs. Madison*?

James St. Clair, the attorney who represented President Nixon before the Supreme Court.

WHAT ARE THE LEVELS OF STATE COURTS?

Objectives: After reading this section, you will be able to:

- Describe the three different levels of state courts.
- Distinguish between misdemeanors and felonies.
- Understand why district court judges must be well trained in many aspects of the law.

While court systems may be different in different states, most states have three levels of courts. The lowest level are called justice-of-the-peace courts and deal with smaller crimes or civil cases. District or circuit courts handle more important cases, and the appellate or state supreme courts are primarily concerned with appeals.

Justice-of-the-peace courts

The judge who presides over the lowest state court usually is called a justice of the peace or city judge. This title varies in different communities. The duties of the justice-of-the-peace courts and the district courts are carefully divided. Cases of lesser

Have a student list three crimes that would be heard by justice-of-the-peace courts: 1. Traffic violations 2. Minor civil cases 3. Minor crimes.

What are small claims courts? How do they work and why are they important? 1. If the claim is over $20.00 and under $750.00, you are entitled to a court hearing. 2. They ease the load for the courts.

importance are tried before the justice of the peace. Civil cases are brought before the justice of the peace when the amount in controversy is small. A justice of the peace may also perform marriages and carry out other duties.

Criminal cases are also divided between the courts. The justice-of-the-peace courts and city judges try only *misdemeanors* while the district or circuit courts try persons charged with *felonies*. Misdemeanors are minor crimes such as disturbing the peace, speeding on the highway, or trespassing on another's property, usually punishable by a fine or imprisonment for a maximum of one year. Felonies are more serious crimes such as murder, kidnapping, or robbery, usually punishable by imprisonment for a longer period of time.

The qualifications for a justice of the peace do not necessarily include a wide knowledge of law. If a legal error is made in a justice-of-the-peace court, it can be corrected through an appeal to a higher state court. Many cases can be settled in these courts. This lowers the case load on higher courts and allows faster action.

Hollywood movies often feature a starry-eyed couple being married by a justice of the peace, a typical duty of such officials.

The number of cases brought before a justice of the peace in a rural township is small. He or she may not need to hold court oftener than two or three days a month or for more than two or three hours a day. In some of the areas the person does not receive a fixed salary but is paid only for the

Try to find out how many cases were heard in the district court of your county last year. Discuss with students whether they feel this is too heavy a load.

As the sign proclaims ("Law West of the Pecos"), Judge Roy Bean was the only judicial officer in this area of Texas in the 1880's.

time served. Part of the costs are paid by the people found guilty.

Usually a justice of the peace does not summon a jury to try cases. But when a prisoner demands a trial by jury or when the parties to a civil suit want a jury, one is called. In most of the states that employ this practice, such a jury consists of six persons.

District or circuit court

The next court level is the *district court.* This court is usually held at the county seat. The presiding officer is called the district judge. Many counties with small populations may be combined into a single district with one judge. The district judge holds court in one county for a few weeks or months, then in the next county, and so on until court has been held in all the counties in the district. Since the judge travels in a kind of circle, or circuit, the name *circuit court* is applied to the district court in many of the states.

The district court is the chief trial court of cases that concern state laws. The presiding judge must be well trained in law to preside over such an important court. Every person brought to trial before a district judge has the right of trial by jury. The judge must be able to instruct the jurors regarding the points of law involved in the trial.

In some states one type of district court judge tries criminal suits and another judge tries civil suits. But in most states the same judge tries both kinds of suits. Among the civil suits that may be tried in a district court are disputes over the ownership of property, contracts, and claims for damage due to injuries. Any controversy that involves a large sum of money is tried in a district court.

All felonies and some misdemeanors are tried in a district court. Appeals from the police courts and the justice-of-the-peace courts also are tried by a jury with the guidance of the judge. In each state the district courts handle most of the criminal cases which are brought to trial in that state.

Special courts

Questions of the inheritance of property, divorce, rights of children, and other matters that concern the family are tried in special courts in some states. These special courts may be called probate courts, family courts, or juvenile courts.

State supreme court

Above all other state courts is the state supreme court. It is the highest court in the state. The state supreme court is not a trial court, except for special cases. It is created as a court of appeal to correct any error that may have occurred in a lower court.

Cases may be appealed to a higher court after a decision has been made in a lower court. The higher court reviews the case and either upholds or refuses to uphold the decision of the lower court. It may order the lower court to hold a new trial.

Most of the cases brought before the state supreme court have been appealed to it from the county or circuit courts. In some states appeals courts relieve the burden on the supreme court by hearing most of the appeals from lower courts. Appeals that have been turned down by the appeals court may be carried to the state supreme court. Finally, appeals may be made from these courts to the U.S. Supreme Court.

Police court

Police courts are created for the cities. The presiding official of the police court is either the police judge or city judge magistrate.

Have a committee of three give a short report on the workings of your state supreme court.

Police courts handle matters such as this traffic violation, which resulted in an accident.

This person is a local officer. The police court may be called municipal court or magistrate's court.

The police judge tries persons charged with the violation of city ordinances. Among the violations that are most commonly brought to trial in police courts are such offenses as violations of traffic ordinances, disturbing the peace, disorderly conduct, or operating a business without a license.

Check for Understanding: Now that you have completed this section, you should be able to answer these questions:

1. What are the three different levels of state courts?
2. What is the difference between a misdemeanor and a felony?
3. Why must a district court judge be well trained in different aspects of the law?
4. What are the duties of a state supreme court? Of a police court?

WHAT PROBLEMS FACE OUR COURTS?

Objectives: After reading this section, you will be able to:

- See why so many of our courts are overworked.
- Understand that there is no easy solution to the problems that face our courts.
- Tell why some people would like to alter the power of the courts.

An overworked system

One problem that faces all the courts of the United States is that of being overworked.

Have members of the class attend a session of your local court and report on it to the class.

As more crimes are committed and more people have differences, more trials come to courts. Many of these trials take a long time to settle. The result is that there are more cases appearing before the courts than they can handle.

Chief Justice Warren Burger of the Supreme Court has frequently called attention to this problem of overworked courts. He believes that cases such as those of child adoptions, child custody, divorce, title research, and automobile accidents could be handled by government agencies rather than by the courts.

There have been many possible solutions presented for this problem. Some would merely create more courts and more judges, including special courts to handle certain types of cases. Other suggestions do even more. They include reducing the size of the jury, since a smaller jury might mean less time to select the jury members and to decide the case.

Another problem facing the courts is people's desire from time to time to change the courts' power to decide certain cases, including the right to appeal. Throughout American history, public opinion has been felt within the court system. For example, in 1867 an act of Congress prohibited the Supreme Court from hearing cases on habeas corpus arising from the Civil War. The

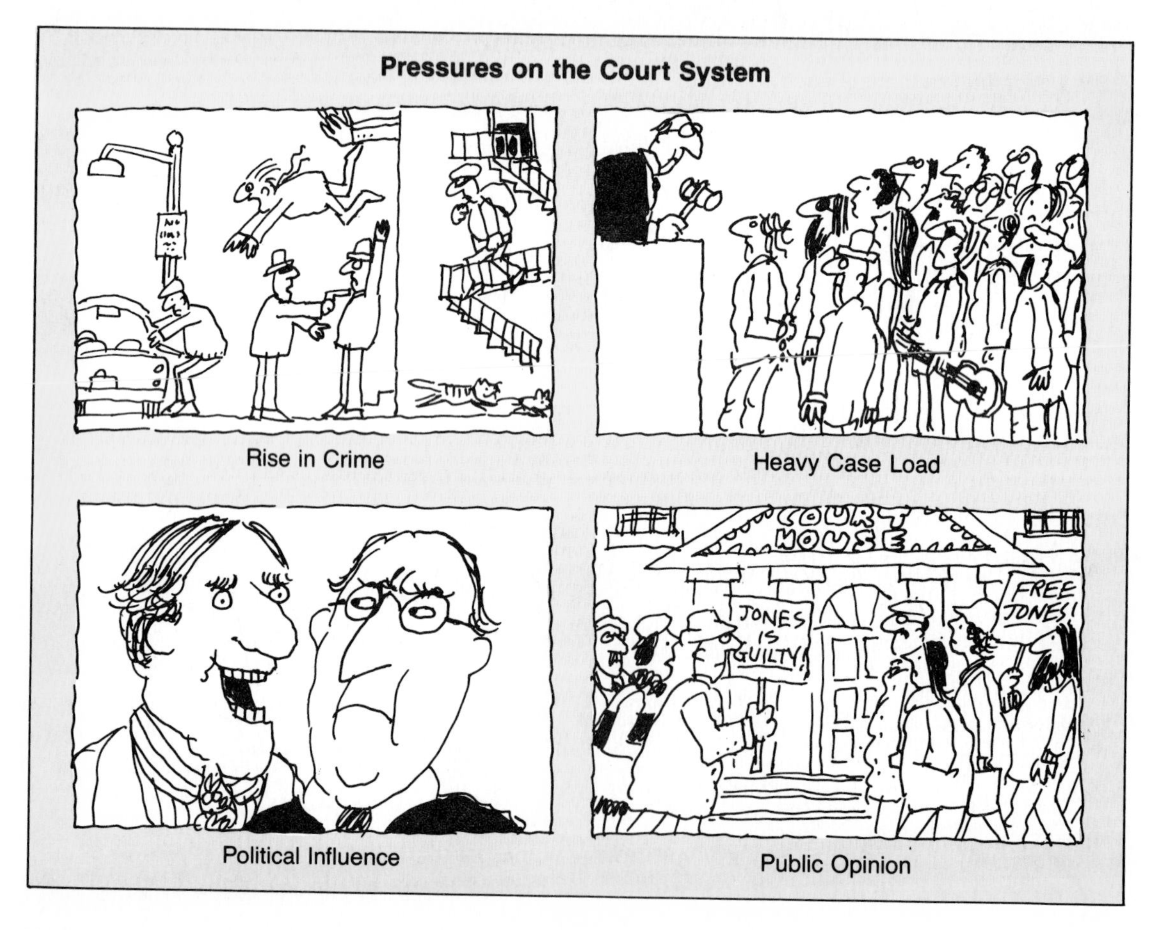

Have a student report on the working day of the judges. Do they work five days a week? Are the courts crowded because of work schedules? Are there enough judges to handle the load?

Supreme Court agreed that Congress had such power. However, three years later, in 1870, the Supreme Court did not hesitate to strike down a law of Congress that forbade them to hear property cases from those who had been pardoned during the Civil War. Today, there are many persons who did not like the Supreme Court's ruling on such issues as abortion, busing, and school prayer. One proposed solution to the problem would be to limit the Supreme Court's right to hear these kinds of cases.

It is almost a national custom to blame the courts for all the ills of society. However, the courts cannot do everything to please everybody. Whenever the courts do something unpopular, often citizens forget that the courts are doing what they were designed to do: safeguarding the fundamental rights of the individual against the attitudes of the majority.

Check for Understanding: Now that you have read this section, you should be able to answer these questions:

1. Why are the courts in our country so overworked?
2. Why isn't there one easy solution to the problems that face our courts?
3. Why do some people want to alter the power of the courts?
4. What kind of cases might be handled by agencies rather than courts?

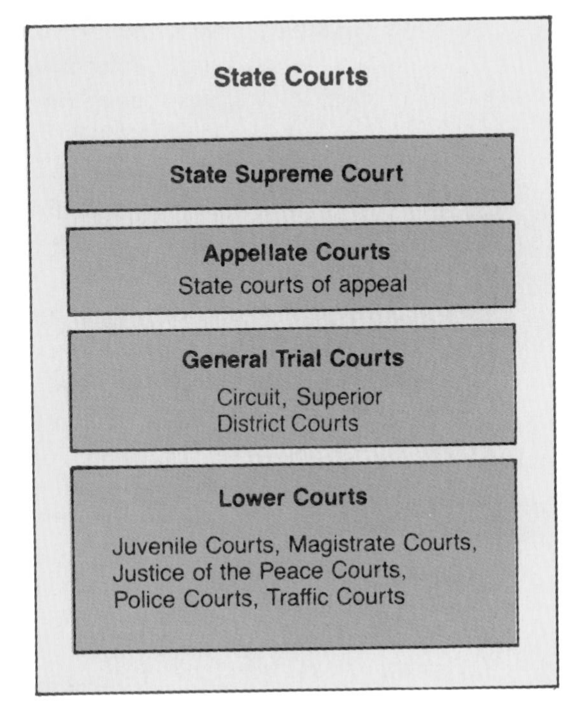

SUMMARY

Cases may be tried in federal, state, or city courts depending on the laws that are involved. The cases may be either criminal cases or civil cases. Most federal cases are first tried in a district court. Appeals are handled by the federal court of appeals. The U.S. Supreme Court is the highest interpreter of the laws and the Constitutionality of laws.

There are usually three levels of state courts. Justice-of-the-peace courts handle most misdemeanors and small civil cases. The district or circuit courts try criminal and civil cases before a jury. The appellate or supreme court deals with most state appeals.

Police or municipal courts handle cases that involve violations of city ordinances, such as traffic offenses.

Two problems facing the nation's courts are too large a load of cases that have to be dealt with, and attempts to limit the court's authority in certain cases, including the right of appeal.

Issues in Civics: Has the Supreme Court overstepped its boundaries in recent years? Have any of its decisions been attempts to set policy rather than interpret the law? Is an "activist Court" a good thing?

BUILDING SKILLS IN CIVICS

THINKING SKILLS

1. Give examples of three problems that might be considered in a civil case. What about a criminal case?
2. How is it determined if a federal, state, or city court will hear a case?
3. Edit the following paragraph and create a title that tells the main idea.

    As more crimes are committed and more people have conflicts, more trials come to court. Many of these trials take a long time to settle. Interpretation of the law is not the same thing as judicial review. Two problems facing the nation's courts are overworked dockets, and attempts to limit the court's authority in certain cases.

VOCABULARY SKILLS

Match the term with its definition. If you need help, use the Glossary.

a. criminal case
b. circuit court
c. unconstitutional
d. misdemeanor
e. appeal
f. felony
g. plea bargaining
h. judicial review

1. A major crime such as murder, punishable by imprisonment for a long time.
2. A court presided over by a federal district judge.
3. Court action brought by the government to determine the guilt and possible punishment of a person accused of a crime.
4. A minor crime such as trespassing, punishable by a fine or short imprisonment.
5. A request on the part of the losing party in a trial to have the case heard before a higher court.
6. Contrary to the Constitution.
7. Settled by the prosecutor, the defense lawyer, and the police working out an agreement.
8. The power of the courts to declare a law unconstitutional.

STUDY SKILLS—LEARNING FROM NEWS BROADCASTS

The news story is only one part of the regular *news broadcast.* Do you remember the definition of a news story? What six questions will it answer? Does it include the reporter's opinion? There are many kinds of reports and stories on a newscast. Which of the following have you seen on the evening television newscast?

1. THE NEWS STORY
2. THE FEATURE STORY: A report that is interesting today and will probably be of interest in the future, too. It is intended to inform, instruct, and entertain. For example, it might be about how people are working together to solve a problem, different ways people use resources, a new invention, etc.
3. SPORTS: Information on teams, scores, and interviews are included during the sports segment of the newscast.
4. WEATHER: This part of the newscast informs the public about current and predicted weather on the local and national scene.
5. EDITORIALS: These stories express the opinions of identified groups, the TV station, or individuals, about an event, person, or issue.
6. REVIEWS: These reports provide a reviewer's opinion about a movie, play, special attraction, book or restaurant.
7. BUSINESS AND CONSUMER REPORTS: These provide factual information about the stock market and current business trends, as well as advice and warnings for the consumer.

Activity: Prepare a checklist of the different kinds of stories and reports. Watch the evening news and tally both the kind and how many of each were included in the newscast. Which included opinions? Whose opinions?

BEYOND THE BOOK

1. As you watch the news, compile a list of the different kinds of cases and the different courts that are mentioned.
2. Interview people who are involved in some kind of trial work. What skills are needed for the job? Does the job seem interesting to you? Why?/Why not?

CHAPTER TWENTY-THREE TEST

VOCABULARY CHECK

Some words in the sentences below are misused. Write "True" if the underlined word is correctly used. If not, select a word from the list to replace it.

plea bargaining	appeal	criminal case	judicial review
unconstitutional	misdemeanor	circuit court	felony

1. If a person convicted of a crime in one court believes the court made a wrong decision, that person has the right of misdemeanor.
2. A criminal case is a case brought by the government to determine guilt and punishment of a person accused of a crime.
3. The Supreme Court has ruled that plea bargaining is constitutional.
4. There is at least one circuit court in each county.
5. If a law does not agree with the Constitution it can be declared unconstitutional.
6. Felonies are minor crimes usually punishable by a fine or short imprisonment.
7. Criminal cases are more serious crimes such as robbery, murder, or kidnapping.
8. The power of the courts to declare a law unconstitutional is called plea bargaining.

COMPREHENSION CHECK

1. Which of these are problems that face modern U.S. courts?
   a. increasing number of crimes committed
   b. overworked dockets
   c. desire to change the court's power to decide certain cases
2. Since the judge can travel from place to place in a kind of circle, the name ______ is applied to this district court.
   a. Circuit Court
   b. Court of Appeals

SKILL BUILDERS—INTERPRETING PHOTOGRAPHS AND PAINTINGS

In this book you have been using different kinds of artwork to gain information. *Photographs* are used to show you the actual place and event. Photographs can show action as it is happening or can be "set up" or posed, to show particular content. Skim the book and find examples of both action and set-up photos. How does each type of photo help you gain information?

Photographers and artists select details they want to include or exclude in their visual statement. They can use lighting, angle, color, and focus to affect the way you perceive something. *Paintings* or drawings can tell us about a particular subject, and can also tell us something about the artist. The artist will paint or draw something the way *he or she* sees it. This perception is strongly influenced by the experiences, viewpoints, and purpose of the individual doing the artwork.

Activity: Go through the book and analyze several different drawings by different artists—for example, those on pages 361, 362, and 370. Can you tell how a particular artist felt about a subject by the way the picture is drawn? Give examples to support your opinions. Then do the same with several photos.

BUILDING WRITING SKILLS

1. Write an editorial about one of the following topics:
   a. Overworked Courts
   b. Size of Juries
   c. Plea Bargaining
   In your first sentence, state your viewpoint and the problem. Include at least four sentences that state facts and one sentence that is based on opinion.
2. Select one kind of court and write a paragraph describing its responsibilities.
3. Compile a list of factual sentences to support this generalization: "All courts seek to give fair hearings in order to protect our rights."

Chapter Twenty-Four · The Process of Justice

Document: The Constitution of the United States

Amendment V. No person shall be held to answer for a capital, or otherwise infamous crime, unless on a presentment or indictment of a Grand Jury, except in cases arising in the land or naval forces, or in the Militia, when in actual service in time of War or public danger; nor shall any person be subject for the same offence to be twice put in jeopardy of life or limb; nor shall be compelled in any criminal case to be a witness against himself, nor be deprived of life, liberty, or property, without due process of law; nor shall private property be taken for public use, without just compensation.

Amendment VII. In Suits at common law, where the value in controversy shall exceed twenty dollars, the right of trial by jury shall be preserved, and no fact tried by a jury, shall be otherwise re-examined in any Court of the United States, than according to the rules of the common law.

Amendment VIII. Excessive bail shall not be required, nor excessive fines imposed, nor cruel and unusual punishments inflicted.

To do justice, a government must enforce laws that treat each individual fairly and morally. In the United States, government bodies such

The illustration shows a man being arrested by plain-clothes policemen. What do students think will happen to the man in the next step of the judicial process?

as courts and police departments see that the laws are obeyed. The law establishes certain rules that define a citizen's rights and duties, and if those rules are violated, penalties must be set to protect the rights of the innocent. As you can see by the content of the Amendments above, the process by which the aims of justice are served starts at the moment an individual is accused of an offense, and does not let up until guilt or innocence is decided by a jury of one's peers.

FOCUSING IDEAS

- Modern law enforcement departments protect us by sending officers to check out complaints, and by compiling the evidence needed to solve crimes.
- A modern law enforcement department uses the latest electronic equipment to obtain information and check out law violators.
- When a juvenile goes to court, the evidence against him or her is heard by a judge, a judgment of delinquency is decided, and a determination on the method of correction is made.
- When a lawyer prepares a defense for a client, he or she must obtain the facts of the case, interview witnesses, look into the chain of custody, and defend the client to the best of his or her ability.

This court scene illustrates several rights guaranteed in the Constitution and its amendments. Discuss these rights with your students.

PRE-TEST

1. How does a modern law enforcement department protect our rights?
2. What role does a juvenile officer play in our system of justice?
3. How does a modern law enforcement department operate?
4. What happens to a juvenile in court?
5. What process must a lawyer go through in order to prepare a good defense for a client?

HOW DOES A MODERN LAW ENFORCEMENT DEPARTMENT PROTECT US?

Objectives: After reading this section, you will be able to:

- See why the gathering of evidence is so important in solving a crime.
- Understand the role of the grand jury in the indictment process.
- Understand why judges post bail during arraignment.

An understanding of justice requires a knowledge of the steps involved in the protection of the rights of an individual. In the following story you will observe some of these steps.

You'll remember the fictional characters Mary Gentry and Sam Elliott from the story about them in Chapter 11, Kermit Ross' election campaign. In this chapter, their teacher has assigned them to give a report on the process of justice for the annual Citizenship Day in their school. The information in this chapter is based on actual fact, although the names and places are

Mary Gentry met with Chief of Police Anderson to begin her tour of the law enforcement offices.

Building vocabulary:
grand/petit jury *(398)* • indictment *(398)* • arraignment *(398)* • bail *(398)* • juvenile *(399)* • burden of proof *(403)* • probation *(403)* • defendant/plaintiff *(404)*

---

ficitious. The chief of police in their town has arranged for them to observe the work of the law enforcement department.

The briefing room and the daily blotter

Sam and Mary arrived at the Clinton Law Enforcement Department at 8:00 A.M.; just in time to join Lt. Johnson and Sgt. Thomas in the briefing room. "Here law enforcement officers learn, or 'are briefed' on what happened since they were last on duty," explained Lt. Johnson. "Because the law enforcement department functions twenty-four hours a day, including holidays, people work in three eight-hour periods called 'shifts'. The shifts are from 8 A.M. to 4 P.M., from 4 P.M. to 12 midnight, and from midnight to 8 A.M. Each shift has a lieutenant and a sergeant who are in charge."

"Telephone calls are received in the communications room and recorded on the daily blotter." Sam, Mary, and Lt. Johnson looked at the blotter for the previous shift. When Lt. Johnson finished briefing the officers, he suggested that Sam and Mary talk to Detective Sergeant Martin about a midnight burglary charge that appeared on the blotter.

How evidence is obtained

Sam asked Sgt. Martin about the importance of evidence. "Let me give you an example of how important evidence is in solving a crime," Sgt. Martin replied. "Let's say there's a man who burglarizes grocery stores. He might have the habit of drinking some milk out of a carton which he leaves. This bit of information might be completely overlooked by the detectives when they look over the scene of his first two or three burglaries. But when his habit of drinking milk and leaving the carton is noticed, it becomes valuable evidence for them."

Mary and Sam looked at the file of suspects prepared by Sgt. Thomas.

The process of indictment

"What happens when you identify a suspect?" inquired Mary. "What are the steps that you take next?"

"Suppose I have suspects at large, such as the two men who burglarized the Metro Plaza," Sgt. Martin answered. "I've arrived at the conclusion that John Doe and Al Long have committed this act. I type up my case report setting out my facts and stating why these two men should be arrested. I present this to a justice of the peace. He reads my report, and if he feels that I have

Contact a law enforcement officer and ask him about gathering evidence. Report to the class on how it is done and the restrictions in gathering it.

Detective Sgt. Martin showed the students some information from a case he was working on.

established what we call 'probable cause,' he'll issue a warrant for the arrest of these men. My detective partner and I will find and arrest them, and then the case report on the burglary will be filed with the district attorney's office."

Sgt. Martin explained that the district attorney (D.A.) or his assistant compiles the case and talks with all of the witnesses. He refines his case until it is ready to be presented to a grand jury. There are two kinds of juries. The *grand jury* is so named because it is the larger of the two. A grand jury is usually composed of twenty-four persons. The other kind of jury is called a *petit jury*, from the French word "petit" meaning "small." It has twelve members and is a trial jury.

"In this case," Sgt. Martin said, "I'll go before the grand jury to present my evidence. If the grand jury feels there is enough 'probable cause' to establish that the men are guilty of the crime, they'll give what is called a *true bill of indictment*. An indictment does not mean the men are guilty, but merely that there is sufficient evidence against them to justify bringing them to trial.

"If the grand jury feels the case is not strong enough or that the evidence has been improperly gathered, such as through an illegal search of the men, then they return a *no bill of indictment*. The men would then be freed from our custody and could not be brought to trial.

"If they've been indicted by the grand jury, the men can be released after appearing before a district judge. The act of appearing before a judge in court to answer an indictment is called *arraignment*. The judge would set a date for trial and fix the amount of *bail*. Bail is a guarantee in the form of money that they'll be available at the time of the trial. Sometimes it's called a 'bond' or 'bail bond."

Check for Understanding: Now that you have completed this section, you should be able to answer these questions:

1. Why is evidence so important in solving a crime?
2. What role does the grand jury play in the indictment process?
3. Why do judges post bail during arraignment?
4. What is "probable cause"?

Have your students research the county Grand Jury. When does it meet? Where? How are the jurors selected?

Interview a bail bondsman. Report to the class on the problems he has, his rates, and some of his more interesting cases.

WHAT DOES A JUVENILE OFFICER DO?

Objectives: After reading this section, you will be able to:

- Understand the term "juvenile."
- Explain how juvenile offenders are dealt with by the police.
- See that parents also have a responsibility when their son or daughter is charged with a delinquent act.

A crime by a juvenile

Next Sam and Mary went to talk with Mr. Dobbs, the juvenile officer. Officer Dobbs volunteered, "You might be interested in the case of a fourteen-year-old boy who was picked up last night with marijuana in his possession. In our state the law defines a *juvenile* as any boy or girl who has reached his or her tenth birthday but has not reached his seventeenth birthday in the case of a boy, or her eighteenth birthday in the case of a girl," explained Officer Dobbs.

"A juvenile who has been arrested or picked up for any delinquent act will be sent to me along with the arrest records. Normally, what I do with a first-time offender brought in for small theft or as a runaway is talk to the juvenile. Then I'll have the parents come in and we'll try to work things out by talking to each other. Usually, I release the juvenile to the family for correction at home."

"Possession of marijuana is a serious offense, isn't it?" asked Sam.

"In our state it's either a felony or misdemeanor, depending on the amount of marijuana involved," Officer Dobbs said.

Officer Dobbs, the juvenile officer, described the legal status of a juvenile offender.

Discuss with students the legal definition of a juvenile in your state and other states.

Serious juvenile offenders

Officer Dobbs continued his description of the handling of serious juvenile cases. "We can detain a juvenile in a jail cell for a few hours, or at least until his parents pick him up. By law we must provide separate jail cell blocks from those of adult prisoners in order to protect a young person from the influence of older lawbreakers. If it is a case like this one, possession of marijuana, we would complete the paperwork necessary to transfer the boy to the County Juvenile Home."

A parent's responsibility

Officer Dobbs then told Sam about a state law that had to do with parent's responsibility for the delinquent acts of their children.

"You mean that if I did something wrong, my parents would be charged?" Sam asked.

"They wouldn't actually be charged with the crime itself, but they might have to pay for any damages involved in the crime. The intent of the law is to involve the parents in the consequences of delinquent acts committed by their children," explained Officer Dobbs.

"Well, suppose someone is angry with his parents and damages something just to get them in trouble. What would you do about that?" asked Mary.

"I have to explain to the child that he could be sent to the juvenile home for an act of this kind," replied Officer Dobbs. "Also, in such a case I might charge the child, instead of making the parents responsible for damages."

Check for Understanding: Now that you have completed this section, you should be able to answer these questions:

1. Who does the term "juvenile" refer to?
2. How are juvenile offenders dealt with by police?
3. What responsibility do parents have when their son or daughter is charged with a delinquent act?
4. Why are juveniles separated from adult lawbreakers in jail cell blocks?

HOW DOES A MODERN LAW ENFORCEMENT DEPARTMENT WORK?

Objectives: After reading this section, you will be able to:

- See how modern electronic equipment aids law enforcement officers.
- Explain the role of the National Crime Information Center.
- Understand why education is important to a law enforcement officer.

The communications room

Next Sam and Mary went into the communications room, where they met Officer Phillips. He explained the equipment used in the room. "We check out law violators by using the latest electronic devices," said Officer Phillips. "As you can see, we have a teletype machine and a computer terminal. They connect our department with a regional police computer and with the National Crime Information Center in Washington, D.C."

Officer Phillips then showed them the computer terminal. He described the kind of information that was obtainable from the National Crime Information Center. He said, "If an individual had an FBI number, if he has ever been booked, fingerprinted, or arrested, the NCIC will have his record

Issues in Civics: "Juvenile laws are too lenient, and therefore, not effective." Debate this issue.

Have a student interview the local juvenile officer. Are parents really required to pay damages? How often? Is it fair?

in Washington, D.C. If he has a record, then the information sent back to us would include a complete physical description and a list of the charges brought against the individual."

"Who has the right to this information?" questioned Sam.

Officer Phillips replied, "Only certified civilians and law enforcement officers have the right to see this information, because it's confidential. If someone else gets a person's record, they could use it against that individual."

Training of a law enforcement department

From the communications room Sam and Mary went to meet Chief of Police Anderson in his office. "Have you had an informative day with us?" asked Chief Anderson.

"It's been great, and everyone has been so helpful. We've learned a lot," Sam answered.

"Chief Anderson, would you tell us about a law enforcement officer's training?" asked Mary.

"Law enforcement officers are required to have training beyond a high school diploma," said Chief Anderson. "In this department, an officer has to have the equivalent of two years of college training. Our citizens are better educated today, and there have been important changes in the law in recent years. You can't have a law-enforcement officer who knows less than the average citizen knows about the law and about civil liberties. If we don't know the constitutional rights of an individual when we make an arrest or prepare to testify in court, we could have our evidence thrown out later by the court. Psychology classes are being conducted for law enforcement officers in many cities."

Sam and Mary visited the police communications room to see the computer system in action.

Check for Understanding: Now that you have completed this section, you should be able to answer these questions:

1. How does modern electronic equipment aid law enforcement officers?
2. What training is a law enforcement officer required to have?
3. What information does the NCIC provide?
4. Who has the right to this information?

Have a student interview the chief of police. What are the requirements for joining your local police department. Are there women officers on the force?

WHAT HAPPENS TO A JUVENILE IN COURT?

Objectives: After reading this section, you will be able to:

- Explain the process involved in preparing for a juvenile court hearing.
- Understand what happens to a juvenile when he or she appears in court.
- Recognize the difference between a felony and a misdemeanor.

Work of a juvenile court

Sam and Mary crossed the street to the county courthouse to keep their appointment with Sarah Colvin, the juvenile judge. "We'd like you to describe the process involved in judging a juvenile," they asked her.

Judge Colvin met with Mary in her courtroom at the county courthouse.

"Usually the juvenile officer and the probation officer meet with the prosecuting attorney once a week," Judge Colvin began. "They review all the cases that have come to the attention of the authorities during the past week. They all participate in the discussion about the child, telling what they know about the person and the home situation. The prosecuting attorney is the one who has to make the final decision as to whether or not there is sufficient evidence to warrant a court hearing. The prosecuting attorney may be a District Attorney or County Attorney in our state.

"Assuming there is sufficient evidence, each person involved then has a job to do. The school supplies the school records about the child's attendance, grades, and test scores. The law enforcement officers locate the witnesses, and the prosecuting attorney talks with the witnesses and prepares the evidence. If the child is on probation, then the probation officer meets with the parents and gives us the social history of the child—where the person lives, family, hobbies, sports, and so on."

The meaning of proof

"Then we have the prosecuting attorney present in court, and he prepares the papers to present in the case against the juvenile. When I first came into this office, the juvenile hearings were very informal. The young person, parents, and the juvenile officer were usually the only ones present. Recent Supreme Court decisions have established the rights of a juvenile to be the same as those of an adult. It's difficult now to tell whether the juvenile court is a criminal court or a civil court. While the law in most states still regards a juvenile court as a

Issues in Civics: "If a juvenile has the same rights as an adult, then he should have the same responsibilities and punishment." Discuss this issue.

The Burden of Proof

Civil Case
Only a slight burden required.

Criminal Case
A heavy burden is required.

civil court, the standard of proof must be the same as in a criminal court."

"What do you mean by 'standard of proof'?" inquired Mary.

Judge Colvin explained, "In a civil case, proof must be established by the evidence. Think of a set of scales. The prosecutor must present enough evidence to tip the scales slightly in his favor. That is his *burden of proof*. But in a criminal case the burden of proof is much greater. The scales must be completely tipped down by the prosecutor's evidence. It must be proof beyond a reasonable doubt."

A juvenile in court

"Once a young person is in court, what happens then?" asked Sam. "Does he need a lawyer?" asked Mary. "What if the family doesn't have enough money to hire one?

"If the parents can't afford an attorney, then I appoint one for them," replied Judge Colvin. "At the hearing, we listen to the evidence about the child. Cross-examination can be made and witnesses can be questioned. A court reporter is present to record the testimony. At the end of this part of the hearing, a court judgment of delinquency is made. The child either is or is not declared a delinquent. The second half of the hearing will determine what kind of correction the child needs. This usually means placing the child on probation in his home or with some friend or relative. *Probation* means suspending a stronger sentence, such as sending the juvenile to a state training school, and granting the person provisional freedom on good behavior. The last resort, of course, would be commitment to the state training school."

Issues in Civics: "You must be found guilty beyond a reasonable doubt." What does this mean, and why is it important?

Sam had another question. "What about the marijuana case that Mr. Harris told us about? Would a fourteen-year-old boy caught with the possession of an illegal drug be sent to the state training school?"

"That's either a felony or misdemeanor in our state," answered the judge. "A misdemeanor is a lesser crime, such as a fine or short jail term at the local level, for which a person is not sent to a state institution. A felony is a serious crime, such as murder or burglary, for which a person may be sent to a state institution. If this case could be proven against him, he would probably be declared a juvenile delinquent by the court. But the court would also want to know if this act was just a thing he was doing to show off. If he could stay out of trouble at home, in the community, and at school, he would probably receive probation. But if it can be proven that he is selling drugs to other young people, this might mean that he would be committed to the state training school."

"Would the same thing happen if he were eighteen years old or older?" Mary wanted to know.

"No," replied the judge. "If an eighteen-year-old were faced with a felony charge, he would be indicted by a grand jury. He would be tried in district court. There the judge's options are adult probation, the penitentiary, or a hospital."

Check for Understanding: Now that you have completed this section, you should be able to answer these questions:

1. What preparations are made before a juvenile has a court hearing?
2. What actually happens once the juvenile appears in court?
3. How does a felony differ from a misdemeanor?
4. What is "burden of proof"?

HOW DOES A LAWYER PREPARE A DEFENSE FOR A CLIENT?

Objectives: After reading this section, you will be able to:

- See that the inquiry process is a crucial part of a lawyer's defense preparation.
- Understand that a lawyer-client relationship is dependent on honesty and trust.
- Explain how our system of checks and balances promotes a just judicial system.

The inquiry process in defense preparation

Sam and Mary went across the street to meet with Mr. William Cason, an attorney who was a friend of Judge Colvin's.

"How can I help you?" inquired Mr. Cason.

"Judge Colvin said that you might be able to give us some information for a school report we're doing. We'd like to know how you would defend a fourteen-year-old boy who was accused of the possession of an illegal drug," Sam and Mary told him.

"In defending a case like this," answered Mr. Cason, "I would be concerned with two things: First, did the young man or *defendant* (the person against whom an action in court is brought) think he was guilty of the offense with which he was charged, and, second, can the state or *plaintiff* (the person or party, such as the state, that brings an action in a court) prove its case under the juvenile code? I would want to

Give a short report on your Juvenile Court. Is it overcrowded? Do you have enough probation officers to hear each case fully? Are "minor" offenses let off because of these shortages?

interview my client—in this case the young man. I would talk to him about the charge against him and see what he could tell me about the circumstances as he knew them to be."

"Is it his responsibility to tell you the truth?" Sam asked.

"Yes, it is," answered Mr. Cason. "An attorney can't provide his client with the best defense possible unless the client tells him the truth. Suppose I prepare a defense based on one set of facts, and then find out later in court that the truth was something else? Of course, when you talk to any person charged with a crime, you must assure him that anything he says to his lawyer is confidential, and won't be brought out in public if he doesn't want it to be."

"Does the boy need to know his rights under the law?" Mary inquired. "This seems important."

"This young man must know exactly what his rights are," said Mr. Cason. "Once he understands his rights, you can proceed to the decision-making stage to see what should be done in his case. If a decision is made to admit to the charge of possession of a dangerous drug, you can try to get the court to accept probation as the best thing for the boy."

"Wouldn't this admission be giving up his rights?" questioned Sam.

"Before any decision were made to admit the charge, I'd be sure the young man knew that it was his right not to do it," responded Mr. Cason. "Now, going a step further, I would interview the witnesses from the information given me by the boy. I would want to know if the charge against him were a proper one."

"What is a proper charge?" asked Sam.

"For example, suppose that the 'dangerous drug' our young man was charged with possession of was several small white pills, and after a laboratory examination these white pills turned out to be Vitamin 'C' tablets. Then this would not be a proper charge," the lawyer replied.

"Or, let's suppose that the laboratory analysis does show that the pills were in fact

William Cason talked about the proper role of an attorney in the law enforcement process.

Read the Fifth Amendment and explain your rights under the Fifth to the class.

The Process of Justice

1. A Crime Is Committed

2. The Police Examine the Evidence

3. They Arrest a Suspect

4. The Grand Jury Returns an Indictment

5. A Trial Date Is Set

6. The Prosecution and The Defense Present Their Case

7. The Jury Returns a Verdict

8. The Defendant Is Found Innocent or Guilty

Analyze the stages of justice outlined above. Ask students if they feel any particular step in the process could be omitted, or if any other step should be added.

a dangerous drug. I could then look into the "chain of custody" of the drug to see who had it at different times," continued Mr. Cason. "Did someone else put it in his pocket? Did the state handle the drug properly as it was being analyzed? If the drug was found in a car and there were two people in the car, how would it be proven that my client was the one who had the drug? Did the young man make a statement to the law enforcement officer? If he did, I would want to know what the statement was, and whether he had been told of his constitutional rights before making it. If any one of my questions results in a favorable reply for my client, the prosecutor might fail to prove his case beyond a reasonable doubt."

The meaning of justice

"Does this method of defense really produce justice?" asked Sam. "This is one thing I've never understood about a defense lawyer. It seems as if you're working hard to free someone who might be guilty, especially when you know things about the case that he's told you, things that don't always come out in court."

"Sam, a defense attorney's job is to present his client's case in the best possible way, just as the prosecuting attorney's job is to do the same thing for the prosecution's case. Neither of us is supposed to decide whether the defendant is guilty or not. That's up to the judge or the jury. In my opinion justice occurs when you have someone representing the defendant in the best light and someone doing the same for the state or plaintiff," replied Mr. Cason. "It is when these two points of view are really on an equal basis that justice can be done."

That evening, as Sam and Mary were preparing their report on the meaning of the process of justice, it occurred to them that our judicial system, like other parts of our government, was one of checks and balances. They also realized that every step in the process of justice used the method of inquiry. The need to learn how to think logically became very real to them.

Check for Understanding: Now that you have completed this section, you should be able to answer these questions:

1. How does the inquiry process aid a lawyer in the preparation of a defense?
2. Why are honesty and trust so crucial to a successful lawyer-client relationship?
3. How does our system of checks and balances promote a just judicial system?
4. What is the "chain of custody," and how might it affect the charge against an individual?

SUMMARY

Law enforcement agencies protect us by sending a trained officer to check out every complaint call. Detectives gather evidence to present to judicial officers or bodies such as the justice of the peace and the grand jury. Only by indictment can a person be brought to trial for a crime. Modern machinery and advanced courses of study for law enforcement officers help them to protect the rights of citizens better. Today in Juvenile Court young people have the same rights as adults. Lawyers are necessary in our system of justice to defend the rights of an accused person. The real meaning of justice is the demand for proof of a person's guilt beyond a reasonable doubt.

Issues in Civics: Is the proper role of an attorney to be simply an advocate, as described above by the fictitious Mr. Cason, or should he or she make judgments about a client's guilt? What do students think of lawyers who specialize in defending members of organized crime, or political radicals?

BUILDING SKILLS IN CIVICS

THINKING SKILLS

1. Identify the activities and jobs you would see on a visit to a law enforcement department.
2. How is evidence used? What methods are used to obtain it?
3. What is the job of the juvenile officer? Give examples of his or her work.
4. Who has the right to information from the National Crime Information Center? Why?
5. What training is required to be a law enforcement officer?
6. Create a flow chart to show the steps in the indictment process.
7. Identify items that would fit in this category: "A Lawyer's Preparation of a Good Defense."

VOCABULARY SKILLS

Fill in each blank below with the word in parentheses that best fits the sentence.

1. The grand jury decides if enough "probable cause" was established to issue a true bill of ______. (burden of proof - indictment)
2. At the ______ the judge sets a date for trial and fixes the amount of the bail. (probation - arraignment)
3. If you are under the age of 18, you are considered a ______ in most states. (juvenile - plaintiff)
4. The ______ is the person or party that brings an action in a court. (plaintiff - defendant)
5. In a criminal case the ______ is much greater and proof must be beyond a reasonable doubt. (burden of proof - indictment)
6. Granting a person provisional freedom on the basis of good behavior is called ______. (arraignment - probation)
7. At the time of arraignment, the judge posts ______, which is a guarantee in the form of money that the indicted person will be available at the time of trial. (probation - bail)
8. The ______ hears a trial and decides whether the defendant is guilty or not. (grand jury - petit jury)

STUDY SKILLS—COMPARING MEDIA SOURCES

You probably get your opinions from a number of *sources.* The media or news sources such as radio, TV, newspapers and magazines help you form opinions. So do your friends, neighbors, parents and other family members, and teachers. To be a well-informed citizen, you need to be able to use different sources and know which sources will help you gain information as needed.

WHICH WOULD YOU USE TO . . .	TV	Radio	Newspaper	Weekly Magazine
1. get a summary of the day's news?				
2. learn the most "up-to-date" information?				
3. hear about an event as it happens?				
4. see an event happening?				
5. see people and places that are part of the news?				
6. hear the actual people and sounds of the event?				
7. choose only the stories that interest you?				
8. gain information any time of the day or night?				
9. re-study information at your own pace?				
10. get continuing coverage of an event, story, or issue?				

Activity: Prepare a chart like the one above to use as you analyze and compare media sources. Identify one advantage and disadvantage of each source.

BEYOND THE BOOK

1. Plan a visit to your local law enforcement department. Prior to the visit, make a list of jobs and activities you expect to see. Use this as a checklist during your visit.
2. Invite a juvenile officer to your class to discuss his or her job, special training skills, and concerns.
3. Skim the newspaper for additional news and feature stories about the court system, law enforcement agencies and other legal matters. Compile a list of factual information.
4. Use information from the library to learn more about the requirements for becoming a lawyer.

CHAPTER TWENTY-FOUR TEST

VOCABULARY CHECK

Match each term with the correct definition.

a. indictment
b. arraignment
c. juvenile
d. probation
e. defendant
f. burden of proof
g. bail
h. grand jury

1. The prosecutor's responsibility to present enough evidence to show guilt beyond a reasonable doubt.
2. Issued as a result of a grand jury's belief that there is enough evidence to justify a trial.
3. The act of appearing before a judge to answer an indictment.
4. A person against whom a court case is brought.
5. Someone not yet of adult age.
6. The process of suspending a stronger sentence.
7. The group of people who decide if enough probable cause is established to issue an indictment.
8. A guarantee in the form of money that an indicted person will be available at the time of trial.

COMPREHENSION CHECK

1. True or False: Bail is a guarantee in the form of money that a person will be available at the time of trial.
2. True or False: If the grand jury feels the case is not strong enough or that the evidence has been improperly gathered they will return a "no bill of indictment" decision.
3. True or False: Recent Supreme Court decisions have established the rights of a juvenile to be the same as those of an adult.
4. Which of the following are things that a lawyer would do to "Prepare a Good Defense"?
   a. Interview the client.
   b. Make sure the client knows his or her rights.
   c. Advise in the decision-making stage.
   d. Interview witnesses.
   e. Investigate the chain of custody.

SKILL BUILDERS—INTERPRETING A STORYBOARD

A *storyboard* is a series of pictures and captions that show the sequence and intended content of a program, commercial, or film. The storyboard provides the visual and verbal "plan" needed for the actual filming. It does not include *all* the pictures and actions. Like a timeline and a flow chart, it only provides the information needed to understand the work as a whole.

Activity: Above is the illustrated part of a storyboard for a feature story on the "Process of Indictment." Study each picture. What action is being shown? Write a caption for each picture that tells the camera crew and cast what that part should show.

BUILDING WRITING SKILLS

1. Create your own storyboard (pictures and captions) for a feature story for the evening news on one of the following topics from this chapter:
   a. Visit to a law enforcement department.
   b. Responsibilities of a juvenile officer.
   c. Juvenile court.
2. Which factual statements would you use to support this generalization: "Lawyers are necessary in our system of justice to defend the rights of an accused person."

Chapter Twenty-Five
Great Decisions For Justice

Document: The Constitution of the United States

Article III, Section 2. . . . In all Cases affecting Ambassadors, other public Ministers and Consuls, and those in which a State shall be Party, the supreme Court shall have original Jurisdiction. In all the other Cases before mentioned, the supreme Court shall have appellate Jurisdiction, both as to Law and Fact, with such Exceptions, and under such Regulations as the Congress shall make.

Amendment IV. The right of the people to be secure in their persons, houses, papers, and effects, against unreasonable searches and seizures, shall not be violated, and no Warrants shall issue, but upon probable cause, supported by Oath or affirmation, and particularly describing the place to be searched, and the persons or thing to be seized.

This chapter is entitled "Great Decisions for Justice," because the decisions that were reached in each case insure the preservation of a freedom set forth in the Bill of Rights.

Supreme Court decisions have great importance, as once a decision has been reached by the Court, all other courts in the country must follow the decision in similar cases.

This illustration describes the freedoms of religion, speech, and the press described in the First Amendment. Discuss with students how life would be different if we were denied these basic freedoms.

The complete text of the Bill of Rights can be found in the Appendix on pages 575–76.

One of the fundamental duties of the Supreme Court is to determine whether federal, state, and local governments are acting in accordance with the rules laid down by the Constitution. Although each state court is also headed by a supreme court, the U.S. Supreme Court may review state high court decisions if a particular decision involves the Constitution or acts of Congress.

FOCUSING IDEAS

- Before a Supreme Court decision is made, there must be a full discussion of the case, each justice must state his or her decision on the issue, and the case must be decided by majority vote.
- The legal rights of individuals include protection during search and seizure, the right to a speedy trial, the right to counsel, "Miranda" rights, the right to an impartial judge and jury, the right to confront witnesses, and the right against self-incrimination.
- Freedom of speech is a right of all citizens provided that the "clear and present danger" test is not violated.
- Protection of one's person and property from arbitrary search and seizure is a Constitutional right.
- A citizen has certain rights regarding trial and arrest that insure that the process of justice will be served.

Issues in Civics: How are the legal rights of individuals protected? Discuss the problems involved in their protection.

PRE-TEST

1. What steps are involved in the making of a Supreme Court decision?
2. What legal rights do individuals in our society have?
3. What are the major rights of free speech that all individuals in our country are entitled to?
4. What major rights do individuals have regarding search and seizure?
5. What are the rights involved in the trial and arrest process?

HOW ARE SUPREME COURT DECISIONS MADE?

This symbol of "blind justice" has been used since ancient times to represent the legal process.

Objectives: After you read this section, you will be able to:

- Understand how a case comes to be heard by the Supreme Court.
- Describe the process by which the Supreme Court arrives at its decision.
- See why electronic equipment is a valuable aid to the Supreme Court.

Ideal justice, meaning equal treatment for both sides in a dispute, is something people have sought since ancient days. Justice is often represented as a woman with a blindfold over her eyes and a pair of scales in one hand. What do you think this representation is meant to say about justice?

The Supreme Court of the United States is the final body to hear an appeal from a lower court. The real meaning of justice to all the people is often decided in this Court. Thus, the manner in which a decision is reached is important to us.

Building vocabulary:
Writ of Mandamus *(415)* • appellate jurisdiction *(415)* • original jurisdiction *(415)* • dissenting opinion *(416)* • concurring opinion *(416)* • due process *(417)* • procedural right *(424)*

The members of the Supreme Court in 1981, including Sandra Day O'Connor, the first woman justice.

How cases reach the Supreme Court

Appeals reach the Supreme Court by way of an order from a lower court, called a *Writ of Mandamus*. The term "Mandamus" comes for a Latin word meaning "we require." This then means that the lower court is required to send its transcript of the trial proceedings to the Supreme Court. However, there are thousands of appeals sent to the Supreme Court every year. If the Court took each one, the justices would still be hearing cases that originated in 1920. Therefore, the justices of the Supreme Court must be selective in the cases that they take. The Supreme Court can hear any case on appeal, or *appellate jurisdiction*. The term *jurisdiction* means "the authority to interpret or apply the laws." The Court has *original jurisdiction* in cases involving ambassadors, maritime accidents, and disputes between states. These cases the Court must take.

The decision by the justices to hear an appeal is usually based upon its potential national meaning. For example, if a point of law could be made clearer for all the courts, then this case would likely be heard. Sometimes the case has implications for extending the rights of individuals. These decisions eventually become great decisions for justice.

Reaching decisions

In reaching a conclusion about a case, arguments are brought before the Court. The Solicitor General, or lawyer for the government, is presented along with the lawyers representing the other party. Any one of the nine justices can ask questions of the law-

Have a student do research to determine how the issuing of a Writ of Mandamus was a concern in the *Marbury v. Madison* case of 1803.

Sandra Day O'Connor is the first woman justice of the Supreme court in our history. Have a student give a full report on her.

yers. In one recent case, they interrupted eighty-four times in 120 minutes. Usually the spoken arguments are presented first and then the justices ask questions.

The law clerks in each justice's office assist the justice in preparing a decision. Each Friday the justices meet in conference. During the week they have heard the oral arguments, read and studied the briefs, and examined the petitions. The justices bring their votes and records in locked briefcases. During the week they have also privately sought the opinions of their fellow justices about the case being considered.

Although the procedure is not the same every time, the Chief Justice usually opens with a summary of the case to be decided. The justices are then polled separately, with the senior one speaking first and each one afterward in order until the most recent appointee to the Court speaks last. After full discussion, a vote is taken with the least senior justice voting first.

The case is decided by majority vote, and one justice is assigned the task of writing the opinion. If the Chief Justice votes with the majority, he or she decides who writes the opinion. If he does not, the senior justice among the majority makes the decision as to the writer. Justices who were among the minority normally select one of their group to write a *dissenting opinion*. If a justice agrees with the majority but differs on the reasoning, he or she writes a *concurring opinion*.

Use of computers

The Supreme Court, in an attempt to cut down on paperwork, has decided to use computers to speed up its work. Law clerks, secretaries, and even some of the justices have computerized their work habits as part of this movement. Several word processors have been installed at the Supreme Court building in Washington D.C. Supreme Court opinions—together with law clerk memoranda, opinion drafts, headnotes, speech texts and correspondence—now are composed on word processors. The opinions are published in final form by electronically transferring the information to typesetting computers.

These computers, known as word processors, are used to process information for the Supreme Court.

Check for Understanding: Now that you have completed this section, you should be able to answer these questions:

1. What steps take place before a case is heard by the Supreme Court?
2. How does the Supreme Court reach a decision in a case?
3. Why has electronic equipment become such a valuable aid to the Court?
4. What is the difference between a "dissenting opinion" and a "concurring opinion"?

Ask students to research a recent Supreme Court decision. What was the issue? On what basis was it decided?

WHAT ARE THE LEGAL RIGHTS OF INDIVIDUALS?

Objectives: After you read this section, you will be able to:

- List the major legal rights of individuals as stated in the Bill of Rights.
- Understand that the Bill of Rights applies to both the national government and to the states as well.
- See the difference between an absolute right and a relative right.

Individual rights

Since it is not possible within this textbook to look at each major decision of the Court, only a few will be examined. These decisions will be on the First Amendment rights of free speech and assembly, *due process* of law, and major legal rights. The major legal rights of an individual are: protection during search and seizure, the right to a speedy trial, the right to counsel, "Miranda" rights, the right to an impartial jury and an impartial judge, the right to confront and cross-examine witnesses, the right to be able to call one's own witnesses, and the right against self-incrimination.

The Bill of Rights originally applied only to the national government. This was decided during the time of Chief Justice John Marshall and has never been challenged since that time. However, most states include within their own constitutions a bill of rights granting the same rights contained in the national Constitution. With the adoption of the Fourteenth Amendment and its Due Process Clause, legal rights in the Bill of Rights have been extended gradually to include the states.

The rights of free speech and assembly are not absolute rights. They were never intended to be. They are relative and depend upon the rights of others. As the saying goes, "Your right to swing your arms around stops one inch short of another person's nose."

Chief Justice Oliver Wendell Holmes formulated the "clear and present danger" test for issues of free speech.

Check for Understanding: Now that you have completed this section, you should be able to answer these questions:

1. What are the major legal rights which you possess under the Bill of Rights?
2. How has the Bill of Rights come to apply to the states as well as to the national government?
3. Why are the rights of speech and assembly not considered to be absolute rights?
4. What did the Fourteenth Amendment and its Due Process Clause allow for?

The complete text of the Bill of Rights can be found in the Appendix on pages 575–76.

Two of the great Chief Justices have been John Marshall and Oliver Wendell Holmes. Have a student report on each Justice.

WHAT ARE THE RIGHTS OF FREE SPEECH?

Objectives: After reading this section, you will be able to:

- Understand how the "clear and present danger" test applies to the right of free speech.
- See that even "silent" or "symbolic" speech might constitute a clear and present danger.
- See why symbolic speech that is peaceful in nature is considered Constitutional.

Free speech

The decision reached by the Supreme Court in *Schenck vs. U.S.* (1919) established the "clear and present danger" test. By this test the limit of tolerance for free speech was determined. Schenck had been convicted of circulating pamphlets urging men who had been drafted to refuse to serve. By the "clear and present danger" test it was decided that if an act were of such a nature to bring about an immediate threat to the country, it was unlawful. Because Schenck's act took place during World War I, the Court held that advocating resistance to the draft was an attempt to obstruct the nation's war effort. Schenck's conviction was upheld by the Supreme Court.

Some would consider the limit of free speech to be saying that the government should be overthrown. In *Dennis vs. U.S.*, (1951) this question was considered.

History of Freedom of Speech and the Press in the United States

1791:	First Amendment guarantees freedom of speech and the press.
1798:	Alien and Sedition Acts outlaw writing or speaking that causes discontent with government.
1860:	Federal laws make it illegal to mail immoral material.
1919:	Courts begin ruling that speech or writing must present a "clear and present danger" before being banned.
1940:	Smith Act makes it illegal to publish or distribute material for the overthrow of U.S. government.
1957:	Roth vs. U.S. Supreme Court decision says First Amendment does not apply to what may be considered immoral material.
1967:	Freedom of Information Act makes it possible for individuals to obtain much government information that was formerly not available to the public.
1973:	Miller vs. California sets guidelines for what is considered to be immoral.

Facts—Dennis vs. the United States

The Smith Act of 1940 made it a crime to knowingly advocate a violent overthrow of the government by any means—through a speech or through printed literature, or by organizing or belonging to such an anti-government group. In 1948 the top eleven leaders of the American Communist Party were indicted for willfully saying the government should be overthrown by force or violence. They were convicted by the lower court and the conviction was upheld by the Court of Appeals. When the case reached the Supreme Court, they limited its scope to free speech under the First Amendment.

Issues—Dennis vs. the United States

The issue was whether or not the eleven presented a danger, since they were too small in number to actually overthrow the United States government. Does it constitute sufficient danger that a group may

List three major cases the Supreme Court has decided. How did they change things? For example: 1. Segregation—Eliminates school discrimination. 2. Dred Scott—Upheld slavery. 3. Marbury vs. Madison—Gave Supreme Court right of Judicial Review.

A father and son register together for the draft in World War I. Schenck distributed circulars telling such men to refuse to serve in the war.

overthrow the government at a later time? Is free speech in a favorable position to be considered above all other freedoms? Does a party's activities come under the rest of clear and present danger, since these would not be literature or speech itself.

Opinions—Dennis vs. the United States

The Court affirmed the decision of the Court of Appeals. Four judges decided that the danger need not be immediate. It was sufficient that a group was willing to overthrow the government. The time element was read out of the test. One justice said that free speech did not have a favorable position.

One justice, in a concurring opinion, said that a party's activities were sufficient danger and that "speech" as referred to in the First Amendment meant literature and speeches. Two justices dissented. They said the clear and present danger test was being destroyed.

The case of *Tinker vs. Des Moines Community School District* (1969) opened a new dimension to the meaning of free speech. In this unique court decision, speech was interpreted to mean "silent" or "symbolic speech."

Make a bulletin board depicting some of your basic rights to freedom of speech.

Tinker vs. Des Moines dealt with the question of whether wearing a symbol of protest is in effect "silent speech."

Facts—Tinker vs. Des Moines Community School District

John F. Tinker, 15 years old, and Christopher Eckhardt, 16 years old, were high school students in Des Moines, Iowa. Mary Beth Tinker, John's sister, was a 13-year-old student in junior high school.

During the Vietnam War controversy, a group of adults and students in Des Moines planned a protest movement. They decided to wear black armbands to show their support for a Vietnam truce during the holiday season. The school principals learned about the protest. They met and adopted a policy to suspend any student who refused to remove an armband and to retain such suspension until that student returned to school without one.

On December 16 Mary Beth and Christopher wore black armbands to their schools. John Tinker wore his the next day. They were all sent home. They did not return to school until after the holidays, which was the time period planned for the truce. Charging that their First Amendment rights had been violated, the students sought an injunction in district court to prohibit their school board from carrying out the suspensions.

Issues—Tinker vs. Des Moines School District

Were the students being restricted unfairly, when others had been permitted to wear political buttons and even an Iron Cross (a German military medal awarded during World War I and World War II) to school? Were their First Amendment rights being violated?

Opinions—Tinker vs. Des Moines School District

The justices ruled that the wearing of an armband was symbolic speech. Therefore, it was an expression of free speech. They said the suspension of the students was an unlawful act, since they were peaceful in their behavior. The Tinkers were being treated unfairly if they could not express dissent about the Vietnam War, even if such a dissent was distasteful to the school officials.

Check for Understanding: Now that you have completed this section, you should be able to answer these questions:

1. How does the "clear and present danger" test apply to the right of free speech?
2. How might "silent" or "symbolic" speech constitute a clear and present danger?
3. Why is symbolic speech that is carried out peacefully considered to be Constitutional?
4. In the *Tinker vs. Des Moines School District* case, why did the students feel that their First Amendment rights had been violated?

Issues in Civics: To what extent should the rights of free speech and assembly be restricted? Discuss this with the class.

WHAT ARE THE RIGHTS AGAINST SEARCH AND SEIZURE?

Objectives: After reading this section, you will be able to:

- See that protection of privacy is a basic right of Americans.
- Tell why unlawful search and seizure offends the codes of decency and fairness for U.S. citizens.
- Understand how the case of *Ker vs. California* set a standard for reasonable search and seizure in our states.

William Pitt, prime minister of England, made a famous speech on the right to privacy. (See page 588.)

Search and seizure

The English law concept that "a person's home is a castle" has led America to the protection of privacy as a basic right. Nowhere is this right more evident than in the protection of one's person and property from arbitrary search and seizure as outlined in the Fourth Amendment.

Through the years the courts have tried to determine what evidence to admit. Sometimes they have been shocked at the manner in which evidence has been gained. In *Rochin vs. California* (1952) "being shocked" came out as a test in the decision reached in the case.

Facts—Rochin vs. California

Antonio Rochin lived in a two-story dwelling in the country of Los Angeles with his mother, wife, brother, and sisters. Three deputy sheriffs of Los Angeles County had information that Rochin was selling narcotics. They entered his home through an open door. They forced open the door to Rochin's bedroom on the second floor of the house.

Rochin was sitting on the side of the bed. Upon the night stand were two capsules that he immediately swallowed. The police jumped on him to force the capsules from his mouth. They did not succeed. They then handcuffed Rochin and took him to a hospital.

Against his will the doctor pumped his stomach. When the materials were extracted and examined, they were found to be morphine, a dangerous drug. Rochin was brought to trial before a California Superior Court, sitting without a jury, on the charge of possessing a preparation of morphine in violation of the California Health and Safety Code. The chief evidence at the trial was the two capsules.

William Pitt's statement was cited by Senator Herman Talmadge of the Senate's Watergate Investigative Committee in attacking the illegal break-ins of the White House "Plumbers" group. He said Pitt's words were "still a good principle of law." Do your students agree with him?

Issues—Rochin vs. California

Did the deputy sheriffs enter Rochin's home legally? Can one extract evidence from a person's stomach without the person's consent? Did the method for obtaining evidence offend the codes of decency and fairness for people of the United States? Is trial by jury a rigid requirement for justice in the state court?

Opinions—Rochin vs. California

The question of entry into Rochin's home was not debated by the court. The majority decision held that due process was violated. And the evidence was obtained by a means that indeed did shock the conscience of many people. Trial by jury is considered a requirement of justice. Evidence forcefully extracted from a defendant, either from his mind by confession or physically from his body as it was in this case, cannot be used against him in court.

State standards of search and seizure

In 1963 in *Ker vs. California* eight justices agreed that federal constitutional standards of reasonableness of search and seizures is the same for states as it is for federal courts under the Fourth and Fourteenth Amendments.

Check for Understanding: Now that you have completed this section, you should be able to answer these questions:

1. Why is the protection of privacy a basic right of Americans?
2. Why does unlawful search and seizure offend the common decency of Americans?
3. How did *Ker vs. California* affect the search and seizure laws in the states?
4. Why was due process violated in the *Rochin* case?

WHAT ARE THE RIGHTS OF TRIAL AND ARREST?

Objectives: After reading this section, you will be able to:

- See why *Gideon vs. Wainright* had a profound effect on individual rights.
- Explain why the law now requires law enforcement officers to inform a suspect of his or her rights before questioning begins.
- Understand that the rights of both the accused and the accuser must be safeguarded in order to ensure justice.

Right to an Attorney

By the time of *Gideon vs. Wainwright* (1963) the rights contained in the First, Fourth, and Eighth Amendments had been extended to cover procedures in state courts. This case incorporates yet another amendment.

Facts—Gideon vs. Wainwright

Clarence Earl Gideon was charged in a Florida state court with breaking and entering a poolroom with intent to commit a misdemeanor. The offense of breaking and entering was a felony under Florida law. Gideon appeared in court without funds and without a lawyer. When he requested counsel be appointed, this dialogue took place: "The Court: Mr. Gideon, I am sorry, but I cannot appoint Counsel to represent you in this case. Under the laws of the State of Florida the only time the Court can appoint Counsel to represent a Defendant is when that person is charged with a capital offense. I am sorry, but I will have to deny your request to appoint Counsel to defend you in this case."

Even the poorest person has the right to counsel. Have two student teams debate: "The law is not fair because wealthy people can hire the best lawyers and poor people have to take a court-appointed lawyer who is not likely to be as good."

Clarence Earl Gideon studying law books in preparation for serving as his own attorney.

"The Defendant: The United States Supreme Court says I am entitled to be represented by Counsel."

Clarence Gideon conducted his own defense. Without knowledge of the law, he did as well as could be expected. He made an opening statement to the jury, cross-examined the state's witnesses, presented witnesses in his own defense, declined to testify for himself, and made a short closing argument emphasizing his innocence.

The jury found Clarence Earl Gideon guilty. The judge sentenced him to five years in state prison. Gideon asked the Supreme Court of Florida for a writ of *habeas corpus*, meaning "show just cause why and by what offense he was being charged." But the writ was denied, and Gideon began his prison term.

While in prison, Gideon prepared and submitted a five-page "pauper's petition," asking the United States Supreme Court to review his case. Gideon said his conviction violated the Due Process Clause of the Fourteenth Amendment.

Issues—Gideon vs. Wainwright

Is a poor person entitled to have the state pay counsel for a trial as a guaranteed right from the federal Constitution? Is it a trial by "due process" if a lawyer for defense is not present during the trial?

Opinions—Gideon vs. Wainwright

The right of counsel is fundamental to the concept of justice. And it is of such a nature that without it due process is not followed in the court. The Court stated:

". . . reason and reflection require us to recognize that in our adversary system of criminal justice, any person hailed into court, who is too poor to hire a lawyer, cannot be assured a fair trial unless counsel is provided for him. This seems to be an obvious truth." One justice concurred but did not believe the Fourteenth Amendment "due process" clause made Sixth Amendment rights binding upon the states. This was stated in his written opinion.

Other rights

After the Gideon case the incorporation of other rights into the state courts came rapidly. In 1964 the Court in *Malloy vs. Hogan* incorporated the Fifth Amendment privilege against self-incrimination. This action was followed by extending the right to confront one's accusers (*Pointer vs. Texas*,

Issues in Civics: Why did the Court feel that Gideon's conducting his own defense was not an adequate protection of his rights? Our tradition provides for a person's right to serve as his or her own counsel. Why did the Court interpret "right to counsel" to mean "right to *professional* counsel"?

According to *Miranda vs. Arizona,* the police must advise this suspect that he has the right to an attorney before they may begin questioning him.

1965) speedy trial (*Klopfer vs. North Carolina*, 1967), an impartial jury (*Parker vs. Gladden*, 1967), the right to subpoena defense witnesses (*Washington vs. Texas*, 1967), and the protection against double jeopardy (*Benton vs. Maryland*, 1969).

Facts—Miranda vs. Arizona

The Fifth Amendment right to remain silent and Sixth Amendment right to counsel reached a climax in the case of *Miranda vs. Arizona* (1966). On March 3, 1963 an 18-year-old girl was kidnapped near Phoenix, Arizona. Ten days later, Ernesto Miranda was arrested and taken to the police station. At this time Miranda was 23 years old, poor, and educated to the extent of completing half of ninth grade. He had been examined previously by a doctor and found to be suffering from an emotional illness. However, the doctor stated Miranda was capable of standing trial for the crime.

At the police station the victim picked out Miranda from a lineup. Two officers then took him to a separate room to question him. Though at first denying his guilt, within a short time Miranda gave a detailed oral confession and then wrote out in his hand a written confession that he signed. This was done without any threats or force by the police.

At Miranda's trial the two officers testified before a jury that during Miranda's interrogation he admitted to the crime. Then they asked him to prepare a written statement, which he did. At the beginning of the statement, he was given warning that anything he might write could be used against him, and he proceeded with the full knowledge of his legal rights. The officer who read this statement aloud to Miranda admitted that it did not say anything about a right to an attorney.

Miranda was found guilty. He was sentenced to 20 to 30 years in prison. He appealed his case to the Arizona Supreme Court. That Court affirmed his conviction.

Issues—Miranda vs. Arizona

Can evidence be admitted in court that was obtained in a manner violating "due process?" At which point in police custody do *procedural rights* (the rights of the legal process) begin? What procedural rights are guaranteed in the Fifth and Sixth Amendments? Under what circumstances can an individual waive his constitutional rights? Are Fifth Amendment rights absolute?

Evidence taken from Miranda was held by the Court to be inadmissable. Chief

Have students ask a local policeman about the *Miranda* decision. How does it affect his job? Does the decision make it more difficult?

Justice Warren in writing the majority stated: ". . . the prosecution may not use statements, whether *exculpatory* (tending to prove guilt) or *inculpatory* (free from guilt), stemming from custodial interrogation of the defendant unless it demonstrates the use of procedural safeguards effective to secure the privilege against self-incrimination. By *custodial interrogation*, we mean questioning initiated by law enforcement officers after a person has been taken into custody or otherwise deprived of his freedom of action."

"Prior to any questioning, the person must be warned that he has a right to remain silent, that he has a right to the presence of an attorney, either retained or appointed. The defendant may *waive* effectuation of these rights, provided the waiver is made voluntarily, knowingly, and intelligently."

The right to remain silent is absolute, since the individual may start answering questions and then refrain from further participation until his or her attorney is present.

The meaning of justice

At the beginning of this chapter, you were asked to give your meaning of the figure of justice represented blindfolded and holding scales. The cases chosen in this chapter represent the rights of the accused on one scale. These would be balanced on the opposite scale as the rights of the accuser. Justice then is the protection of the innocent as well as punishment for the guilty.

In pursuit of justice our system seeks to protect the rights of the individual. Evidence obtained and the trial conducted must be done in such a manner that those rights are safeguarded. To destroy rights to bring about a conviction is not in keeping with our heritage. The maintenance of this concept of justice in the future is in the hands of you, the citizen.

Check for Understanding: Now that you have completed this section, you should be able to answer these questions:

1. What effect did the *Gideon* case have on the rights of the individual?
2. Why does the law require that a law enforcement officer inform a suspect of his or her rights?
3. Why is it important for there to be a balance between the rights of the accused and that of the accuser?
4. What are a defendant's "procedural rights"?

SUMMARY

Justice is an ideal to be realized within the conduct of law enforcement officers, the courts, and the protection afforded the individual of his rights. Justice must also include the protection of the rights of the accuser and society. Ours is an adversary system where the balancing of these rights is important to the concept of justice. Through the years a number of notable United States Supreme Court cases have extended the rights of the individual. Originally these rights applied to the federal courts as interpreted in the U.S. Bill of Rights if they were not spelled out in state constitutions. But the Fourteenth Amendment Due Process Clause has been the means to extend federal rights to states. The protection of our American system of justice in the future is the responsibility of each citizen.

Issues in Civics: "It is better that ten guilty persons go free than one innocent person be convicted." Have students write a paragraph explaining this issue. (See also page 588)

BUILDING SKILLS IN CIVICS

THINKING SKILLS

1. What rights are protected by the First Amendment? Fourth Amendment? Fifth Amendment?
2. Use an outline format to organize chapter information on the topic "Free Speech." Use the headings: a. First Amendment b. Clear and Present Danger c. Silent or Symbolic Speech d. Court Decisions
3. Which of the following does not belong in the category "Reaching Supreme Court Decisions"? a. Arguments are heard from both sides. b. Nine justices can ask questions of the lawyers. c. A jury is selected. d. Arguments are read and briefs are studied. e. Thousands of appeals are sent every year. f. Case is decided by majority vote.

VOCABULARY SKILLS

Some words below are misused. Write True if the underlined word is correctly used. If not, select a word to replace it.

concurring opinion	Writ of Mandamus	original
appellate jurisdiction	procedural right	jurisdiction
due process	dissenting opinion	

1. Appeals reach the Supreme Court by way of a written order from the lower court called a Writ of Mandamus.
2. A dissenting opinion is written by a Supreme Court justice and states why the minority disagrees with the majority.
3. The Supreme Court has the authority to hear any case on appeal because of appellate jurisdiction.
4. A Writ of Mandamus is written if a justice agrees with the majority but differs on the reasoning.
5. The Supreme Court has original jurisdiction in cases involving ambassadors and disputes between states.
6. A concurring opinion is one of the rights guaranteed an accused criminal when he is taken into custody.
7. The judicial system exercises procedural rights in trying all accused criminals.

STUDY SKILLS—USING DIFFERENT SOURCES OF INFORMATION

Reporters depend on different *sources* to get information about an event or issue. As you watch a newscast, you need to be aware of the reporter's source and to decide if it is a dependable one. The next time you watch a newscast, identify which of the following sources were used.

1. THE PRIMARY SOURCE: These are the people directly involved in an event. If the story involves a disagreement, it is important that the reporter interview primary sources from both sides.
2. INFORMED SOURCES: These are people who know about the event. They may work with or for the primary source, or be family members, friends, or associates. They may also be people who were at the location when the event occurred.
3. EXPERTS: These people are sought because of their recognized expertise in a particular area. They are used to provide opinions and give additional information.
4. REFERENCE WORKS: The content of books, magazines, newspaper articles, and television shows may be used as a resource for the reporter. Often, historical film will be shown to provide a background for an event or issue.

Activity: Choose a recent news story. Give examples of how each source can be used as a resource.

BEYOND THE BOOK

1. Prepare a list of questions that would help you gain factual information about one of the following subjects.
   a. Being a Supreme Court justice
   b. Being a defense lawyer
   c. Being a prosecuting attorney
   d. Being an arresting officer
2. Prepare a news story on one of the cases included in this chapter. Be sure your story tells the "5 W's and 1 H." Keep a week-long tally of the different sources used on a TV newscast. Present your findings to the class orally.

CHAPTER TWENTY-FIVE TEST

VOCABULARY CHECK

Fill in each blank with the correct definition.

concurring opinion	Writ of Mandamus	original
appellate jurisdiction	procedural right	jurisdiction
due process	dissenting opinion	

1. The Supreme Court has ______ in cases involving ambassadors, maritime accidents, and disputes between states.
2. Every year thousands of appeals are sent to the Supreme Court which has ______ on any case.
3. The written order to send a lower court transcript of a trial to the Supreme Court is called ______.
4. A ______ agrees with the decision reached by the majority but shows that a justice differs on the reasoning.
5. ______ refers to legal proceedings carried out in accordance with the established rules.
6. Accused criminals are guaranteed ______ when they are taken into custody.
7. A ______ disagrees with the decision reached by the majority and states the reasons why.

COMPREHENSION CHECK

Write True if the question and answer match. If they do not, write a correct answer to match the question.

1. What is the meaning of justice?—Justice is the protection of the innocent as well as punishment for the guilty.
2. What kind of evidence cannot be used in court?—Evidence forcefully extracted from a defendant, either from his mind by confession or physically, cannot be used against him in court.
3. What are three legal rights which you possess under the Bill of Rights?—The protection of justice in the future is the responsibility of each citizen.
4. What is involved in the making of a Supreme Court decision?—The Supreme Court is the final body to hear an appeal from a lower court.

SKILL BUILDERS—INTERPRETING CARTOONS

Newspapers and magazines frequently use *cartoons* to express a point of view and to try to influence public opinion. A political or editorial cartoon is a comment on a significant event or important issue. Cartoons have the following characteristics:

1. They focus on one central idea, event, or issue.
2. They use symbols and physical characteristics that are quickly recognized.
3. They make use of exaggeration.

Both the art and the copy are vital in order to understand a cartoon's intent. As is the case with other visuals, you must be alert to all details.

Activity: Choose an editorial or political cartoon that you see in a newspaper or magazine. Then answer these questions:

1. How do the art and text complement each other?
2. What point is the cartoonist trying to convey?
3. How effective is the cartoon in conveying this point?
4. Why do you think this is so?

BUILDING WRITING SKILLS

1. Explain the meaning behind the following quotations about legal rights.

   "Your right to swing your arms around stops one inch short of another person's nose."
   ". . . a person's home is a castle"
   "The defendant may waive effectuation of these rights, provided the waiver is made voluntarily, knowingly, and intelligently."

2. Use facts to support this generalization:
   "To destroy rights to bring about a conviction is not in keeping with our heritage."
3. Do you know anyone who has ever been involved in a court case? If so, explain the nature of the case and what the results were. If not, write about a case that you have heard of through the media or through friends.

UNIT SIX TEST

U.S. Court System

Name	Composition
Supreme Court	One Chief Justice, eight Associate Justices
Courts of Appeals	Eleven judicial circuits with three to nine judges in each
Court of Claims	One Chief Judge, four Associate Judges
Court of Customs and Patent Appeals	One Chief Judge, four Associate Judges
District Courts	Over 340 District Judges
Court of Military Appeals	One Chief Judge, two Associate Judges

A. Study the chart above. Then answer the following questions:

1. Why do you think it's necessary to have so many different levels of courts in our country?
2. Do you think that the structure of the court system could be changed to make it more efficient? Why or why not?
3. Are there any levels of courts that you think are unnecessary? Do you think any levels should be added? Explain.
4. Do you think that the U.S. court system protects our basic freedoms? Why do you say so?

B. Write an editorial for a TV newscast on one of the following subjects:

1. The overworked court system.
2. Why judges must be independent.
3. Why unreasonable search and seizure offends our code of decency.
4. Parental responsibility and juvenile delinquency.

C. Based on facts from Unit Six, do you think that *you* would be interested in a career in law enforcement? Why or why not? Do you think that law enforcement officers receive adequate training? Do you think that the use of electronics in law enforcement violates the privacy of citizens, or do you think it's a valid means of seeking out law violators?

Unit Seven · Cooperating In Our Republic

The problems that affect our society are numerous, but we, as individuals can join forces with the powers of government to help solve them. One way to do this is by sharing and conserving the resources that are essential to us. For example, one river has the potential to be used for transportation and recreation; as a means of providing water for farmlands and electrical power for industry; and as a source of fish and minerals. But it is only through mutual cooperation that we will *all* be able to take advantage of the natural and human resources at our disposal.

The river is an example of cooperating in our republic, because the one river's resources must be shared by many different segments of our society, since it serves for transportation, industry, recreation, etc.

Chapter Twenty-Six • Promoting the General Welfare

Document: The Constitution of the United States

Preamble. WE THE PEOPLE of the United States, in Order to form a more perfect Union, establish Justice, insure domestic Tranquility, provide for the common defence, promote the general Welfare . . .

Article I, Section 8. The Congress shall have Power To lay and collect Taxes, Duties, Imposts and Excises, to pay the Debts and provide for the common Defence and general Welfare of the United States . . .

The Constitution gave Congress the power to collect taxes to provide for the general welfare of the United States. "Welfare" is the term used when government and private programs provide money, food, and other necessities for those in need.

There are two types of welfare programs: social insurance and public assistance. Public assistance programs provide benefits based on an individual's need, no matter how much the person has earned or paid in taxes. Social insurance programs pay benefits to people and their families, who have worked and paid certain taxes in the past.

There has been much criticism of the welfare system due to the taxes that people must pay to support such programs, and the belief by

The bread line illustrated above was typical during the Depression of the 1930's. Have your students ask older friends or relatives if they remember those times of hardship.

The complete text of the Constitution can be found in the Appendix, beginning on page 564.

some individuals that people who receive public assistance are not always worthy of the benefits. As a result of such criticism, many experts have proposed alternate programs.

The United States also helps to promote the general welfare by setting up agencies and commissions that help protect the environment and conserve our national resources. As Theodore Roosevelt once said, "To waste, to destroy, our natural resources, to skin and exhaust the land instead of using it so as to increase its usefulness, will result in undermining in the days of our children the very prosperity which we ought by right to hand down to them.

FOCUSING IDEAS

- When governments "promote the general welfare," they provide certain goods and services to people, or to society as a whole.
- Under communism and socialism, governments promote the general welfare by controlling important areas of the economy. Under such systems, freedom of choice is limited.
- The United States has promoted the general welfare by setting up federal programs in health, education, and human development.
- Our government helps to conserve many natural resources, including soil, water, wildlife, forests, air, and mineral resources.

Issues in Civics: Government plays a major role in promoting the general welfare. This illustration shows men who were put to work by government-created jobs in the 1930's. Discuss the consequences of too much intervention by the government in the general welfare.

PRE-TEST

1. What is the meaning of the term "promoting the general welfare"?
2. How have other governments worked to promote the general welfare?
3. What government programs in the U.S. help to promote the general welfare today?
4. What resources does our government help to conserve and protect?

WHAT IS "PROMOTING THE GENERAL WELFARE"?

Objectives: After reading this section, you will be able to:

- Realize there is no easy solution to problems that affect the general welfare.
- Explain the "How?" and "How Much?" questions that are important to the issue of promoting the general welfare.
- Understand that government cannot be responsible for every problem that affects the general welfare.

In this chapter you will read about many ways that your government is working to promote the general welfare of people. Promotion of the *general welfare* occurs when government takes an action that makes some people better off, or able to live better.

Governments generally promote the general welfare in one of two ways. One way is to directly provide goods, services, or even money to people in need. For example, the government provides food and education to the poor, money to older people, and medical care to some people that could not otherwise afford it.

The second way in which the government may work for the general welfare is to pass laws that require people to do things that help others or not do things that hurt others. For example, our government has laws concerning the purity of foods and the safety of aviation and highways. In the same way, our government also has laws requiring people to take responsible action to protect the environment.

The basic problem of "promoting the general welfare" can be shown by an example. You and your classmates would probably agree that it would be a good idea to reduce the number of automobile accidents. Certainly, this is a good thing to do for people and would promote the general welfare.

You could begin to make a list of the things that might be done by governments to stop accidents from taking place. Your list might include some of the following:

Building Vocabulary:
general welfare *(434)* • welfare state *(438)* • depression *(438)* • pension *(439)* • Medicare *(441)* • Medicaid *(441)* • natural resources *(441)* •

Issues in Civics: Discuss the question of whether or not laws that help people or prevent people from hurting others restrict our freedoms. Examples: Smog control, nuclear waste, pesticides/herbicide use, sewage/sanitation control.

1. Put more police on streets and highways to enforce the laws.
2. Lower the speed limit.
3. Place speed bumps on local streets.
4. Not allow cars to be built that will go over a certain speed.

Finally, someone in your class might add: "Let's outlaw all private automobiles." That may seem to be an extreme solution, but one place, Mackinac Island in Michigan, has done actually this. Obviously, they have not had to worry about automobile accidents and deaths.

Now, go back and review the actions that were listed above, plus any that you may have added. You will begin to find problems and additional expenses with each action on the list. If we put more police on the streets, we would have to pay more taxes to hire additional members of the department. Or, we would have to give up other things that the police might be doing instead of controlling traffic, such as solving more serious crimes like burglary and murder.

If we were to lower the speed limits to very low speeds, it would take people much more time to travel from place to place. If we were to put up speed bumps, it would certainly reduce traffic accidents, but it would also jolt our cars and slow us down. We would have to pay more for car repairs because of the wear and tear caused by the bumps.

If we limit the speed that cars can go, then we would have all the problems caused by using more time for traveling, and we would have to give up the freedom of ever going faster under any conditions. Finally, if we gave up automobiles altogether, we would be using the law to greatly restrict our freedom to purchase automobiles and use them in ways that are helpful to us.

People on Mackinac Island must travel by some other means than the automobile, because cars are not permitted.

This would certainly change the way that we live today.

This example shows some of the problems involved in government's trying to act for the welfare of people. It is not a question of whether a purpose is good or bad, or of whether or not it should be done. Certainly, automobile accidents are bad for people and lowering the number of them is a good thing to do. We would all agree to that. So those who would argue against doing those things are not saying that it is not good to do. They would have other questions.

Every time we decide to do something good for the welfare of people, it is going to cost us something in one way or another. It may cost us in tax money, or it may cost us

Ask students what they might do if they were given the mandate of trying to reduce traffic accidents.

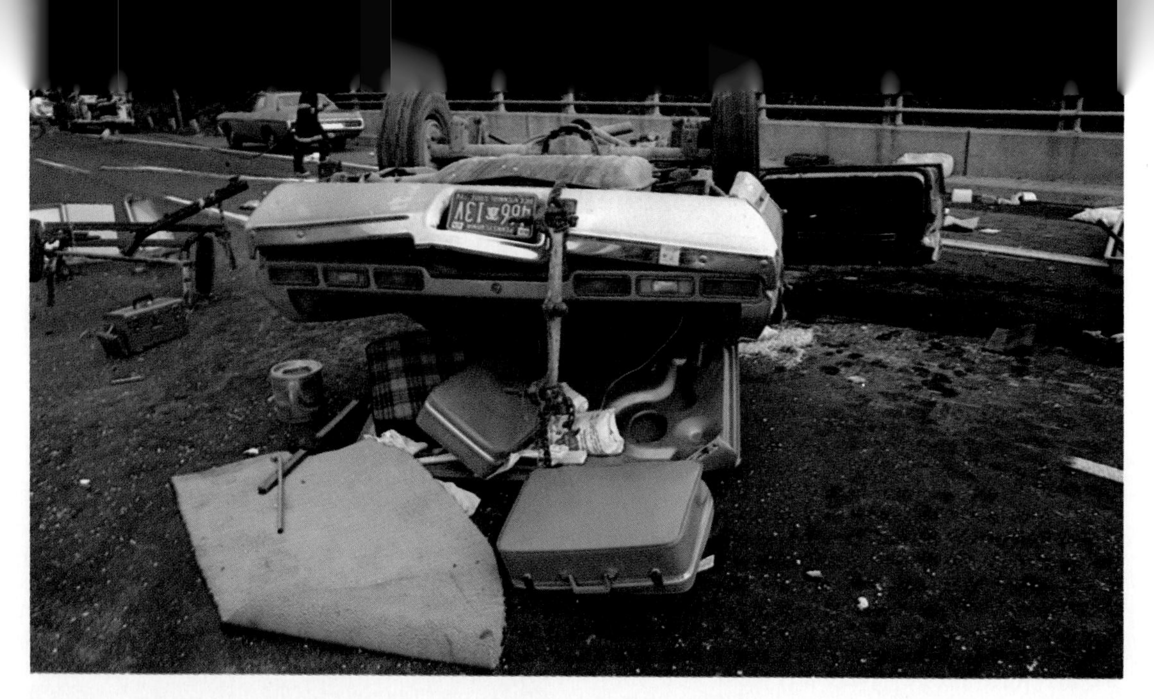

Everyone agrees that car accidents are harmful, but people don't agree on what steps the government should take to prevent them.

in the things that we give up and in the higher prices for the things we buy. Also, once we decide how to do something, we will usually restrict our freedoms in one way or another.

For example, let us look at the fact that the slower automobiles go, the fewer accidents occur. When the speed limit was 70 miles per hour, there were fewer accidents than when people could drive at any speed they wanted. When the speed limit was lowered to 55 m.p.h., the number of accidents was reduced ever further. If we were to lower the speed to 45 m.p.h., we would have still fewer accidents. But if we did so, we would restrict the freedom of people to use their cars and cause them to spend much more time traveling. We could lower the speed limit to 35, to 25, to 15, or finally, as in Mackinac Island, not even allow people to drive cars at all. Each time we took one step further in this way, we would, we can assume, lower the number of traffic accidents. But each time we did this we would also have less freedom and more cost for all the people.

At some point, the loss of freedoms and the cost to people would be more important than the reduction in accidents. So how much of a good thing we can do always comes down to the question of when we reach the point where the cost is greater than the good that is done.

Check for Understanding: Now that you have completed this section, you should be able to answer these questions:

1. Why isn't there one easy solution to the problems that affect the general welfare?
2. Why are the "How" and "How Much" questions important to the general welfare issue?
3. Why can't we expect government to take care of every problem that affects us?
4. Why does the cost of providing extra services for the general welfare often cost everyone more in the long run?

Issues in Civics: Is the 55 mile limit a good idea? It was originally intended not to reduce accidents, but to conserve energy. Does it really reduce accidents? How faithfully do motorists in your state obey it?

HOW HAVE OTHER GOVERNMENTS PROMOTED THE GENERAL WELFARE?

Objectives: After reading this section, you will be able to:

- Explain the purpose of The Code of Hammurabi.
- Define the term "welfare state," and give two general examples.
- Explain some of the advantages and disadvantages of welfare states.

Historic codes

Through all of history, governments have been concerned with the general welfare of people. Each government has, therefore, had to answer the questions of "How do we do it?" and "How much do we do?" Even today, you will find different answers to those questions.

As long ago as about 1800 B.C., one of the earliest-known codes of law included rules for promoting the general welfare. The Code of Hammurabi (a king of the ancient empire of Babylonia) drew many of its ideas from even earlier groups of people. The code was based upon the principle that "the strong shall not take advantage of the weak." It provided laws to govern family and business life, trade, and government. It provided for a fair way to collect taxes. It set a maximum of hours for work. More than 3000 years ago, this code of laws provided for a minimum wage. This idea, that all members of a group should share in the group's standard of living, is an important part of many different governments' systems for promoting the general welfare.

Communism

One extreme type of government involvement in the general welfare is communism. Under communism, the government may decide where persons may live, what their work will be, how many children they may have, and what clothing they will wear. The government also runs the businesses and collects the profits. It supplies medical care, housing, food, and other basic needs to the people. A system like this exists in most communist countries today. In some of them, however, individual freedom of choice has been increasing a little in recent years. Some private enterprise has been encouraged also.

Another system for providing for the general welfare today is socialism. There are many kinds of socialism, but most are based

In Communist countries, medical services such as this Chinese acupuncture treatment are provided by the government.

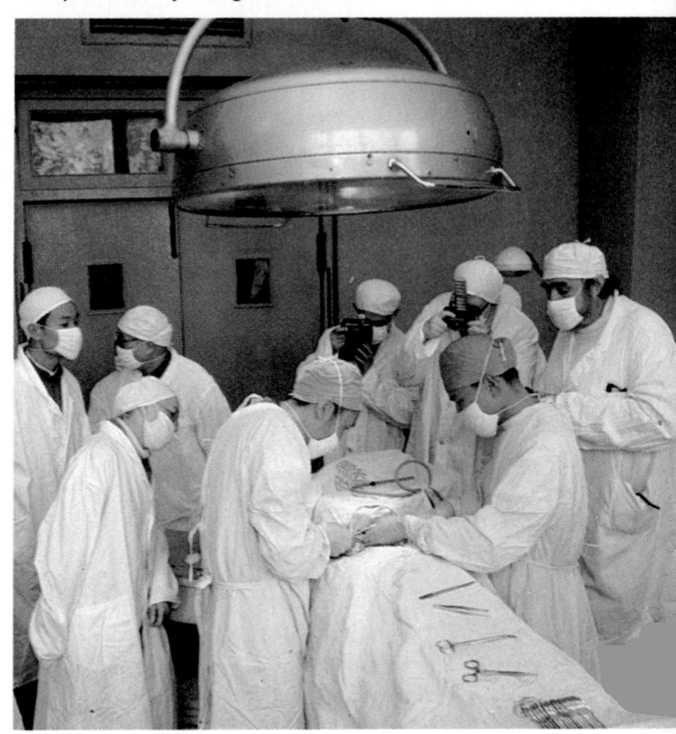

Have a student research and report on the meaning of the terms "Communism" and "Socialism" as they apply to governments.

upon the idea that the national government should control important areas of the economy. Usually, the government owns and operates the major industries and takes care of providing for the physical needs of the people who are citizens of the country.

At one time socialism and communism were considered to be very much alike, in that both are *welfare states.* This idea is no longer common. Most socialists, especially in the non-Communist countries, believe in democratic elections and programs.

In most democratic socialist countries, the social welfare system is extensive. In Sweden, it includes subsidized housing, education, medical care, high retirement pensions, and even, in some cases, subsidized vacations. People are free to make personal decisions without interference from the government. Their democratic participation in government is also very well developed. However, some people feel that in socialist countries there is too much security, and no basis for individual ambition and pride in accomplishment.

Check for Understanding: Now that you have completed this section, you should be able to answer these questions:

1. What was the purpose of The Code of Hammurabi?
2. Why might socialist and communist governments be considered "welfare states"?
3. What are some advantages and disadvantages of welfare states?
4. Why is Sweden's social welfare system considered very advanced?

HOW HAS THE UNITED STATES PROMOTED THE GENERAL WELFARE?

Objectives: After you have read this section, you will be able to:

- Explain why the federal government became more interested in welfare after 1930.
- List the programs that the government provides to promote the general welfare.
- Understand that the problem of medical care and insurance for our citizens is a controversial issue.

Before the 1930's, there were not many federal programs in this country to promote the general welfare. In the great *depression* that began in 1929, the American economy suffered as never before or since. This economic hardship made great changes in the social system in America, and in many other countries as well. Masses of people without jobs, income, food, and shelter presented greater social problems than the towns or even the state governments could handle. Finally, after the election of Franklin D. Roosevelt in 1932, the federal government became involved.

The Preamble to the Constitution states that one of the major goals in the establishment of our government is "to promote the general Welfare." From the beginning, Americans have been dedicated to building a society that is good for all its citizens. Americans have also had a strong tradition of independence. A person's ability to take care of her or his own needs is a source of pride. The beginnings of government programs that provided for jobs, food, and

Discuss in class: What does "subsidize" mean? In countries like Sweden, where do the subsidies come from? Do the people get what they pay for?

Unemployed men in the early 1930's receive a free meal from a private sponsor. President Roosevelt (below), through the Social Security Administration, enacted government programs to deal with the problems of the Depression.

shelter were looked on unfavorably by many people. The problems of the 1930's were so great, however, that the majority believed that the new government programs were necessary, and Roosevelt was re-elected in 1936 with the greatest number of electoral votes in history.

Social Security

The 1930's saw the beginning of the Social Security Administration. The federal government entered the areas of unemployment insurance and retirement pensions. Many people thought that private individuals and business should handle *pensions,* which provided income to people after they retired. However, more thought that there were too many people without jobs and without income after they retired. The government programs expanded.

Issues in Civics: Ask your students if they think there are solutions to the problems the Social Security program has had lately.

Under the G.I. Bill, these veterans of World War II studied at the University of Maryland in 1946.

Other Federal programs

In the 1940's, after World War II, another major increase in government programs occurred. Veterans were provided with help to get jobs, low-cost loans for housing, medical programs, and other benefits under the G.I. Bill. These programs were expanded with the Korean War and the Vietnam War.

In the 1960's, federal programs increased greatly. The War on Poverty was a major new social welfare program with many new benefits and costs. It included food stamp programs, the Job Corps, Headstart, and the Office of Economic Opportunity. Many of these programs helped minority groups and the very young or the very old, and were badly needed. There were problems, however, and the programs were criticized by many people. They also increased taxes at a time when government costs were very high.

The Department of Health and Human Services (HHS) is responsible for many of the federal programs to promote social welfare. HHS includes four major divisions:

1. The Social Security Administration
2. The Public Health Service
3. Health Care Finance Administration
4. The Office of Human Development

The Social Security Administration

This division provides funds for retirement, for survivors of wage earners who have died, and for disabled wage earners. Wage earners and their employers pay into the Social Security funds while they are employed. Benefits are paid when workers are unable to work. Self-employed persons also pay into this fund. Other federal social insurance programs include Unemployment Insurance, Workers' Compensation, and Medicare. Amounts and kinds of benefits vary.

The Public Health Service

This large group includes the Food and Drug Administration (FDA), the Health Services Administration, the National Institute of Health, and many other health agencies. The Food and Drug Administration sets standards of purity and safety, and it enforces laws that govern the contents of foods and drugs. The Health Resources Administration, National Institutes of Health, and Center for Disease Control find disease causes and plan prevention and control programs.

Have students write a paragraph answering the following questions: 1. Were the increased federal programs products of Democratic or Republican Presidents and Congresses? 2. What people would be helped by these programs?

The Health Care Finance Administration

Medicare and Medicaid are under the control of this administration. The *Medicare* program provides hospital care for retired persons and low-cost insurance for some additional medical costs. *Medicaid* provides payments for medical costs of people on welfare.

One of the most hotly debated questions about the general welfare today is that of a national insurance program for medical care. Many of the Western democracies, such as Great Britain, have such insurance, which is handled by the government. The majority of United States citizens have not yet expressed a desire for such a program.

Human Development

This office was set up in 1973. It provides training and opportunities for people who need to develop new or special skills. This includes people from minority cultures, people whose native or first language is not English, young people, old people, and some physically handicapped people. Most of the programs of this kind are run on the local level.

Check for Understanding: Now that you have completed this section, you should be able to answer these questions:

1. Why did the federal government develop programs for the general welfare after 1930?
2. What are some of the government programs that are intended to benefit the general welfare?
3. Why do you think the problem of medical insurance is a controversial issue?
4. What does the Office of Human Development provide for?

WHAT RESOURCES DOES OUR GOVERNMENT HELP TO CONSERVE AND PROTECT?

Objectives: After reading this section, you will be able to:

- List six of our natural resources that we are working to conserve and protect.
- Tell which services and agencies in the U.S. work to enforce environmental standards.
- See why the conservation of natural resources is vital to a healthy society.

Soil

The United States has many natural resources. It contains major *natural resources* of the world. These are the land upon which living things grow, the water which gives moisture to the land, sunlight, and the air. The United States also has a great deal of wildlife and thick, rich forests. Our country has large amounts of minerals, too. These are used in our industries.

When there is farming, the soil becomes subject to erosion. Wind blows away the topsoil. Rain washes it into the nearest stream. The few inches which make up the topsoil are precious, because topsoil is needed to grow things. The United States Soil Conservation Service, with the cooperation of the farmers, has worked to preserve the land.

There was little rain in the Midwest during the 1930's. Many high winds swept the topsoil away. Parts of the Midwest became known as the "dust bowl." To help hold what soil was left, the Soil Conservation Service developed special pellets. They contained drought-resistant grass

Ask a student to report on a program of the Office of Human Development. Who does it help? When was it begun?

Ask a student to give a short report on the local mental health program.

A farm in Oklahoma during a dust storm in the 1930's. The government provided programs to deal with the crisis in the Dust Bowl.

seeds with fertilizer. The service spread them over the prairie lands of the Midwest.

The service taught the farmers to leave plant stubble in their fields instead of plowing it under. This helped to keep the topsoil from eroding and to absorb any rain or snow that might fall. The plant stubble also protected the topsoil when farmlands received too much rainfall over short periods.

Water

Protecting the water requires as much attention as conserving the soil. With other agencies, the Water Resources Board, a branch of the Department of the Interior, and the Army Corps of Engineers work to keep our water systems clean.

The Water Resources Board requires that cities and towns purify all sewage before it is drained into any body of water. Many factories have strong chemicals and other injurious byproducts in their waste. The board insists that factory waste be processed so that it is acceptable to be put into the environment. Then the purified waste can be discharged into a body of water.

The Army Corps of Engineers constructs dams and canals to use some of our water resources. They provide irrigation and hydroelectric power. However, dams change the ecology by covering usable land with water and by diverting the course of many surrounding rivers.

Nuclear resources

Nuclear power plants, if improperly operated, can pollute our water, land, and air. They can emit many kinds of radioactive waste products.

The federal Nuclear Regulatory Commission makes and checks on safety standards for nuclear power plants. However, Pennsylvania's Three Mile Island nuclear reactor crisis of 1979 highlighted the urgent need for further knowledge and increased controls by the commission. This crisis drew national attention to the danger of unforeseen accidents in these power plants.

There are different types of radioactive waste. Short-lived radioactive waste remains radioactive for only a short amount of time. High-level radioactive waste remains harmful to life forms for hundreds of years.

Have a student report on the potential problems of nuclear reactors.

Fort Peck Dam, built in the 1930's, is an example of government efforts to protect water resources.

The Nuclear Regulatory Commission has discovered various ways to dispose of radioactive wastes. For example, it has ruled that nuclear power plants must store shortlived waste until it is harmless and can be put into the environment. The commission requires that nuclear power plants should send high-level waste to reprocessing plants. There, much of the high-level material is taken out to be reused. The reprocessing plants must ship remaining high-level waste to government areas where it is stored.

Disposal of radioactive waste is an urgent problem. Government agencies do not yet have a completely safe or satisfactory solution. For this reason, few reprocessing plants have been built, and some nuclear power research is being postponed.

Wildlife

The United States Fish and Wildlife Service, a branch of the Department of the Interior, is responsible for the management of the wildlife in the United States. Wild animals are observed by the service to record their numbers, food supplies, health, andmigrations. The Wildlife Serv-

The Three Mile Island incident in 1979 prompted people to call for tighter controls on nuclear plants.

Have a student report further on the Three Mile Island reactor crisis.

ice enforces laws passed by Congress to protect endangered species. Hunting restrictions on federal lands are also enforced by the service.

Air

Each human being breathes about 15,000 quarts of air each day. This air is sometimes polluted, and it affects all of us. The National Oceanic and Atmospheric Bureau, a section of the Department of Commerce, and the Council on Environmental Quality work to keep our air and oceans free of pollution.

Both the Atmospheric Bureau and the Council on Environmental Quality examine samples of the air for purity. They require factories to use processes that purify the gases that they release. Gases are broken down into less harmful compounds before they are released into the air. Both agencies have imposed strict standards for the control of exhaust fumes on car makers.

Forests

One of our great natural resources is our forests. The Forest Service, a branch of the Department of Agriculture, looks after our national forests. Forest Service rangers work to guard our forests against fire, disease, and insects. A system of lookout stations, roads, and trails have been built to give rangers access to the forests. The rangers help to preserve the wildlife in forests. They also protect camping areas.

The lumber in the forests is used to build many things our country needs. Trees are a renewable resource. That is, they can be replaced. However, unless the cutting in the forest is done wisely, the forest will not grow again. The Forest Service works with lumber companies to help develop better ways of logging. It also encourages the planting of new trees.

Minerals

The United States has many mineral resources. They are needed by our industries. The minerals upon which the United States depends heavily include petroleum, natural gas, and coal. These are fossil fuels. Millions of years were needed to form these fuels from decayed matter. There is only a limited supply of fossil fuels and all other minerals. Because of this, the Department of Energy seeks to find new sources of energy and to conserve existing sources.

The branches of the Department of Energy help it to carry out its responsibilities. The Energy Information Administration gathers facts on the amount of fossil fuels used. It also figures out how much these energy sources will produce in the future. The Section of Energy Technology directs efforts to create new energy sources. The Section of Conservation and Solar Applications heads programs that try to conserve the use of gasoline, natural gas, and electricity. It also carries out experiments with solar energy, which comes directly from the sun. The Section of the Environment finds out how energy programs affect the environment. Other agencies of the Department of Energy help to plan and regulate uses of energy forms.

Many minerals which are used in the United States must be mined. The Bureau of Mines, an agency of the Department of the Interior, works to keep mining safe and efficient. It sees that minerals are conserved and not wasted when mined. The Bureau of of Mines does research to find mining methods which will increase the amount of minerals mined. It gathers facts on the mining and use of minerals throughout the world. This information is used to help the United States know which minerals are becoming scarce and which are plen-

Ask an interested student to do a report on air pollution in a major United States city (For example—Los Angeles, Denver, Pittsburgh).

Discuss with your class: What local industries are dependent upon fossil fuels? What alternative fuels exist?

tiful. The Bureau of Mines also works to stop mining methods that can be harmful to the environment and to recycle unused minerals.

Check for Understanding: Now that you have completed this section, you should be able to answer these questions:

1. What are some of the natural resources that our country is striving to protect?
2. Which services and agencies in our country enforce environmental standards?
3. Why is the conservation of natural resources so vital to our society?
4. Why are fossil fuels so important to us?

SUMMARY

The Constitution of the United States provides for promoting the general welfare of the people, or taking actions that make people's lives better. There are two basic ways of doing this. One is to provide goods and services directly. The other is to pass and enforce laws that will either improve certain conditions or protect people from certain kinds of harm. Whenever the government takes an action for the general welfare, it must consider the consequences of its action. These are often things like loss of freedoms, higher taxes, and over-regulation. Private agencies and citizens can sometimes do more to promote the general welfare than the government can.

The Code of Hammaurabi, which dates from 1800 B.C., is the earliest example we have of a government's concern for the general well-being of its people. It included laws to govern family, business and government, to collect taxes, to set maximum work hours per week, and a minimum wage. An extreme example providing for the general welfare is found in communist countries, where the government not only provides all the essential services, but also decides which citizens will use the services and how. Another system providing for the general welfare is socialism. There are many kinds of socialism. One example of a socialist country is Sweden, which has both an extensive social welfare system and a high degree of participation in the democratic process.

The 1930's, the years of the Great Depression, saw the beginning of social welfare programs in this country. The Social Security Administration, which was started by President Franklin D. Roosevelt, began providing unemployment insurance and retirement pensions. In the 1940's, government programs started providing benefits to veterans. They were expanded with the Korean and Vietnam wars. Another major expansion of social programs took place in the 1960's. This included food stamps and job programs for the poor. These programs were criticized because they increased taxes. The agency of social welfare in the U.S. is the Department of Health and Human Services. Many state and local agencies offer social programs.

One important way our government works to protect us is by protecting our environment. The Soil Conservation Service teaches farmers to preserve valuable topsoil. Other agencies work to protect our water supply, to regulate nuclear power plants, to protect wildlife, to maintain a supply of clean air, and to encourage the wise use of our natural resources.

Issues in Civics: Did the New Deal help or hurt? Was it necessary at the time? Did it help the country out of the Depression? What effect does it have on the role of government today? Will the government ever return to its "hands-off" social philosophy of the 1920's and earlier?

BUILDING SKILLS IN CIVICS

THINKING SKILLS

1. How do governments promote the general welfare?
2. What are the disadvantages of government involvement in the general welfare?
3. Read through the chapter and locate five factual sentences that support this generalization:

   "Whenever the government takes an action for the general welfare, it must consider the consequences of its action."
4. Edit this paragraph to eliminate any unnecessary information. Then rewrite it and write a title to go with it.

   One important way our government works to protect us is by protecting our environment. The Supreme Court teaches farmers to preserve valuable natural gas. Other courts work to protect our water supply, protect wildlife, and to regulate nuclear power plants. They also encourage the careless use of our natural resources.

VOCABULARY SKILLS

Match each term with the correct definition.

a. pension	c. Medicaid	e. general welfare	g. welfare state
b. Medicare	d. Depression	f. natural resources	

1. Provides hospital care costs for retired people.
2. Provides medical cost payments for people on welfare.
3. A period of very low economic activity and very high unemployment.
4. Payment to a person, or his or her family, after he or she has retired or stopped working due to injury.
5. A method of providing for the general welfare in which the government controls important areas of the economy.
6. The good of the people.
7. Materials that we use in industry that are found in the environment.

STUDY SKILLS—LEARNING FROM NEWS SHOWS

Press conferences, televised debates and interview shows can help you be well-informed about issues and events in our society. Each one allows you to see and hear people in the news give their opinions on the topics of the day.

Activity: As you read the descriptions of each type of program, think about these questions:

1. How are the programs alike? How are they different?
2. How much is prepared ahead of time? By whom?
3. How could each type of program be helpful to you?

PRESS CONFERENCES: Reporters from the various forms of the media are invited to attend a meeting. The meeting usually begins with a statement by the political leader, candidate, celebrity, or concerned party. Questions from the media follow.

TELEVISED DEBATES: Debates are formal arguments in which people representing opposing viewpoints try to persuade others to accept their views. Definite time constraints are established ahead of time and adhered to for the debate. Each side is given equal time to present its viewpoint and to reply to the comments expressed by the other side.

INTERVIEW SHOWS: This format involves a guest and an interviewer. Frequently, a panel of reporters representing the different media will be selected to ask a guest questions about a particular issue or about the guest's past or future actions.

BEYOND THE BOOK

1. Participate in a debate on one of the topics in this chapter. Decide who will speak for the affirmative viewpoint and who will speak for the negative side. Use a variety of sources to gain factual data to support your opinion.
2. Make a poster that will inspire people to help conserve a particular natural resource of our country. Write a slogan to accompany the art.
3. With other class members, present a mock television interview with the head of one of the agencies in this chapter. Prepare your list of questions carefully, using library resources.

CHAPTER TWENTY-SIX TEST

VOCABULARY CHECK

Some of the words below are misused. Write True if the word is correctly used. If not, replace it with a word from the list.

pension	general welfare	depression	natural resource
Medicare	welfare state	Medicaid	

1. Medicaid provides hospital care for retired persons.
2. Pensions provide income to people after they retire.
3. Medicare provides medical payments of people on welfare.
4. Our government strives to improve the welfare state of the people.
5. The U.S. has many natural resources, including land, water, forests, and wildlife.
6. A depression is a method of providing for the people in which the government controls important areas of the economy.
7. Low economic activity and high unemployment are the chief characteristics of a depression.

COMPREHENSION CHECK

1. Which is *not* an example of a way to promote the general welfare?
   a. Providing food for the poor.
   b. Medicare and Medicaid.
   c. The "dust bowl."
2. The two basic ways that government works to promote the general welfare are by: (1) directly providing goods, services, and money and (2)
   a. providing Medicare and Medicaid.
   b. passing laws that require people to do things that help or not hurt others.
3. The Code of Hammurabi was based on the principle ______
   a. "The strong shall not take advantage of the weak."
   b. "All private automobiles should be outlawed."

SKILL BUILDERS—INTERPRETING A TABLE

The *table* below shows the sources of U.S. budget receipts and outlays in 1980. Using this information and also the material covered in Chapter 26, answer the following questions:

1. How does the amount of net budget receipts compare to the amount of net budget expenses.
2. Do you see any departments in the outlay section that you think should be abolished in order to make a more balanced budget?
3. How does the table relate to the concept of promoting the general welfare?
4. Which of the following would be an appropriate caption?
   —The United States has many natural resources.
   —Every time we decide to do something good for the welfare of people, it is going to cost us something.

Sources of U.S. Budget Receipts and Outlays—1980
*(in thousands of dollars)

Receipts	Outlays	
Individual income taxes	Legislative Branch	Justice Dept.
Corporation income taxes	Judicial Branch	Labor Dept.
Social insurance taxes	Executive Office	State Dept.
Other insurance and retirement	Funds appropriated to President	Transportation Dept.
Excise taxes	Agriculture Dept.	Treasury Dept.
Estate and gift taxes	Commerce Dept.	Environmental Protection Agency
Customs duties	Defense Dept.	General Services Administration
Deposits of earnings-Federal Reserve banks	Energy Dept.	National Aeronautics and Space Administration
Miscellaneous	Health, Education and Welfare Dept.	Veterans Administration
*Net Budget Receipts—520,049,919	Housing and Urban Development Dept.	Independent agencies
	Interior Dept.	*Net Budget Outlays—579,011,294

BUILDING WRITING SKILLS

1. Write facts to support the generalization:
   "One important way our government works to protect us is by protecting our environment."
2. Summarize ways that governments have answered the questions of "How do we do it?" and "How much do we do?" when promoting the general welfare.

Chapter Twenty Seven
Facing Our Energy Problem

Document: The Constitution of the United States

Article I, Section 8. . . . "The Congress shall have the Power . . . To regulate Commerce with foreign nations, and among the several States . . .

An eighteenth century poet, William Cowper, once wrote: "Our wasted oil unprofitably burns, Like hidden lamps in old sepulchral urns." Now, while it is unlikely that Cowper was referring to the energy crisis in the twentieth century, it seems like a fitting comment for the problems our country faces regarding oil and related energy concerns.

Congress has acted in facing our energy problem by controlling the prices of oil and natural gas. But even though Congress has the power **to** *regulate* such commerce, the fact that more than 60% of the world's oil reserves lie in the Middle East and North Africa means that we rely considerably on other nations to *supply* this valuable energy source.

However, conservation of our energy supplies can greatly relieve the problems we face. The use of insulation in buildings, public transpor-

The illustration depicts a common occurrence at the gas pumps in 1974. Ask your students if they remember when gas was in limited supply, and discuss what caused the shortage.

tation, smaller cars, and other conservation actions might provide the time needed for additional energy research. Scientists though, have many problems to overcome before new energy sources become practical. And, even if new sources of energy appeared suddenly, United States citizens would still have to use energy efficiently to keep costs down and reduce the environmental problems that almost all sources of energy create.

FOCUSING IDEAS

- Our nation has a limited supply of energy resources. As a result, we must depend on other countries as sources of energy. The actions of these countries directly influence how we spend our money, the amount of energy we use, and the cost of the goods that we buy.
- In order to solve our energy problem we can find new ways to conserve the energy we already have or approach the problem by using general, large-scale or local, small scale methods.
- As a result of the energy crisis, the government took certain emergency steps, and also established the Department of Energy to help manage the nation's energy resources.

This picture shows the gasoline situation today. We *do* have enough gas, but the price has increased enormously. Discuss the ways in which Americans have had to modify their consumption due to reduced energy resources.

PRE-TEST

1. Why is the energy problem such an important issue in our society?
2. What are some of the ways that we can solve this problem?
3. What is the role of government in finding solutions to the energy problem?

WHAT IS OUR NATION'S ENERGY PROBLEM?

Objectives: After reading this section, you will be able to:
- Explain how the U.S. and other countries became so dependent on oil usage.
- Define the role of OPEC and tell which countries originally created it.
- Tell how the energy problem has affected all of our lives.

Each day of your life is involved with the use of energy. *Energy* is the ability to do work or to cause movement. Therefore every time you work or move, you are using energy. Each day you have to eat food, which provides you with the energy to keep moving and working. Without this food as a fuel, your body would soon have no more energy.

In the same way, all the machines that work for us are using energy—such as cars, which move us around. This is also true of those moving machines which produce the goods we use. This includes most of those machines, or turbines, that generate electricity. Each of those machines must use, or burn fuel, if it is to continue to produce energy.

Whenever you perform any kind of physical activity, you are using energy.

In the 1960's, 63% of all the world's energy depended upon oil as a fuel. Some machines used oil made into gasoline, others used fuel oil or diesel fuel.

Building Vocabulary:
energy *(452)* • OPEC *(454)* • conserve *(456)* • synfuel *(458)* • solar power *(459)* • renewable resource *(459)*

Issues in Civics: What sources of energy are now used in the United States? Which is the most economical source of energy to generate electricity?

You can also see how important oil is when you see the many ways that we use the energy provided by oil. We use it to move from place to place in cars and airplanes. It drives many of the machines that work for us. In addition, oil is the raw material from which many plastic goods are made. This gives us a better idea of how much we depend upon oil in our day-to-day world. It also gives us an idea of the problems we face when oil and energy become scarce and the price increases rapidly.

Not so many years ago, oil and the products made from it were very abundant and cheap. Gasoline, for example, sold for around 20¢ a gallon not too long ago; it now sells for more than five times that price. The low price of oil was made possible because of the large supplies of oil that came from overseas. Over 50% of the oil used by this country came from outside of our borders. The same situation was true in other industrial nations throughout the world.

Most of this oil was exported to the United States and industrial nations from nations in the Middle East. The largest producer was the nation of Saudi Arabia. These oil exporting nations could sell oil at a very low price because they had so much of it. Since each of many nations had a lot of oil to export, they all kept their price low. That way they could sell as much as they could produce. As oil was very inexpensive, so was the energy it produced. As a result, the United States and many other countries became large users of oil. It was easier to use more energy to heat our homes than to put in extra insulation. Our automobiles were very fast and heavy, with large motors. They provided a lot of comfort, but they used large amounts of gasoline. People didn't care much, because gasoline was not very expensive.

Oil also produced much of our electricity. Other ways of producing electricity were expensive or had problems. Nuclear power was expensive and was considered to be

Before the energy crisis people didn't worry much about the price of gasoline. Now the cost of fuel is a concern to all of us.

Write a list on the blackboard of machinery and modes of transportation that do *not* use oil directly (and indirectly).

Have students interview parents and other adults to find out what the mileage of American-made cars averaged in the late 50's and in the 60's. How does this compare with today's mileage?

dangerous. Coal had to be moved long distances and could pollute the air when it was burned. Many people didn't worry about other ways to get energy. They knew oil was available at low costs. In this way, we developed a whole way of life based on the use of oil. But it was a way of life that was coming to an end in the 1970's.

OPEC

In 1960, five countries that were producing and exporting oil or petroleum got together in a group. These countries were Saudi Arabia, Iran, Venezuela, Kuwait, and Iraq. They formed an association called *OPEC*, or the Organization of Petroleum Exporting Countries. For years, OPEC did not take any strong action to change the price of oil.

Major Oil-Producing Nations

Nation	Production[1]	% Total World Production
USSR	4,277,800	19.7
*Saudi Arabia	3,613,500	16.7
United States	947,905	4.3
*Iraq	917,610	4.2
*Venezuela	790,955	3.6
China	771,610	3.6
Nigeria	750,075	3.5
Mexico	707,005	3.3
*Libya	652,255	3.0
*United Arab Emirates	623,785	2.9
*Iran	606,630	2.8
*Kuwait	604,440	2.8
United Kingdom	592,030	2.7
*Indonesia	575,605	2.7
Canada	519,760	2.4
*Algeria	369,380	1.7
*Qatar	172,280	0.8

[1](in thousands of barrels–1980) *OPEC nation

By 1970, however, there were thirteen nations belonging to OPEC. Now these countries supplied over half of the world's oil. They also supplied most of the oil imported into the United States. In October of 1973, these nations began to hold back much of their oil. They did not export it to other nations. As they did this, the price of oil began to rise. Other countries, including the United States, still needed oil. As it became scarce, they were willing to pay more for it. The OPEC countres had found that by getting together to hold back the supply of oil, they could raise the price. This would let them make more money. They continued to hold regular meetings during the year. At almost every meeting, the OPEC countries raised the price of oil. In 1973, oil was selling for $3.60 per barrel. By 1980, this price had risen to over $30 per barrel. This higher price and smaller supply was the cause of the energy problem in our nation and the world.

It affected all parts of the country

The shortage of oil and its high cost affected all parts of the country, because this was a nation that had built its machines and way of living on low-priced oil. Now, using all those machines began to cost us much more. Many changes began to occur. Automobiles that had once been large and powerful now became small, with smaller engines. Because agriculture used large amounts of oil to run machines for planting and harvesting crops, the price of food began to rise. Houses became very expensive to heat and many people began to put in insulation. The price of airline tickets went up as jet fuel rose in price. Suddenly, many things that had been inexpensive and available now became high-priced and

On a world map, indicate the OPEC nations. Have a student or students research the following and indicate on the map: which nations export oil to the United States, and how much oil these countries export.

Discuss the ways the oil shortage could affect us (other than inconvenience).

A meeting of the OPEC ministers to determine the price that will be charged by the group in the international market.

gy itself became more expensive. Energy costs caused the price of many other goods to rise.

The problem affected more than just energy and the goods we use. It also began to affect our international relationships. As the price of oil began to rise, we began to send large amounts of money to OPEC countries. The actions of these countries became a very important part of our foreign policy. By cutting off oil supplies, they could take away much of the energy in our country. The energy situation began to affect the lives of every citizen. Today it is still affecting us, and it will continue to do so throughout our lives. How you spend your money, how much energy you use, and what other goods you buy will be influenced by the cost of oil and the energy problem.

Check for Understanding: Now that you have completed this section, you should be able to answer these questions:

1. How have the U.S. and other countries become so dependent on oil usage?
2. What countries formed OPEC, and what is OPEC's role?
3. How have we all been affected by the energy crisis?

WHAT CAN BE DONE TO SOLVE THE ENERGY PROBLEM?

Objectives: After reading this section, you will be able to:

- List several different approaches to solving the energy problem.
- Give specific examples of each approach and tell the advantages and disadvantages of each.
- Explain how the balanced approach would combine various methods to solve the energy problem.

You will read below about three general approaches to solve the energy problem. Some people argue that we should use only one of these approaches. Others say that we should select one as the main approach to

Issues in Civics: Some people argue that OPEC's actions have simply been acceptable free enterprise, in which the goal is to charge whatever price customers are willing to pay. Others say that since oil is so essential, unrestricted price increases should not be allowed to prevail. Discuss this issue.

the problem. Most people, however, would probably agree we will try many ways to provide new sources of energy and to conserve its use. But each of these general approaches has its advantages and disadvantages. This means that we cannot solve the energy problem without having to face some disadvantages.

The conservation approach

Conservation is one approach to the energy problem. To *conserve* means "to save." We save energy by finding ways to get by with less energy than we once used. One example is our automobiles. In 1972, the average new automobile could go 14 miles on a gallon of gas. In 1980, the average new automobile went about 24 miles on a gallon of gas. There are other examples. We can conserve by keeping our homes cooler in the winter and warmer in the summer. We can also put more insulation in them so they are easier to heat.

Industry could also find many ways to produce goods with less energy. One person has estimated that such conservation would allow us to double the size of our economy by the year 2010 without using more energy than we do today. Whether this is true or not remains to be seen, but it does show the importance of conservation.

Conservation has great advantages. It also amounts to real savings in the use of energy. As somebody has said "Conservation is the cheapest fuel of all." If we conserve fuel, we are less dependent upon the OPEC countries. We also have less need to develop other ways of generating electricity.

Conservation also has disadvantages, in that it will change our life style. In most ways we can conserve energy, it will mean a less comfortable and convenient life.

The large-scale approach

Other approaches to the energy problem will look for new supplies and sources of energy. One way to do this is by using what is called a general large-scale solution. These solutions are called large-scale because they would require large plants and industries costing millions of dollars.

These large "gas guzzlers" sit unsold on a dealer's lot because the cost of gas makes them too expensive to operate.

Approaches to the Energy Problem

Conservation

Smaller Cars

Home Insulation

55 mph Limit

Less Heat in Winter

"General, Large-Scale" Solutions

Coal

Synfuels

Nuclear Power

Offshore Drilling

"Local, Small-Scale" Solutions

Solar Power

Wind Power

Water Power

Have the class make a list of products that conserve more energy than they previously did or are specifically designed to conserve energy.

These large plants and industries would then supply energy to large parts of the country. They would seek to replace oil as a source of energy.

There are many examples of these large-scale solutions. One approach would be to use coal. The United States has at least 435 billion tons of coal in reserve that we could use. We could build more coal plants to generate electricity. Some coal and a rock called shale could be made into oil and natural gas. This approach is called *synfuel,* short for "synthetic fuels." Coal now supplies about 7% of our energy needs. It is estimated that in the future it could provide almost 30% and be the largest single source of our energy.

Sources of Our Energy		
Major U.S. Energy Sources (in % of type)		
	1973	1980
Coal	17%	19%
Natural gas	29%	26%
Petroleum	45%	44%
Hydro-electric Power	4%	4%
Nuclear electric power	1%	3%

U.S. Petroleum Imported Directly From OPEC Countries (thousand barrels per day)	
Year	Total OPEC
1970	1,334
1971	1,673
1972	2,063
1973	2,993
1974	3,280
1975	3,601
1976	5,066
1977	6,193
1978	5,751
1979	5,637
1980	4,233

Another "large" solution would be nuclear power. At one time it was thought that nuclear power would eventually be the primary source of energy in the United States. One of the problems with nuclear power is the high cost. The Pilgrim Nuclear Plant near Plymouth Rock, Massachusetts, was first estimated to cost 65 million dollars. The final cost was over 239 million dollars in 1972. Still, in the 1980's, nuclear power is being used in many parts of the country. There are over 70 nuclear power plants in the United States. Together they provide about 9% of all the electricity in the United States.

Another "large" approach to the energy problem is to produce more oil and natural gas. This would involve drilling for oil that is found deep down in the ground. It would also call for drilling off the seashore of many parts of the country. All of this would require huge drilling rigs, both on land and at sea. Many people believe that there is still a lot of oil that can be made available if we will do everything possible to find it. The state of Texas has already produced about 45 billion barrels of oil since oil was first discovered there, but some people believe that there are still about 118 billion barrels to be found in the state. So this country could, by drilling for more oil and natural gas, become less dependent upon the OPEC countries for some time to come.

There are many advantages to using large-scale solutions. Together they could supply this nation with all the energy that it could ever use. Central supplies would always be available. But there are, of course, disadvantages to the large-scale solutions. All of these ways are very expensive. They would give us energy, but the cost would be high. Many of them also involve problems with the environment. The use of coal would

Discuss in class the ecological problems that are caused by strip mining and offshore drilling.

Developing our own sources of oil requires huge drilling operations.

mean mining large areas of what is now wilderness. The burning of coal tends to pollute the air, unless very expensive measures are taken.

Nuclear power is not only expensive, but many people believe it is also dangerous. In 1979, a nuclear plant, Three Mile Island in Pennsylvania, had a radiation leak. No one was killed or hurt in this accident, but it alarmed many people. They were afraid that if a nuclear plant were to leak radiation into the air, it would hurt or kill a large number of people. Since that time, measures have been taken to make nuclear plants safer. Some people in the nuclear industry claim that they have now achieved a very safe way to produce electricity. However, the state of Maine outlawed nuclear plants in 1981, and the people in Austin, Texas, recently voted to sell their shares in a nuclear plant being built near their community.

The small-scale approach

There are other ways to get electricity than by using large, expensive plants. Another way is called the small-scale solution. It is called this because there would be many small plants scattered throughout the country. Each would provide a little bit of energy. There are many examples of small-scale ways to produce energy. *Solar power* is one. We already know that we can produce electricity by the heat from the sun. This cannot now be done in large plants that serve many homes. Instead it would mean that individual buildings would have their own solar plants. Today, some houses heat their water by use of the sun's heat. President Carter installed a solar heating system in the White House.

Some people feel that a large number of these small plants is one answer to our energy problem. Windmills are another example. At one time, in many rural parts of the country, each home had its own windmill to produce energy. Some people believe that, in the future, homes will have windmills to generate small amounts of electricity. But all of these approaches use many small plants. The primary advantage to the small-scale plants is that they will produce much less expensive energy. Most of them will be built right into buildings and houses. There will be no pollution problems. Since they will use nature's energy—sun, wind, and water—we would never run out of supplies. They would depend on a *renewable resource.* Renewable resources are those that have no limits such as coal and oil do, but will be with us forever.

Issues in Civics: What resulted from the Three Mile Island incident? How many people were directly or indirectly affected? How long did the problem last? What caused the leak?

Have a student or students research the cost of home solar heating units and windmills, then report to the class on the initial outlay for a unit.

One disadvantage of this approach is that these energy sources are less reliable. They cannot be used now to produce large amounts of electricity. Many people argue that they will never provide all the energy we would want. They say that we will still have to learn to get by with much less energy or have other energy sources, and just use these sources to provide a part of our needs.

A balanced approach

One government official has said, "The true energy problem is that no one really agrees on what the energy problem is." He meant that people disagree on how to solve the problem.

A balanced approach would use parts of all of these solutions. It would include conservation, so that we would be able to get by with less energy. It would provide some large-scale plants that would substitute coal or synfuels for oil. It would also include drilling with larger rigs for oil and natural gas. Finally, there would be many small energy plants located around the country. They would not provide all of our energy needs, but would help to provide some of them.

Check for Understanding: Now that you have completed this section, you should be able to answer these questions:

1. What are three different approaches to solving the energy problem?
2. What is one specific example of each approach and the advantages and disadvantages of it?
3. How would a balanced approach attempt to solve the energy problem?
4. What happened at Three Mile Island in 1979?

WHAT IS THE ROLE OF GOVERNMENT IN THE ENERGY PROBLEM?

Objectives: After reading this section, you will be able to:

- List some emergency actions taken by our government to conserve fuel.
- List some of the functions of the Department of Energy.
- Name other ways in which the government has tried to act to solve the energy problem.

Emergency action

The energy problem came to the United States very suddenly. It first started in 1973 when the OPEC nations began to hold back supplies of oil and the price rose rapidly. In 1979, Iran became involved in a civil war. At that time, Iran was the second largest oil exporting country. During the civil war, Iran closed down almost all of its oil production. This caused another shortage in the world supply of oil and another increase in price.

In each of these cases, governments took emergency action to help people adjust to the problem. For example, the federal government determined where fuel oil could be used in our country. It made sure that supplies were available to heat homes in the colder northern parts of our country. In 1979, President Carter established temperature controls for most public buildings. In office buildings, schools and other places, temperatures were to be kept low in the winter and high in the summer to conserve

The energy crisis caused increased prices and short supplies. Because of this, car pools became popular. Poll the class on people they know who carpool to work. How does this conserve energy?

energy. The recommended temperatures were 78 in the summer and 65 in the winter. When there was a shortage of gasoline, many state governments established rationing. They set up rules as to who could buy gasoline and how much they could buy. One common system allowed people whose license plates ended in an even number to buy gasoline on even-numbered days of the month. Those whose plates ended in an odd number could buy it on odd-numbered days of the month.

Acting together, the federal and state governments determined who would be given electricity if power companies ran short. They established that hospitals would be given first use, then homes would be next, and then industries. Other government agencies provided people with money to pay their high heating bills if they needed it. In many ways, governments worked together to take those emergency actions that would help people get through sudden problems.

Gas lines like this were a common sight throughout the U.S. during the OPEC oil embargo, because of the shortage it created.

President Carter worked in a sweater after he lowered the White House thermostat.

The Department of Energy

In 1977, Congress created the Department of Energy. Many duties and responsibilities were taken from other departments and given to this new department. It also created some new duties and responsibilities. This department was to help manage the nation's scarce energy resources.

Among the rules set by this department are those that determine the price of natural gas and oil. The department tries to set prices that will lower the hardship for people who must pay for oil. It also tries to encourage people to spend large amounts of money for drilling to discover new oil and natural gas.

Has your school adjusted its maximum/minimum thermostat temperature according to the federal guidelines? Has this made a difference in comfort? Do students think this practice is a worthwhile form of conservation?

The Department of Energy has two other important roles. The first is to increase the conservation of energy. The second is trying to find new ways to develop energy supplies. The Department goes about its job in many ways. It can also provide grants of money to people and to businesses to do this job. One of the important duties of the department is the development of synfuels. In these many ways, the Department of Energy is primarily responsible for helping the government solve its problems.

Other departments, agencies, and laws

Just as the energy problem is involved in all parts of our lives, so are all parts of the government involved in trying to solve this problem. One example is highway speed limits. For many years, each state established its own speed limit on highways. Most states had a limit of 60 or 65 miles per hour, but some states allowed speeds of up to 80 miles per hour on major highways. In certain unpopulated areas there was no specific limit at all; the speed limit was what was "reasonable and proper." In order to conserve gasoline, the federal government established a 55-mile per hour speed limit on all highways. It did this by saying it would withhold money grants to build highways from any state that did not have a 55 m.p.h. speed limit. Now most states use this speed limit to conserve energy, and new cars have a special indication on the speedometer at 55 miles per hour.

You have read that the Department of the Interior controls many federal lands owned by the federal government. Many of these lands are now sources of coal, oil, or shale. Therefore, this department is trying to determine how much of these resources should be used. This is difficult, because increased use for energy will harm the wilderness environment. This is another example of the difficult choices to be made involving energy problems.

The high speed limits that were common before the energy crisis have been eliminated by the national limit of 55.

Have students check with local automobile dealers (American-made cars) to see how close to the 1985 E.P.A. requirements the cars are now.

In 1975, Congress passed the Energy Policy and Conservation Act. One part of this act established the number of miles per gallon of gasoline for new cars. The act calls for the figure to reach 27 miles per gallon by 1985. In this way, the government and the automobile industry are cooperating to conserve energy.

The energy problem is everybody's problem. It reaches all of our lives in many ways. You can see examples of this problem all around you. You have also seen how all governments, in all parts of the country, are working to solve the problem. They are also supported by the people, doing many things to conserve energy. In this way, the energy problem provides a very good contemporary example of cooperation in our republic.

Check for Understanding: Now that you have completed this section, you should be able to answer these questions:

1. What are some emergency actions that have been taken by our government as a result of the energy crisis?
2. What are the functions and responsibilities of the Department of Energy?
3. In what other ways has the government tried to solve the problem?
4. What function does the Department of the Interior serve in regards to energy?

SUMMARY

The U.S. and other countries became heavily dependent on oil because it is used to run machines, it is the raw material that plastics are made of and it is used to produce electricity. Until a few years ago oil was cheap and plentiful so no efforts were made to conserve it. OPEC, the Organization of Petroleum Exporting Countries, changed that. In order to force the price of oil up, they produced less, until in 1980 the price of a barrel of oil was almost ten times as much as it had been in 1973. This forced conservation practices such as insulating houses and setting speed limits at 55 miles per hour.

The three basic approaches to dealing with the energy crisis are: conservation, the large-scale solution, and the small-scale solution. Conservation amounts to a real savings in the use of energy. The general, large-scale solutions require big investments. They are such things as mining more coal, creating synfuel, producing more oil and gas, and using nuclear power. Solar power and windmills are examples of the local, small-scale approach. Each approach has supporters. A balanced approach would use parts of all these solutions.

As a result of the energy crisis, the government took certain emergency steps. They included setting temperature controls for public buildings and rationing gasoline in some states. Had the crisis been worse, the government would have decided who could use electricity and who could not.

The Department of Energy was established in 1977 to help manage the nation's energy resources. The Department of Interior is trying to determine how much the material resources on federally controlled lands should be used as additional energy supplies. The government and the automobile industry are cooperating to increase the miles per gallon of American automobiles.

Discuss in class how much the issue of "mile per gallon" is taken into consideration in buying a car.

BUILDING SKILLS IN CIVICS

THINKING SKILLS

1. What are some of the many ways in which we use the energy provided by oil? In what way did we develop a way of life based on our consumption of oil?
2. What was the cause of our nation's energy problem, and how were we all affected by it?
3. Do you think that solar energy and windmills are realistic solutions to the energy problem in our country? Why?/Why not?
4. Read the paragraph. Then choose the statement that best explains the main idea.

   During the energy crisis, the government determined where fuel oil could be used in our country. It made sure that supplies were available to heat homes in the colder northern parts of our country. The government also set up rules as to who could buy gasoline and how much they could buy.

   a. The government took certain emergency steps to help people adjust to the energy shortage.
   b. The Department of Energy was established to help manage the nation's energy resources.

VOCABULARY SKILLS

Choose the term that best completes each sentence.

conserve	renewable resource	synfuel
OPEC	solar power	energy

1. One way to ______ is to insulate our homes.
2. The ______ countries decided to hold back their oil.
3. The Department of Energy was established in 1977 to help manage the nation's ______ resources.
4. Sun, wind, and water are examples of ______.
5. The approach called ______ is derived from the fact that coal and shale can be made into oil and natural gas.
6. ______ is a form of energy that was used by President Carter in the White House.

STUDY SKILLS—USING THE YELLOW PAGES

Look in the *yellow pages* of your telephone book under "Solar Energy." See what research development companies and commercial firms are in the business of providing access to this alternative energy source. Call or write several of the companies to find out the exact services that are being offered, how much they cost, and the reasoning behind them. If your Yellow Pages refers you to related topics that may provide you with additional information, follow up on these leads as well. After gathering this information, form an opinion as to whether you think the services that a particular company provides are worthwhile. Explain why you either are or aren't in favor of the services or products of different firms and report back to your class.

BEYOND THE BOOK

1. Using information that you and your class members have gotten from the newspaper, news magazines, TV, radio, and public opinion, form two opposing groups and debate the merits and disadvantages of nuclear energy as a power source in our country. Make sure you have facts to back up your opinions.
2. Think about the ways in which you use energy every day. What could you do in your home and school to start conserving it? How would your life be affected by your new approach to energy use?
3. Make a table with three columns in it: one for the energy use of the past, one for the present, and another for the future. List the methods and resources that were, are, and might be used for energy sources in each of these three time periods. Do you think that life is better now than it was in the past? Will it be better or worse in the future? How does energy usage play a part in your answer?
4. Did you know that it costs 55¢ a day to keep a refrigerator running? Do you know how much it costs every time you watch TV or play the radio or use a hairdryer? Write to your local gas and electric company to see if they have any brochures that detail daily electrical expenses.

CHAPTER TWENTY-SEVEN TEST

VOCABULARY CHECK

Some of the underlined words in the sentences below are used correctly, but others are not. If the underlined term is used correctly, write True. If it is not, replace it with the best choice from the list.

synfuel	solar power	renewable resource
OPEC	energy	conserve

1. Some of the oil exporting countries such as Kuwait, Iraq, and Iran, are members of OPEC.
2. When he was in the White House, President Carter installed a synfuel system.
3. A renewable resource is one that will never be used up.
4. One way to conserve energy is through home insulation.
5. There are many ways in which we use the energy provided by oil.
6. The approach called solar power is derived from the fact that coal and shale can be made into oil and natural gas.

COMPREHENSION CHECK

1. Which of these countries is *not* an OPEC country?
   a. Saudi Arabia　c. Kuwait
   b. Canada　d. Iraq
2. Which of the following statements describes the effect that the energy crisis had on our country?
   a. Oil produced much of our electricity.
   b. Many things that had been inexpensive became high-priced and scarce.
   c. The New York Stock Exchange closed its doors.
   d. The price of airline tickets went down.
3. In 1973, oil was selling for ______ a barrel.
   a. $97　c. $30
   b. $12.50　d. $3.60

4. Why did many people start to put insulation in their houses?
   a. Houses became very expensive to heat.
   b. Insulation keeps roofs from leaking during the winter months.
   c. The government ordered all citizens in northern areas to insulate their homes.
   d. The price of insulating one's home dropped considerably during the 1970's.
5. Which of the following is *not* a renewable resource?
   a. wind   c. water
   b. coal   d. sun

SKILL BUILDERS—INTERPRETING CARTOONS

Look at the *cartoon* on page 457. Which of the three approaches looks the most appealing to you? Why? Which approach do you think would be best for our country in the long run? Which do you think would be worst? Make a cartoon of your own showing the ways that you think the energy problem should be solved. Your cartoon should show the following points:

a. How individuals can work to solve the energy problem.
b. How the nation as a whole can help find solutions.
c. What the results might be if we don't come up with a workable solution in the near future.

BUILDING WRITING SKILLS

1. Explain why OPEC has had such a major effect on the energy situation in our country.
2. Write several reasons that explain why the price of food rose as a result of the energy crisis.
3. Write a short paragraph that would go with one of the following titles:
   a. Energy: The Conservation Approach
   b. The Advantages of the Large-Scale Approach
   c. Government's Role in the Energy Problem
4. Why is it difficult for the Department of the Interior to determine how much of our energy resources should be used?

Chapter Twenty-Eight • Education in America

Document: The Constitution of the United States

Amendment XIV, Section 1. All persons born or naturalized in the United States, and subject to the jurisdiction thereof, are citizens of the United States and of the State wherein they reside. No State shall make or enforce any law which shall abridge the privileges or immunities of citizens of the United States; nor shall any State deprive any person of life, liberty, or property, without due process of law; nor deny to any person within its jurisdiction the equal protection of the laws.

Brown v. Board of Education of Topeka: To separate (Negro children) from others of similar age and qualifications solely because of their race generates a feeling of inferiority as to their status in the community that may affect their hearts and minds in a way unlikely ever to be undone . . . We conclude that in the field of public education the doctrine of "separate but equal" has no place. Separate educational facilities are inherently unequal. (Earl Warren, 1954)

"To furnish the means of acquiring knowledge is . . . the greatest benefit that can be conferred upon mankind. It prolongs life itself and enlarges the sphere of existence." (John Quincy Adams, 1846)

The picture depicts the type of educational facility used in Abraham Lincoln's era. Ask students to tell some of the ways that education has progressed since that time.

The Constitution states that each person shall be provided "equal protection of the laws." The right to a free and equal education is now guaranteed to all as a result of several Supreme Court decisions.

By obtaining a good education, an individual is able to select the field that he or she wants to enter regardless of his or her economic background or social position. Many people regard education as a "great equalizer" of all peoples, and as a means of stimulating character development and intellectual discipline.

FOCUSING IDEAS

- The first public schools in the United States originated in the Massachusetts Bay Colony in 1647. Since that time public school systems have been started in every state in the union.
- The federal government contributes to the educational process in America by providing funds for schools and related programs.
- Educational systems are organized on the federal, state, and local levels.
- The three levels of government support higher education through aid in the form of scholarships and loans, and through the creation of state and community colleges.

As the picture shows, people of every background and ethnic group are free to get a good education, but education *can* be expensive. Ask students if they think the government should play a larger role in education by providing more funds to the system.

PRE-TEST

1. What is the historical background of the U.S. educational system?
2. What role does the federal government play in the educational process?
3. In what way are educational systems organized?
4. Through what means does the government support higher education?

WHAT IS THE HISTORY OF EDUCATION IN THE UNITED STATES?

Objectives: After reading this section, you will be able to:

- Explain the development of public schools in the U.S.
- See how education was a factor in unifying our country in its early days.
- Understand the importance of the Land Grant Act.

No matter how rich a country's natural resources, they cannot be developed without human resources. A nation's human resources are its people. Without the talents of business people, scientists, technicians, farmers, and others the United States would not have many of the things it enjoys today.

It is the responsibility of education to develop the human resources of the United States. This challenge includes seeing that all people have a chance to learn how to use the resources of our society to earn a good living. Free education that will produce informed, thinking people has been a concern of our nation since colonial times.

Massachusetts' colonial public schools

In the early days of our colonies, the few schools that were in existence were organized and run by churches. Only about one out of ten children went to these schools. Some wealthy colonists hired tutors to educate their children at home. Others sent their children to England to study. Many children became apprentices to learn trades such as shipbuilding, blacksmithing, or ironmaking.

In 1642 the Massachusetts Bay Colony passed a law stating that parents had to teach their children to read. In 1647 this state began the first *public schools.* These schools taught religion as did other schools. However, they were aided in part by public funds. All towns in which there were at least one hundred families had to start a Latin grammar school. At that time the study of Latin was considered to be the most important part of early education. These schools were attended by students who planned to go on to a college or

Building vocabulary:
public school *(470)* • compulsory *(472)* • segregated *(473)* • real tax *(474)* • personal tax *(474)* • tuition *(475)* • vocational *(476)*

The U.S. is unique in having a history of providing a free public education for every young person. What strengths does this practice contribute to our nation?

A typical grammar school of the colonial period.

university. Boston Latin School, which was founded in Boston in 1635 and is still in existence, was the first Latin grammar school and secondary school in the thirteen colonies.

Education to unify the country

After the United States became a nation in 1776, Americans were concerned with creating a unified country. They believed that education should teach children information and values that Americans should hold in common. Textbooks were written that taught students patriotism and the virtues of honesty, thrift, and hard work. They also helped to give Americans the common spelling and pronounciation of words, and to standardize the American English language and make it distinct from British English. One such textbook was "The Blue-Backed Speller," by Noah Webster (editor of the famous *Webster's Dictionary*) which was published in 1783. It remained in use in schools for more than 150 years and at one time sold over one million copies a year when the population of the entire country was less than twenty million. Another was the series of *Eclectic Readers* by William McGuffey, which were first published in 1837 and are still being used today. These sold a total of over 120 million copies and in the mid-1800's were used in virtually every public school classroom in the country.

Have your students write a paragraph explaining why they think all citizens *must* be educated in a democracy.

Public school systems were started in each state. In 1837 Massachusetts established the first State Board of Education. In 1852 it passed the first *compulsory* school attendance law. This law required children of a certain age to attend school.

Land Grant schools

In 1862 Congress passed the Morrill, or Land Grant, Act. This act granted each state land for establishing agricultural and technical colleges. Sixty-nine colleges were founded under this law. The second Morrill Act, passed in 1890, granted federal money to each state to help support its land grant colleges. These programs have enabled many colleges and universities to expand.

Check for Understanding: Now that you have completed this section, you should be able to answer these questions:

1. How did public schools develop in the U.S.?
2. What part did education play in unifying our country in its early days?
3. Why was the Land Grant Act important?
4. Why do you think compulsory school attendance is important?

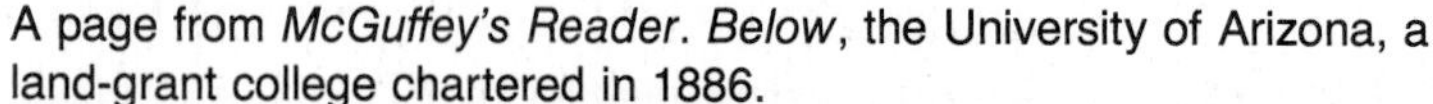
A page from *McGuffey's Reader*. *Below*, the University of Arizona, a land-grant college chartered in 1886.

HOW IS THE FEDERAL GOVERNMENT INVOLVED IN EDUCATION?

Objectives: After reading this section, you will be able to:

- Explain the influence of federal funds on the educational system in our country.
- Explain the result of the Supreme Court case of *Brown vs. the Board of Education of Topeka*.
- List other ways in which education is financed.

Federal government funds and schools

The federal government does not directly control school systems in the states. However, it has funded many schools and school programs. In 1917 Congress passed the Smith-Hughes Act. This act authorized federal funds for career education in agriculture, home economics, and industrial arts. Since 1940 the federal government has greatly increased the money it gives to education. Today almost all public schools depend upon federal funding for portions of their budgets.

The Supreme Court and the schools

The Supreme Court can judge the actions of the nation's school systems. For example, in 1954 the Supreme Court ruled that *segregated* schools were unconstitutional. These are schools that do not have in their student body a mixture of races or religions that is roughly proportionate to the mixture in the general population of the community that the school serves. In the case of *Brown*

A segregated classroom in Georgia in 1942. Before the *Brown vs. Board of Education* decision in 1954, students in many states were required by law to attend segregated schools.

Check with your school district and report to the class how much federal money your school receives. Are there any strings attached to this money?

vs. the Board of Education of Topeka, the Supreme Court stated that segregated schools violated the fourteenth amendment. This amendment says that all people have equal protection under the law. Segregated schools were unequal in quality with other schools. Before this decision, many states had separate school systems for white and black students.

Education is financed in many ways

Most school systems in the United States are large and need large sums of money. There were 88,025 schools in the United States in 1981. The number of students was about 57.5 million. The total amount spent on education in 1981 was $198 billion. Of this sum, more than 10% was funded by the federal government. Clearly most of the money came from state and local taxes. The people spent between $2,000 and $2,200 on each pupil.

Federal funds

All of the money that the federal government gives to education must first be approved by Congress. The funds are then passed to the Department of Education. In 1979, the Department of Education was established as a separate part of the President's cabinet. It distributes most of the federal education funds to the states.

State funds

States manage the money they give to their school districts in different ways. For example, some states furnish all textbooks and supplies.

In all states there are many aid programs for schools and students. One program provides money to buy meals for children of low-income families. The aid program also includes teaching and health aides.

Howard Jarvis' Proposition 13 has affected educational funding throughout the country.

Local funds

Most of the public money spent on schools comes from *real* property taxes, or taxes on houses, buildings, businesses, and land. In some places schools are also funded by *personal* property taxes, or taxes on property owned by people which is not real estate.

In recent years the property tax in many places has increased rapidly. There has been a great deal of protest because of this. A law was recently passed in California, known as "Proposition 13," that limits the amount of property taxes to be paid. It therefore also limits the amount of money available for funding public education. Many people have agreed with Proposition 13 because it restricts taxation, while others object to it because it seriously reduces school budgets.

Make a "pie" graph showing how the education dollar is spent. How much for salaries, equipment, textbooks, etc.?

Private funds

Many schools are financed by private funds. These are private schools and are at all levels of education. They include preschools, elementary and high schools, and colleges. They receive their money in many ways. Much of it comes from *tuition,* which is a fee paid by a student to attend that particular school. Other funds may be in the form of gifts from supporters of private education or from people who have formerly attended the school. Some private schools are associated with churches or religious groups. In these cases the church or religious group may collect donations to support the school.

Check for Understanding: Now that you have completed this section, you should be able to answer these questions:

1. What influence has federal funding had on our nation's educational system?
2. What was the result of *Brown vs. the Board of Education of Topeka*?
3. What are some other ways in which education is financed?
4. What is the role of the Department of Education?

HOW ARE EDUCATIONAL SYSTEMS ORGANIZED?

Objectives: After reading this section, you will be able to:

- Tell how the federal government is involved in the organization of our educational systems.
- See the function of the state boards of education.
- Understand the importance of local boards of education.

Three different levels of government are involved in various ways with our elementary and secondary school systems. The three are the federal and state governments and the local communities.

Federal level

The federal government created the Department of Education to deal with our school systems on a national level. This department works to improve the quality of education throughout our country. It gives funds to the states and gathers facts about education from various parts of the country.

The migrant student program is also managed by the federal government. This

The children of migrant workers such as these are aided by a federal education program.

Issues in Civics: Taxes are too high. Discuss how we could eliminate government waste and reduce taxes.

program keeps track of the school records of the children of migrant workers. These are farm workers who move from one part of the country to harvest crops according to the season. The school in which the children are presently enrolled can find out what they have been studying through this program.

State level

Some states have a State Board of Education and a State Commissioner or State Superintendent of Education. These people set some standards for the local school systems and administer the state school funds. The structure of the board and the role of the commissioner may vary from state to state.

Each state manages a program for people who did not finish high school. There are special classes for them. These people can earn a high school diploma, which is required on many jobs. This program is called G.E.D. and gives a General Education Diploma.

Local community level

Locally, public schools are directed by a Board of Education. This consists of members of the community who are elected for set terms. The terms may vary in each state. The members serve without pay. It is the board members' duty to make rules for the school system and hire the system's administrative staff. This staff in turn runs the school system. It hires teachers, decides on the school courses, and keeps up the school properties and grounds.

School districts in different areas may vary. They usually cover the elementary and secondary schools. In some parts of our country, there is one board for the elementary schools and another for high schools. In large cities there may be several school districts, each with a board and administrative staff.

Some school boards have started *vocational* high schools. These are high schools where a trade may be learned. There are also vocational programs in general high schools that provide business education and industrial training. In these programs students work in their trade part time while attending high school. Each school that has a vocational program also has an advisory committee. This group is made up of people from the school district. They counsel students and help manage the vocational program.

At the local community level people can have the most influence on the schools and on education. In local elections people may vote for the school board members they want. People select the members of the State Board of Education in general elections. In some states the State Commissioner of Education is also elected. The people in local school districts can control the amount of money given to schools in their districts. They can vote to pass or reject school bond programs, which provide funds for local schools. The PTSA, or Parent Teacher Student Association, is a group in which people work to improve education.

Check for Understanding: Now that you have completed this section, you should be able to answer these questions:

1. How is the federal government involved in the organization of our educational system?
2. What function do state boards of education perform?
3. Why are local boards of education important?
4. What are vocational schools, and what function do they serve?

Interview a local school board official and report to the class what the most recent issues before the board have been. Discuss these issues.

Issues in Civics: How should education be financed? Discuss the present system in comparison with proposed alternatives such as the voucher system.

HOW DO GOVERNMENTS SUPPORT HIGHER EDUCATION?

Objectives: After reading this section, you will be able to:

- See how the federal government supports higher education.
- Understand how state colleges are funded.
- Explain how community colleges are established and what their functions are.

All governments contribute

As our society becomes more advanced and work depends more on the use and understanding of computers and other machines, a greater number of jobs require people to have college educations. For this reason, more and more Americans are attending colleges and universities. The federal and state governments and local school districts all support higher education in various ways.

Federal support of colleges

The federal government gives aid to most colleges and universities. The amount of money it gives depends on certain factors. The factors are the number of students in scholarship and loan programs and the number of graduate students and veterans at the college. The federal government also gives aid to colleges for many of their research programs.

The federal government supports all of the military service academies. These are four-year colleges that are run by the various branches of the military to prepare people to become officers. These schools include the U.S. Military Academy (West Point), the U.S. Naval Academy (Annapolis), the Air Force Academy, and the Coast Guard Academy.

State colleges

Each state has at least one state college or university. Many state colleges in larger states have a system of schools. Such a system has branches of the main college in different parts of the state. State colleges

The U.S. Military Academy is located on a bluff above the Hudson River north of New York City.

Education is all-important if students are to become responsible citizens.

are mainly funded by state and local taxes. Student tuition or fees are not the major source of income for these colleges. State colleges are managed by boards of trustees or, in some states, regents appointed by the governors of the states. In other states they are elected by the people.

State universities offer four-year programs in many fields of study. Students must meet certain academic requirements. Then they are given bachelor's degrees. At some universities students can continue to study to obtain advanced degrees.

Private universities

There are many private colleges and universities in the United States. These schools are often funded by tuition payments or by gifts. Many of these schools also receive some grants from the federal government for special projects. In addition, some states will help pay the tuition of students.

Community colleges

The people of a local school district may vote to establish a community college. The community college is funded by local taxes. There is a board of trustees to manage the college. This board is elected by the people who live in the community.

Community colleges offer various types of programs. Most programs can be completed in two years. Vocational education and on-the-job training in many fields are offered. Many students can start work on a bachelor's degree at community colleges. Adult education courses are also given at these schools. Community colleges give associate's degrees when their two-year programs have been finished.

Developing thinking people

The Constitution states that the people are the main source of power in our govern-

U.S. Public School Statistics

	1870	1900	1920	1940	1960	1980
Population 5–17 years of age	12,055	21,573	27,556	30,150	43,881	49,010
% Pop. 5–17 enrolled	57	71	78	84	82	88
*High School Graduates		62	231	1,143	1,627	2,825
Average School Term (in days)	132	144	161	175	178	178
*Teachers, librarians; Men:	78	127	93	195	402	795
Women:	123	296	565	681	985	1,557
Percent Men:	38	29	14	22	29	33
Average Annual Teacher Salary	$189	$324	$2,130	$3,894	$8,213	$14,700
Expenditure per capita total pop.	$2	$3	$24	$48	$138	$374

*in thousands

Point out to students that one hundred years ago only a little over half of the school-age population actually attended schools, because of the greater presence of children in the labor force. Now nearly all school-age children are in attendance. What effect has this change had on the nature of the schools?

ment. The right to vote on issues concerning our country gives us this power. People can read and use radio and television to inform themselves about important issues. Studying the political issues is necessary to make sound decisions and to vote wisely. Thomas Jefferson realized the importance of informed, involved citizens when he said, "Educate and inform the whole mass of people. No other sure foundation can be devised for the preservation of freedom and happiness."

The federal government works to promote education in the United States. It tries to give all children an equal opportunity for a good education. It funds educational programs when they help the whole nation.

Check for Understanding: Now that you have completed this section, you should be able to answer these questions:

1. How does the federal government support higher education?
2. How are state colleges funded?
3. How are community colleges established, and what kinds of courses do they offer?
4. How might government also help support private universities?

SUMMARY

Free education has always been a concern of our nation. The first public schools in the U.S. originated in 1647 in the Massachusetts Bay Colony. After the United States became a nation in 1776, Americans became even more concerned with the education of the general public. They saw the educational process as a means of unifying the new country through the teaching of common values.

The federal government contributes to the educational process through the funding of schools and related programs. The Supreme Court also has an effect on the educational process in that it makes judgments on the actions of school systems.

Education is financed through federal, state, and local funds. All federal government funding must first be approved by Congress and is then distributed to the states by the Department of Education. Local funds come from taxes on real property, while funding for private schools comes from tuition.

The three levels of government are involved in our educational system in many ways. The federal government created the Department of Education to deal with our school system on a national level; many states have boards of education to set their respective standards; and locally, public schools are directed by local boards of education.

The federal, state, and local governments all support higher education in many ways. The federal government gives aid in the form of scholarships and loans and supports all of the military service academies. Each state has state colleges funded by state and local taxes, and many local districts have established community colleges.

The federal government realizes the importance of educated, informed citizens to the preservation of our republic, and it does everything in its power to give United States citizens an opportunity to acquire a good education.

Issues in Civics: Jefferson and Lincoln, among others, believed that a system of general public education was the best way to produce responsible, free-thinking citizens. Critics of our educational system, on the other hand, say that it instead conditions people to accept society as it is rather than to strive for improvement. Discuss this issue.

BUILDING SKILLS IN CIVICS

THINKING SKILLS

1. How were children educated in the early days of our colonies?
2. What was the compulsory school attendance law? Which state was the first to pass it?
3. Why did the federal government create the Department of Education?
4. Read the following paragraph. Then select the generalization that applies to it.

   No matter how rich a country's natural resources, they cannot be developed without human resources. A nation's human resources are its people. Without the talents of business people, scientists, technicians, farmers, and others, the United States would not have many of the things it enjoys today.

   a. Natural resources are the most important elements of our society.
   b. Although natural resources are vital to a society, human resources are what make a country thrive.
   c. There should be more vocational programs for farmers, technicians, and others.

VOCABULARY SKILLS

Match each term below to the definition that goes with it.

a. tuition
b. public school
c. segregated
d. vocational
e. compulsory
f. real tax
g. personal tax

1. Massachusetts established the first one in 1837.
2. These are schools that do not have a mix of races and religions in their student body.
3. These are high schools where a trade may be learned.
4. This type of school attendance law required children of a certain age to go to school.
5. These are taxes on houses, buildings, businesses, and land.
6. These are taxes on property which is not real estate.
7. This is a fee paid by a student to attend a particular school.

STUDY SKILLS—USING DIFFERENT SOURCES OF INFORMATION

Vocational schools teach high school age students various trades to prepare them for the working world. There are also vocational programs in general high schools that provide business education and industrial training.

Activity: Using different *sources of information* that you obtain in your school office, library, or telephone directory, make a list of the vocational programs in your school district. Use books, catalogs, newspapers, and advertisements to gather information. What skills are taught in the programs? Would you be interested in learning one of the trades that is taught in one of these programs? Why?/Why not?

BEYOND THE BOOK

1. The first textbooks that were written in our country taught students patriotism and the virtues of honesty, thrift, and hard work. Think about the textbooks that you use in *your* classes. Other than teaching a specific subject, what values or concepts do the books try to get across to you? Do you think that the books try to persuade you to think in a certain way, or are they neutral? Give examples for your opinions.
2. Interview a friend or family member who is employed in a profession that interests you. Find out what that person's educational background is and how he or she decided on that profession. After learning the requirements for a particular field, form an opinion as to whether it is a profession that you would be interested in pursuing.
3. In 1980, almost 9% of the 16- and 17-year-olds in our country were high school dropouts, although statistics show that people who do not finish high school are severely limited in terms of securing good jobs. Make a poster that might inspire a would-be high school dropout to stay in school. You might divide the poster into two sections to show one situation featuring a high school dropout and another showing someone who has completed his or her education.

CHAPTER TWENTY-EIGHT TEST

VOCABULARY CHECK

Choose the term that completes each of the following statements.

1. Today, almost all ______ depend on federal funding for portions of their budgets. (amendments, colonies, public schools)
2. ______ school attendance laws require children of a certain age to go to school. (Agricultural, Compulsory, Segregated)
3. A ______ is a tax on housing, businesses, buildings, and land. (real tax, personal tax, income tax)
4. ______ is a fee paid by a student to attend a particular school. (Tuition, Real tax, Personal tax)
5. A ______ school is a high school where a trade may be learned. (compulsory, vocational, public)
6. If a school is ______, it does not have a mix of races and religions. (segregated, vocational, compulsory)
7. A ______ is a tax on property owned by people which isn't real estate. (real tax, personal tax, income tax)

COMPREHENSION CHECK

Write True if the question and answer match. If not, write an answer to the question.

1. Other than by tuition, how do many private schools receive financing? —Other funds may be in the form of gifts from people who have formerly attended the school.
2. What power does the right to vote on issues concerning our country give us? —It gives us the power to judge the actions of the nation's school systems.
3. What are personal property taxes? —They are taxes on houses, buildings, businesses, and land.
4. What is a General Education Diploma? —It is a diploma given to people who attend a special state-managed program for those who did not finish high school.
5. What is one function of the Department of Education? —The Department helps give Americans the common spelling and pronunciation of words.

SKILL BUILDERS—INTERPRETING TABLES

Before you look at the *table* below, answer the following questions based on your general knowledge and on information you have retained from the text. After you have looked at the table, go back and answer the questions again. How accurate were your original answers?

a. In what field were the most Bachelor's degrees conferred in the past few years?
b. Name a field that very few people have received degrees in recently.
c. Name a field that few people received Bachelor's degrees in, but a lot of people received Master's degrees in recently. Why do you think this is so?

Field of Study	Bachelor's*	Master's*
Agriculture and natural resources	22.7	4.0
Biological Sciences	51.5	6.0
Business and Management	161.3	40.5
Communications	25.4	3.3
Education	136.1	110.6
Engineering	55.7	16.4
Health professions	59.4	14.3
Law	.7	1.0
Library Sciences	.7	6.9
Mathematics	12.6	3.4
Military Sciences	.4	.45
Physical Sciences	23.0	5.6
Public affairs and Services	37.2	20.0
Social Sciences	113.2	14.6
Theology	6.3	3.3

(*in thousands—1978)

BUILDING WRITING SKILLS

1. Write a paragraph explaining the issues in the *Brown vs. Board of Education of Topeka* case and tell why it was so important to our nation's educational system.
2. Choose two of these four pairs of words and write sentences explaining the difference between them.
   a. real property taxes—personal property taxes
   b. public schools—private schools
   c. state colleges—private universities

Chapter Twenty-Nine
Religion in America

Documents: The Constitution of the United States
Jefferson's First Inaugural Address (March 4, 1801)

Amendment I. Congress shall make no law respecting an establishment of religion, or prohibiting the free exercise thereof; or abridging the freedom of speech, or of the press; or the right of the people peaceably to assemble, and to petition the government for a redress of grievances.

"Freedom of religion; freedom of the press, and freedom of person under the protection of the *habeas corpus,* and trial by juries impartially selected. These principles form the bright constellation which has gone before us, and guided our steps through an age of revolution and reformation. The wisdom of our sages and the blood of our heroes have been devoted to their attainment. They should be the creed of our political faith, the text of civil instruction, the touchstone by which we try the services of those we trust; and should we wander from them in moments of error or alarm, let us hasten to retrace our steps and to regain the road which alone leads to peace, liberty, and safety.

The picture shows the early settlers of our country pursuing their quest for religious freedom. Discuss the concept of religious freedom with students and ask them how important this freedom is in *their* lives.

The complete text of the Bill of Rights can be found in the Appendix on pages 575–76.

Freedom of religion means that an individual has the right to believe in and practice whatever faith he or she chooses. The quest for religious freedom was one of the major reasons why Europeans first settled in this country. The Puritans and other groups came to America to escape religious persecution.

Today, freedom of religion is still an issue in America. There are various court rulings that interpret the First Amendment to the satisfaction of some people, but to the extreme displeasure of others. In any case, the Supreme Court has ruled that all states must uphold the principles of the First Amendment and not promote or give special treatment to any one religion.

FOCUSING IDEAS

- Freedom of religion assures individuals of their right to believe in and practice the faith of their choice.
- Separation of church and state means that the government can not set up a church or pass laws that favor one religion, aid all religions, or prefer one religion to another.
- There are limits on religious freedom, in that a group or individual may not practice a religion that calls for breaking the law.

Issues in Civics: There has been much conflict in recent years regarding the separation of church and state. Ask students how they feel about this issue and how they think it can be resolved.

PRE-TEST

1. What is meant by the concept of religious freedom?
2. What is the history of freedom of religion in our country?
3. Why is the separation of church and state such an important issue?

WHAT IS FREEDOM OF RELIGION?

Objectives: After reading this section, you will be able to:
- Define freedom of religion.
- Tell how the law places certain limitations on religious freedom.
- Understand why the state may decide to interfere in some religious cases.

"Congress shall make no law respecting an establishment of religion, or prohibiting the free exercise thereof . . ."

Since long before recorded history, religion has been important in people's lives. In most societies religions grew a little at a time generation after generation. However,

These are examples of various houses of worship in our country.

Building Vocabulary:
state religion *(487)* • religious freedom *(487)* • separation of church and state *(489)* • parochial school *(489)* • evolution *(491)*

Do students feel that they have complete religious freedom in this country? Why or why not?

in some societies a strong ruler or group of rulers would decide what form religion should take and impose certain restrictions on religious worship. The people of these societies would have to follow these restrictions without question.

We call a religion that is enforced by the government a *state religion*. Almost all the countries of Europe had state religions at one time. People were allowed to worship only in the state church. Those who did not obey were sometimes arrested, tortured, or killed.

When people are ruled by what someone else wants, some of them will always continue to try to make up their own minds. When the printing press was invented in Europe, more books could be read by many of the people. People's ideas could spread faster. They could find out about more things and think more for themselves. In England many decided that they did not agree with the state religion. Some hid their different beliefs. However, many endured the consequences of refusing to conform to the state religion.

King Henry VIII established a state religion—the Church of England.

Some left their homes to live in a land where they could worship in their own ways. The Puritans left their homelands and came to the New World so that they could worship as they wished. Strangely enough, they were not willing to give others in the Massachusetts Bay Colony the same *religious freedom* that they had wanted for themselves. Rhode Island, Maryland, and Pennsylvania were the only colonies that allowed religious freedom in the beginning. In fact, the colony of Rhode Island was first settled by people who left Massachusetts because of the restrictions on religious freedom there. Other colonies punished or expelled people whose beliefs differed.

By the time the Constitution was written, the desire for religious freedom had become widespread. A declaration of religious freedom was the first item in the Bill of Rights. However, some of the states continued to control religious practices until the Fourteenth Amendment was adopted. It begins, "No state shall make or enforce any law that shall abridge the privileges or immunities of citizens of the United States; . . ." Religious freedom means that people may believe as they choose. They may practice their beliefs as long as they do not violate the law. Our government supports no church and taxes no one to support a church.

Limitations on freedom

There are limits to religious freedom, however, If a person's religion calls for breaking a law, that part of the religion cannot be

Have interested students research the provisions in the Maryland Toleration Act of 1649, which was designed to protect Maryland from religious intolerance.

Discuss with students the ways in which other nations in other times have handled the subject of religion. Why do students think there have been so many cases of intolerance throughout world history?

Roger Williams, here meeting with Indian chiefs, left Massachusetts to found Rhode Island, a new colony with religious freedom.

practiced. If a religion calls for stealing or for hurting another person or the person's property, that will not be allowed. Such laws are not passed to prevent worship but to maintain law and order. While people are free to worship as they please, they must obey other laws as well.

A religious group may not have meetings that harm or disturb people who live nearby. In one case a church was ordered by the court not to have loud music late at night.

In recent years, as well as in the past, some new religious groups have formed around magnetic leaders. If a leader gains such control over the followers that their own welfare is threatened, the state must decide whether or not to interfere. This has been done in cases where medical treatment (such as setting a child's broken bones) has been refused for religious reasons. Is it a right of the government to interfere in such cases? The question is argued from other sides.

The Amish people observe very traditional religious and social practices.

Have an interested student do research on the Amish people and the customs that they practice.

Check for Understanding: Now that you have completed this section, you should be able to answer these questions:

1. What is meant by the term "freedom of religion"?
2. How does the law limit this freedom?
3. When might government decide to interfere in a religious case?
4. Do you think the government should have this right? Why?/Why not?

WHAT DOES SEPARATION OF CHURCH AND STATE MEAN?

Objectives: After reading this section, you will be able to:

- Explain the meaning of the separation of church and state.
- See the ways in which government and religion relate to each other.
- Tell how the Supreme Court has influenced the issue of religion and its place in public schools.

The *separation of church and state* is an important principle in religious freedom in the United States. As Supreme Court Justice Hugo Black said, it means that "Neither a state nor the federal government can set up a church or pass laws which aid one religion, aid all religions, or prefer one religion to another."

Government recognition of God

Religious expressions occur throughout the fabric of our government. Our coins and paper money carry the motto, "In God We Trust." Our elected officials take the oath of office with a hand on the Bible, and conclude with the phrase, "So help me, God." Each session of Congress is opened with prayer. The Supreme Court opens each session with the prayer, "God save the United States and this Honorable court." Chaplains of various religions are appointed and paid by the government to officiate in Congress and the armed forces, including military hospitals.

Religion and taxation

All property used for religious purposes is tax exempt. This includes places of worship, education, and recreation as well as the dwelling furnished by a church for its leaders. All religious schools, hospitals, and church retirement homes are not taxed by the government. Also, gifts to these institutions may be deducted from income tax.

If parents choose to send children to religious schools instead of public schools, they may do so. However, they must still pay taxes for support of the public schools. The state governments require *parochial schools*, those operated by religious institutions, to teach the same basic courses that are required of other schools in that state.

Government regulation of conduct

Sunday closing of businesses is a very old custom. The idea came originally from the Bible, which said that every seventh day should be a day of rest. From the 13th century there have been laws in Europe concerning work on Sunday. The laws were passed under Christian governments to allow workers to attend church services, and to "keep the Sabbath holy." Now it is simply accepted as providing a necessary break in the weekly routine. Now, however, although offices and smaller stores still close on Sundays, some large stores remain open seven days a week.

Issues in Civics: Many people feel that Sunday closing laws are antiquated. Ask students if they feel this way. Are there Sunday closing laws in the area where they live?

The government has banned polygamy (having more than one husband or wife) from the United States, even though it has been strongly encouraged by at least one large religious organization.

Religion in the public schools

The Supreme Court has had to decide many hard questions. Some of these have concerned religion and the public schools. Is it legal to ask children to salute the flag in school, if it is against their religion to salute an image such as a flag? Can schools legally ask that prayers be said or that the Bible be read in a classroom? Is a public school system able to give a part of the school day for religious teaching? Can it do so at the school itself, or outside the school property?

The Supreme Court has ruled that all of these actions violate the First Amendment. However, the court has also ruled that the Constitution does not prohibit non-devotional use of the Bible, teaching about scriptures, or studying about the similarities and differences between religious groups in classes in literature or in history.

The Supreme Court has also ruled that parochial schools may receive governmental aid as do the public schools. This includes transportation by bus, free lunches, free milk, and medical inspection and services. Also, scholarships and tuition from governmental funds may be used in religious schools.

In 1925, the State of Tennessee passed a law prohibiting the teaching in public schools of theories contrary to the belief in the creation of human beings as related in

The "Scopes Monkey Trial" dealt with a religious issue that is still with us today, the teaching of the theory of evolution.

Ask students how they feel about prayer in the classroom. Do they think it should be mandatory, or do they think it should be banned? Or should everyone have the freedom of choice?

the Bible. John T. Scopes, a biology teacher, was tried for teaching the Darwinian theory of *evolution*, and convicted. The theory got its name from Charles Darwin, an English scientist who stated that humans and other animals developed, or evolved, gradually over millions of years from lower forms of life. The Supreme Court later released him on a technicality. This famous case drew much attention to the topics of freedom of speech and religion.

Check for Understanding: Now that you have completed this section, you should be able to answer these questions:

1. What is meant by "separation of Church and state"?
2. In what ways do government and religion inter-relate?
3. How has the U.S. Supreme Court influenced the role of religion in the public schools?
4. What are parochial schools?

SUMMARY

Throughout history, religion has been a vital part of people's lives. Societies in every culture have placed various religious restrictions on their people. The Puritans came to the New World so that they could worship as they wished, and the first settlers of several other colonies were people who were striving for religious freedom.

The writers of the Constitution recognized the importance of the issue and made the declaration of religious freedom the first item in the Bill of Rights. Although our government does not support any one church, it does place certain limits on religious freedom if it feels that the public welfare is threatened by a particular religious practice.

The separation of church and state is an important part of religious freedom because it means that the government cannot pass laws to aid one religion over another. Nevertheless, religious expression is a part of all our lives through the recognition of God as expressed by our government in various ways.

Although property used for religious purposes is tax exempt, parents who send their children to parochial schools are still required to pay taxes in support of public schools. The government has also passed laws regulating conduct on certain days, although those restrictions are gradually being weakened.

The Supreme Court has had to make many crucial decisions regarding the question of religion. Some of these cases deal with the teaching of religious doctrine in the public schools, the question of governmental aid to non-public schools, and the relationship of free speech and religion in the educational system.

U.S. Religious Groups

Group	Members (approx.)
Protestant	73,000,000
Roman Catholic	50,000,000
Jewish	6,000,000
Eastern Rite	4,000,000
Other	2,000,000
	Total: 135,000,000

This represents about 60% of the total U.S. population

Discuss the evolution controversy with your students. How do they feel about this issue? Do they think that it was right for John T. Scopes to be tried for teaching this theory in a public school?

BUILDING SKILLS IN CIVICS

THINKING SKILLS

1. What used to happen to people in Europe when they did not agree to worship in state churches?
2. Do you think it's strange that the Puritans weren't willing to give other people religious freedom? Why?/Why not?
3. What does "freedom of religion" mean?
4. What are some of the limits to religious freedom? Do you think they are reasonable? Why?/Why not?
5. What does the "separation of church and state" mean?
6. Read the paragraph below. Then select a title.

   Each year the President proclaims a day of Thanksgiving and a national day of prayer. Our coins and paper money carry the motto, "In God We Trust." Our elected officials take the oath of office with a hand on the Bible, and conclude with the phrase, "So help me, God."

   a. State Religions in America
   b. The Recognition of God by the Government

VOCABULARY SKILLS

If the underlined terms in the statements below are used correctly, write True. If not, replace them with the correct term.

state religion	parochial	separation of church and state
religious freedom	evolution	

1. John T. Scopes was tried in the 1920's for teaching <u>state religion</u> in the public schools.
2. A religion that is enforced by the government is called an <u>evolution</u>.
3. The Supreme Court has ruled that <u>parochial</u> schools may receive governmental aid as do the public schools.
4. The <u>separation of church and state</u> is an important part of religious freedom.
5. <u>Religious freedom</u> gives citizens the opportunity to practice the religion of their choice.

STUDY SKILLS—USING SKIMMING TECHNIQUES

In order to find information on a particular subject, it is not always necessary to read an entire book, article, or even a whole chapter of a text. *Skimming* is a technique that allows you to pick out key words that pertain to the subject you're researching without reading an entire selection. For example, in order to find information on parochial schools in Chapter 29, you need only let your eyes pass quickly over the chapter until you find the word "parochial." Then you can go back to the beginning of the paragraph that contains that word and find the facts that you need.

Activity: Practice your skimming techniques by using an encyclopedia to research the Buddhist religion. Don't read the entire section; just skim through the "Religion" article quickly until you find the key word.

BEYOND THE BOOK

1. In Chapter 29, there is a table on the major religions in the U.S. Use an almanac, encyclopedia, or other reference book to make a table of the major religions of the world. See how the estimated number of members in each religion in the world compares to the number of members in the U.S. Are you surprised by your findings? Why?/Why not?
2. How often does the subject of religion come up in our daily lives? In order to get a general idea about this question, you might pay particular attention to radio news stories, TV reports, information in news magazines, and to conversations of those around you for one particular week. Every time you hear the subject of religion discussed, write down the source and the context of the discussion. At the end of the week, see how many times you heard religion mentioned and what particular issue was being mentioned. Was there a lot of repetition? Do different sources discuss different aspects of the subject?

CHAPTER TWENTY-NINE TEST

VOCABULARY CHECK

Match each term in the list with the definition or statement that it refers to.

parochial	state religion	evolution
religious freedom	separation of church and state	

1. The theory that says that man and other animals developed gradually over millions of years from lower forms of life.
2. A religion that is enforced by the government.
3. This means that people may practice their beliefs in any way they choose as long as they do not violate the law.
4. It means that the government may not set up a church or pass laws that aid any one religion over another.
5. These are schools that are operated by religious institutions.

COMPREHENSION CHECK

1. True or False: The Supreme Court has prohibited schools from studying about the similarities between religious groups.
2. True or False: Sunday closing of businesses is a custom.
3. True or False: Our coins and paper money carry the motto, "In God We Trust."
4. Read the two categories below. Then put each of the six statements under the correct heading.

   Categories: a. Limitations on Religious Freedom
   b. Religion and Taxation

   Statements:
   —A religious group may not have meetings that harm or disturb other people.
   —Gifts made to religious institutions may be deducted from income.
   —Parents who send children to religious schools must pay taxes for support of public schools.
   —A certain religion may not call for stealing from or hurting another person.

SKILL BUILDERS—INTERPRETING PHOTOGRAPHS

Look at the photograph on page 488 that shows characteristics of the Amish way of life. What evidence can you see in the picture that reflects the following facts about the Amish people? Which facts surprise you?

a. The Amish teach separation from the world.
b. Their members are forbidden to go to war, swear oaths, or hold public office.
c. Amish men wear beards and wide-brimmed hats and the women wear long dresses without ornamentation and bonnets.
d. The Amish limit education to the eighth grade.
e. They till the soil with horses, and their rules forbid the use of telephones and electricity.
f. Their religious doctrine requires farming and personal simplicity as a way of life.

BUILDING WRITING SKILLS

1. Write a paragraph detailing some of the decisions that the Supreme Court has had to make concerning religion.
2. Put the statements below into the correct sequence and then write them in paragraph form to match this title: The Evolution Controversy.
   a. The Supreme Court released Scopes on a technicality.
   b. John T. Scopes was tried and convicted for teaching evolution in the public schools.
   c. The State of Tennessee passed a law prohibiting the teaching of theories contrary to the creationist beliefs that were stated in the Bible. They did this in 1925.
   d. English scientist Charles Darwin theorized that man evolved over millions of years from lower forms of life.
3. Write a question to go with this answer:
   It was adopted to ensure that no state would make or enforce any law that would abridge the privileges or immunities of the United States.
4. Do you think religion should be taught in the public schools? Why?/Why not?

UNIT SEVEN TEST

A. Look at the photo above of a Fourth of July celebration in Brooklyn in 1915. Then answer the following questions:

1. How do you think the educational system has changed since the early 1900's—the period of the photo above? Do you think people receive better educations today, or worse?
2. What federal programs have been created since the eraly 1900's to promote the general welfare? Do you think these programs have improved the quality of life? Why or why not?
3. Through the use of modern energy sources, we have many advantages that people in past generations did not have. But there are also disadvantages that result from modern technology. What are they? Do you think people in our generation are happier as a result of technological advances? How has our environment been affected by science?

B. Write a paragraph explaining how you feel about the use of nuclear resources in this country. What are the advantages and disadvantages of nuclear power?

Unit Eight · Our Free Enterprise Economy

The economy of the United States is a free enterprise, or capitalist system. Citizens choose the items they wish to buy and sell, and businesses compete to sell their goods at the lowest possible prices. We all play a vital part in our economic system. because as consumers we vote, in a sense, for the products and services that are on the market. Although the economic situation is always changing, one constant that consumers must be aware of is the importance of being well-informed. In this way, both buyers and sellers can take advantage of the opportunities our economy affords us.

The illustration symbolizes the condition of free competition that exists in our economy, including both U.S. and foreign companies. Ask students to think of other industries that have a large number of sellers. Would the U.S. auto industry be healthier if we had only one nationalized company?

Chapter Thirty
How Our Economy Works

Document: The Constitution of the United States

Amendment V. No person shall . . . be deprived of life, liberty, or property, without due process of law; nor shall private property be taken for public use, without just compensation.

The right of individuals to own property is one of the fundamental principles of the free enterprise system in America. For, without the right to own land, one cannot own the means of production. In a free enterprise system, people may use their property as they see fit and profit from it.

Although our country has a free enterprise system, the government has always had some influence on the economic system. The government regulates foreign trade, provides for our defense, and makes economic changes that attempt to improve the welfare of the masses.

Profits and losses also play an important part in a free enterprise economy. A business will only profit if it provides a good that people are willing and able to buy. So, the desire for profit is a way of assuring consumers that sellers will provide the goods that people want and need.

The picture shows an example of a major industry in America. Ask students if they think that government should take more or less interest in the affairs of big business. Why do they think so?

In any free enterprise system, people have the same basic problem: making choices as to the quantity and type of goods to produce. They must also decide which of the goods is most important to them, and who, of all the people who demand certain goods and services, should get them. Whatever the outcome of their decisions, people who live in a free enterprise system at least have the satisfaction of knowing that they made their own choices.

FOCUSING IDEAS

- Nations need an economic system to provide citizens with income to spend, and goods and services to spend their money on.
- Other countries function under traditional, planned, or combined economic systems.
- A free market economy involves the right to free choice and ownership of private property, as well as a competitive market system.
- All economies face the problems of recession and inflation, which often result in unemployment and loss of production.

This picture shows an example of small businesses in America. Ask students if they think our system of competitive markets is fair to the small business owner. Why or why not?

PRE-TEST

1. Why is the economy such an important part of our lives?
2. Why do nations need a sound economic system to survive?
3. How do other economic systems work?
4. How does a free market economy work?
5. What are some of the problems that face all economies?

WHY DO NATIONS NEED AN ECONOMIC SYSTEM?

Objectives: After reading this section, you will be able to:

- Define the term "economic scarcity."
- Understand that an economic system must decide what goods to produce.
- See that the question of who gets the goods that are produced is important to all of us.

Can you imagine three trillion dollars? If you were to write that in figures, it would be $3,000,000,000,000. If you were to spend that much money, you would have to spend $100,000 every minute for the rest of your life. Obviously this is a lot of money. But three trillion is less than the size of our economy in one year. This means that over three trillion dollars worth of goods and services are bought and sold in the United States in each year.

People do most of that spending as consumers, when they buy goods and services. Goods are things that you buy for your use. A service is when you pay someone else to do something for you. But government and business also buy goods and services, and foreign customers buy some things in our economy. Together, they all spend more than three trillion dollars a year.

The economy is not only large, it is also an important part of your life. You depend upon the economy whenever you buy anything. You also depend upon the economy when you work and earn money. Our economic system provides you and your family with income or money to spend and the goods and services that you may spend money on.

Scarcity

Make a list of all the things you know of that are free—all those things that do not cost you, your family, or others any money. You will find some very important things on that list—the air you breathe to live, friendship, beauty, and others. But you will also find that most goods and services are not on that list, because they have a price and cost money. All these things not on your list are made available by the economy.

Those things that are not on your free list will have a price and cost money because they are scarce. There is not as much of them available as people want. It is the job

---

Building Vocabulary:
economic scarcity *(501)* • traditional/planned economy *(503)* •
free enterprise *(506)* • private property *(507)* • competitive market *(507)*
mixed practice *(510)* • recession *(510)* • inflation *(512)*

Ask students if they think that availability of a certain good decreases or increases its price on the market? Why is this so?

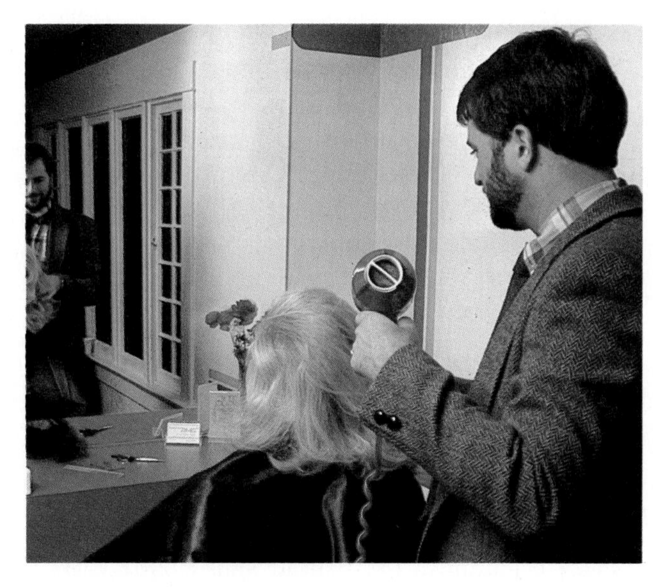

Economic activity consisting of buying *goods,* such as these foods, and *services,* such as this hairdresser is providing.

of the economy to provide people with all goods that are scarce. This means that economics has to do with the way that scarce goods are made available to people.

Most goods and services have economic scarcity. *Economic scarcity* means there is less of something available than people want or need. Both the amount of something available and the amount that people want determine economic scarcity. For example, air is free. People need air in order to live. But no matter how much we need, there is always plenty available. Therefore air is not scarce. There is also quite a bit of food available in the world. But there is less food than people want. So food is scarce and has a price. You can see that part of scarcity depends upon how much of something people want. Another part of scarcity is how much is made available.

A line of people waiting to buy food at a supermarket in Gdansk, Poland.

Have students discuss a time when they saw long lines of people waiting in line to take advantage of a good or service.

We need an economy because of the limits that are provided by nature. There is not enough land, metals, energy, natural resources, workers, and machines to bring us all of the things that we want. Since natural things are scarce, all goods and services are also scarce. But we must find some way to see that we have the things that we want, even though they are scarce.

Nature forces us to choose

Because of the limits of nature, we have to choose among all the goods that we want and need. We need a system that tries to make those choices that will be best for the largest number of people. Just as the government in the United States has a system of elections and parties to arrive at national choices, so do we have an economic system that provides for us to make choices. There are two major choices or questions that an economic system has to answer. Both of these involve choosing how to use the scarce means made available by nature.

Deciding what goods to produce

Perhaps the most important question in an economic system is "What goods to produce?" There are many kinds of goods that we could produce with what is given us by nature. We could use our land to grow wheat and nothing else. Or we could use it to grow wheat, corn, vegetables, and other food that we eat. We could also use it to build homes and other buildings. But if we use it for just one of these things, we cannot use it for other things at the same time. The same is true of all other natural resources. If we use them to produce anything, we have given up using them to produce something else. This means that every time you buy something in a store, the economic system has decided to produce it and make it available to you.

Who gets the things that are produced?

Another important question for an economic system is to decide who gets the goods that are produced. For you, this is a very important question. The answer as to how many goods you get is determined in many ways, such as by the amount of money you or your family has to spend and by what goods your family provides to you. You can see that who gets what is produced is important to you.

Goods are produced in a free society according to what the people want to buy.

You can also see that how these questions are answered by the economic system is very important. The answers determine what kinds of goods you will be able to buy. They also determine how much of those goods you, as an individual, can expect to have as your own.

Can students think of any goods or services that they want or need that are not available on the market? If so, what are they?

Check for Understanding: Now that you have completed this section, you should be able to answer these questions:

1. What does the term "economic scarcity" mean?
2. Why must an economic system decide what goods to produce?
3. Why is the basic question of who gets the goods that are produced important to all of us? How is this question answered?
4. In what way does nature force us to make a choice among the goods we need?

HOW DO OTHER ECONOMIC SYSTEMS WORK?

Objectives: After reading this section, you will be able to:

- Explain the theory behind a "traditional economy" and understand what its limitations are.
- Understand why it is that a totally planned economy is not really possible in a free country.
- See how a governmental system and an economic system can work together to solve the economic questions that all societies have.

Traditional economies

One type of economy is called a *traditional economy*. This means that the two basic economic questions or choices are decided by the history of the society or group. What will be produced today is the same as that which has always been produced within that group. Once goods have been produced, they will be distributed to people according to the laws of the group. Things will not change because they are traditionally done that way.

The American Indians' tribal society was an example of a traditional economy, as shown in this 19th-century painting by George Catlin.

Lead a discussion on the pros and cons of a traditional economy. If we had this type of economy in our country, how do students think their lives would be different?

The Communist countries of Eastern Europe have planned economies in which a person's job is determined by the government.

Many years ago, nearly all economies were traditional economies. This was in the days when people were organized into tribes, clans, or kingdoms. Year after year they did the same things that they had learned in the days before. Early American Indian tribes were traditional economies. If the tribe farmed, they continued to farm for a living. If they were hunters, they continued to hunt for a living. In each tribe, it was carefully determined what people would do. If you were born as a male, you would become a farmer or a hunter. If you were a woman, you would probably prepare food and make cloth. The goods from the crop or the hunt were distributed in various ways among the tribe.

One of the problems of the traditional economy is that things change very little and the economy grows very slowly. Only a few goods are available and these are carefully rationed out among the tribe. Because of this lack of change in ways of doing things, very few traditional economies are left in the world today. These are usually found in more isolated places where technological changes have not taken place.

Plannned economies

A *planned* economy is one in which the government determines the answer to the two basic economic questions. A group within the government determines what goods will be produced and who shall receive them. All communist countries are planned economies. The plan is established by a group of national planners. They first decide what goods shall be produced. They start with a list of all goods that will be produced within the year. They then de-

Have students name several countries which have planned economies. If they have ever visited any of these countries, what similarities and differences did they note between their economy and ours?

cide what resources will be needed. This means they determine where people will live and work, how land will be used, and what natural resources are needed to provide goods and services.

The planners also decide how the goods will be distributed among the people. They determine how much income each person will have. Then if they want more people to have a particular item, they set the price very low. If they want an item restricted to a few people, they will make the price very high. They command, through the government's plan, what shall be done in the country's economy.

As you can see, a planned economy is a very complex thing. It takes many months and many people to put the plan together. It also takes a large amount of control to be sure that the plan is carried out. The size of a plan and the need to control it cause two problems. The first problem is to be sure that everything goes right. A mistake or problem can cause the whole plan to go wrong. And when the plan goes wrong, many goods and services are not available to people.

A second problem of a planned economy is the need to control it. For the government to control the plan, it must control the actions and the work of people. It must be able to command people as well as goods. If the government cannot tell people how to work, where they should live and work and what goods to consume, then it cannot plan the economy. This means that a planned economy does not allow very much freedom for its citizens.

Combining the political and economic systems

As you read about the traditional and planned economies, you might also have noticed something about their political sys-

Members of the Polish union Solidarity demonstrate in support of farmers' demands for an independent trade union. The government denied the request.

Have an interested student research the struggle of Lech Walesa and the Polish union Solidarity.

tems. A traditional economy works in a tribal system with tribal leaders and accepted ways of behavior. A planned economy must have a totalitarian state that is able to dictate much of what people are to do. Governments and economic systems must work together. This means that the economic system as well as the government determines how much freedom people have. Governments establish your right to have freedom of speech and religion, fair trials, and free elections. Economic systems establish your freedom to work as you choose and to buy those goods and services that you want. In this way, your freedom depends upon both the governmental system and the economic system under which you live.

Check for Understanding: Now that you have completed this section, you should be able to answer these questions:

1. What is a "traditional economy" and what are its limitations?
2. Why couldn't a planned economy exist in a free country?
3. How can governmental and economic systems work together?
4. Why were almost all economies "traditional" in the past?

HOW DOES A FREE MARKET ECONOMY WORK?

Objectives: After you have finished this section, you will be able to:

- Understand the components of a free market economy.
- See the importance of competition in a free market economy.
- Explain why every economy has mixed practices.

Freedom of choice

A *free enterprise* economy is sometimes called a *free market* economy. This is because questions of economic choice are answered by people being free to choose what to buy and sell.

You will not be surprised to find that your economy works much like your government. There are necessary parts to a free government. Some of these are the right of citizens to hold free elections, to cast secret ballots, to organize political parties and to express their ideas. You will now find out that there are certain necessary rights and responsibilities that you must have to enjoy economic freedom. It is the combination of political freedom and economic freedom that makes you a free individual.

If people are to have this economic freedom, there are two necessary parts. These are free choice and private property. Without them, there is no true free market.

Necessary parts

Free choice is one necessary part of a free economy. You are free to choose where you will work in this country. You are also free to choose the type of goods that you will buy and decide if you are willing to pay the price asked. There is no group of planners determining where you will work and what you will buy.

Free economic choice is much like free elections. To be politically free, people must be able to select those officials who will best represent them. Economic freedom means that one is able to select the goods, the store, and the brands that one prefers. When citizens exercise their free choice, it is like voting for those particular goods and services. They tell the market

Issues in Civics: Although our economy is a free market system, we still have some restrictions. Do students think this is a contradiction in terms? Why or why not?

In a free market economy shoppers make their own decisions as to which variety of a product they prefer.

that they want one thing and not another. For example, people in the United States changed from wanting large cars to wanting small cars that used less gas. They voted for small cars by buying them. They voted against large cars by not buying them. As a result of exercising their free choice, they were able to get the size of cars they wanted. Just as free elections are important in a democracy, so is free economic choice important in a free enterprise economy.

Private property

Private property is another necessary part of the free market economy. *Private property* means that most things are owned by idividual people rather than by the government. You may think of private property as being only people owning land, factories, and business firms. But private property is important to people who do not own any of these things. People have the right to own their homes and other goods that they buy and use. They have the right to own their labor, skills and tools. In this way, the right of private property gives people the right to sell their work to whomever will hire them. They may quit one job and go to a better job if they wish to do so. This is not always possible under a planned economy.

Private property is necessary in a free economy if people are able to exercise free choice. If you do not own your own business, you cannot determine what it is you will sell. If you do not own your labor or skills, you cannot determine how you will use them. In the same way, if you are not able to own the things you buy, they are not very much use to you. Without private property, there is very little economic freedom.

Competitive markets

Competitive markets mean there are many buyers and sellers for goods and services. When you decide to select one store or shop over another and one brand over another, you are being a competitive buyer. You are

Ask students to name several advantages of owning private property. How would their lives be different if the government owned private property?

Three Kinds of Economic Systems

Traditional Economy

Planned Economy

Free Market Economy

trying to get the thing that is best for you at the best price. In the same way, when people search for a job and go to work, they are sellers. They are trying to sell their work to the company that will pay them the best income. When many people are trying to buy the same thing and many people are trying to sell that thing, that is a competitive market.

Through competitive markets people are free to make the economic choice of "what will be produced." Once people began to choose their cars on the basis of trying to save gasoline, they were saying they wanted smaller cars. They bought fewer large cars, and soon not many of these cars were available for sale, because the companies could no longer produce them if they could not sell them. Through competition people determined the type of cars they wanted.

These same competitive markets also allow people to choose "who will get what is produced?" This question is answered by how much people have to spend and are able to buy. And that depends on the income that a person or family might have. We receive income from selling labor and other things. This means that the amount of income we have is determined by the price of what we sell. As a student, your labor is likely to sell at a low wage per hour. That is because you have few skills that have high value or price. As you learn more skills and receive more training, you will become more valuable to other people and earn a higher income.

Our incomes are set by the value of what we sell in a competitive market. The more we are able to contribute to the economy, the more people will want what we sell.

Mixed practices occur in China, which has a planned economy, but allows private farms. In the U.S., the government agreed to Chrysler Chairman Lee Iacocca's request to guarantee private loans for his company to stay in business.

Discuss with students the effect that foreign competition has had on the auto industry in this country. How has this competition affected our economy?

Then our incomes will be higher. If the size of our incomes are established by the economy, then the choice of who receives the goods that are produced is determined by the working of the economy.

Mixed practices

You will very likely have some questions about the free economy. You may be saying "But I am not always free to choose." There are taxes that have to be paid. There are things that governments provide. There are things, such as telephones and electricity, that have only one seller, not many.

Every economy, even a free market economy, has some *mixed practices*. Our economy includes some features of traditional economies and of planned economies. For example, many people make part of their living by receiving tips, such as waiters and waitresses and taxicab drivers. They do not determine how much they will be paid for their services. This is an example of a traditional economic practice in the United States. We pay these people through tips simply because that is what we have done in the past.

In the same way, some parts of our economy are planned or controlled. You must pay taxes for the things that governments provide you. This is done by the command of the government, even though it is a freely-elected government. When gasoline was in short supply and rationing was used, that was a command practice. The actions of the government determined when you could buy gasoline and how much you could pay.

Each economy has some mixed practices

In communist or planned economy countries, there are some elements of free markets. Some farmers are allowed to determine which crops they will raise, and they are able to sell them at whatever price people will pay. Democratic socialist countries make a great use of mixed practices. Parts of their economies are command, or planned. The rest work through a free market. Even if all economies are somewhat mixed, the important thing is how the main part of the economy works.

Check for Understanding: Now that you have completed this section, you should be able to answer these questions:

1. What are the components of a free market economy?
2. Why is competition so important in such an economy?
3. Why does energy economy have some mixed practices?
4. What are some examples of command practices in the U.S. economy?

WHAT PROBLEMS DO ALL ECONOMIES FACE?

Objectives: After you have read this section, you should be able to:

- Name the two major problems facing all economies.
- Explain how a recession can start and what the results of one often are.
- Explain why it is difficult for governments to solve an inflation problem quickly.

Recession

All economies face two major problems: one of these is *recession*. A recession occurs when an economy fails to work in making

What do students think of traditional economic practices such as tipping? What other evidence of mixed practices can they see in our economic system?

jobs and incomes available to people. Many people are out of work, or unemployed. Then they are not able to buy the goods and services that they need and want. Life becomes very difficult for those who are unemployed.

A recession will start when people stop buying large numbers of goods. When people quit buying goods, then workers are no longer needed to produce them. These workers lose their jobs and become unemployed. But as people lose their jobs and income, they have less money to spend. Unemployed people stop buying goods and services. This means that still other people will be out of work and have less to spend. Things may continue to get worse and worse.

For example, in 1980 and 1981, people stopped buying large numbers of automobiles and other things. This started a recession, and at one time over 8 million workers were unemployed.

A recession will continue until buying or spending starts again. Then things turn around the other way. As goods are being sold, workers will go back to work. They will also begin to spend as they now have jobs and incomes. Soon things will return to normal. The economy will be working well once again.

Recessions may start for many reasons. In a free market economy, people may decide to save their money, or they may not want some goods that are being produced. In a planned economy, the planners may make a mistake. Or, the people may not want what the planners provide. But in all economies, a recession has two bad results. One of these is, of course, unemployment. People

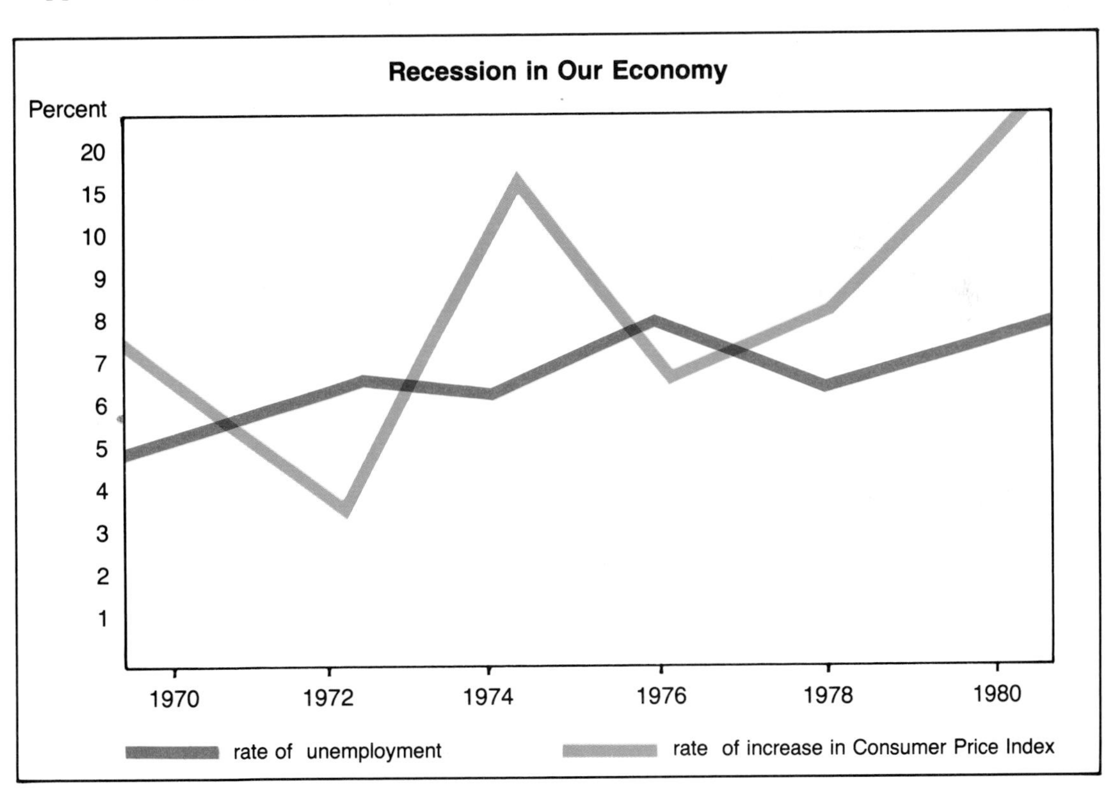

Ask an interested student to do research on the current unemployment rate. How does this rate compare to the 25% unemployment during the Depression?

are out of work, with little to spend and face suffering and hardship.

A second bad result is that the economy has lost production. If people, machines, and factories are not working, the economy has lost forever what they would have produced. Even when they go back to work, they cannot make up for the time that was lost.

Inflation

Inflation is another problem that all economies face. *Inflation* means that the prices of all goods and services are rising rapidly. If you see many of the things you buy costing more from month to month, that is inflation. Inflation has become a very serious problem in the United States and other countries. For example, one dollar today will buy less than half of what it would have bought ten years ago. In an inflationary economy, the prices of goods keep rising, and they become more expensive to buy almost every year.

Inflation starts because there is more money available than there are goods. Inflation has been defined as "too much money chasing too few goods." After all, when you see the price of something, the price tells you how much money you will trade for that thing. As more money becomes available, people are willing to trade more money for goods. This causes prices to rise and inflation to occur.

You may be wondering why governments allow inflation to continue. You might ask "Couldn't a government reduce the amount of money available, and stop inflation?" The answer is: "Yes, a government can stop inflation, but doing so would also cause other problems." If a government were to make less money available, this would not cause prices to fall immediately. At first,

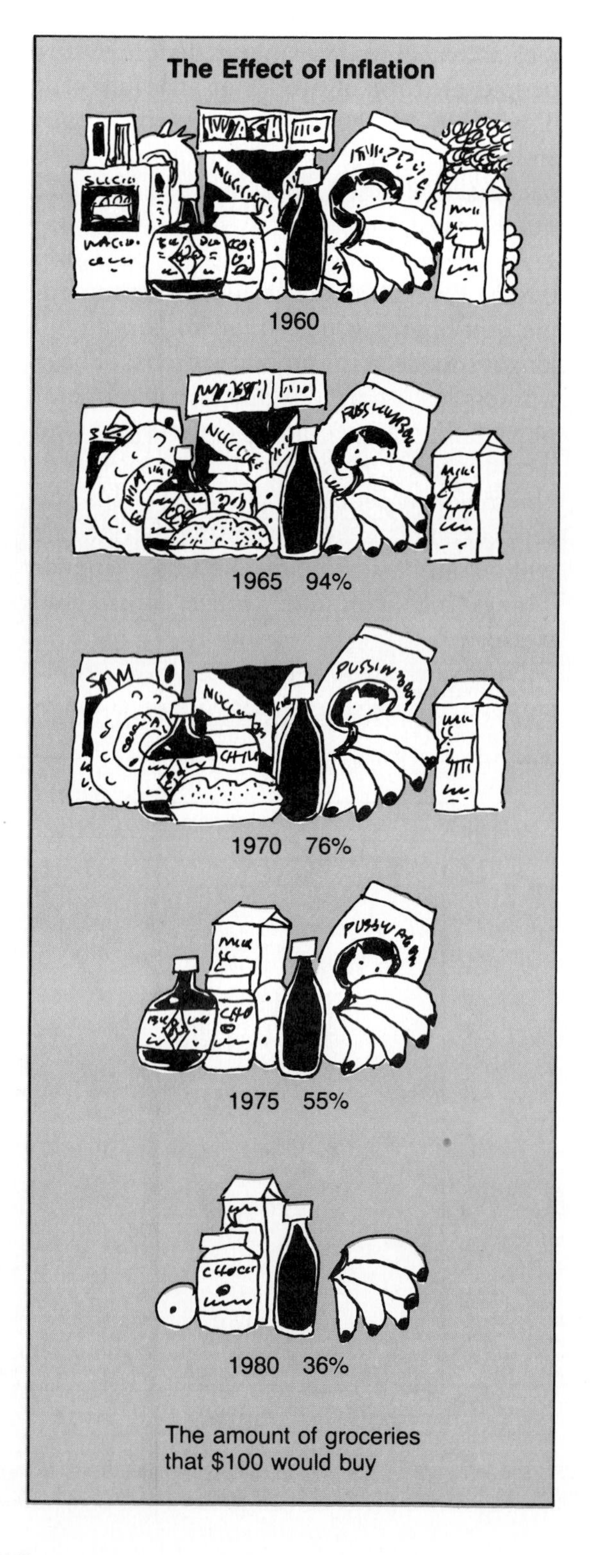

Have students choose another country that has a free market economy and compare the rate of inflation of that country with that of ours.

people would spend less money and buy fewer goods. And this, as you have read, is how recessions start. This means that it would likely take a recession to quickly stop inflation.

Stopping inflation, then, is like stopping a speeding car, or stopping when you have been running fast. It must be done slowly. If you stop too quickly, you may have more problems. Therefore governments try to stop inflation slowly, so as not to cause a bad recession.

Check for Understanding: Now that you have completed this section, you should be able to answer these questions:

1. What two major problems face all economies?
2. How can a recession start, and what can result from one?
3. Why do governments find it difficult to act quickly to deal with an inflation problem?
4. What two bad results do recessions have?

SUMMARY

The economic system of a country is the way in which goods and services are produced and paid for. In the U.S. the total work of the economic system is over three trillion dollars. But goods and services are not unlimited, and one of the roles of the economic system is to make choices about which ones will be available. The two main questions that an economic system answers are: "What goods will be produced?" "Who will benefit from those goods and services?"

Not all economies have the same answer to these questions. Traditional systems continue to produce in the ways that the group has always produced. These economies move more slowly and generally refuse to modernize. As a result there are few left in the world today.

Planned economies exist when a central group within a nation's government makes the basic economic decisions: What will be produced and how the results will be distributed. Planning an economy is a complex job, and a mistake in the planners' judgement can deny goods and services to a large number of people. In order to have an effective planned economy, the government needs control over the lives of its citizens.

In a free enterprise economy, or a free market economy, people choose what to buy and sell. The two things that are necessary for such a system are the right to free choice and private property. Another feature of a free market economy is competitive markets—many buyers and sellers for goods and services. In this way consumers vote by buying the products they want. Although the United States has what is basically a free market economy, most economies, including our own, combine features of all three of the basic economic systems.

The two major problems facing all economies are recession and inflation. A recession is a slow economy—fewer people buy goods, and fewer goods are produced. Unemployment and loss of production result. Inflation means prices are rising rapidly because there is more money than goods. Controlling inflation is dangerous because a recession can result if the controls are too severe.

Discuss with students the problems that could arise if a government tried to stop inflation too rapidly.

BUILDING SKILLS IN CIVICS

THINKING SKILLS

1. Why do we have to choose among all the goods that we want and need?
2. What are the two major questions that an economic system must answer?
3. What is the difference between a traditional economy and a planned economy?
4. How does a free market economy get its name?
5. Why is private property necessary in a free economy?

VOCABULARY SKILLS

Choose the term that best completes each statement below.

1. ______ means there is less of something available than people want or need. (Inflation, Economic scarcity, Recession)
2. A ______ economy must have a totalitarian state that dictates much of what people do. (planned, traditional, tribal)
3. ______ means that most things are owned by individual people rather than by the government. (Recession, Natural resources, Private property)
4. When a free market economy includes some features of traditional economies and some of planned economies, it is said to have ______. (a balanced budget, a socialist government, mixed practices)
5. A ______ occurs when an economy fails to work in making jobs and incomes available to people. (stock market crash, recession, mixed practice)
6. One dollar today will buy less than half of what it would have bought ten years ago. This is called ______. (income tax, personal income, inflation)
7. In a ______, businesses compete with each other to sell goods at the lowest prices. (planned economy, traditional economy, competitive economy)
8. In a ______ economy, people can choose the goods they wish to buy and sell. (free enterprise, planned, traditional)

STUDY SKILLS—USING PERIODICALS

There are hundreds of *periodicals* published in the United States each year. One advantage of our democratic way of life is that each publication is free to choose the issues it wishes to feature and also to select the particular viewpoint it wishes to express.

These days, you can open almost any magazine and find numerous references to the economy with differing viewpoints being expressed in each different periodical.

Activity: With this in mind, go to your library and read through at least four different periodicals. Note the articles that pertain to the economy in our country. How do different magazines treat the subject? Are they critical of the government or in favor of current policy? Is the subject of the economy discussed in a humorous manner or in a serious one? Write down any other observations you make.

BEYOND THE BOOK

1. With other students in your class, stage a mock TV press conference. Choose one student to play some prominent politician in our country and prepare questions on the economic situation that this person must address. In order to stage a press conference effectively, both the questioners and the respondent must be adequately prepared.
2. Look through your daily newspaper for cartoons that pertain to the economy. How does the cartoonist portray the characters and the issues? Do you think it is done effectively? Why?/Why not? If you were going to draw a political cartoon about the economy, how would you express your opinions?
3. Interview the manager or owner of a store in your neighborhood. Ask him or her how the problems in the economy have affected business in the store, the cost of the products sold, and the general mood of the customers. Does the manager/owner think that the economy will improve in the future or get worse? What does he or she think the results will be if it doesn't get better? What other comments does this person make about the economy?

CHAPTER THIRTY TEST

VOCABULARY CHECK

If the underlined term in the statement is used correctly, write True. If not, replace it with the proper term.

free enterprise	traditional	competitive market	inflation
mixed practice		economic scarcity	recession

1. In a planned economy, the government determines the answer to the two basic economic questions.
2. A private property means that there are many buyers and sellers for goods and services.
3. Free enterprise means there is less of something available than people want or need.
4. Because our economy has some features of traditional economies and some of planned economies, it is said to have inflation.
5. Inflation starts because there is more money available than there are goods.
6. A mixed practice occurs when an economy fails to work in making jobs and incomes available to people.
7. In a free enterprise economy, people choose the items they wish to buy and sell.

COMPREHENSION CHECK

1. Which of the following is not a cause of recession?
   a. People have less money to buy goods.
   b. Workers lose jobs and become unemployed.
   c. People spend all their money on material goods.
2. Why can't a government just reduce the amount of money available in order to stop inflation?
   a. Because to do so would cause other problems such as recession.
   b. The U.S. Mint has to make the same amount of money at all times.
   c. The limits of nature would make this impossible.
   d. This is only possible in a traditional economy.

SKILL BUILDER–INTERPRETING TABLES

Look at the *table* below showing how Americans spent their dollar in 1960, 1970, and 1980. Then compare the information from this table to the chart in Chapter 30: The Effect of Inflation. Can you see why the amounts for consumer spending have risen so drastically in the past decade? Are you surprised about any of the ways that consumers spent their money? Why?/Why not? What other observations can you make about the dollar and its relationship to Americans' spending habits?

How U.S. Consumers Spend Their Dollar
(in billions, rounded off)

	1980	1970	1960
Food	303	120	71
Tobacco	20	11	7
Alcohol	43	20	11
Clothing, etc.	124	56	32
Personal care	23	11	5
Housing	272	94	48
Household operation	229	84	46
Medical care	166	50	20
Personal business	90	32	14
Transportation	243	81	42
Recreation	106	41	18
Private education and research	25	10	4
Religious and welfare activities	23	9	5
Foreign travel and other	4	4	2

BUILDING WRITING SKILLS

1. Write a paragraph to go with one of the following titles:
   a. A Planned Economy vs. A Free Market Economy
   b. Why There is Economic Scarcity
   c. The Causes and Effects of Recession
2. Explain why each economy has some mixed practices. Do you think this is a good idea? Why?/Why not?
3. In what ways has the current economic situation affected various Americans? How are they trying to overcome any problems that they've encountered? Do you have any suggestions for solving economic problems?

Chapter Thirty-One
Competition In Our Economy

Document: The Constitution of the United States

Article I, Section 8. The Congress shall have Power To lay and collect Taxes, Duties, Imposts and Excises, to pay the Debts and provide for the common Defence and general Welfare of the United States; but all Duties, Imposts and Excises shall be uniform throughout the United States; To borrow Money on the credit of the United States; To establish . . . uniform Laws on the subject of Bankruptcies throughout the United States; To coin Money, regulate the Value thereof, and of foreign Coin, and fix the Standard of Weights and Measures . . .

"A monopoly granted either to an individual or to a trading company has the same effect as a secret in trade or manufactures. The monopolists, by keeping the market constantly understocked, by never fully supplying the effectual demand, sell their commodities much above the natural price, and raise their emoluments, whether they consist in wages or profit, greatly above their natural rate." (Adam Smith, *Wealth of Nations*, 1776)

Every time you spend money for a good of your own choosing, you play a part in competition and its role in the business process. A free economy such as ours depends on competition to make sure that

This picture presents another example of competition in our economy. Ask students how *they* choose among all the sellers who provide similar goods and services. Do they think there is too much competition in our country or too little?

businesses charge reasonable prices. For example, if there was only one seller of home appliances, the seller might charge exorbitant prices for these products as soon as the demand for them rose. But, if there were many sellers, each one would have to compete with the other. If one seller charged too much, a consumer could simply buy the product from another businessperson. Laws have been passed in this country to prohibit such monopolies—that is, markets that only have one seller.

FOCUSING IDEAS

- A capitalist economy is one in which enterprise is based on exchange of money for goods and services, and where buildings, land, and the things that produce goods and services are privately owned by citizens.
- Our government protects competition by outlawing monopolies and trusts and by regulating public utilities.
- Changes in the economy have brought about major changes in other aspects of our lives in the past two hundred years. The increasing use of technology will continue to change our lives in the future.
- Our economy affects us by making varied opportunities available in different professions and in different areas of the country.

The complete text of the Constitution can be found in the Appendix, beginning on page 564.

Issues in Civics: Discuss the problems that monopolies can cause to both buyers and sellers. How do students think monopolies should be dealt with?

PRE-TEST

1. What is involved in the workings of a capitalist economy?
2. How does our government work to maintain competition in business?
3. How did the changes in our economic system come about?
4. How does our modern economy affect the way you live and work?

WHAT IS A CAPITALIST ECONOMY?

Objectives: After you have read this section, you will be able to:

- Define capitalism and explain how it is different from communism.
- Explain what happens to the money that businesses receive from their sales.
- See why profits are necessary for a business to continue to stay open.

You have seen that one of the many rights you enjoy as an American citizen is that of a free economy. You can buy or sell at any price that is agreeable to the other party. You can hire out your own labor, or work, as you wish. You can invest or spend your income as you please. All of these rights are part of your economic freedom.

Maintaining a free and healthy economy is one of the first concerns of good government. Sometimes the government must take strong actions to protect the economic freedom of the people. But in a free economy, the government's role is usually limited to as few controls as possible. In this way the economic freedom of individual citizens is preserved.

The New York Stock Exchange is a central part of our capitalist economy.

Building Vocabulary:
capitalism *(521)* • communism *(521)* • socialism *(521)* • profit *(522)* • monopoly *(523)* • trust *(523)* • public utility *(524)* • automation *(529)*

Have an interested student do research on the New York Stock Exchange and its effect on our capitalist society.

Capitalism

You have learned that our type of economy has many names. It has been called a free enterprise or free market economy. In the same way, other economies are called planned economies. Still another name for our kind of economy is *capitalism.* This means that the economy is based on exchange of money, or capital, for goods and services. Buildings, land, and the things that produce goods and services are privately owned by citizens. This is different from *communism*, where these things are owned by the government. It is also different from *socialism*, or a mixed economy, where some things are owned privately by people and others are owned by the government. The practice of private ownership means that people have the opportunity to enter business or buy into a business as they wish. They may also seek to improve or enlarge their private business as they see fit. There are no controls upon them as long as they break no laws.

Competition is what drives athletes to perform at their best.

Competition

People always seem to enjoy a good game. There is a thrill in seeing who will finally win. The players on each team try to do better than their opponents. When you see such a game, you are seeing competition in action. Competition means that people are making every effort to surpass others at some activity.

Competition in a sport makes each athlete try to do her or his best, and it is the same with business. In order to make a profit, each business tries to outsell its competitors. It attempts to do this by providing customers the best service or product at the lowest possible price.

In order to provide a lower price, the business can operate so that its costs are less than those of its competitors. Or it may offer a product of higher quality at the same or a slightly higher price. In either case, it must be efficient in order to keep a balance between quality and price.

People gain from competition in business. Prices are kept low so that more goods may be bought for the money. When competing businesses operate efficiently, the customers do not have to pay for waste in the goods they buy.

The business process

The business process consists of people or businesses trying to sell something for more than what it costs them. Costs include all the money that was spent before the good

Have students discuss the differences between communism and capitalism and how the issue of private ownership relates to each practice.

or service was sold to the buyer or customer. Therefore, the costs include money spent for rent, raw materials, equipment, and many other things. Costs also include the wages and salaries of all those who work for the business. In this way, the costs of business firms also provide income to most of the people in the United States.

A business earns a *profit* if it receives more money from its sales than it spends on its costs. If it spends more money than it receives, it has a *loss*. Each business tries to avoid a loss and to make as high a profit as is possible. Therefore, businesses try to spend as little as they can on costs, including wages and salaries. But they cannot pay too little. Competition is also at work here. If one business pays too low a wage, workers will leave it and go to work for a competing company that pays better. If the business tries to spend too little on costs, it will not be able to produce goods and services that are as attractive to customers as those of its competitors.

Competition and the business process work together to set prices and wages at near what they are worth to all people and all businesses. If prices are too high, the goods will not be sold until the price is lowered. If wages are too low, people will not work for a business until it raises its wages. Thus competition works throughout the economy.

A business can sell more goods by lowering prices. It can hire more and better workers by raising wages. But each of these mean greater expenses for the business, so this process places a control or limit on the profits the business can make. All businesses in the United States average about 5¢ profit after taxes out of every $1.00 in sales. The other 95¢ out of each dollar goes to pay many costs, including the wages and salaries of workers. Of course, some businesses

One company may do well while a competitor goes out of business, according to their profit-and-loss performances.

Have an interested student investigate the profits and loss statements of several of our country's biggest companies. Are profits generally going up or down?

make a higher profit. Still, others make less than 5¢ out of each dollar, and some even have losses. When you see a business close or shut down, it has very likely had too many losses. When you see a business remain in place or even grow, it has very likely had good profits.

One expert has said, "Profit is another name for the cost of staying in business." By this he meant that the owners must make a profit in order for it to be worthwhile for them to keep the business going. Suppose a business does not pay the cost of the goods it sells. It would then have nothing to sell, because its suppliers would refuse to furnish the things necessary for it to manufacture these goods. If it did not pay its workers, they would not show up to work. In the same way, if the owners do not receive a profit, they will not be there to keep the business open.

Check for Understanding: Now that you have completed this section, you should be able to answer these questions:

1. What is capitalism and how does it differ from communism?
2. What happens to the money that businesses receive from their sales?
3. Why are profits necessary if a business is to stay open?
4. How does competition relate to the business process?

HOW DOES OUR GOVERNMENT PROTECT COMPETITION?

Objectives: After you have read this section, you will be able to:

- Define "monopoly" and "trust," and explain the purpose of anti-trust laws.
- Tell why public utilities are lawful monopolies.
- See why government deregulation has an affect on costs and services.

Outlawing monopolies and trusts

Sometimes businesses have acted to eliminate competition. When there is only one firm, it is called a *monopoly*. Monopoly comes from the Greek words *mono*, meaning "one," and *polein*, meaning "to sell." It means "one seller." To have only one seller is not good, because the customer has no other firm to turn to for better quality or lower prices.

Some companies in a certain line of business may try to eliminate competition by unfair methods. These businesses agree not to compete. They give control over their prices and selling practices to a small group called a *trust*. The trust acts on their behalf. Without competition, it has a free hand to raise prices.

At one time trusts in this country ran thousands of businesses. These totalled billions of dollars in value. Oil, sugar, steel, and many other important goods came under the control of the trusts. Soon people became concerned with the absence of competition in business. Congress then passed *antitrust* laws to outlaw monopolies and trusts.

The antitrust laws require businesses to compete fairly. Thus buyers have a choice of goods and prices. These laws forbid firms to agree to fix prices or to restrict competition. Those who break these laws may be fined or jailed. The people who are hurt by

Issues in Civics: Ask students if Congress acted responsibly when it passed anti-trust laws to outlaw monopolies and trusts.

John D. Rockefeller became one of the wealthiest people in the country through the monopoly established by his Standard Oil Company.

illegal practices may sue to receive up to three times the value they were overcharged.

The anti-trust laws are like stop signs. Their primary purpose is to make offenders stop, rather than to punish those who violate the laws. Often the attorney general, who enforces these laws, will try to get businesses who might be violating them to stop their practices voluntarily. Firms that are so big that they either have no competition or have complete control over their prices may be forced to sell some of their operations to competing firms. In this way competition may be established again.

It is hard to tell how effective the anti-trust laws have been. Some people say that very few companies have been brought to court in violation of these laws. However, it is likely that most businesses seek to keep competition rather than be brought to court. They believe that their best interests lie in maintaining competition with other companies.

Regulating public utilities

If you look around your own community, you will see many cases in which there is only one firm selling a particular thing or providing a particular service. For example, there is only one telephone company you can go to. You must buy your electricity and usually your water and gas from only one firm. Governments have not overlooked these firms. Instead, they control them as public utilities. A *public utility* is a firm that acts as a monopoly in a community, state, or other area.

Do students think thtat it's fair that a public utility can act as a monopoly in a community or state? Why or why not?

In the case of public utilities it is cheaper and easier for customers to have only one firm providing the service. Think of what it would be like if there were five to six telephone companies in a particular area. How would you call a friend if his or her phone were part of a different system?

The same is true of gas, water, and electricity, where all the users share the costs of bringing these resources to the entire city. Almost all public utility monopolies have this in common—the customer is better off if there is only one firm serving the area.

Another thing about the services of public utilities is that they are all highly important to the customer. We depend upon electricity for convenience, comfort, and even life itself. When the electricity goes off, large cities are brought to a standstill. We depend upon water for sanitation and health. Public transportation is of the utmost importance, especially to the people in large cities. Years ago it became clear that people would have to pay very high prices if there were only one utility in a community. At the same time, if there were more than one firm, there would be duplication and waste. The decision was made to control prices by public utility boards. These boards consist of citizens who may be elected or appointed by the government.

A return to competition

There are other rates that have been controlled by the federal government. Airline fares and the price of oil and natural gas are some of these. But recent decisions have been made by which the government no longer controls these prices. Over the years more businesses have competed in these areas. Under these conditions, lower prices

The "Great Blackout" of 1965, as seen in this view of New York City, showed how much our society depends on electrical services.

Discuss with students the services provided by the various public utility firms in their area. How useful do they think these services are?

and better service might come from competition rather than regulation.

Often new ways of doing things will bring about changes in government regulation of the economy. For many years American Telephone and Telegraph (AT&T) had a monopoly on long distance telephone services. Its prices and services were regulated by the Federal Communications Commission. AT&T provided this service by long telephone lines and cables across the country. In recent years, more long distance calls were sent through the air by microwave signals. But other companies also provided the microwave service. So the decision was made to deregulate much of the long distance service. This was made possible by discovering new ways of providing an old service.

In the future you may see more government deregulation. This means that the governments no longer regulates industry as it once did. As these changes take place, you should watch for their effect on prices and services. If airline fares fall and oil and gas shortages ease, you will see competition at work. You will also see our government taking the stand that competition, when it works, can better serve the people than can government regulation.

Check for Understanding: Now that you have completed this section, you should be able to answer these questions:

1. What are monopolies and trusts? What's the purpose of anti-trust laws?
2. Why are public utilities lawful monopolies?
3. What effect does government regulation have on costs and services?
4. How is AT&T's monopoly on long-distance telephone services changing?

HOW DID CHANGE TAKE PLACE IN OUR ECONOMY?

Objectives: After you have read this section, you will be able to:

- See that from colonial times to the present, there have been major changes in lifestyles.
- See that your way of life depends on the economy.
- Describe the effect that machines have had on our economy.

Little change for over 2000 years

Suppose we could take two people from ancient Rome in 200 B.C. and place them in the United States just after the American Revolution. We would be moving them about 2000 years forward in time.

Surprisingly, they would not feel too uncomfortable. They would recognize most of the things they would see. The large ships in the harbor would only be bigger and have more sails than a Roman galley. Carriages would be better than chariots, but they would still be carts pulled by horses. Light and heat would still come from fires. Horses and people would work the fields. Clothing would be sewn by hand.

Change has come quickly since then

Now suppose we could take two people from the time of the American Revolution and place them in the 1980's. We would be moving them forward about 200 years in time, or only about one-tenth as much.

These people would neither recognize nor understand many of the things they

Issues in Civics: Ask students if they think there should be more or less government regulation of industry? How do they think government deregulation will affect prices and services?

Changes in Transportation

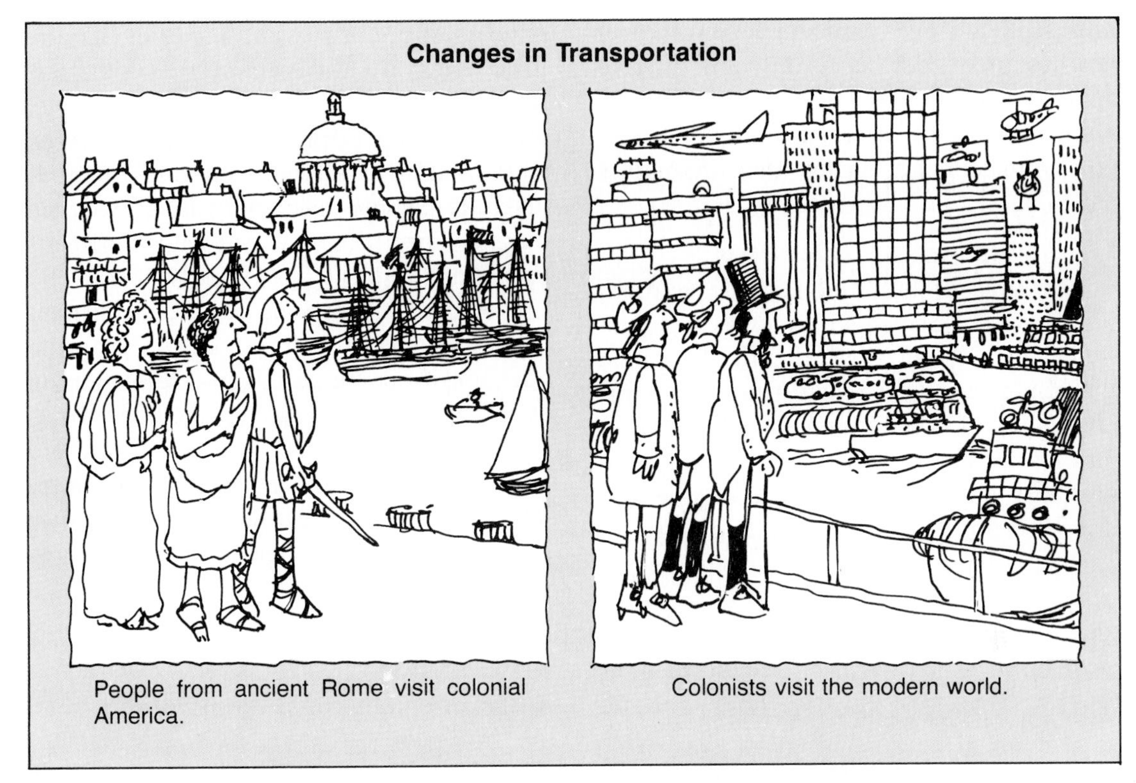

People from ancient Rome visit colonial America.

Colonists visit the modern world.

would see. Carriages would run without horses. Strange machines would fly in the air. Ships would move without sails. Light and heat would be made without fire. People would buy their clothing and food from huge, modern stores.

Our lives change

When we look at the economy in this way, we can learn many things. We can understand how important the economy is in determining the way we live. The things that we take for granted every day come from our ability to produce new and abundant goods.

Many things you use today have been invented in your lifetime. Many things you will use as an adult haven't been invented yet. Your way of life depends on the economy, and it is changing more quickly than ever.

The age of handcrafts

For thousands of years people lived in the age of handcrafts. Production was carried on with tools. A tool is any instrument—such as a hammer, a plow, or a broom—that requires a worker, or perhaps an animal, to provide power. When people depended on tools, many workers were needed on farms to produce enough food for everyone. Consequently, nearly everybody had to work at raising food. In 1790 the first census showed that nine-tenths of the American people lived on farms.

The work of knowledge

The age of handcrafts existed for many centuries with little change. Many people in the world today still live a similar way of life. All of the natural resources we use today have been available throughout history. This shows that economic conditions do not usually change because people discover new resources, but because people learn to apply new knowledge to natural resources. Human knowledge is therefore more important to economic change than are natural resources.

The invention of machines

At the time of the American Revolution, James Watt, a Scotsman, invented the first steam engine. This was the first machine that could do work without using the natural power of wind, water, or animal or human strength. Later other engines were invented, such as the gasoline engine and the electric motor. These additions to knowledge changed the work of the world.

Engines and machines gave rise to power tools, or machines—such as bulldozers, electric saws, and sewing machines—that provide their own power. They will do almost continuous work, and they require little effort on the part of the operators. Machines have a distinct advantage over tools in doing work. They can do heavier work, and do it faster and for longer periods of time. People have only to provide an engine, turn the tool on, and direct its operation.

Machines are making important changes in our economy. Almost every year the number of people working on farms and in factories is a smaller percentage of all workers. But almost every year, our farms and factories produce more goods than before. This is possible because machines, rather than people, are doing more and more of the work.

Automation

While machines could do more work than

The role of machines in today's economy is shown by comparing the way steel was made in the Colonial period and in the 19th century with the current method.

tools, they still needed people to operate them. This meant that the amount of work a machine could do was often determined by the person who controlled it. A sewing machine could not run faster than an operator could handle the cloth, for example. But many of these limits on machines were removed with the development of *automation*, or the ability for machines to control themselves.

Automated machines do all the work that power machines do, yet they have a special advantage. This advantage is called *feedback*. Automated machines with feedback not only perform the work of power machines, but they measure the work that has been done and determine the next step to take. The machine "feeds back" to itself information concerning what has been accomplished. It uses this information to determine what to do next.

Robots are an example of automation. These are machines that are programmed to work much like people. They are able to determine by feedback devices when to start and stop work. Many factories in Japan and the United States are using robots. They are doing much of the work that was once done by people.

Just as engines gave rise to power tools, electronic devices and computers gave rise to automation. Automation allows work to be done much faster with rapid control. These machines can be operated quickly and accurately.

Check for Understanding: Now that you have completed this section, you should be able to answer these questions:

1. In what ways have lifestyles changed since the colonial days?
2. In what way does your life depend on the economy?
3. What effect has machinery had on our economy?
4. Why has knowledge been more important than resources in causing economic change?

HOW DOES A MODERN ECONOMY AFFECT YOU?

Objectives: After you have read this section, you will be able to:

- Define, and give an example of a trend.
- Explain how a modern economy produces leisure time as well as goods.
- Describe two changes that have taken place in terms of career opportunities.

These changes in the economy establish new career or job trends. A trend is a change that is taking place now, and will continue in the future. For example, we are now, and will continue, to replace people with robots and other automated machines. This causes another job trend. There will continue to be fewer jobs in which people directly work to produce goods, and more jobs in which they control the devices that produce goods. In planning for the future, people look for trends. This way they can expect to find new jobs and be prepared for them. If you watch for trends, you may be prepared for the changes that will affect your life.

The hours you will work

One trend is for people to work fewer hours and to produce more. Inventions and competition have reduced costs, so that workers today own things that only the rich could afford years ago. But another benefit to workers has come through reducing the

Do students think the trend toward automation will have a positive or negative effect on our economy? Why do they think as they do?

Have interested students do reports on current business trends such as the four-day workweek and the use of computers in the professional fields.

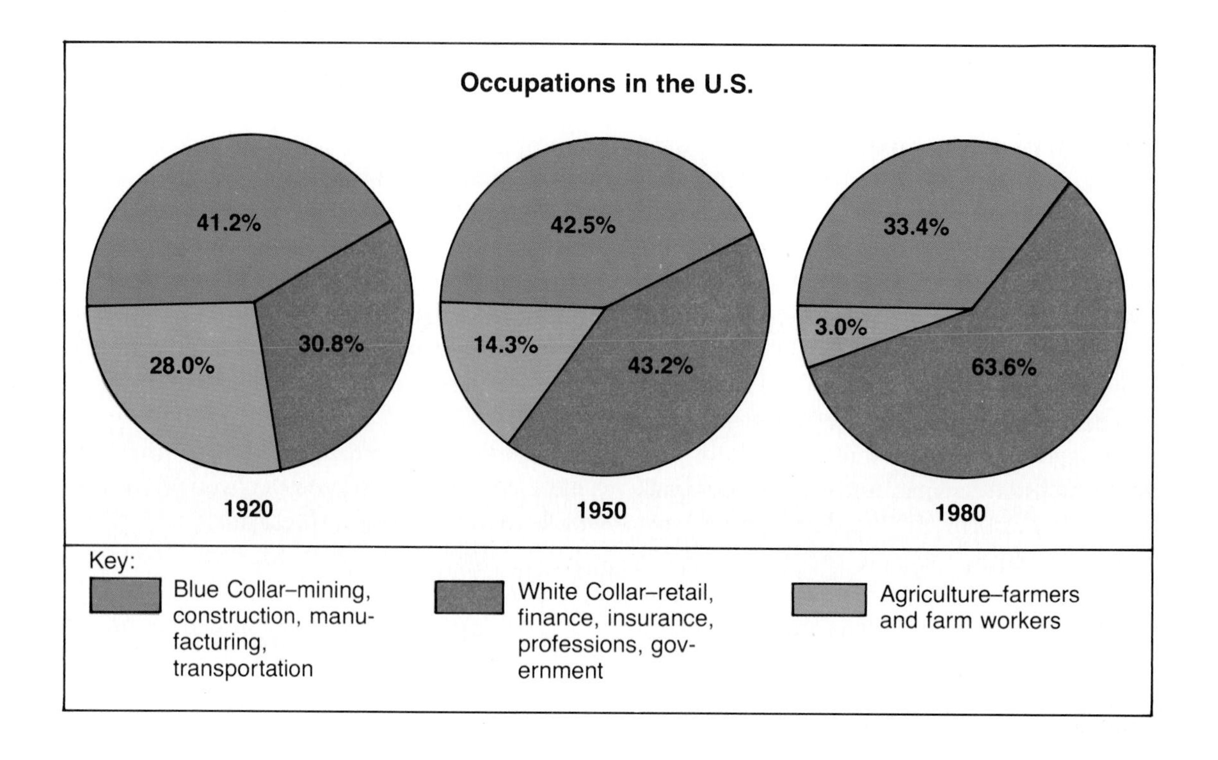

hours of labor. Years ago people worked long hours. Twelve to fourteen hours was the length of a general workday, and people worked six days a week instead of five as they do now. Today few people work longer than an eight-hour day and a forty-hour week, and a thirty-five hour week is standard in many businesses.

Some firms are trying out a four-day work week. Their employees work ten hours a day for four days and then have three days off. As people use modern equipment to make more things in less time, they can earn more money per hour. By working fewer hours, people trade money they could earn for the time off. Thus our modern economy produces more leisure time as well as more goods.

The careers you may choose

Our changing economy has established two new trends in finding a job or career, and the kind of work you will do. In the days of handcrafts, you would probably have gone to work on a farm when you left school. In the age of power tools, you would probably have gone to work in a factory or in a store selling factory goods. Now, when you graduate, you are likely to find a job with government, a store, or a professional office. Fewer people are finding work in manufacturing. New career opportunities in health, finance, recreation, and other areas are developing each day.

A second trend is in the kind of work that people are doing. They are running more complicated machines. Fewer jobs are available that require little skill and hard work. Even in factories, many workers are running computers and other equipment that performs and regulates work. People in offices are using minicomputers and word

Ask your students about families they know of in which both parents are working. Is this a result of the current status of the economy? Have them explain their answers.

processors. In health fields they are also using complicated equipment. Whatever job you end up having, you are likely to use complicated, expensive equipment.

The skills and training you will need

As people do more complicated work with complicated machinery, they need more skills and training. Many jobs that used to require few skills are now called "*paraprofessional.*" The word para means "beside" or "alongside" as in the word "parallel"—parallel lines are alongside each other. Paraprofessionals work alongside professional people. Examples of paraprofessionals are ambulance workers and dental and doctor's assistants, as well as those who work with lawyers and accountants. All of these paraprofessional jobs require some kind of specialized training.

The need for this training makes education more important. That is why more and more young people are completing high school. Many more continue on to community college or university training. The education you receive today will be very important in the career you find tomorrow.

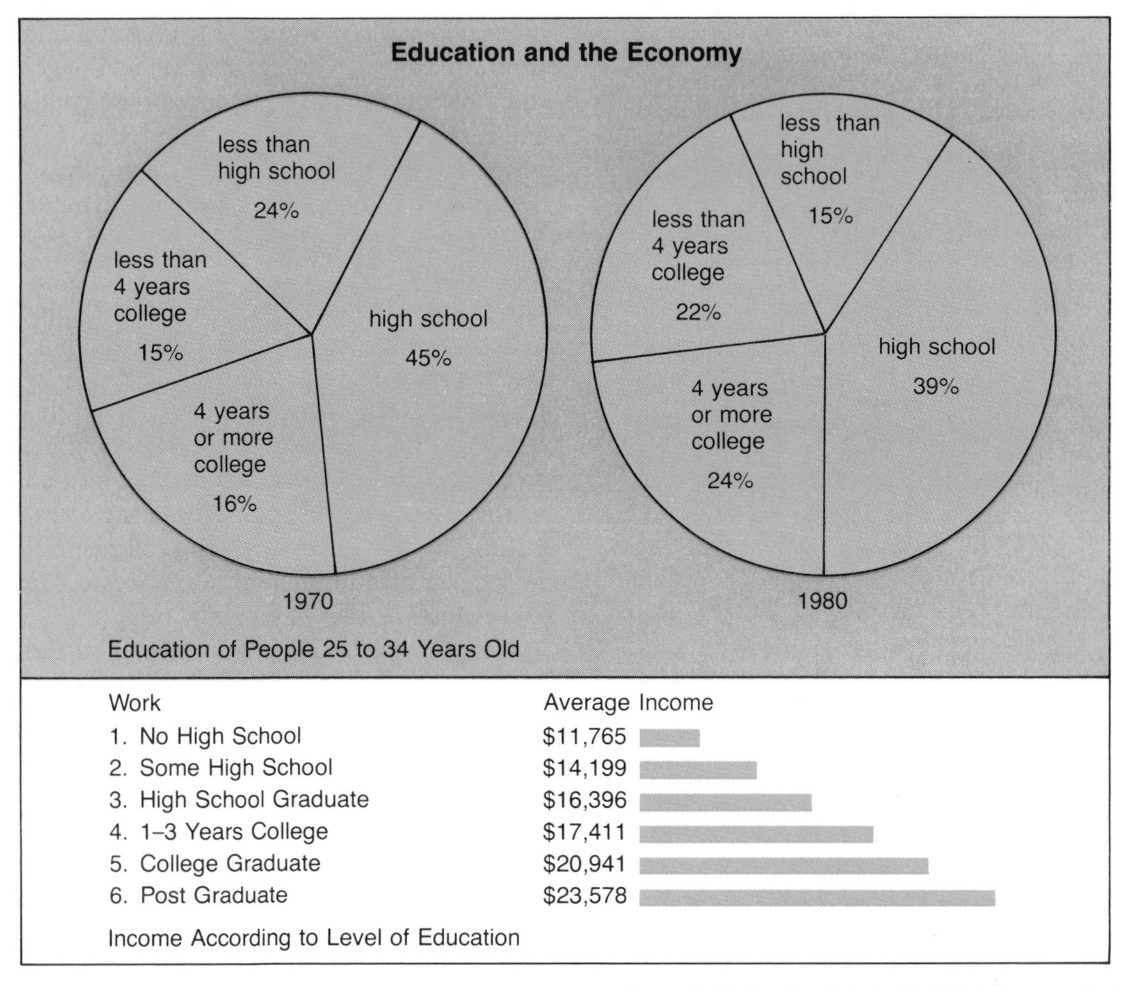

Issues in Civics: Do students think that the amount of education that a person receives really has an effect on that person's professional success, or do they think education has little to do with it?

Who you will work with

Many years ago, the type of person you were would often determine the work you would do. If you were a woman, you were likely to be a housewife, secretary, teacher, or nurse. If you were black or Hispanic, you would likely work on a farm or in a factory. Today, this no longer needs to be true.

In 1981, over one half of the families in the United States had both the husband and wife working. Many women are doing different types of work today. They hold skilled jobs in factories and in construction. Some become managers and accountants, while still others own and manage their own businesses.

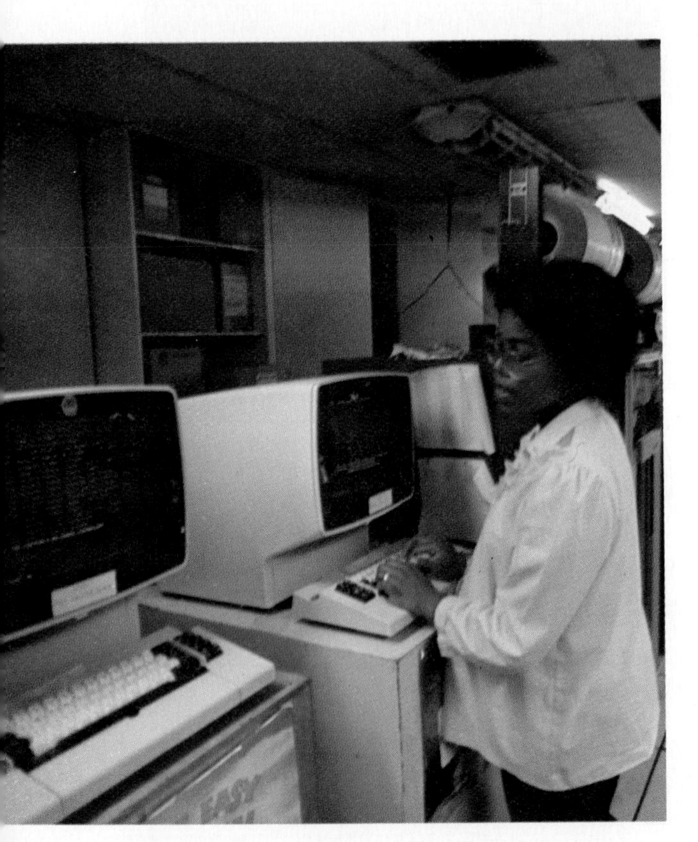

Our modern economy has opened up new business opportunities for women and minorities.

This same trend is also true for blacks, Hispanics and other minorities. As our ideas and our economy changes, it opens up new opportunities. Our changing economy needs trained, skilled people. Less attention is being paid to the question of a person's race or sex. This means that you are very likely to work with a different mix of people in the future. You will be working with people who have similar skills.

The area in which you will work

Our economy is changing in many ways. One of these changes is where new jobs are becoming available. Years ago, you would very likely have spent your working life in or near the place where you grew up and went to school. Today, this is no longer true. As our economy produces new goods and services, it also decides where they will be produced. This may cause new jobs in new places. Many people may have to move if they are to hold those new jobs and start new careers.

Years ago, most of the factories in our nation produced shoes and clothing. Many of these factories were located in the New England states. Years later, new factories developed to produce steel, automobiles, and large goods. Most of these were located in the north central states, near the Great Lakes. In the same way, most of the nation's manufacturing jobs were located in these states.

With the increasing importance of oil and energy, the state of Texas has become a growth area for new jobs. Oklahoma and Colorado are also growing because of energy. California has grown as our economy changed. It has become the center for the electronic and computer industries. People wanting careers in these fields must go where the jobs are available.

Issues in Civics: Do students think that women should be allowed to work in all fields that a man works in? Should women and men be paid on an equal basis?

A rapidly growing part of our country is the "Sun Belt." This is a nickname for the southern and southwestern part of our country. The Sun Belt is growing because companies have decided to open new plants and businesses in these areas of the country. And this creates new jobs.

As our economy changes, it brings about changes in where different types of jobs are located. But one advantage of a free economy is that you own your own labor. It is your private property. You may move and work where you please. And our changing economy may provide you with many career opportunities in many different locations.

Check for Understanding: Now that you have completed this section, you should be able to answer these questions:

1. What is an example of a trend?
2. How does a modern economy produce leisure time as well as goods?
3. What changes have affected career opportunities in our society?
4. What are paraprofessionals? Name some examples of them.

SUMMARY

Our economy in the United States is organized around private ownership of land and production. This type of economy is known as capitalism. An economic system in which land and the means of production are owned by the state is known as communism.

In a capitalist economy, competition is freely at work. Businesses compete to sell quality goods at the lowest possible prices. They often compete for workers as well by offering fair wages. As long as a company is able to sell its goods at a higher total price than its total cost for doing business, it makes a profit. Generally, the more successful business is, the healthier the economy is.

However, sometimes businesses have acted against the best interests of the country as a whole. They have joined together in trusts to eliminate competition and raise prices. They have been merged to form a small number of huge, powerful corporations, or monopolies. Government has acted in these situations to break up and outlaw monopolies and trusts.

Under some circumstances government has limited competition in certain areas for the benefit of the people. Public utilities are monopolies whose prices and services are carefully controlled. Some industries, such as the airlines, have been regulated by the government, too. A trend toward deregulation may be developing in many of these areas as government allows free competition to determine prices.

Changes in the economy have brought great changes in our life in the past two hundred years and the increasing use of technology will continue to affect our lives in the future. The trends are for more people to work fewer hours and produce more, and for people to seek career opportunities outside of manufacturing. More training is required to do most jobs than in the past. Many professions need paraprofessionals. The kind of work people do is less restricted by their sex or ethnic origin than in the past. Our changing economy will continue to make opportunities available in different jobs and in different parts of the country.

Have an interested student do research on the economic boom that is occurring in the Sun Belt and have him or her report back to the class.

BUILDING SKILLS IN CIVICS

THINKING SKILLS

1. What does the business process consist of?
2. How does competition work within the business process?
3. What are some examples of public utility monopolies? Why are the services they provide so important to us?
4. What is the reason that economic conditions usually change?
5. At one time, what kind of important goods came under the control of trusts? What did Congress do as a result of this lack of competition?
6. Look at the photo in Chapter 31 that shows competition in sports. How is this similar to competition in business?

VOCABULARY SKILLS

Fill in the blank in each statement with the correct term.

public utility	capitalism	trust	socialism
automation	monopoly	communism	profit

1. ______ means that machines have the ability to control themselves.
2. When an economy is based on the exchange of money for goods or services, it's called ______.
3. Under ______, government, buildings, land, and the things that produce goods and services are owned by the government.
4. A business earns a ______ if it receives more money from its sales than it spends on its costs.
5. A small group called a ______ sometimes takes control of the prices and selling practices of businesses.
6. A firm that acts as a monopoly in a community, state, or other area is a ______.
7. A ______ occurs when there is only one firm that sells a certain product.
8. ______ is unlike communism in that people believe in democratic elections although the government controls the economy.

STUDY SKILLS–USING THE ENCYCLOPEDIA

In a capitalist government, buildings and land are privately owned by citizens. Ina communist government, these things are owned by the government, and under socialism, some things are privately by people and others are owned by the government. As you know, the United States is a capitalist government. But what about other countries in the world?

Activity: In order to research government influence on the economy in various countries, use a general *encyclopedia* such as *World Book*. Choose a country that you aren't very familiar with and find out if it has a capitalist, communist, or socialist government. How does the type of government that a country has affect the amount or kind of goods and services it produces? How much freedom do the people have? Give examples to support your statements.

BEYOND THE BOOK

1. Do any of your relatives or friends come from countries that have a different economic system than that of the United States? If so, interview them to find out their opinions of that system and how they compare it to our capitalist system. Do you agree with the person's opinions? Why?/Why not?
2. Participate in a debate with other students in your class. Form two opposing groups—one advocating the use of automation as a means of increasing the efficiency in a company, the other group opposing the replacement of employees with machines. Do research beforehand so that you have factual information to back up your opinions.
3. Imagine that you are the owner of a small food or appliance store. Lately, you have realized that you are only averaging about 3¢ profit after taxes out of every $1.00 in sales. Write a sales report detailing the costs and expenditures of your store's operation and prepare a new budget that will once again give you an acceptable profit and loss statement. In your report, take into account the number of employees you have, their salaries, your hours of operation, use of utilities, and, of course, the price of your goods.

CHAPTER THIRTY-ONE TEST

VOCABULARY CHECK

Choose the term in parentheses that best completes each statement.

1. For many years, AT&T had a ______ on long distance telephone services. (monopoly, trust, trend)
2. ______ means that machines can control themselves. (Deregulation, Automation, Taxation)
3. Under ______, an economy is based on the exchange of money for goods and services. (capitalism, recession, inflation)
4. A ______ is a firm that acts as a monopoly on a local level and provides a product all citizens use. (public utility, trust, trend)
5. Under ______, the government controls the economy, but democratic elections are permitted. (capitalism, socialism, automation)
6. Under ______, the government controls the means of production in the name of the workers. (communism, capitalism, monopoly)
7. A business earns a ______ if it receives more money from its sales than it spends on its costs. (loss, profit, trust)
8. A ______ is a small group that takes control of the prices and selling practices of businesses. (trust, monopoly, profit)

COMPREHENSION CHECK

Write True if the question and answer match. If not, write the correct answer to the question.

1. What would happen if a business did not pay the cost of the goods that it sold?—It wouldn't have anything to sell, because its suppliers would refuse to furnish the things necessary to manufacture these goods.
2. What happened when people became concerned with the absence of competition in business?—Congress passed the Fourteenth Amendment.
3. Who do public utility boards consist of?—They consist of citizens who may be elected or appointed by the federal, state, or local governments.

SKILL BUILDERS–INTERPRETING TABLES

The *table* below shows the average weekly earnings and hours worked for certain industries in 1958 and in 1981. Is it true that we work fewer hours these days but make more money? Which professions tend to work the longest hours? Why do you think this is so? Do you think any of the weekly earnings for a particular profession are too high? Too low? Why?

	Earnings*		Hours Worked	
Industry	1958	1981	1958	1981
Metal mining	$95	$455	38.6	40.4
Telephone communications	$79	$372	38.4	39.8
Radio and TV broadcasting	$100	$302	38.0	37.9
Electric, gas, and sanitary services	$98	$409	40.9	41.9
Transportation	$87	$285	43.0	39.2
Wholesale trade	$84	$289	40.2	38.5
Retail trade	$54	$156	38.1	30.0
Hotels, tourist motels	$41	$147	39.7	30.7
Laundries and dry cleaning	$45	$161	38.7	33.7
Genl. building contracting	$97	$342	35.5	35.9

*rounded off

BUILDING WRITING SKILLS

1. Explain the nature of the business process and how competition plays a vital role in it.
2. Write five facts that apply to the following generalization: "Some companies in a certain line of business may try to eliminate competition by unfair methods."
3. Explain some of the effects that deregulation might have on our society.

Chapter Thirty-Two
Living in a Free Economy

"Consumption is the sole end and purpose of production; and the interest of the producer ought to be attended to only so far as it may be necessary for promoting that of the consumer." (Adam Smith, *Wealth of Nations*, 1776)

"The chief business of the American people is business." (Calvin Coolidge, 1925)

"Let the buyer beware." (Anonymous proverb)

In a capitalist system such as ours, we have many privileges and opportunities. However, in order to take full advantage of our free enterprise system, we must be responsible, informed consumers. In the United States, there are many federal, state, and local laws that are designed to protect the consumer. Consumer groups, schools, and government agencies also help in consumer education.

A well-informed consumer is the best defense against dishonest business practices. In recent years, consumer movements have become

During the holiday season, consumers are apt to buy more products and be subject to more advertising by sellers. Ask students how freedom of choice in buying practices relates to the concept of being informed as a consumer.

widespread, and many large cities have consumer protection offices. By paying attention to warnings from such groups, judging product advertisements objectively, and then, spending money wisely, consumers can reap maximum benefits from living in a free economy.

FOCUSING IDEAS

- A consumer's responsibilities include choosing among the ways of spending, making careful budgets, being informed, using shopping aids before making purchases, and understanding the nature of contracts and warranties.
- A consumer can prepare for the future by saving money, placing money in a pension fund, investing in stocks, spending money on various types of insurance, and by buying durable goods.
- Before signing a contract, a person should be fully aware of the nature of the contract, understand the financial terms, and be aware of the penalties involved if scheduled payments are not made.

Issues in Civics: Ask students how they generally feel about the products they buy and use. Do they usually perform as promised? If not, what can they, as consumers, do to protect themselves?

PRE-TEST

1. What is a consumer's responsibility?
2. How does a consumer become informed?
3. How does a consumer prepare for the future?
4. What should you look for in a contract?

WHAT ARE A CONSUMER'S RESPONSIBILITIES?

Objectives: After you have read this section, you will be able to:

- Understand the problems that we face when we spend money.
- See the value of budgeting and planning ahead as a means of spending wisely.
- Explain why it is so important for a consumer to be informed.

No matter what job you have or what other role you play in the economy, you will always be a *consumer*. Consumers are people who buy goods and services for their own use or that of their families.

People often pay too little attention to themselves as consumers, while working very hard to make the money they spend. To be a good consumer is hard work, but it is usually worth the effort.

Choosing among ways of spending

We often think of money as the solution to our problems. We should realize it can also cause problems. Having money forces us to make a choice between the many ways we might use it. Too often we think only of the one thing we buy and forget we made a choice to give up other things. And it is a final choice. We cannot make it again until we have more money.

The problem of spending has been with us ever since we were first able to provide more than our daily needs for food and shelter. The more we have, the greater the problem becomes.

Being responsible to yourself

A good citizen lives up to many responsibilities. Most of the time these are responsibilities to your country, to other citizens, or to the world community. Your responsibility as a consumer is somewhat different. As consumers we are primarily responsible to ourselves and our families. There are many ways to meet these responsibilities wisely.

One way to make a wise choice in spending is to avoid *impulse buying*. An impulse is a sudden action taken without thought. How many times have we bought something because it looked great, would taste good, or be exciting. Later we realize that our decision was unwise, and that we might have used the money better.

Building Vocabulary:
consumer *(540)* • impulse buying *(540)* • budget *(541)* • warranty *(546)* • interest/principal *(546)* • contract *(548)* • garnishee *(550)* • repossess *(550)*

Ask students if they can think of a time when they bought something on an impulse. Do they regret their actions? Why or why not?

Before buying a car, this couple weighed their decision very carefully because of the amount of money involved.

If we spend money today, we give up our chance to buy something tomorrow or the days after. In the same way, if we borrow money and promise to pay it back later, we also give up future choices. This doesn't mean we should never spend or borrow money. It means that we should always think about what we might want or need in the future as well as what we want or need today.

A Family Budget

Monthly Income	$1,800
Federal Income Tax	310
Social Security	120
State Taxes	50
Take Home Pay	$1,320
Expenses	
Rent	350
Food	300
Car payment	250
Car operation	70
Clothing	60
Insurance	90
Medical	25
Other	
Savings	100
Recreation and Charity	75
Total	$1,320

Making a budget

One way to think about future needs is to make a *budget* or plan for spending. In this way we avoid the temptation of impulse buying.

The Foster family allowed for taxes to be taken from their income. They figured out what they had to spend on food, housing, clothing, and transportation. From what was left, they made their choices for savings,

Have an interested student do research on a particular item to determine which brand of the product is the best buy. Suggest that the student use consumer magazines to aid in his or her research.

The purchase of a house is the largest single buying decision most people make.

recreation, and charity. They started off each month with what looked like a lot of money. But if they had not budgeted their money wisely, they might not have been able to buy the things they really needed. Using their budget, they were able to avoid impulse spending and prepare for the future.

Being informed

Our most important responsibility to ourselves when spending money is to be informed. Business people or experts on consumer affairs will tell us the most important thing in buying is to know how much we spend and what it is we buy. This is not as simple as it seems.

Most of us can remember buying something that did not last long, did not work as we thought it should, or did not suit our needs. We have all learned the hard way. We can avoid this experience by being informed at the moment of purchase.

Knowing when to be informed

We cannot learn all we would like to know about everything we buy. If we tried, we would not have time to do anything else but shop. On the other hand, it is obvious that buying a television set is a more important purchase than buying a candy bar because more money is involved. The more important the purchase, the more important it is to know what it is we buy.

A purchase becomes important for two reasons. The first is when we plan to use or enjoy the product for months or years and will not be able to replace it easily during that time. Examples are a car, a house, or a TV set. The second is when we spend a lot of money we are forced to give up other things now and in the future. Examples are vacation trips and expensive dinners.

Some people spend many dollars without thinking about it at all, an others do not spend a cent without worrying about it first. Being able to judge the importance of a purchase can help us find a reasonable compromise between these extremes of spending behavior.

Check for Understanding: Now that you have completed this section, you should be able to answer these questions:

1. What problems do we face when we spend money?
2. How does budgeting and planning ahead help you become a wise spender?
3. Why is it so important for consumers to be informed?
4. What is "impulse buying"?

Have students ask their parents if there was a time that they bought something that they later regretted buying as a result of not being informed about the product to begin with.

HOW DOES A CONSUMER BECOME INFORMED?

Objectives: After you have read this section, you will be able to:

- See that advertising can be a useful aid to the consumer.
- See how other forms of the media can help consumers to make wise purchasing decisions.
- Understand that as a buyer, we should take the total cost of an item into consideration.

Using advertising

Most businesses use advertising to let people know what is for sale. Advertising suggests ways to spend money. If used wisely, it can help us make the right decision.

Some advertising tries to make us want one thing very much and forget the other choices we have. Some advertisements want us to "keep up with the crowd," to use things because famous people use them, or to use one brand simply because we hear its name over and over on radio and television.

Some advertisements are deceptive, or not entirely truthful. The advertiser may say that prices have been "marked down" when they have not been changed at all. Advertisers will claim an advantage for a product it does not have or give a sensational or scientific name for something common and simple.

Television commercials like the one being filmed here have a strong influence on consumers' buying decisions.

Have students clip advertisements from magazines and newspapers that show both slanted approaches to selling and forthright approaches. Which ads do they think are the most appealing?

Advertisements tell us many things. The most important things they tell us are what is for sale, what the item does or what it looks like, how long it will last, where it is available, and how much it costs. Most other things in advertisements are designed to get our attention.

Using shopping aids

Many other aids besides advertising give us information about things we want to buy. Most newspapers, magazines, and TV stations provide consumer information. Reading and watching these can be helpful in making spending choices.

This person read several consumer magazines before making his choice of the particular radio he wanted to buy.

The federal government and some states publish pamphlets that provide information about certain goods and services. Before making an expensive purchase, we should see if there is a government pamphlet written about the product.

Finally, there are special magazines concerned only with consumer affairs. Each month they carry articles about many goods and give advice about spending. They are usually available in libraries, or through subscription. When making an important buying decision, it helps to refer to these magazines.

Knowing the total cost

It may seem strange to talk about knowing the price of something when you buy it. However, there are many things to consider in the total price or cost of a good or service that are not always immediately obvious.

For example, in buying a transistor radio we need to know if the price includes batteries. Even if bought separately, they are part of the total price or cost of a working radio. Total cost involves all the other things we must buy after the first purchase. Sometimes a certain article is only the first part of the complete product we want. In buying some kinds of goods, we should ask ourselves if we are paying the total cost or just the first of many costs.

There are other things which go into the total cost. If we expect an item to last a long time, we should learn a particular brand's average lifetime. What we are paying for are the hours or months of use and enjoyment. For example, a two hundred dollar record player that lasts ten years is in effect less expensive than one for seventy-five dollars that lasts only two years. This kind of information is not always easy to find. But it is information we should consider.

Discuss the idea of "total cost" with your students and help them understand the importance of this concept when buying a good or service.

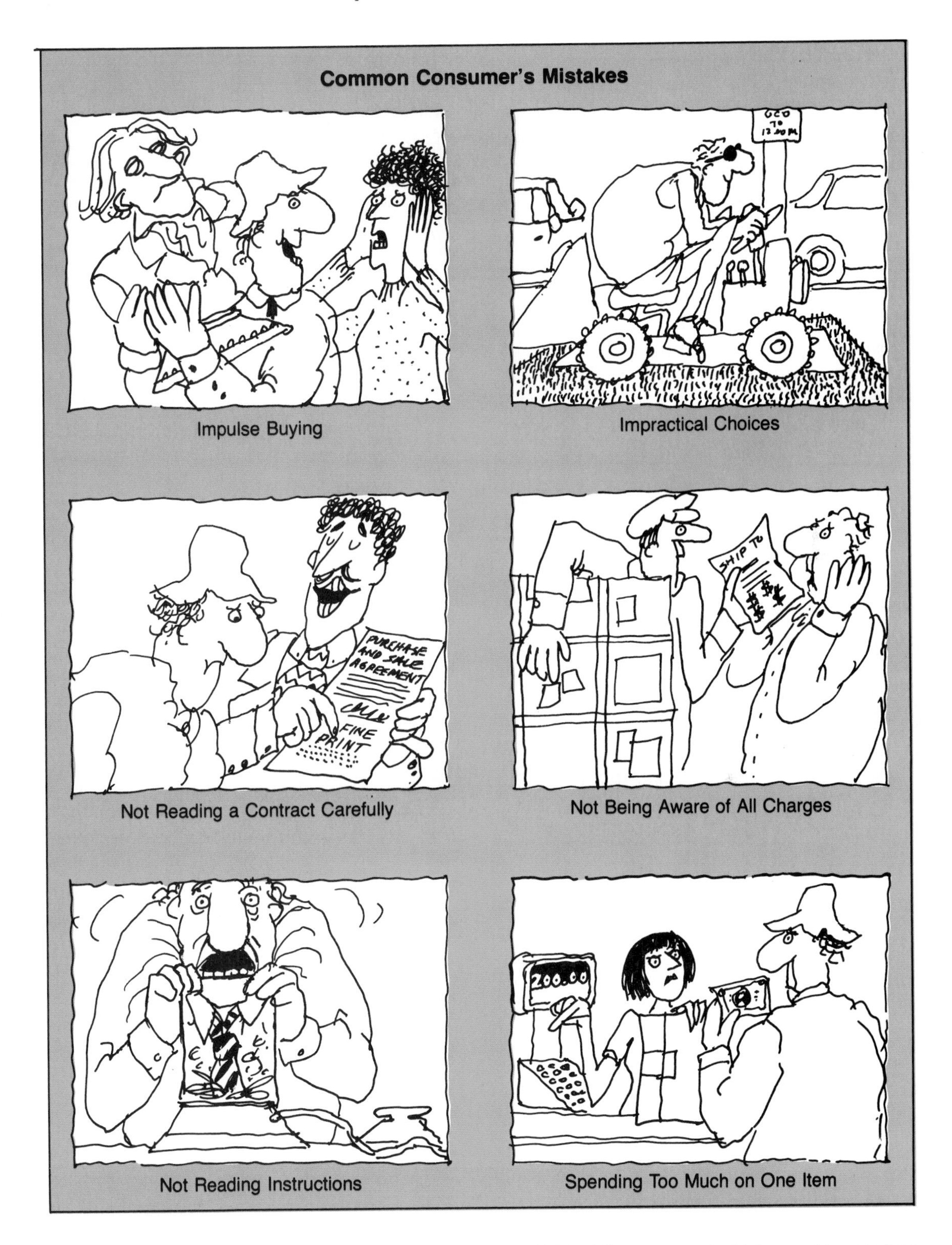

Common Consumer's Mistakes

Impulse Buying

Impractical Choices

Not Reading a Contract Carefully

Not Being Aware of All Charges

Not Reading Instructions

Spending Too Much on One Item

Which of the consumers' mistakes on this page have students been guilty of? Do they think they would make these mistakes again? Why?

Fair advertising

Most businesses use fair and legal advertising. They want us to be good consumers and to buy their products. A few businesses may try to use unfair and deceptive advertising, breaking federal and state laws which make such advertising illegal. The laws state generally that any statement of fact or promise must be true.

Warranties

Many items we buy have a *warranty*—a written guarantee or promise that the item will work for a certain period of time. If it fails to work, it will be replaced or repaired by the seller. Sellers do not have to provide warranties. Nor do they have to exchange goods or provide refunds. They do this for what they sell because they want good customer relations.

Check for Understanding: Now that you have completed this section, you should be able to answer these questions:

1. In what way can advertising help the consumer?
2. What other forms of the media help us make wise purchasing decisions?
3. Why should a buyer take the total cost of an item into consideration?
4. What is an example of deceptive advertising?

HOW DOES A CONSUMER PREPARE FOR THE FUTURE?

Objectives: After you have read this section, you will be able to:

- See that there are several ways in which an individual can prepare for his/her financial future.
- Understand the risks and benefits associated with various investments.
- List three types of insurance and tell what each type will pay for.

Saving

One way to prepare for the future is to save or put off spending money until some future time. Some people save part of their income every month. They save for many reasons. When they do decide to spend some of their savings, they will find that the amount they put aside has grown.

Banks pay *interest* on money deposited in savings accounts. While your money is on deposit, the bank uses it. Interest is what the bank pays you for their use of your money. Suppose that you have a hundred dollars in a savings account that pays 5½% simple interest a year. You do not take out the interest that is added to your account, but leave it in the bank with the original amount, or *principal.* You let your money work for you. At the end of thirteen years the money will have more than doubled.

There are many ways to save other than using savings accounts in banks. Some people save through a plan where the money for savings is taken from their pay before they receive it. Many companies do this automatically. Money is held out every payday and placed in a pension fund. When the worker retires, the pension fund continues to pay the person, even though he or she is no longer working for the company.

Investing

After a person has saved an amount of money over and above what might be needed for emergencies, he or she may wish to invest the money. Such money may be

Issues in Civics: Do students think that warranties are really an adequate protection for the consumer, or do they think that they are merely empty promises?

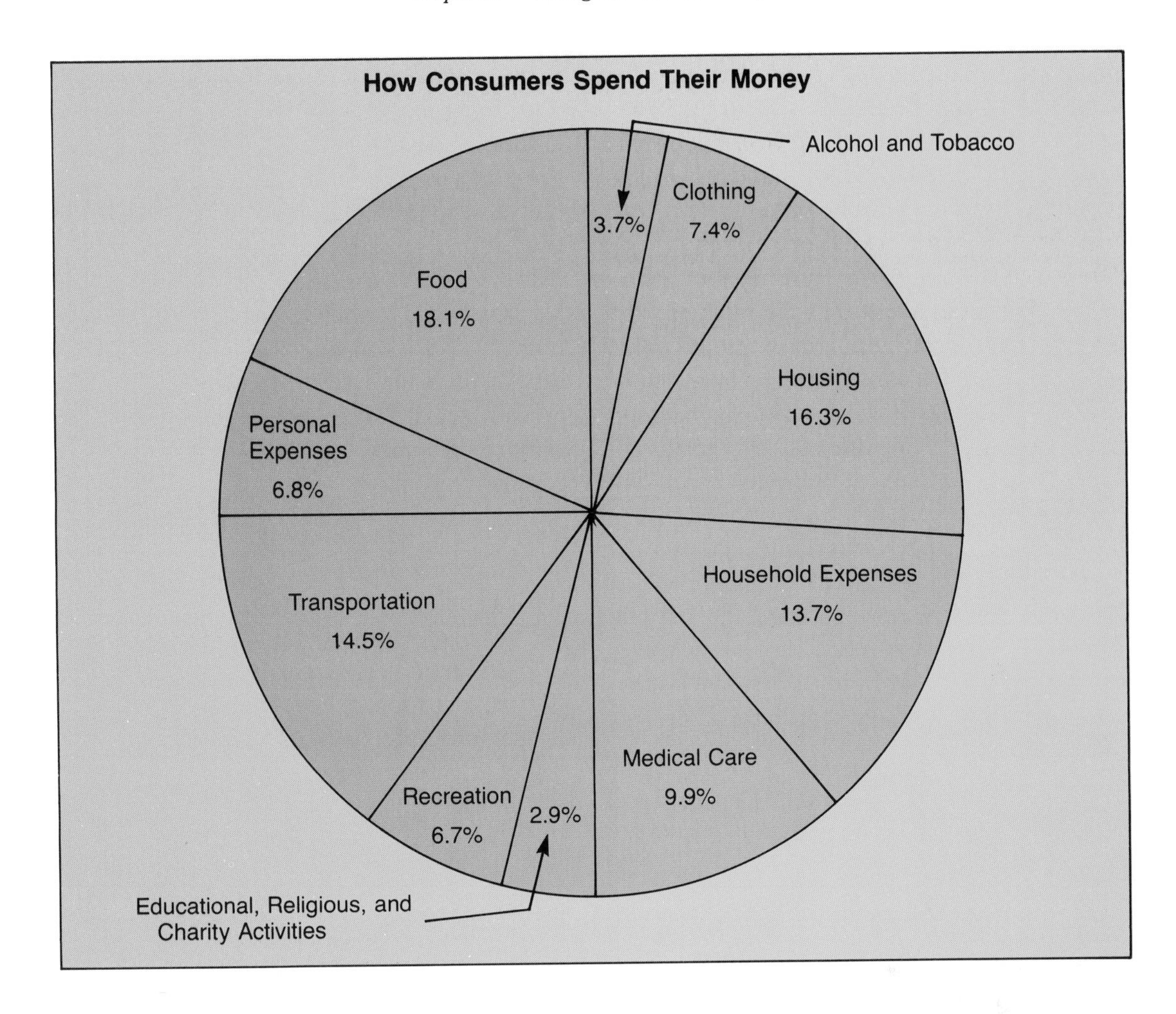

invested where the returns can amount to more than those gained in an ordinary savings account. One way to do this is to buy shares of stock in corporations.

Shares of stock may pay dividends amounting to more than the interest paid by the bank. In addition, the value of the stock may increase over the years if the worth of the companies increase. The stock may also decrease in value if the company does poorly. For this reason, investing in stocks is not as safe as saving in a bank or other savings institution. Investors should remember that the higher the return, the greater the risk.

Insurance

Some people also spend part of their income on insurance. Insurance is used for protection against a loss that might occur in the future. Part of the insurance money may go to buy life insurance. Originally, all life insurance policies were paid at death. A person would pay a set amount in annual payments. Upon death the spouse, children, or other person named would receive the amount of the insurance. Now there are other uses for life insurance.

Today life insurance may be taken out to help pay for a home or for an education. If a

Do any of your students have parents or relatives who have invested in the stock market? What were their experiences? Do they recommend this form of investment?

parent dies, money is provided to pay for the home or the children's schooling. However, if people buy more life insurance than they need, they will not have as much money to invest in other ways.

Everyone who owns or drives a car should consider buying automobile insurance. Many states require that a driver who is involved in an accident show proof of the ability to pay for any damage. If a car is destroyed or a person is seriously hurt or killed, the costs can run into thousands of dollars. As the cost of medical care and automobiles increases, automobile insurance becomes more important.

Another important form of insurance is health and accident insurance. It pays a daily or weekly amount in case of sickness or an accident. This kind of insurance may also pay for hospital and medical expenses.

Buying durable goods

A large part of preparing for the future is investing in a savings account on a regular basis. Another part of preparing for the future is buying durable goods. These are things that last a long time, such as houses, cars, furniture, and television sets.

The problem with durable goods is that they cost a great deal of money. A house may cost more money than a family earns in four or five years. A car may cost as much as many months' earnings. Even a television set can cost as much as a family earns in a month. We cannot go without food and other things for a month, much less for four or five years. Thus, there are many decisions to be made when we want to buy expensive durable goods.

Check for Understanding: Now that you have completed this section, you should be able to answer these questions:

1. What are some of the ways in which an individual can prepare for his or her financial future?
2. What are the risks and benefits associated with the various investments mentioned?
3. What are three types of insurance and what function does each type serve?
4. How does a pension fund work?

WHAT SHOULD YOU LOOK FOR IN A CONTRACT?

Objectives: After you have read this section, you will be able to:

- Explain the nature of a written contract and what it provides for.
- See that installment buying is a contractual obligation that must be upheld.
- Understand the penalties involved in the breaking of a contract.

The nature of a contract

When people borrow money they will have to sign a *contract.* A contract is an agreement between two or more persons or groups of persons.

A spoken contract has the disadvantage of being no better than the memories and honesty of the parties concerned, since there is no permanent record. It is wiser to make a written contract. A written contract cannot easily be mistaken. The signatures of the parties are evidence that each party knew, or had the opportunity to know, the terms of the contract. Such a contract is binding under the law.

Why do students think that many states require a driver to carry auto insurance? Do they think this is a good practice?

Now that the couple has finally decided which car to buy, they examine the sales contract very carefully.

How much to pay

People may learn about interest and other charges the first time they sign a contract to buy a used car. If the price of the car is $4,000, they may make a down payment of $500 and agree to pay the rest in monthly payments of $180 for two years. Later, they may figure out what they had really paid for the car. The figures are:

Down payment	$ 500
24 payments of $180	4,320
Total cost of car	$4,820

They had agreed to pay $820 more than the price of the car.

There is an explanation for the two not-so-obvious factors included in the cost. One is the two years of interest at twenty percent on the $3,500 borrowed. The other is $32 for credit life insurance. The two costs combined equals the difference of $820 which may not be readily noticed.

The interest was the charge for borrowing the money. The credit life insurance was to pay off the loan if the buyers died. The result was that the car cost $820 more because the money was borrowed. In this case, this amount is almost as much as the down payment that the purchasers made.

What happens if payments due are not made

What happens if a contract is broken? A contract is broken if the borrower fails to make the payments as agreed upon. Let's assume that the purchasers bought too many things on credit. Later they found that they could not afford them all, and they stopped making payments on the car. They would have broken the contract.

The lender might write or call them to avoid going to court. If they did not start to make their payments, they could be taken into court. The courts might say that the

Discuss with students the consequences that could result if a buyer fails to make the agreed-upon payments set forth in a contract.

contract was broken and they owed all the remaining money at once. If they could not pay, they might be made to sell some of their household goods to raise the money.

In certain states a worker's wages may be *garnisheed*. This means that the court orders his employer to take a certain amount out of his pay and give it to the lender. Once it was possible to garnishee a person's wages without letting them know about it until they received their smaller paycheck. In 1969 the Supreme Court ruled this illegal. Now a person must be called into court to have the opportunity to explain why the contract was broken. But if the explanation is not accepted, the wages may be garnisheed. As a citizen, you should know if wages can be garnisheed in your state.

If the Fosters failed to make payments on the car, the company might *repossess*, or take back the car. The car could be taken with a court order. The company would then resell the car. Suppose they still owed $500 on the car, and it was repossessed and resold for $400. The Fosters would have no car, and they would still owe $100. If the car were resold for more than $500, the company would have to pay them the difference.

Read the contract and know the terms

We have seen that many undesirable things can happen if a buyer breaks a contract. Wise buyers know this, so they are careful. They know how much they will pay back each time they borrow money. They use a budget to see if they can continue to make all of their payments.

They also read every contract before they sign it. They know that it does no good to say they didn't understand the terms of the contract after the contract is signed.

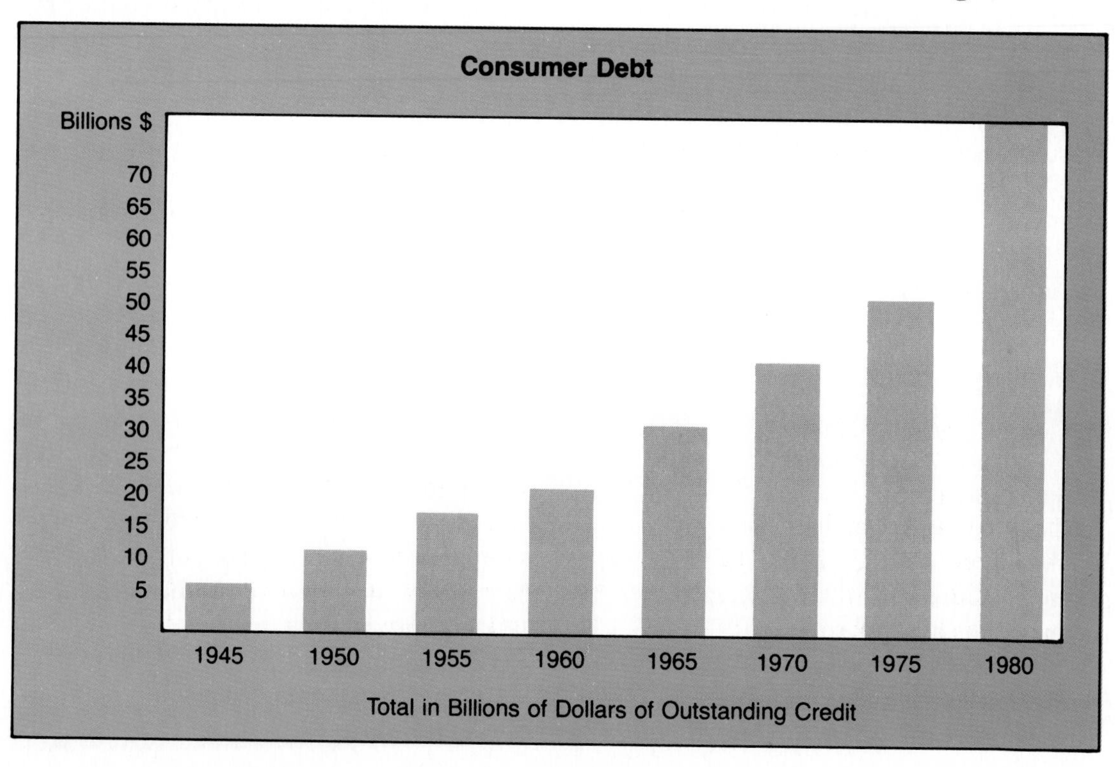

Do students know of anyone who had an item repossessed by a bank or company? What were the circumstances that caused this action?

Trust and honesty

The best protection for both buyers and seller is the trust and honesty of most people. When you order a hamburger or soft drink in a restaurant, you don't promise to pay when you are finished eating. There is a trust on the part of both parties that you will pay the check when you leave. In the same way honest sellers will exchange goods when they are not what they are supposed to be.

Many laws have been passed to protect consumers. A federal law called the "Truth in Lending Act" requires sellers and other lenders to put into writing the total amount that is paid for credit. It also required that the yearly rate of interest be put in writing.

Check for Understanding: Now that you have completed this section, you should be able to answer these questions:

1. What does a written contract mean to the two parties who sign it?
2. Why must an individual sign a contract when buying an item on an installment plan?
3. What are the penalties that result from a contract being broken?
4. Under what circumstances might a worker's wages be garnisheed?

SUMMARY

All of us will always spend money and be consumers. This involves certain responsibilities to ourselves to plan ahead and be well-informed. This is especially true when committing large amounts of money for major purchases such as a house or an automobile.

One way of being informed is to read advertisements. They tell us what goods are for sale, where to find them and how much they cost. Advertising can be deceptive, however, so it must always be evaluated critically. Other shopping aids are pamphlets from the government, and special consumer magazines. The well-informed consumer always finds out the total cost of an item, including extras and taxes, before making the decision to buy. For major purchases the existence or not of a warranty is an important part of making a decision.

One way to prepare for the future is to save money. As money makes money, it is a good idea to keep your savings in a bank or some other financial institution that pays you a good rate of interest on your principal. Pension funds are another way of saving money. There are several ways of investing extra money. Buying shares of stock in a corporation is one way, buying insurance is another. Insurance is not only an investment. Many states require automobile insurance.

Buying durable goods is also a way of investing in your future.

If you borrow money to purchase items you will have to sign a contract. It should be read very carefully before it is signed, otherwise you might find yourself in an agreement you are not happy with. Breaking a contract can have serious consequences. Almost the best protection for both buyers and sellers is trust and honesty. There is a federal law that requires sellers and other lenders to put in writing the total amount paid for credit charges.

Do students have a better understanding of the phrase, "Let the buyer beware" after reading the material in this unit? Discuss this topic as a group.

BUILDING SKILLS IN CIVICS

THINKING SKILLS

1. How is money a cause of problems as well as a solution to them?
2. Why is it so important to be an informed consumer?
3. What are some ways to save money other than by using savings accounts in banks?
4. Why is it required in many states to have automobile insurance? How can this type of insurance protect you?
5. Why is it better to make a written contract than a spoken contract?

VOCABULARY SKILLS

If the underlined terms in the statements below are used correctly, write True. If not, replace it with the proper term.

impulse buying	garnishee	budget	contract
consumer	interest	warranty	repossess

1. Banks pay dividends on money deposited in savings accounts.
2. A contract is broken if the borrower fails to make the payments as agreed upon.
3. A person may be called into court to explain why a contract has been broken, but if the court doesn't accept the explanation, the person's wages may be budgeted.
4. One way to make a wise choice in spending is to avoid impulse buying.
5. A contract is a written guarantee that an item that we buy will work for a certain period of time.
6. If a person buys a particular item but fails to make the payments, the company he/she bought the item from might repossess it.
7. Garnishees are people who buy goods and services for their own use or that of their families.
8. A budget is a detailed plan for spending within the limits of a given income.

STUDY SKILLS–USING A GLOSSARY AND DICTIONARY

The vocabulary words in this chapter are all defined in the *Glossary* in terms of how they are used in this particular context, that is, the way in which we participate in our free economy. However, several of the vocabulary words have other meanings that do not relate to this subject, for example, the word "interest." Many even function as other parts of speech when used in other contexts.

Activity: Go through the chapter carefully and pick out any word that has multiple meanings. Use your *dictionary* and the Glossary in this book to find all the possible definitions for a particular word. When you have finished, share your findings with other class members to see if they have found words or definitions that are not in your list.

BEYOND THE BOOK

1. Investigate the differing costs of a particular durable good that you or a family member might be interested in purchasing. Comparison shop to find out which store sells the item at the lowest price. Does the cost of the item include any accessories that may be needed for its operation, such as batteries or bulbs? Does the warranty cover a reasonable period of time? What do consumer magazines say about the brand of good that you are thinking of buying? Make sure you take all of these factors into consideration before purchasing the item.
2. Before a consumer buys an item on credit, a credit application must be filled out. The consumer must provide the seller with information that will assure him or her that future payments will be made according to the terms of the contract. Go to any bank or department store and obtain a blank credit application form. What kind of information is requested on the form? Can you understand why the information is vital to the protection of the seller? If you were a merchant, would you require that your customers fill out a credit application? Why?/Why not?

CHAPTER THIRTY-TWO TEST

VOCABULARY CHECK

Fill in the blank in each statement below with the correct term in parentheses.

1. The original amount of money that you put into a savings account is called the ______. (share, stock, principal)
2. One way to think about future needs is to make a ______ for spending. (budget, contract, warranty)
3. A ______ is a written guarantee that if an item fails to work within a certain period of time, it will be replaced or repaired. (warranty, dividend, durable good)
4. A ______ buys a good or service for his/her own use or for someone else's. (consumer, budget, garnishee)
5. One way to avoid poor spending practices is to avoid ______. (interest, principal, impulse buying)
6. A ______ is broken if a borrower fails to make the agreed-upon payments. (budget, warranty, contract)
7. A company may ______ an item if a person fails to make the proper payments. (repossess, garnishee, contract)
8. A person's wages may be ______ if the court does not accept the reasons that caused a person to break a contract. (repossess, garnishee, warranty)

COMPREHENSION CHECK

If the question and answer match, write True. If not, write the correct answer to the question.

1. How can consumers avoid buying items that do not live up to our expectations?—We can avoid this by being informed at the moment of purchase.
2. What are some of the things that advertising tells us?—It tells us how much money we must pay each month for a particular item.
3. What does the federal government do in order to provide consumers with information?—The government publishes pamphlets about certain goods and services.

4. How is making a budget useful to a consumer? It allows the consumer to "keep up with the crowd."
5. What is "impulse buying"?—It means that a consumer buys an item or service without thinking carefully about his or her actions beforehand.

SKILL BUILDERS–INTERPRETING CHARTS

Look at the *chart* in Chapter 32 called "Education and the Economy." Then answer the following questions:

a. What do the graphs at the top of the page show you?
b. How does the number of people who attended college in 1970 compare to that of 1980?
c. Are people more educated today than they were ten years ago? Why do you think this is so?
d. What information does the bar graph give you?
e. Do the incomes that apply to different levels of education surprise you?
f. Do you think the information on this page would have any effect on someone who is considering dropping out of high school? Why?/Why not?

BUILDING WRITING SKILLS

1. Write a paragraph detailing the preparation that would take place before a couple purchased a refrigerator on credit.
2. Explain the different ways that an individual or family can save money, and tell which method you are in favor of.
3. Write at least four statements to support this generalization: "One of the most important responsibilities of a consumer is to be informed."
4. What did the Supreme Court rule in 1969 regarding the garnisheeing of a person's wages? How did this law come about?

UNIT EIGHT TEST

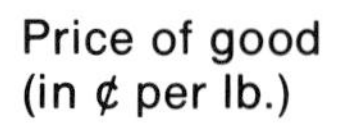

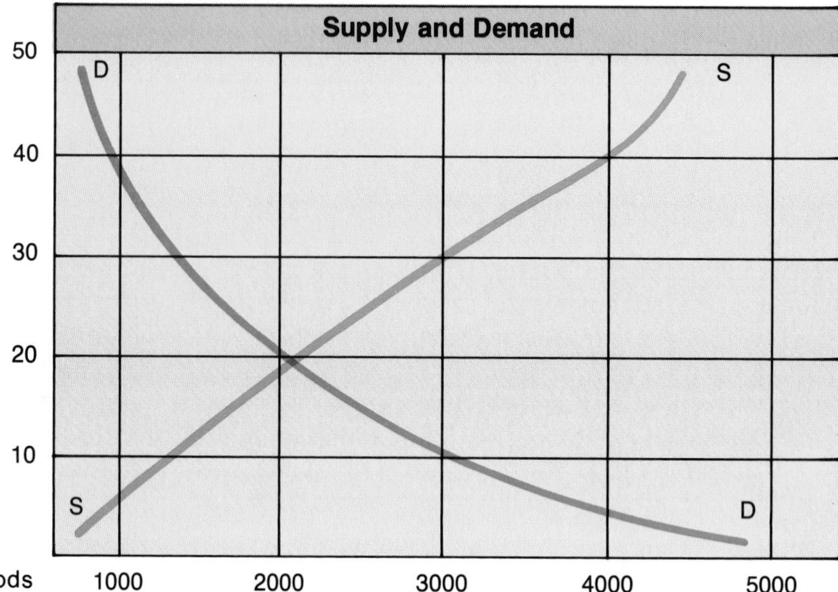

Quantity of goods produced (in lbs.)

A. The graph above shows the relationship of supply and demand in our economy. As you can see, the Supply Curve shows the number of pounds of a product that suppliers will produce at different prices. The demand Curve shows how much of a product customers want to buy at each price. Based on this information, answer the following questions:

1. Why do you think that the higher a certain price is, the greater the supply will be?
2. Is demand lower or higher when prices are high?
3. At what point on the graph would both sellers and buyers be satisfied? Why?

B. Imagine that the government has just decided that they are going to take control of all private property in the country. Write a letter to your congressman telling him or her why this action should not be taken and what the results would be if it is carried out.

C. Make a storyboard showing the steps that a consumer should take before spending money on a durable good.

Appendix

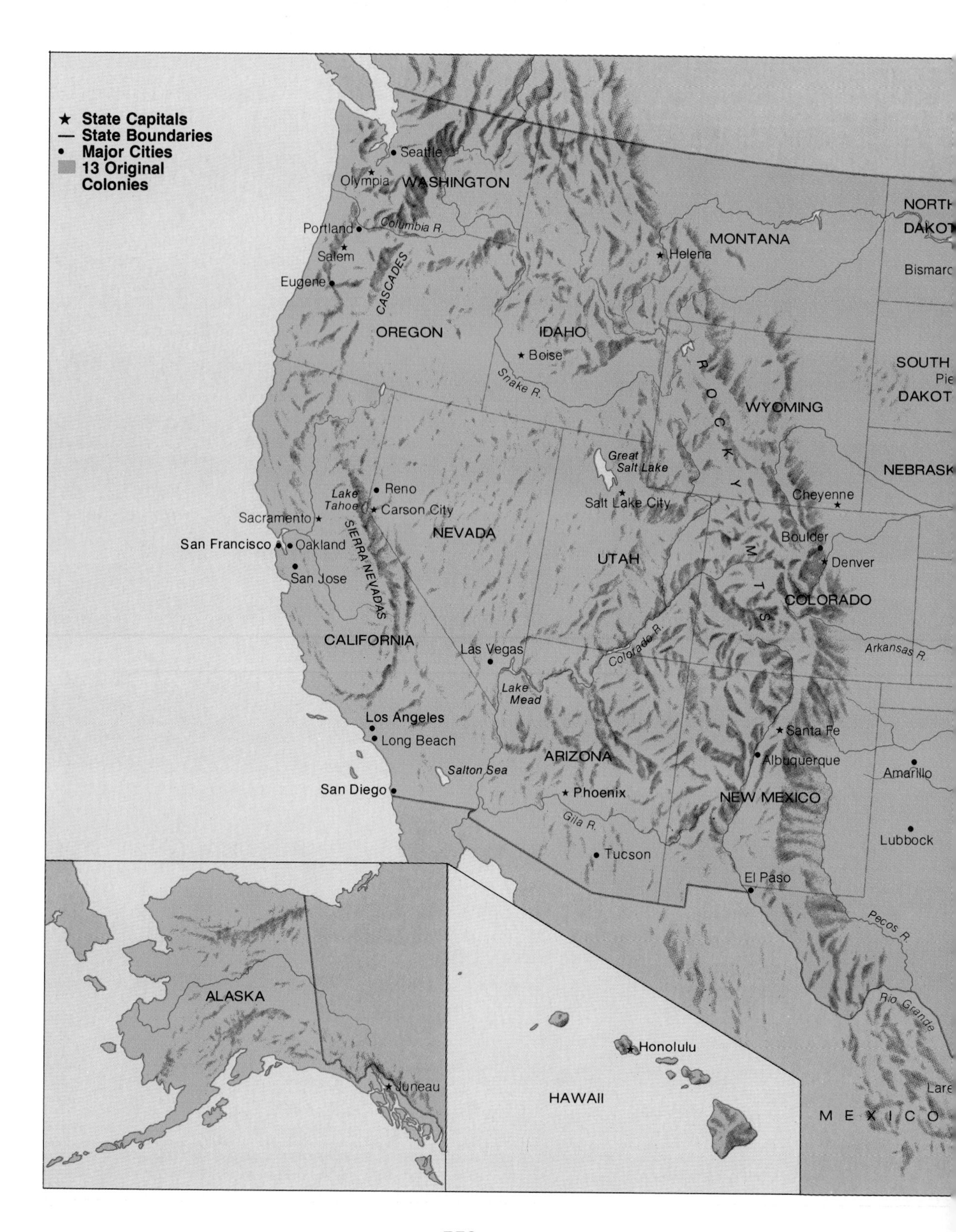

★ State Capitals
— State Boundaries
• Major Cities
13 Original Colonies
Seattle
Olympia
WASHINGTON
Portland
Columbia R.
Salem
Eugene
CASCADES
OREGON
IDAHO
Boise
Snake R.
MONTANA
Helena
WYOMING
ROCKY MTS
Great Salt Lake
Salt Lake City
Cheyenne
NEBRASK
SOUTH DAKOT
NORTH DAKOT
Bismarc
Reno
Lake Tahoe
Carson City
Sacramento
San Francisco
Oakland
San Jose
SIERRA NEVADAS
NEVADA
UTAH
Boulder
Denver
COLORADO
CALIFORNIA
Las Vegas
Colorado R.
Arkansas R.
Lake Mead
Los Angeles
Long Beach
Salton Sea
ARIZONA
Santa Fe
Albuquerque
Amarillo
San Diego
Phoenix
NEW MEXICO
Gila R.
Tucson
Lubbock
El Paso
Pecos R.
Rio Grande
ALASKA
Juneau
Honolulu
HAWAII
MEXICO

Map of the United States

Great Documents of the United States

THE DECLARATION OF INDEPENDENCE
In Congress, July 4, 1776.

THE UNANIMOUS DECLARATION OF THE THIRTEEN UNITED STATES OF AMERICA.

When in the Course of human events, it becomes necessary for one people to dissolve the political bands which have connected them with another, and to assume among the Powers of the earth, the separate and equal station to which the Laws of Nature and of Nature's God entitle them, a decent respect to the opinions of mankind, requires that they should declare the causes which impel them to the separation.

We hold these truths to be self-evident, that all men are created equal, that they are endowed by their Creator with certain unalienable Rights, that among these are Life, Liberty and the pursuit of Happiness. That to secure these rights, Governments are instituted among Men, deriving their just powers from the consent of the governed, That whenever any Form of Government becomes destructive of these ends, it is the Right of the People to alter or to abolish it, and to institute new Government, laying its foundation on such principles and organizing its powers in such form, as to them shall seem most likely to effect their Safety and Happiness. Prudence, indeed, will dictate that Governments long established should not be changed for light and transient causes; and accordingly all experience hath shown, that mankind are more disposed to suffer, while evils are sufferable, than to right themselves by abolishing the forms to which they are accustomed. But when a long train of abuses and usurpations, pursuing invariably the same Object evinces a design to reduce them under absolute Despotism, it is their right, it is their duty, to throw off such Government, and to provide new Guards for their future security. — Such has been the patient sufferance of these Colonies; and such is now the necessity which constrains them to alter their former Systems of Government. The history of the present King of Great Britain is a history of repeated injuries and usurpations, all having in direct object the establishment of an absolute Tyranny over these States. To prove this, let Facts be submitted to a candid world.

The spelling and punctuation of the original documents are used here.

He has refused his Assent to Laws, the most wholesome and necessary for the public good.

He has forbidden his Governors to pass Laws of immediate and pressing importance, unless suspended in their operation till his Assent should be obtained; and when so suspended, he has utterly neglected to attend to them.

He has refused to pass other laws for the accommodation of large districts of people, unless those people would relinquish the right of Representation in the Legislature, a right inestimable to them and formidable to tyrants only.

He has called together legislative bodies at places unusual, uncomfortable, and distant from the depository of their Public Records, for the sole purpose of fatiguing them into compliance with his measures.

He has dissolved Representative Houses repeatedly, for opposing with manly firmness his invasions on the rights of the people.

He has refused for a long time, after such dissolutions, to cause others to be elected; whereby the Legislative Powers, incapable of Annihilation, have returned to the People at large for their exercise; the State remaining in the mean time exposed to all the dangers of invasion from without, and convulsions within.

He has endeavoured to prevent the population of these States; for that purpose obstructing the Laws for Naturalization of Foreigners; refusing to pass others to encourage their migration hither, and raising the conditions of new Appropriations of Lands.

He has obstructed the Administration of Justice, by refusing his Assent to Laws for establishing Judiciary Powers.

He has made Judges dependent on his Will alone, for the tenure of their offices, and the amount and payment of their salaries.

He has erected a multitude of New Offices, and sent hither swarms of Officers to harass our people, and eat out their substance.

He has kept among us, in times of peace, Standing Armies without the Consent of our Legislature.

He has affected to render the Military independent of and superior to the Civil Power.

He has combined with others to subject us to a jurisdiction foreign to our constitution, and unacknowledged by our laws; giving his Assent to their acts of pretended Legislation:

For quartering large bodies of armed troops among us:

For protecting them, by a mock Trial, from Punishment for any Murders which they should commit on the Inhabitants of these States:

For cutting off our Trade with all parts of the world:

For imposing taxes on us without our Consent:

For depriving us in many cases, of the benefits of Trial by Jury:

For transporting us beyond Seas to be tried for pretended offences:

For abolishing the free System of English Laws in a neighboring Province, establishing therein an Arbitrary government, and enlarging its Boundaries so as to render it at once an example and fit instrument for introducing the same absolute rule into these Colonies:

For taking away our Charters, abolishing our most valuable Laws, and altering fundamentally the Forms of our Governments:

For suspending our own Legislature, and declaring themselves invested with Power to legislate for us in all cases whatsoever.

He has abdicated Government here, by declaring us out of his Protection and waging War against us.

He has plundered our seas, ravaged our Coasts, burnt our towns, and destroyed the lives of our people.

He is at this time transporting large armies of foreign mercenaries to compleat the works of death, desolation and tyranny, already begun with circumstances of Cruelty & perfidy scarcely paralleled in the most barbarous ages, and totally unworthy the Head of a civilized nation.

He has constrained our fellow Citizens taken Captive on the high Seas to bear Arms against their Country, to become the executioners of their friends and Brethren, or to fall themselves by their Hands.

He has excited domestic insurrections amongst us, and has endeavoured to bring on the inhabitants of our frontiers, the merciless Indian Savages, whose known rule of warfare, is an undistinguished destruction of all ages, sexes and conditions.

In every stage of these Oppressions We Have Petitioned for Redress in the most humble terms: Our repeated Petitions have been answered only by repeated injury. A Prince, whose character is thus marked by every act which may define a Tyrant, is unfit to be the ruler of a free people.

Nor have We been wanting in attention to our British brethren. We have warned them from time to time of attempts by their legislature to extend an unwarrantable jurisdiction over us. We have reminded them of the circumstances of our emigration and settlement here. We have appealed to their native justice and magnanimity, and we have conjured them by the ties of our common kindred to disavow these usurpations, which, would inevitably interrupt our connections and correspondence. They too have been deaf to the voice of justice and of consanguinity. We must, therefore, acquiesce in the necessity, which denounces our Separation, and hold them, as we hold the rest of mankind, Enemies in War, in Peace Friends.

We, therefore, the Representatives of the united States of America, in General Congress, Assembled, appealing to the Supreme Judge of the world for the rectitude of our intentions, do, in the Name, and by Authority of the good People of these Colonies, solemnly publish and declare, That these United Colonies are, and of Right ought to be Free and Independent States; that they are Absolved from all Allegiance to the British Crown, and that all political connection between them and the State of Great Britain, is and ought to be totally dissolved; and that as Free and Independent States, they have full Power to levy War, conclude Peace, contract Alliances, establish Commerce, and to do all other Acts and Things which Independent States may of right do. And for the support of this Declaration, with a firm reliance on the protection of Divine Providence, we mutually pledge to each other our Lives, our Fortunes and our Sacred Honor.

JOHN HANCOCK

BUTTON GWINNETT
LYMAN HALL
GEO. WALTON
WM. HOOPER
JOSEPH HEWES
JOHN PENN
EWARD RUTLEDGE
THOS. HEYWARD, JUNR.
THOMAS LYNCH, JUNR.
ARTHUR MIDDLETON
SAMUEL CHASE
WM. PACA
THOS. STONE
CHARLES CARROLL OF CARROLLTON
GEORGE WYTHE
RICHARD HENRY LEE
TH. JEFFERSON
BENJ. HARRISON

THOS. NELSON, JR.
FRANCIS LIGHTFOOT LEE
CARTER BRAXTON
ROBT. MORRIS
BENJAMIN RUSH
BENJA. FRANKLIN
JOHN MORTON
GEO. CLYMER
JAS. SMITH
GEO. TAYLOR
JAMES WILSON
GEO. ROSS
CAESAR RODNEY
GEO. READ
THO. M'KEAN
WM. FLOYD
PHIL. LIVINGSTON
FRANS. LEWIS

LEWIS MORRIS
RICHD. STOCKTON
JNO. WITHERSPOON
FRAS. HOPKINSON
JOHN HART
ABRA. CLARK
JOSIAH BARTLETT
WM. WHIPPLE
SAML. ADAMS
JOHN ADAMS
ROBT. TREAT PAINE
ELBRIDGE GERRY
STEP. HOPKINS
WILLIAM ELLERY
ROGER SHERMAN
SAM'EL HUNTINGTON
WM. WILLIAMS
OLIVER WOLCOTT
MATTHEW THORNTON

THE CONSTITUTION OF THE UNITED STATES OF AMERICA

PREAMBLE

WE THE PEOPLE of the United States, in Order to form a more perfect Union, establish Justice, insure domestic Tranquility, provide for the common defence, promote the general Welfare, and secure the Blessings of Liberty to ourselves and our Posterity, do ordain and establish this Constitution for the United States of America.

ARTICLE I

THE LEGISLATIVE DEPARTMENT

SECTION 1. All legislative Powers herein granted shall be vested in a Congress of the United States, which shall consist of a Senate and House of Representatives.

[How the House of Representatives Is Formed]

SECTION 2. The House of Representatives shall be composed of Members chosen every second Year by the People of the several States, and the Electors in each State shall have the Qualifications requisite for Electors of the most numerous Branch of the State Legislature.

No Person shall be a Representative who shall not have attained to the Age of twenty five years, and been seven Years a Citizen of the United States, and who shall not, when elected, be an Inhabitant of that State in which he shall be chosen.

Representatives and direct Taxes shall be apportioned among the several States which may be included within this Union, according to their respective Numbers, [which shall be determined by adding to the whole Number of free Persons, including those bound to Service for a Term of years, and excluding Indians not taxed, three fifths of all other Persons.] The actual Enumeration shall be made within three Years after the first Meeting of the Congress of the United States, and within every subsequent Term of ten Years, in such Manner as they shall by Law direct. The Number of Representatives shall not exceed one for every thirty Thousand, but each State shall have at Least one Representative; [and until such enumeration shall be made, the State of New Hampshire shall be entitled to chuse three, Massachusetts eight, Rhode-Island and Providence Plantations one, Connecticut five, New-York six, New Jersey four, Pennsylvania eight, Delaware one, Maryland six, Virginia ten, North Carolina five, South Carolina five, and Georgia three.]

Note: Brackets [ ] indicate parts of the original Constitution that no longer apply due to amendments or changes.

When vacancies happen in the Representation from any State, the Executive Authority thereof shall issue Writs of Election to fill such Vacancies.

The House of Representatives shall chuse their Speaker and other Officers; and shall have the sole Power of Impeachment.

[How the Senate Is Formed]

SECTION 3. The Senate of the United States shall be composed of two Senators from each State, chosen [by the Legislature thereof,] for six Years; and each Senator shall have one Vote.

Immediately after they shall be assembled in Consequence of the first Election, they shall be divided as equally as may be into three Classes. The Seats of the Senators of the first Class shall be vacated at the Expiration of the second Year, of the second Class at the Expiration of the fourth Year, and of the third Class at the Expiration of the sixth Year, so that one third may be chosen every second Year; [and if Vacancies happen by Resignation, or otherwise, during the Recess of the Legislature of any State, the Executive thereof may make temporary Appointments until the next Meeting of the Legislature, which shall then fill such Vacancies.].

No Person shall be a Senator who shall not have attained to the Age of thirty Years, and been nine Years a Citizen of the United States, and who shall not, when elected, be an Inhabitant of that State for which he shall be chosen.

The Vice President of the United States shall be President of the Senate, but shall have no vote, unless they be equally divided.

The senate shall chuse their other Officers, and also a President pro tempore, in the Absence of the Vice President, or when he shall exercise the Office of President of the United States.

The senate shall have the sole Power to try all Impeachments. When sitting for that Purpose, they shall be on Oath or Affirmation. When the President of the United States is tried, the Chief Justice shall preside: And no Person shall be convicted without the concurrence of two thirds of the Members present.

Judgment in Cases of Impeachment shall not extend further than to removal from Office, and disqualification to hold and enjoy any Office of honor, Trust or Profit under the United States: but the Party convicted shall nevertheless be liable and subject to Indictment, Trial, Judgment and Punishment, according to Law.

[Congressional Elections: Time of Assembling]

SECTION 4. The times, Places and Manner of holding Elections for Senators and Representatives, shall be prescribed in each State by the Legislature thereof; but the Congress may at any time by Law make or alter such Regulations, [except as to the Places of chusing Senators].

The Congress shall assemble at least once in every Year, [and such Meeting shall be on the first Monday in December, unless they shall by Law appoint a different Day].

[Rules and Procedure of Congress]

SECTION 5. Each House shall be the Judge of the Elections, Returns and Qualifications of its own Members, and a Majority of each shall constitute a Quorum to do Business; but a smaller Number may adjourn from day to day, and may be authorized to compel the Attendance of absent Members, in such Manner, and under such Penalties as each House may provide.

Each House may determine the Rules of its Proceedings, punish its Members for disorderly Behaviour, and, with the Concurrence of two thirds, expel a Member.

Each House shall keep a Journal of its Proceedings, and from time to time publish the same, excepting such Parts as may in their Judgment require Secrecy; and the Yeas and Nays of the Members of either House on any question shall, at the Desire of one fifth of those Present, be entered on the Journal.

Neither House, during the Session of Congress, shall, without the consent of the other, adjourn for more than three days, nor to any other Place than that in which the two Houses shall be sitting.

[Privileges and Restrictions of Members of Congress]

SECTION 6. The Senators and Representatives shall receive a Compensation for their Services, to be ascertained by Law, and paid out of the Treasury of the United States. They shall in all Cases, except Treason, Felony and Breach of the Peace, be privileged from Arrest during their Attendance at the Session of their respective Houses, and in going to and returning from the same; and for any Speech or Debate in either House, they shall not be questioned in any other Place.

No Senator or Representative shall, during the Time for which he was elected, be appointed to any civil Office under the Authority of the United States which shall have been created, or the Emoluments whereof shall have been encreased during such time; and no Person holding any Office under the United States, shall be a Member of either House during his continuance in Office.

[How Federal Laws Are Made]

SECTION 7. All Bills for raising Revenue shall originate in the House of Representatives; but the Senate may propose or concur with Amendments as on other Bills.

Every Bill which shall have passed the House of Representatives and the Senate, shall, before it become a Law, be presented to the President of the United States; if he approve he shall sign it, but if not he shall return it, with his Objections to that House in which it shall have originated, who shall enter the Objections at large on their Journal, and proceed to reconsider it. If after such Reconsideration two thirds of the House shall agree to pass the Bill, it shall be sent, together with the Objections, to the other House, by which it shall likewise be reconsidered, and if approved by two thirds of that House, it shall become a Law. But in all such Cases the Votes of both Houses shall be determined by yeas and Nays, and the Names of the Persons voting for and against the Bill shall be entered on the Journal of each House respectively. If any Bill shall not be returned by the President within ten Days (Sundays excepted) after it shall have been presented to him, the Same shall be a Law, in like Manner as if he had signed it, unless the Congress by their Adjournment prevent its Return, in which Case it shall not be a Law.

Every Order, Resolution, or Vote to which the Concurrence of the Senate and House of Representatives may be necessary (except on a question of Adjournment) shall be presented to the President of the United States; and before the Same shall take Effect, shall be approved by him, or being disapproved by him, shall be repassed by two thirds of the Senate and House of Representatives, according to the Rules and Limitations prescribed in the Case of a Bill.

[Powers Granted to Congress]

SECTION 8. The Congress shall have Power To lay and collect Taxes, Duties, Imposts and Excises, to pay the Debts and provide for the common Defence and general Welfare of the United States; but all duties, Imposts and Excises shall be uniform throughout the United States;

To borrow Money on the credit of the United States;

To regulate Commerce with foreign Nations, and among the several States, and with the Indian Tribes;

To establish a uniform Rule of Naturalization, and uniform Laws on the subject of Bankruptcies throughout the United States;

To coin Money, regulate the Value thereof, and of foreign Coin, and fix the Standard of Weights and Measures;

To provide for the Punishment of counterfeiting the Securities and current Coin of the United States;

To establish Post Offices and post Roads;

To promote the Progress of Science and useful Arts, by securing for limited Times to Authors and Inventors the exclusive Right to their respective Writings and Discoveries;

To constitute Tribunals inferior to the supreme Court;

To define and punish Piracies and Felonies committed on the high Seas, and Offences against the Law of Nations;

To declare War, grant Letters of Marque and Reprisal, and make Rules concerning Captures on Land and Water;

Further explanation of the powers listed above can be found in Chapter 15, "The Powers and Limits of Congress", beginning on page 222.

To raise and support Armies, but no Appropriation of Money to that Use shall be for a longer Term than two Years;

To provide and maintain a Navy;

To make Rules for the Government and Regulation of the land and naval Forces;

To provide for calling forth the Militia to execute the Laws of the Union, suppress Insurrections and repel Invasions;

To provide for organizing, arming, and disciplining, the Militia, and for governing such Part of them as may be employed in the Service of the United States, reserving to the States respectively, the Appointment of the Officers, and the Authority of training the Militia according to the discipline prescribed by Congress;

To exercise exclusive Legislation in all Cases whatsoever, over such District (not exceeding ten Miles square) as may, by Cession of particular States, and the Acceptance of Congress, become the Seat of the Government of the United States, and to exercise like Authority over all Places purchased by the Consent of the Legislature of the State in which the Same shall be, for the Erection of Forts, Magazines, Arsenals, dock-yards, and other needful Buildings;—And

To make all Laws which shall be necessary and proper for carrying into Execution the foregoing Powers, and all other Powers vested by this Constitution in the Government of the United States, or in any Department or Officer thereof.

[Powers Denied to Federal Government]

SECTION 9. [The Migration or Importation of such Persons as any of the States now existing shall think proper to admit, shall not be prohibited by the Congress prior to the Year one thousand eight hundred and eight, but a Tax or duty may be imposed on such Importation, not exceeding ten dollars for each Person.]

The Privilege of the Writ of Habeas Corpus shall not be suspended, unless when in Cases of Rebellion or Invasion the public Safety may require it.

No Bill of Attainder or ex post facto Law shall be passed.

No Capitation, [or other direct,] Tax shall be laid, unless in Proportion to the Census or Enumeration herein before directed to be taken.

No Tax or Duty shall be laid on Articles exported from any State.

No Preference shall be given by any Regulation of Commerce or Revenue to the Ports of one State over those of another: nor shall Vessels bound to, or from, one State, be obliged to enter, clear or pay Duties in another.

No Money shall be drawn from the Treasury, but in Consequence of Appropriations made by Law; and a regular Statement and Account of the Receipts and Expenditures of all public Money shall be published from time to time.

Issues concerning federal and state governments are covered in Chapter 8, beginning on page 122.

No Title of Nobility shall be granted by the United States: And no Person holding any Office of Profit or Trust under them, shall, without the Consent of the Congress, accept of any present, Emolument, Office, or Title, of any kind whatever, from any King, Prince, or foreign State.

[Powers Denied to State governments]

SECTION 10. No State shall enter into any Treaty, Alliance, or Confederation; grant Letters of Marque and Reprisal; coin Money; emit Bills of Credit; make any Thing but gold and silver Coin a Tender in Payment of Debts; pass any Bill of Attainder, ex post facto Law, or Law impairing the Obligation of Contracts, or grant any title of Nobility.

No State shall, without the Consent of the Congress, lay any Imposts or Duties on Imports or Exports, except what may be absolutely necessary for executing its inspection Laws: and the net Produce of all Duties and Imposts, laid by any State on Imports or Exports, shall be for the Use of the Treasury of the United States; and all such Laws shall be subject to the Revision and Controul of the Congress.

No State shall, without the Consent of Congress, lay any duty of Tonnage, keep Troops, or Ships of War in time of Peace, enter into any Agreement or Compact with another State, or with a foreign Power, or engage in War, unless actually invaded, or in such imminent Danger as will not admit of delay.

ARTICLE II

THE EXECUTIVE DEPARTMENT

[The President and Vice-President]

SECTION 1. The executive Power shall be vested in a President of the United States of America. He shall hold his Office during the Term of four Years, and, together with the Vice-President, chosen for the same Term, be elected, as follows

[The Electoral College]

Each State shall appoint, in such Manner as the Legislature thereof may direct, a Number of Electors, equal to the whole Number of senators and Representatives to which the State may be entitled in the Congress: but no Senator or Representative, or Person holding an Office of Trust or Profit under the United States, shall be appointed an Elector.

[The Electors shall meet in their respective States, and vote by Ballot for two Persons, of whom one at least shall not be an Inhabitant of the same State with themselves. And they shall make a List of all the Persons voted for, and of the Number of Votes for each; which List they shall sign and certify, and transmit sealed to the Seat of the Government of the United States, directed to the President of the Senate. The President of the Senate shall, in the Presence of the Senate and House of Representatives, open all the Certifi-

Unit Five, "Our Nation's Executives," fully explains the nature of Article II.

cates, and the Votes shall then be counted. The Person having the greatest Number of Votes shall be the President, if such Number be a Majority of the whole Number of Electors appointed; and if there be more than one who have such Majority, and have an equal Number of Votes, then the House of Representatives shall immediately chuse by Ballot one of them for President; and if no person have a Majority, then from the five highest on the List the said House shall in like Manner chuse the President. But in chusing the President, the Votes shall be taken by States, the Representation from each State having one Vote; A quorum for this Purpose shall consist of a Member or Members from two thirds of the States, and a Majority of all the States shall be necessary to a Choice. In every Case, after the Choice of the President, the Person having the greatest Number of Votes of the Electors shall be the Vice President. But if there should remain two or more who have equal Votes, the Senate shall chuse from them by Ballot the Vice President].

The Congress may determine the Time of chusing the Electors, and the Day on which they shall give their Votes; which Day shall be the same throughout the United States.

[Qualifications, Succession, Salary, and Oath of the President]

No Person except a natural born Citizen, [or a Citizen of the United States, at the time of the Adoption of this Constitution,] shall be eligible to the Office of President; neither shall any Person be eligible to that Office who shall not have attained to the Age of thirty five Years, and been fourteen Years a Resident within the United States.

In Case of the Removal of the President from Office, or of his Death, Resignation, or Inability to discharge the Powers and Duties of the said Office, the Same shall devolve on the Vice President, and the Congress may by Law provide for the Case of Removal, Death, Resignation or Inability, both of the President and Vice President, declaring what Officer shall then act as President, and such Officer shall act accordingly, until the Disability be removed, or a President shall be elected.

The President shall, at stated Times, receive for his Services, a Compensation, which shall neither be encreased nor diminished during the Period for which he shall have been elected, and he shall not receive within that Period any other Emolument from the United States, or any of them.

Before he enter on the Execution of his Office, he shall take the following Oath or Affirmation:—"I do solemnly swear (or affirm) that I will faithfully execute the Office of President of the United States, and will to the best of my Ability, preserve, protect and defend the Constitution of the United States."

[Military and Pardoning Powers of the President]

SECTION 2. The President shall be Commander in Chief of the Army and Navy of the United States, and of the Militia of the several States, when called into the actual Service of the United States; he may require the

Do students think that any of the qualifications for the Presidency are unfair? Discuss.

Opinion, in writing, of the principal Officer in each of the executive Departments, upon any Subject relating to the Duties of their respective Offices, and he shall have Power to grant Reprieves and Pardons for Offences against the United States, except in Cases of Impeachment.

[Treaties and Appointments Made by The President and Senate]

He shall have Power, by and with the Advice and Consent of the Senate, to make Treaties, provided two thirds of the Senators present concur; and he shall nominate, and by and with the Advice and Consent of the Senate, shall appoint Ambassadors, other public Ministers and Consuls, Judges of the Supreme Court, and all other Officers of the United States, whose Appointments are not herein otherwise provided for, and which shall be established by Law: but the Congress may by Law vest the Appointment of such inferior Officers, as they think proper, in the President alone, in the Courts of Law, or in the Heads of Departments.

The President shall have Power to fill up all Vacancies that may happen during the Recess of the Senate, by granting Commissions which shall expire at the End of their next Session.

[The Executive and Other Duties of the President]

SECTION 3. He shall from time to time give to the Congress Information of the State of the Union, and recommend to their Consideration such Measures as he shall judge necessary and expedient; he may, on extraordinary Occasions, convene both Houses, or either of them, and in Case of Disagreement between them with Respect to the Time of Adjournment, he may adjourn them to such Time as he shall think proper; he shall receive Ambassadors and other public Ministers; he shall take Care that the Laws be faithfully executed, and shall Commission all the Officers of the United States.

[Removal of Executive Officers from Office]

SECTION 4. The President, Vice President and all civil Officers of the United States, shall be removed from Office on Impeachment for, and Conviction of, Treason, Bribery, or other high Crimes and Misdemeanors.

ARTICLE III

THE JUDICIAL DEPARTMENT

[The Federal Courts and Judges]

SECTION 1. The judicial Power of the United States, shall be vested in one supreme Court, and in such inferior Courts as the Congress may from time to time ordain and establish. The Judges, both of the supreme and inferior Courts, shall hold their Offices during good Behaviour, and shall, at stated

Discuss the privileges and drawbacks associated with the U.S. Presidency. Refer to the photographic chart on page 300.

Times, receive for their Services, a Compensation, which shall not be diminished during their Continuance in Office.

[Jurisdiction of Federal Courts in General]

SECTION 2. The judicial Power shall extend to all Cases, in Law and Equity, arising under this Constitution, the Laws of the United States, and Treaties made, or which shall be made, under their Authority;—to all Cases affecting Ambassadors, other public Ministers and Consuls;—to all Cases of Admiralty and maritime Jurisdiction;—to Controversies to which the United States shall be a Party;—to Controversies between two or more States; [—between a State and Citizens of another State;]—between Citizens of different States,—between Citizens of the same State claiming Lands under Grants of different States, and between a State, or the Citizens thereof, and foreign States, [Citizens or Subjects].

[Jurisdiction of Supreme Court]

In all Cases affecting Ambassadors, other public Ministers and Consuls, and those in which a State shall be Party, the supreme Court shall have original Jurisdiction. In all the other Cases before mentioned, the supreme Court shall have appellate Jurisdiction, both as to Law and Fact, with such Exceptions, and under such Regulations as the Congress shall make.

[Trial by Jury]

The Trial of all Crimes, except in Cases of Impeachment, shall be by Jury; and such Trial shall be held in the State where the said Crimes shall have been committed; but when not committed within any State, the Trial shall be at such Place or Places as the Congress may by Law have directed.

[Treason: Definition and Punishment]

SECTION 3. Treason against the United States, shall consist only in levying War against them, or in adhering to their Enemies, giving them Aid and Comfort. No Person shall be convicted of Treason unless on the Testimony of two Witnesses to the same overt Act, or on Confession in open Court.

The Congress shall have Power to declare the Punishment of Treason, but no Attainder of Treason shall work Corruption of Blood, or Forfeiture except during the Life of the Person attainted.

ARTICLE IV

RELATIONSHIP BETWEEN STATES AND FEDERAL GOVERNMENT

[Each State Recognizes Laws of Other States]

SECTION 1. Full Faith and Credit shall be given in each State to the Public Acts, Records, and judicial Proceedings of every other State. And the

Refer to Unit 6, "Justice Under the Law" beginning on page 361 for further explanation of Article III.

Have students do research on an individual who has been convicted of treason in our country.

Congress may by general Laws prescribe the Manner in which such Acts, Records and Proceedings shall be proved, and the Effect thereof.

[Interstate Cooperation Regarding Citizens and Fugitives]

SECTION 2. The Citizens of each State shall be entitled to all Privileges and Immunities of Citizens in the several States.

A person charged in any State with Treason, Felony, or other Crime, who shall flee from Justice, and be found in another State, shall on Demand of the executive Authority of the State from which he fled, be delivered up, to be removed to the State having Jurisdiction of the Crime.

[No Person held to Service or Labour in one State, under the Laws thereof, escaping into another, shall, in Consequence of any Law or Regulation therein, be discharged from such Service or Labour, but shall be delivered up on Claim of the Party to whom such Service or Labour may be due.]

[Admission of New States to the Union]

SECTION 3. New States may be admitted by the Congress into this Union; but no new States shall be formed or erected within the Jurisdiction of any other State; nor any State be formed by the Junction of two or more States, or Parts of States, without the Consent of the Legislatures of the States concerned as well as of the Congress.

[Congress Makes Rules Respecting Government Property]

The Congress shall have Power to dispose of and make all needful Rules and Regulations respecting the Territory or other Property belonging to the United States; and nothing in this Constitution shall be so construed as to Prejudice any claims of the United States, or of any particular State.

[Federal Protection to States]

SECTION 4. The United States shall guarantee to every State in this Union a Republican Form of Government, and shall protect each of them against Invasion; and on Application of the Legislature, or of the Executive (when the Legislature cannot be convened) against domestic Violence.

ARTICLE V

PROVISIONS FOR AMENDMENTS

The Congress, whenever two thirds of both Houses, shall deem it necessary, shall propose Amendments to this Constitution, or, on the Application of the Legislatures of two thirds of the several States, shall call a convention for proposing Amendments, which, in either Case, shall be valid to all Intents and Purposes, as Part of this Constitution, when ratified by the Legislatures of three fourths of the several States, or by Conventions in three fourths thereof, as the one or the other Mode of Ratification may be proposed by the Congress; Provided [that no Amendment which may be made prior to

Refer to the chart on page 126 of Chapter 8, "Federal and State Government" for more information on the division of power in the federal system.

the Year One thousand eight hundred and eight shall in any Manner affect the first and fourth Clauses in the Ninth Section of the first Article; and] that no State, without its Consent, shall be deprived of its equal Suffrage in the Senate.

ARTICLE VI

CONSTITUTION THE SUPREME LAW OF THE LAND

[Prior Debts]

All Debts contracted and Engagements entered into, before the Adoption of this Constitution, shall be as valid against the United States under this Constitution, as under the Confederation.

[The Supreme Law of the Land; Obligation of State Judges]

This Constitution, and the Laws of the United States which shall be made in Pursuance thereof; and all Treaties made, or which shall be made, under the Authority of the United States, shall be the supreme Law of the Land; and the Judges in every State shall be bound thereby, any Thing in the Constitution or Laws of any State to the Contrary notwithstanding.

[Federal and State Officers Bound by Oath to Support the Constitution]

The Senators and Representatives before mentioned, and the Members of the several State Legislatures, and all executive and judicial Officers, both of the United States and of the several States, shall be bound by Oath or Affirmation, to support this Constitution; but no religious Test shall ever be required as a Qualification to any Office or public Trust under the United States.

ARTICLE VII

PROVISION FOR RATIFICATION BY STATES

[The Ratification of the Conventions of nine States, shall be sufficient for the Establishment of this Constitution between the States so ratifying the Same.]

DONE in Convention by the Unanimous Consent of the States present the Seventeenth Day of September in the Year of our Lord one thousand seven hundred and Eighty seven and of the Independence of the United States of America the Twelfth. In witness whereof We have hereunto subscribed our Names,

Go. Washington—Presidt. and deputy from Virginia

Attest William Jackson, Secretary

An explanation of the Amendment process can be found in Chapter 7, "Amending the Constitution" beginning on page 108.

AMENDMENTS TO THE CONSTITUTION

[The first ten amendments went into effect November 3, 1791]

AMENDMENT I

[Freedom of Religion, Speech, and the Press: Right of Assembly and Petition]

Congress shall make no law respecting an establishment of religion, or prohibiting the free exercise thereof; or abridging the freedom of speech, or of the press; or the right of the people peaceably to assemble, and to petition the government for a redress of grievances.

AMENDMENT II

[Right to Keep and Bear Arms]

A well regulated Militia, being necessary to the security of a free State, the right of the people to keep and bear Arms, shall not be infringed.

AMENDMENT III

[Quartering of Soldiers]

No soldier shall, in time of peace be quartered in any house, without the consent of the Owner, nor in time of war, but in a manner to be prescribed by law.

AMENDMENT IV

[Freedom from Unreasonable Search and Seizure]

The right of the people to be secure in their persons, houses, papers, and effects, against unreasonable searches and seizures, shall not be violated, and no Warrants shall issue, but upon probable cause, supported by Oath or affirmation, and particularly describing the place to be searched, and the persons or things to be seized.

AMENDMENT V

[Protection for Persons and Property]

No person shall be held to answer for a capital, or otherwise infamous crime, unless on a presentment or indictment of a Grand Jury, except in cases arising in the land or naval forces, or in the Militia, when in actual service in time of War or public danger; nor shall any person be subject for the same offence to be twice put in jeopardy of life or limb; nor shall be compelled in any criminal case to be a witness against himself, nor be deprived of life, liberty, or property, without due process of law; nor shall private property be taken for public use, without just compensation.

An explanation of the historical background of the Bill of Rights begins on page 112 of Chapter 7, "Amending the Constitution."

Ask students if they think Amendment III is or could be pertinent in these times.

AMENDMENT VI

[Rights of Persons Accused of Crime]

In all criminal prosecutions, the accused shall enjoy the right to a speedy and public trial, by an impartial jury of the State and district wherein the crime shall have been committed, which district shall have previously ascertained by law, and to be informed of the nature and cause of the accusation; to be confronted with the witnesses against him; to have compulsory process for obtaining witnesses in his favor, and to have the Assistance of Counsel for his defence.

AMENDMENT VII

[Right of Trial by Jury in Suits at Common Law]

In Suits at common law, where the value in controversy shall exceed twenty dollars, the right of trial by jury shall be preserved, and no fact tried by a jury, shall be otherwise re-examined in any Court of the United States, than according to the rules of the common law.

AMENDMENT VIII

[Protection Against Excessive Bail, Fines and Punishments]

Excessive bail shall not be required, nor excessive fines imposed, nor cruel and unusual punishments inflicted.

AMENDMENT IX

[Constitution Does Not List All Individual Rights]

The numeration in the Constitution, of certain rights, shall not be construed to deny or disparage others retained by the people.

AMENDMENT X

[Powers Reserved to the States and the People]

The powers not delegated to the United States by the Constitutiton, nor prohibited by it to the States, are reserved to the States respectively, or to the people.

AMENDMENT XI [Jan. 8, 1798]

[Limitation of Power of Federal Courts]

The Judicial power of the United States shall not be construed to extend to any suit in law or equity, commenced or prosecuted against one of the United States by Citizens of another State, or by Citizens or Subjects of any Foreign State.

See pages 367–68 for information on how the Bill of Rights safeguards our liberties.

Discuss the purpose of setting bail with students. Do they think that bail serves its purpose?

AMENDMENT XII [Sept. 25, 1804]

[Regulation of Electoral College]

The Electors shall meet in their respective states, and vote by ballot for President and Vice-President, one of whom, at least, shall not be an inhabitant of the same state with themselves; they shall name in their ballots the person voted for as President, and in distinct ballots the person voted for as Vice-President, and they shall make distinct lists of all persons voted for as President, and of all persons voted for as Vice-President, and of the number of votes for each, which lists they shall sign and certify, and transmit sealed to the seat of the government of the United States, directed to the President of the Senate;—The President of the Senate shall, in the presence of the Senate and House of Representatives, open all the certificates and the votes shall then by counted;—The person having the greatest number of votes for President, shall be the President, if such number be a majority of the whole number of Electors appointed; and if no person have such majority, then from the persons having the highest numbers not exceeding three on the list of those voted for as President, the House of Representatives shall choose immediately, by ballot, the President. But in choosing the President, the votes shall be taken by states, the representation from each state having one vote; a quorum for this purpose shall consist of a member or members from two-thirds of the states, and a majority of all the states shall be necessary to a choice. And if the House of Representatives shall not choose a President whenever the right of choice shall devolve upon them, [before the fourth day of March next following,] then the Vice-President shall act as President, as in the case of the death or other constitutional disability of the President.—The person having the greatest number of votes as Vice-President, shall be the Vice-President, if such number be a majority of the whole number of Electors appointed, and if no person have a majority, then from the two highest numbers on the list, the Senate shall choose the Vice-President; a quorum for the purpose shall consist of two-thirds of the whole number of Senators, and a majority of the whole number shall be necessary to a choice. But no person constitutionally ineligible to the office of President shall be eligible to that of Vice-President of the United States.

AMENDMENT XIII [Dec. 18, 1865]

[Abolition of Slavery]

SECTION 1. Neither Slavery nor involuntary servitude, except as a punishment for crime whereof the party shall have been duly convicted, shall exist within the United States, or any place subject to their jurisdiction.
SECTION 2. Congress shall have power to enforce this article by appropriate legislation.

Do students think that the electoral college is outdated? Why?/Why not?

See the Emancipation Proclamation on pages 585–86 for historical reference.

AMENDMENT XIV [July 28, 1868]

[Full Rights to All Citizens]

SECTION 1. All persons born or naturalized in the United States, and subject to the Jurisdiction thereof, are citizens of the United States and of the State wherein they reside. No State shall make or enforce any law which shall abridge the privileges or immunities of citizens of the United States; nor shall any State deprive any person of life, liberty, or property, without due process of law; nor deny to any person within its jurisdiction the equal protection of the laws.

[Penalty for Denial of Right to Vote]

SECTION 2. Representatives shall be apportioned among the several States according to their respective numbers, counting the whole number of persons in each State, excluding Indians not taxed. But when the right to vote at any election for the choice of electors for President and Vice-President of the United States, Representatives in Congress, the Executive and Judicial officers of a State, or the members of the Legislature thereof, is denied to any of the male inhabitants of such State, being twenty-one years of age, and citizens of the United States, or in any way abridged, except for participation in rebellion, or other crime, the basis of representation therein shall be reduced in the proportion which the number of such male citizens shall bear to the whole number of male citizens twenty-one years of age in such State.

[Denial of Public Office]

SECTION 3. No person shall be a Senator or Representative in Congress, or elector of President and Vice-President, or hold any office, civil or military, under the United States, or under any State, who, having previously taken an oath, as a member of Congress, or as an officer of the United States, or as a member of any State legislature, or as an executive or judicial officer of any State, to support the Constitution of the United States, shall have engaged in insurrection or rebellion against the same, or given aid or comfort to the enemies thereof. But Congress may by a vote of two-thirds of each House, remove such disability.

[Public Debts]

SECTION 4. The validity of the public debt of the United States, authorized by law, including debts incurred for payment of pensions and bounties for services in suppressing insurrection or rebellion, shall not be questioned. But neither the United States nor any State shall assume or pay any debt or obligation incurred in aid of insurrection or rebellion against the United States, or any claim for the loss or emancipation of any slave; but all such debts, obligations and claims shall be held illegal and void.

SECTION 5. The Congress shall have power to enforce, by appropriate legislation, the provisions of this article.

Refer to pages 4–6 of Chapter 1, "Freedom Through Responsible Citizenship" for a discussion of the meaning of citizenship.

AMENDMENT XV [March 30, 1870]

[Suffrage Not Denied Because of Race, Color, or Servitude]

SECTION 1. The right of citizens of the United States to vote shall not be denied or abridged by the United States or by any State on account of race, color, or previous condition of servitude.

SECTION 2. The Congress shall have power to enforce this article by appropriate legislation.

AMENDMENT XVI [February 25, 1913]

[Power to Levy Income Taxes]

The Congress shall have power to lay and collect taxes on incomes, from whatever source derived, without apportionment among the several States and without regard to any census or enumeration.

AMENDMENT XVII [May 31, 1913]

[Election of Senators by Direct Vote; Vacancies in Senate]

The Senate of the United States shall be composed of two Senators from each State, elected by the people thereof, for six years; and each Senator shall have one vote. The electors in each State shall have the qualifications requisite for electors of the most numerous branch of the State legislature.

When vacancies happen in the representation of any State in the Senate, the executive authority of such State shall issue writs of election to fill such vacancies: *Provided,* That the legislature of any State may empower the executive thereof to make temporary appointments until the people fill the vacancies by election as the legislature may direct.

[This amendment shall not be so construed as to affect the election or term of any Senator chosen before it becomes valid as part of the Constitution.]

AMENDMENT XVIII [January 29, 1919]

[Prohibition of Liquor]

[**SECTION 1.** After one year from the ratification of this article, the manufacture, sale, or transportation of intoxicating liquors within, the importation thereof into, or the exportation thereof from the United States and all territory subject to the jurisdiction thereof for beverage purposes is hereby prohibited.

SECTION 2. The Congress and the several States shall have concurrent power to enforce this article by appropriate legislation.

SECTION 3. This article shall be inoperative unless it shall have been ratified as an amendment to the Constitution by the legislatures of the several States, as provided in the Constitution, within seven years from the date of the submission hereof to the States by the Congress.]

Ask students to explain why voting is such an important way of influencing government. Refer to Chapter 12, beginning on page 190.

AMENDMENT XIX [August 26, 1920]

[Suffrage Granted to Women]

The right of citizens of the United States to vote shall not be denied or abridged by the United States or by any States on account of sex.

The Congress shall have power by appropriate legislation to enforce the provisions of this article.

AMENDMENT XX [February 6, 1933]

[Terms of Office of President, Vice-President; Time Congress Shall Assemble]

SECTION 1. The terms of the President and Vice-President shall end at noon on the 20th day of January, and the terms of Senators and Representatives at noon on the third day of January, of the years in which such terms would have ended if this article had not been ratified; and the terms of their successors shall then begin.

SECTION 2. The Congress shall assemble at least once in every year, and such meeting shall begin at noon on the third day of January, unless they shall by law appoint a different day.

SECTION 3. If, at the time fixed for the beginning of the term of the President, the President-elect shall have died, the Vice-President-elect shall become President. If a President shall not have been chosen before the time fixed for the beginning of his term, or if the President-elect shall have failed to qualify, then the Vice-President-elect shall act as President until a President shall have qualified; and the Congress may by law provide for the case wherein neither a President-elect nor a Vice-President-elect shall have qualified, declaring who shall then act as President, or the manner in which one who is to act shall be selected, and such person shall act accordingly until a President or Vice-President shall have qualified.

SECTION 4. The Congress may by law provide for the case of the death of any of the persons from whom the House of Representatives may choose a President whenever the right of choice shall have devolved upon them, and for the case of the death of any of the persons from whom the Senate may choose a Vice President whenever the right of choice shall have devolved upon them.

[**SECTION 5.** Sections 1 and 2 shall take effect on the 15th day of October following the ratification of this article.

SECTION 6. This article shall be inoperative unless it shall have been ratified as an amendment to the Constitution by the legislatures of three-fourths of the several States within seven years from the date of its submission.]

See page 116 of Chapter Seven, "Amending the Constitution" for a discussion of Women's Suffrage.

AMENDMENT XXI [December 5, 1933]

[Repeal of Prohibition]

SECTION 1. The eighteenth article of amendment to the Constitution of the United States is hereby repealed.

SECTION 2. The transportation or importation into any State, Territory, or possession of the United States for delivery or use therein of intoxicating liquors, in violation of the laws thereof, is hereby prohibited.

[**SECTION 3.** This article shall be inoperative unless it shall have been ratified as an amendment to the Constitution by conventions in the several States, as provided in the Constitution, within seven years from the date of the submission hereof to the States by the Congress.]

AMENDMENT XXII [February 26, 1951]

[Term of Office of the President]

SECTION 1. No person shall be elected to the office of the President more than twice, and no person who has held the office of President, or acted as President for more than two years of a term to which some other person was elected President shall be elected to the office of the President more than once. [But this Article shall not apply to any person holding the office of President when this Article was proposed by the Congress, and shall not prevent any person who may be holding the office of President, or acting as President, during the term within which this Article becomes operative from holding the office of President or acting as President during the remainder of such term.

SECTION 2. This article shall be inoperative unless it shall have been ratified as an amendment to the Constitution by the legislatures of three-fourths of the several States within seven years from the date of its submission to the States by the Congress.]

AMENDMENT XXIII [March 29, 1961]

[Inhabitants of District of Columbia Given Right to Vote in Presidential Elections]

SECTION 1. The District constituting the seat of Government of the United States shall appoint in such manner as the Congress may direct: A number of electors of President and Vice-President equal to the whole number of Senators and Representatives in Congress to which the District would be entitled if it were a State, but in no event more than the least populous State; they shall be in addition to those appointed by the States, but they shall be considered, for the purposes of the election of President and Vice-President, to be electors appointed by a State; and they shall meet in the District and perform such duties as provided by the twelfth article of amendment.

Discuss Amendment XXI with students. Ask them if there are any other amendments that they believe should be repealed.

Do students think that the length of Presidential terms is sufficient? Why? Why not?

SECTION 2. The Congress shall have power to enforce this article by appropriate legislation.

AMENDMENT XXIV [January 24, 1964]

[Poll Tax Abolished]

SECTION 1. The right of citizens of the United States to vote in any primary or other election for President or Vice-President, for electors for Vice-President or President, or for Senator or Representative in Congress, shall not be denied or abridged by the United Staes or any State by reason of failure to pay any poll tax or other tax.

SECTION 2. The Congress shall have power to enforce this article by appropriate legislation.

AMENDMENT XXV [February 10, 1967]

[Presidential Succession and Vacancy]

SECTION 1. In case of the removal of the President from office or of his death or resignation, the Vice President shall become President.

SECTION 2. Whenever there is a vacancy in the office of the Vice President, the President shall nominate a Vice President who shall take office upon confirmation by a majority of both Houses of Congress.

SECTION 3. Whenever the President transmits to the President pro tempore of the Senate and the Speaker of the House of Representatives his written declaration that he is unable to discharge the powers and duties of his office, and until he transmits to them a written declaration to the contrary, such powers and duties shall be discharged by the Vice President as Acting President.

Thereafter, when the President transmits to the President pro tempore of the Senate and the Speaker of the House of Representatives his written declaration that no inability exists, he shall resume the powers and duties of his office unless the Vice President and a Majority of either the principal officers of the executive department or of such other body as Congress may by law provide, transmit within four days to the President pro tempore of the Senate and the Speaker of the House of Representatives their written declaration that the President is unable to discharge the powers and duties of his office. Thereupon Congress shall decide the issue, assembling within forty-eight hours for that purpose if not in session. If the Congress, within twenty-one days after receipt of the latter written declaration, or, if Congress is not in session, within twenty-one days after Congress is required to assemble, determines by two-thirds vote of both Houses that the President is unable to discharge the powers and duties of his office, the Vice-President shall continue to discharge the same as Acting President; otherwise, the President shall resume the powers and duties of his office.

Have interested students do research to determine when and why the provisions in Section 1, Amendment XXV have been put into practice in our nation's history.

AMENDMENT XXVI [July 1, 1971]

[Eighteen-year-olds given the right to vote]

SECTION 1. The right of citizens of the United Sates, who are eighteen years of age or older, to vote shall not be denied or abridged by the United States or by any State on account of age.
SECTION 2. The Congress shall have power to enforce this article by appropriate legislation.

PROPOSED AMENDMENT TO PROVIDE FOR REPRESENTATION OF THE DISTRICT OF COLUMBIA IN CONGRESS*

SECTION 1. For purposes of representation in the Congress, election of the President and the Vice-President, and Article V of this Constitution, the District constituting the seat of the government of the United States shall be treated as though it were a state.
SECTION 2. The exercise of the rights and powers conferred under this article shall be by the people of the District constituting the seat of the government, and as shall be provided by the Congress.
SECTION 3. The twenty-third article of amendment to the Constitution of the United States is hereby repealed.
SECTION 4. This article shall be inoperative unless it shall have been ratified as an amendment to the Constitution by the legislatures of three-fourths of the several States within seven years from the date of its submission.

**Submitted to the states for ratification; not yet approved by a three-fourths majority*

Ask students if they believe they will eventually take advantage of the provisions in Amendment XXVI. Why?/Why not?

THE MAYFLOWER COMPACT

In the name of God, Amen, We, whose names are underwritten, the Loyal Subjects of our dread Sovereign Lord, King *James,* by the grace of God, of *Great Britain, France* and *Ireland,* King, *Defender of the Faith,* &,
Having undertaken for the Glory of God, and Advancement of the christian Faith, and the Honour of our King and Country, a voyage to plant the first colony in the northern Parts of Virginia; do by these Presents, solemnly and mutually in the Presence of God and one of another, covenant and combine ourselves together into a civil Body Politick, for our better Ordering and Preservation, and furtherance of the ends aforesaid; And by Virtue hereof to enact, constitute, and frame, such just and equal Laws, Ordinances, Acts, Constitutions and Offices, from time to time, as shall be thought most meet and convenient for the General good of the Colony; unto which we promise all due Submission and Obedience.
In Witness whereof we have hereunto subscribed our names at *Cape Cod* the eleventh of *November,* in the Reign of our Sovereign Lord, King *James* of *England, France* and *Ireland,* the eighteenth, and of *Scotland* the fifty-fourth. *Anno Domini,* 1620.

John Carver
Digery Priest
William Brewster
Edmund Margesson
John Alden
George Soule
James Chilton
Francis Cooke
Moses Fletcher
John Ridgate
Christopher Martin
William Mullins
Thomas English
John Howland
Stephen Hopkins
Edward Winslow
Gilbert Winslow
Miles Standish
Richard Bitteridge
Francis Eaton
John Tilly
John Billington
Thomas Tinker
Samuel Fuller
Richard Clark
John Allerton
Richard Warren
Edward Liester
William Bradford
Thomas Williams
Isaac Allerton
Peter Brown
John Turner
Edward Tilly
John Craxton
Thomas Rogers
John Goodman
Edward Fuller
Richard Gardiner
William White
Edward Doten

THE MONROE DOCTRINE

[December 2, 1823]

"In the discussions to which this interest has given rise, and in the arrangements by which they may terminate, the occasion has been deemed proper for asserting as a principle in which rights and interests of the United States are involved, that the American continents, by the free and independent condition which they have assumed and maintain, are henceforth not to be considered as subjects for future colonization by any European power. . . . We owe it, therefore, to candor and to the amicable relations existing between the United States and those powers to declare that we should consider any attempt on their part to extend their system to any portion of this hemisphere as dangerous to our peace and safety. With the existing colonies or dependencies of any European power we have not interfered and shall not

See pages 337–38 of Chapter 20, "Setting a Foreign Policy" for information related to the Monroe Doctrine.

Refer to the photo and explanation on pages 79–80 of Chapter 5, "Our Government Before the Constitution" for further explanation of the Mayflower Compact.

interfere. But with the governments who have declared their independence and maintain it, and whose independence we have, on great consideration and on just principles, acknowledged, we could not view any interposition for the purpose of oppressing them or controlling in any other manner their destiny by any European power in any other light than as the manifestation of an unfriendly disposition toward the United States."

LINCOLN'S GETTYSBURG ADDRESS

[November 19, 1863]

Fourscore and seven years ago our fathers brought forth on this continent a new nation conceived in liberty and dedicated to the proposition that all men are created equal. Now we are engaged in a great civil war testing whether that nation, or any nation so conceived and so dedicated, can long endure. We are met on a great battlefield of that war. We have come to dedicate a portion of that field as a final resting-place for those who here gave their lives that that nation might live. It is altogether fitting and proper that we should do this. But, in a larger sense, we cannot dedicate, we cannot consecrate, we cannot hallow this ground. The brave men, living and dead, who struggled here have consecrated it far above our poor power to add or detract. The world will little note nor long remember what we say here, but it can never forget what they did here. It is for us the living rather to be dedicated here to the unfinished work which they who fought here have thus far so nobly advanced. It is rather for us to be here dedicated to the great task remaining before us—that from these honored dead we take increased devotion to that cause for which they gave the last full measure of devotion—that we here highly resolve that these dead shall not have died in vain, that this nation under God shall have a new birth of freedom, and that government of the people, by the people, for the people shall not perish from the earth.

THE EMANCIPATION PROCLAMATION

[January 1, 1863]

By the President of the United
States of America

Whereas on the 22d day of September, A.D. 1862, a proclamation was issued by the President of the United States, containing, among other things, the following, to wit:

"That on the 1st day of January, A.D. 1863, all persons held as slaves within any State or designated part of a State the people whereof shall then be in rebellion against the United States shall be then, thenceforward, and forever free; and the executive government of the United States, including the military and naval authority thereof, will recognize and maintain the

Have students do research in order to determine which famous sources and speeches inspired the American's Creed.

Refer to page 29 of Chapter 2, "Government of the People" for a discussion of the Gettysburg Address.

freedom of such persons and will do no act or acts to repress such persons, or any of them, in any efforts they may make for their actual freedom.

"That the executive will on the 1st day of January aforesaid, by proclamation, designate the States and parts of States, if any, in which the people thereof, respectively, shall then be in rebellion against the United States; and the fact that any State or the people thereof shall on that day be in good faith represented in the Congress of the United States by members chosen thereto at elections wherein a majority of the qualified voters of such States shall have participated shall, in the absence of strong countervailing testimony, be deemed conclusive evidence that such State and the people thereof are not then in rebellion against the United States."

Now, therefore, I, Abraham Lincoln, President of the United States, by virtue of the power in me vested as Commander-in-Chief of the Army and Navy of the United States in time of actual armed rebellion against the authority and government of the United States, and as a fit and necessary war measure for suppressing said rebellion, do, on this 1st day of January, A.D. 1863, and in accordance with my purpose so to do, publicly proclaimed for the full period of one hundred days from the first day above mentioned, order and designate as the States and parts of States wherein the people thereof, respectively, are this day in rebellion against the United States the following, to wit:

Arkansas, Texas, Louisiana (except the parishes of St. Bernard, Plaquemines, Jefferson, St. John, St. Charles, St. James, Ascension, Assumption, Terleans, including the city of New Orleans), Mississippi, Alabama, Florida, Georgia, South Carolina, North Carolina, and Virginia (except the forty-eight counties of Berkeley, Accomac, Northhampton, Elizabeth City, York, Princess Anne, and Norfolk, including the cities of Norfolk and Portsmouth), and which excepted parts are for the present left precisely as if this proclamation were not issued.

And by virtue of the power and for the purpose aforesaid, I do order and declare that all persons held as slaves within said designated States and parts of States are, and henceforward shall be, free; and that the Executive Government of the United States, including the military and naval authorities thereof, will recognize and maintain the freedom of said persons.

And I hereby enjoin upon the people so declared to be free to abstain from all violence, unless in necessary self-defense; and I recommend to them that, in all cases when allowed, they labor faithfully for reasonable wages.

And I further declare and make known that such persons of suitable condition will be received into the armed service of the United States to garrison forts, positions, stations, and other places, and to man vessels of all sorts in said service.

And upon this act, sincerely believed to be an act of justice, warranted by the Constitution upon military necessity, I invoke the considerate judgement of mankind and the gracious favor of Almighty God.

See page 197 of Chapter 12, "People Influence Their Government" for further information on the slavery issue.

Discuss the text of the Emancipation Proclamation with students. Ask them which Amendment was ratified as a result of it. (Amendment XIII)

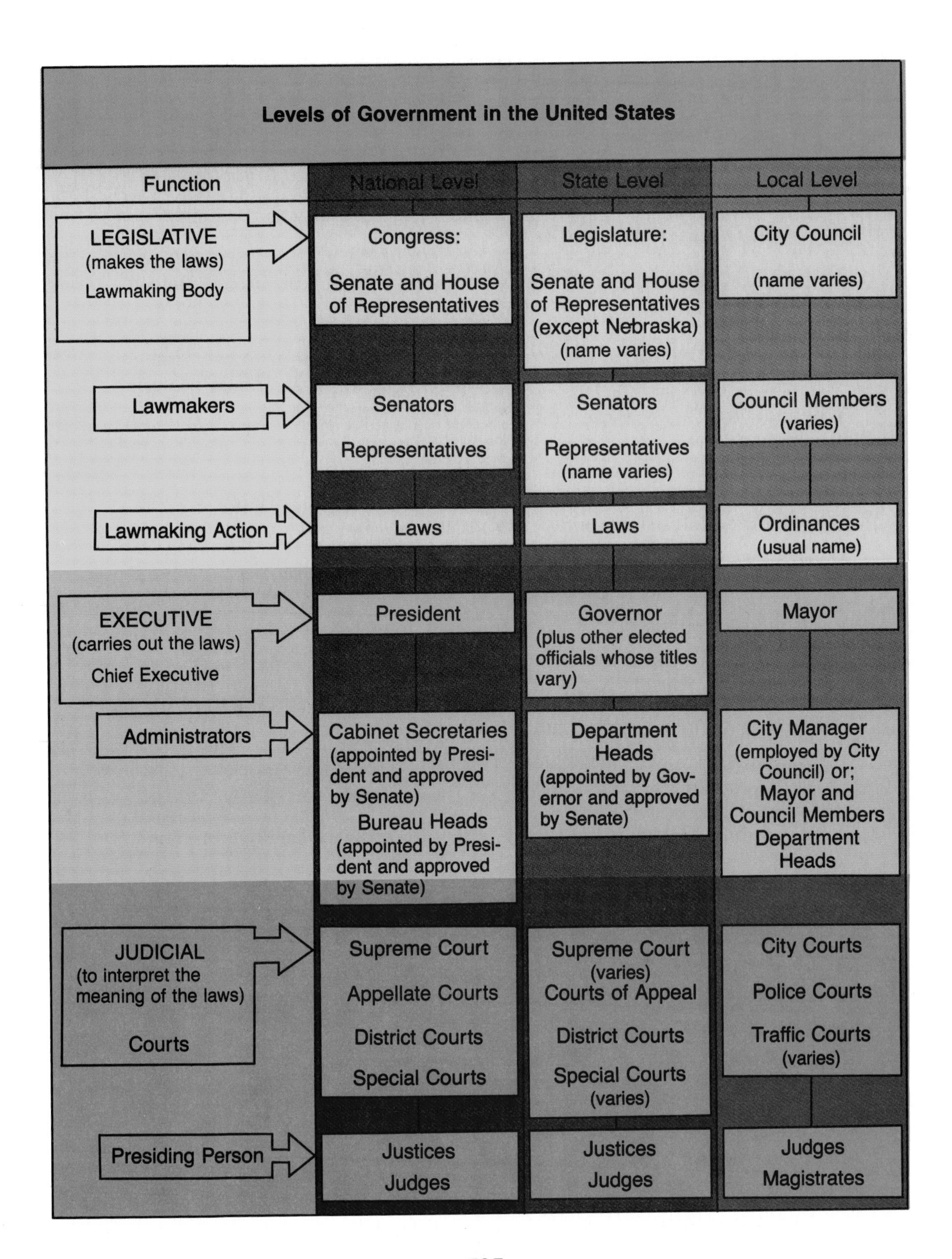

Levels of Government in the United States

Function	National Level	State Level	Local Level
LEGISLATIVE (makes the laws) Lawmaking Body	Congress: Senate and House of Representatives	Legislature: Senate and House of Representatives (except Nebraska) (name varies)	City Council (name varies)
Lawmakers	Senators Representatives	Senators Representatives (name varies)	Council Members (varies)
Lawmaking Action	Laws	Laws	Ordinances (usual name)
EXECUTIVE (carries out the laws) Chief Executive	President	Governor (plus other elected officials whose titles vary)	Mayor
Administrators	Cabinet Secretaries (appointed by President and approved by Senate) Bureau Heads (appointed by President and approved by Senate)	Department Heads (appointed by Governor and approved by Senate)	City Manager (employed by City Council) or; Mayor and Council Members Department Heads
JUDICIAL (to interpret the meaning of the laws) Courts	Supreme Court Appellate Courts District Courts Special Courts	Supreme Court (varies) Courts of Appeal District Courts Special Courts (varies)	City Courts Police Courts Traffic Courts (varies)
Presiding Person	Justices Judges	Justices Judges	Judges Magistrates

Thoughts on Free Government

Aristotle (384–322 B.C.): The basis of a democratic state is liberty.

William Shakespeare (1564–1616): Every subject's duty is the king's; but every subject's soul is his own.

John Milton (1608–1674): No man who knows aught, can be so stupid to deny that all men naturally were born free.

Benjamin Franklin (1706–1790): They that can give up essential liberty to obtain a little temporary safety deserve neither liberty nor safety.

William Pitt, Earl of Chatham (1708–1778): The poorest man may in his cottage bid defiance to all the forces of the Crown. It may be frail—its roof may shake—the wind may blow through it—the storm may enter—the rain may enter—but the King of England cannot enter—all his force dares not cross the threshold of the ruined tenement!

Voltaire (François Marie Arouet) (1694–1778): I disapprove of what you say, but I will defend to the death your right to say it. (attributed)

Sir William Blackstone (1723–1780): It is better that ten guilty persons escape than one innocent suffer.

Edmund Burke (1729–1797): The only thing necessary for the triumph of evil is for good men to do nothing. (attributed)

George Washington (1732–1799): The basis of our political system is the right of the people to make and to alter their constitutions of government.

John Adams (1735–1826): Liberty cannot be preserved without a general knowledge among the people.

Thomas Paine (1737–1809): Those who expect to reap the blessings of freedom must, like men, undergo the fatigue of supporting it.

Thomas Jefferson (1743–1826): If a nation expects to be ignorant and free, it expects what never was and never will be.

John Marshall (1755–1835): The people made the Constitution, and the people can unmake it. It is the creature of their own will, and lives only by their will.

Tecumseh (1768–1813): Sell a country? Why not sell the air, the clouds and the great sea, as well as the Earth? Did not the Great Spirit make them all for the use of his children?

In 1776, Thomas Paine wrote "Common Sense," a work which summed up the political sentiments of the day. Have an interested student report on the content of this historical pamphlet.

Although historians do not know the text of patriot Nathan Hale's last speech before his execution, his final quote is very well known: "I only regret that I have but one life to lose for my country." Have students research the events that led up to these moving last words.

John C. Calhoun (1782–1850): The very essence of a free government consists in considering offices as public trusts, bestowed for the good of the country, and not for the benefit of an individual or a party.

Daniel Webster (1782–1852): The people's government, made for the people, made by the people, and answerable to the people.

Abraham Lincoln (1809–1865): Those who deny freedom to others deserve it not for themselves, and, under a just God, cannot long retain it.

Henry David Thoreau (1817–1862): Any man more right than his neighbors constitutes a majority of one.

Frederick Douglass (1817–1895): Where justice is denied, where poverty is enforced, where ignorance prevails, and where any one class is made to feel that society is in an organized conspiracy to oppress, rob, and degrade them, neither persons nor property will be safe.

Susan B. Anthony (1820–1906): Here, in the Declaration of Independence, is the assertion of the natural right of all to the ballot; for how can "the consent of the governed" be given, if the right to vote be denied?

Ulysses S. Grant (1822–1885): I know no method to secure the repeal of bad or obnoxious laws so effective as their stringent execution.

Oliver Wendell Holmes, Jr. (1841–1935): If there is any principle of the Constitution that more imperatively calls for attachment than any other it is the principle of free thought—not free thought for those who agree with us but freedom for the thought that we hate.

Woodrow Wilson (1856–1924): The flag is the embodiment, not of sentiment, but of history. It represents the experiences made by men and women, the experiences of those who do and live under that flag.

Theodore Roosevelt (1858–1919): No man is above the law and no man is below it; nor do we ask any man's permission when we require him to obey it. Obedience to the law is demanded as a right, not asked as a favor.

Albert Einstein (1879–1955): My political ideal is democracy. Everyone should be respected as an individual, but no one isolated.

Franklin D. Roosevelt (1882–1945): The truth is found when men are free to pursue it.

Adlai Stevenson (1900–1965): The most American thing about America is the free common school system.

John F. Kennedy (1917–1963): And so, my fellow Americans, ask not what your country can do for you; ask what you can do for your country.

Patrick Henry (1736–1799) is remembered most for the words: "Give me liberty or give me death." Have students do research to find out when and why these words were spoken.

Facts about the Presidents

	President (Party)	Born–Died	State of Birth/ State Elected From	Term of Office	Runner-Up	Vice President
1.	George Washington[1]	1732–1799	Virginia	1789–1797	John Adams (1789, 1792)	John Adams (1789–1797)
2.	John Adams(F)	1735–1826	Massachusetts	1797–1801	Thomas Jefferson (1796)	Thomas Jefferson (1797–1801)
3.	Thomas Jefferson(DR)	1743–1826	Virginia	1801–1809	Aaron Burr (1800) Charles C. Pinckney (1804)	Aaron Burr (1801–1805) George Clinton (1805–1809)
4.	James Madison(DR)	1751–1836	Virginia	1809–1817	Charles C. Pinckney (1808) De Witt Clinton (1812)	George Clinton (1809–1812) Elbridge Gerry (1813–1814)
5.	James Monroe(DR)	1758–1831	Virginia	1817–1825	Rufus King (1816) No opposition second term	Daniel D. Tompkins (1817–1825)
6.	John Qunicy Adams(DR)	1767–1848	Massachusetts	1825–1829	Andrew Jackson (1824)	John C. Calhoun (1825–1829)
7.	Andrew Jackson(D)	1767–1845	South Carolina/ Tennessee	1829–1837	John Q. Adams (1828) Henry Clay (1832)	John C. Calhoun (1829–1832) Martin Van Buren (1833–1837)
8.	Martin Van Buren(D)	1782–1862	New York	1837–1841	William H. Harrison (1836)	Richard M. Johnson (1837–1841)
9.	William H. Harrison(W)[2]	1773–1841	Virginia/Ohio	March 1841	Martin Van Buren (1840)	John Tyler (1841)
10.	John Tyler(W)	1790–1862	Virginia	1841–1845	None[4]	—
11.	James K. Polk(D)	1795–1849	North Carolina/ Tennessee	1845–1849	Henry Clay (1844)	George M. Dallas (1845–1849)
12.	Zachary Taylor(W)[2]	1784–1850	Virginia/ Louisiana	1849–1850	Lewis Cass (1848)	Millard Fillmore (1849–1850)
13.	Millard Fillmore(W)	1800–1874	New York	1850–1853	None[4]	—
14.	Franklin Pierce(D)	1804–1869	New Hampshire	1853–1857	Winfield Scott (1852)	William R. King (1853)
15.	James Buchanan(D)	1791–1868	Pennsylvania	1857–1861	John C. Frémont (1856)	John C. Breckenridge (1857–1861)
16.	Abraham Lincoln(R)[3]	1809–1865	Kentucky/ Illinois	1861–1865	Stephen A. Douglas (1860) George B. McClellan (1864)	Hannibal Hamlin (1861–1865) Andrew Jackson (1865)
17.	Andrew Johnson(U)	1808–1875	North Carolina/ Tennessee	1865–1869	None[4]	—
18.	Ulysses S. Grant(R)	1822–1885	Ohio/Illinois	1869–1877	Horatio Seymour (1868) Horace Greeley (1872)	Schuyler Colfax (1869–1873) Henry Wilson (1873–1875)
19.	Rutherford B. Hayes(R)	1822–1893	Ohio	1877–1881	Samuel J. Tilden (1876)	William A. Wheeler (1877–1881)
20.	James A. Garfield(R)[3]	1811–1831	Ohio	March–Sept. 1881	Winfield S. Hancock (1880)	Chester A. Arthur (1881)
21.	Chester A. Arthur(R)	1830–1886	Vermont/New York	1881–1885	None[4]	—
22.	Grover Cleveland(D)	1837–1908	New Jersey/ New York	1885–1889	James G. Blaine (1884)	Thomas A. Hendricks (1885)

23. Benjamin Harrison(R)	1833–1900	Ohio/Indiana	1889–1893	Grover Cleveland (1888)	Levi P. Morton (1889–1893)
24. Grover Cleveland(D)	1837–1908	New Jersey/ New York	1893–1897	Benjamin Harrison (1892)	Adlai E. Stevenson (1893–1897)
25. William McKinley(R)[3]	1843–1901	Ohio	1897–1901	William J. Bryan (1896, 1900)	Garret A. Hobart (1897–1899) Theodore Roosevelt (1901)
26. Theodore Roosevelt(R)	1858–1919	New York	1901–1909	Alton B. Parker (1904)	Charles W. Fairbanks (1905–1909)
27. William H. Taft(R)	1857–1930	Ohio	1909–1913	William J. Bryan (1908)	James S. Sherman (1909–1912)
28. Woodrow Wilson(D)	1856–1924	New Jersey	1913–1921	Theodore Roosevelt (1912) Charles E. Hughes (1916)	Thomas R. Marshall (1913–1921)
29. Warren G. Harding(R)[2]	1865–1923	Ohio	1921–1923	James M. Cox (1920)	Calvin Coolidge (1921–1923)
30. Calvin Coolidge(R)	1872–1933	Vermont/ Massachusetts	1923–1929	John W. Davis (1924)	Charles G. Dawes (1925–1929)
31. Herbert C. Hoover(R)	1874–1964	Iowa/California	1929–1933	Alfred E. Smith (1928)	Charles Curtis (1929–1933)
32. Franklin D. Roosevelt(D)[2]	1882–1945	New York	1933–1945	Herbert Hoover (1932) Alfred M. Landon (1936) Wendell L. Willkie (1940) Thomas E. Dewey (1944)	John N. Garner (1933–1941) Henry A. Wallace (1941–1945) Harry S. Truman (1945)
33. Harry S. Truman(D)	1884–1972	Missouri	1945–1953	Thomas E. Dewey (1948)	Alben W. Barkley (1949–1953)
34. Dwight D. Eisenhower(R)	1890–1969	Texas/Kansas	1953–1961	Adlai E. Stevenson (1952, 1956)	Richard M. Nixon (1953–1961)
35. John F. Kennedy(D)[3]	1917–1963	Massachusetts	1961–1963	Richard M. Nixon (1960)	Lyndon B. Johnson (1961–1963)
36. Lyndon B. Johnson(D)	1908–1973	Texas	1963–1969	Barry M. Goldwater (1964)	Hubert H. Humphrey (1965–1969)
37. Richard M. Nixon(R)[5]	1913–	California	1969–1974	Hubert H. Humphrey (1968) George S. McGovern (1972)	Spiro T. Agnew (1969–1973) Gerald R. Ford (1973–1974)
38. Gerald R. Ford(R)	1913–	Nebraska/Michigan	1974–1977	None[6]	Nelson A. Rockefeller (1974–1977)
39. James E. Carter, Jr.(D)	1924–	Georgia	1977–1981	Gerald R. Ford (1976)	Walter F. Mondale (1977–1981)
40. Ronald Reagan(R)	1911–	Illinois/ California	1981–	James E. Carter, Jr. (1980)	George H. Bush (1981–)

KEY:

(D) - Democratic (F) - Federalist (DR) - Democratic-Republican (R) - Republican (W) - Whig (U) - Union

[1]No party for first election. The party system in the U.S. originated during Washington's first term.
[2]Died in office.
[3]Assassinated in office.
[4]Succeeded to presidency upon death of President.
[5]Resigned August 9, 1974.
[6]Inaugurated August 9, 1974 to replace Nixon.

Facts about the States

State	Date Entered Union (Rank)	Nickname	1980 Population (Rank)	Reps. in Congress	Area: Sq. mi./ (Rank)	Capital/ Largest City
ALABAMA	Dec. 14, 1819 (22)	Yellowhammer State	3,890,061 (22)	7	50,708 (28)	Montgomery/ Birmingham
ALASKA	Jan. 3, 1959 (49)	The Last Frontier	400,481 (50)	1	566,432 (1)	Juneau/ Anchorage
ARIZONA	Feb. 14, 1912 (48)	Grand Canyon State	2,717,866 (29)	5	113,417 (6)	Phoenix
ARKANSAS	June 15, 1836 (25)	Land of Opportunity	2,285,513 (33)	4	51,945 (27)	Little Rock
CALIFORNIA	Sept. 9, 1850 (31)	Golden State	23,668,562 (1)	45	156,361 (3)	Sacramento/ Los Angeles
COLORADO	Aug. 1, 1876 (38)	Centennial State	2,888,834 (28)	6	103,766 (8)	Denver
CONNECTICUT	Jan. 9, 1788 (5)	Constitution State	3,107,576 (24)	6	4,862 (48)	Hartford/ Bridgeport
DELAWARE	Dec. 7, 1787 (1)	Diamond State	595,225 (47)	1	1,982 (49)	Dover/ Wilmington
FLORIDA	March 3, 1845 (27)	Sunshine State	9,739,992 (7)	19	54,090 (26)	Tallahassee/ Jacksonville
GEORGIA	Jan. 2, 1788 (4)	Peach State	5,464,265 (13)	10	58,073 (21)	Atlanta
HAWAII	Aug. 21, 1959 (50)	Aloha State	965,000 (39)	2	6,425 (47)	Honolulu
IDAHO	July 3, 1890 (43)	Gem State	943,935 (41)	2	86,677 (11)	Boise
ILLINOIS	Dec. 3, 1818 (21)	Prairie State	11,418,461 (5)	22	56,400 (23)	Springfield/ Chicago
INDIANA	Dec. 11, 1816 (19)	Hoosier State	5,490,179 (12)	10	36,097 (38)	Indianapolis
IOWA	Dec. 28, 1846 (29)	Hawkeye State	2,913,387 (27)	6	55,491 (24)	Des Moines
KANSAS	Jan. 29, 1861 (34)	Sunflower State	2,363,208 (32)	5	81,787 (13)	Topeka/ Wichita
KENTUCKY	June 1, 1792 (15)	Bluegrass State	3,661,433 (23)	7	39,650 (37)	Frankfort/ Louisville
LOUISIANA	April 30, 1812 (18)	Pelican State	4,203,972 (18)	8	44,930 (33)	Baton Rouge/ New Orleans
MAINE	March 15, 1820 (23)	Pine Tree State	1,124,660 (38)	2	30,920 (39)	Augusta/ Portland
MARYLAND	April 28, 1788 (7)	Old Line State	4,216,446 (19)	8	9,891 (42)	Annapolis/ Baltimore
MASSACHUSETTS	Feb. 6, 1788 (6)	Bay State	5,737,037 (11)	11	7,826 (45)	Boston
MICHIGAN	Jan. 26, 1837 (26)	Wolverine State	9,258,344 (8)	18	56,817 (22)	Lansing/ Detroit
MINNESOTA	May 11, 1858 (32)	North Star State	4,077,148 (21)	8	79,289 (14)	St. Paul/ Minneapolis
MISSISSIPPI	Dec. 10, 1817 (20)	Magnolia State	2,520,638 (31)	5	47,296 (31)	Jackson
MISSOURI	Aug. 10, 1821 (24)	Show-me State	4,917,444 (15)	9	68,995 (18)	Jefferson City/ St. Louis

State	Date Entered Union (Rank)	Nickname	1980 Population (Rank)	Reps. in Congress	Area: Sq. mi./ (Rank)	Capital/ Largest City
MONTANA	Nov. 8, 1889 (41)	Treasure State	786,690 (44)	2	145,587 (4)	Helena/ Billings
NEBRASKA	March 1, 1867 (37)	Cornhusker State	1,570,006 (35)	3	76,483 (15)	Lincoln/ Omaha
NEVADA	Oct. 31, 1864 (36)	Sagebrush State	799,184 (43)	2	109,889 (7)	Carson City/ Las Vegas
NEW HAMPSHIRE	June 21, 1788 (9)	Granite State	920,610 (42)	2	9,027 (44)	Concord/ Manchester
NEW JERSEY	Dec. 18, 1787 (3)	Garden State	7,364,158 (9)	14	7,521 (46)	Trenton/ Newark
NEW MEXICO	Jan. 6, 1912 (47)	Land of Enchantment	1,299,968 (37)	3	121,412 (5)	Santa Fe/ Albuquerque
NEW YORK	July 26, 1788 (11)	Empire State	17,557,228 (2)	34	47,831 (30)	Albany/ New York City
NORTH CAROLINA	Nov. 21, 1789 (12)	Tar Heel State	5,874,429 (10)	11	48,798 (29)	Raleigh/ Charlotte
NORTH DAKOTA	Nov. 2, 1889 (39)	Flickertail State	652,695 (46)	1	69,273 (17)	Bismarck/ Fargo
OHIO	March 1, 1803 (17)	Buckeye State	10,797,419 (6)	21	40,975 (35)	Columbus/ Cleveland
OKLAHOMA	Nov. 16, 1907 (46)	Sooner State	3,025,266 (26)	6	68,782 (19)	Oklahoma City
OREGON	Feb. 14, 1859 (33)	Beaver State	2,632,660 (30)	5	96,184 (10)	Salem/ Portland
PENNSYLVANIA	Dec. 12, 1787 (2)	Keystone State	11,866,728 (4)	23	44,966 (32)	Harrisburg/ Philadelphia
RHODE ISLAND	May 29, 1790 (13)	Ocean State	947,154 (40)	2	1,049 (50)	Providence
SOUTH CAROLINA	May 23, 1788 (8)	Palmetto State	3,119,208 (25)	6	30,225 (40)	Columbia
SOUTH DAKOTA	Nov. 2, 1889 (40)	Coyote State	690,178 (45)	1	75,955 (16)	Pierre/ Sioux Falls
TENNESSEE	June 1, 1796 (16)	Volunteer State	4,596,750 (17)	9	41,328 (34)	Nashville/ Memphis
TEXAS	Dec. 29, 1845 (28)	Lone Star State	14,228,383 (3)	27	262,134 (2)	Austin/ Houston
UTAH	Jan. 4, 1896 (45)	Beehive State	1,461,037 (36)	3	82,096 (12)	Salt Lake City
VERMONT	March 4, 1791 (14)	Green Mountain State	511,456 (48)	1	9,276 (43)	Montpelier/ Burlington
VIRGINIA	June 25, 1788 (10)	The Old Dominion	5,346,279 (14)	10	39,780 (36)	Richmond/ Norfolk
WASHINGTON	Nov. 11, 1889 (42)	Evergreen State	4,130,163 (20)	8	66,570 (20)	Olympia/ Seattle
WEST VIRGINIA	June 20, 1863 (35)	Mountain State	1,949,644 (34)	4	24,070 (41)	Charleston
WISCONSIN	May 29, 1848 (30)	Badger State	4,705,335 (16)	9	54,464 (25)	Madison/ Milwaukee
WYOMING	July 10, 1890 (44)	Equality State	470,816 (49)	1	97,203 (9)	Cheyenne/ Casper

Flag Etiquette

(Excerpted from the United States Code)

The national anthem

During rendition of the national anthem when the flag is displayed, all present except those in uniform should stand at attention facing the flag with the right hand over the heart. Men not in uniform should remove their headdress with their right hand and hold it at the left shoulder, the hand being over the heart. Persons in uniform should render the military salute at the first note of the anthem and retain this position until the last note.

Display of the flag

It is the universal custom to display the flag only from sunrise to sunset on buildings and on stationary flagstaffs in the open. However, when a patriotic effect is desired, the flag may be displayed twenty-four hours a day if properly illuminated during the hours of darkness. The flag should be hoisted briskly and lowered ceremoniously.

The flag should be displayed daily on or near the main administration building of every public institution. It should be displayed in or near every polling place on election days. It should be displayed during school days in or near every schoolhouse.

Discuss the text of the "Star-Spangled Banner" with students. Have a student report on the historical events that led up to the song's creation.

Position of the flag

The flag, when carried in a procession with another flag or flags, should be either on the right, or, if there is a line of other flags, in front of the center of that line. No other flag or pennant should be placed above, or, if on the same level, to the right of the flag of the United States of America. The flag of the United States of America should be at the center and at the highest point of the group when a number of flags of states or localities or pennants of societies are grouped and displayed from staffs. When the flags are flown from adjacent staffs, the flag of the United States should be hoisted first and lowered last. No such flat or pennant may be placed above the flag of the United States or to the United States flag's right.

When the flag of the United States is displayed from a staff projecting horizontally or at an angle from the window sill, balcony, or front of a building, the union of the flag should be placed at the peak of the staff unless the flag is at half staff. When the flag is suspended over a sidewalk from a rope extending from a house to a pole at the edge of the sidewalk, the flag should be hoisted out, union first, from the building. When displayed either horizontally or vertically against a wall, the union should be uppermost and to the flag's own right, that is, to the observer's left. When displayed in a window, the flag should be displayed in the same way, with the union or blue field to the left of the observer in the street.

Flying the flag at half-staff

The flag, when flown at half-staff, should be first hoisted to the peak for an instant and then lowered to the half-staff position. The flag should be again raised to the peak before it is lowered for the day. By order of the President, the flag shall be flown at half-staff upon the death of principal figures of the United States Government and the Governor of a State, territory, or possession, as a mark of respect to their memory. In the event of the death of other officials or foreign dignitaries, the flag is to be displayed at half-staff according to Presidential instructions or orders, or in accordance with recognized customs or practices not inconsistent with law.

Uses of the flag

No part of the flag should ever be used as a costume or athletic uniform. However, a flag patch may be affixed to the uniform of military personnel, firemen, policemen, and members of patriotic organizations. The flag represents a living country and is itself considered a living thing. Therefore, the lapel flag pin, being a replica, should be worn on the left lapel near the heart.

The flag should form a distinctive feature of the ceremony of unveiling a statue or monument, but should never be used as the covering for the statue or monument. When the flag is used to cover a casket, it should be so placed that the union is at the head and over the left shoulder. The flag should not be lowered into the grave or allowed to touch the ground.

Disposal of the flag

The flag, when it is in such condition that it is no longer a fitting emblem for display, should be destroyed in a dignified way, preferably by burning.

Respect for the flag

No disrespect should be shown to the flag of the United States of America; the flag should not be dipped to any person or thing. Regimental colors, state flags, and organization or institutional flags are to be dipped as a mark of honor. The flag should never be displayed with the union down, except as a signal of dire distress in instances of extreme danger to life or property. The flag should never touch anything beneath it, such as the ground, the floor, water, or merchandise. The flag should never be carried flat or horizontally, but always aloft and free. The flag should never be used as wearing apparel, bedding or drapery. It should never be festooned, drawn back, nor up, in folds, but always allowed to fall free.

The flag should never be fastened, displayed, used, or stored in such a manner as to permit it to be easily torn, soiled, or damaged in any way. The flag should never be used as a covering for a ceiling. The flag should never have placed upon it, nor on any part of it, nor attached to it any mark, insignia, letter, word, figure, design, picture, or drawing of any nature. The flag should never be used as a receptacle for receiving, holding, carrying, or delivering anything. The flag should never be used for advertising purposes in any manner whatsoever. It should not be embroidered on such articles as cushions or handkerchiefs and the like, printed or otherwise impressed on paper napkins or boxes or anything that is designed for temporary use and discard. Advertising signs should not be fastened to a staff or halyard from which the flag is flown.

Glossary

administer To manage a government; to act as an administrator. [313]

administrator A person who carries out laws according to the orders of an executive. [346]

agenda A list of matters to be acted on in a council meeting. [267]

alien A citizen of one country who lives in another country. [11]

allegiance Loyalty to your country. [4]

ambassador The highest representative of the State Department of the U.S. to another country. [315]

amendment An addition to the Constitution. The first ten amendments are called the Bill of Rights. [103]

apellate jurisdiction The authority of a court to interpret or apply the law in any case on appeal. [415]

appeal A request to have a case heard again before a higher court. [383]

arraignment The act of appearing before a judge in court to answer an indictment. [398]

article One of the sections following the Preamble in the Constitution that establish the basic structure of American government. [98]

Articles of Confederation A Constitution drawn up by the Continental Congress that provided for a congress to be elected by the legislatures of the states. It did not call for a president. [85]

automation The ability of machines to control themselves and work on their own. [529]

bail A guarantee in the form of money that an indicted person will be available at the time of trial. [398]

biennial Every other year. [259]

bill A proposed law that is presented to Congress. [240]

bill of attainder A bill passed by a legislature that convicts a person of a crime without a trial. [232]

Bill of Rights The first ten amendments to the Constitution, which state the basic human rights of the people. [112]

budget A plan for spending. [541]

burden of proof The obligation that a prosecutor has to present enough evidence to make a jury decide in his favor. [403]

bureaucracy A group of appointed government officials. [299]

cabinet The heads of the executive departments, who are appointed by the President with the approval of the Senate. [313]

calendar The order of business appearing before a legislative session. [262]

campaign manager A person who is hired by a candidate to be in charge of the campaign. [178]

capitalism An economic system based on the exchange of money, or capital, for goods and services which are owned by private citizens. [512]

censure The official criticism by Congress of a member of Congress who is considered guilty of misconduct or wrongdoing. [217]

census A count of the population of the United States, that is taken every ten years. [100]
centralization The condition of more power in the federal government than the states. [134]
charter A document issued by the state government that sets the boundaries, governmental powers and functions, and method of finance of a city. [266]
checks and balances Limits of power placed on each of the executive, legislative, and judicial branches of the government by the other two branches. [303]
chief of state The President's role as the leader of the country. [301]
circuit court One of the courts presided over by a district judge. There is usually one in each county, each of which the district judge visits. [386]
citizenship The state of being a citizen, which provides certain rights and requires certain duties and responsibilities. [6]
city manager A person who is hired to run a city. [352]
civics The study of government and the rights and duties of citizens. [23]
civil case A suit between people, brought to court by an individual and involving rights and privileges. [380]
Civil Service The civilian employees in the executive branch of the government. [304]
commander-in-chief The title of the President, stated in the Constitution, that delegates to him or her the power to declare and plan war. [296]
committee A group of people who study a bill before it goes before the house. [241]
communism An economic system in which buildings, land, and the things that produce goods and services are owned by the government. [521]
competitive market A market in which there are many buyers and sellers for goods and services. [507]
compromise Settling differences in such a way that each side makes concessions or gives up something. [46]
compulsory Required or demanded by law. [472]
concurrent powers The powers held by both the states and the federal government. [129]
concurring opinion An opinion written by a Supreme Court justice who agrees with the majority in deciding a case, but who disagrees with the reasoning of their decision. [416]
confederation A national government in which states keep most of the power and give the central government only limited authority. [124]
congressional districts The areas into which states are divided according to population, each of which sends one representative to the house. [211]
conservative A person who prefers that government change society slowly or not at all. [181]
conserve To save, or use as little as possible. [456]
consul A representative of the State Department of the United States who looks after American business interests abroad. [315]
consumer A person who buys goods and services for his or her own use or that of his or her family. [504]
Continental Congress A meeting in Philadelphia in 1774 of delegates from twelve colonies to protest several new tax laws. [81]
contract An agreement that is made between two or more persons or groups of persons. [548]

county board The legislative body of a county. [144]

criminal case A case brought by the government to determine guilt and punishment of a person accused of a crime. [380]

cruel and unusual punishment A punishment that is too severe for the crime it is given for. [368]

decentralization The condition of more power in the individual states. [134]

defendant The person against whom an action in court is brought. [404]

delegated powers The authority given by the states to the federal government. [129]

democracy A country in which people make their own laws, either directly or indirectly through representatives. [26]

depression A condition of low economic activity and high unemployment. [438]

detente A diplomatic relationship of peaceful competition, which has been used in an attempt to relax relations between the Soviet Union and the United States. [332]

dictatorship A form of government in which one person establishes and enforces all the laws. [28]

diplomacy The art of establishing relations between countries that both sides can accept as useful and beneficial. [330]

dissent Having an opinion that disagrees with existing policy. [46]

dissenting opinion An opinion, written by a Supreme Court justice who is in the minority in deciding a case, stating the minority's reasons for disagreeing with the majority. [416]

district An area of a community where a special service is needed, such as a school, hospital, port, or the like. [149]

doctrine of implied powers The idea that Congress has powers that are not specifically described in the Constitution, but that are necessary in order to exercise those described. [229]

donor A wealthy person who supports candidates by giving large sums of money. [183]

due process Legal proceedings carried out in accordance with the established rules. [417]

duty One of the things that citizens must do, such as obeying laws. [541]

economic scarcity A condition where there is less of something available than people want or need. [501]

elastic clause A clause in Article I, Section 8 of the United States Constitution that gives Congress authority to exercise powers not specifically stated in the Constitution. [235]

elector One of the people chosen by his or her state to elect a President and Vice President; a member of the electoral college. [280]

electoral college The group of people selected by the individual states to elect a President and Vice President. [280]

embargo Refusal by a nation or group of nations to trade any or all of its products with another nation or nations. [333]

energy The ability to do work or to cause movement. [452]

ethnic group A group of people who have in common such things as national origin, religion, language, customs, etc. [40]

evolution The theory, conceived by Charles Darwin, that humans developed gradually over millions of years from lower forms of life. [491]

ex post facto A Latin phrase meaning "after the fact," which refers to the idea that laws are not to be applied to things that people did before the laws were passed. [232]

executive A person who orders laws to be carried out. [346]

executive power Having the power to carry out laws, which in the case of the national government belongs only to the President. [276]

expel To remove a member of Congress from office because of misconduct or wrongdoing. [217]

extradition Sending an accused criminal from a state to which he or she has fled to the state where he or she is wanted. [130]

federalism A form of government in which authority is divided between the central government and the self-governing states. [125]

felony A serious crime tried by a district or circuit court. [385]

filibuster Long speeches, made by senators who are in the minority, which force the majority to make a compromise in the passing or failure of a bill. [249]

foreign aid Goods, services, or funds given to help other nations. [335]

founding fathers The people who wrote the Constitution of the United States. [94]

free enterprise An economy in which questions of economic choice are answered by people being free to choose what to buy and sell. [506]

Free World The countries of the world that are not communist bloc nations or non-aligned nations; the self-governing "first world" nations. [337]

garnishee To take money out of an employee's paycheck by order of a court, and give it to a lender to whom the employee owes money and has not paid it. [550]

general welfare The decent conditions for the people that the government strives to provide; the good of the people. [434]

gerrymander To maneuver for an advantage in redistricting a state, done by the party in power. [261]

government The way people have organized to make rules or laws by which they can live together in peace. [5]

grand jury The larger of the two types of jury, usually made up of 24 people, who hear a case and decide whether there is sufficient evidence to indict the accused person or persons. [398]

grant-in-aid Money given by the federal government to the states for the general welfare. [132]

home rule The status of government in a city, granted by a state government, where the city has much to say about its own government. [147]

House of Burgesses The original legislature of the State of Virginia, the first body of lawmakers to be elected in the English way anywhere in the New World. [79]

immigrant A person who comes from one country to live in another. [8]

impeachment The process by which a public official is accused of wrongdoing by the House of Representatives. [227]

impulse buying Buying something without thinking about it. [540]

inauguration The ceremony in which the President-elect is sworn into office. [278]

incumbent The person who already holds the office he or she is running for. [179]

indictment A ruling by a grand jury that there is sufficient evidence to bring an accused criminal to trial. [398]

indirect participation To influence government without doing it directly, such as by trying to get your representative to support a certain law. [192]

inflation An economic condition where

prices are rising rapidly because there is more money available than there are goods. [512]

influence To get somebody to think as you do or to act as you think they should act. [192]

inherent power Powers of the presidency not stated in the Constitution, but assumed by some presidents in times of crisis. [301]

inherent right A right that all people have and that cannot be justly taken away. [31]

initiative An extension of the right of petition that allows the people to bring bills before a lawmaking body for consideration. [142]

insurgent A member of a party who refuses to vote with the party on a particular issue. [195]

interest The amount of money that a bank pays you for their use of your money when it is on deposit in a savings account. [546]

interest group People who share a common interest and who try to influence government officials to support laws that favor their interest. [196]

investigative committee A committee organized by Congress to study how laws are being enforced or where new ones are needed. [230]

isolationism The concept of being involved as little as possible with other nations. [331]

jeopardy A situation in which one is in danger of losing one's liberty. [370]

judicial review The power of the courts to declare a law unconstitutional. [383]

jurisdiction The power to apply the law. [115]

jury system A judicial system in which a group of people hear evidence to decide a case. [366]

justice The condition of being fair or equal according to the principles of right and wrong. [354]

juvenile A legal term for a young person, usually under the age of 18. [399]

lame duck A term applied to members of Congress during the months between election and when they left office, used because they had very little influence during this time. [115]

law A rule made by government. [20]

legislative Having to do with laws or the passing of laws. [210]

liberal A person who wants society to change, and wants the government to help bring this about. [81]

lobbyist A person whose job is to try to influence government for an organization or interest group. [199]

Magna Carta A document signed by King John of England in 1215 that gave certain rights to the English people. [77]

majority More than one half of all the votes, or more votes than all other candidates combined. [160]

majority party The party with the most members in each house. [215]

majority report The recommendation that a bill be passed or not passed by the larger group of committee members for or against the bill. [248]

Mayflower Compact A document drawn up by English settlers in Massachusetts in 1620 that stated that laws would be made for the general good of the people. [79]

Medicaid A program that provides payments for the medical cost of people on welfare. [441]

Medicare A program that provides hospital care and low-cost insurance to retired persons. [441]

minimum wage The lowest amount of money allowed by law to be paid by firms to their employees. [246]

minister A representative of the State Department of the U.S. to another country who is of lesser rank than an ambassador. [315]

minority The group of people that does not constitute enough votes for control. [45]

minority party The party with the smallest number of members in each house. [215]

minority President A President who was elected by a majority of the electoral vote, but a minority of the popular vote. [286]

minority report The recommendation that a bill be passed or not by the smaller group of committee members for or against the bill. [248]

misdemeanor A minor crime tried by justice-of-the peace courts and city judges. [385]

mixed practice An economic practice using features of traditional and planned economies as well as free enterprise. [510]

modify To change or make less strong. [46]

monarchy A form of government in which one person becomes head of the government by birth. [28]

monopoly A firm that controls the entire market for one good or service. [523]

Monroe Doctrine A statement made by President James Monroe in the early 1820's declaring that foreign powers were not to establish colonies in the Western Hemisphere or to interfere with the affairs of the countries in the Americas. [337]

municipality A self-governing town or city. [146]

natural resources Materials that we use that come from the environment. [441]

naturalization The granting by Congress of citizenship to a person who has come from another country. [11]

nominee A person who is selected by his or her party to run for a certain office. [164]

officer One of the people responsible for making and enforcing laws. [20]

ombudsman A watchdog or grievance commissioner. [348]

OPEC The Organization of Petroleum Exporting Countries. [454]

opinion campaign A campaign by a lobbyist to get people to write to their representatives for or against a certain bill. [200]

opinion poll A poll that is taken to determine how people feel about a certain issue. [201]

ordinance A law passed by a city government. [146]

original jurisdiction The authority of a court to interpret or apply law in the first hearing of a case. [415]

override To obtain two-thirds of the votes in each house in favor of a bill that the president has vetoed, and thus make it a law without his or her approval. [241]

parochial Operated by a religious institution. [489]

patronage The distribution of jobs or favors on a political basis. [262]

pension An allowance paid to a person by his or her employer after he or she has retired or left work because of injury. [439]

personal tax A tax on property owned by people which is not real estate. [475]

petit jury The smaller of the two types of jury, made up of twelve persons, who hear the evidence in a trial and decide whether the accused person is guilty or not. [398]

petition A list of signatures from registered

voters requesting a certain person to run for an office. [177]

petition A written request to a public official. [367]

plaintiff The person or party that brings an action to court. [404]

planned economy An economy where the questions of what is to be produced and how it is to be distributed are determined by the government. [503]

platform A party's statement of principles. [285]

plea bargaining Settling a case in a agreement between the prosecutor, the defense lawyer, and the police. [381]

plurality More votes than any other candidate, but not necessarily more than half the total votes. [160]

political machine An organized bloc of voters who vote the way they are told to vote by a political boss. [59]

popular vote The votes actually cast by the people in an election, as opposed to electoral votes. [280]

posterity Future generations. [98]

preamble The title of the statement introducing the Constitution. It comes from a Latin word meaning "to walk or go before." [96]

precinct The smallest unit of organization in a political party. [162]

president pro tempore A representative who serves as President of the Senate when the Vice President is absent or cannot serve. [215]

press secretary A member of the White House office who holds press conferences for reporters. [322]

primary An election held by members of one political party to nominate a candidate for a general election. [164]

principal The original amount of money that you deposit in a savings account. [546]

private property Property owned by individual people, not the government. [507]

probation Suspending a stronger sentence and granting the person provisional freedom on good behavior. [403]

procedural right One of the rights guaranteed by an accused criminal in the process of his being accused and taken into custody. [424]

profit A larger amount of money received from sales than is spent on costs. [522]

Prohibition The nineteenth amendment to the Constitution, which prohibited the sale, manufacture, or transportation of any kind of alcoholic beverage. It was repealed in 1933. [113]

propaganda Putting an idea in a favorable light in order to persuade people to accept it. [64]

public opinion How people feel and think about issues. [62]

public school A school that is aided in part or in full by public funds. [470]

public utility A firm that acts as a monopoly in a community, state, or other area, as to provide electrical service. [524]

push card Calling cards with a picture and the name of a candidate that he or she hands out when meeting people so that they will remember him or her. [179]

ratification Approval by the states of an amendment. [110]

real tax A tax on real property, such as houses, buildings, businesses, and land. [474]

reapportion To change the boundaries of districts in order to keep the populations equivalent. Districts are reapportioned after each census. [260]

recall A plan under which an officer of a state's government may be removed by an election called by the governor. [143]

recession An economic condition where there is high unemployment. [510]

recognize To accept a nation's government as the sovereign government of its people, and to accept that nation as a political equal in international affairs. [334]

referendum A vote by which a majority opinion is determined. [143]

regulatory authority The authority held by the more than fifty independent, specialized agencies which help regulate interstate commerce. [323]

religious freedom The freedom to practice whatever faith you choose, as long as you do not violate the law. [487]

renewable resource A resource that will never be used up, such as the sun, wind, or sea. [459]

repeal To take away an amendment or a law. [113]

repossess To take an item back because the buyer has failed to pay for it. [550]

representative-at-large A representative who is not from a particular district, but is elected by all the people of a state. [212]

republic A form of government in which people govern themselves through elected representatives. [5]

reserved powers The authority held by the states for themselves alone. [129]

responsibility One of the things that citizens ought to do, such as voting. [58]

right The privilege of being able to do or have something. [57]

runoff An election between the two candidates who have received the most votes in a primary election where no candidate got a majority. [164]

segregated Not having a mixture of ethnic groups and religions that is proportionate to the mixture in the general population of the community it serves. [473]

self-government Government ruled by the people through representatives. [39]

self-incrimination Being proven guilty by testifying against oneself. [370]

seniority Consecutive length of time in office in Congress, which determines a member's privileges in office. [262]

separation of church and state The principle that holds that the government shall not aid or support any or all religions. [489]

sheriff The main legal officer in a country, who, with his or her staff, maintains law and order and apprehends those who break the law. [350]

socialism An economic system where some things are owned privately by people but major areas of the economy are controlled by the government. [521]

solar power Energy generated from the sun's heat. [459]

special district A unit of local government created by an act of legislature to perform limited functions. [353]

spoils system The practice of firing government employees and appointing political supporters to replace them. [303]

Stamp Act Congress A meeting in New York City in 1765 of delegates from the colonies who protested taxation without representation by the King of England in a new tax law. [81]

state religion A religion that is enforced by the government. [487]

strategy The way a campaign is planned so that the candidate wins. [179]

suffrage The right to vote. [116]

summit conference A meeting between the President and top leaders of other nations. [334]

sunset law A law that requires all boards, commissions, agencies, and departments to be reviewed after a certain period of time to see if they are still necessary. [348]

synfuel Synthetic fuels, such as oil taken from shale. [458]

tax Money collected from people by the government to pay for public services. [56]

third party A political party that is not one of the two major parties. [160]

Third World The countries of the world that are not directly associated with the Free World or the Soviet Union and other communist bloc nations. [338]

tolerance Allowing people to express beliefs with which we disagree. [46]

totalitarian Controlled by only one authority or party, and allowing no opposition. [27]

traditional economy An economic system where the questions of what is to be produced and how it is to be distributed are determined by the history of the society. [503]

tranquility Peacefulness or quiet in a society, which is insured by the Constitution, as stated in the Preamble. [97]

treason Attempting to overthrow a government or otherwise harm the country or help its enemies. [12]

treaty An agreement signed by representatives of two or more nations. [333]

trial by ordeal An unfair method of determining whether a person is guilty or innocent by putting him or her in some kind of contest. [365]

trust A small group that represents a number of companies in a certain line of business who agree not to compete with each other. [523]

tuition A fee paid by a student to attend a particular school. [475]

tyrant An absolute ruler who rules in a cruel and unjust way for his or her own benefit. [77]

unconstitutional Not agreeing with the Constitution. [383]

uniform laws Laws that are written to apply in the same way to all states. [130]

unitary state A single central government that has complete legal control over all the territory within its borders. [124]

veto The rejection by the President of a bill. [241]

vocational Training students in a trade or skill. [476]

warranty A written guarantee or promise that an item will work or last for a certain period of time. If it doesn't, the manufacturer will replace or repair it. [546]

welfare state A method of providing for the general welfare in which the government controls important areas of the economy. [438]

whip The assistant to a majority or minority leader. [216]

writ of habeas corpus An order given by a judge to either bring a prisoner to court to be formally accused, or to require police to let him or her go free. [232]

Writ of Mandamus A request to the Supreme Court by a lower court that it hear an appeal from the lower court. [415]

Index

An entry in **boldface** indicates a "Building Vocabulary" item.
A page number in *italics* indicates an illustration.

Sequence of Skills

CHAPTER	STUDY SKILLS	VISUAL SKILLS
1	Using a Glossary	Graphs
2	Using Facts to Support Generalizations	Maps
3	Using an Index	Illustrations
4	Using Forms	Tables
5	Using Documents	Time Lines
6	Outlining	Charts
7	Using an Appendix	Time Charts
8	Using a Card Catalog	Maps
9	Outlining	Illustrations
10	Using an Encyclopedia	Graphs
11	Recognizing Techniques of Persuasion	Advertisements
12	Using the Newspaper	Illustrations
13	Topic Outlining	Illustrations
14	Using the Almanac	Flow Charts
15	Editing	Flow Charts
16	Making a Formal Outline	Atlases
17	Editing	Comic Strips
18	Making a Sentence Outline	Postage Stamps
19	Preparing a First Draft	Photographs
20	Using the *Reader's Guide*	Global Projections
21	Presenting Book Reports	Diagrams
22	Watching Television News Shows	Collages
23	Listening to News Broadcasts	Photographs and Paintings
24	Comparing Media Sources	Storyboards
25	Using Different Sources of Information	Cartoons
26	Learning from News Shows	Tables
27	Using the Yellow Pages	Cartoons
28	Using Different Sources of Information	Tables
29	Using Skimming Techniques	Photographs
30	Using Periodicals	Tables
31	Using the Encyclopedia	Tables
32	Using a Glossary and a Dictionary	Charts

Acknowledgments

Editorial Consultants: Robert Bell; Johnnie Prather; James Wilson

Editorial Research: Marilyn Cooley; Erma Underwood

Illustrator, Frontispiece and Unit Openers: Robert Steele

Illustrators, Chapter Openers: Konrad Hack (Chapters 1, 2, 3, 5, 6, 28); Helen Tullen (Chapters 4, 10, 22); Ron Himler (Chapters 7, 12, 16); Jas Syzgiel (Chapters 8, 20, 23, 25, 30, 32); Jon Friedman (Chapters 9, 13, 18); Tom Leonard (Chapters 14, 15, 19, 31); Al Fiorentino (Chapters 21, 27, 29); Simon Galkin (Flag Etiquette pgs. 594–597)

Cartoons: Mark Kelley

Charts and Graphs: Kirchoff/Wohlberg, Inc.

Maps: Richard Sanderson

Special Photography: Stephen McCarroll (Pages 4, 11, 22, 64, 177, 179, 180, 183, 199, 241, 247, 263, 265, 305, 348, 355, 365, 372, 396, 397, 398, 399, 401, 402, 405, 478, (tl)502, 507, 532, 541, 544, and 549)

Photo Research: Judy Greene

Photo Credits Key: (t)top; (c)center; (b)bottom; (l)left; (r)right

Unit 1: Page 5(tl), James Amos, Photo Researchers, Inc.; 5(tlc), S. L. Craig, Bruce Coleman, Inc.; 5(trc), Richard Hutchings, Photo Researchers, Inc.; 5(tr), Thomas D. W. Friedman, Photo Researchers, Inc.; 5(bl), Paul Kuhn, Bruce Coleman, Inc.; 5(blc), Henry Bradshaw, Photo Researchers, Inc.; 5(brc), David Madison, Bruce Coleman, Inc.; 5(br), Bill Brooks, Bruce Coleman, Inc.; 13, Culver Pictures, Inc.; 21, The Bettmann Archive, Inc.; 27, Eastfoto; 29(tl), The Bettman Archive, Inc.; 29(tr), The Bettmann Archive, Inc.; 29(bl), The Bettmann Archive, Inc.; 29(bc), The Bettmann Archive, Inc.; 29(br), Sovfoto; 38(l), Eunice Harris, Photo Researchers, Inc.; 38(r), R. Rowan, Photo Researchers, Inc.; 39(l), Katrina Thomas, Photo Researchers, Inc.; 39(r), Bill Belknap, Photo Researchers, Inc.; 41(tl), Jeff Lowenthal, Woodfin Camp & Associates; 41(tc), Dan Budnick, Woodfin Camp and Associates; 41(tr), Russ Kinne, Photo Researchers, Inc.; 41(bl), Herman Kokojan, Black Star; 41(bc), Lester Sloan, Woodfin Camp and Associates; 41(br), Lawrence Schiller, Photo Researchers, Inc.; 44, Stan Pantovic; 45, Stan Pantovic; 59, Tom McHugh, Photo Researchers, Inc., National Portrait Gallery-Smithsonian Institution; 60, Tom McHugh, Photo Researchers, Inc., National Portrait Gallery-Smithsonian Institution.

Unit 2: Page 76, The Bettmann Archive, Inc.; 77, The Bettmann Archive Inc.; 78, The Bettmann Archive, Inc.; 79, The Bettmann Archive, Inc.; 81, Historical Pictures Service, Inc.; 82, The Bettmann Archive, Inc.; 83, The Bettmann Archive, Inc.; 86, The Bettmann Archive, Inc.; 94, Tom McHugh, Photo Researchers, Inc., National Portrait Gallery-Smithsonian; 95(l), Francis G. Mayer, Photo Researchers, Inc., National Portrait Gallery-Smithsonian; 95(c), Tom McHugh, Photo Researchers, Inc.; 95(r), Francis G. Mayer, Photo Researchers, Inc.; 96, The Bettmann Archive, Inc.; 97(tl), Joe Bilbao, Photo Researchers, Inc.; 97(tc), Fred Ward, Black Star; 97(tr), Fred Maroon, Photo Researchers, Inc.; 97(bl), Don Morgan, Photo Researchers, Inc.; 97(bc), Rigmor Mason, Photo Researchers, Inc.; 97(br), Russ Kinne, Photo Researchers, Inc.; 103(l), The Bettmann Archive, Inc.; 103(r), Bruce Frisch, Photo Researchers, Inc.; 112, Scala/EPA Archives, Inc.; 113, The Bettmann Archive, Inc.; 114(tl), The Bettmann Archive, Inc.; 114(tr), The Bettmann Archive, Inc.; 128, The Bettmann Archive, Inc.; 129, Guy Gillette, Photo Researchers, Inc.; 131, The Bettmann Archive, Inc.; 145, Farrell Grehan, Photo Researchers, Inc.; 146, Roger A. Clark, Jr., Photo Researchers, Inc.; 150, The Bettmann Archive, Inc.

Unit 3: 160(l), The Bettmann Archive, Inc.; 160(r), The Bettmann Archive, Inc.; 161(tl), The Bettmann Archive, Inc.; 161(tr), Photo Researchers, Inc.; 161(bl), The Bettmann Archive, Inc.; 161(br), Rick Friedman, Black Star; 164, Dennis Brack, Black Star; 165, The Bettmann Archive, Inc.; 166(t), Sam Pierson, Photo Researchers, Inc.; 166(b), Sam Pierson, Photo Researchers, Inc.; 167(tl), The Bettmann Archive, Inc.; 167(tc), The Bettmann Archive, Inc.; 167(tr), The Bettmann Archive, Inc.; 167(b), Charles Moore, Black Star; 168(tl), The Bettmann Archive, Inc.; 168(b), The Bettmann Archive, Inc.; 193, Dennis Brack, Black Star; 196, Andrew Sacks, Black Star; 197, The Bettmann Archive, Inc.; 200, Dennis Brack, Black Star.

Unit 4: Page 211, Dennis Brack, Black Star; 213(l), Jack Fields, Photo Researchers, Inc.; 213(r), Tom Hollyman, Photo Researchers, Inc.; 215, Dennis Brack, Black Star;

216, John Troha, Black Star; 225, The Bettmann Archive, Inc.; 228, Jim Tuten, Black Star; 229, Wide World Photos, Inc.; 233, Lowell Georgia, Photo Researchers, Inc.; 249, The Bettmann Archive, Inc.; 258, Catherine Ursillo, Photo Researchers, Inc.; 259, Nancy Zimmerman, Photo Researchers, Inc.; 260, Robert Carter; 261, The Bettmann Archive, Inc.; 264, The Bettmann Archive, Inc.; 264, The Bettmann Archive, Inc.; 266, The Bettmann Archive, Inc.

Unit 5: Page 276, Dennis Brack, Black Star; 277, Boccon-Gibod/Black Star-Sipa Press; 279(l), Black Star; 279(r), Fred Ward, Black Star; 281, The Bettmann Archive, Inc.; 296, John S. Tarkey, Black Star; 297, Wide World Photos, Inc.; 298, Dennis Brack, Black Star; 300(tl), Dennis Brack, Black Star; 300(tr), John Troha, Black Star; 300(cl), D. B. Owen, Black Star; 300(cr), Dennis Brack, Black Star; 300(bl), Dennis Brack, Black Star; 300(br), Alan Clifton, Black Star; 302, The Bettmann Archive, Inc.; 303, The Bettmann Archive, Inc.; 304, The Bettmann Archive, Inc.; 312, The Bettmann Archive, Inc.; 316, The Bettmann Archive, Inc.; 317, Wide World Photos, Inc.; 318, Steve van Matue, Photo Researchers, Inc.; 319, Herman J. Kokojan, Black Star; 322, Bill Ray, Black Star; 331, Wide World Photos, Inc.; 332, Wide World Photos, Inc.; 333, Wide World Photos, Inc.; 335, Dennis Brack, Black Star; 336, Wide World Photos, Inc.; 346, The Bettmann Archive, Inc.; 347, Wide World Photos, Inc.; 353, Russ Kinne, Photo Researchers, Inc.

Unit 6: Page 360, D. B. Owen, Black Star Photos; 364, The Bettmann Archive, Inc.; 366, The Bettmann Archive, Inc.; 367, The Bettmann Archive, Inc.; 369, The Bettmann Archive, Inc.; 383, The Bettmann Archive, Inc.; 384, Dennis Brack, Black Star; 385(tr), Culver Pictures, Inc.; 385(b), Bettmann Archives, Inc.; 414, The Bettmann Archive, Inc.; 415, Black Star; 416, Joseph Nettis, Photo Researchers, Inc.; 417, The Bettmann Archive, Inc.; 419, The Bettmann Archive, Inc.; 420, Wide World Photos, Inc.; 421, The Bettmann Archive, Inc.; 423, Flip Schulke, Black Star; 424, John Running, Black Star.

Unit 7: Page 435, William Carter, Photo Researchers, Inc.; 436, Martin A. Levien, Black Star; 437, George Holton, Photo Researchers, Inc.; 439(t), The Bettmann Archive, Inc.; 439(b), The Bettmann Archive, Inc.; 440, Wide World Photos, Inc.; 442, The Library of Congress; 443(t), Margaret Bourke-White/Life Magazine (c)-1936 Time, Inc.; 443(b), Jim Anderson, Black Star; 452, Stan Pantovic; 453 (bl), David Krasnor, Photo Researchers, Inc.; 453(br), Stan Goldblatt, Photo Researchers, Inc.; 455, Black Star, Sipa Press; 456, Sam Pierson, Photo Researchers, Inc.; 459, Ron Church, Photo Researchers, Inc.; 461(tr), Dennis Brack, Black Star; 461(bl), Wide World Photos, Inc.; 462(l), David Krasnor, Photo Researchers, Inc.; 462(r), Georg Gerster, Photo Researchers, Inc.; 471, The Bettmann Archive, Inc.; 472(t), The Bettman Archive, Inc.; 472(b), G. Whitely, Photo Researchers, Inc.; 473, The Bettmann Archive, Inc.; 474, Ken Rogers, Black Star; 475, Bob Fitch, Black Star; 477, Ted Spiegel, Black Star; 486(l), Eunice Harris, Photo Researchers, Inc.; 486(c), Susan McCartney, Photo Researchers, Inc.; 486(r), Guy Gillete, Photo Researchers, Inc.; 487, The Bettmann Archive, Inc.; 488(t), The Bettmann Archive, Inc.; 488(b), Thomas B. Hollyman, Photo Researchers, Inc.; 490, The Bettmann Archive, Inc.; 496, Dorothy Wild.

Unit 8: Page 501, Wide World Photos, Inc.; 503, The Bettmann Archive, Inc.; 504, Thomas D. W. Friedman, Photo Researchers, Inc.; 505, Wide World Photos, Inc.; 509(l), George Holton, Photo Researchers, Inc.; 509(r), Wide World Photos, Inc.; 520, George E. Jones III, Photo Researchers, Inc.; 521, Wide World Photos, Inc.; 522(l), Wide World Photos, Inc.; 522(r), Alan Reininger, D.P.I.; 524(l), The Bettmann Archive, Inc.; 524(r), Wide World Photos, Inc.; 525, Wide World Photos, Inc.; 528(l), The Bettmann Archive, Inc.; 528(c), The Bettmann Archive, Inc.; 528(r), M. E. Warren, Photo Researchers, Inc.; 542, Earl Roberge, Photo Researchers, Inc.; 543, Wide World Photos, Inc.

A Note on How This Book Was Made

The text of *We the People* is set in a typeface known as *Caslon.* This is a modern film version of one of the first machine typefaces. It was named in honor of William Caslon (1692–1766), the great English type designer. The Caslon typeface was selected for *We the People* by the publisher because of its patriotic association with the United States. Benjamin Franklin, a printer by trade, introduced this type in the American colonies, where it soon became the most widely accepted face. It was in fact the first typeface ever used in the new country of the United States, since the official copies of the Declaration of Independence were printed in Caslon.

We the People was designed by Kirchoff/Wohlberg, Inc., Madison, Connecticut. The book was typeset by Black Dot, Inc., Crystal Lake, Illinois. The illustrations were photographed for printing by the Color Division of Black Dot. The book was printed and bound by Kingsport Press, Kingsport, Tennessee, using a stock of paper known as Warren Matte, manufactured by S. D. Warren Company, Boston, Massachusetts.

We the People

of the United States, in Order to form a more perfect Union, establish Justice, insure domestic Tranquility, provide for the common defence, promote the general Welfare, and secure the Blessings of Liberty to ourselves and our Posterity, do ordain and establish this Constitution for the United States of America.

Article I

Section. 1. All legislative Powers herein granted shall be vested in a Congress of the United States, which shall consist of a Senate and House of Representatives.

Section. 2. The House of Representatives shall be composed of Members chosen every second Year by the People of the several States, and the Electors in each State shall have the Qualifications requisite for Electors of the most numerous Branch of the State Legislature.

No Person shall be a Representative who shall not have attained to the Age of twenty five Years, and been seven Years a Citizen of the United States, and who shall not, when elected, be an Inhabitant of that State in which he shall be chosen.

Representatives and direct Taxes shall be apportioned among the several States which may be included within this Union, according to their respective Numbers, which shall be determined by adding to the whole Number of free Persons, including those bound to Service for a Term of Years, and excluding Indians not taxed, three fifths of all other Persons. The actual Enumeration shall be made within three Years after the first Meeting of the Congress of the United States, and within every subsequent Term of ten Years, in such Manner as they shall by Law direct. The Number of Representatives shall not exceed one for every thirty Thousand, but each State shall have at Least one Representative; and until such enumeration shall be made, the State of New Hampshire shall be entitled to chuse three, Massachusetts eight, Rhode-Island and Providence Plantations one, Connecticut five, New-York six, New Jersey four, Pennsylvania eight, Delaware one, Maryland six, Virginia ten, North Carolina five, South Carolina five, and Georgia three.

When vacancies happen in the Representation from any State, the Executive Authority thereof shall issue Writs of Election to fill such Vacancies.

The House of Representatives shall chuse their Speaker and other Officers; and shall have the sole Power of Impeachment.

Section. 3. The Senate of the United States shall be composed of two Senators from each State, chosen by the Legislature thereof, for six Years; and each Senator shall have one Vote.

Immediately after they shall be assembled in Consequence of the first Election, they shall be divided as equally as may be into three Classes. The Seats of the Senators of the first Class shall be vacated at the Expiration of the second Year, of the second Class at the Expiration of the fourth Year, and of the third Class at the Expiration of the sixth Year, so that one third may be chosen every second Year; and if Vacancies happen by Resignation, or otherwise, during the Recess of the Legislature of any State, the Executive thereof may make temporary Appointments until the next Meeting of the Legislature, which shall then fill such Vacancies.

No Person shall be a Senator who shall not have attained to the Age of thirty Years, and been nine Years a Citizen of the United States, and who shall not, when elected, be an Inhabitant of that State for which he shall be chosen.

The Vice President of the United States shall be President of the Senate, but shall have no Vote, unless they be equally divided.

The Senate shall chuse their other Officers, and also a President pro tempore, in the Absence of the Vice President, or when he shall exercise the Office of President of the United States.

The Senate shall have the sole Power to try all Impeachments. When sitting for that Purpose, they shall be on Oath or Affirmation. When the President of the United States is tried, the Chief Justice shall preside: And no Person shall be convicted without the Concurrence of two thirds of the Members present.

Judgment in Cases of Impeachment shall not extend further than to removal from Office, and disqualification to hold and enjoy any Office of honor, Trust or Profit under the United States: but the Party convicted shall nevertheless be liable and subject to Indictment, Trial, Judgment and Punishment, according to Law.

Section. 4. The Times, Places and Manner of holding Elections for Senators and Representatives, shall be prescribed in each State by the Legislature thereof; but the Congress may at any time by Law make or alter such Regulations, except as to the Places of chusing Senators.

The Congress shall assemble at least once in every Year, and such Meeting shall be on the first Monday in December, unless they shall by Law appoint a different Day.

Section. 5. Each House shall be the Judge of the Elections, Returns and Qualifications of its own Members, and a Majority of each shall constitute a Quorum to do Business; but a smaller Number may adjourn from day to day, and may be authorized to compel the Attendance of absent Members, in such Manner, and under such Penalties as each House may provide.

Each House may determine the Rules of its Proceedings, punish its Members for disorderly Behaviour, and, with the Concurrence of two thirds, expel a Member.

Each House shall keep a Journal of its Proceedings, and from time to time publish the same, excepting such Parts as may in their Judgment require Secrecy; and the Yeas and Nays of the Members of either House on any question shall, at the Desire of one fifth of those Present, be entered on the Journal.

Neither House, during the Session of Congress, shall, without the Consent of the other, adjourn for more than three days, nor to any other Place than that in which the two Houses shall be sitting.

Section. 6. The Senators and Representatives shall receive a Compensation for their Services, to be ascertained by Law, and paid out of the Treasury of the United States. They shall in all Cases, except Treason, Felony and Breach of the Peace, be privileged from Arrest during their Attendance at the Session of their respective Houses, and in going to and returning from the same; and for any Speech or Debate in either House, they shall not be questioned in any other Place.

No Senator or Representative shall, during the Time for which he was elected, be appointed to any civil Office under the Authority of the United States, which shall have been created, or the Emoluments whereof shall have been encreased during such time; and no Person holding any Office under the United States, shall be a Member of either House during his Continuance in Office.

Section. 7. All Bills for raising Revenue shall originate in the House of Representatives; but the Senate may propose or concur with Amendments as on other Bills.

Every Bill which shall have passed the House of Representatives and the Senate, shall, before it become a Law, be presented to the President of the

We the People

[illegible]

Article 1

[illegible]